Robert Mar

Claire A. Pittman

Kate Reilly

Wooten-Hawkins

Ardis Hatch

May Steele

Gerald Barrax

Ellen Turlington Johnston-Hale

Peggy Hoffmann

Gladys Owings Hughes

Kathryn Stripling Byer

Germaine Todd

Frances Gray Patton

Grace L. Gibson

Suzanne Newton

Our Words, Our Ways

Reading and Writing in North Carolina

Our Words, Our Ways

Reading and Writing in North Carolina

Sally Buckner

Professor of English
Peace College

CAROLINA ACADEMIC PRESS
Durham, North Carolina

Carolina Academic Press
700 Kent Street at Duke University Road
Durham, North Carolina 27701
(919) 489-7486

OUR WORDS, OUR WAYS:
Reading and Writing in North Carolina

An Open Letter to North Carolina Students

Greetings:

For the past several years, you have been very much on my mind. As I have worked to put this book together, I have tried to picture you: students of all sizes and races, in all sorts of settings—biking along sandy plains, jogging on city sidewalks, dashing through surf at the coast, climbing red clay Piedmont hills, sledding down a mountain slope. Of course I couldn't meet you all, but I have visited classrooms and asked some of you what you like to read and what interests you. I have also asked a number of your teachers to review my plans for this text and the writings I have chosen. They have told me what readings you prefer and what they would find useful to enrich your classes in literature or North Carolina history.

For this anthology I have chosen a wide variety of readings—wide in kind (fiction, poetry, biography, journalism, etc.), in complexity, in topic, and in mood. Reading these selections, you may sometimes enjoy a good belly laugh. You may sometimes feel a lump in your throat. You may cheer as you encounter courage and perseverance. You may chill at the wickedness of which some human beings are capable—and you may glow when you see the goodness of others.

This book contains a broad cross section of human life as it has been written about by authors in this state. It also contains works which can be of practical value in your lives—writings which can in one way or another make your lives better.

Why Read North Carolina Literature?

That's a reasonable question. I suggest three answers:

1. *Because at this point in your education you're studying North Carolina history.* Literature can make dramatic and personal the information which history presents in cold, objective facts. For example, reading an excerpt from John Ehle's novel *Time of Drums*, we learn more than the fact that an important Civil War Battle was fought at Chancellorsville. We see what it's like to prepare men to fight, to see men in the fury of battle—some acting courageously, others foolishly. Another example: in her poem, "Carolina Boat People," Rebecca Rust does not give us the dimensions of the ship, the number of passengers, the names of the crew—material we can find in historical documents. Instead, she helps us to experience something of the nervousness as well as the excitement of those settlers who came to Roanoke Island.

2. *Because you're a North Carolinian and this is your heritage.* Whether you were born here of a family that has inhabited this soil for

generations or you are a newcomer still trying to accustom yourself to Tar Heel dialects, you are influenced by the ideas, beliefs, customs, and attitudes current in this state. You will agree with some—even cherish them. You may reject others absolutely. Either way, they affect your thinking and believing and behaving.

This is a special period in your lives, one in which you are making important decisions about what you think, what you believe, and what you want to do with your life. You can best make those decisions if you understand what is influencing you. In other words, understanding your heritage helps you to understand yourself and control your life.

3. *Because it is important to recognize that good writing is not done in some far-off mythical city, but right down the highway, maybe even in the house next door.* Good poems and stories and articles are created not by strange geniuses who produce words only when under some supernatural inspiration, but by your neighbors and kinfolk—by teachers and farmers, nurses and secretaries, homemakers, business managers, and lawyers. And someday they may be produced by you.

A Wealth of Writing

In putting this book together—always with you in mind—I have reviewed over one thousand writings by North Carolina authors: stories, novels, biographies, poems, articles, essays, reports, tall tales, and legends. You may be amazed at that number. Actually, I could have reviewed ten thousand pieces and not covered all the possible material. North Carolina has a rich literary history, and right now this state is undergoing what some call a "literary renaissance"—that is, a rebirth of interest in writing. New works are pouring off the presses at a record rate. Our writers are attracting not just local, but national attention. In 1990, the North Carolina

Poetry Society had 200 members and the North Carolina Writers' Network had over 1300.

Who is a North Carolina Writer?

In a country in which people move around a great deal, it isn't always easy to decide whether a writer qualifies as a North Carolinian or not. For the purposes of this book, I have designated as North Carolina writers not merely those who have spent their entire lives here—people like John Charles McNeill, Doris Betts, and Fred Chappell. I have also included writers who meet either of two qualifications:

1. They spent most of their early lives—the years which formed their attitudes, values, and personalities—in this state. Thomas Wolfe spent his adult life mostly in New York and Europe, but because he grew up in Asheville and graduated from the University of North Carolina in Chapel Hill, we claim him as our own.

2. Although they did not grow up here, they have spent such a large part of their lives here that they can be said to have absorbed the North Carolina experience and/or to have contributed a great deal to the Tar Heel literary scene. Thus we include Lee Smith, who grew up in Virginia, but who lives and works in Chapel Hill and Raleigh, and Stephen E. Smith, a native of Maryland, who has taught for many years at Sandhills Community College in Moore County.

All of these writers created works that can help us to grow in positive ways.

I wish you good reading!

Sincerely,

Sally Buckner

Sally Buckner

How to Use This Book

Unless they are reading a novel, good readers do not simply open a book to page one and read straight through. They preview the book to see how it is organized and what features are included.

The Organization of
Our Words, Our Ways

This book is organized into two main sections:

1. **Heritage:** Writings that deal with our past—from the time this land was just being settled through the mid 1970s. These works are arranged chronologically.

2. **Home:** Writings which deal with North Carolina now (since about 1975)—our people, our land, our problems, our beliefs and customs.

Also included is **A Showcase of Other North Carolina Writers:** Brief sketches of writers whose works could not be included, but with whom you, as a North Carolinian, should certainly be familiar.

Hints and Helps for
Efficient Reading

Because we all have a number of things we want to do, all of us like to work efficiently. If we're reading, we don't enjoy stumbling over passages, stopping and starting repeatedly.

The following are provided to help your reading be as pleasant and as productive as possible:

1. *Preview*

Most of us prefer to see a movie or television show that we've heard something about. We feel more comfortable if we know ahead of time whether it's going to be a comedy or a mystery or whether it focuses on American teenagers or Chinese soldiers. For this reason, you will be given a brief preview for each work. These previews are designed to provide context, just as a movie or television preview does. They will also alert you to special problems, such as strange customs or unfamiliar references.

2. *An opportunity to "Meet the Author"*

Any writing should stand on its own merit, regardless of the writer's age, sex, race, or history. However, we usually find that the writing fits into our own experience better if we know something about the author. Biographical sketches are provided for every author represented.

3. *Language Alert*

This section will point out words that are outdated or whose meanings have changed. It will spotlight dialect and help you become acquainted with words that may be unfamiliar.

4. *Reflecting*

We rarely get the entire message from a piece of writing just by reading through it. Usually if we take time for reflection, we will find new angles to explore, and the work will have more meaning for us.

Our memories work something like the process involved in creating good snapshots. We snap the images onto film, then, during the developing process, use a "fixative" to make sure the images remain permanent. It's a pity to take good pictures, then have them fade because a fixative was not used. It's a pity to read and enjoy good material, then not be able to recall (and use) that material simply because we haven't taken time to "fix" it in our memories. The "Reflecting" activities, provided after each reading, are intended to act as fixatives.

Taking Control of Your Own Education

A good text can be a valuable resource in helping you to learn. With the help of many people who have your best interests at heart, I have tried to make this a text you will enjoy as well as one from which you can learn.

A good teacher is an even better resource. He/she can clear up fuzzy passages and orga-nize the class so that all activities relate to one another and to our lives, and inspire us to learn.

But there is one other important ingredient without which even the best of texts and the most magnificent of teachers cannot be successful: a learner who is determined to take full advantage of every learning experience. You can make your study hours worthwhile if you recognize that learning is a tool for mastery—that it will give you the power to make the most of your abilities, and will help you understand the world so that you can deal with it better.

One way to get the most from your reading is to talk back! The best readers read as if they were having a conversation with the writer. They think (ever so quickly and subconsciously) "Hey, that's terrific!" or "How dumb!" or "That reminds me of...." Sometimes they take notes or write responses (like journal entries) expressing their feelings and ideas about a piece of writing. You will find that talking back to the writer, whether in your mind or with a pencil, can make reading more fun, more meaningful—and finally more helpful as you take more control of your own learning and your own life.

Some Words about Words

Our Ever Changing Language

Language is not set in stone, but is fluid as water—constantly changing over years of everyday use. This change is reflected in pronunciation, spelling, vocabulary, and all the parts of speech. Some words retain their original meanings and stay with us for centuries. Others are popular for a time, then suddenly fall out of usage and are forgotten. Even in our own lives, we can see slang words and catchwords move in and out of the language very quickly. Still other terms may remain in use, but their meaning gradually changes. Words that once were taboo and forbidden may over time grow acceptable in polite conversation. By contrast, frequently used words may later come to be considered insulting and improper.

The literary selections in this book are for the most part presented to you precisely as they were originally published. In the very first selection, written by one of the earliest sixteenth-century explorers, you will find several old, out-of-date spellings. Notes and hints have been given to help you understand what these old words mean.

As you move toward more modern works, you may notice that over time our language has tended to become less and less formal. A hundred years ago, stories, poems, articles, and even speeches and conversation were often expressed in an ornate, flowery language. Today we use a simpler, more direct style. The simplicity of modern language

does not mean that vocabulary is limited or that all sentences are short. It does indicate that in an effort to attract larger audiences, speakers and writers have avoided unnecessarily complicated sentences and out-of-date terms. Today's reader must have patience with the language of writers from earlier times and remember that they were just writing in the style of their own day. The fact that we use language differently now should not stop us from understanding and enjoying their work.

You will also notice major changes in the language used to refer to minorities. Before the Civil Rights movement of the 1960s, the polite term for a black person was *Negro* or *colored person*; slang terms included *darky* and *nigger*, used rudely to belittle blacks, and showing the ignorance and thoughtlessness of racial prejudice. Since the 1960s, when "Black is beautiful" became a proud slogan, the preferred term in most cases has become *black*. (*Negro* is still used occasionally, however, as in *United Negro College Fund*.) Another example of changing terms is that until recently, the original inhabitants of this land were called *Indians*. Today we usually say *Native Americans* to distinguish them from the Indians of India and to pay respect to their historical roots.

It is important for readers to recognize that the use of these varied terms in a work, like the use of archaic language or slang, reflects the time in which the work was written. In fictional pieces, language also reflects the personality and attitudes of the character who speaks it, not necessarily of the author who is recording that speech. In fact, an author who wants to attack prejudice may have one of his characters use a rude or derogatory term simply to show the ignorance or cruelty of that character.

Dialects

Many writings in this collection feature dialects. Dialects are varieties of speech common to one region or community of people. We find them in all world languages. Dialects are marked by differences in pronunciation, in vocabulary, and in the way words are strung together to make phrases. These differences may be based on nationality, race, and/or geography. Although television and radio have helped to develop what is called the "standard dialect," we still recognize distinctive dialects: the South (think of the voice of Andy Griffith); Boston (the voice of John or Robert Kennedy); the Bronx; or Texas. As you travel across North Carolina, you will notice marked differences in dialect. For instance, natives of the Outer Banks speak very differently from those who have spent their lives in the Blue Ridge Mountains.

Within a given group or community, dialects help people to communicate with one another in colorful ways. However, it is often difficult for people who speak one dialect to fully understand another, so it is important that we also have a standard dialect—one which is understood by everyone in the nation, regardless of geography, race, or national origin. Thus for formal writing (essays at school, newspaper articles, scientific reports, and all the writing done in the business and professional world), we use Standard American English and obey the rules described in grammar books.

But dialects should be considered different from, not inferior to the standard language. They are not less useful than the standard language; they are simply unique to a particular region or group. They provide flavor and richness to the national culture, and demonstrate how each group and region is distinctive.

In stories written before the middle of this century, spelling often reflects pronunciation of a dialect: for example, *goin'* instead of *going* for a story using a Southern dialect. If a large number of words are spelled to reflect special pronunciation, the reader may find it difficult to understand all the language. Recognizing this difficulty, modern writers have changed the way they reflect dialect: instead of using phonetic spelling, they depend on word choice and sentence structure to provide the flavor of regional speech.

HERITAGE

In conversation we often use the word *heritage* to refer to property that has been handed down through the generations: for example, a farm, a house, a tool, a shawl. But our heritage consists of much more than property. It includes our traditions, laws, moral standards, literature, art—the entire culture passed on from earlier times.

In the following pages we will look at our heritage through the eyes of some of our state's best writers. If we are to understand ourselves and our present society, it is important to understand our heritage—for in order to know where we are, we need to know where we have been. As we review the heritage of this state, we will find situations of which we are not proud: events and persons marked by bigotry and cruelty and ignorance. We will also find occasion for pride as we see courage and integrity and consideration for others. Reviewing the mistakes in our past, perhaps we can learn how to avoid repeating them. Seeing our best ideals brought to life, perhaps we can use those persons and those ideals as models, to build better lives for ourselves and coming generations.

Beginnings

We tend to think of our state as "beginning" when the first English explorers came to these shores. Actually, we would have to go to geologists to examine the origins of this state, for the land was here long before explorers "discovered" it. For that matter, Native Americans—those whom Columbus, thinking he was in India, misnamed "Indians"—had been on this soil for perhaps ten thousand years or more when European and British ships first touched these shores.

We have no written records before the sixteenth century, but American Indian legends, handed down orally through the generations, have been collected, so we will begin with these. (Although they were not written down, we can regard them as the compositions of our first native authors.) Then we will turn to the reports which some of the early explorers prepared to submit to their queen—Elizabeth I. Next we will consider the first settlers—those who braved a long and difficult voyage to attempt to establish a new home on Roanoke Island. Finally, we will see both Native Americans and settlers through the eyes of John Lawson, our state's first historian.

Preview: Native American Myths

Have you ever sat outdoors and looked at the world around you—at river waters tumbling over brown rocks on their way to the sea; at tall pine trees stretching toward the sky; wild roses spilling over fences; turtles scrunching inside their shells—and wondered how it all came to be? If so, you're not alone. Almost every person with normal curiosity has at some time wondered how this earth came into existence. In our technological age, astronomers, physicists, and geologists have provided some scientific information, although no one has anything close to a full explanation. Long before we had the tools to measure chemical and physical forces, people were seeking answers to the mystery of creation. In fact, almost every culture and every religion have their own explanations of how the world was created, of how the earth functions as part of the universe, of how human beings came to exist, and of how good and evil coexist in the same world.

Here are two creation stories from two different American Indian tribes of North Carolina—the Tuscarora and the Cherokee. Before reading, think about the explanations with which you may already be familiar, such as the biblical account of the Garden of Eden; the Greek or Norse myths of creation; or the "Big Bang" theory favored by some scientists. Then, as you read, look for ways in which the Tuscarora and Cherokee legends differ from (or are similar to) those other accounts. (For example, in the Cherokee story, watch for similarities to the biblical story of Noah.)

How the World Began: the Cherokee Myth

James Mooney

The earth is a great island floating in a sea of water, and suspended at each of the four cardinal points by a cord hanging down from the sky vault, which is of solid rock. When the world grows old and worn out, the people will die and the cords will break and let the earth sink down into the ocean, and all will be water again. The Indians are afraid of this.

When all was water, the animals were above in Gălûñ′lătĭ, beyond the arch: but it was very much crowded, and they were wanting more room. They wondered what was below the water, and at last Dâ-

From *Myths of the Cherokees*, by James Mooney; extract from the Nineteenth Annual Report of the Bureau of American Ethnology, Government Printing Office, Washington, DC, 1902.

This authentic re-creation of an 18th-century seven-sided Council House is part of the Oconaluftee Indian Village at Cherokee, NC.

yuni′sĭ, "Beaver's Grandchild," the little Water-beetle, offered to go and see if it could learn. It darted in every direction over the surface of the water, but could find no firm place to rest. Then it dived to the bottom and came up with some soft mud, which began to grow and spread on every side until it became the island which we call the earth. It was afterward fastened to the sky with four cords, but no one remembers who did this.

At first the earth was flat and very soft and wet. The animals were anxious to get down, and sent out different birds to see if it was yet dry, but they found no place to alight and came back again to Găl-ûñ′lătĭ. At last it seemed to be time, and they sent out the Buzzard and told him to go and make ready for them. This was the Great Buzzard, the father of all the buzzards we see now. He flew all over the earth, low down near the ground, and it was still soft. When he reached the Cherokee country, he was very tired, and his wings began to flap and strike the ground, and wherever they struck the earth there was a valley, and where they turned up again there was a mountain.

5

When the animals above saw this, they were afraid that the whole world would be mountains, so they called him back, but the Cherokee country remains full of mountains to this day.

When the earth was dry and the animals came down, it was still dark, so they got the sun and set it in a track to go every day across the island from east to west, just overhead. It was too hot this way, and Tsiska′gĭlĭ′, the Red Crawfish, had his shell scorched a bright red, so that his meat was spoiled; and the Cherokee do not eat it. The conjurers put the sun another hand-breadth higher in the air, but it was still too hot. They raised it another time, and another, until it was seven handbreaths high and just under the sky arch. Then it was right, and they left it so. This is why the conjurers call the highest place Gûlkwâ′gine Di′gălûñ′lătiyûñ′, "the seventh height," because it is seven hand-breadths above the earth. Every day the sun goes along under this arch, and returns at night on the upper side to the starting place.

There is another world under this, and it is like ours in everything—animals, plants, and people—save that the seasons are different. The streams that come down from the mountains are the trails by which we reach this underworld, and the springs at their heads are the doorways by which we enter it, but to do this one must fast and go to water and have one of the underground people for a guide. We know that the seasons in the underworld are different from ours, be-cause the water in the springs is always warmer in winter and cooler in summer than the outer air.

When the animals and plants were first made—we do not know by whom—they were told to watch and keep awake for seven nights, just as young men now fast and keep awake when they pray to their medicine. They tried to do this, and nearly all were awake through the first night, but the next night several dropped off to sleep, and the third night others were asleep, and then others, until, on the seventh night, of all the animals only the owl, the panther, and one or two more were still awake. To these were given the power to see and to go about in the dark, and to make prey of the birds and animals which must sleep at night. Of the trees only the cedar, the pine, the spruce, the holly, and the laurel were awake to the end, and to them it was given to be always green and to be greatest for medicine, but to the others it was said: "Because you have not endured to the end you shall lose your hair every winter."

Men came after the animals and plants. At first there were only a brother and sister until he struck her with a fish and told her to multiply, and so it was. In seven days a child was born to her, and thereafter every seven days another, and they increased very fast until there was danger that the world could not keep them. Then it was made that a woman should have only one child in a year, and it has been so ever since.

MEET THE AUTHOR:
James Mooney (1861 – 1921)

Born in Indiana in 1861, James Mooney was working as a newspaperman when he met John Wesley Powell, who had founded the Bureau of American Ethnology and whose interest in native Americans was contagious. For the remainder of his life Mooney studied American Indians, recording their history and collecting their myths. Of all the tribes, he was most interested in the Cherokee.

James Mooney was not himself a North Carolinian. However, he so carefully recorded the myths of the Cherokees that we can consider his versions to have been spoken by Native Americans who inhabited western North Carolina (as well as eastern Tennessee; northern Georgia, South Carolina, and Alabama; and southern Virginia and West Virginia). The Cherokee myths included here are among the many which he preserved for us.

Language Alert

1. *cardinal*: central, chief
2. conjurers: A *conjurer* is one who *conjures*.
   In fairy stories, witches and goblins are often portrayed as *conjuring* magical happenings. Today in the real world, we may use the term *conjure up*, as in "I think I'll see if I can *conjure up* some supper." Can you guess what *conjure* means and how it differs from *conjure up*? Now check your guess by using the dictionary.

How the World Began: the Tuscarora Myth

F. Roy Johnson

For several centuries the Tuscarora Indians lived upon the North Carolina Coastal Plains before removing to the north to be with their brethren the Five Nations of the Iroquois. Their culture was quite similar to that of their Carolina Indian neighbors. The following is their story of creation as recorded by Elias Johnson, a native chief:

The Tuscarora tradition opens with the notion that there were originally two worlds, or regions of space, that is an upper and lower world. The upper world was inhabited by beings resembling the human race. And the lower world, by monsters, moving on the surface and in the waters, which is in darkness.

When the human species were transferred below, and the lower sphere was about to be rendered fit for their residence, the act of their transference is by these ideas: that a female who began to descend into the lower world, which is a region of darkness, waters, and monsters, she was received on the back of a tortoise, where she gave birth to male twins, and there she expired. The shell of this tortoise expanded into a continent, which, in English is called "island," and is named by the Tuscaroras, *Yowanook*.

One of the children was called *Got-ti-gah-rak-quasht*, or Good Mind, the other *Got-ti-hah-rak-scnh*, or Bad Mind. These two antagonistic principles were at perpetual variance, it being the law of one to counteract whatever the other did. They were not, however, men, but gods, or existences, through whom the Great Spirit or Holder of the Heavens, carried out his purposes.

The first work of Got-ti-gah-rah-quasht was to create the sun out of the head of his dead mother, and the moon and stars out of other parts of her body. The light these gave drove the monsters into the deep waters to hide themselves. He then prepared the surface of the continent and fitted it for human habitation, by making it into creeks, rivers, lakes and plains, and by filling them with the various kinds of animals and vegetable kingdom. He then formed a man and a woman out of the earth, gave them life, and called them *Onwahonwa*, that is, *real people.*

Meanwhile the Bad Mind created mountains, waterfalls, and steeps, caves, reptiles, serpents, apes, and other objects supposed to be injurious to, or in mockery to mankind. He made an attempt also to conceal the land animals in the ground, so as to deprive man of the means of subsistence. This continued opposition to the wishes of the Good Mind, who was perpetually at work, in restoring the effects and displacements, of the wicked devices of the other, at length led to a personal combat, of which the time and instrument of battle was agreed on. They fought two days; the Good Mind using the deer's horn, and the other using wild flag leaves, as arms. Got-ti-gah-rah-quasht, or Good Mind, who had chosen the horn, finally prevailed. His antagonist sank down into a region of darkness, and became the Evil Spirit of the world of despair. Got-ti-gah-rah-quast, having obtained his triumph, retired from the earth.

MEET THE AUTHOR:
F. Roy Johnson (1911 – 1988)

A native of Bladen County in the southeastern part of the state, F. Roy Johnson began writing in high school and never stopped. At Duke University, he worked on the staff of the student newspaper. After graduation, he was associated with newspapers from 1937, when he became publisher of the *Surry Herald* in Virginia, until 1964, when he sold the *Roanoke-Chowan News.* During those years he also interviewed older residents of North Carolina and Virginia, collecting legends, stories, and historical facts that might otherwise have been lost forever. He used that first-hand research as material for more than sixty books dealing with folklore, biographies, and historical events of the region.

Eventually he left newspaper publishing in order to devote himself full time to his books. E. Frank Stephenson, who coauthored four books with Johnson, tells how he worked: "One of the incredible things about this man is that he researched the books, he wrote them, he set the type, he printed them, he bound them by hand, and he sold them. He was a one-man show. I don't know another like him."

In 1976 Johnson was honored by the NC Folklore Society for his contributions to folk-lore nationally. He was honored in 1987 by the Murfreesboro Historical Association and in 1988 by the town of Murfreesboro, both times for his contributions to the Roanoke-Chowan region.

The Tuscarora legends are typical of the material F. Roy Johnson collected and published.

Language Alert:

1. *antagonistic*: having to do with opposing sides
   Two football teams engaged in a game are *antagonists*; so are two people arguing differing viewpoints. Strictly speaking, *antagonism* merely means *opposition*. However, in everyday language, we often use the word to indicate that the two sides are hostile toward each other.
2. *perpetual*: ongoing, lasting forever
   In conversation, we often use *perpetual* to refer to things which only seem to last forever. For example, we may say that two children engage in a *perpetual* quarrel.
3. *variance*: differing
   This word is similar to *antagonism*, but not quite the same. *Variance* may mean a slight difference—*antagonism* refers to major differences.
4. *subsistence*: remaining existent, staying alive
   If someone earns just enough money to *sustain* himself—to purchase only necessary food and shelter and clothing—we would say that he receives only *subsistence* wages.

Reflecting

Now that you have read the two stories, think about the following:
1. Which story seems the most imaginative to you? Why?
2. Which makes the world seem a friendlier, more comfortable place? What makes it seem so?
3. Does the fact that the Tuscaroras lived mainly in the coastal area explain how they characterize mountains in paragraph 6?

The Animals, the Plants, the Human Beings: A Cherokee Myth

James Mooney

Preview

You will recall that in the Cherokee story of creation, animals were given credit for creating firm land on a watery earth, for sculpting the mountains and valleys, and for setting the sun on a track to move across the earth each day. In this myth, the animals hold a conference to consider what to do about human beings, who are not only becoming numerous, but are also beginning to kill animals.

Myths are meant not merely to entertain us with imaginative stories, but also to offer explanations for natural phenomena. As you read the animals' various plans and actions, notice how they account for the behavior and/or physical traits which animals display. Be sure also to look for explanations concerning human beings: (a) certain customs observed by deer hunters; (b) certain kinds of dreams.

In the old days the beasts, birds, fishes, insects, and plants could all talk, and they and the people lived together in peace and friendship. But as time went on the people increased so rapidly that their settlements spread over the whole earth, and the poor animals found themselves beginning to be cramped for room. This was bad enough, but to make it worse Man invented bows, knives, blowguns, spears, and hooks, and began to slaughter the larger animals, birds, and fishes for their flesh or their skins, while the smaller creatures, such as the frogs and worms, were crushed and trodden upon without thought, out of pure carelessness

From *Myths of the Cherokees*, by James Mooney; extract from the Nineteenth Annual Report of the Bureau of American Ethnology, Government Printing Office, Washington, DC, 1902.

or contempt.[1] So the animals resolved to consult upon measures for their common safety.

The Bears were the first to meet in council in their townhouse under Kuwâ'hĭ mountain, the "Mulberry place," and the old White Bear chief presided. After each in turn had complained of the way in which Man killed their friends, ate their flesh, and used their skins for his own purposes, it was decided to begin war at once against him.

Some one asked what weapons Man used to destroy them., "Bows and arrows, of course," cried all the Bears in chorus.

"And what are they made of?" was the next question.

"The bow of wood, and the string of our entrails,"[2] replied one of the Bears.

It was then proposed that they make a bow and some arrows and see if they could not use the same weapons against Man himself. So one Bear got a nice piece of locust wood and another sacrificed himself for the good of the rest in order to furnish a piece of his entrails for the string. But when everything was ready and the first Bear stepped up to make the trial, it was found that in letting the arrow fly after drawing back the bow, his long claws caught the string and spoiled the shot. This was annoying, but some one suggested that they might trim his claws, which was accordingly done, and on a second trial it was found that the arrow went straight to the mark.

But here the chief, the old White Bear, objected, saying it was necessary that they should have long claws in order to be able to climb trees. "One of us has already

died to furnish the bowstring, and if we now cut off our claws we must all starve together. It is better to trust to the teeth and claws that nature gave us, for it is plain that man's weapons were not intended for us."

No one could think of any better plan, so the old chief dismissed the council and the Bears dispersed[3] to the woods and thickets without having concerted[4] any way to prevent the increase of the human race. Had the result of the council been otherwise, we should now be at war with the Bears, but as it is, the hunter does not even ask the Bear's pardon when he kills one.

The Deer next held a council under their chief, the Little Deer, and after some talk decided to send rheumatism to every hunter who should kill one of them unless he took care to ask their pardon for the offense. They sent notice of their decision to the nearest settlement of Indians and told them at the same time what to do when necessity forced them to kill one of the Deer tribe. Now, whenever the hunter shoots a Deer, the Little Deer, who is swift as the wind and can not be wounded, runs quickly up to the spot and, bending over the blood-stains, asks the spirit of the Deer if it has heard the prayer of the hunter for pardon. If the reply be "Yes," all is well, and the Little Deer goes on his

1. contempt: scorn, ridicule, disgust

2. entrails: guts

3. dispersed: broken up, scattered

4. concerted: agreed upon

12

way; but if the reply be "No," he follows on the trail of the hunter, guided by the drops of blood on the ground, until he arrives at his cabin in the settlement, when the Little Deer enters invisibly and strikes the hunter with rheumatism, so that he becomes at once a helpless cripple. No hunter who has regard for his health ever fails to ask pardon of the Deer for killing it, although some hunters who have not learned the prayer may try to turn aside the Little Deer from his pursuit by building a fire behind them in the trail.

Next came the Fishes and Reptiles, who had their own complaints against Man. They held their council together and determined to make their victims dream of snakes twining about them in slimy folds and blowing foul breath in their faces, or to make them dream of eating raw or decaying fish, so that they would lose appetite, sicken, and die. This is why people dream about snakes and fish.

Finally the Birds, Insects, and smaller animals came together for the same purpose, and the Grubworm was chief of the council. It was decided that each in turn should give an opinion, and then they would vote on the question as to whether or not Man was guilty. Seven votes should be enough to condemn him. One after another denounced Man's cruelty and injustice toward the other animals and voted in favor of his death.

The Frog spoke first, saying: "We must do something to check the increase of the race, or people will become so numerous that we shall be crowded from off the earth. See how they have kicked me about because I'm ugly, as they say, until my back is covered with sores;" and here he showed the spots on his skin.

Next came the Bird—no one remembers now which one it was—who condemned Man "because he burns my feet off," meaning the way in which the hunter barbecues birds by impaling[5] them on a stick set over the fire, so that their feathers and tender feet are singed off. Others followed in the same strain. The Ground-squirrel alone ventured to say a good word for Man, who seldom hurt him because he was so small, but this made the others so angry that they fell upon the Ground-squirrel and tore him with their claws, and the stripes are on his back to this day.

They began then to devise[6] and name so many new diseases, one after another, that had not their invention at last failed them, no one of the human race would have been able to survive. The Grubworm grew constantly more pleased as the name of each disease was called off. He rose up in his place and cried: "Wadâñ! [Thanks!] I'm glad some more of them will die, for they are getting so thick that they tread on me." The thought fairly made him shake with joy, so that he fell over backward and could not get on his feet again, but had to wriggle off on his back, as the Grubworm has done ever since.

When the Plants, who were friendly to Man, heard what had been done by the

5. impaling: piercing

6. devise: invent, plan

animals, they determined to defeat the latters' evil designs. Each Tree, Shrub, and Herb, down even to the Grasses and Mosses, agreed to furnish a cure for some one of the diseases named, and each said: "I shall appear to help Man when he calls upon me in his need." Thus came medicine; and the plants, every one of which has its use if we only knew it, furnish the remedy to counteract[7] the evil wrought by the revengeful animals. Even weeds were made for some good purpose, which we must find out for ourselves. When the doctor does not know what medicine to use for a sick man the spirit of the plant tells him.

Reflecting

This myth is many centuries old, but several segments describe conditions that are of serious concern today. Review the first paragraph and the frog's speech in paragraph 12, and find and list statements that apply to our own time.

7. counteract: cancel, act against

The Legend of Raven Rock

F. Roy Johnson

Preview

You may have visited Raven Rock State Park near Lillington. It was designated as a park because of the spectacular rock formation (especially spectacular in an area of the state that for the most part is rather flat and sandy). Perhaps the following legend was composed by a Native American who, struck by the unusual stone outcropping, was inspired to devise an equally unusual story—one filled with danger, intrigue, and romance. Or perhaps it was based on a true incident.

Six miles west of Lillington in Harnett County lies 2,700-acre Raven Rock State Park. Its main attraction is an 152-foot-high boulder called Raven Rock, which towers above the Cape Fear River.

According to legend, before coming of white settlers the rock was named for Raven, son of Hancock, the Tuscarora Indian chief who led his warriors against the English during the Tuscarora War of 1711–13. A second explanation is that once this was a favorite roosting place for ravens.

The rock leans forward, forming at its base a sheltered pavilion with a smooth stone floor. Without the long stairway leading to its top, it could be a dark and hopeless prison, as the legend holds that it was for the young Tuscarora brave.

Before the Indians retired from the Cape Fear country, the Catawbas ruled to the south of the river, and the Tuscaroras held sway over the north of it. In the legend, one Black Jack was the powerful Catawba chief who had a beautiful daughter, White Fawn.

The Catawbas and Tuscaroras were traditional enemies. Few years passed without the young braves of one of the two tribes going to war against the other.

One time Chief Black Jack became very angry when his warriors found a group of Tuscaroras hunting in Catawba country. During the ensuing battle, Raven was captured by Fleet Deer, a Catawba brave, and brought to his camp.

White Fawn was sitting with Eagle Eye, chief Black Jack's sister, as Black Jack and

Fleet Deer emerged from the forest with Raven between them. The maiden was struck by his noble and fearless appearance. She was so smitten that she jumped to her feet and spilled the beads she was making into a chaplet[1]. Although she recognized the prisoner as a hated Tuscarora, she felt a strange attraction to him. Then when Raven's eyes met hers, a new singing entered her heart. Then she turned and saw that Eagle Eye was watching her suspiciously. Then, day after day, as White Fawn looked out over the river and the forest, the newly arriving springtime had new beauty.

Meanwhile Raven was made to hunt and fish for his captors, and one day White Fawn told her father that she would gladly guard the prisoner as he sought food for the village. This would relieve one of his braves; so he agreed.

The days and weeks passed. Each morning White Fawn led Raven back to camp when the dusk began to fall. Soon both became prisoners of a deep love. Spring had changed into summer and summer into autumn when they knew they could not live without each other. And while discussing their plans, they saw a silhouette figure move against the dusk. It was Eagle Eye, who hastened to tell her brother Black Jack of their love. So when they reached camp, Black Jack was waiting with Fleet Deer beside him.

Black Jack told White Fawn to take Fleet Deer's hand, that he was publicly betrothing her to him.

"No," she protested, "I shall marry no one but Raven."

Black Jack grew so angry that he, assisted by Fleet Deer, immediately led Raven to Raven Rock. Tying a strong deer hide rope about his arm pits, they dropped him over the cliff, straight down the perpendicular wall to the narrow ledge of the cave.

Turning to White Fawn, Black Jack said, "No daughter of mine shall marry a Tuscarora; but if your warrior can live in that cave a year without food and water, then you may claim him."

Before another sun had set, White Fawn devised a plan to keep Raven alive. If she was careful not to be discovered, she might let down food and water to him with a rope.

After that, White Fawn secreted half of her food beneath her blanket, and when night came and all the camp was asleep, she darted through the forest to Raven Rock. Wrapping the food in a doe skin, she tied it to the end of the rope and let it down to the ledge of the cave. Then she let down jugs of water, blankets, twigs, and a flint. Then when the wind had ceased to stir the forest, she would call to her lover with mourning love cry of the dove, and he would answer with the hoarse call of the mating raven.

With winter the ravens came, seeking protection against the cold; and the young Indian made friends with them. But after first snow White Fawn could no longer go to the cliff with food, lest her footprints be discovered, and then Raven would be slain. Her heart was filled with fear for him, alone and cold in the barren cave.

1. *chaplet*: a string of beads.

But Raven had his flint and a generous heap of faggots White Fawn had let down before the snow began, and he scooped snow from the cave's ledge for water. The ravens had made their nests in the cave, and soon there was an abundance of eggs. These Raven cooked over his fire, and he killed some of the birds and broiled them over the coals.

Spring followed winter; then summer and autumn again. The year was spent, and Black Jack and Fleet Deer went once more to Raven Rock. They found White Fawn waiting for them, her eyes sparkling with happiness. She watched them uncoil their leather rope and slide it over the cliff. In a moment there was a tug at the rope; then there was another tug. They began to pull, and within a few moments Raven stood before them well and sound. White Fawn flung herself into his arms.

True to his promise, Black Jack gave his only daughter to Raven. They were married at the Catawba camp and then went in their bridal canoe up the Cape Fear to the camp of the Tuscaroras. They were followed by Black Jack and his braves. Once the lovers were safely at their new home, the Catawbas sent their canoes back down stream to their camp fires on the south bank of the Cape Fear.

Now after nearly three centuries, story tellers say, the spirits of the two lovers may be heard at Raven Rock. Upon a warm spring night, if a visitor listens quietly, he may hear the call of the dove, and he may even hear the lover's answer—the hoarse mating call of the raven.

Eugenia Johnson

The illustration, which first appeared in F. Roy Johnson's book, *North Carolina Indian Legends and Myths*, is by Johnson's daughter-in-law, Eugenia Johnson. She illustrated several of his books. A native of Waynesville, Eugenia Johnson received her undergradu ate degree at Berea College in Kentucky and her master's degree at East Carolina University. Currently she lives in Almond and teaches commercial art at Southwestern Community College near Sylva.

Language Alert: Understanding in Context

See if you can figure out the meanings of the italicized words, given in context as they appear in the story. You are given three choices for each:

1. During the *ensuing* battle, Raven was captured by Fleet Deer. . . . "
   a. vicious   b. following   c. long
2. "[The maiden] was so *smitten* that she jumped to her feet. . . . "
   a. suddenly frightened   b. utterly overjoyed   c. affected by sharp feeling
3. "Raven had his flint and a generous heap of *faggots*. . . . "
   a. bundles of sticks   b. seasonings for food   c. warm clothing

Reflecting

This legend is based on a situation that has appeared many times in very different writings: the love between two young people from warring or feuding families. Mark Twain tells a similar story in his famous novel, *Huckleberry Finn*. Shakespeare used the situation in *Romeo and Juliet*. In Twain's story, the feuding families renew bloodshed when they discover the young couple has eloped. In Shakespeare's, after the lovers both die, the two families, grown wiser through their tragedy, make peace. Can you tell from this legend whether the love between White Fawn and Raven has any permanent effect on their families?

Exploring the New Land

First Voyage to Roanoke

Arthur Barlowe

Preview

Imagine yourself to be a sixteenth-century Englishman. You live in a land whose culture has been richly influenced by Europe and even by trade with the Orient. The large stretches of farm acreage and woodland are broken up by many small hamlets and several large cities. (By modern standards, none of those cities were quite metropolitan. London, the largest, could boast only about 100,000 citizens—far less than Charlotte or Raleigh in the 1980s. In fact, all of England had about a million fewer citizens than North Carolina does today.)

Your nation has survived many internal squabbles and is now united under a royal family and governing body. It boasts a great navy. In London, theaters present plays by Christopher Marlowe and William Shakespeare. The queen dresses in silks and velvets. On special occasions she wears a golden crown adorned with shimmering jewels.

You now have been sent all the way across the Atlantic to what is referred to as the New World—a place sparsely inhabited by small clusters of people whose appearance, language, and traditions are markedly different from your own. The natives live in settlements, but there are no cities; they have canoes, but no ships; their dress and houses, even their food and crops, are strange to you. Can you imagine yourself stepping onto the shores of Roanoke Island and seeing sights no Englishman has ever seen before?

Published in Old South Leaflets, No. 92. New York: Burt Franklin Research and Work Series.

The second of July we found shole water, where we smelt so sweet, and so strong a smel, as if we had bene in the midst of some delicate garden abounding with all kinde of odoriferous flowers, by which we were assured, that the land could not be farre distant: and keeping good watch, and bearing but slacke saile, the fourth of the same moneth we arrived upon the coast which we supposed to be a continent and firme lande, and we sayled along the same a hundred and twentie English miles before we could finde any entrance, or river issuing into the Sea. The first that appeared unto us, we entred, though not without some difficultie, & cast anker about three harquebuz-shot within the havens mouth on the left hand of the same: and after thanks given to God for our safe arrivall thither, we manned our boats and went to view the land next adjoyning, and to take possession of the same, in the right of the Queenes most excellent Majestie. . . . We viewed the land about us, being, whereas we first landed, very sandie and low towards the waters side, but so full of grapes, as the very beating and surge of the Sea overflowed them, of which we found such plentie, as well there as in all places else, both on the sand and on the greene soile on the hils, as in the plaines, as well on every little shrubbe, as also climing towardes the tops of high Cedars, that I thinke in all the world the like abundance is not to be found. . . .

The Native Americans Arrive

The next day there came unto us divers boates, and in one of them the Kings brother, accompanied with fortie or fiftie men, very handsome and goodly people, and in their behaviour as mannerly and civill as any of Europe. His name was Granganimeo, and the king is called Wingina, the countrey Wingandacoa. . . . The manner of his comming was in this sort: hee left his boates altogether as the first man did a little from the shippes by the shore, and came along to the place over against the shipes, followed with fortie men. When he came to the place, his servants spread a long matte upon the ground, on which he sate downe, and at the other ende of the matte foure others of his companie did the like, the rest of his men stood round about him, somewhat a farre off: when we came to the shore to him with our weapons, hee never mooved from his place, nor any of the other foure, nor never mistrusted any harme to be offered from us, but sitting still he beckoned us to come and sit by him, which we performed: and being set hee made all signes of joy and welcome, striking on his head and his breast and afterwardes on ours to shew wee were all one, smiling and making shewe the best he could of al love, and familiaritie. After hee had made a long speech unto us, wee presented him with divers things, which hee received very joyfully, and thankefully. None of the company durst speake one worde all the time: only the four which were at the other end, spake one in the others eare very softly. . . .

Visiting the Indian Village

The evening following wee came to an Island which they call Roanoak. . . . And at the North end thereof was a village of nine houses, built of Cedar, and fortified round about with sharpe trees, to keepe out their enemies, and the entrance into it made like a turnepike very artificaly; when wee came towardes it, standing neere unto the waters side, the wife of Granganimo the Kings brother came running out to meete us very cheerfully and friendly, her husband was not then in the village; some of her people shee commanded to drawe our boate on shore. . . . others she appointed to cary us on their backes to the dry ground, and others to bring our oares into the house for feare of stealing. When we were come into the utter roome, having five roomes in her house, she caused us to sit downe by a great fire, and after tooke off our clothes and washed them, and dryed them againe: some of the women plucked off our stockings and washed them, some washed our feete in warme water, and she herselfe tooke great paines to see all things ordered in the best maner shee could, making great haste to dress some meate for us to eate....

We were entertained with all love and kindnesse, and with much bountie, after their maner, as they could possibly devise. We found the people most gentle, loving and faithfull, voide of all guile and treason, and such as live after the manner of the golden age. The people onely care howe to defend themselves from the cold in their short winter, and to feed themselves with such meat as the soile affoordeth.... While we were at meate, there came in at the gates two or three men with their bowes and arrowes from hunting, whom when wee espied, we beganne to looke one towardes another, and offered to reach our weapons: but assoone as shee espied our mistrust, shee was very much mooved, and caused some of her men to runne out, and take away their bowes and arrowes and breake them, and withall beate the poore fellowes out of the gate againe.

When we departed in the evening and would not tary all night she was very sorry, and gave us into our boate our supper halfe dressed, pottes and all, and brought us to our boate side, in which wee lay all night, remooving the same a prettie distance from the shoare: she perceiving our jealousie, was much grieved, and sent divers men and thirtie women, to sit all night on the banke side by us, and sent us into our boates five mattes to cover us from the raine, using very many wordes, to entreate us to rest in their houses: but because wee were fewe men, and if we had miscaried, the voyage had bene in very great danger, wee durst not adventure any thing, although there was no cause of doubt: for a more kinde and loving people there can not be found in the worlde, as far as we have hitherto had triall.

Arthur Barlowe (no known dates)

Strictly speaking, Arthur Barlowe is not a North Carolinian, but he was one of the first English explorers to set foot on North Carolina soil, and through his vivid description we can see how this land and its inhabitants looked before colonization forever changed the landscape and the life of Native Americans.

We know little of Barlowe except that he was a member of the household of Sir Walter Raleigh, who supported the Virginia Expedition of 1584, and that he served as second captain to Philip Amadas, leader of the expedition. The exploration lasted from the end of April through mid-September. When he and Amadas returned to England, they took two Indian leaders, Manteo and Wanchese, back with them.

Language Alert

A. Antiquated Spelling:

This selection has been printed with the original spelling; for example, *where* is spelled *wher*; *month* is spelled *moneth*. Furthermore, some words which we spell as two words, Barlowe spells as one: for example, *assoone* (as soon). The reverse is also true: what Barlowe writes as *a farre*, we would write as *afar*. (You may have heard that English spelling was not made regular until the eighteenth century. In fact, William Shakespeare spelled his last name several different ways!)

Think of this material as something written in code; see if you can guess—from context or from pronunciation—what the words are. You will, of course, read more slowly than if the selection were "translated" into modern spelling, but you may find it amusing to test your wits as you figure out the words. Perhaps you can work in pairs or groups to decode the explorers' account of their adventure.

B. Key Words:

1. *abounding*: great in number or supply (This word has the same root as our more common word *abundant*.)
2. *shole*: (modern spelling: *shoal*) a shallow place in a body of water, a sandbar
3. *harquebus*: a heavy but portable gun invented during the fifteenth century (spelled *harquebuz* in the explorers' account)
4. *divers*: various (Notice the similarity to our word *diverse*, which means unlike, having variety.)
5. *durst*: dared

Reflecting

1. Notice the ways in which the explorers express their delight with this new world. Jot down the phrases which praise the beauty or the abundance.
2. Although the Indians could not communicate through language, they made it clear that they welcomed the strangers and wanted to live in peace. List the things they did to communicate these messages.
3. The Indians lived much more simply than the English, but even in these short selections, we have evidence that they were an intelligent people with many skills and with sophisticated traditions. List items that provided this evidence. (Hint: Look at what they wear; at the ceremony surrounding the King; at their hospitality to strangers; at what they have built; and at the evidence that they understood the need for sanitation and health care.)

Carolina's Boat People

Rebecca Rust

Is the land so unloving,
so hostile a host,
that they choose this gnawed hull
and the anarchy of the sea?
So many, so many
ride the splintered ark,
press the bow, jam the stern.
Their bones scrape the deck,
the oils of their bodies mingle,
one flesh quickening.

Heavy they ride, rise and fall,
their hopes, the sea.
With each oncoming wave
the throat of the sea widens,
swallowing, swallowing.

quickening: coming to life

Preview

Are you familiar with the term "boat people"? In recent years it has been used to refer to refugees from Vietnam and other Southeast Asian countries, people who were fleeing invaders of their lands. Crowded together on small ships, many underwent long, dangerous voyages as they sought refuge in free nations.

If you have seen in Manteo the Elizabeth II, a replica of the ship which brought those first English settlers to this land, you know that they were also crammed tightly together in very cramped quarters. No plush cruise ship here; no private quarters with soft beds and baths; no gourmet dinners in glossy dining rooms!

As you read, try to imagine why anyone would leave his/her homeland and undertake a long, difficult, dangerous journey to an unknown land.

MEET THE AUTHOR:
Rebecca Rust (1928–   )

Rebecca Rust, who began writing a weekly Girl Scout column in *The Raleigh Times* when she was only twelve, now lives in Raleigh where she works as a writer, editor, and publisher. Her own poems, published in many lands, have earned numerous awards, not only in North Carolina but in Hawaii, Japan, New Zealand, and the People's Republic of China. Tar Heel writers probably know her best for her work with the North Carolina Haiku Society, which she helped found in Raleigh in 1979. The society now includes seventy-three members from fifteen states and Canada, and their work has appeared in publications over the world.

Ms. Rust graduated from Duke University with a degree in psychology and worked for some years as an exhibits curator for the Hall of History at the North Carolina Department of Archives and History. One day while shopping in a department store, she came

across a book on haiku. It sparked an interest which has never diminished. In addition to composing her own poetry and working with the Haiku Society, she has written a book describing the techniques for writing haiku: *The Outside of a Haiku.*

Ms. Rust gives two bits of advice to those who wish to write well:
1. Write only about what excites your interest; and
2. Learn grammar so that you can say what you really mean.

Language Alert

The poet uses the phrase "the anarchy of the sea." *Anarchy* is a term commonly associated with organizations and governments. Look it up and consider how it might be appropriately applied to the sea.

Reflecting

1. Notice that Rebecca Rust calls this boat a "splintered ark." In what way are the passengers like those animals who crowded together in Noah's ark? (Think of why the animals were on the ark.)
2. Rebecca Rust not only creates vivid pictures with the meanings of words; she also uses the sounds of words to create a kind of *word music* in the following ways:
   a. repeated initial sounds (alliteration): **h**ostile a **h**ost
   b. repeated words or phrases:
      So many, so many
      swallowing, swallowing
   c. similar rhythms:

      press the bow, jam the stern
      Heavy they ride, rise and fall

   Marking the beat of these lines, you get:
      /-/, /-/   /--/, /-/

   (Notice how those rhythms imitate the rhythm of rising and falling waves.)

From *North Carolina's 400 Years: Signs Along the Way,* ed. Ronald H. Bayes. Copyright © 1986 by North Carolina Poetry Society. Reprinted by permission of the author and the North Carolina Poetry Society.

Croatoan

Kate Kelly Thomas

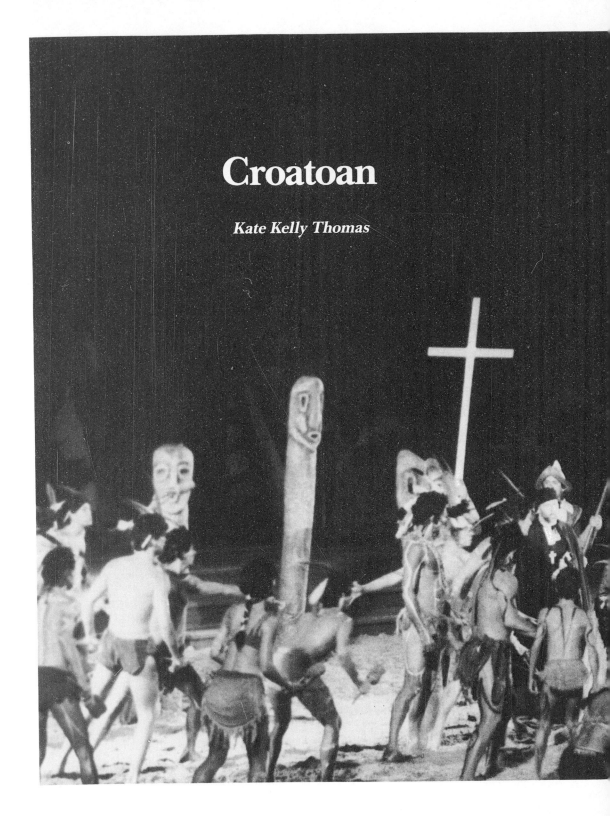

We scan the seascape for ships
that never come
and tread cobblestones
of hunger and death.
A hollow cough leaves our young men
weak and yellow,
our children cry
our women whisper, "What will we do?"

I keep the watch all day.
Specks on the horizon
bring shouts of joy, but hope falls
heavy as burial dirt.
The ocean is a monument
of cold wet winds
and wolves are howling in the west.

The Brown Man points to tall trees
fishing waters and fertile ground.
I carve the message. . . .

Preview: Croatoan

Have you ever, even for a few minutes, felt lost and abandoned? Perhaps you got separated from your family in the middle of a large, strange city, or found yourself momentarily alone in a park, with the rest of your group out of sight. Remember how you felt exposed to whatever dangers might be nearby? Perhaps you even experienced a moment of panic, afraid that you would fail to find your way to familiar surroundings and friendly people.

How much more desolate the settlers of the so-called Lost Colony must have felt during the long months—months that stretched into three years—while they waited for their leader, Governor John White, to return from England with supplies. They were in a strange land which had not even been mapped. They lacked medicine and equipment. Some of the natives were hostile.

Imagine yourself on Roanoke Island, as one of the younger people among the settlers. An Indian chieftain has just convinced the people in your settlement that you must all move with him to another area. How would you react? What might you expect? What might you fear? How do you think the other settlers would respond to this situation?

MEET THE AUTHOR:
Kate Kelly Thomas (1919–   )

Kate Kelly Thomas has never lived far from her Harnett County birthplace, but through her imagination and her gift for words, she has explored widely.

She began writing poetry while she was a student at Benhaven High School, and studied writing at Sandhills Community College and Central Carolina Technical College. A story she wrote while at CCTC won two awards. She began writing consistently in 1974, after her five children were all grown and had moved away from the Lee County farm which she and her husband developed.

Using her original poetry as her talent, she was crowned the first "Ms. Senior Citizen of North Carolina." She especially enjoys writing humorous verse. Because her best thoughts seem to come at night, she sometimes leaves her bed "to catch them on paper." She has read her poems on radio and television as well as in a public series, "Poetry under the Stars," at Morehead Planetarium in Chapel Hill. Her work has appeared in three anthologies and a collection, *Both Sides of the Page*. She continues writing as she enjoys her eleven grandchildren and five great-grandchildren.

Reflecting

1. Did your feelings and expectations resemble those expressed in Kate Kelly Thomas's poem? In what ways did they differ? (Consider mood and details about the condition of the settlers.) Notice the last three lines of the poem. Do they sound hopeful? Fearful? Resigned?

2. Review the poem to notice the phrases and words that paint a vivid picture. For example, instead of *telling* us "Our young men are sickly," she *shows* us: "A hollow cough leaves our young men / weak and yellow."

   Instead of *making a direct statement*, "we lost hope," she *uses a simile* to make hope seem concrete: "... hope falls / heavy as burial dirt."

From *North Carolina's 400 Years: Signs Along the Way,* ed. Ronald H. Bayes. Copyright © 1986 by North Carolina Poetry Society. Reprinted by permission of the author and the North Carolina Poetry Society.

The Legend of the White Doe

Two Versions

In human history, when you find a mystery you frequently find a legend built around it. The mysterious disappearance of the Lost Colony has never been satisfactorily explained. Especially haunting is the fact that one of the citizens of that colony was Virginia Dare, the first European settler's child born in America. A Native American legend centers on Virginia Dare as a beautiful young woman. It is such a fascinating story that it has been retold repeatedly by a variety of writers, each of whom devised his/her own form for the telling.

The White Doe

The Fate of Virginia Dare

Sallie Southall Cotten

Preview

For her version of the story, Sallie Southall Cotten adapted the rhythms
and style of the most famous poem ever written about a Native American.
Here are her opening lines. Can you name the other poem which sounds
so much like this one? (Try reading this aloud; it seems to echo the beat of
tribal drums!)

In the Land-of-Wind-and-Water,
Loud the sea bemoaned its sameness;
Dashing shoreward with impatience
To explore the landward mysteries.
On the sand the waves spread boldly,
Vainly striving to reach higher;
Then abashed by vain ambition,
Glided to their ordained duty.
There the pine-tree, tall and stately,
Whispered low the ocean's murmur;
Strove to soothe the restless water
With its lullaby of sighing.

If you said this poem resembles Henry Wadsworth Longfellow's "Hiawatha," you guessed right. The style is very much Longfellow's, but the
story is very different from that of the young Indian, Hiawatha.

Because this poem is very long and complex, the version below offers a
prose summary in brackets (which will provide the basic action) inter-
spersed with segments of Sallie Southall Cotten's poem (which will give
you the picturesque details and the flavor of her tale).

[While Governor White was still in England trying to get supplies for the colony, Chief Wanchese led his tribe to destroy Fort Raleigh, planning to kill everyone there. During the attack, Chief Manteo, who had been friendly to the colonists, persuaded survivors—including Eleanor Dare and her infant daughter, Virginia—to come with him to his village, where he and his tribe would protect them. We return to the poem at the point when Eleanor Dare and Manteo prepare to get into his boat:]

As her sad eyes turned upon him
Man-te-o was moved with pity
For the brave and tender woman,
Friendless in the land without him.

On the brow of Pale-Face baby
First he made the Holy Cross-Sign;
Then upon the sad-eyed mother
Traced the sign her people taught him;
Then again the sacred symbol
Outlined on his own dark forehead;
And with open hand uplifted
Sealed his promise of protection;
Linking thus his pledge of safety
With her faith in Unseen Power.

Mute with grief, she trusted in him;
In his boat they crossed the water,
While the night fell like a mantle
Spread in mercy to help save them.

When in Cro-a-to-an they landed,
There they found the few survivors
Of that day of doom to many,
Glad once more to greet each other.
Man-te-o within his wigwam
From the cold wind gave them shelter,
Shared with them his furry bear-skins,
Made them warm, and warmth gave courage
To meet life's relentless duties.

Then he summoned all the people.
Called the old men and the young men,
Bade the squaws to come and listen,
Showed the papoose to the women.
They gazed on its tender whiteness,
Stroked the mother's flaxen tresses;
" 'Tis a snow-papoose" they whispered,
"It will melt when comes the summer."

Man-te-o said to the warriors:
"Ye all know these Pale-Face people
Whom Wan-ches-e sought to murder,
They have often made us welcome.
Brave their hearts, but few are living,
If left friendless these will perish;
We have store of corn and venison,
They are hungry, let us feed them;
They have lightning for their arrows,
Let them teach us how to shoot it.
They with us shall search the forest,
And our game shall be abundant;
Let them teach us their strange wisdom
And become with us one people."

And the old men, grave in counsel,
And the young men, mute with deference,
While the uppowoc[1] was burning
Pondered on his words thus spoken,
And to Man-te-o gave answer:
"All your words are full of wisdom;
We will share with them our venison,
They shall be as our own people."

[Thus were the surviving colonists received and protected. As the years passed, Virginia Dare grew to be a beautiful young woman whom the Indians called "Winona-Ska." Their admiration was so great that they regarded her almost as a priestess.

1. Uppowoc: tobacco

One brave, Okisko, not only admired her, but loved her deeply. Despite the fact that she felt only sisterly love towards him, he waited devotedly, hoping that eventually she would choose him for a mate. Another Indian also fell in love with her—Old Chico, the magician and witch doctor. A jealous and evil man, he decided that if he could not have her, no one else could either. So he devised a plan. From the shallow waters he collected mussel-pearls which he knew imprisoned the spirits of water nymphs who had displeased the King of the Sea. He knew, too, that these nymphs would be grateful enough to do anything for him if he freed them. So Old Chico made a magic necklace from the pearls. Then he built a new canoe and asked Winona to go with him to Roanoke:]

Where the waves are white with blossoms,
Where the grapes hang ripe in clusters
Come with me and drink their juices.

[As they floated across the water, he gave her the pearl necklace, which he had already bewitched so that once they were on land, he could work his evil magic. Then they came to shore:]

Lithe and happy she sprang shoreward,
When, from where here foot first lightly
Pressed the sand with human imprint,
On—away—towards the thicket
Sprang *a White Doe,* fleet and graceful.

[The mourning Indians searched long and diligently for their beloved Winona-Ska but, finding no trace, gave her up as having met some mysterious end. In the meantime, braves began to tell of an equally mysterious white doe in the woods of Roanoke. She was exquisitely beautiful and had become a leader of the other deer. She also seemed impervious to hunters: no arrow, from even the most skillful hunter, could strike her. The women of the tribe, adding these two mysteries together—and knowing of both Chico's love and his black magic—wove a story explaining that Winona-Ska still lived, but as doe rather than woman.

Encouraged by this news, Okisko went to Roanoke repeatedly, but although he saw the doe frequently, he could not capture her. So he turned to another mighty magician, Wenaudon, who hated Chico and was delighted with the opportunity to humiliate his rival. He gave Okisko directions for making a magic arrow. It was a very complicated task:]

"In a shark's tooth, long and narrow
In a closely wrought triangle,
Set three mussel-pearls of purple,
Smooth and polished with much rubbing.
To an arrow of witch-hazel,
New, and fashioned very slender,
Set the shark's tooth, long and narrow,
With its pearl-inlaid triangle.
From the wing of living heron
Pluck one feather, white and trusty;
With this feather wing the arrow,
That it swerve not as it flyeth.
Fashioned thus with care and caution,
Let no mortal eye gaze on it;
Tell no mortal of your purpose;
Secretly at sunset place it
In the spring of magic water.
Let it rest there through three sunsets;
Then when sunrise gilds the tree-tops
Take it dripping from the water,
At the rising sun straight point it,
While three times these words repeating:
Mussel-pearl arrow, to her heart go;
Loosen the fetters which bind the White Doe;
Bring the lost maiden back to O-kis-ko.
With this arrow hunt the White Doe,
Have no timid fear of wounding;
When her heart it enters boldly
Chi-co's charm will melt before it."

[With the hope of releasing his beloved from Chico's spell, Okisko hurried home and began doing just as he had been instructed. Soon he was ready once more to seek the white doe. Unfortunately, at the same time, two other braves decided to hunt the fabled animal. Wingina, a chieftain, boasted that he could do what no other hunter had done: kill the white doe, feast on her meat, and use her skin for his cloak. Meanwhile, young Wanchese, son of old Chief Wanchese,

came to Roanoke for the same purpose as the other two. Like
Wingina, he boasted of his valor and skill; like Okisko, he possessed
what he believed to be a magic arrowhead—a silver one presented
to him by Queen Elizabeth when he had visited England.

As luck would have it, the three men, aided by other Indians who
were to stalk the deer, all arrived on Roanoke and spotted the beautiful white doe at the same instant.]

Where the deer were wont to wander
All the hunters took their stations,
While the stalkers sought the forest,
From its depths to start the deer-herd.

Near the shore Win-gin-a lingered
That he first might shoot his arrow,
And thus have the certain glory
Of the White Doe's death upon him.

By a pine tree stood Wan-ches-e
With his silver arrow ready;
While O-kis-ko, unseen, waited
Near by in his chosen ambush,
Where he oft had watched the White Doe,
Where he knew she always lingered.

Soon the stalkers with great shouting
Started up the frightened red deer;
On they came through brake and thicket,
In the front the White Doe leading,
With fleet foot and head uplifted,
Daring all the herd to follow.

Easy seemed the task of killing,
So Win-gin-a twanged his bow-string,
But his arrow fell beside her
As she sprang away from danger.

Through the tanglewood, still onward,
Head uplifted, her feet scorning
All the wealth of bright-hued foliage
Which lay scattered in her pathway.
Up the high sand-dunes she bounded,
In her wake the whole herd followed,
While the arrows aimed from ambush
Fell around her ever harmless.

On she sped, towards the water,
Nostrils spread to sniff the sea-breeze;
Through the air a whizzing arrow
Flew, but did not touch the White Doe;
But a stag beside her bounding
Wounded fell among the bushes,
And the herd fled in confusion,
Waiting now not for the leader.

On again, with leaping footsteps,
Tossing head turned to the sea-shore,
For one fatal minute standing
Where the White Man's Fort had once stood;
In her eyes came wistful gleamings
Like a lost hope's fleeting shadow.

While with graceful poise she lingered,
Swift, Wan-ches-e shot his arrow
Aimed with cruel thought to kill her;
While from near and secret ambush,
With unerring aim, O-kis-ko
Forward sent his magic arrow,
Aimed with thought of love and mercy.

To her heart straight went both arrows,
And with leap of pain she bounded
From the earth, and then fell forward,
Prone, amidst the forest splendor.

O-kis-ko, with fond heart swelling,
Wan-ches-e, with pride exultant,
To the Doe both sprang to claim it,
Each surprised to see the other.

Suddenly, within the forest,
Spread a gleaming mist around them,
Like a dense white fog in summer,
So they scarce could grope their pathway.
Slowly, as if warmed by sunbeams,
From one spot the soft mist melted,
While within its bright'ning dimness,
With the misty halo 'round her,
Stood a beautiful white maiden,
Stood the gentle, lost Wi-no-na.

Through her heart two arrows crosswise
Pierced the flesh with cruel wounding;
Downward flowed the crimson blood-tide,
Staining red the snow-white doe-skin
Which with grace her form enveloped,
While her arms with pleading gesture
To O-kis-ko were outstretching.

As they gazed upon the vision,
All their souls with wonder filling;
While the white mist slowly melted,
Prostrate fell the wounded maiden.

Then revealed was all the myst'ry,
Then they saw what had befallen.
To her heart the magic arrow
First had pierced, and lo! Wi-no-na
Once more breathed in form of maiden.

But while yet the charm was passing
Came the arrow of Wan-ches-e;
To her heart it pierced unerring,
Pierced the pearl-inlaid triangle,
Struck and broke the shark's tooth narrow,
Charm and counter-charm undoing;
Leaving but a mortal maiden
Wounded past the hope of healing.

Woe to love, and hope, and magic!
Woe to hearts whom death divideth!
While upon her bleeding bosom
Fatal arrows made the Cross-Sign,
Wistful eyes she turned to Heaven;
"O forget not your Wi-no-na,"
Whispered she unto O-kis-ko,
As her soul passed to the silence.

[So as Wenaudon had planned, Okisko's arrow had transformed the doe back to human form, but Wanchese's arrow, striking an instant later, had killed the young woman. The grieving Okisko, hoping yet to save the woman he loved, ran back to the enchanted spring into which he had dipped the arrow earlier and plunged his arrow into it. To his surprise, the bubbling waters vanished, the arrow took root, and green leaves began to appear as the arrow turned into the stem of a vine. This plant became a sturdy grapevine from which cuttings were taken to be transplanted throughout the country.]

The legend of the White Doe may be at least half fantasy, but the grapevine is not only real—it still exists! Known as the Mother Vineyard, it is said to be 300 years old. We know that it was already a very old vine in 1750. Those who do not believe in magic but still like to give the Mother Vineyard a legendary basis claim that it was planted by colonists from the Lost Colony.

And what about Winona? Okisko ran back to look for her body, and although it had disappeared, in the distance a white doe bounded away. To this day it is rumored that she wanders the woods of Roanoke and the nearby mainland. True believers vow that, as of old, she cannot be captured or wounded—and woe befalls any who try to harm her.

The "Old Mother Vineyard" on Roanoke Island.

MEET THE AUTHOR:
Sallie Southall Cotten (1846–1929)

Although she was born fifteen years before the Civil War, Sallie Southall Cotten was in many ways a very modern woman. After attending public school in Murfreesboro, she graduated from Greensboro Female College and taught school before marrying Robert Randolph Cotten. She not only helped her husband manage two plantations in Pitt County and rear nine children, but she organized a school and became a distinguished Episcopalian churchwoman. In 1893, Governor Elias Carr appointed her as one of the North Carolina managers for the Chicago World's Fair. She traveled the state gathering materials to display. One of her exhibitions, a collection of books written by North Carolina women, won a World's Fair medal and diploma.

Somehow Sallie Cotten also found time to write and publish a number of articles and poems, of which "The White Doe" is her most famous. She wrote the poem in 1901, donating it as a fund-raising project for the North Carolina Federation of Women's Clubs, which she had helped found and for which she had served as first president.

Toward the end of her life, at a gathering of women in Boston, Sallie Southall Cotten was introduced as the "Julia Ward Howe of the South,"[1] and received a standing ovation. Two university dormitories (at East Carolina University and at UNC-G) are named for her. Perhaps more unusual, during World War II her contributions to our state and nation were recognized by the naming of a Liberty freighter for her. The ship was christened in 1943 by her granddaughter.

Sincerely Yours
Sallie Southall Cotten

[1] Julia Ward Howe (1819–1910): a writer, lecturer, and social reformer known best for writing the lyrics to "The Battle Hymn of the Republic."

Preview

One of the reasons legends live for centuries is that frequently their chief characters are said to exist even after death and appear to people throughout the years. You have read how it is believed that the White Doe still inhabits the forests near Roanoke. At the turn of this century, Benjamin Sledd wrote a poem in which he shows us how the legend lives on, coming as a vision to a hunter drowsing by his campfire. He uses words we seldom use now—*raiment*, instead of *clothing*; *woe*, instead of *sorrow*; *steed* instead of *horse*—but otherwise, those of us with vivid imaginations can picture the same event happening today.

The Vision of the Milk-White Doe

Benjamin Sledd

The hunter by his lonely fire
Wakens in sweet, unknown desire,
To watch by the dim, delusive light
What seems a woman in raiment white,
Among the forest shadows go:—
Lingering it goes, and backward turns,
Like some sad spirit that vainly yearns
To break the bonds of its voiceless woe;
But the light flares up from the dying brands,
And gazing out of the darkness stands
Only a milk-white doe.

A moment he marks her large dark eyes
Gazing in mournful human wise,
Then falters and sinks the faithless light.
Again the gleam as of raiment white,
The woods are stirred with a footfall slight;
And like the dawn-wind wandering by,
The presence fades with a deep drawn sigh,
As breaks a far-heard, phantom sound
Of galloping steed and baying hound—
Then only the silence and the night.

delusive: tending to delude, deceive, or mislead
wise: a way of doing something

46

Benjamin Sledd (1846—1940)

Benjamin Sledd was an English professor at Wake Forest College in the early part of this century. A native of Virginia, he had begun studying for a Ph.D. at Johns Hopkins University in Baltimore, Maryland, when his eyesight began to fail. Doctors advised him that he must take care to preserve his sight—that the close study required to obtain a Ph.D. was out of the question. A few years later, his hearing, too, began to fail.

A lesser man might have retired in self-pity. Instead, Benjamin Sledd undertook a teaching career at Wake Forest College, serving there for over fifty years. He was greatly beloved by his students, who fondly called him "Old Slick." Among those students were John Charles McNeill (see p. 000) and Gerald W. Johnson, both of whom became well-known writers.

Benjamin Sledd was widely known as a master teacher of poetry. He also wrote and published two collections of his own verse.

Reflecting

Assume that, as the legend tells us, the white doe still wanders the woodlands of Roanoke. Of course, today those woodlands are not as thick and flourishing as they were in the sixteenth century. Manteo is now a thriving town. Nags Head and surrounding areas are bustling tourist areas. The broad highways on Roanoke Island are lined with restaurants, motels, shops, and row upon row of beach cottages.

Write a story in which the white doe leaves the woods one night to move about in this much-changed area. You might write from the doe's point of view. (What does she think of the changes? How does she feel?) Perhaps, like Benjamin Sledd, you might create a person who encounters this ghostly deer. See if you can do what both Sallie Southall Cotten and Benjamin Sledd did—create an air of mystery about this fabled creature.

From *The Watchers of the Hearth,* by Benjamin Sledd, published by Gorham Press, Boston. Copyright © 1897 by Benjamin Sledd.

Our Earliest State History

From *A New Voyage to Carolina*

MEET THE AUTHOR:
John Lawson (Birthdate unknown—1712)

We don't know much about the early life of John Lawson, whose book is the only North Carolina contribution to American colonial history. We do know that he began life as an English gentleman and that he was well educated. We also know that on a journey to Rome, he met a man who had been to the New World. Inspired by his companion's stories, John Lawson gave up his comfortable status in England to try adventures on these shores.

Once here, he proved to be a leader. He was one of the incorporators of Bath Town, the first town established in North Carolina. Later he served as trustee of the Bath library, the first public library in North Carolina. His book was published in 1709.

Two years later he began his last journey in this country. With a Swiss adventurer, two blacks, and two trusted Native Americans, he began exploring the Neuse River to determine whether it could be navigated. Unfortunately, the Indian tribes of the area, led by the Tuscaroras, were in the process of organizing for battle against the whites. Lawson, who had always dealt fairly with the Indians, must have believed that he was immune to their anger, for he continued his journey, though it required him to be in repeated contact with the Indians.

His party was going up the river when they were surrounded and seized by Indians who took them to King Hencock's town, Catechna. They were tried and acquitted; in fact, they were ordered to be set free the next day. However, some other Indians who arrived in the settlement questioned why these white men should be set at liberty. So Lawson and DeGraffenreid were tried again and sentenced to death. DeGraffenreid somehow managed to talk his way out of this horrible fate, but Lawson was tortured and killed. What irony that this man, who had always treated the Native Americans well and had written so kindly of them in his book, should die a cruel death at their hands!

John Lawson and his companions are captured by the Indians.

North Carolina Pioneers

Preview

If a magician were to come to your community and decide to restore it to frontier—that is, turn back the clock almost three hundred years—what would he have to change? Think of all the items which would disappear: televisions, refrigerators, telephones, electric lights, airplanes, and automobiles. You would have no paved roads, no modern medicine, no air conditioning and no supermarkets. For the most part you would be supplying your own food. How would your house be different? Your clothing?

Try to predict what your life would be like as a young person on this frontier. Living in very small communities, or perhaps on an isolated frontier, what duties do you think you might have? If you are a girl, what kind of future can you envision? (Lawson gives a great deal of attention to the lives of the women and young girls.)

As for those of our own Country in Carolina, some of the Men are very laborious, and make great improvements in their Way; but I dare hardly give them that Character in general. The Easy way of living in that plentiful Country makes a great many Planters very negligent, which, were they otherwise, that Colony might now have been in a far better Condition than it is, (as to Trade and other Advantages) which an universal Industry would have led them into.

The Women are the most industrious Sex in that Place, and, by their good Housewifery, make a great deal of Cloath of their own Cotton, Wool and Flax; some of them keeping their Families, (though large,) very decently appareled, both with Linnens and Woollens, so that they have no occasion to run into the Merchants Debt, or lay their money out on Stores for Cloathing. . . .

From *A New Voyage to Carolina,* by John Lawson, published 1709.

They marry very young; some at Thirteen or Fourteen; and She that stays till Twenty is reckoned a stale Maid. . . . Both Sexes are generally spare of Body and not Cholerick nor easily cast down at Disappointments and losses, seldom immoderately grieving at Misfortunes, unless for the Loss of their nearest Relations and Friends, which seems to make a more than ordinary impression upon them. Many of the Women are very handy in Canoes and will manage them with great Dexterity and Skill, which they become accustomed to in this watery Country. They are ready to help their Husbands in any servile Work, as Planting, when the Season of the Weather requires Expedition; Pride seldom banishing good Housewifery. The Girls are not bred up to the Wheel and Sewing only, but the Dairy, and affairs of the House they are very well acquainted withal; so that you shall see them, whilst very young, manage their Business with a great deal of Conduct and Alacrity. The Children of both Sexes are very docile and learn any thing with a great deal of Ease and Method, and those that have the Advantages of Education, write very good Hands, and prove good Accountants, which is most coveted, and indeed, most necessary in these Parts. The young Men are commonly of a bashful, sober Behaviour; few proving Prodigals to consume what the Industry of their Parents has left them, but commonly improve it.

Language Alert

Lawson's history was published 125 years after the report of explorers Amadas and Barlowe. You will notice that the spelling is much more like ours, though Lawson's wording, like the explorers', seems quaint to modern ears. You will also notice that Lawson capitalizes all nouns and some other words as well.

Here are some words and phrases that are either not in use or are used somewhat differently from the way we use them today.

1. *laborious*: Lawson uses this as a synonym for hardworking; we use it mainly to describe work that requires a great deal of labor—i.e., a *laborious* task.
2. *stale Maid*: a woman who is unmarried and is likely to remain so.

The following words have retained the meaning they had in Lawson's time. Can you guess the meanings?

1. "Both Sexes are . . . not *Cholerick,* nor easily cast down at Disappointments." (Note: the modern spelling is *choleric*.)
   a. bad tempered   b. lazy   c. unfriendly

2. "Many of the Women are very handy in Canoes and will manage them with great *Dexterity* and Skill. . . ."
   a. ability to use the hands well   b. strength   c. determination
3. Lawson also describes the females of the household as working with great *alacrity*.
   a. determination   b. grumbling, complaint   c. enthusiasm, vigor
4. Lawson tells us that few young men prove to be "*Prodigals* to consume what the Industry of their Parents has left them." (Hint: Do you know the story of the Prodigal Son?)
   a. wicked   b. recklessly wasteful   c. hot tempered

Reflecting

Notice that for the most part Lawson seems to approve of these pioneers and the way they live. Do you? If you visited North Carolina during the early eighteenth century, how well would you fit into colonial life? What parts of it might make you uncomfortable? Why?

The Indians of North Carolina

Preview

You have already read Arthur Barlowe's description of the Native Americans whom he encountered while exploring the North Carolina coastline. Barlowe's acquaintance with them was brief. Lawson spent much more time with the Indians and studied them in more detail. In the excerpts below he provides descriptions of their bodies, their skills, and their celebrations. Some of what he says will fit our common picture of native Americans, built and reinforced by movies, videos, and novels of frontier days. But you may find some surprises.

Immediately you will notice Lawson's kindly attitude toward those who were called American "Indians." He finds much to admire in them and their way of life. Before you read what Lawson says, can you predict (from your own knowledge of Native Americans) the things he admired? Make a list of your predictions; as you read, check off the items you correctly predicted, and add those you didn't think of.

The Indians of North Carolina are a well shaped clean-made People, of different Statures, as the Europeans are, yet chiefly inclined to be tall. They are a very straight People, and never bend forward or stoop in the Shoulders, unless much overpowered by old Age. Their Limbs are exceeding well shaped. As for their Legs and Feet, they are generally the handsomest in the World. Their Bodies are a little flat, which is occasioned by being laced hard down to a Board in their infancy. This is all the Cradle they have, which I shall describe at large elsewhere. . . .

Their Eyes are commonly full and manly, and their Gate sedate and majestic. They never walk backward and forward as we do, nor contemplate on the Affairs of Loss and Gain, the things which daily perplex us. They are dexterous and steady, both as to their Hands and Feet, to Admiration. They will walk over deep Brooks and Creeks on the smallest Poles, and that without any Fear or Concern. Nay, an Indian will walk on the Ridge of a Barn or House and look down the Gable-end, and spit upon the Ground as unconcerned as if he was walking on Terra firma. In Running, Leaping, or any such other Exercise, their Legs seldom miscarry and give them a Fall; and as for letting any thing fall out of their Hands, I never yet knew one Example. They are no Inventers of any Arts or Trades worthy mention; the Reason of which I take to be, that they are not possessed with the Care and Thoughtfulness, how to provide for the Necessaries of Life as the Europeans are; yet they will learn any thing very soon. I have known an Indian to stock Guns better than most of our Joiners, although he never saw one stocked before and besides, his Working-Tool was only a Sorry Knife. . . .

They let their Nails grow very long, which, they reckon, is the use Nails are designed for, and laugh at the Europeans for pairing theirs, which, they say disarms them of that which Nature designed them for.

They are not of so robust and strong Bodies as to lift great Burdens, and endure Labour and Slavish Work, as the Europeans are; yet some that are Slaves, prove very good and laborious. But for themselves, they never work as the English do, taking care for no farther than what is absolutely necessary to support Life. In Traveling and Hunting, they are very indefatigable, because that carries a Pleasure along with the Profit. I have known some of them very strong; and as for Running and Leaping, they are extraordinary Fellows, and will dance for several Nights together with the greatest Briskness imaginable, their Wind never failing them.

Their Dances are of different Natures;

and for every sort of Dance they have a Tune, which is allotted for that Dance; as, if it be a War-Dance, they have a war-like Song, wherein they express, with all the Passion and Vehemence imaginable, what they intend to do with their Enemies; how they will kill, roast, scalp, beat, and make Captive, such and such Numbers of them; and how many they have destroyed before. All these Songs are made new for every Feast; nor is one and the same Song sung at two several Festivals. Some one of the Nation, (which has the best Gift of expressing their Designs,) is appointed by their King and War Captains to make these Songs.

Others are made for Feasts of another Nature; as, when several Towns, or sometimes different Nations have made Peace with one another; then the Song suits both Nations, and relates how the bad Spirit made them go to War and destroy one another; but it shall never be so again; but that their Sons and Daughters shall marry together, and the two Nations love one another, and become as one People.

They have a third sort of Feasts and Dances, which are always when the Harvest of Corn is ended and in the Spring. The one to return Thanks to the good Spirit for the Fruits of the Earth; the other, to beg the same Blessings for the succeeding Year. And to encourage the young Men to Labour stoutly in planting their Maize . . . , they set a sort of an Idol in the Field, which is dressed up exactly like an Indian, having all the Indians Habit, besides abundance of Wampum and their Money, made of Shells, that hangs about his Neck. The Image none of the young Men dare approach; for the old ones will not suffer them to come near him, but tell them that is some famous Indian Warriour that died a great while ago, and now is come amongst them to see if they work well, which if they do, he will go to the good Spirit and speak to him to send them Plenty of Corn, and to make the young Men all expert Hunters and mighty Warriours. All this while, the King and old Men sit round the Image and seemingly pay a profound Respect to the same. One great Help to these Indians in carrying on these Cheats, and inducing Youth to do what they please, is, the uninterrupted Silence which is ever kept and observed with all the Respect and Veneration imaginable.

Language Alert

A. You have probably noticed in the earlier excerpt how Lawson's spelling and punctuation differs from ours. For example, he spells *gait* as *gate* and *paring* as *pairing*.
B. Some special terms to watch for:
   1. *perplex*: puzzle
   2. *terra firma*: solid ground (The literal translation of these Latin words is *firm land*.)
   3. *sorry*: When Lawson describes a *sorry* knife, he means one which is worthless.
   4. *volatile*: This may mean either *easily vaporized* or *explosive*. When Lawson describes turpentine, he uses the first meaning.
   5. *indefatigable*: untiring, not easy to fatigue
   6. *veneration*: profound respect
   7. *cheats*: tricks (This term is used to describe a situation in which the older men of the tribe are playing a trick on the younger.)

Reflecting

1. Notice in the second paragraph the description of how firmly Indians walked on narrow poles over creeks or ridges of barns and houses with no quivering and no fear. Did you know that Indian workers are still prized today for work on scaffolding on skyscrapers?
2. Which Indian habits, customs, beliefs, behaviors seem very similar to those of settlers—or for that matter, to our own? Which seem very different?

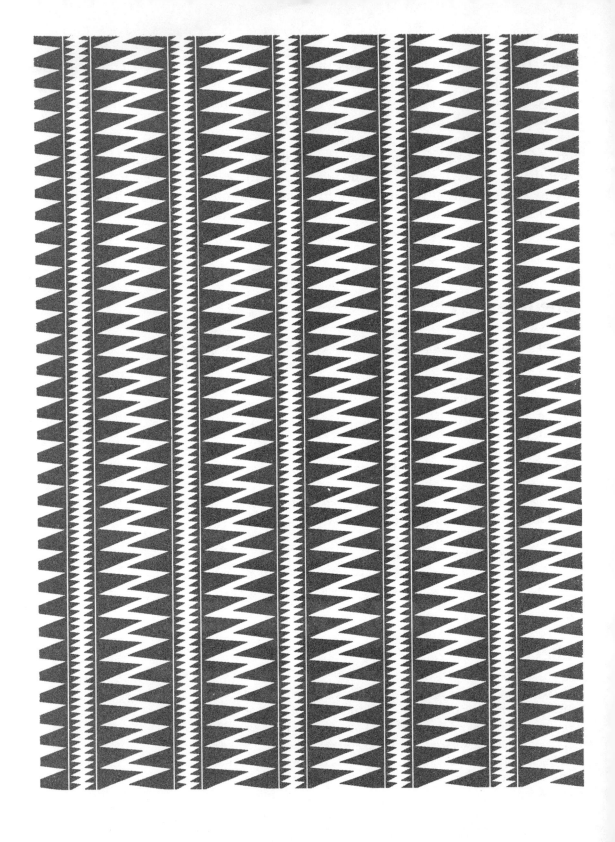

Becoming a Nation

Every Fourth of July we celebrate the event which led to our becoming an independent nation. Since we have celebrated more than two hundred national birthdays, it is difficult for us to realize what a giant step our forefathers took: separating themselves from the Mother Country, declaring themselves a new nation, and—most startling of all—organizing that nation as a democracy ruled by most of the people, not by a few. To take that step required, first of all, original thinking. It also required determination and courage—for it led to war.

The war touched many people, and it touched them in different ways. In the following pages we will get glimpses of some ladies in Edenton, a planter, an Indian, a spunky girl on the Outer Banks, and the most important British officer during the Revolutionary War.

Preview

When you hear the term "tea party," you probably picture a group of women in their silkiest dresses, sitting in a formal living room, munching wafer-thin cookies and sipping tea from fragile china.

During pre-Revolutionary days, while the colonists were protesting various aspects of British rule, there were at least two "tea parties." The most famous took place in Boston. In December 1773, a band of about forty men, using war paint and feathers to disguise themselves as Indians, boarded three British ships and tossed the contents of 342 cartons of tea overboard into the bay. Ten months later, forty-eight women from several counties conducted their own tea party in Edenton, North Carolina. There they signed a resolution supporting the actions of the First Provincial Congress, which at an earlier meeting in New Bern had opposed British taxation and endorsed a boycott of British goods. The following poem provides us with a glimpse of that second party.

Edenton Tea Party
October 25, 1774

Helen Goodman

There's a stillness
As Edenton's gentleladies gather.
Sweetgum's crimson leaves dance at their feet
As silken skirts rustle across the dry grass.

Disdaining paint and feathers
Worn by Boston brethren,
The women step forward to sign their names
And the sound of the scratching quill is heard in London.

They lift a last cup of British tea,
Then spill out their rebellion on Carolina soil.

disdaining: rejecting
quill: an old-fashioned quill pen, made from a stiff wing or tail feather of a bird.

From *North Carolina's 400 Years: Signs Along the Way*, ed. Ronald H. Bayes. Copyright © 1986 by North Carolina Poetry Society. Reprinted by permission of the author and the North Carolina Poetry Society.

MEET THE AUTHOR:
Helen Goodman (1932–)

Helen Goodman, a registered nurse in Polkton, grew up in Otsego, Michigan, and moved to North Carolina in 1958. In 1972, while she was studying at UNC-Charlotte, she decided to take a writing class to complete her curriculum. That class whetted her appetite for poetry, and she has been writing ever since.

She has had a long and varied career as a nurse, both at Union Memorial Hospital in Monroe and with the Carolina Medical Review. However, she continues to write about those things which deeply concern her—currently a number of her poems focus on the natural environment—and recently she has branched out into fiction. She is one of the founders of the Anson County Writers' Club.

Ms. Goodman's poetry has won a number of local and state awards. This poem appears in *North Carolina's 400 Years: Signs Along the Way.*

Reflecting

This poem upsets our expectations. The title does not hint at rebellion. The words and images in the first stanza create a placid scene of a quiet social gathering. In fact, it isn't until the last line of the poem that we recognize that this is no ordinary "tea party," but a revolutionary act.

The effectiveness of any piece of writing—poem, letter, speech, story, or essay—depends on very subtle matters. The contrast of stillness in the first line and rebellion in the last line creates a nice surprise for the reader. Observe other ways in which this writer has created special effects:

1. Notice the other words—or parts of words—in the first stanza which reinforce the feeling of stillness (for example, *gentle-ladies, sweetgum, dance, silken*).

2. Read the first stanza aloud. Notice all the *s* sounds—and how they create the effect of silken skirts rustling across dry grass.

3. The peacefulness of the first stanza is broken in the second by the word *disdaining* and the reference to paint and feathers—very much out of keeping at a tea party. We realize something important is going on when we're told "the sound of the scratching quill is heard in London"—a physical impossibility, of course, but the effects of those signatures were certainly felt in London and elsewhere.

4. Notice that the ladies lift their cups of tea—as in a toast—and that this is their last cup, another reference to the finality of their rebellious act.

The Sound of Drums

James Boyd

Preview

Critics have praised James Boyd's *Drums* as the best novel ever written
about the American Revolution. In contrast to many historical novels
which are overly romantic and historically inaccurate, *Drums* is the result
of the author's careful historical research. It has also been praised for its
realistic characters.

Drums centers on a young man, Johnny Fraser, who grows up in North
Carolina in the years just before and during the Revolutionary War. In
those days, good schools were scarce, and a young man or woman in
search of an education often had to go away from home to "boarding
school." In this excerpt, young Johnny is getting ready to return to school
in Edenton. On Johnny's last evening home in Little River, an old Indian
comes to visit—not for just a friendly call, but for a solemn conference
with Johnny's father.

The Indian, Long Thought, talks frequently of "the Long Knives," who
have evidently been in conflict with his tribe. Can you guess who they are?
He speaks indirectly, almost poetically, but Squire Fraser has no trouble
comprehending his message. Can you understand it?

Two evenings later Johnny Fraser saw
a thread of smoke and three tufts of
lodge-poles rising from the hollow down
by the branch. That was where the Indians once or twice before had camped,
and now again they had stolen in and set
up their teepees without a sound and

without, as Mrs. Fraser coldly remarked,
a by-your-leave.

"A-weel," said Squire Fraser from the
porch, drying his big square hands for
supper. "We can afford them a one night
camping ground. We've got a continent
frae them. Ye might bid Sofa, though," he

added reflectively, "tae shut up the hens."

Johnny Fraser was not thrilled by this barbaric visitation. Indeed he felt that this wandering Cherokee encampment added the final touch of savagery to a background already far too crude for a young gentleman of his pretensions. What would the Tennants say if they knew that his home, which he had tried to picture to them as a country gentleman's estate, was looked on as free camping ground by casual Indians? Yet he must have a look at them. He wandered down the lane, down the road till the weathered hides of the teepees showed beneath the shoulder of the hill. A bundled squaw hung over a tiny fire; a buck smoked on an elk-hide before a door-flap; a mangy lemon-colored cur with yellow eyes licked an impassive baby; three wretched skewbald ponies, loosely hobbled, grazed down towards the swamp. Into his nostrils came an odor, greasy, musky, acrid, a smell revolting, yet like the scene, subtly intriguing, disturbing, barbarous and strange. Half disgusted, half uneasy he turned back home.

Seated at the table in the corner, breathing laboriously, Squire Fraser had just finished the letter which Johnny was to carry back to Dr. Clapton. Ignorant of the finer points of etiquette, he sealed it firmly with his ring.

"Ye might snuff the candle out, son. There's light enough frae the fire. Caroline, ye shouldna grieve."

"Would you like to see me happy, then, with Johnny going back to Edenton?"

"Ye could be satisfied. We're paying out good money for his schooling."

"I know, I know. But he'll not be a boy for long now."

"Well, then, let's make a man o' him. Would ye keep him at your skirts?" She twined her hands.

"I'm afear of the times. There might be a war, they say."

"That's Wylie Jones. Well, my lass, what's tae trouble ye? There will always be braggarts everywhere. And when a' the rest are gone there will still be plenty in America."

They fell silent, listening to the wind.

A cold gust passed over them, twisted the flames; they turned. In the open doorway stood an old Indian wrapped in a red trade-blanket, his free arm raised stiffy in salutation.

"Greeting, white brother." The cracked voice, still touched with liquid music, brought hazy memories to Johnny. John Fraser rose.

"Long Thought, I give ye welcome."

The Indian closed the door.

"Peace to this house."

He opened his blanket; his pinched bare chest was painted ceremonial vermilion.

"Draw tae the fire."

He reached the fire in a stride, sank slowly to the floor, stretched his claw hands to the blaze.

"Caroline, will ye just bring Long Thought a plate of provender and a dram."

Without enthusiasm, Johnny's mother went into the kitchen.

"It's six year," his father continued, "since I've seen ye."

"Seven. I come from over the mountains now."

"Ah! And where are ye bound?"

"Here, I come to make council talk."

"Ah! Well, I'm real glad tae see ye."

"I come because in the old days, when my Cherokee people hunted these forests, my white brother was not as the other Long Knives. He was wise to give talk and to hear talk."

"Aye, between us we stopped a deal o' trouble. A few more like us and there'd have been no trouble at all."

"The wise are few."

Mrs. Fraser came in with the plate and cup. Reaching up his thin arms, Long Thought took them without acknowledgment. He drained the cup. His eye brightened. He demolished the heaped yams and mutton voraciously. From beneath his blanket he produced a pipe, its reed stem browned with use, the tip of a wolf's brush hanging from the black stone bowl.

"We smoke. Then will be time for council talk."

He glanced significantly at Mrs. Fraser. She flushed and flashed an angry look into the ancient, cryptic face.

"I'll go above stairs, John," she said.

"Vera well. And take Johnny."

"Let the young man hear the talk, that he may learn from the wisdom of the old men," a wintry smile just touched the Indian's face, "and from their folly."

He lit the pipe, passed it to John Fraser, who puffed gravely during many minutes, then gave it back.

The pipe was finished.

"And now, Long Thought, what is in my brother's mind?"

"As my white brother knows, we once hunted here. Now the Long Knives hold it. Then we hunted the mountains. Now the Long Knives hunt there. We are beyond the mountains, seeking peace. But still the Long Knives come and there is no peace. But many troubles. The young men would fight the Long Knives, but they know not how. The old men would save the people, but they know not how. And I who in old days led the people with wise talk am come to nothing."

He bowed his head.

"I lie drunken in the street of the bark houses. The children mock me. My horse is gone to buy rum. My beaded council dress is gone to buy rum. My power is gone, to buy rum. This is a hard talk to say."

He was silent.

"Why, my brother, I'm sorry indeed. Ye were never so in the old days."

"In old days I had hope and great dreams. I would save my people, make them brothers to the Long Knives."

His black hair fell about his toothless, bitter mouth.

"Hope went, then came the rum." He touched the cup. "Rum brings dreams."

"So now," he went on, "I am mocked. And yet when a new trouble now comes to my people and they will send chiefs to the governor who never hears, I say, 'I will pass back across the mountains to my white brother. Again we will make talk and I will bring new wisdom to my people.' "

"I'll do the best I can, my friend. But I'm no sae sure as I used tae be when we were younger."

"Nor I, brother."

"Well, then?"

"War-drums, drumming, drumming. At night I walk on the hills to hear what the Great Spirit says to me. But I only hear drums. All the earth, from the Father of Waters to the sea, is filled with drums—drums to Northward, in the Long House of the Six Nations, drums to Southward in Seminole lagoons, drums to Eastward in the Long Knives' stone towns. All night they drum."

"Ye think it means an Indian war?"

"I do not know, but in this drumming Long Knife drums against Long Knife, Indian against Indian."

A pause followed.

"Well, there has been talk of some trouble between the provincials and Britain. But it's talk, only just."

Long Thought shook his head wearily.

"My brother is wise. But he has not heard the drums. I am now an old man. I have not heard such drums before."

"Let us put it thus, then, brother. If ye are wrong, which God grant ye may be, then your troubles are naught. And if ye are right, what is it ye would ask?"

"I ask: When Long Knife fights Long Knife, what shall my people do?"

"They'll try tae bring ye intae it, I've nae doubt."

The Indian nodded.

"And if ye would know whether the rebels or the King would win, I think I can tell ye, having once been a rebel myself.'" He grinned.

"'I would know," answered Long Thought simply, "what is best for my people."

"Aye, and I would tell ye, my friend. It's thus: If there's a war and ye are on the wrong side, ye'll be massacred, and if ye are on the right side, ye'll be neglected and forgotten, having made enemies o' the losers wi'out making friends of the winners. Both sides will try threats and bribes and promises. But just ye bide in your towns and when it's over they'll respect ye the more."

He checked himself.

"I talk as though there was tae be a war. But that was merely tae answer your question, my brother. There will be no war."

The Indian rose, went to the door. From the porch he beckoned. John Fraser joined him.

"What does my white brother hear?"

"I hear the wind."

Long Thought's old head craned forward intently beneath his huddled blanket.

"Listen—you hear?—Drums."

James Boyd (1888–1944)

As a boy, James Boyd, a native of Pennsylvania, visited his grandfather in Moore County many times, but he did not call North Carolina "home" until he was an adult. However, once Boyd came to live in Southern Pines, he made a substantial impact on his adopted state—an impact that is still felt.

Boyd's health, which had been fragile, was further damaged by his experience in World War I. He came to Southern Pines to recover and to try a five-year apprenticeship at writing fiction. He began selling short stories, then started extensive research for a historical novel, not only checking historical documents, but reading diaries and letters of the Revolutionary period to learn the right dialect. After publication of his historical novel, *Drums*, he became one of the most noted writers in the state, with short stories, articles, and books appearing regularly. He also became editor/publisher of the Southern Pines *Pilot*, and was an active citizen participating in local, state, and national affairs.

James Boyd and his family hosted many famous writers in their home, Weymouth, which was set in a tall forest of pines. Long after his untimely death in 1944, he and his home continue to influence the arts in this state. Weymouth has become an arts center. Lectures and concerts are now held in the large, gracious drawing room, and during week-long stays, writers, artists, and musicians write, paint, and compose.

Language Alert

A. Language from the Old Country

The Frasers, like so many North Carolina settlers, are of Scotch-Irish descent, and some of their words still echo the dialect of the land of their origin. Notice the following, which occur early in the story: *a-weel* (well), *shouldna* (shouldn't), *frae* (from), and *tae* (to). Be alert to others.

B. Good Words to Know

Choose the best definition.

1. A mangy dog licked an *impassive* baby.
   a. weak   b. unemotional   c. crying
2. Johnny smelled a greasy, *musky* odor coming from the Indian fire.
   a. a powerful animal odor   b. a bitter odor, painful to the nostrils
3. Coming in the door, the Indian raised his arm in *salutation*.
   a. warning   b. greeting   c. threat
4. Long Thought's chest was painted *vermilion*.
   a. black   b. yellow   c. red
5. Given supper, Long Thought devours it *voraciously*.
   a. with a greedy appetite   b. gratefully   c. resentfully
6. We are told that Long Thought's face is *cryptic*.
   a. emotionally revealing   b. handsome, dignified   c. mysterious, secretive

Check your answers either in a dictionary or with your teacher.

Reflecting

Because of James Boyd's skill as a writer, even in such a very short excerpt from his novel, we get remarkably clear profiles of two characters: Mr. Fraser and Long Thought. Reread the story, concentrating on one of the two. Make notes as you find words or behavior that leads you to understand your chosen character. Then consider the following:

1. Mr. Fraser may be considered typical of many colonists in that place and that time. What are his values; that is, what does he consider important? What kind of relationship does he have with his wife and son? How has he dealt with Indians in the past? How does he deal with Long Thought? How does he view the threat of war?

   Write a profile of Mr. Fraser—the kind you often see as a feature story in the newspaper or a popular magazine like *People* or *Newsweek*. Include information concerning the questions above.

2. Although Long Thought's visit is short and he came mainly to talk about the possibility of war, not about himself, we learn a good deal about him. We learn about the role he has played in his tribe and with the white colonists, about his personal troubles, and about what troubles him.

   Assume the role of Johnny Fraser. Write one of your friends at school, describing Long Thought and his mission. What reactions to this experience would you expect Johnny to have?

From **Betsy Dowdy's Ride**

The Ghost Ship

Nell Wise Wechter

Preview

The following story is from the first chapter of Nell Wise Wechter's novel, *Betsy Dowdy's Ride*. Betsy Dowdy was a real person who lived in the Carolina colony during the Revolution; in fact, when she was only fifteen years old, she was considered a heroine. A number of versions of her adventures have been handed down through the years, although there are no factual documents. Ms. Wechter has chosen details from those versions to build a novel which captures the spirit of a brave young girl in a difficult time.

This excerpt tells of the appearance of a weird ship in the treacherous waters off the Outer Banks. From this story, you will not only get acquainted with a genuine North Carolina heroine, but learn about the life of those who depend on the sea for their livelihood. You will also be introduced to the dialect of the "high-tiders" of that time—the people who lived and worked on the Outer Banks.

An Englishman is the unfittest person on earth to argue another Englishman into slavery.

EDMUND BURKE

"The Ghost Ship is breaking up!" Betsy Dowdy gasped, watching the mountainous seas beat the three-master from stem to stern. "I must go after Pa like he said." But the girl seemed glued to the hillock of sand on which she had been keeping watch for hours. She found it absolutely impossible to move or to take her eyes from the scene of destruction before her.

For two days, the natives on the North Banks of Currituck had watched the strange antics of a full-rigged three-masted schooner which, when it appeared, had not been more than a mile off shore. The howling northeaster which followed the vernal equinox had kicked up such seas that it had been impossible for the Bankers to launch their small boats through the great breakers of the

Atlantic, row out to the schooner, and investigate the strange goings-on.

Betsy and her father, Joe Dowdy, had been rounding up horses on the south end of Currituck Beach the day before, when Betsy had suddenly espied the schooner. It was so close to the shore that, for a second, the girl was stunned into speechlessness. Almost within the same second, Joe Dowdy saw the ship. It was sailing north, rising and falling with every rough sea and trough. Before either of them could find his voice, the ship came about and began to sail southward.

"By the King's realm!" Joe Dowdy exclaimed in astonishment. "Where did that vessel come from? And what's the matter with the helmsman? Don't he know he's courting disaster, coming in so close to shore when the seas are as rough as they are!"

"Pa," Betsy shivered, "there's something mighty peculiar about that ship. I feel it in my bones. We've been working out here on the beach all day, and we've not seen even a sail. Then all at once we look up, and there's a full-rigged vessel close enough to touch. Gives me goose pimples all over."

"I'm going to git Sammy Jarvis and Jess Pinner," Joe Dowdy said, forgetting all about the horses he and Betsy were herding. "You ride down and tell Haley Morris to git out here in a hurry. There's something mighty strange about this."

Before they could get off, the schooner came about again, this time on a course straight toward the beach. As if bent on hastening the destruction of the vessel, the wind increased suddenly, sending flying sand into the faces of Betsy and her father with such stinging blows that they were forced to take cover behind the red calico kerchiefs they wore about their necks.

Betsy turned her marsh pony and took off down the beach. Joe Dowdy wheeled his mount and sent him galloping in the opposite direction toward Sammy Jarvis's.

"Folks don't usually fear things that's visible," Betsy said to herself. "It's the unseen that people dread. And there's something unseen about that ship. She acts just like she's sailing by herself, no crew, no nothing, except the screaming sea gulls a-hovering over her and that flock of Mother Carey's chickens a-skimming the water line."

In less than an hour almost every man, woman, and child on Currituck Beach was standing on the shore watching in awe the strange sailing pattern of the schooner. The wind blew a gale, and the screeching gulls added to the din. But the watchers were very subdued. Because of the mystery surrounding the sudden appearance of the craft, they began to call her the Ghost Ship. When the vessel was less than half a mile from shore, she suddenly slackened speed without apparent reason.

"She's grounded on the shoals!" Sammy Jarvis yelled. But almost immediately, the schooner wheeled again. This time her course was north. The crowd watched in muted amazement as she knifed her way through the mountainous waves. Look as they might, the Currituck-ers could see no human being aboard the ship. Betsy could feel the electric tension in the air. It was like a magnetic field, holding the crowd in some invisible line of force. The screaming wind added to the eerie scene.

When darkness drove most of the islanders from the shore back to their homes, Joe Dowdy, Sammy Jarvis, Jess Pinner, and Haley Morris set up watch on the beach.

"Please, can I stay too, Pa?" Betsy begged. "I'll get in the lea of that hill. But I'll just bust with curiosity if you make me go home."

"Female women!" Joe Dowdy snorted. "What do you think, wife?"

"Let her stay, Joseph," Elizabeth Dowdy said serenely. "She'd not sleep a wink at the cabin and would pester the life out of me."

"Thank you, Ma," Betsy said, hugging her mother. "I've got a funny, scary feeling about that schooner, but I reckon my curiosity is just as strong to see what happens to her tonight."

"You go on back to the house, Elizabeth," Joe Dowdy told his wife. "Scare us up some victuals jest in case we git hungry before morning. One of us will ride down and bring them back. Come, men, let's tether the horses behind that sand dune. That ship beats me," he went on. "Fifty-odd years I've lived, and thirty years or longer I've been a wrecker, but I ain't never seen a sailing craft behave in such a crazy fashion." The men nodded in solemn agreement. But still they stood watch just in case the vessel broke up in the night and there was salvaging to do.

The watch was a cold, miserable one to Betsy. She took cover from the wind behind a dune. Before she settled down, she spread an old bed quilt over Bess, her marsh pony, and made sure that the animal was tied securely to a scrub oak in the lea of the hill. Bess snorted, not liking the cumbersome covering. But Betsy knew the cold sea wind would chill animals and humans alike.

Her father and the men piled driftwood and made a roaring fire. Once or twice Betsy ventured from behind the hill to get some warmth, but the stinging sand, whipped up by the wind, struck her face so sharply that she wondered whether the trips were worthwhile. Inside she was churning with doubts and fears. In the darkness, the ship could not be seen. Once Betsy came up to the fire just in time to hear Sammy Jarvis say:

"That cunner ain't carryin' no runnin' lights or ridin' lights . . . no lights of no kind, Joseph. Hit's dark as Egypt out here, and as close as that vessel is to the shore, iffen she had lights on her, they'd show up bigger than a Caroliny moon. I tell you, she's un'arthly, that's what she is . . . a regular spook ship, I'm thinkin'. Plum makes my scalp prickle up like hit's been stuck with bear grass."

"Strange happenings ain't no novelty on the Caroliny Banks," Haley Morris said solemnly. "Only thing, right now, with all this trouble 'twixt the colonies and the Mother Country, that ship acting like a graveyard ha'nt a-prancing back and forth like it's doing—well, sir, it does give a body the creeps. Why, it wouldn't surprise me nary a bit to see a Redcoat pop

68

right out of the middle of that fire, take a bead on us, and shoot us all right through the eyeballs."

"Haley Morris, watch your words!" Joe Dowdy snapped.

"You're crazier than a bedbug tryin' to get away from turpentine," Sammy snorted. "You know that ain't no fittin' talk to say around Mistress Betsy."

"It's all right, Uncle Sammy, Pa," Betsy answered, shoving a piece of driftwood on the fire. "Master Haley's just saying out loud how he feels. Reckon I feel mixed up inside too. Times are mighty fogerty, with Tories and Redcoats a-worrying the colony to death. Now that Ghost Ship has to come a-sailing off our Banks like a banshee to finish worrying the living lights out of us."

"Well, the life of wreckers ain't no bed of violets," Joe Dowdy observed. "Like I said, I've been salvaging vessels a long time, and I've seen some terrible things happen to cargo and people aboard ships, but that crazy schooner out there has got me up a tree. Why, a body don't know if she's a Colonial, a Britisher, or a craft full of cutthroats all set to murder the lot of us if they come ashore."

"Now, Joseph Dowdy, you know that cunner ain't got no crew on her," Sammy Jarvis told him. "Friend er foe, no ship captain wouldn't be crazy enough to drive his vessel up and down this shore like that one's been a-goin'. I tell ye, she's a Ghost Ship!"

Betsy scrunched up under the quilt she had wrapped about her. Her shoulders were shaking. She moved in nearer to the fire, taking a seat close to her father.

"As I was a-saying," Haley Morris went on, as if he hadn't been called down a few minutes before, "I reckon all of us is right familiar with the stories we've heared all our lives about headless horsemen rushing pell-mell through the darkness out here on the Banks, their ghosty bodies sticking to the saddles of their horses like pitch to pine bark. And every one of you has heered bloodcurdling yells in the dead of night. Ghosts of departed loved ones, that's what they be! I agree with Sammy. That schooner out there ain't human. She's a regular Flying Dutchman."

"The night wind has addled your brains, Haley. Yours too, Sammy. Maybe you call her a Ghost Ship, but she's real enough. You jest wait and see. If this northeaster keeps up, she'll pile up sooner or later. Now, I agree there's something mighty strange about the way she's been acting. But if she don't have nobody a-piloting her, how else can she act but crazy? Something's happened to her crew. That's the ghosty part, I'm thinking. But that vessel's real enough," Joe Dowdy argued.

Betsy rose and quietly made her way back to the lea of the hill. She preferred the cold to being near the fire where all the scary talk was going on. Like her father, she knew the ship was real. But what had happened to the crew aboard? What had brought about their disappearance?

Somehow, the long, grim night passed. Nothing happened. By daylight, the strange ship began to draw the crowd back to the shore. The wind continued to blow a gale. After a while the watchers rode back to their homes to do their daily chores. When Betsy had eaten her breakfast, her father instructed her to take up the watch again. She was to ride after him and the others, immediately, if the ship came ashore or began to break up. Uneasiness still beset her, as it did everyone else who came down to the water's edge, Betsy chose a sand dune on which to watch. It lay a hundred yards or more from the breakers and on it was a water oak to which she tied Bess so that the pony would not wander off.

"I'm achey and sore," the girl said, stretching her shoulders and pushing her legs out in front of her. "But not sleepy a bit, It's too exciting a time to sleep. Besides, I reckon I'd have nightmares about that crazy schooner if I did close my eyes."

The vessel continued her pattern of first sailing north, then south, and then heading toward the beach, wheeling back and forth until a body got dizzy watching. By noon, the natives who had come back to watch again left the shore, and Betsy found herself alone. She watched the sea gulls as they flew madly against the wind and hovered over the ship. Their shrill cries made her wince. "Them gulls are wondering why somebody aboard that ship don't throw some slop overboard for them to eat," she thought.

By noon, the vessel had come abreast of the shore opposite Betsy's sand dune. A blast of rising wind spun the schooner around like a wind clatter. As if in a nightmare, Betsy watched the whirling waves and the spinning ship come toward her with the speed of a musket ball. Less than five hundred yards from the beach, the craft came to a grinding halt, and the air was torn with a tremendous crash like a hundred claps of giant thunder!

"I've got to go," Betsy said. But she couldn't move. She felt as if she would stifle for want of breath. Her body seemed paralyzed, and yet, deep down within her, there was a feeling of relief. There was still no sign of a living soul aboard the vessel.

The schooner groaned and whined under the terrific beating of the sea. Betsy saw the timbers splinter and be hurled by the wind into the swirling breakers. The mizzenmast shattered and cracked like lightning as it tumbled into the sea. The flapping of the canvas sails against the wind hurt her eardrums when the noise hit them. The breaking, splitting sounds of the ship's ribs made her grab her own sides. But still she was powerless to make her feet move. It was as if the Day of Doom had transfixed and petrified her. Yardarms and crosstrees tore loose; stanchions cracked and broke; davits ripped away, sending small boats hurling across the wreckage, where they promptly sank into the sea.

When the gunwales of the vessel were even with the breakers, Betsy closed her eyes against the horror and prayed for motion to return to her. It was only when a hatch cover was tossed nearly to her feet on the dune and the wailing of a cat struck her ears that she found she could move.

"It's a hideous, unearthly nightmare I'm having," she gasped, as she began to walk like one in a trance toward the piece of wreckage. "A Ghost Ship piloted by a cat!" Her own hysterical laughter against the northeaster brought the girl to her senses.

There was a cat!

The animal was clinging precariously to the hatch cover, which was now being tossed hither and yon in the shallow seas wallowing on the shore.

"Sooky! Poor Sooky! Little Sooky!" Betsy sing-songed like a Poll parrot, gathering up the bedraggled, half-drowned animal and sticking him inside her cloak. "Now, to ride for Pa," she said, trying to run. But her legs were too wobbly to buck the sand and wind. Once she fell. The cat let out a fearful yowl. She finally managed to get her pony untied. Once she was mounted and riding away, the shock began to leave her. Inside her cloak she could feel the cat's purring.

"Poor little Sooky, what happened aboard that vessel?" she asked. "Was it pirates that forced the crew to walk the plank? Was it sea prowlers of another breed . . . like Britishers, maybe? Oh, if you could only talk!" The cat meowed blissfully and purred harder, keeping behind his green eyes the secret of the Ghost Ship!

Thus, the saga of the strange schooner came to an end. Betsy helped her father and the other wreckers salvage what was left. By the end of the first week in April, 1775, the salvaging had been completed. Betsy had worked like a beaver. Now, on the last day of their work, she stood on the sand under a spring sun, which was already belting Currituck Beach with its hot rays. She wiped the sweat from her forehead with the big square of red calico she carried in the pocket of the faded old breeches she had appropriated from her father. She bent down to scratch the back of her legs where the flannel underwear chafed her. Out of the corner of her eye she saw her father wrestling with a cask near the water's edge. That, and the stool which she held, were the very last pieces of cargo to be salvaged. Other things might wash ashore later, she knew. But the usable things had already been carted away by the wreckers.

"Well, Ghost Ship," she sighed, "I reckon your secrets are safe in Davy Jones's locker. Nothing alive but a cat, and no sign of anybody dead!"

"Ready, daughter?" Joe Dowdy bellowed in his great voice.

"Coming, Pa," she answered, grasping the stool. "I'll help you roll the cask. Wonder what's in this one?"

"Black strap molasses, more than likely," her father answered.

"Well, I could lay away a good sopping of it," Betsy laughed. "I'm as hungry as a Dismal Swamp bear. I reckon Ma thinks we've been swallowed up by quicksand, captured by Redcoats, or spirited off by the ghosts on the schooner."

"Aye, I reckon so," Joe Dowdy said, stopping to wipe his forehead. "That ship will be speculated about on these Banks fer a long time to come. Like Haley said, she was a real Flying Dutchman all right. I shore wish we could have boarded her before she broke up. Reckon we'll not know what her registry was, her name, ner nothing else about her fer a long time to come . . . maybe never."

Nell Wise Wechter (1913–1989)

When Nell Wise of Stumpy Point was a little girl, her fisherman father praised her compositions written for school and encouraged her to become a writer. She began her professional writing career when she was only nineteen, composing features for the *Coastland Times* in Manteo. Later she taught school in Northampton County and Cape Hatteras. After the war, she and her husband, Robert Wechter, completed their education at East Carolina and UNC-Chapel Hill. Both taught in the public schools in Greensboro until they retired.

In 1957, using both her writing and her teaching experience, Nell Wise Wechter began writing books for middle-school readers. Her first novel, *Taffy of Torpedo Junction*, a World War II tale set in Cape Hatteras, won an award for the best book for young readers published in North Carolina that year. Her other novels also focus on critical historical events—the Revolutionary War, the Lost Colony, the piracy of Edward Teach (Blackbeard), the Civil War. Thus these books inform readers as well as entertain them.

Language Alert

A. Several terms have to do with the sea and sailing—

1. *shoals*: shallow places in a body of water, sandbars (Usually these are dangerous for navigation.)
2. *schooner*: a ship with two or more masts
3. *cunner*: a marine fish (In this story, the word is used to refer to ships.)
4. *Flying Dutchman*: a legendary mariner (It was told that he was condemned to sail the seas against the wind until Judgment Day. His ghostly ship was said to appear in storms.)
5. *mizzenmast*: the third mast aft on large sailing ships.

6. *stanchion*: an upright pole or support
7. *davits*: small cranes, used on ships to hoist boats, anchors, and cargo
8. *yardarms*: either end of a yard of a square sail
9. *crosstrees*: horizontal crosspieces at the upper ends of lower masts
10. *gunwale*: the upper end of a ship's side

B. Words which aren't used as frequently now as they once were:

1. *victuals*: food
2. *tether*: to secure with a rope or chain (as with a horse or dog, for example)
3. *banshee*: in Gaelic folklore, female spirit whose wailing is believed to indicate a death
4. *nary*: not one
5. *lea*: meadow or grassland

C. Strong words to add to your vocabulary

1. *muted*: to muffle or soften sound (Trumpeters sometimes insert a device inside the throat of their instrument to *mute* the sound.)
2. *precarious*: dangerously insecure or unstable (A climber might have a *precarious* foothood on the mountainside; an investor who has made bad investments may find himself or herself in a *precarious* financial situation.)
3. *speculated*: thought about, considered (When you are trying to figure out why or how something happened, you are *speculating*.)
4. *transfixed*: made motionless, usually through amazement or terror
5. *petrified*: frozen or made numb by terror or shock (Literally this word means *to be turned to stone*.)

Reflecting

1. The currents and shoals at the Outer Banks are very dangerous, so until modern times, shipwrecks in those waters were not at all uncommon. What *is* uncommon is the fact that this ship is abandoned. Notice the varied explanations the Currituck natives give for the disappearance of the crew.
2. Notice the responsibilities that Betsy takes and the way that the adults treat her. What does this information tell you about the lives of children when North Carolina was only a colony?

Preview

Does the title "Lord Cornwallis and a Carolina Spring" seem strange to you? Two very different things are juxtaposed (placed together): an important British general in the Revolutionary War and one of the gentlest seasons of our year. Lord Cornwallis and his troops were engaged in one of their most difficult battles in just that season: the Battle of Guilford Courthouse, fought on March 15, 1781, just as the Carolina countryside was beginning to turn green again.

The previous autumn, Carolina Patriots had given Lord Cornwallis an unpleasant surprise at the Battle of King's Mountain, where Cornwallis lost his trusted aide, Colonel Patrick Ferguson, and more than one hundred soldiers. He spent the next few months in South Carolina preparing for a battle in which he expected to defeat North Carolina once and for all. At the same time, General Nathaniel Greene enlisted and trained troops and took a stand at Guilford Courthouse.

As you read the following poem, imagine yourself as Lord Cornwallis, traveling through greening forests. Headed for what is now Greensboro, Cornwallis expects to make quick work of General Nathaniel Greene and his country-bred Patriots and then to march on triumphantly to Wilmington.

General Nathaniel Greene

Lord Cornwallis and a Carolina Spring

Helen Bevington

Cardinals were singing in this wood
(And Greene was clamoring for his blood)

As Lord Cornwallis rode through the spring.
Green was the shimmer of everything,

Of mimosa leaf, of loblolly pine,
The tangled growth of the muscadine,

Of great dark magnolias where he rode,
Caught in an American episode,

Posting through April, on the run,
Hoping to get to Wilmington—

Mocked by the enemy Greene, by fate.
With spring and his honor to contemplate,

Lord Cornwallis rode softly by,
Greene in his thought and green in his eye.

muscadine: a grape (and its vine)

MEET THE AUTHOR:
Helen Bevington (1932–   )

Helen Bevington, who taught English at Duke University for many years, has won a national reputation for her poetry, especially her light and humorous verse. Born in New York, the daughter and granddaughter of Methodist ministers, she received her Ph.D. at the University of Chicago, then came to Duke University, where she and her husband, Dr. Merle Bevington, both taught English.

About her writing, she has said, "I began writing verse, some of it very light verse, probably because of the particular pleasure of living in the country in North Carolina." Many of her poems were published in major periodicals, such as *The New Yorker*. Her first collection of poetry was published in 1946, and she has written several other books— both poetry and prose—since. The excellence of her writing has been recognized by several prizes, including the North Carolina Award for Literature (1973).

Reflecting

Notice how this poem is built on contrasts—peace and beauty *vs.* war and blood:

First couplet: (red) cardinals singing *vs.*
                Greene "clamoring" for (red) blood

Twelfth line: contemplating spring *vs.*
                contemplating honor won through battle

Last line: green (of springtime) *vs.*
              Greene (the general)

These contrasts are **ironic**: that is, they cause a surprising mismatch; they upset our expectations. (The evil of war seems out-of-place in the season of rebirth and beauty.) Watch for examples of **irony** in other readings in this book.

JAMES FORTEN, BOY HERO

Burke Davis

Preview

The following excerpt from Burke Davis's *Black Heroes of the American Revolution* is taken from a chapter entitled "Two Famous Patriots." You will see that James Forten earned the titles *hero* and *patriot* not once, but several times.

When offered his freedom and a life of ease in England, the young black sailor from Philadelphia replied, "No, I'm a prisoner for my country, and I'll never be a traitor to her."

Just before the end of the Revolution, a fifteen-year-old black youth signed on as a powder boy aboard the American privateer[1] *Royal Louis*, a small ship commanded by Stephen Decatur, Sr.

The youngster was James Forten, who had been born free in Philadelphia, where he had attended the school of an anti-slavery Quaker. This slender young volunteer was to become one of the wealthiest men in Philadelphia after the war. He was already a war veteran, for he had served as a drummer in the army.

The *Royal Louis* put to sea to prey on British shipping, with the hope of dividing captured prizes among the officers and crew. Of her crew of two hundred, twenty were black. The first cruise was bloody but successful, and Captain Decatur's ship forced a British Navy brig to surrender. The

---

1. privateer: a ship that is privately owned and managed, but has been given authority from the government to attack and/or capture enemy vessels

second cruise ended in disaster. A heavily armed enemy frigate,[2] the *Amphyon*, with the aid of two other warships, battered the *Royal Louis* so fiercely that Decatur was forced to surrender.

It was a bad moment for James Forten. The British seldom exchanged black prisoners who fell into their hands, but usually sold them in the West Indies to serve as plantation laborers under cruel overseers and the merciless tropical sun. But James Forten was one of the lucky prisoners aboard the *Amphyon*. He met the captain's son, a boy of his own age, and the two became friends at once. The English boy was so fond of the quick-witted black American, and so impressed by his skill at playing marbles, that he persuaded his father to offer Forten a life of ease in England. Forten refused, declaring he would not be a traitor to his country.

Rather than shipping him to the West Indies, the British captain sent Forten to the prison ship *Jersey,* which was anchored off Long Island. "Thus," James Forten wrote later, "did a game of marbles save me from a life of West Indian servitude."

There were days when Forten felt that he had not been so lucky after all, for he was shoved deep into the hold[3] of the ship with a thousand other prisoners, forced to live on wormy meat, crusts of moldy bread and foul water, gasping for breath in the stinking, overcrowded quarters. Each day, fresh bodies were hauled out of the hold for burial in the sand dunes ashore. During the war more than 10,000 American prisoners died on the rotting hulk of this prison ship.

James Forten once had a chance to escape when a patriot officer, who was to be exchanged for a British prisoner, left the *Jersey* with his chest. Forten had planned to crawl into the officer's chest and be carried to freedom, but stood aside to allow a younger white boy to hide instead. Forten helped to carry the chest over the side of the ship into a waiting boat and watched his smaller companion escape.

After enduring seven months in the floating hell of the *Jersey,* James Forten was set free in an exchange of prisoners and walked to his home in Philadelphia. During the next fifty years of his life, Forten was to become one of the best-known men of his city. He began to make sails for ships and was soon the head of a business employing scores of people. James Forten became an inventor as well as a manufacturer, gave much of his wealth to aid poor and struggling blacks, and became a founder of the Abolition movement to help end American slavery. Among his friends was

2. frigate: a sailing war vessel used during the seventeenth to nineteenth centuries

3. hold: the interior of a ship, located below the decks; cargo is often stored here

the famous white orator William Lloyd Garrison, who befriended many of the country's blacks.

Garrison won Forten's heart in his early speeches attacking slavery when he said, "I never rise to address a colored audience, without feeling ashamed of my own color, ashamed of having been identified with a race of men who have done you so much injustice."

James Forten lived to see his sons and grandsons become leaders in the anti-slavery crusade, but never regretted the years he spent as a drummer, powder boy, and prisoner during the Revolution.

Still, as he said in 1830 when it appeared that black slavery would never be stamped out, the war he had fought in was an incomplete revolution, and the country faced a real crisis, "The spirit of Freedom is marching with rapid strides and causing tyrants to tremble; may America awake . . . "

MEET THE AUTHOR
Burke Davis (1913–)

Burke Davis is noted both for the quality and for the variety of his writing. He has forty-seven books to his credit, including novels, biographies, historical accounts, and over a dozen books for young readers (both fiction and non-fiction). His historical novels are recognized both for their realism and their accuracy. They are based on painstaking research into such details as weather, exact routes of marches, and the precise timing of battles. Rather than glorify heroes, as many novelists do, he has chosen to portray his characters as realistic human beings with recognizable flaws.

Born in Durham, Burke David grew up in Greensboro. While still in high school he began writing—poetry, short stories, and essays. His essay on snakes, "My Experiences as a Snake Man in the Boy Scouts," won an award from the North Carolina Academy of

Science. Encouraged by his mother and a high school writing teacher, he continued writing through his years at Guilford College, Duke University, and branches of the University of North Carolina at Chapel Hill and Greensboro.

For a number of years Davis was a journalist, working with newspapers in Charlotte, Baltimore, and Greensboro. In 1960 he moved to Virginia to work with Colonial Williamsburg, Inc. Already he was a writer of wide reputation. His first novel, *Whisper My Name*, had appeared in 1949 and was quickly followed by a number of historical novels. Published in 1956, *Roberta E. Lee*, his first book for young readers, featured as its heroine a Chatham County rabbit who was a southern belle.

Davis's book *To Appomattox: Nine April Days, 1865*, won the Mayflower Award in 1959. In 1973 he was presented the North Carolina Award for Literature, and in 1990 the North Caroliniana Society honored him for his contributions to the cultural life of the state.

Reflecting

We learn that after James Forten became a wealthy and influential citizen of Philadelphia, he did several more things that would qualify him for the title *patriot*. List those actions, then look back at the story of his wartime experience. What qualities do we see in the young James Forten that would help us predict the kind of man he became?

A Young State in a Young Nation

After October 18, 1781, the United States was independent from British rule. Now it was up to us to determine our own destiny—to settle this wilderness (we had no idea how large it was!) and build our own homes and communities. We had to establish our own government, our own way of life, without either the rules or the protections of a powerful nation like England.

Think about what the young state of North Carolina was like during the eighty years between the Revolution and the Civil War. There were only about 350,000 people in the entire state—just about as many as the city of Charlotte had in the 1980s! The land was beautiful and rich with natural resources. However, without the kinds of transportation, communication, and machinery we take for granted, developing those resources took tremendous effort. In most families everyone from little children to the elderly had chores to do. Schools—when they existed at all—operated only a few months a year, because the children were needed to work on the farm.

The most serious problems in this state involved not physical labor, but human relationships. Two major issues darkened this state (and this nation) like huge shadows: the question of slavery and the issue of native Americans and their claims to this land.

The selections in this section spotlight a number of very different people: a political leader; two Indian chiefs; two slaves with gifts for writing; two men who loved the mountains (each in his own way); and some children living in this interesting and difficult time.

Nathaniel Macon

Sam Ragan

It's time to move on, he said,
When you can hear your neighbor's dog bark.
Old Nathaniel Macon lived
Far out in the country,
And he didn't stay in Washington
Any more than he had to—
He was Jefferson's friend,
And there were letters between them.
He had power in Washington
As Speaker of the House,
But Warren was his home,
And it was where he returned.
He didn't want any funeral when he died,
And no monument on his grave.
But, he said, if anyone should pass this way
And think kindly of me,
Let them toss a stone on my resting place.

That was long ago, and there's
A big pile of rocks in Warren County.

Preview

Important political figures are usually remembered for the important contributions they made to the law and/or the history of their area. Nathaniel Macon (1758-1837), a native of Warren County, is noted for having served thirty-seven years in Congress—first in the House of Representatives, where eventually he became speaker of the House, and later in the Senate, where he chaired important committees. Macon was considered one of our most influential politicians of that time. In fact, at one time he was even mentioned as a candidate for vice-president. After returning to North Carolina, he continued to serve the state, presiding over the state convention of 1835, which proposed reforms for the state constitution.

Macon County (on the North Carolina/Georgia border in the western part of the state) and the town of Macon in Warren County (northeast of Raleigh) are both named for Nathaniel Macon. In our neighboring state, Virginia, Randolph-Macon College bears his name along with that of his friend, another congressman, John Randolph of Virginia.

Sometimes the personal, colorful stories about such persons tell us as much—or more—about them than does the formal record of achievements. In this poem, Sam Ragan takes note of Macon's national reputation, but he also gives us a glimpse of the man's personality.

MEET THE AUTHOR:
Sam Ragan (1915–)

"Read and write, look and listen to the world around you," Sam Ragan, Poet Laureate of North Carolina, advises students— and he has followed this advice himself, as his long and distinguished career clearly illustrates.

Born in Granville County, Sam Ragan decided in the third grade that he wanted to be a writer. Immediately after graduating from Atlantic Christian College, he began his journalistic career, which has included serving as editor of two major newspapers, the Raleigh *News and Observer* and the Southern Pines *Pilot*, of which he is also publisher.

But his career has involved more than journalism. During World War II, Sam Ragan served in military intelligence in the Pacific. During the 1970s, he was named North Carolina's first secretary of the Department of Cultural Resources. He has also helped start and/or support many local and statewide programs relating to the arts. Because of his encouragement and help, many North Carolina writers consider him a sort of "literary godfather."

Throughout his lifetime Sam Ragan has written poetry, publishing five collections. His excellence as journalist, poet, and public servant has been recognized by many awards, including the North Carolina Award in Fine Arts.

When he received the North Caroliniana Society Award, he summed up his philosophy and his career this way:

"Robert Frost talked about having a lover's quarrel with the world. Well, I've had a love affair with North Carolina for lo these many years, and it continues. I am greatly pleased, and I applaud when North Carolina and its people advance and show their humanity, and I suffer pain when it is less than humane. I've sort of taken as a criterion for journalism—and I once said so on the 'Good Morning' show—that as an editor you never go wrong if you are on the side of humanity."

Reflecting

1. Poetry is concentrated; it condenses a great deal of material into fewer words than would be used in prose. Assume that this poem is the only record we have of Nathaniel Macon. What facts do you know about his life? What can you infer about what kind of man he was, about his personality? What can you infer about how well he was regarded by his community?

2. In his weekly column in *The Spectator*, "As I Recall It," writer Noel Yancey tells us the following about Macon's death:

"In 1837, when he sensed the approach of death, Macon was ready. He selected a grave site atop a hill on his plantation, ordered a plain pine coffin built, paid the carpenter and dressed himself as he wished to be buried. A few hours later he was dead."

What does this information tell you about Macon's character?

3. Read the following very short poem by Sam Ragan. What does it say about what writers try to do? About how successful most of them are at doing it? About the importance of every person? How does the message of this poem apply to Ragan's work in composing "Nathaniel Macon"?

The One Small Singing

Sam Ragan

Novelists deal with the time of man—
Birth and death, and in between a little living
That barely breathes and seldom bleeds.
And poets, too, but rarely find
The shining moment
Or the one small singing
Of every man.

From *The Tree in the Far Pasture,* by Sam Ragan, published by John Blair, Publisher. Copyright © 1964 by Sam Ragan. Reprinted by permission of the author.

The Original
Carolina Mountaineers

When we hear the term *mountaineers*, we may picture a farmer (straw hat, overalls, corncob pipe, jug of homemade whiskey) and his wife (calico dress, apron, sunbonnet) sitting on the front porch of their log cabin. In the background are an orchard and a field with a mule, some cattle, and perhaps a dog or so. In other words, the term *mountaineer* may bring to mind a stereotyped—and very inaccurate—image of relatively poor but fiercely independent farmers descended from English or Scotch-Irish settlers.

What we forget is that the North Carolina mountains were settled long before travelers from England and Europe reached these shores. Native Americans had occupied that area for generations. Judge Felix Alley called the Cherokees "the original Carolina mountaineers."

Below are two accounts of those original mountaineers. Both reports are written by Caucasians who were deeply interested in the history and culture of this state. Both have told stories about notable Cherokee chieftains, and in these stories have included speeches made by these Indian leaders.

From *Random Thoughts and the Musings of a Mountaineer*

Old Tassel

Felix Alley

Preview

Assume that you are Old Tassel, a Cherokee chief, conferring with a white colonel. You are trying to end recent wars between Indians and whites and trying to get white settlers off lands that have by treaty been declared Cherokee areas.

Make the following decisions, then write the speech you would make.

1. Every speech begins with a *term of address*: for example, "Ladies and gentlemen," or "Fellow Democrats," or "Students and Faculty of _____ School." What *term of address* will you use for the white men?
2. What *approach* will you take? Will you beg and plead? Make demands? Make threats? Prove your claim?
3. What *tone*—attitude—will you take? Will you openly show anger? Will you be conciliatory (agreeable, trying to soothe feelings)? Or submissive (surrendering, giving in to others)? Or aggressive (pushy and hostile)? Or assertive (forceful in a self-confident, nonthreatening way)?

Briefly list the things you will say, then write your speech. Share your writings with others in the class. Be able to explain your decisions.

After reading Old Tassel's speech, you will want to compare your words to his. What does he ask for? What is the basis of his plea? Can you explain his choice of tone and language? How do you think Colonel Martin will respond?

Continue to read the remainder of the article in which Judge Alley explains what happened after Old Tassel's speech.

From *Random Thoughts and the Musings of a Mountaineer,* by Felix Alley, published by Rowan Printing Company. Copyright © 1941 by Felix Alley. Reprinted by permission of Betty Jean Alley.

"Brother, I am now going to speak to you.... We are a poor, distressed people that is in great trouble, and we hope our elder brother will take pity on us and do us justice.

Your people from Nolichucky are daily pushing us out of our lands. We have no place to hunt on. Your people have built houses within one day's journey of our town. We do not want to quarrel with our elder Brother; we therefore hope our elder Brother will not take our lands from us that the Great Man above gave us. He made you and He made us; we are all His children, and we hope our elder Brother will take pity on us, and not take our lands that our Father gave us, because he is stronger than we are. We are the first people that ever lived on this land; it is ours, and why will our elder Brother take it from us! We hope that you will take pity on your younger Brother, and send Colonel Sevier, who is a good man, to have all your people moved off our lands."

From the plea of Old Tassel, of Echota, to the Governor of North Carolina and Virginia, delivered September 25, 1782, at a conference with Colonel Joseph Martin.

World's Best Orations, Volume 7, page 2569.

It may be stated here that the foregoing eloquent plea of Old Tassel went unheeded, and those who had encroached upon the Indian land, in violation of the treaty concluded at Long Island, were not required to move. The time came, too, when Old Tassel had ample reason to believe that he was mistaken in his opinion that John Sevier was a good man. After the little war between John Sevier and John Tipton had ended in the latter's favor, and the State of Franklin, of which Sevier was Governor, had come to an end, Sevier led a band of about forty men against the Indian town of Chilhowa. The Indians put out a white flag; and the whites also raised one. One of the Indians, who had crossed the river in a boat, was induced to row Sevier and his men to the other side. Old Tassel was there, and it was well known that the Indians of this town were friendly to the whites. Old Tassel himself had for years been foremost in the endeavor to prevent Indian raids on the white settlers. However, after disarming the Indians, Sevier put them in a hut, and John Kirk, one of Sevier's troops, whose mother, sisters, and brothers had been killed by other Indians who had no connection with the Indians in question, went into the hut with his tomahawk, brained, killed, and scalped every one of these chiefs, while his comrades looked on and made no effort to prevent this horrible butchery of innocent and defenseless men.

The frontiersmen everywhere were outraged by this atrocity, and public sentiment became so aroused that Sevier's followers scattered. The Continental Congress passed a resolution condemning the outrage, and the justices of the Court at Abbeville, South Carolina, led by Andrew Pickens, wrote to the people settled on the Nolichucky, the French Broad, and the Holston, and scathingly denounced Sevier and his men. The Governor of North Carolina, upon hearing the horrible story, ordered that Sevier and his men be at once arrested for treason against the State. Sevier was brought to jail at Morganton, but he escaped and was never tried. In 1789, Washington County, in the present State of Tennessee, but then in North Carolina, elected Sevier to the North Carolina Legislature, and toward the end of the session he was permitted to take his seat, and the charge of treason was dropped. He was a representative in Congress from North Carolina—from March, 1789, to March, 1791—and was the first Governor of the new State of Tennessee.

Sevier no doubt rendered signal service both in the field and in the councils of the State and Nation. History refers to him as a pioneer statesman, and the great State of Tennessee still sings his praises, and honors his memory as one of their greatest men; but let me ask, Who sings the praises of Old Tassel, the great Indian Chief, who always advocated peace between the Indians and their "Elder Brother," and who asked nothing more than that his people be permitted to retain their own land, the peaceable possession of which had been guaranteed to them by the joint treaty of the Colonies of Virginia and North Carolina, and the Cherokee Nation, at the Long Island of the Holston on the second day of July, 1777?

MEET THE AUTHOR:
Felix Alley (1873–1957)

Felix Alley was born in Whiteside Cove in Jackson County and grew up on a farm there. His pioneer family was poor, and so was the community. Children had schooling for only six weeks out of every year. When young Felix was seventeen, his family sent him to what is now Western Carolina University. At that time it was only a high school, but it offered ten months of education a year. Later, the young man went to UNC-Chapel Hill, but financial problems made it impossible for him to go straight through college and law school, as he desired to do. By studying nights, eventually he passed the bar examination and began practicing law in the mountain town of Webster.

In 1905, just two years after becoming a lawyer, Felix Alley was elected to the General Assembly. Later, he became solicitor of the 20th Judicial District, and from 1933 to 1948 he served as a superior court judge.

Judge Alley had two major hobbies. One was music: he was a skilled banjo player and composed "Kidder Cole," a song which gained wide popularity. The second involved studying his beloved mountain region. Eventually from these studies came his book, *Random Thoughts and the Musings of a Mountaineer.*

Language Alert

1. If someone has *encroached* on your territory, what has he done?
   a. abused it   b. intruded on it   c. improved it
2. When you have been *induced* to do something, you have been
   a. persuaded   b. forbidden   c. forced
3. An *atrocity* is an act that is extremely
   a. kind, generous   b. bold, courageous   c. evil, cruel
4. A *scathing* remark is one which
   a. compliments generously   b. criticizes severely   c. complains
5. One who *advocates* a plan
   a. argues for it   b. argues against it   c. wants to discuss it

Can you determine each word's meaning from its use in the story? If not, check your answers with a dictionary or with your teacher.

Reflecting

1. You may want to read further about John Sevier. As Judge Alley points out, Sevier regained his good name after the first bad publicity and even served in major offices in North Carolina and Tennessee.
2. Re-read the last paragraph from Judge Alley's report. Then, taking a cue from the judge's comments, write a "song of praise" for Old Tassel—perhaps as a poem, perhaps as a **eulogy** (a speech to be read at his funeral).

John Sevier

Yonaguska

Letter XIV, Qualla Town, North Carolina, May 1848

Charles Lanman

Preview

In Felix Alley's story of Old Tassel, you saw how the settlers often dealt dishonestly with Native American's and how some Native Americans responded to the situation. After Old Tassel's death, new treaties continued to be written, signed, and broken. Eventually, the federal government made the Cherokees an offer. If the Cherokees would abandon their territory east of the Mississippi and move west, the government would pay them for the land they abandoned and guarantee them good land in what is now Oklahoma. In 1835 one group of Cherokees signed a treaty to that effect, but many others refused to accept that treaty.

The following letter, written by Charles Lanham in May 1848 and collected in his book, *Letters from the Alleghany Mountains,* tells of a Qualla chieftain, Yonaguska, and his response to the government offer.

In the present letter I purpose to give you a brief historical account of certain celebrated Cherokee Indians, who are deservedly considered as among the bright particular stars of their nation. Some of them are dead, and some still living, but they were all born in this mountain land, and it is meet that I should award to each a "passing paragraph of praise."

The first individual that I would mention is *Yo-na-gus-ka,* or the *Drowning Bear.* He was the principal chief of the Qualla Indians, and died in the year 1838, in the seventy-fifth year of his age. When the Cherokees were invited to remove west of the Mississippi in 1809, he petitioned President Jefferson that he might be permitted to remain with his followers, among his native mountains, and his

From *Letters from the Allegheny Mountains,* by Charles Lanman, published by George P. Putnam and Sons, 1849.

prayer was granted. He was eminently a peace chief, but obstinately declined every invitation of the Government to emigrate, and would probably have shed his blood and that of all his warriors in defending his rights. When about sixty years of age he had a severe fit of sickness, which terminated in a trance; this apparent suspension of all his faculties lasted about twenty-four hours, during which period he was supposed to be dead. It so happened, however, that he recovered, and on resuming his speech, told his attendants that he had been to the spirit land, and held communion with his friends who had been long dead, that they were all very happy. He also stated that he had seen many white men, and that some of them appeared to be unhappy. The Great Spirit talked with him, and told him his time was not yet come to leave the world; that he had been a good and honest man, and that he must return to his people, and govern them with great care and affection, so that he might finally come and live with the Great Spirit for ever.

Subsequently to that time his people gave him a new name, which was *Yon-na-yous-ta*, or *How like an Indian*. He governed his people like a father, and was universally beloved. It was at his suggestion that Mr. Thomas was adopted into the Cherokee nation; the prominent reasons assigned for such a desire on his part being that Thomas had proved himself to be the Indian's friend, and was alone in the world, having no father or brother. Mr. Thomas exerted a great influence over him, and among the measures which the former recommended was the adoption of a temperance society for the improvement of himself and people, who were all addicted to the intoxicating bowl.

He was a true patriot at heart, and on being reasoned into a correct state of mind, he expressed his determination to create a reform. He first reformed himself, and then summoned a council of all his people, ostensibly but secretly, for the purpose of establishing a temperance society. At this council he made a speech to the effect that they knew he had been an intemperate man, and had discouraged the use of strong drink, which he was confident was rapidly annihilating his nation; he expected to be with his people but a short time, and to extricate them from the great evil he had mentioned was the real purpose of the Great Spirit in prolonging his life; he also spoke of the many evils to families and individuals resulting from intemperance; and when he concluded, it is said that his entire audience were in tears. Taking advantage of this triumph, he called his scribe, (for he himself was an illiterate man,) and requested him to write these words upon a sheet of paper: "The undersigned drink no more whiskey;" to which pledge he requested that his name should be attached. Every member of the council appended his name to the paper, and thus was established the first temperance society among the Cherokees, which has already accomplished wonders. Among the regulations which he afterwards proclaimed, was one that each Indian should pay a fine of two shillings for every offence committed in breaking the pledge, and that the money thus collected should be expended in extending the boundaries of their territory. And here it may be well to mention the fact, that though this "father of temperance" among the Indians had been extremely dissipated during a period of thirty years, he was never known, even in *the way of medicine,* to touch a drop of spirits after his first temperance speech.

The reputation of Yo-na-gus-ka as an orator was co-extensive with his entire nation. He not only understood the art of working upon the feelings and clothing his thoughts in the most appropriate imagery, but the thoughts themselves were invariably sound, and his arguments unanswerable. From many examples of his reasoning I select one. When once invited by the officers of Government to remove westward, even after he and his people had become citizenized, he was informed that in the West he would have an abundance of the most fertile land, with plenty of game; also a government of his own; that he would be undisturbed by the whites, and that the United States Government would ever protect him from future molestation. In replying to this invitation, as he stood in the midst of armed soldiers, he remarked in substance as follows:

"I am an old man, and have counted the snows of almost eighty winters. My hair, which is now very white, was once like the raven's wing. I can remember when the white man had not seen the smoke of our cabins westward of the Blue Ridge, and I have watched the establishment of all his settlements, even to the Father of Waters. The march of the white is still towards the setting sun, and I know that he will never be satisfied until he reaches the shore of the great water. It is foolish in you to tell me that the whites will not trouble the poor Cherokee in the Western country. The white man's nature and the Indian's fate tell a different story. Sooner or later one Government must cover the whole continent, and the red people, if not scattered among the autumn leaves, will become a part of the American nation. As to the white man's promises of protection, they have been too often broken; they are like the reeds in yonder river—they are all lies. North Carolina had acknowledged our title to these lands, and the United States had guaranteed that title; but all this did not prevent the Government from taking away our lands by force; and, not only that, but sold the very cow of the poor Indian and his gun, so as to compel him to leave his country. Is this what the white man calls justice and protection? No, we will not go to the West. We wanted to become the children of North Carolina, and she has received us as such, and passed a law for our protection, and we will continue to raise our corn in this very land. The people of Carolina have always been very kind to us, and we know they will never oppress us. You say the land in the West is much better than it is here. That very fact is an argument on our side. The white man must have rich land to do his great business, but the Indian can be happy with poorer land. The white man must have a flat country for his plough to run easy, but we can get along even among the rocks on the mountains. We never shall do what you want us to do. I don't like you for your pretended kindness. I always advise my people to keep their backs for ever turned towards the setting sun, and never to leave the land of their fathers. I tell them they must live like good citizens; never forget the kindness of North Carolina, and always be ready to help her in time of war. I have nothing more to say."

When Yo-na-gus-ka was about to die, he summoned his chiefs and warriors by his bed-side, and talked to them at great length upon the importance of temperance, and in opposition to the idea of their emigrating to the West, and made them swear that they would never abandon the graves of their fathers, or his own grave, which is now marked by a pile of stones on the margin of the Soco. In personal appearance he was very handsome, and left two wives. He was the owner of considerable property, and among his possessions was an old negro named *Cudjo*. This man is now living, and on questioning him about his former master he replied: "If Yo-na-gus-ka had had larning, I b'lieve he'd been a very great man. He never allowed himself to be called *master*, for he said Cudjo was his brother, and not his slave. He was a great friend o' mine, and when he died, I felt as if I didn't care about living any longer myself; but Yo-na-gus-ka is gone, and poor old Cudjo is still alive and well."

Charles Lanman (1819–1895)

Like explorers Arthur Barlowe and John Lawson, Charles Lanman was not a native North Carolinian, but like them he traveled here and recorded his travels carefully. His writings fill important gaps in our history.

Lanman was born in Michigan, and traveled and worked widely. Much of his professional life was spent in Washington, DC, where at one time he was secretary to Daniel Webster. During his travels, he collected significant historical facts and intriguing stories, including material about the Cherokee Indians in the western part of our state.

Language Alert

1. Yonaguska "*obstinately* declined every invitation of the Government to *emigrate*." (That is, he stubbornly turned down every invitation to leave his country.)
2. His sickness "*terminated* in a trance." (It ended in a trance.)
3. "This *apparent suspension of his faculties* lasted about twenty-four hours." (To put it another way: For about twenty-four hours his skills and powers seemed to be interrupted.)
4. Because he believed that strong drink was *annihilating* his people, he began a *temperance society*. (He believed that alcoholic beverages were completely destroying his people, so he began an organization which encouraged people not to drink alcohol.)
5. Yonaguska wanted to *extricate* his people from evil. (He wanted to untangle and free them from evil.)
6. Eventually Yonaguska's reputation as an orator was "*co-extensive* with his entire nation." (A modern writer would probably say that Yonaguska's reputation spread throughout the nation.)

Did you notice that some of Charles Lanman's paragraphs are very long? This style was very common in older writings.

Reflecting

1. Review the story to find the following:
   a. Evidence that Yonaguska had firm religious beliefs
   b. His efforts to reform first himself, then his people
   c. His response to the federal government's offer to move to the West and his attitude toward the North Carolina government
   d. Evidence that Yonaguska—like Thomas Jefferson, who wrote our Declaration of Independence—believed in the equality of all human beings
2. The chief of a tribe, the president of a nation, the chairperson of a club—all should possess certain qualities of leaders. Find details that indicate that Yonaguska possessed the following traits:
   a. honesty
   b. courage
   c. the willingness to lead by example as well as by word
   d. respect for others
   e. the ability to express himself effectively
3. Notice how poetic Yonaguska's language is. To make his points, he uses concrete images that the listener can visualize. Find the image he uses to express each of the following:
   a. I am eighty years old.
   b. My hair was once black.
   c. I can remember when the white man did not know of our settlements west of the Blue Ridge.
   d. I have seen the white man move westward, even to the Mississippi.
   e. We may become separated as a people.
   f. The government took our possessions and our weapons.
   g. We will continue to farm here.
   h. The white man can farm only on flat land.
   i. I advise my people not to consider going West.

Sequoyah's Gift

Julia Montgomery Street

Preview

True stories about two Cherokee chiefs—Yonaguska and Old Tassel—appear earlier in this section. In the following excerpt from Julia Montgomery Street's novel, *Moccasin Tracks*, Yonaguska presides over a tribal council as chief of the tribe. During the meeting, another Indian refers to Old Tassel.

Another real person appears in this story: Sequoyah, a Cherokee who became so fascinated with the way white people communicated by writing that he invented a system of writing for his own people. He completed the task in 1821 after twelve years of strenuous work. The giant sequoia redwood trees in California—among the largest and the oldest living things on earth—were named for this distinguished Cherokee Indian.

We pick up this story one evening when Timothy, an orphaned boy from a family of settlers, comes with his friend Suyeta, Yonaguska's son, to a tribal meeting. All the tribe is gathered in the council-house: boys and men in one area; women, including Adaleei, Yonaguska's wife, in the other. Timothy is hoping that his friend's tribe will adopt him. However, tonight the Indians have other matters on their mind: the new writing devised by Sequoyah.

Can you predict how the Indians will react to Sequoyah's work?

As he entered the seven-sided council house through the door in the eastern wall, Timothy saw all the people of Kituwah assembled there, dressed in their brightest turbans and best beaded and fringed buckskin trousers and skirts. Following close to Suyeta, he looked about him in awe. The flickering light from the sacred fire in the center of the building made the seven pillars holding up the peaked roof seem to reach to the sky. These polished, gleaming tree trunks, stripped of bark, were decorated with ugly, grinning dancing-masks, ceremonial eagle-feather fans, gourd rattles and other sacred symbols.

Opposite the door, in front of the central pillar, sat Yonaguska, majestic, resplendent in an eagle-feather robe and pure white doeskin trousers and moccasins, which were beautifully beaded and fringed. On his head was a magnificent crown of white crane feathers and egret plumes, and about his neck hung a string of wolves' teeth. On his breast, suspended by a silver chain, gleamed a large, round silver medal, beautifully engraved.

"My father wears a new silver gorget, in place of his old stone one," Suyeta whispered, pointing to the gleaming necklace. "It must be a gift from Sequoyah. I have not seen it before."

"Oh! I forgot to give your family the gifts I fetched," Tim whispered back. "I hadn't even thought about them since you fright—since you took me to your house from the forest."

Suyeta pointed out a seat to Tim on the lowest tier of benches, near the eastern door, and walked up to the sacred fire, directly in front of his father. He bowed low seven times, once to each of the seven pillars; then stood erect, waiting for a signal from the chief. Yonaguska nodded and Suyeta sat down on the ground, cross-legged, near the foot-high cone of earth, the hollowed-out top of which held the everlasting fire. With great concentration he began to arrange a lattice work of small sticks around the cone, from which to replenish the fire.

Timothy, feeling deserted, lonely and almost fearful, gazed around. On each side of the chief were seats made from large sections of logs, and behind him, covering the walls of the council house, hung mats and curtains woven of the finest splints of river cane, in beautiful designs and colors. On the posts on either side hung the red and the yellow ceremonial costumes Suyeta had told him about—the yellow always worn when a new chief was selected and the red always used by a war chief. Both sets of garments were faded and dusty now, for Yonaguska had long been chief and Kituwah had not gone to war for many years.

Spotting Adaleei and Atalsta where they sat on the east side of the building, Timothy wished he might join them, but he noted that only women and girls sat on the tiers of mat-covered benches on that side. On his own, the west side, sat all the men and boys of the town.

Everyone was as still as a fallen wind, waiting for the chief to speak.

Yonaguska rose, folded his arms, bowed to each of the seven posts in turn, then picked up a brightly painted gourd from among the jars, baskets and rattles on a bench near him and shook it. It rattled loudly.

All the people rose and bowed to each of the seven pillars; but Timothy sat like a stone, too awed to move, though no one seemed to notice him, as they all sat down.

The chief spoke:

"I, Yanugunski, Drowning Bear, who walk in the moccasin tracks of the Great Yanegwa, Big Bear, make talk with you, my people."

All the people bowed their heads and murmured, "*Ha-yu, ha-yu!*"

Yonaguska rattled the gourd again, softly, and continued:

"Now, when *Nunda*, the Sun, has dropped below the vault of the sky, and the dark has raised its sheltering curtain; now when the sacred fire burns brightest, I, the Peace Chief of all the Mountain Cherokee, who live in brotherhood with their neighbors the palefaces, bring you a message."

Timothy, listening closely, thought, "Now he is going to call me up and tell them he is adopting me as his son." But the tall, stately chief did not even glance his way.

Suddenly old Agawela shouted from her high seat among the women, "Down with the palefaces! Give them the arrow!" And Tim shrank down in his seat, wishing he could become invisible, as several other old women echoed, "Give them the arrow!" But Yonaguska did not even notice the interruption.

"The last important talk that I made with you," he continued in a voice like the rumbling of a rushing river, "was to bring you a message from the Spirit World, whither I had gone for a sun and a moon, but this talk I make now, is a talk from the world of the living."

"That time I told you how, after my long sickness, I ascended into the realm of *Asgaya-Galun-Lati*, The Man Above, and talked with Him, and with our fathers who had gone before. I brought you word that the Great Spirit, seeing the harm the white man's firewater was doing to His children, forbade you to drink it."

The people rose as one, shouted "*Ha-yu! Ha-yu!*" and reseated themselves.

"That time," said the chief, "I came to the council house to take something harmful from you. This time I come to give you something good."

"Now," thought Timothy, sitting up eagerly as the chief walked forward, and he half-rose to meet him, but Yonaguska passed him by without a glance. The people turned in their seats and watched Yonaguska's progress to the door of the council house, where he greeted Sequoyah and little Eye-o-kah, then led them to the seats on each side of his own.

"Gosh! I forgot all about Sequoyah, I was so taken with this place," Timothy said to himself, scrunching down in his seat. "No wonder they've not got around to me, yet."

Yonaguska spoke again, in his deep voice, "Before the curtain of darkness fell, you greeted our brother Sequoyah in the town square. Now I bring him to you in all honor in our council house, as the greatest man the *Ani-yun-wiya* have ever had among them. Our brother has sought out, and found, a way to capture Cherokee words, so that we may keep them, even as the white man captures his words and keeps them."

Yonaguska moved forward a step, drew himself to his full, towering height and said, "Sequoyah has found a way to *write* and *read*! He has discovered a way to accomplish this in *our own tongue!* Even as the palefaces read and write in their tongue."

A screech sounded from among the old women. "He's a witch! Kill him! He makes bad medicine!"

An old man called from the top row on

the men's side. "He will make fools of all the Cherokees. What do we want with captured words? We have our tongues to speak with! Already we have too many of the white man's ways. We have taken his goods and his clothes, his cats and his cows, his beds and his tables, his guns and his hoes. Now you would have us take his books!"

"*Ha-yu! Ha-yu!*" agreed a feeble voice here and there, and, encouraged, the tottery old man, wrapped in a ragged blanket, stood up to be heard better.

"The Great Spirit is already angry with his Cherokee children. We have offended His Great White Deer, and the game is leaving our hunting grounds. Bear and deer are no longer plentiful, and the wild doves no longer abound, delighting our ears with their musical cries of '*gule, gule* (acorns, acorns).' For even those acorns are scarce, since we cut the trees to build lodges like the Long Knives. The streams are drying up and our people are dying of the white devils' sicknesses. We must put off paleface ways and be Indians again!" He dropped in his seat, exhausted.

Timothy shrank deeper into his own seat, trying to be so still that no one would notice him. "What's going to happen," he thought, "will they kill me? Suyeta says the old men and women are always obeyed when they speak in the council. These old folks are saying to kill the white people. I know they are, by their looks and what words I can make out: Now Unacata's getting up! I'm scared!"

Unacata (White Man Killer), another old man whom Timothy had always avoid-

ed because of his angry manners, rose. Although he was feeble and trembly, his voice ran out:

"Our brother, Old Tassel, was right when he said we must drive the white man back whence he came! White ways are not Indian ways. The Great Spirit made us two separate peoples. He stocked their lands with cows and sheep; ours with deer; theirs with hogs, ours with bear; his animals are tame and easily killed; ours are wild and need much space and hard hunting. Old Tassel bade us keep our land and our Indian ways, and not take on the white man's. Now this witch, Sequoyah, comes among us and bids us take on their books and their writing, as well as their ways!"

Unacata looked all about as if trying to find someone, and when his eyes finally lighted on Timothy he made a horrible face, then folded his blanket around him and sat down.

Timothy shrank even lower in his seat. He noticed that little Eye-o-kah had crept to her father and leaned against his side, while the old men and women spoke against him.

Suddenly Yonaguska blew a shrill blast on his eaglebone whistle, and all the people shifted in their seats, then became as quiet as a smoke cloud.

"*Tsi-wani-hu* (I am speaking, now)!" said the chief in a moderate, but firm, tone. "Although we all may not think it is good, our white brothers have come to the land of the *Tsalagi* to stay. We have lived in peace with them for many seasons, now, and the war hatchet has long been buried in Kituwah. We will continue to

Sequoyah.

live in peace with our paleface neighbors. Our ancient ones are wise, and we must respect their counsel, when their counsel is good, but times are different now, from the days of their youth, and it is no longer wise to strike the hatchet on the war post for the white man."

Suyeta threw a handful of sticks on the fire, causing it to blaze brightly; and Timothy straightened up in his seat. The glow of the blaze on Yonaguska's white raiment and on the iridescent feathers of his cloak and crown made him look like some shining spirit.

The chief pulled out a carved, whitestone peace pipe, held a long stick to the glowing fire and lighted it.

"Now let us smoke the pipe of peace," he said in a deep, calm voice, "and proceed to the purpose for which we have met in Council."

He took a deep draw and sent a great puff of smoke toward the ceiling.

"Now, from the pipe of peace, we will send our petition upward on its smoke to *Yo-He-Wah!*" His eyes followed the ascending smoke. "O, Great Spirit, give us wisdom!"

Yonaguska handed the pipe to Sequoyah, who also blew a puff of smoke toward the ceiling, and murmured some words that Timothy could not understand. After Sequoyah, the pipe went to the old men who, each in turn, blew a puff upward, then passed it on to his neighbor. None dared refuse the peace pipe.

While the smoking was in progress Suyeta crept over to Timothy. "Do not be afraid, my brother," he whispered, "we are your friends. The ancient ones quickly forget their threats and go to sleep. See, most of them are dozing now. My father says the hoary-headed ones are often transported in their minds to the days of their youth, and for the moment would have all Cherokee as they were then. He says we must listen with respect to their talk, but we must act for the best. He says we must not heed those who would have us make war, but must walk in the ways of peace. Do not be afraid, Timothy."

Suyeta slipped back to his place by the sacred fire, and Timothy tried to put his fears away.

"Now," said Yonaguska, when the white-stone pipe had gone to every man and returned to him, and been put aside, "now, we will proceed. Our brother Sequoyah has brought a great gift to Kituwah, and we will all listen while he makes talk." He exchanged seats with Sequoyah.

Eye-o-kah unfastened the thongs that bound the large, deerskin-wrapped package that her father held, and he began to remove from it sheets of white hide, marked in strange symbols. Pieces of bark, and some stones, followed the sheets of hide, all covered with the markings, and the people craned forward to see and to murmur approvingly; but here and there an old man or woman muttered, "Bad Medicine."

Timothy was no longer afraid, but, like everyone else, was eager to see the wonderful new writing.

In Kituwah, the morning after Sequoyah and his little girl had demonstrated the wonderful Cherokee alphabet, all the people were in a stew of excitement. Each

was trying to out do the other, with his marks on skin, bark, stone—anything that would take a mark made with a piece of charcoal or a pointed stick. Some even wrote in the dust.

"Look! I write!"

"See, I write my own name!"

"I read, I write!"

"I, too, can write, and read!"

Men, women, boys and girls, and even the old people, quickly learned to write and read a few words, so simple was Sequoyah's method; and all were very proud of their new knowledge.

The great man himself was sleeping late, tired out, and Timothy would not stir from in front of Yonaguska's lodge, for fear Sequoyah might get away before he spoke to him. But, all the time he waited, he practiced writing and reading, drawing the characters of the Cherokee alphabet on a board with a piece of burnt stick, scrubbing them off in the sand, then writing again. Sometimes he forgot a letter and made a mental note of it, that he might study it later.

The sun had reached the height of heaven and started toward the west, and still Sequoyah slept on, while Suyeta tried to lure Tim to the town square, where most of the villagers were gathered, practicing their skill.

"You were so eager to learn to write in our tongue," he twitted Timothy, "I'd think you would want to show off your accomplishment to the rest of us. But here you sit, alone. Truly, white men are strange and stubborn people. Look, you make those characters wrong!"

"I plan to stay here and speak to

Sequoyah."

"Come on down to the square. There I will teach you the correct way to write!" Suyeta was impatient to show off Timothy's and his writing skill before the townspeople.

"I can't. I have to talk to Sequoyah about something important. What did you do with your panther skin, Suyeta?"

"*Ha-yu!* I had forgotten all about it. Now I must go call my father and all the people and show them *my* great deed." Suyeta ran around the cabin, and returned, dragging the stiffened pelt with him. "Perhaps I'd better take it to the square and show it," he said boastfully. "Is this not a beautiful trophy?"

"I don't believe I would, Suyeta. Anyway, here comes your father and your mother now."

Yonaguska, followed by Adaleei, came striding up the trail to the lodge, with the two little girls behind them, and old Agawela bringing up the rear.

"*Si-yu!*" called Suyeta, running to meet them. "At last perhaps you will notice my great deed!" He ran back and picked up the panther skin and waved it. "See, my Father, my Mother, I am a hero, too! I have killed a Cat of God!"

Yonaguska frowned. "Boasting is not becoming to the son of a chief," he chided. "Have you ever heard the story of the possum's tail? You, Suyeta, as well as the possum, should be called *Awaniski* (he who talks too much)."

Suyeta answered nothing, but hung his head and backed toward the lodge, pulling the pelt along in the leaves.

"Wait, my Son!" ordered Yonaguska.

"Let us all sit upon these fallen tree trunks, and I will tell you that story, as the old men told it to me. Come, Timothy-*Usdi*, and join us, while I relate to Suyeta the story of 'Why The Possum's Tail Is Bare.' "

Timothy sat down on a log, facing Yonaguska, Adaleei and Suyeta, who was still sulking, while the two little girls ran in and out among the trees, playing a game. Agawela panted up and sat down at the other end of the log from Timothy, not seeming to notice him at all.

Yonaguska began his story:

"The Possum used to have a long bushy tail, and was so proud of it that he combed it out every morning, and sang about it at the dance, until Rabbit, who had had no tail since the Bear pulled it out, became very jealous, and made up his mind to play Possum a trick."

"There was to be a great council and a dance at which all the animals were to be present. It was Rabbit's business to send out the news, so as he was passing Possum's place he stopped and asked him if he intended to be there. Possum said he would come if he could have a special seat, 'Because I have such a handsome tail I ought to sit where everyone can see me.' The Rabbit promised to attend to it, and send someone to comb and dress Possum's tail for the dance. Possum was very pleased.

"Then Rabbit went over to Cricket, who is such an expert haircutter that the Indians call him 'The Barber,' and told him to go next morning and dress Possum's tail for the dance. He told Cricket just what to do; then went on about some oth-

106

er mischief."

"In the morning, when Cricket arrived and said he had been sent to dress Possum's tail for the dance, Possum stretched out with his eyes shut, while Cricket combed out his tail and wrapped a red string around it to keep it smooth till night.

"When it was night, Possum went to the dance, and found the best seat waiting for him, just as *Tsistu*, the Rabbit, had promised. When his turn to dance came, he loosened the string from his tail and stepped into the middle of the floor. The drummers began to drum, and the Possum began to sing, 'See my beautiful tail.' Everybody shouted and danced around the circle and sang. They shouted again, and Possum danced around another time singing, 'See how it sweeps the ground.' The animals shouted louder, and Possum was delighted.

"He danced around again and sang, 'See how beautiful the fur is.' Then everybody laughed so loud that Possum wondered what they meant. He looked around the circle of animals and saw that they were all laughing at him. Then he looked down at his beautiful tail, and saw there was not a hair left upon it. Cricket had snipped off every single hair! Possum was so astonished and chagrined that he fell down and rolled over, and sulked, even as he does to this day."

As Yonaguska finished his story, merry laughter from the cabin caused them all to look up and see Sequoyah, who had finally awakened, standing there.

"*Ha!*" he said. "That is a good tale. I have heard it many times from the old men. Now I shall write it down so that it can never be lost from the Cherokee language." He went into the lodge and came out with his packet of writing materials, and proceeded to make a great many marks upon a large piece of white doeskin. His watchers were fascinated, and even old Agawela crowded close to see.

Finally, he laid down his piece of charcoal and held out the script to Suyeta, saying, "This is a gift to you, Suyeta, son of my friend, Yonaguska. Preserve it carefully. It is the very first one of the Cherokee tales that has ever been written in our own tongue. I honor you. A youth of your years who has killed a panther, even a small one, deserves to be honored in some fashion."

Suyeta took the script reluctantly, thinking, "Is Sequoyah making fun of me, too?"

Everybody looked at Suyeta, whose head was bowed in confusion. Then Yonaguska patted his shoulder and said, "My Son, you are indeed the Chosen One. Sequoyah brings great honor to our family when he entrusts you with the keeping of our first myth in writing. Stand up. Hold your head high."

Then Suyeta knew that they were not laughing at him. He stood tall, and bowed to Sequoyah, saying "*Wadan*, Sequoyah. I shall try to prove worthy of your trust."

Julia Montgomery Street
(1898–   )

Born in Concord, NC, Julia Montgomery Street grew up in Apex. She began her writing career in 1959, when she was already a grandmother. Now retired in Winston-Salem, Mrs. Street has written four novels for young readers, all of them based on some aspect of North Carolina history. She has covered topics ranging from the driving of farm animals down the Buncombe Turnpike to the appearance of enemy submarines in the waters near Cape Lookout during World War I.

Before composing her stories, Julia Montgomery Street did a great deal of research to make sure her facts were accurate. She later collected and published folk legends and, with Richard Walser, coauthored *North Carolina Parade*, a collection of legends and true stories about North Carolina people. She also published articles on North Carolina history. Three times her books won the AAUW[1] Award for the best book for young readers written by a North Carolina author.

Language Alert

In the earlier account of Yonaguska (see page 94), we saw how eloquent, even poetic, his speech became at times. Notice how Julia Montgomery Street has managed to capture this same style when Yonaguska and his people speak—especially in formal situations such as the council meeting.

Reflecting

1. Why do you think other Indians in the tribe reacted as they did to Sequoyah's work? Knowing what you do of Yonaguska (see page 94), can you explain his reaction?
2. Notice the skill with which Yonaguska taught his son that it is unbecoming to boast. He does not yell or preach. Instead, he tells an entertaining legend which gets his point across—a story so entertaining that Sequoyah, who overhears it, laughs.

   Think of an occasion when you observed a child—maybe a younger brother or sister—doing something wrong or foolish. Can you make up a legend which would teach a lesson about that behavior without embarrassing the child? Can you even make it humorous?

1. American Association of University Women

The Professor and the Hunter

Wilma Dykeman

Preview

Dr. Elisha Mitchell, a brilliant university professor with such wide knowledge that his students call him "the walking encyclopedia"; and Big Tom Wilson, a backwoods mountain man who spends more time reading footprints than books—what could these two have in common? Wouldn't they feel contempt for each other—the professor scoffing at the mountaineer's lack of cultural and scientific education, the mountaineer ridiculing a man who had "nothing but book-larnin"?

This true story, included in Wilma Dykeman's *The French Broad*, tells of two very different men whose lives crossed in unexpected ways in the North Carolina mountains during the years just preceding the Civil War. As you read, you will certainly be struck by the contrasts in the two men, but look, too, for surprising similarities. See if you can tell how the two felt about each other.

The farm was only a minute human patch laid at the foot of the great wooded mountains in the midst of hundreds of acres of unexplored wilderness. There was a house—two rooms and a kitchen with a porch across the front and a loft above—and clustered nearby were the open-air barn and squat spring-house, all the color of weather: wind and sun and rain.

On a July afternoon in 1857, Big Tom Wilson sat on his porch and enjoyed the fresh breeze that occasionally drifted down from the heights around him. Chickens wallowed lazily in the dust near the barn, and out in the pasture between the blackberry vines the sound of the cowbell was slow and long. His bear dogs had long since stretched out in the cool shadows under the house. At one end of the porch a loom stood with a half-finished piece of cloth in its intricate maze; fish rods leaned limp against the wall. From inside the house there was the sound of children.

The lethargy[1] of late afternoon was broken by two visitors. As the men came up to the porch from the narrow rough trail, children clustered in the open doorway and the dogs bristled till they heard their owner's voice. "Howdy, John Stepp."

"How are you, Tom? This here's Charley Mitchell, the Professor's boy."

With good-natured manners, the tall sinewy mountain man shook the young stranger's hand.

"My father," Charles Mitchell said, "has my father been here, Mr. Wilson? Have you seen him in the last four days?"

"No. I ain't seen him since his last exploring trip up here." And Big Tom looked at John Stepp.

"Last Saturday, the twenty-seventh I reckon it was, the boy here parted company with his father at the Patton House, over on the south side of the Black Mountain. They'd come up from Swannanoa and the Professor wanted to go back up to the peak where you'd taken him nigh thirteen year ago."

Big Tom nodded. He remembered Dr. Mitchell, with all his learning and his measuring apparatus, as clear as he did that bear track he'd found this morning down in the cornfield among his tender roasting ears.

"Well," John Stepp went on, "he started up the mountain alone about noontime last Saturday. Nobody's laid eyes on him since. Monday, Charley and me was supposed to meet him up on the Elizabeth Rock where he was going to do some more surveying and measuring. We went up to the rock Monday but he never did come."

"We can't find a trace of him," Charles Mitchell said.

Big Tom looked up toward the Black Mountain and the Black Brothers that ranged there beyond it, looked at the cap of giant fir and balsam that had given the peaks their name. There were vast stretches in there that had never been explored by white men. Clear rushing Cane River that wound through his farm here drew its waters from a dozen streams webbed like crooked veins up into the hidden recesses[2] of those mountains, and no man had traced them to their source. Bear and "painters" and lesser varmints roamed undisputed in this tangled domain. It was a wild dark region. He'd better tell it to the boy plain out.

"If the Professor ain't been here, and if he ain't come back to where he was supposed to have met you, then he's dead on those mountains."

Nobody said anything for a little bit, while the sound of Cane River and the cowbell took over. Then Charley Mitchell asked, "Would you help us look for him?"

Big Tom Wilson said he would help. It was not in the nature of mountain men to

---

1. lethargy: lacking energy
2. recesses: hollow places

refuse a person in need. And within two days, in that sparsely settled region which had no system of communication, one hundred and fifty men had answered the call for searchers. Twice that many were eventually to volunteer. They could not be just any men, either, for the job they offered to undertake would demand the last ounce of their physical strength. It was not only that the mountains were steep and trailless, or that the contours of every slope shaped a unique ruggedness, but the thick mazes of twisted laurel made every climb and descent a battle with tough interlocking limbs and roots. Nevertheless they came as gladly and freely as one who said, "When I heard that Professor Mitchell was lost on the mountain somewhere, I was plowing, but I dropped my plow and took out to find him."

Who was this lost stranger they went in search of?

Elisha Mitchell was about as different from these men as could easily be imagined. He was as different from Big Tom Wilson as a Doberman is from a bear dog, but there is one virtue common to both and that is intelligence. Developed along different lines, with unlike methods and varying uses, the intellects of these two men were drawn together because of mutual need. Each represented a sort of mind that seems peculiarly American, and without either the development of the country would have been far different and much less interesting.

One more thing that the professor and the hunter had in common, the factor that gave them ground for understanding: interest in the natural world around them. Keen curiosity to know about creatures and inanimate creation as well, quickness to see what was to be seen, alertness to make judgments and draw conclusions from observations. The curious interweaving of Wilson's and Mitchell's life and death seems a parable of each man's worth in his own particular sensibility.[3]

Born in Connecticut, a graduate of Yale University, Elisha Mitchell had received an education for the ministry from a New England seminary before he came to the University of North Carolina as a professor of mathematics. His variety of interests and abilities soon became legendary. In addition to mathematics, he taught natural history, chemistry, botany, surveying, agriculture, geology, and geography; his university students called him "the walking encyclopedia." Besides writing books for his students to study, he taught his own family of five children. Almost every Sunday he preached either at the Chapel Hill village church or in the college chapel. He was also the college bursar, a justice of the peace, a farmer, a commissioner for the village and at times its magistrate of police. It is self-evident that he was a man who, as one of his friends said, "enjoyed being busy. Neither laziness nor idleness entered into his composition, so that he always had something which he was doing heartily." There was nothing he did more heartily than study the birds and animals, the trees

3. sensibility: mental or emotional responsiveness to something

and plants, the rocks and sands and clays of North Carolina. He had said once in a sermon that God is a part of nature and nature a part of God.

While on an exploration in the Western mountains years before this trip with his son, he had measured the Black Mountain and discovered that it was higher than Mount Washington in New Hampshire, at that time considered the highest peak in the East. A few years later he and Thomas Clingman, also an avid[4] explorer of this region, made a trip together through the Balsam and Black Mountains as well as the Great Smokies, measuring and making scientific studies. But when Clingman issued the news that he had discovered a peak higher than Dr. Mitchell's Black—a peak called the smoky Dome which would later be renamed for its discoverer—a scientific feud flared between the two men. Each published his findings and made his claims and the public was left to wonder about the "accuracy" of science.

But not for long. Dr. Mitchell was not one to let such a controversy run on without verification of his own figures. It was this necessity to establish, without doubt or falsification, the claim he made for his mighty Black that had sent him on this last journey into the mountains. When he had struck off alone toward its summit, he had gone to find the marked balsam under which he had stood years before and made his first exciting measurement. Somewhere between that pinnacle and the overnight hiker's cabin on one side of the range and Big Tom Wilson's farm on the other side, the Professor had become

lost or injured.

As the party of volunteer searchers increased and was organized, a natural division separated them into two groups: the Men of Buncombe and the Men of Yancey they called themselves, men from the two westernmost North Carolina counties whose boundaries were among these mountains. The Buncombe Men were led by two of their famous old bear hunters, Eldridge and Frederick Burnett. The Burnetts directed the early part of the search, mostly on the south side of the mountain.

For days they toiled and looked. One party followed the east fork of the Cane River and another took the west. More scenic, more difficult terrain would be hard to imagine. Through the July heat they combed the undergrowth, working higher and higher, across the gaps, and finally late one afternoon, hungry and exhausted, they met at the Patton House on the Buncombe road from the pinnacle. They looked at one another and shook their heads and there was no need for comment or explanation. They were bone-tired and there was nothing for them to eat.

Zeb Vance, who in a few years would become the famous Civil War governor of North Carolina, was one of the searchers. When he arrived at the house and saw the situation, he promptly directed some of the men to drive up a fat heifer that was grazing in one of the mountain pastures nearby. A skilled marksman named Ephraim Glass put a bullet through her

4. avid: enthusiastic

The falls where Elisha Mitchell slipped to his death.

head, and the sharp hunting knives soon had the meat divided and roasting on long sticks over an open fire. A few of the men were too famished to wait, and they ate the chunks raw, without even the savor of salt. Vance had also started a party down toward the settlement of Swannanoa to get flour, salt and a little "extract of corn."

When they returned, far up in the night by the light of pine torches, the jug of "corn extract" made the rounds from one thirsty mouth to another. The older hunters began to compare details of the day's search and plan the next day's route, and finally they launched into a few tales of past hunts and hardships. There was no one who could equal Big Tom in telling about the woods and bears and the ways of both. The men listened, reassured, as his calm, low voice recounted dangers he had overcome, not once or twice but many times. He described bears individually, like people, familiar with their habits and oddities, and he called his dogs, past and present, by apt affectionate names. The bear who turned, finally, and stood his ground tenaciously[5] against assault by pack and hunter, the dog who hung on to the trail no matter how many days it took to bring their bear to bay, these were victim and victor Big Tom admired. The men shared their experiences and knowledge of the woods. They slept, at last, by the chunky coals of the fire that felt good at night in this high altitude.

Monday was another hard fruitless day and that night the pessimism in the camp was so solid it seemed almost tangible.

After eating a chunk of crude bread made of the flour brought up the night before, and some of the leftovers of beef, they discussed plans for tomorrow. When someone suggested the hunt be postponed for three or four days until birds of prey might begin to gather and point out the location of the corpse, there was almost unanimous agreement. The size of the area to be combed, its dense tangle and generally unknown terrain, made the task of finding one small man seem hourly more hopeless. But young Charley Mitchell could not abandon his father so completely, even for a few days. He pleaded with these worn realistic mountain men to continue for even a little longer.

Then Big Tom took over. Soft as rain on moss but firm as granite, he explained: "Now I've talked with the men who gave Professor Mitchell his directions regarding the way to my house, and I've talked with William Wilson who guided the Professor the first time he ever visited that peak. Turning what both these fellers have told me in my mind, I'm certain that if any trace of the Professor is ever found, it'll be somewhere between a little garden patch that opens out just before you get to the top of the peak, and my house."

He paused but there was no comment.

"Now, Mr. Vance," the tall rawboned mild-mannered man went on, "up to this time I've been letting the old men and you men from Buncombe search. Now I'm going to search. Any of you men want to come with me, that's all right too. I'm going up to the cabin on the mountain to-

5. tenaciously: stubbornly

114

night. From there we can get a soon start in the morning."

He stood up and four of the Yancey men joined him, four of the keenest who had trailed many a mile in these woods: Adoniram and James Allen, Berton Austin and Bryson McMahan. They took scanty rations from what was left of the flour and beef. That night they climbed to the cabin—jumping-off-place for any exploration of the Black.

Big Tom Wilson who had always walked quietly beside the Professor's learning and scientific instruments, who had stood aside a little awed at the university air that clung to the older man, open and friendly though he was—this Wilson now became the leader, putting *his* learning to the test. That learning was a mixture of reading the lost man's mind, observing every detail in the woods he searched, judging distances and possibilities and correlating small separate fields to a significant whole.

Several years later, Big Tom gave his own account of the following eventful day. Tuesday, the seventh of July, ten days after the Professor was last seen alive by his son, the last intensive search began.

We Ate our breakfast at Day break consisting of some Beef and Biscuit and took enough along for our dinner and started off in the direction that we Supposed Dr. Mitchel would have gon from the top of the peak to my house and had only gon som 2 or 3 hundred yards When Mr. A.D. Allin Said, 'Come here Big Tom I believe I have found his track.' calling all the party together We followed the impressions in the moss resembleing the foot prints of a man Some 200 yards and found the marks of a Shoe heel on a small balsam root and was Satisfied then that we were on the track As we could See the print of the tacks on the root then we held a hurried consultation and agreed to return and backtrack to where he had left the top of the mountain and give the whole force. Notice of our success doing so and finding a complete track under a fallen Balsam which formed a Shelter for the foot print in the Soft loose earth beneath . . . then Big Tom over anksose to spread the good tiding Whooped long and loud makeing the mountain wring for miles away with the echoes of his Stentorious voice then retraceing our Stepps . . . without hesitation or delay traced the tracks to the heel print on the rock thence we must follow the dim foot prints of the lone man after the laps of 10 days . . . Big Tom leads the way and Said com on boys here hes went Mr. Bob Patton said how can you say here hes went when we could not track a horse here for the laurel! Come Said Tom and I will show you how at the Same tim pulling off a branch of Laurel Said do you see the top of the leaf is dark green and the underside is white look now I can see the white side of the leaf up turned for 20 yds go ahead Said Patton you are better than any old hound that ever Jumped on a track So I did goe a head only looseing the track one time then it was found by Bob Patton and all stood stock still and called the old hound Big Tom and set him on the track as you would your fox hound.

The "hound" remained steady at his tracking throughout the afternoon. When he stopped at one place and said this was where night had overtaken the Professor, his companions demanded once more "how he could tell." His explanation was as simple and logical as any of the best of Sherlock Holmes—and just as neglected by the less observing eyes of those around him.

"Don't you see," Big Tom said, "back there among the laurels the doctor picked the best ways and crept through the open places, and here he ran up against a bush and there he fell over a rock. Don't you see where he slid down and this shows he couldn't see his way any longer?"

When they came to a creek soon afterward, Tom went down in the creek bed and found scratches on the jutting rocks made by those same tacks in the heels of the Professor's shoes. They crossed, as he had done, to the opposite side of the creek, certain now that he had decided to follow this water route down the mountain and to some eventual settlement. But Big Tom had already seen the signs and heard whispers of the menace that lay just ahead. As he joined the others he said, "There's a high fall in the creek just below. I wouldn't be surprised if he's found right there."

Only a short distance farther they came to the precipice over which the stream plunges forty feet. Crawling to its edge, Big Tom looked over into the pool. The dark water was impenetrable, but on a driftwood log lodged at one side lay a familiar soft fur hat. Crumpled and water-soaked, it lay like a black period marking the end of a search and a life.

"I've found the hat. Come and see," Big Tom called to his companions.

At the base of the falls was a pool fifteen feet deep, and at one side a rock ledge shelved over part of it, deadening some of the sound of the falls. This had probably helped deceive the Professor as to the height of the falls. When he worked his way around the slippery rocks in the darkness, he had turned too soon back to the channel of the stream he was trying to follow, while he was still above the pool. Tom crawled and clung and slipped around the falls and back up to the pool. Now he could make out the body, caught by a log about halfway between the bottom of the water and the top, floating face down with outstretched arms. The watch he wore had stopped at nineteen minutes past eight o'clock. Big Tom's estimate of where night had overtaken the Professor was correct.

Big Tom Wilson lived on to become a legend in his own lifetime. The many visitors who came to visit Mount Mitchell, once its supremacy was established, hired him as guide and helped furnish support for the ten children born to him and his wife Niagara Ray. He was a fine sampling of the finest sort of mountain person— the six-feet-two, spare, sinewy, bearded man whose naïveté oftèn overshadowed for strangers the shrewd wisdom that kept him alive. The Professor had been given degrees attesting to his learning, yet Tom Wilson knew something that meant the difference between living and dying in this mountain country, and that was respect for the unmeasured power of any adversary, mountain or bear or stream or even the darkness of night. If the splendid old man could have been, for that one night of June twenty-seventh, only a little less busy and zealous. If that once he could have assumed some of the mountain leisureliness that is supposed to be laziness but often masks caution and awareness, if he could simply have let the mountain and the night have their time and waited until daylight to break his hazardous path, the steep little falls would never have had their victim.

The falls are still there, at the head of Cane River before it becomes the Nolichucky before it becomes the French Broad. The falls and the wonderful dark pool, cold and hidden, under a mountain thick with pathless undergrowth and pungent with the smell of ancient leaf mold. The cupped stones where constant water has swirled and rounded their contours and hewn them into a basin holding the still water that does not reveal its bottom but seems only quiet and waiting, like some ancient sacrificial well, the ferns in the ledges along the perpendicular sides of the falls, the nervous water bugs and the resilient moss, all are still there.

The Wilsons are there too. A grandson of Big Tom's talks to you in a voice so mild it is difficult to hear above the sound of the water—and he carries a mammoth pistol on the belt at his hip. He wears a neat businessman's tie with his crisp brown Game Warden's shirt—and tells you that last week he saw twenty-one places back on the mountain where bear

had just crossed the path. His house is small and unpainted, but it sits at the edge of sixteen thousand acres of Wilson land. His grandfather killed 114 bears during his lifetime. He's killed only fifty-seven. There are still remnants of the "differences" between the Yancey Wilsons and the Buncombe Burnetts. You tell this man that you talked with a Burnett a few months ago who'd choked a bear to death. He gives you a quick blue-eyed glance. "I'm not that husky," he chuckles quietly and winks. "The moon's got to be just right for that sort of hunting."

A new highway now runs almost to the summit of Mount Mitchell. The doctor lies there among the frequent clouds and constant evergreens of 6,684 feet. Nearby, and only 126 feet less than its mighty brother, is the peak called Big Tom. So the professor who could be bound by no classroom and the hunter who was learned in his own way have in death what they had in life: a common earth and an uncommon awareness of all its marvels.

117

MEET THE AUTHOR:
Wilma Dykeman (1920–   )

Asheville native Wilma Dykeman has traveled around the world, but her writing has always focused on her beloved Appalachian Mountain region. Her first book, *The French Broad*, is a collection of stories and essays about the land and people around the French Broad River, which runs through the western part of our state. In all, Ms. Dykeman has published over sixteen books—both novels and nonfiction—some of which are coauthored with her husband, James Stokely, or their sons, Jim and Dykeman.

Wilma Dykeman is also widely known as a lecturer and as the author of essays, articles, and book reviews which have appeared in major newspapers, magazines, and the *Encyclopedia Britannica*. She and her family were among the first to speak out strongly against such matters as racial injustice and environmental destruction. Her writings and lectures have won her many awards, including the North Carolina Award for Literature and the Hillman Award for the best book published in this country on race relations or world peace.

Ms. Dykeman traces her interest in writing to the stories her parents read aloud to her when she was a child. By the time she was in elementary school, she was making up her own stories, plays, and poems, and in Grace High School (now Ira B. Jones School) in Asheville, she was editor of the class annual. She continued her interest in writing while at Northwestern University.

She urges students to learn to listen and look at the world with keen eyes and ears, then apply themselves diligently. She also draws a keen distinction between *aptitude* and *attitude*. "The talent comes from developing the aptitude," she has said. "The writer comes from developing the attitude."

Language Alert

1. Some phrases which would be entirely familiar to mountaineers of the last century may be unfamiliar to many of us now. The term "roasting ears" doesn't refer to corn that is actually being cooked; it means good tasty ears fit for "roasting" for a meal. Corn extract, which the men drink from a jug, is not a flavoring or a medicine; it is homemade corn whiskey. Late in the story Big Tom Wilson tells us that he called out in a *stentorious* voice; he meant *stentorian*—very loud.

2. Toward the end of the story you will see how Big Tom Wilson told his own story. Apparently he never mastered capitalization, punctuation, or spelling, so you will have to make a game of figuring out where sentences begin and end and even what some words are. (*Anxious* turns out as *anksose* in Wilson's account.) But we should recognize that however unskilled he was at the mechanics of getting words onto paper, Big Tom was a good storyteller with a wide vocabulary capable of expressing his meanings precisely.

3. Following Big Tom's example, we should all continue to develop our vocabularies. Below are some words you may not use often. Try to guess what the italicized words mean. Try using them in your own sentences. As you read the story, check your guesses to see if they are correct.

   a. His chickens wallowing lazily nearby, the dogs stretched out in the shadows, Big Tom Wilson sits on his front porch enjoying the *lethargy* of late afternoon.

   b. The Cane River is fed by many streams hidden in the *recesses* of the mountains.

   c. Wilma Dykeman speaks of each man's "particular *sensibility*."

   d. Professor Mitchell and Thomas Clingman were *avid* explorers who made repeated trips into the Smoky Mountains.

   e. When cornered by dogs and hunters, a bear "stood his ground *tenaciously*."

Reflecting

After reading this story, what do we know that we didn't know before about:

1. How three mountain peaks in North Carolina were named?
2. How a laurel thicket can disclose the path a person takes?
3. How one can "read" a trail?
4. Two different kinds of education?

From Incidents in the Life of a Slave Girl

The Slave Child

Harriet Jacobs (Linda Brent)

Preview

Of course you know that slavery was once legal in this nation, and that thousands of blacks were brought from African homelands in chains to work (mostly as servants and field hands). You know that slaves were considered the property of their owners. This meant that they could be bought, sold, or exchanged—just like horses or furniture or wagons. You've probably heard of the cruel punishment some slaves had to undergo or the poverty under which many lived. But have you ever tried to imagine what the daily life of a slave might have been like?

For a moment, imagine yourself as a child growing up in slavery. How do you think your family life might differ from the way it is now? What would your educational possibilities have been? How would you feel toward your "masters" and "mistresses"? How would you deal with having to obey others, never having the privilege of arguing or saying "no"?

As you read, think of how your own life compares to that of Harriet Jacobs.

I was born a slave; but I never knew it till six years of happy childhood had passed away. My father was a carpenter, and considered so intelligent and skillful in his trade, that, when buildings out of the common line were to be erected, he was sent for from long distances, to be head workman. On condition of paying his mistress two hundred dollars a year, and supporting himself, he was allowed to work at his trade, and manage his own affairs. His strongest wish was to pur-

From *Incidents in the Life of a Slave Girl,* by Linda Brent (Harriet Jacobs), ed. L. Maria Child. Published for the author in 1861.

chase his children; but, though he several times offered his hard earnings for that purpose, he never succeeded. In complexion my parents were a light shade of brownish yellow, and were termed mulattoes. They lived together in a comfortable home; and, though we were all slaves, I was so fondly shielded that I never dreamed I was a piece of merchandise, trusted to them for safe keeping, and liable to be demanded of them at any moment. I had one brother, William, who was two years younger than myself—a bright, affectionate child. I had also a great treasure in my maternal grandmother, who was a remarkable woman in many respects. She was the daughter of a planter in South Carolina, who, at his death, left her mother and his three children free, with money to go to St. Augustine, where they had relatives. It was during the Revolutionary War; and they were captured on their passage, carried back, and sold to different purchasers. Such was the story my grandmother used to tell me; but I do not remember all the particulars. She was a little girl when she was captured and sold to the keeper of a large hotel. I have often heard her tell how hard she fared during childhood. But as she grew older she evinced so much intelligence, and was so faithful, that her master and mistress could not help seeing it was for their interest to take care of such a valuable piece of property. She became an indispensable personage in the household, officiating in all capacities, from cook and wet nurse to seamstress. She was much praised for her cooking; and her nice crackers became so famous in the neighborhood that many people were desirous of obtaining them. In consequence of numerous requests of this kind, she asked permission of her mistress to bake crackers at night, after all the household work was done; and she obtained leave to do it, provided she would clothe herself and her children from the profits. Upon these terms, after working hard all day for her mistress, she began her midnight bakings, assisted by her two oldest children. The business proved profitable; and each year she laid by a little, which was saved for a fund to purchase her children. Her master died, and the property was divided among his heirs. The widow had her dower in the hotel, which she continued to keep open. My grandmother remained in her service as a slave; but her children were divided among her master's children. As she had five, Benjamin, the youngest one, was sold, in order that each heir might have an equal portion of dollars and cents. There was so little difference in our ages that he seemed more like my brother than my uncle. He was a bright, handsome lad, nearly white; for he inherited the complexion my grandmother had derived from Anglo-Saxon ancestors. Though only ten years old, seven hundred and twenty dollars were paid for him. His sale was a terrible blow to my grandmother; but she was naturally hopeful, and she went to work with renewed energy, trusting in time to be able to purchase some of her children. She had laid up three hundred dollars, which her mistress one day begged as a loan, promising to pay her soon. The reader probably knows that no promise or writing given to a slave is legally binding; for, according to Southern laws, a slave, *being* property, can *hold* no property. When my grandmother lent her hard earnings to her mistress, she trusted solely to her honor. The honor of a slaveholder to a slave!

To this good grandmother I was indebted for many comforts. My brother Willie and I often received portions of the crackers, cakes, and preserves, she made to sell; and after we ceased to be children we were indebted to her for many more important services.

Such were the unusually fortunate circumstances of my early childhood. When I was six years old, my mother died; and then, for the first time, I learned, by the talk around me, that I was a slave. My mother's mistress was the daughter of my grandmother's mistress. She was the foster sister of my mother; they were both nourished at my grandmother's breast. In fact, my mother had been weaned at three months old, that the babe of the mistress might obtain sufficient food. They played together as children; and, when they became women, my mother was a most faithful servant to her whiter foster sister. On her death-bed her mistress promised that her children should never suffer for any thing; and during her lifetime she kept her word. They all spoke kindly of my dead mother, who had been a slave merely in name, but in nature was noble and womanly. I grieved for her, and my young mind was troubled with the thought who would now take care of me and my little brother. I was told that my home was now to be with her mis-

tress; and I found it a happy one. No toilsome or disagreeable duties were imposed upon me. My mistress was so kind to me that I was always glad to do her bidding, and proud to labor for her as much as my young years would permit. I would sit by her side for hours, sewing diligently, with a heart as free from care as that of any freeborn white child. When she thought I was tired, she would send me out to run and jump; and away I bounded, to gather berries or flowers to decorate her room. Those were happy days—too happy to last. The slave child had no thought for the morrow; but there came that blight, which too surely waits on every human being born to be a chattel.

When I was nearly twelve years old, my kind mistress sickened and died. As I saw the cheek grow paler, and the eye more glassy, how earnestly I prayed in my heart that she might live! I loved her; for she had been almost like a mother to me. My prayers were not answered. She died, and they buried her in the little churchyard, where, day after day, my tears fell upon her grave.

I was sent to spend a week with my grandmother. I was now old enough to begin to think of the future; and again and again I asked myself what they would do with me. I felt sure I should never find another mistress so kind as the one who was gone. She had promised my dying mother that her children should never suffer for any thing; and when I remembered that, and recalled her many proofs of attachment to me, I could not help having some hopes that she had left me free. My friends were almost certain it would be so. They thought she would be sure to do it, on account of my mother's love and faithful service. But, alas, we all know that the memory of a faithful slave does not avail much to save her children from the auction block.

After a brief period of suspense, the will of my mistress was read, and we learned that she had bequeathed me to her sister's daughter, a child of five years old. So vanished our hopes. My mistress had taught me the precepts of God's Word: "Thou shalt love thy neighbor as thyself." "Whatsoever ye would that men should do unto you, do ye even so unto them." But I was her slave, and I suppose she did not recognize me as her neighbor. I would give much to blot out from my memory that one great wrong. As a child, I loved my mistress; and, looking back on the happy days I spent with her, I try to think with less bitterness of this act of injustice. While I was with her, she taught me to read and spell; and for this privilege, which so rarely falls to the lot of a slave, I bless her memory.

She possessed but few slaves; and at her death those were all distributed among her relatives. Five of them were my grandmother's children, and had shared the same milk that nourished her mother's children. Notwithstanding my grandmother's long and faithful service to her owners, not one of her children escaped the auction block. These God-breathing machines are no more, in the sight of their masters, than the cotton they plant, or the horses they tend.

Dr. Flint, a physician in the neighborhood, had married the sister of my mistress, and I was now the property of their little daughter. It was not without murmuring that I prepared for my new home; and what added to my unhappiness, was the fact that my brother William was purchased by the same family. My father, by his nature, as well as by the habit of transacting business as a skillful mechanic, had more of the feelings of a freeman than is common among slaves. My brother was a spirited boy; and being brought up under such influences, he early detested the name of master and mistress. One day, when his father and his mistress both happened to call him at the same time, he hesitated between the two; being perplexed to know which had the strongest claim upon his obedience. He finally concluded to go to his mistress. When my father reproved him for it, he said, "You both called me, and I didn't know which I ought to go to first."

"You are *my* child," replied our father, "and when I call you, you should come immediately, if you have to pass through fire and water."

Poor Willie! He was now to learn his first lesson of obedience to a master. Grandmother tried to cheer us with hopeful words, and they found an echo in the credulous hearts of youth.

When we entered our new home we encountered cold looks, cold words, and cold treatment. We were glad when the night came. On my narrow bed I moaned and wept, I felt so desolate and alone.

I had been there nearly a year, when a dear little friend of mine was buried. I heard her mother sob, as the clods fell on the coffin of her only child, and I turned away from the grave, feeling thankful that I still had something left to love. I met my grandmother, who said, "Come with me, Linda;" and from her tone I knew that something sad had happened. She led me apart from the people, and then said, "My child, your father is dead." Dead! How could I believe it? He had died so suddenly I had not even heard that he was sick. I went home with my grandmother. My heart rebelled against God, who had taken from me mother, father, mistress, and friend. The good grandmother tried to comfort me. "Who knows the ways of God?" said she. "Perhaps they have been kindly taken from the evil days to come." Years afterwards I often thought of this. She promised to be a mother to her grandchildren, so far as she might be permitted to do so; and strengthened by her love, I returned to my master's. I thought I should be allowed to go to my father's house the next morning; but I was ordered to go for flowers, that my mistress's house might be decorated for an evening party. I spent the day gathering flowers and weaving them into festoons, while the dead body of my father was lying within a mile of me. What cared my owners for that? He was merely a piece of property. Moreover, they thought he had spoiled his children, by teaching them to feel that they were human beings. This was blasphemous doctrine for a slave to teach; presumptuous in him, and dangerous to the masters.

The next day I followed his remains to a humble grave beside that of my dear mother. There were those who knew my father's worth, and respected his memory.

My home now seemed more dreary than ever. The laugh of the little slave-children sounded harsh and cruel. It was selfish to feel so about the joy of others. My brother moved about with a very grave face. I tried to comfort him, by saying, "Take courage, Willie; brighter days will come by and by."

"You don't know any thing about it, Linda," he replied. "We shall have to stay here all our days; we shall never be free."

I argued that we were growing older and stronger, and that perhaps we might, before long, be allowed to hire our own time, and then we could earn money to buy our freedom. William declared this was much easier to say than to do; moreover, he did not intend to *buy* his freedom. We held daily controversies upon this subject.

Little attention was paid to the slaves' meals in Dr. Flint's house. If they could catch a bit of food while it was going, well and good. I gave myself no trouble on that score, for on my various errands I passed my grandmother's house, where there was always something to spare for me. I was frequently threatened with punishment if I stopped there; and my grandmother, to avoid detaining me, often stood at the gate with something for my breakfast or dinner. I was indebted to *her* for all my comforts, spiritual or temporal. It was *her* labor that supplied my scanty wardrobe. I have a vivid recollection of the linsey-woolsey dress given me every winter by Mrs. Flint. How I hated it! It was one of the badges of slavery.

While my grandmother was thus helping to support me from her hard earnings, the three hundred dollars she had lent her mistress were never repaid. When her mistress died, her son-in-law, Dr. Flint, was appointed executor. When grandmother applied to him for payment, he said the estate was insolvent, and the law prohibited payment. It did not, however, prohibit him from retaining the silver candelabra, which had been purchased with that money. I presume they will be handed down in the family, from generation to generation.

My grandmother's mistress had always promised her that, at her death, she should be free; and it was said that in her will she made good the promise. But when the estate was settled, Dr. Flint told the faithful old servant that, under existing circumstances, it was necessary she should be sold.

On the appointed day, the customary advertisement was posted up, proclaiming that there would be a "public sale of negroes, horses, &c." Dr. Flint called to tell my grandmother that he was unwilling to wound her feelings by putting her up at auction, and that he would prefer to dispose of her at private sale. My grandmother saw through his hypocrisy; she understood very well that he was ashamed of the job. She was a very spirited woman, and if he was base enough to sell her, when her mistress intended she should be free, she was determined the public should know it. She had for a long time supplied many families with crackers and preserves; consequently, "Aunt Marthy," as she was called, was generally known, and every body who knew her respected her intelligence and good character. Her long and faithful service in the family was also well known, and the intention of her mistress to leave her free. When the day of sale came, she took her place among the chattels, and at the first call she sprang upon the auction-block. Many voices called out, "Shame! Shame! Who is going to sell *you*, aunt Marthy? Don't stand there! That is no place for *you*." Without saying a word, she quietly awaited her fate. No one bid for her. At last, a feeble voice said, "Fifty dollars." It came from a maiden lady, seventy years old, the sister of my grandmother's deceased mistress. She had lived forty years under the same roof with my grandmother; she knew how faithfully she had served her owners, and how cruelly she had been defrauded of her rights; and she resolved to protect her. The auctioneer waited for a higher bid; but her wishes were respected; no one bid above her. She could neither read nor write; and when the bill of sale was made out, she signed it with a cross. But what consequence was that, when she had a big heart overflowing with human kindness? She gave the old servant her freedom.

At that time, my grandmother was just fifty years old. Laborious years had passed since then; and now my brother and I were slaves to the man who had defrauded her of her money, and tried to defraud her of her freedom.

Harriet Jacobs (Linda Brent) (1813–1896)

In Harriet Jacobs's early years, we find little that would lead us to predict that some day she would write an important book. But eventually she wrote her life story—a story more astounding than much fiction.

Born a slave in Edenton, she led the difficult and sometimes dangerous life borne by most slaves. When she was only a child, her mother died. Later her owner died and willed her to a three-year-old child. The child's mother and father both made young Harriet's life miserable. When she was a young woman with two small children, she finally ran away. For almost seven years she hid in her free grandmother's house, spending much of the time in the narrow crawl space above a room. Her children's father, a white lawyer, purchased their children's freedom, and they, too, lived with the grandmother, although they did not have to hide as their mother did.

After Harriet Jacobs finally escaped to New York, she was still threatened with capture and re-enslavement by her former owner. She worked as a nursemaid in the household of Nathaniel and Mary Willis and devoted much time working to abolish slavery. Finally, Mrs. Willis purchased Harriet's freedom and convinced her to write her story to make the world aware of the evils of slavery.

Fearful of endangering herself and others, Harriet Jacobs wrote under the pen name Linda Brent and used false names for all persons in her story. Two white friends interested in helping the antislavery cause helped her to write, polish, and publish her book. Today, her book, *Incidents in the Life of a Slave Girl*, is considered one of the most notable of what are called "slave narratives."

Language Alert

Like others who have used reading and writing as a way of dealing with the harshness of their lives, Harriet Jacobs treasured her language skills. You will see that she uses an extensive vocabulary. Here are some important words from this story; be sure that they become a part of your own active vocabulary:

1. *indispensable*: essential (A company executive may consider his secretary to be *indispensable*.)
2. *officiating*: to perform the duties and functions of an office. (As president of the class, Jake is *officiating* at the class meeting this afternoon.)
3. *diligently:* done with industrious effort (Athletes must practice *diligently* if they are to develop their abilities.)
4. *blight*: something that withers growth, dreams, or hopes (*Blight* killed our corn crop last year. First slavery, then discrimination, was a *blight* on the dreams of many black Americans.)
5. *chattel*: This word is a synonym for *slave*.
6. *bequeathed*: willed (The mistress *bequeathed* freedom to her slave.)
7. *blasphemous*: dishonors God or his work (Since some slaveowners felt that God approved of slavery, it seemed *blasphemous* for anyone to question slavery.)
8. *insolvent*: unable to pay debts (When a business becomes *insolvent*, the owner may declare bankruptcy.)
9. *hypocrisy*: pretending feelings or beliefs, insincerity. (When someone says something we know he does not believe, we accuse him of *hypocrisy* and may call him a *hypocrite*.)

Reflecting

Later in her book, Harriet Jacobs tells us of many cruelties and indignities which slaves had to bear: whippings, imprisonment, threats, deprivations. Because she had a kind mistress, Harriet escaped such treatment the first few years of her life. But, as we have seen, after her mistress died, Harriet either experienced or witnessed situations which showed how the owners treated their slaves as less than worthy human beings. Make a list of these experiences, beginning with Harriet's being willed to another mistress as if she were a piece of jewelry or furniture.

Learning, Learning

George Moses Horton

Preview

Imagine yourself as a slave whose master doesn't "set much store" in books, and certainly sees no reason to provide education for slaves. You have no schoolroom, no trained teachers, no textbooks, flashcards, notebook, or television aids. However, you are determined to learn to read. How might you go about fulfilling this ambition? Where would you find materials? How could you learn? If you did learn to compose your own pieces, what subjects would you choose for your compositions?

The first selection presented here includes the story, told in his own words, of how such a slave—George Moses Horton—nourished his love of reading and writing. Next are two poems: "The Slave's Complaint" from his first book, *The Hope of Liberty*, written and published while he was a slave; and "George Moses Horton, Myself," written when he was much older and at last a free man. As you read each selection, try to put yourself in the place of the writer—first as a child trying desperately, against incredible odds, to learn how to read; then as a slave frustrated with your condition in life; and finally, as an older man considering what you have and have not done, what yet you might do.

I here became a cow-boy, which I followed for perhaps ten years. . . . In the course of this disagreeable occupation, I became fond of hearing people read; but being nothing but a poor cow-boy, I had but little or no thought of ever being able to read or spell one word or sentence in any book whatever. My mother discovered my anxiety for books and strove to encourage my plan; but she, having left her husband behind, was so hard run to make a little shift for herself that she could give no assistance in that

From "The Life of George Moses Horton, The Colored Bard of North Carolina" in *The Poetical Works of George Moses Horton,* originally published by D. Heartt, 1845.

case. At length I took a resolution to learn the alphabet at all events; and lighting by chance at times with some opportunities of being in the presence of school children, I learnt the letters by heart, and fortunately afterwards got hold of some old parts of spelling books abounding with these elements, which I learnt with but little difficulty. . . .

And by this time my brother was deeply excited by the assiduity which he discovered in me to learn . . . ; and some of his partial friends strove to put him before me. . . . But still my brother never could keep time with me. He was indeed an ostentatious youth, and of a far more attractive person than myself, more forward in manly show, and early became fond of popularity to an astonishing degree for one of his age and capacity. He strove hard on the wing of ambition to soar above me, and could write a respectable fist before I could form the first letter with a pen or barely knew the use of a goose-quill. And I must say that he was quite a remarkable youth, as studious as a judge, but much too full of vain lounging among the fair sex.

But to return to the earlier spring of my progress. Through blundering, I became a far better reader than he; but we were indeed both remarkable for boys of color and hard raising. . . .

On well nigh every Sabbath during the year did I retire away in the summer season to some shady and lonely recess, where I could stammer over the dim . . . syllables in my old black and tattered spelling book, sometimes a piece of one and then of another; nor would I scarcely spare the time to return to my ordinary meals, being so truly engaged with my book. . . . Hence I had to sit sweating and smoking . . . , almost exhausted by the heat of the fire, and almost suffocated with smoke; consequently from Monday morning I anticipated with joy the approach of the next Sabbath, that I might retire to the pleasant umbrage of the woods, whither I was used to dwell or spend the most of the day with ceaseless investigation over my book.

A number strove to dissuade me from my plan and had the presumption to tell me that I was a vain fool to attempt learning to read with as little chance as I had. Play boys . . . insisted on my abandoning my foolish theory, and go with them on streams, disport, and sacrifice the day in athletic folly, or . . . levity. Nevertheless did I persevere with an indefatigable resolution, at the risk of success. . . .

But with defiance I accomplished the arduous task of spelling (for thus it was with me), having no . . . assistance. From this I entered into reading lessons with triumph. I became very fond of reading parts of the New Testament, such as I could pick up as they lay about at random; but I soon became more fond of reading verses, Wesley's old hymns, and other pieces of poetry from various authors. . . .

After encountering poetry I became fond of it to that degree that whenever I chanced to light on a piece of paper . . . lying about, I would pick it up in order to examine it whether it was written in that curious style or not. If it was not, unless some remarkable prose, I threw it aside; and if it was, I as carefully preserved it as I would a piece of money. . . .

At length, I began to wonder whether it was possible that I ever could be so fortunate as to compose in that [poetic] manner. I fell to work in my head and composed several undigested pieces, which I retained in my mind, for I knew nothing about writing with a pen.

MEET THE AUTHOR:
George Moses Horton (1797?–1883?)

When he was very young, George Moses Horton was a slave child tending cows in Chatham County. But his imagination and his desire to better himself led him, in spite of great odds, to become a respected poet and one of the first black people in America to publish a book.

George Moses Horton was born in the late 1790s in Northampton County. As a child, he took advantage of every opportunity to learn to read. As a young man of seventeen, he was sent by his master to sell farm produce in Chapel Hill to the students. Eventually the students recognized his writing talent and hired him to write poems, paying him from twenty-five to seventy-five cents apiece. (They later gave the poems to their sweethearts.) This money enabled him to purchase his own time from his master for twenty-five cents a day, allowing him to write instead of toil in the fields.

Horton's poems eventually attracted the attention of Caroline Lee Hentz, a novelist and poet from Massachusetts who was living in Chapel Hill. She helped him improve his

work and taught him how to write it down instead of depending on others to do so. She also encouraged him to publish his work. Publication of his poetry collection, *The Hope of Liberty,* made Horton the third black person in America to have a book published.

Although publication won him attention, Horton's work never sold enough copies to enable him to buy his own freedom. It did, however, attract the attention of influential persons such as the university president, the mayor of Chapel Hill, and, during the Civil War, a captain from the Union cavalry. Despite their efforts, however, he was never able to obtain his freedom until Lincoln's Emancipation Proclamation freed all slaves. After the war ended, he went north, where he worked as a servant and wrote Sunday School materials. We do not know how he spent the last years of his life or when or where he died and was buried. But we have his poems—a testimonial to the unquenchable spirit of a man who in spite of overwhelming odds became what he most wanted to be: a poet.

Language Alert

1. Some of the terms and some of the spellings which George Moses Horton uses are unfamiliar to us now:
   a. When George Moses Horton speaks of being a *cowboy*, he means a farmhand who looks after cattle, not the kind of range-riding cowboy we associate with the Old West.
   b. *Learnt* is a non-traditional way of spelling *learned*.
   c. To write a *respectable fist* is a way of saying that one has good hand-writing.
   d. Horton uses *umbrage* to mean something that gives shade. That meaning is now considered out-of-date. The word now is used to mean resentment, as in "Although I didn't mean to offend him, he took *umbrage* at my words."
2. You will notice that in the selections from his life story, George Moses Horton uses a very elegant style and many long words of Greek or Latin origin. His writing is quite different from the much simpler style that is preferred by modern writers—a style much closer to everyday speech. Two reasons may account for Horton's style. First, writers during Horton's time frequently used such flowery language. Secondly, in an effort to be taken seriously, Horton probably made his language even more complex than it had to be.

   He also tended to be rather wordy, so the prose selections have been condensed and omissions are marked with ellipses (three or four periods in a row).

Here are definitions of some of the more difficult words he uses:

1. *assiduity*: close and diligent attention
2. *ostentatious*: showy, pretentious
3. *formidable*: difficult to undertake or defeat
4. *dissuade* : discourage, hinder (This is the opposite of *persuade*.)
5. *disport*: play or amusement
6. *levity*: light—not serious—in speech or manner
7. *persevere*: continue, persist
8. *indefatigable*: untiring (Do you see *fatigue* embedded in *indefatigable*?)
9. *arduous*: difficult, strenuous, demanding much effort

Two Poems by George Moses Horton

The Slave's Complaint

Am I sadly cast aside,
On misfortune's rugged tide?
Will the world my pains deride
Forever?

Must I dwell in Slavery's night,
And all pleasure take its flight,
Far beyond my feeble sight,
Forever?

Worst of all, must Hope grow dim,
And withhold her cheering beam?
Rather let me sleep and dream
Forever!

Something still my heart surveys,
Groping through this dreary maze;
Is it Hope?—then burn and blaze
Forever!

Leave me not a wretch confined,
Altogether lame and blind—
Unto gross despair consigned,
Forever!

Heaven! in whom can I confide?
Canst thou not for all provide?
Condescend to be my guide
Forever:

And when this transient life shall end,
Oh, may some kind eternal friend
Bid me from servitude ascend,
Forever!

From *The Hope of Liberty*, by George Moses Horton, published by J. Gales and Sons, 1829.

George Moses Horton, Myself

I feel myself in need
    Of the inspiring strains of ancient lore,
My heart to lift, my empty mind to feed,
    And all the world explore.

I know that I am old
    And never can recover what is past,
But for the future may some light unfold
    And soar from age's blast.

I feel resolved to try,
    My wish to prove, my calling to pursue,
Or mount up from the earth into the sky,
    To show what Heaven can do.

My genius from a boy,
    Has fluttered like a bird within my heart;
But could not thus confined her powers employ,
    Impatient to depart.

She like a restless bird,
    Would spread her wing, her power to be unfurl'd,
And let her songs be loudly heard,
    And dart from world to world.

Reflecting

1. From what you have read both about and by George Moses Horton, what do you know about his character? List as many adjectives as you can think of which describe what kind of person he was. Then choose one and look back over the selections to find evidence which supports your choices. Be ready to present this evidence in class discussion or to write a paragraph characterizing this remarkable man.

(Hint: Choose specific, precise adjectives like "courageous" or "determined," not general ones like "wonderful" or "nice." The former describe traits; the latter merely give your opinion.)

2. What similarities and/or differences do you see in the *experiences* of George Moses Horton and Harriet Jacobs (p. 120)? Do you see any similarities and/or differences in their personalities and characters?

From *Naked Genius,* by George Moses Horton, originally compiled by William H. S. Banks, published by William B. Smith Company, 1865.

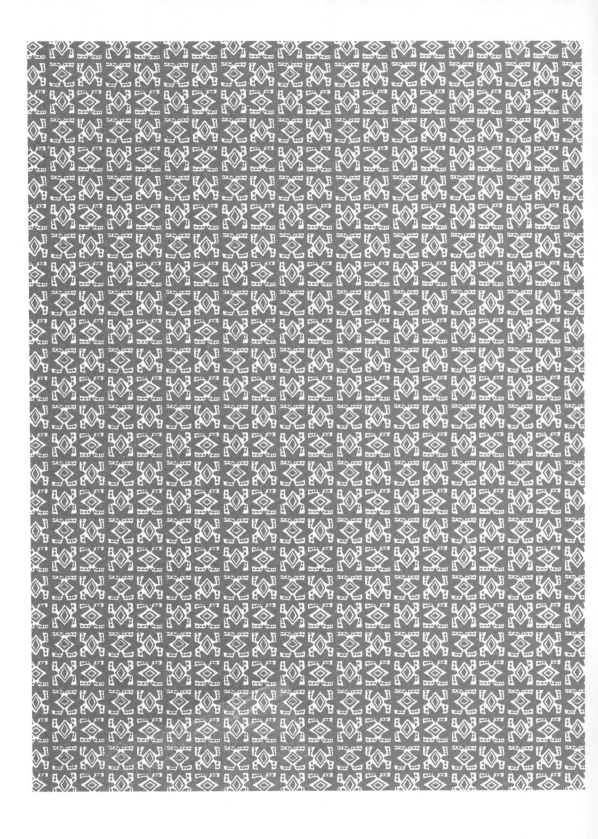

A Nation, and a State, Divided

From 1781, when the Revolution ended, until 1861, when the Civil War began, our nation was involved in two wars: the War of 1812 and a war with Mexico. In neither case was our state a battleground, and relatively few North Carolinians took part in the fighting. Thus we had little experience to prepare us for the bloody conflict that followed our secession from the Union.

This state was almost as divided as the nation itself was. North Carolina, which was made up mostly of small farms, not plantations, had fewer slaves than most Southern states and in the mountains there were very few slaves at all. Thus many North Carolinians did not consider slavery their issue—certainly not one worth war. On the other hand, they felt a fierce loyalty to their state and resented the federal effort to keep North Carolina in the Union.

The selections in this section give us several glimpses of that conflict. We follow a ten-year-old white boy as he tries to figure out what war is all about—and how that war is perceived by the slaves in the household. We also move in and out of battle with the men who wore those gray uniforms.

The Fringe of War

Walter Hines Page (Nicholas Worth)

Preview

Walter Hines Page was only six years old when the Civil War began and ten when it ended. His only novel, *The Southerner* (written under the pen name Nicholas Worth), deals with a young man's life during the Reconstruction. In this, the opening chapter, we see that young man as a boy. The chapter, "The Fringe of War," is well named, for the boy is too young to fight, and the war comes directly to his region only briefly. But through the boy's eyes we discover what it was like for three kinds of people who were living on "the fringe of war."

1. Children (the boy and his "slave, philosopher, and friend") who at first aren't sure that the war isn't just a story someone made up. Notice what first makes the war real to them.
2. The boy's father, who is torn between his feelings about the war and his loyalty to his region and his friends. Notice how he handles these conflicts.
3. The adult slaves, who have been told how wonderful freedom is. What do you think they will do when they are freed?

One day when the cotton fields were white and the elm leaves were falling, in the soft autumn of the Southern climate wherein the sky is fathomlessly clear, the locomotive's whistle blew a much longer time than usual as the train approached Millworth. It did not stop at so small a station except when there was somebody to get off or to get on; and so long a blast meant that someone was coming. Sam and I ran down the avenue of elms to see who it was. Sam was my slave,

From *The Southerner,* by Nicholas Worth (Walter Hines Page), published by Doubleday, Page, 1909.

philosopher, and friend. I was ten years old and Sam said that he was fourteen.

There was constant talk about the war. Many men of the neighborhood had gone away somewhere—that was certain; but Sam and I had a theory that the war was only a story. We had been fooled about old granny Thomas's bringing the baby, and long ago we had been fooled also about Santa Claus. The war might be another such invention, and we sometimes suspected that it was. But we found out the truth that day, and for this reason it is among my clearest early recollections.

For, when the train stopped, they put off a big box and gently laid it in the shade of the fence. The only man at the station was the man who had come to change the mail-bags; and he said that this was Billy Morris's coffin and that he had been killed in a battle. He asked us to stay with it till he could send word to Mr. Morris, who lived two miles away. The man came back presently and leaned against the fence till old Mr. Morris arrived, an hour or more later.

The lint of cotton was on his wagon, for he was hauling his crop to the gin when the sad news reached him; and he came in his shirt sleeves, his wife on the wagon seat with him.

All the neighborhood gathered at the church, a funeral was preached and there was a long prayer for our success against "the invaders," and Billy Morris was buried. I remember that I wept the more because it now seemed to me that my doubt about the war had somehow done Billy Morris an injustice.

Old Mrs. Gregory wept more loudly than anybody else; and she kept saying, while the service was going on, "It'll be my John next." In a little while, sure enough, John Gregory's coffin was put off the train, as Billy Morris's had been, and I regarded her as a woman gifted with prophecy. Other coffins, too, were put off from time to time. About the war there could no longer be a doubt. And, a little later, its realities and horrors came nearer home to us, with swift, deep experiences.

One day my father took me to the camp and parade ground ten miles away, near the capital. The General and the Governor sat on horses and the soldiers marched by them and the band played. They were going to "the front." There surely must be a war at the front, I told Sam that night.

Still more coffins were brought home, too, as the months and the years passed; and the women of the neighborhood used to come and spend whole days with my mother, sewing for the soldiers. So precious became woollen cloth that every rag was saved and the threads were unravelled to be spun and woven into new fabrics. And they baked bread and roasted chickens and sheep and pigs and made cakes, all to go to the soldiers at the front.

My father had not gone into the army. He was a "Union man" and he did not believe in secession. I remember having heard him once call it a "foolish enterprise." But he could not escape the service of the Confederate Government, if he had wished; and, although he opposed the war, he did not wish to be regarded by his neighbors as a "traitor." The Government needed the whole product of his little cotton mill, and of a thousand more which did not exist. He was, therefore, "detailed" to run the mill at its utmost capacity and to give its product to the Government. He received pay for it, of course, in Confederate money; and, when the war ended, there were thousands of dollars of these bills in the house. My mother made screens of one-hundred-dollar bills for the fireplaces in summer.

I once asked her, years afterwards, why my father did not buy something that was imperishable with all this money, while it had a certain value—land, for instance.

"Your father would have regarded it as dishonourable to use money in this way which he knew would lose its value; for this would have been taking advantage of the delusion of his neighbors."

Thus the thread that the little mill spun went to the making of clothes for soldiers and bandages for the wounded— mitigated human suffering somewhat, it is now pleasant to think; and thus it happened that my father was at home when the noise of cannon came. It was in the first soft days of spring. There was a battle at Marlborough, they said. Would they fight here, too? The slaves were terror-stricken. What was going to happen to them? Would they be carried off and shot? Old Aunt Maria, the cook, shouted throughout the day:

"Dey say dat de niggers'll be free. I ain't gwine ter have none o'deir freedom, I ain't. May de good Lord carry me erway in er chariut o' fire."

Officers in gray came to the house all day and all night and all the next day. Their horses pawed the lawn and ate the bark from the mimosa trees. Coming and going, asking for food and drink, all talked loudly, their swords clanking, and big pistols hung from their saddles.

Colonel Caldwell, my father's old friend, was one of these officers; and he and my father sat by the fire a long time that night talking in sad excitement. My mother in after years recalled their conversation to me.

My father said that the war ought immediately to be ended, that our army ought to give up, that there was no chance of success, and that no more men ought to be killed.

"True, true," said Colonel Caldwell, "but they are invading our homes. They are despoiling and starving the innocent. Shall we tamely submit? Shall we be cowards? Your own home, Worth, may be plundered before another night."

"As for me," he went on, "even if I were relieved of my command on this line of retreat, I should not dare be found at home when they come. That would mean death or capture. God knows what will become of my family. My wife expects me to call at home to-morrow to tell her what to do. I can but ride by and go on."

"Sacrificing more men," said my father, "every cruel day."

"Men!" exclaimed the Colonel. "What of it? So long as the conflict goes on, we cannot regard the life of a soldier. Its very cheapness is the basis of all war. We have become used to death. It is better than to go to starve in prison. If I must die, let me die fighting."

"But, after that, what?" my father asked. "Even if we could win, the country is dead. That is the thought that troubles me—the coming anarchy."

Then the roll of musketry was heard down the road.

"God save you, Caldwell"; and the Colonel and his companions rushed to their waiting horses and rode away in the moonlight.

We now all lived in my mother's room. I remember that my father sat by the fire with his face buried in his hands. The bed had been taken from the bedstead and put on the floor, because the floor, being below the windows, was a safer place from bullets. I was lying on it, my brother Charles beside me, and my mother held the baby in her arms.

I had feverishly heard all that had been said; and it seemed to me that the end of the world was about to come. The earth rolled toward me. In a moment it would crush us all. Then, as I held my breath, the great globe became light as air and floated away. The feverish dream came again and I cried out. My mother caressed me. Then she took the baby again and sat at the fire by my father, with one hand on his knee.

And soon after daylight the blue-coated cavalry of the "Yankees" came down the road. They had a little cannon on a horse and they put it on the high ground behind our garden and shot a ball clean through John Root's shanty, far down the road. John's old mother believed the rest of her days that when it struck the house she was killed and went to heaven. She met her husband there, and he told her that they had plenty of rations in the army of the Lord and that they slept in houses with gold window sashes. He had been a carpenter.

And that night the Union officers occupied my father's house. A colonel made his headquarters in the parlor, and he appropriated two bedrooms upstairs. But a good deal of work had to be done during the afternoon to make them comfortable for him; for, before he came, looting cavalry men of his regiment had run their swords through the beds, looking for hidden silver; and the hearth had been torn up on the same quest. I saw one soldier who had three silver pitchers hanging from his saddle.

Old George, a lame slave, a simple old man, hovered during the day about the back porch, to be near the white people, and a Union soldier thrust a pistol in his face.

"Say, old man, tell it quick or I'll blow your head off—where is everything hidden here?"

Old George fell on his knees.

" 'Fore God, Marster don' shoot a poo' old nigger—your 'umble sarvant;" and, in an ashamed, frightened way, he led the "bummer" up the back stairs to the place in the ceiled wall through which many things had been put into the garret of the "ell." The soldiers broke into this hiding place and found food, and little else. In their chagrin they brought out sacks of flour, cut the bags and emptied it on the floor through the bedrooms and down the stairs. Thus the Colonel walked to his bayonetted bed up a stairway strewn and packed with flour, and slept in a room where the bricks that had been torn from the hearth were piled to right and left.

I slept that night on a trundle bed by my mother's, for her room was the only room left for the family, and we had all lived there since the day before. The dining room and the kitchen were now superfluous, because there was nothing more to cook or to eat.

An army corps built its camp-fires under the great oaks and cut their emblems on their trunks, where you may see them to this day; and, while they were there, the news came one day that Lincoln had been killed. I heard my father and the Union General talking about it; and, so solemn was their manner, I remember it clearly. The news that somebody had been killed had become so common that more than the usual solemnity was required to impress any particular death on the mind.

A week or more after the army corps had gone, I drove with my father to the capital one day, and almost every mile of the journey we saw a blue coat or a gray coat lying by the road, with bones or hair protruding—the unburied and forgotten of either army.

Thus I had come to know what war was, and death by violence was among the first deep impressions made on my mind. My emotions must have been violently dealt with and my sensibilities blunted— or sharpened? Who shall say? The wounded and the starved straggled home from hospitals and from prisons. There was old Mr. Sanford, the shoemaker, come back again, with a body so thin and a step so uncertain that I expected to see him fall to pieces. Mr. Larkin and Joe Tatum went on crutches; and I saw a man at the post-office one day whose cheek and ear had been torn away by a shell. Even when Sam and I sat on the river-bank fishing, and ought to have been silent lest the fish swim away, we told over in low tones the stories that we had heard of wounds and of deaths and of battles.

But there was the cheerful gentleness of my mother to draw my thoughts to different things. I can even now recall many special little plans that she made to keep my mind from battles. She hid the military cap that I had worn. She bought from me my military buttons and put them away. She would call me in and tell me pleasant stories of her own childhood. She would put down her work to make puzzles with me, and she read gentle books to me and kept away from me all the stories of the war and of death that she could. Whatever hardships befell her (and they must have been many) she kept a tender manner of resignation and of cheerful patience. There was a time— how long I do not know—while Aunt Maria was wandering about looking for the "freedom" for which she had said she did not care, when my mother did the cooking for the family; and I remember to have seen her many times in the wash-house scrubbing our clothes.

I have often wondered, and no doubt you have, too, at the deficiencies of the narratives that we call history; for, although they tell of what men did with governments and with armies, they forget the pathetic lack of tender experiences that has ever fallen to war-shortened childhood, and the childlessness of women who never had mates because the men who would have wed them fell in battle in their youth. In histories of this very war I have read boasts about the number of men who perished from a single State!

After a while the neighborhood came to life again. There were more widows, more sonless mothers, more empty sleeves and wooden legs than anybody there had ever seen before. But the mimosa bloomed, the cotton was planted again, and the peach trees blossomed; and the barnyard and the stable again became full of life. For, when the army marched away, they, too, were as silent as an old battlefield. The last hen had been caught under the corn-crib by a "Yankee" soldier, who had torn his coat in this brave raid. Aunt Maria told Sam that all Yankees were chicken thieves whether they "brung freedom or no."

The little cotton mill was again started, for I must tell you, in the very beginning, that the river ever ran and the mill kept turning; and I should be ungrateful if I allowed you to forget that on every year, whose events will be told in this book, the cotton bloomed and ripened and opened white to the sun; for the ripening of the cotton and the running of the river and the turning of the mills make the thread not of my story only but of the story of our Southern land—of its institutions, of its misfortunes and of its place in the economy of the world; and they will make the main threads of its story, I am sure, so long as the sun shines on our white fields and the rivers run—a story that is now rushing swiftly into a happier narrative of a broader day.

The same women who had guided the spindles in war-time were again at their tasks—they at least were left; but the machinery was now old and worked ill. Negro men, who had wandered a while looking for an invisible "freedom," came back and went to work on the farm from force of habit. They now received wages and bought their own food. That was the only apparent difference that freedom had brought them.

My Aunt Katharine came from the city for a visit, my Cousin Margaret with her. Through the orchard, out into the newly ploughed ground beyond, back over the lawn which was itself bravely repairing the hurt done by horses' hoofs and tent-poles, and under the oaks, which bore the scars of camp-fires, we two romped and played gentler games than camp and battle. One afternoon, as our mothers sat on the piazza and saw us come loaded with apple-blossoms, they said something (so I afterward learned) about the eternal blooming of childhood and of nature—how sweet the early summer was in spite of the harrying of the land by war; for our gorgeous pageant of the seasons came on as if the earth had been the home of unbroken peace.

Walter Hines Page (1855–1918)

Cary-native Walter Hines Page is best known, not for his novel, *The Southerner,* but for his work as editor, publisher, and diplomat. Born in 1855, he grew up to become a farsighted man whose ideas were frequently ahead of his time. Early in his career he began a small newspaper in Raleigh, hoping to help his region turn from racism and a romantic attachment to a lost cause—the Confederacy. He tried to promote interest in good schools, good roads, rotation of crops, vocational training in public schools—all of which he expected would move this state forward.

Eventually, he became discouraged at what he considered the lack of a forward-looking spirit in his native state. So he moved to the North, eventually becoming editor of *The Atlantic Monthly,* one of the most renowned magazines in the country. He was also a co-founder of two magazines and a successful publishing house, Doubleday, Page, and Company. As a publisher, he helped Charles Chesnutt (see p. 182) get his first book into print.

Page served as ambassador to Great Britain, and handled his duties so well there that when he died in 1918, the British paid him one of their highest honors. They buried him in Westminster Abbey, the great cathedral in which England crowns its royalty and buries its most respected citizens. The inscription on his burial tablet speaks of "his friendship and sympathy in Great Britain's greatest hour of need." Back home, he was honored in 1923 by construction of the Walter Hines Page Vocational Building at Cary High School.

It is interesting that this talented man who had won professional success and worldwide respect cherished his family more than his accomplishments. The father of three sons and a daughter, he once said, "After all, my main business has been in rearing these boys and their younger sister. My family life has given me the greatest joy of all; that's my real life. The rest is incident."

Language Alert

1. You will see two words which seem misspelled. They are spelled the British way.
   a. *neighbourhood* (We spell it *neighborhood*.)
   b. *unravelled* (Americans spell it *unraveled*.)
2. As with most stories written before the middle of this century, dialect is given phonetic spellings and is somewhat hard to read. (Black dialect was not the only dialect to be spelled phonetically. The everyday language of Irish, Jews, Swedes, rural white southerners, mountaineers, and others was often spelled to represent pronunciation.)
3. Key Words and Their Uses
   a. *fathomlessly*: A *fathom* is a measure. The word is also used to mean *understand*. Something that is *fathomless* cannot be measured or understood.
   b. *capacity*: This word may mean *an ability* or *a power*, as in "He has the *capacity* to lead this organization." It may also refer to maximum amount, as in "We filled the truck to its *capacity*."
   c. *delusion*: Illusions and delusions are both false impressions or beliefs, but they differ. An *illusion* usually results from seeing things wrong—perhaps from wishful thinking. A *delusion* often happens when one simply doesn't want to see the truth—or when one is mentally disturbed.
   d. *mitigated*: If something intense or painful has been made milder, we say that it has been *mitigated*.
   e. *anarchy*: When a region is lawless and without political order, we say that it is in a state of *anarchy*. (Sometimes this situation occurs right after a war or revolution.)
   f. *superfluous*: the root word *super* means over; the root word *floere* means flow. *Superfluous* literally means *overflowing*. We use it now to mean *extra*—even *useless* and *excessive*.
   g. *deficiencies*: A starved person has a nutritional *deficiency*. A student who does math poorly may be said to have a *deficiency* in that subject. *Deficiencies* are lacks or weaknesses.

Reflecting

1. Although there were exceptions, most slaves were uneducated and their experience was limited to their immediate surroundings. In this story, Aunt Maria and others have never experienced freedom, so they don't know what to do with it. Pauli Murray explains this situation in her book about her grandfather, *Proud Shoes*. You may want to compare the two works (see p. 166).
2. Toward the end of this chapter, the boy speaks of "the deficiencies of the narratives that we call history," the gaps in the story. He mentions some of the side effects of war—not those felt by soldiers, but those felt by children and women.

   Interview someone you know who has lived through one of the more recent wars: World War II, the Korean War, the Vietnamese War. Instead of concentrating on property destroyed, lives lost, or battles won, ask about the "side effects"—the ways people were affected personally and in their family lives.

From **Time of Drums**

Battle

John Ehle

Preview

What is it like to be in the middle of a war? How does it feel to be a soldier—when you were recently a farmer, student, mechanic, lawyer, or millworker, but are now outfitted in a uniform and trained to kill? Could you enter battle for the first time, commanded to kill human beings with whom you have no personal quarrel, knowing that at any moment a bullet you don't even hear may end your own life?

Most art—literature, films, paintings, sculpture—that deals with war concentrates on either the ferocious action during conflict, the bravery of those involved in battle, or the destruction of land, property, and human beings. Rarely do we get a realistic behind-the-scenes glimpse of what life is like before the battle as soldiers prepare to defend themselves or to attack others.

In this excerpt from his novel, *Time of Drums*, John Ehle gives us just such a glimpse. (Ehle was born sixty years after the Civil War ended, but he served as a rifleman in Europe during World War II, so he knows firsthand what it is like to be a soldier in combat.)

The speaker, Owen, is a colonel in charge of five hundred soldiers. They are about to participate in their first major battle—Chancellorsville. We pick up the story as Owen instructs his men.

I started with a cartridge, which I usually do at such a time. I held one up for them to see. "It's a piece of paper with a lead ball in the smooth end and the gunpowder in the crinkly end; you bite off the crinkly end and put that end first into the muzzle of the musket, is that so?"

They nodded dumbly.

"Then you take the ramrod and push down the bullet and its wadding to hold the powder in place, so that the powder can be lit. Then you do what?"

"You shoot," somebody said.

"Well, you just shot your ramrod at the enemy, soldier," I said, and everybody laughed. "Which most of us have done from time to time," I said. "Now listen, don't fire until ordered to, and fire only when you see an enemy clearly. Fire deliberately. Take your time, don't rush. The war is going to take most all spring."

"A-men," Sergeant Raper said.

"Don't shoot high. Shoot low. Yanks don't live in Heaven. Shoot at the officers first. Aim to wound, not to kill; a wounded man is more of a problem to an army than a dead one. Don't huddle. If you're in a second or third rank, keep behind the man in the first rank to make a single target. You can't shoot anyway until he drops to fire or load his gun, or falls—for whatever reason. In battle when you are signaled forward, follow in random order, that is, about one third of each company moves forward while the others cover them. Stay with your company. If I or Captain Crawford or a sergeant signals for you to fall back, do so in an orderly way. More men are lost retreating than attacking. Don't stop to help the wounded, no matter who he is, except in retreat. Don't stop to help me, for instance. Don't stop to help your brother or the man who bunks with you. The best service you can be to your friend is to push the Yanks back, for they will kill him quicker than your mother would wring a chicken's neck."

I backed off the road to let an ambulance pass, then several mounted men rode by, all going to our left flank as we faced the enemy. The withdrawal, the Lee and Jackson strategy, was beginning now. With half as many men as the Yanks, they were dividing their army. It made no sense, of course, especially to the enemy.

"Don't pick up spoils during the battle," I said to Crawford's men. "If you see a diamond ring as big as an egg, call out and tell me where it is, and you go on."

The men fell to laughing. They were nervous, anyway, and susceptible to humor.

"Now, the hospital corps has convalescents to help with the wounded, and they have litter-bearers and assistant surgeons, and if you get wounded you will see them coming along. You'll find that one of your big needs is water, for you'll be sweating from tension. Don't drink all that you've got in your canteen. If you get wounded in the stomach, don't drink water at all. If you get lost, ask somebody where Manger's brigade is, or ask where I am. We're in Heth's division, Jackson's corps. We're going to be rounding the enemy most all day and that can be dangerous, for we'll be a thin line. If they attack, we're not going to try to hold them. If you get captured, say I told you to go home."

Several of the men laughed.

"Anybody want to go home?"

Nobody said a word. We stood there looking at each other, most everybody smiling except for the smith's men.

"Now, I do want to say one more thing, and those who know me know what it is. I've been put on the honor roll eleven times for past battles, which is a creditable score, and I have four medals, but I didn't get decorated all those times by being a hero all the time. Pick the occasions carefully when you are willing to risk your life."

"Tell 'em, Colonel," Sergeant Raper said.

"If we don't do anything today except find out how to protect ourselves so we can fight tomorrow, that's all right, because I expect there's going to be a fight here tomorrow. So you men who are not sure you want to fight in a sorry place like this can wait out your chances. We don't expect men to fight all the time. It's your army, and you'll find in good time that it's your war. Nobody who fights likes his enemy for very long. Keep your head down, keep your tail down, stay low, love the ground. Crawl if you can. Fire from the ground—I'd rather have that than have you stand out there like a queen's guard and be shot down. Nobody on earth can accurately fire a musket standing up anyway."

"A-men," Sergeant Raper said.

"You'll see some of Jackson's other regiments marching forward, erect and in order, and it looks impressive, but we use a more frontier way, not theirs, not the army-manual way. That's why some of us have eleven honor roll citations and are still around. Now, any questions?"

"I got my cartridges wet last night, Colonel."

"Use your bayonet," I said. "Anything else?"

"Colonel, I got them wet, I tell you."

"Sell him a few rounds, Sergeant Furr," I said. "Anything else?"

"When we going to get our mail?"

"Let's say it'll be tonight," I said. "How do I know?"

"Didn't you once promise we'd have us a band, Colonel?"

"We got one," I said. "It's right down there. One fiddle, two guitars, two banjos, a drum, a bugle, and the bagpipes."

"Seem to be playing for you more'n us."

"Now I notice that some of you still have pets. Is that a dog, Meadows?"

"Yes, sir."

"Well, can she shoot?"

"No, sir. but she can retrieve." He laughed nervously.

"What are you going to do with her?"

"I'll tie her to a tree, sir."

"I think you better give her away to the cavalry, where she'll be safe."

Several men laughed.

"I want to offer a prize of ten dollars to the first man to show me a dead cavalryman of either army," I said. "Last year nobody was able to collect. This year I'm offering the same prize."

"My brother is a cavalryman," a young soldier said defensively.

"Well, once he gets home you'll need to buy him a bigger hat and a wider chair seat."

"Sick call," a man said, "what about that?"

"No sick call today. Most days we're only pretending to be soldiers, but today we are soldiers, and it's a clean feeling, it'll heal you. . . . Now, put your name somewhere on your uniform, pin it to your jacket, inside or out. Nothing to be ashamed of to admit you've got people who'll want to know if something happens to you."

They fell to work at that chore, and I noticed most of the smith's men were preparing the name slips, along with the rest, though they glowered at me moodily, grumbling at me whenever I came near.

I turned into the woods. There was scattered musket fire many miles away, probably as far away as General Lee's army. Between us and that gunfire lay the Yank army, like a lamb's gut full of cheese. I placed my men six feet apart, each company forming three lines, each line about ten feet behind the one in front of it; thus my Company A, with about fifty men, had sixteen men in each of three lines, each line being about forty-five feet long. B Company took its place to the right. In all, my regiment occupied the front for a distance of about 400 feet, with Lieutenant King in charge of the left section, Captain Crawford of the middle, and Lieutenant McGregor of the right. Another North Carolina brigade fell in to my right flank. On our regimental left were Colonel McRuder's men.

I checked my lines. Sergeant Smith was so disturbed he couldn't understand a five-word question, even when I spoke slowly to him. Billy Furr and his men, on the other hand, were eager to be off; it was as if they were expecting to have a race and the starting pistol was about to be fired. I asked for Captain Crawford and found him behind a hickory truck, sitting on the ground, Sergeant Red Raper with him, and he was telling Raper that he wasn't going to accept ever again the sort of insults several of Raper's men had heaped on him that morning.

On my far right I found Lieutenant McGregor's three companies in perfect order. You would think he had used a ruler to measure the distance between his men. He had a command post set up, had even sent a sergeant around to be certain every man had kept his cartridges dry, that the nipple of his musket's firing pin was dry, and that nobody had mud stopping up his musket barrel. He had hot coffee, a canteenful of it, and I drank half a cup, which was all any one person was allowed, he said. I mentioned to him that we had not since dawn had a single message of any sort from General Manger and it appeared I was ostracized[1] for some reason. "If a courier from Heth arrives, I am to be found at once," I said. "It makes no difference what stage the fighting is in."

The men had card games going by now. Several men were trying to read their testaments, even in that dark woods; others were singing softly to themselves. Many were writing letters. One elderly man was eating a piece of corn bread; he had no teeth and the crumbs kept falling out of his mouth. Another was chewing on a raw piece of bacon, which I suppose wasn't good for him, but there's no point in telling a man waiting to go into battle that it's unhealthy to eat raw pork.

A band began to play, a Yank band. Not far away either, and my musicians perked up. The Yanks were playing "The Girl I Left Behind Me." Betsy laughed out loud; music tickles men whenever a battle is brewing. I sent word to my three officers to advance their sections slowly to the

1. ostracized: isolated, shut out, excluded

first field. I crept forward with Company A, with Hal King. Usually I kept to the center of my regiment, but I wanted Crawford to feel the full weight of his responsibility. Ahead of me I could see the little scraggly field. Most all my men were crawling now.

We stopped at the edge of the field. It was about a hundred feet wide. On the other side of it a Yank officer climbed onto a breastwork[2] he and his men had made the night before. It was facing toward our old position, not our new one. We could see other breastworks in a line going into the woods, all facing wrong. To outflank a company or regiment is often done in a battle, but to outflank[3] an army is remarkable and says precious little for their perceptiveness. I suspect their generals were so far removed from the actual battlefield, and their Yank organization so complex, that they didn't know what changes were taking place and they couldn't evaluate[4] what they did know. Jackson, on the other hand, stayed with his men and did much of his own scouting.

A Yank soldier, blue uniformed, wearing good shoes and a peaked hat, walked casually down to a creek and got water in a cup. He returned to his fire.

"That apple tree's going to be pretty in a few weeks," I said to Hal. "It's budding."

"Must have been a homestead here once," Hal said.

A deer appeared, moved out into the field about 150 yards to our left, where McRuder's men were quietly moving to the edge of the woods. Another deer appeared farther down the field. The Yank officer, his hands on his hips, studied about that, looking thoughtfully along the line of woods.

Hal said, "What would you do, Owen, if you were that Yank officer?"

"Get ready to run," I said.

Victor Plover came forward. He had his snare drum strapped over his shoulder. He was a child, really, and was so dumb or scared he couldn't understand what was being said to him. Several of Hal's men on his nod put their muskets to their shoulders. That poor Yank officer was still standing up on his breastwork studying our woods fretfully. You better get down, mister, I thought; you'll soon be food for Virginia tumblebugs if you don't mind.

The drum roll began way off, the long roll, and moved swiftly toward us, and in that instant the muskets fired and the Yank officer was flung upward and backward. My drummer boy was striking his drum now and Hal's men rose with a yell, that infernal[5] Rebel yell, a mingling of challenge and blood-terror, a hunter's sound meant to frighten. His men moved out into the field, walking quickly.

One of them fell. He scrambled to his feet, started back toward where I lay, his hand inside his jacket, a young man, about nineteen, a veteran soldier named Vance. He took his hand out of his jacket.

2. breastwork: a temporary barrier used as a fortification, usually breast high

3. outflank: to get around and behind the flank of the opponent

4. evaluate: to measure the value of

5. infernal: fiendish, vile, relating to hell

Soldiers before battle. This photograph was taken at ceremonies commemorating the Battle of Bentonville near Newton Grove, NC.

His hand was red and dripping, and he said, "Colonel, what does this mean?" and fell dead.

The yell sounded again. As far as one could see were gray men moving through the woods and all about were the shattering noises of our muskets firing. At this close range a ball goes zip. There is no whistle or shriek or whine. It goes zip, with now and then one singing off into space with a villainous, greasy slide. My men were in perfect formation, except as I moved to the right I found that the smith's men were lingering in a mass back a ways.

After a while Yank musket balls began to whistle and whine, and now and then to shriek through the air overhead. They flew past us sounding like swifts. Others sounded like bumblebees.

A man twenty feet away crumpled to the ground. I decided he was acting, that was all. "Get up, mister. On your feet," I said.

He got up slowly, not looking at me.

"Go slow, no hurry," I told him. "Those bees won't sting you." I saw my bagpipe player moving ahead, his pipes on his back, chewing tobacco and spitting and peering forward, hoping to catch a sight of the Yanks. We had crossed the field and were once more in pine woods, where low branches had already been broken by Yanks, so we had to avoid the sharp pointed stubs that were left.

The shelling began, our own artillery opening fire on the body of the Yank army, which was no doubt in confusion enough without this added excitement. Big shells flew overhead, sounding like lo-comotive whistles, and exploded over the woods ahead of us, scattering hunks of metal. The shells had been made of iron from the rails of old North Carolina railroad track, I suspect, and lampposts taken off the streets of Charleston and Atlanta and Memphis and other cities, and black iron cookpots from Alabama, Mississippi, and a thousand other places. The South was breaking iron this afternoon, trying to free itself. Sergeant Smith's men panicked at the noise, started running toward the rear. I decided to ignore them for now. I couldn't outrun them, after all.

"You want to play a tune?" I asked McIlvenna.

"Don't I have to be quiet?" he said, astonished.

"Quiet?" I said, and laughed.

He struck up a tune. He was grinning with such happiness he could scarcely make a steady sound. There he went walking through those pine woods, playing "The Highland Laddie," which tingled in my blood. The Plover boy came running, ready to join in. The sound of the artillery seemed less dangerous now.

When we came upon wounded Yanks, we walked on past them. To step over wounded men adds to the feeling of omnipotence[6] which a soldier gets in battle; the more wounded men a soldier sees the less likely he is to be afraid of being hit, for each one is a credit to his infalli-

6. omnipotence: unlimited power (*omni* means all, *potence* refers to power)

bility.[7] We didn't hear most of their cries, anyway, because of the rapid musket fire around us and the artillery shells overhead, and my band playing.

Colonel McRuder came hurrying through the woods, proud and big, puffing for breath and patting his huge belly. "Owen, where did you get that bagpipe player?" he asked. "I want him. I'd rather have him than my own cannon."

"No, no," I said, "you'll not get him, Mac."

"I'll give you two scouts that can find their way home blindfolded."

We laughed and listened to him play, and walked along in the deep woods, neither of us having lost many men yet—though I had lost a few to the rear apparently.

Captain Crawford came up to me. "They—it's getting late, Colonel," he began, almost incoherently,[8] "and the men want to attack." He was shirt-ripped and had powder marks all over his face, marks daubed on by his fingers, I could tell, not put there by biting cartridges. "Billy Furr wants to advance," he said. "He wants to go forward faster."

"Every man stays in line, Captain," I said.

At once he nodded and started away, staggering, so frightened that his legs were wobbly.

Our cannons were still lobbing shells over us and we were moving forward steadily. There were scores of prisoners. The Yank army couldn't get organized to turn to meet us, and time after time pockets of men would have to surrender. We would disarm them and wave them toward the rear. All was going well, but I suppose Billy Furr was afraid the battle was going to end before he could get in the thick of it, so he and his men spurted forward in a charge. Sergeant Raper and I tried to overtake them. We saw them stop at one point, baffled, confused, for they had thought in a battle there were two lines, one always pushing at the other, and here they were, having exposed themselves, offered themselves for combat, but where were the enemy? They began running forward again. Raper and I went chasing after them as best we could, I shouting at them. The tree limbs were raking at our uniforms, but we tore our way through. We got quite far out ahead of our own line, which meant we could conceivably be cut off and captured, but how does one stop a runaway company gone merrily to see the enemy? They were losing their canteens, their cups; I saw one man cut his haversack's straps to let it fall so he wouldn't be delayed by the trees snagging it. "Come back here, you fools!" I shouted at them.

"Forward!" Billy Furr shouted.

"Come here!" I demanded and fired my pistol over his head, but it might as well have been a robin peeping in his noisy place.

A Yank appeared. Billy let out a Rebel yell and went tearing toward him, to choke him to death, I suppose, and the Yank retreated right smartly, Billy's men

---

7. infallibility: inability to fail or to make an error (or, in this case, the inability to be wounded or to die)
8. incoherently: in a confused, muddled, unclear manner

following along a little trail about eight feet wide. Six Yanks appeared, blocking the road, and fired down the road at Billy Furr's company, almost in their very faces. Billy's men reeled, stunned, screaming, some of them hit, of course. Even as this happened another group of Yanks began firing on them from the woods to our left. I shouted for Billy's men to get into the woods to our right. Raper and I ran here and there, trying to collect them, few of my brave Company E being able or even interested now in returning the enemy fire. They were so shocked, scared that all they wanted was to run the other way, and off they went tearing through the woods, as swift in retreat as they had been in attack. Only a few of them helped Billy Furr answer the enemy.

I left those few to fight or retreat as they chose, and took half a dozen less belligerent men back the way we had come, Sergeant Raper joining us with ten men. We entered our lines almost sheepishly, and I saw Lieutenant McGregor watching us, his hands on his hips, a big grin on his handsome face.

"What do you call that maneuver, Colonel?" he asked me.

"Charge and retreat," I said.

"You've got two or three fast runners there," he said.

"I think so," I said.

"You fellows get a look at Washington, D.C.?" he asked them. Billy was still out there firing away.

MEET THE AUTHOR:
John Ehle (1924–   )

One might suspect that there are two John Ehles, for this Asheville native has had a dual career as a writer and as a public servant. In each, he has accomplished more than enough to make a distinguished name for himself. As a writer, he has authored a number of scripts for radio, television, and stage, as well as publishing ten novels and five books of nonfiction. As a public servant, he has helped establish the North Carolina School of the Arts, the Governor's School, and an antipoverty program.

His classes in English and speech at Lee Edwards High School (now Asheville High School) first sparked John Ehle's interest in writing. He developed that interest and his talent at UNC-Chapel Hill under the direc-

tion of Paul Green (see p. 227). While still a student, he wrote radio scripts which were produced by NBC radio in a series called "American Adventures."

All of Ehle's fiction is set in North Carolina, mostly in the mountains in which he grew up and in which he still makes his home. In addition to his books, he has also written an outdoor drama, *The Road to Orange*. His writing has won a number of awards, including the North Carolina Award for Literature and the Lillian Smith Award for Southern Fiction.

John Ehle's popularity is not limited to North Carolina. *The Winter People*, set in the Appalachians, was made into a 1989 movie starring Kurt Russell and Kelly McGillis, and his books have sold well throughout Europe.

Whenever writing, Ehle sticks to a strict schedule, getting up at about 4:30 or 5:00 a.m. and writing until about 7:00 a.m. before stopping for breakfast. Then he resumes writing until he meets his quota: twenty pages a day.

Reflecting

1. This is a very brief passage from a long novel, but we get a clear picture of Owen. List his personality and character traits which are exhibited in this story. Would you want to serve under his command? Why or why not?

2. Imagine that the war is over and Owen has come to your office to apply for a job that has to do with managing people—perhaps as a warehouse manager or the principal of a school. Would you hire him? Why or why not?

3. Did anything surprise you as you read? That is, was there anything that did not fit your own previous ideas about war?

Statue of Henry Lawson Wyatt on Capital Square, Raleigh, NC. Wyatt was the first NC soldier killed in the War between the States.

Preview

Many paintings and novels about war concentrate on action. The authors want you to picture hundreds of men in bright uniforms charging down a hill, their bayonets glinting in the sun, horses rearing on hind legs. They are less likely to focus on the drabness and discomfort of everyday life.

In the following poem, Mary Kratt adapts entries from the diary kept by her mother's grandfather, John Richard Hood. Considering the fact that keeping a diary must have been difficult for a soldier in the middle of a war, we can assume that he wrote only about those matters which most concerned him. Notice what kinds of things those were.

Great-Grandfather Writes Home, 1862–63

Mary Kratt

Each man cooks his own
pound of beef
pound of flour
at Rapidan, Culpeper, Gum Swamp
stirred over the campfire
when we're not marching
and that's not often

John Richard Hood ("Great-Grandfather") in his Confederate uniform.

March fifteen miles at night
march eighteen
march ten
from Crow Creek, Sand Ridge, Shepardstown
cross the Potomac
the Shenandoah
road knee deep in mud
two letters this week from home

Cornmeal and bacon rations
no pay
a letter took four months to come
at Chicahominy, Petersburg
men punished everyday
one stole bacon, had to stand
three days on a stump

We slept in an old church
marched twenty miles in rain
fell out of ranks
for the first time
and from a farmer's wife
bought dinner for a quarter
pair of socks, jar of honey
from Kenansville, Kinston, Goldsboro
Fast Day proclaimed
by Jefferson Davis

The Methodist preacher in town
took his text Psalm 118:1
O give thanks unto the Lord
for he is good, his mercy
endureth for ever.

Mary Kratt (1936–   )

A Charlottean for most of her life, Mary Kratt began writing when she was in junior high school. In fact, she was editor of both her junior high and senior high newspapers, and wrote occasional school news for the *Charlotte Observer*. Most of her writing today takes one of two forms: history (she has written a number of books on Charlotte and Mecklenburg County, including *Legacy, The Myers Park Story,* and *Charlotte: Spirit of the New South*) and poetry (her most recent collection is *On the Steep Side*). Of particular interest is her book *The Imaginative Spirit,* which provides mini-biographies of writers in the Charlotte-Mecklenburg area. Recently she has combined her interests in history and poetry, adapting old journals and letters into poems.

Miss Kratt's historical writing has won recognition from the North Carolina Society of Historians. Her poetry has won a number of prizes, including the Oscar Arnold Young Award for the best poetry book published in North Carolina during 1982.

Reflecting

1. If we assume that John Richard Hood's experience was typical, what does this writing tell us about the daily existence of Confederate soldiers?

2. Mary Kratt tells us that John Richard Hood was wounded in battle near Plymouth, N.C. "He came home limping, claimed his bride, Mary Anne Hunter, and began life with her in his ancestral home in 1864 near Matthews, N.C. and Hood's Cross Roads. He had inherited the frame two-story farmhouse and 200 acres from his father. He cleared the forests, made a good living from the land and sent his children to college." What can you find in the poem that would lead you to predict that he would become what we call "a solid citizen"?

A Soldier's Odyssey

Dennis Rogers

Preview

You are a Confederate soldier engaged in battle with Union troops outside the tiny northeastern North Carolina town of South Mills. The fighting is fierce. Five thousand enemy soldiers are firing at you and your comrades. Suddenly, to your astonishment, you see a young woman and baby running right into the open battlefield, heading for the shelter of an old house. What do you do?

The Confederate soldiers defending this northeastern North Carolina town on April 19, 1862, first saw the woman during the heat of the battle that raged over these swampy fields.

They were dug into the south of the town, facing 5,000 Yankee troops. Between the lines, in an open field, was an old house.

Suddenly the Rebel boys saw the figure of a young woman break from the Union lines. Carrying a baby in her arms, she ran as hard as she could for the safety of the old house in the middle of the battlefield.

Henry Dixon, the aristocratic son of wealthy South Carolina planters, saw the woman and baby reach the house safely. He could also see that the house was being ripped to shreds by the cannon balls and rifle fire.

So the young man—who had left his home in the bloodpounding days when the war was young and every Southerner thought it would be over in a month—dropped his gun and dashed across the open battlefield for the little house.

He was too late. A cannon blast had killed the woman, striking her in the face. But the baby she was carrying was alive, smeared in its mother's blood, trying to wake her up as it sat by her unrecognizable body.

Dixon grabbed the infant and ran back to his lines, somehow making it through the fire to safety. Maybe Providence was on his side. Maybe the enemy soldiers couldn't bring themselves to shoot at Dixon and the baby.

Dixon gave the child to Dr. R. A. Lewis, the unit surgeon, and went back to being a soldier. Lewis eventually took the child, a baby girl, to his home in Richmond where she would live.

But Lewis did something else that fateful day. When the battle was over, he went out looking for survivors and to oversee burial of the dead. He found the woman's body in the house and removed a locket from her breast, slipping it into his pocket and planning one day to give it to the little girl.

Henry Dixon survived the war and returned to South Carolina. But Sherman's army had gotten there first, and the only thing left was blackened rubble and the graves of his parents.

Among the missing was his wife, the former Mary Singleton. No one could tell him what had happened to Mary. All the neighbors knew was that she had left South Carolina during the war, taking their only child with her. Some said she went to Norfolk, looking for Henry.

Dixon went in search of Mary and the baby. He followed her trail to Norfolk, but there it died.

His search and his money ended, Dixon returned to South Carolina and began the long work of rebuilding his plantation and his life. But then there was a windfall of money and the search was on

again.

Back to Norfolk he went, this time for a month, but with the same dead-end result. Mary Singleton Dixon had vanished.

Brokenhearted, Dixon decided to drop in on his old friend Lewis before returning home. On his way to Lewis' Richmond home, Dixon happened by a school while recess was on.

There, in that place of childish laughter, was a little girl playing in the schoolyard.

Dixon asked the little girl her name. She said it was May Darling. He asked her where she lived. She said with Dr. Lewis.

Dixon went to the Lewis home. Lewis told him that May Darling wasn't really her name. It was the little girl Dixon had saved from the battlefield, and since they didn't know her last name, they had taken to calling her May Darling.

Lewis showed Dixon something else that day, the locket he had taken from the dead woman's breast.

Dixon, with shaking fingers, opened the locket.

On one side was a picture of the little girl.

On the other side was a picture of Henry Dixon.

The dead woman with the locket had been Mary Singleton Dixon, Henry's wife. She had gone looking for her husband, and he had found her that bloody day, too late only by the seconds it takes a cannon ball to fly.

The child that Henry Dixon had saved so long ago was his daughter.

Dennis Rogers (1942–   )

Dennis Rogers began writing during the early 1960s while he was a student at Ralph L. Fike Senior High School in Wilson, but it wasn't until he began writing for newspapers in the 1970s that his work was published. In the meantime, he had served with the United States Army in Vietnam and earned a degree in journalism from UNC-Chapel Hill. At the university, his academic record was recognized by initiation into Phi Beta Kappa, and as a journalist, he has been a four-time winner of awards from the North Carolina Press Association.

Many North Carolinians currently look forward each morning to Dennis Rogers's human interest stories in the Raleigh *News and Observer*. Many are humorous; some are touching; almost all arouse feelings. Many of his columns have been republished in four collections of his work. He is also known as an actor, with a number of memorable performances in productions at the Raleigh Little Theater.

Reflecting

1. Unbelievable as this incident is, it is true, though based on the most incredible sequence of coincidences. For example, if the cannonball had not struck the woman in the face, Henry Dixon would have recognized her. What other surprising coincidences contribute to the story?
2. Dennis Rogers travels the eastern part of this state looking for interesting folks and the material for good yarns. But good yarns don't just happen, they are created.

   If you've ever heard someone muddle through a joke or a story which should be exciting, you know that *how* a story is told is almost as important as *what* the story is about. Good yarns are created by master yarn spinners who know
   a. which details to include, which to omit;
   b. when to withhold information to create suspense, and precisely when to furnish that information for best effect;
   c. how to begin a story in such a way as to awaken interest;
   d. how to continue enticing the reader by creating suspense and, when appropriate, including humor or horror or sympathy; and
   e. exactly how to end the story with a memorable crackle.

   Review Dennis Rogers's story to see how he made best use of the material at hand.

A Time of Rebuilding

Any war is costly in terms of human life, property damage, and emotional suffering. The Civil War was unusually destructive and it left the South with many burdens. Many of its finest young men had died in the war. Others were left with severe permanent injuries. Homes, farms, and businesses had been destroyed, livestock and other possessions stolen or damaged. Both families and the states were faced with poverty.

Beyond the physical and financial losses were the psychological effects. Many families had to deal with personal loss and somehow summon the courage and energy to start all over again. The South as a whole had to swallow its pride and admit defeat. And there remained the problem of racial conflict. The Emancipation Proclamation had freed blacks from legal slavery, but it could not free them from prejudice nor from the effects (psychological, educational, financial) of slavery.

In this section, you will catch several glimpses of people in this region as they dealt with everyday life in a difficult time.

My Earliest Recollections

Josephus Daniels

Preview

Although the earliest years are said to be the most important in forming one's personality and character, few of us can consciously remember many events from that part of our lives. In the following excerpt from his autobiography, *Tar Heel Editor*, Josephus Daniels reports his four earliest recollections.

Before reading what he remembers, make a brief list of the earliest things you can recall: perhaps a trip or celebration, perhaps an illness or accident, maybe just a scene that surprised or impressed you. As you read, compare your own recollections to those of Josephus Daniels.

It was in 1865 that my widowed mother with her three small boys reached Wilson to make it home. My oldest brother Frank was seven years old; I was three; and my brother Charles was a baby. Our possessions were almost nil,[1] but we had our never-failing capital of my mother's courageous faith and the welcome by the Griffins and Nadals, the only Wilsonians my mother knew. I was too young to recall the nearly all-night travel on the train and the hardships and long delays of the journey, of which my mother often talked. My father's death threw upon her the sole responsibility of making a living for her little family at a time when the South was prostrate[2] and few openings for women in business existed. When the outlook was dark, there came from her sister Elizabeth, and her sister's husband, George H. Griffin, an invitation to make her home in Wilson, with assurances that she would be received with affection and assistance and that good schools in Wilson would af-

1. nil: nothing
2. prostrate: lying face down, as in humility or humiliation

ford opportunity for the education of her children.

At that time Wilson had a population of less than one thousand. It had been too far out of the war zone to have suffered like the towns on the coast. Resolved[3] to be self-supporting, my mother opened a small millinery and dressmaking establishment and, working often late in the night with her needle, was soon able to earn enough to support herself and her three small boys. A little later she was appointed post mistress.

My earliest clear recollection is the day when I received the scar on my forehead that I shall carry to my grave. My brother Frank, and George and Doug Hackney, and John Pomeroy Clark were digging foundations for a play store in our yard on Tarboro Street, when, as Doug was swinging an ax high, he struck me full on the forehead. I was playing about, and he had not seen me. I fell unconscious and was thought to have been killed, but by the time Dr. Edwin Barnes arrived I had revived, and the gift of a big lump of sugar from Mr. J. V. Blackwell, a neighbor merchant, helped the doctor to bring me around. My mother, always capable, had bathed my wound and the doctor did the rest. Hackney was fearful he had killed me and could not be consoled[4] until the doctor said I was all right. Always afterward when we met, he would say, "Take off your hat and let me see my mark you bear." At that time Mr. Blackwell was the only man in Wilson who made a habit of wearing a silk hat and patent-leather shoes and dressing in a way that attracted attention. I do not recall any other man in Wilson when I was a boy who was very particular with his dress except on Sundays or wedding days. Even on Sundays and holidays, it was a rare thing for a Wilson business man to dress in a way to indicate that he had ever read the fashion plates. Mr. Blackwell was as straight as an Indian. After a time in business in Wilson, he moved away, but I never saw him without thinking pleasantly about that lump of sugar.

My second recollection is that of being awakened by the flames that were consuming our house—the third time my mother was burned out in six years. I was terrified, and I remember "Uncle Anthony" Nadal wrapping me in a blanket and carrying me to his home, where he and "Aunt Sack" gave shelter and home to my mother and her three boys for the night. Soon after, we moved to the home of Uncle Griffin, whose kindness and generosity to my mother and her three orphaned boys were such as to insure him a place with the angels. We lived there as members of his family until Mother rented a place for the post office in a building that provided a home also.

My next recollection is of the time when a horse kicked me, and again Dr. Barnes had to sew up my head. He was the leading physician in Wilson, universally beloved. He never had an office. There were no telephones to call him when his services were needed. If he could not be found at home, he was usually at his favorite drugstore—favorite because interesting people gathered there to swap ex-

3. resolved: determined
4. consoled: comforted

163

periences and tell stories. A paper that was published anonymously now and then, the *Investigator*, to shoot darts at leading figures, invented and printed his advertisement:

E. BARNES, M.D.,
Practicing Physician
Wilson, N.C.
Office At Any Place Where
He May Be Found

Doctor Barnes never sent a bill to a patient or failed to respond to a professional call from those he knew could not or would not pay him. He was the model country-town doctor, responding to all calls, day or night, to distant country homes over bad roads

. . . .

To return to the horse-kicking incident, my Uncle Griffin had warned me not to go near the rear of the horse, but I sought to drive him into the stable, a few steps above ground, when he gave me a kick that for a time rendered me unconscious. My head seemed to be so hard that neither an ax nor the kick of a horse could do more than make a dent in it. Boarding with my aunt was a young man, James E. Shepherd, afterwards Chief Justice, who was among those to give me first aid. He found great delight ever afterward in teasing my mother, between whom and the lawyer-jurist existed a lifelong rare friendship, by telling her that her son was so hardheaded that the kick did not hurt him at all, "but the horse went off limping."

The fourth thing I recollect is a shining silver dime I received for a Christmas present. It was the first piece of silver money I had ever seen. I was about four or five years old. In those days we had what were called shinplasters, paper money, five- and ten-cent pieces, and usually they were dirty and dingy. Paper money is always dirty and dingy away from Washington City, and in those days it was very scarce. I remember on this Christmas morning, after the stockings had been opened, my brother and I and some neighbors were popping crackers[5] on the sidewalk, when Mr. Anthony Nadal, who was then living in the country and whose home was always open to the Daniels boys whenever they wished to come, drove up and we yelled "Christmas Gift" at him. He had come prepared with what we thought was a Croesus gift and handed out a brand-new silver dime to me and to each of my two brothers. The sun shone upon it and made it look more beautiful than anything I thought I had ever seen. I felt richer that day than I have ever felt since, and I would run my hand in my pocket and take out and hold the dime up to the sun again and again. I think we three boys were the only three boys in Wilson who had any silver money and we were very stuck up about it and made our playmates envious of us. I kept it for a long time.

5. "Popping crackers" refers to setting off firecrackers

Josephus Daniels (1862–1948)

A "dynasty" is a family that maintains power or influence for several generations. Usually we use the term to refer to royal or imperial families, such as the Ming dynasty in China. Sometimes, however, the term applies to families who continue a certain powerful tradition—in banking, perhaps, or publishing.

Josephus Daniels could be called the patriarch—the founding father—of a publishing/writing dynasty. After growing up in Wilson, he became editor of the *Wilson Advance* when he was only twenty-two, and soon afterward purchased the paper. Eventually, he purchased the Raleigh *News and Observer*, which has been a property of the Daniels family ever since. His son, Jonathan, succeeded him as editor, three generations of his heirs have managed the business, and his granddaughters have published novels. Looking at the Daniels family, one could almost believe the old cliché that "printer's ink runs in their veins."

Josephus Daniels quickly earned a reputation as a writer/editor with strong and often controversial views, especially on social and

political issues. He favored giving women the right to vote, he supported laws against child labor, and he wrote editorials against the Ku Klux Klan. He was also very active in politics, and served in national positions under three United States presidents. Daniels wrote a number of books, most of which centered on history or his own colorful experiences.

Reflecting

1. Josephus Daniels's first three recollections all involve near-disasters, but it's interesting to notice that the boy was as impressed by people as much as by the danger he faced. In the first incident, he remembers Mr. Blackwell; in the second, "Uncle Anthony" and "Aunt Sack"; and in the third, James E. Shepherd and Dr. Barnes. What personal qualities do these people have in common?

2. Young Josephus was almost overwhelmed by the gift of a piece of silver money. It wasn't a very large sum. Why was he so excited? What amount of money would make a four-year-old equally excited today?

From **Proud Shoes**

Grandfather's Mission

Pauli Murray

Preview

In 1866, the Civil War had been over for one year. Peace reigned in the land, and all blacks had been freed from legal slavery. However, the South was still ravaged by the aftermath of war and the pain of slavery. Young Robert Fitzgerald came to Hillsborough (then spelled Hillsboro) as a missionary, to save souls not through preaching, but through teaching. It was not an easy task.

At twenty-five, Robert Fitzgerald set out to join the "Yankee school-marms" in the South. He carried with him only his Bible, his faith and a few books and charts. Behind him lay a winter of teaching in Delaware and a year of training at Ashmun Institute—now Lincoln University—to become a missionary. Lincoln University students were granted commissions from the Presbyterian General Assembly's Committee on Freedmen to spend their summer vacations among the freedmen as teachers, catechists and licentiates. They assisted ministers in the field and in turn recruited promising young men for enrollment in their school. Among the many changes the war had brought was a reorientation of Ashmun Institute toward missionary work among the freed Negroes in the United States. Symbolic of its new approach was the school's change of name to Lincoln University in 1866. Young Fitzgerald was among the first of its ardent[1] emissaries[2] to carry on this important work.

He had known since his army days that he would return to the South. Emancipation was born in the violent chaos of war; a whole people had been jarred loose, cast up from unspeakable depths of poverty and ignorance and were trying

1. ardent: eager
2. emissaries: messengers, agents

to take the first terrifying step toward becoming free men. He had felt the turbulent[3] force of this event, a force which needed direction. Educating the freedmen was the most urgent task at hand.

Few in those times could fully appreciate the vast release of pent-up emotions among four million people when they realized that at last they were their own masters. They had not owned their bodies and at times doubted that they owned their souls. The accumulated[4] restlessness of a lifetime of unnatural restraints now propelled them in all directions at once. It was a time for casting off every obligation,[5] for turning one's back on the sorrows of the old life and reveling[6] in this new-found thing they had prayed for and which was now more compelling[7] to experience than food or water. It was a time for walking off the plantation with all their belongings in a little bundle slung over the shoulder, for testing the ultimate limits of their freedom. As one former slave told his former master, he had to leave, to go away just to see if he could mind himself and stand on his own two feet.

To those who had borne the worst of slavery, freedom was the end of being nobodies, of being at the beck and call of the tiniest white child. It meant no more work, no curbs of any kind—work and restraints were the earmarks of slavery. It meant the right to roam at will, free as a bird, without carrying the hated "passes" or having to answer to patrols on the roads. Little wonder that in those first luxurious moments of liberty, millions

were in motion following the Union armies. Nor was it strange that those who had watched their masters thought freedom meant that you could loaf all day and be high-toned like rich white folks, that you could pick up your heels and take off whenever the spirit led you, or drink as much corn liquor as you could hold and stay drunk as long as you chose.

In this restless movement were those for whom freedom meant an unending quest for loved ones. Years before, they had been parted; wives sold one way and husbands another, children separated from their parents and aged separated from their children. When the parting came, each had carried with him an image of his loved one and the place where he had left him. All his remaining years he would be inquiring of people if they had heard of a slave called "Black Cato" or "Yellow Sam" or "Sally," and trying to get to that place where they had been separated. He would describe the loved one in the intimate way he had remembered him—a charm worn about the neck, a dimple in the cheek, a certain manner of walking or smiling. It did not matter that children had grown up and lost childish features or that parents had grown old and white haired. The description remained the same.

There were the old and sickly who shrank from freedom. They had prayed

3. turbulent: stormy, tempestuous
4. accumulated: collected
5. obligation: duty, responsibility
6. reveling: celebrating, delighting
7. compelling: forceful, driving

for it longest, but now that it had come they were terrified of it. They wanted only what they knew, the security of a cabin where they could spend their last days in peace and the kindness of a master or a mistress who would feed them and nurse them when they were laid up. There were the children who had no memories of slavery and could not understand what freedom meant. On the other hand there were those lean, hungry, bitter men to whom freedom had meant so much they had taken to the swamps and backlands, living on roots and herbs; desperate bands of hunted men who used to leave the swamps only at night to rob or kill for their needs without passion. Some doubted the freedom word when it came and stayed on in the swamps, preferring death or starvation to being re-enslaved.

There had been those first glorious months after Appomattox when the colored people had seen the coming of the Lord, had left the crops untended, the kitchens and nurseries deserted, had clogged the roads and flocked into the cities. Then hunger and homelessness pressed down upon them and they began to doubt the reality of their triumph. Freedom was not something you could hold in your hands and look at. It was something inside you which refused to die, a feeling, an urge, an impelling force; but it was other things, too, things you did not have and you had to have tools to get them. Few freedmen had tools in 1865; only the feeling, the urge.

Whatever else the freedmen lacked, there was in them a fierce hunger for knowledge. They believed, as perhaps no other people had believed so fervently,[8] that knowledge would make them truly free, for had not their masters taken great pains to withhold it from them? Before freedom, "stealing learning" was a crime for which they could be whipped; now it held the magic of the rainbow after a violent storm. This hunger made itself felt wherever the Union forces appeared in the South. When the soliders halted for a spell, slaves poured into the camps and pretty soon little schools sprouted among the Yankee regiments. The northern men had never seen anything quite like it—ragamuffins coming out of the fields and swarming to whatever place had a teacher. They brought with them old scraps of newspaper, a page from the Bible, a leaf torn from a young master's spelling book, a ragged almanac, a piece of broken slate—anything they thought would help them to learn. They wept tears of joy when they could recite the alphabet or read a line from the Bible or write their names.

Army chaplains who witnessed it were humbled by their hunger and their gratitude. They took these moving tales back to their churches in the North and soon a stream of missionaries flowed into the South in the wake of the armies to begin the redemptive work from slavery. The response was enough to fire anyone's soul. As Booker T. Washington said later, "It was a whole race trying to go to school. Few were too young and none were too old to make the attempt to learn." This almost universal desire for education

8. fervently: passionately, ardently

168

among the freedmen was the most inspiring thing to emerge from the bitterness and misery of war. It struck deep chords in human memory, like the first elemental urge of man to lift himself from all fours and stand face to face with his God.

Grandfather Fitzgerald was on his way to answer this urge in 1866. He had just left the commencement exercises at Lincoln University in which the guest speaker was General O. O. Howard, chief of the newly created Freedmen's Bureau. General Howard had been commander of Pennsylvania troops throughout the war, at Bull Run, Antietam, Malvern, Gettysburg and as leader of Sherman's right wing in the march to the sea. His empty sleeve showing where an arm had been torn off by a Rebel shell gave mute testimony to his contribution, and he had spoken with deep emotion urging the young men of Lincoln "onward and upward" in the advancement of their race, "in this country and in Africa, but particularly in this country." When he finished, the men of Lincoln, many of whom had fought in the war, burst into resounding cheers. Next day Grandfather Fitzgerald resolutely turned toward his summer's work.

Grandfather was so convinced his future lay in North Carolina that, in spite of occasional outbreaks of violence and intimidation of the freedmen, before he left for his summer vacation in 1868 he sent home for his melodeon. It was the only piece of furniture he owned and it was a symbol of home to him. He had it varnished, tuned up and shipped to Hillsboro. He also ordered a bark machine from New York for the tanning business

he and Beverly had set up, and left a sum of money with his partner to develop the work while he was gone.

He had some reason to be encouraged. The North Carolina legislature had met and ratified the Fourteenth Amendment, and Republican Governor W. W. Holden took office on July 4. A week later North Carolina was officially proclaimed to have fulfilled the requirements of the Reconstruction Acts and was re-admitted to the Union. The reports from Rev. F. A. Fiske, Negro superintendent of Freedmen's Bureau's educational work, showed that some sixteen thousand freedmen were attending the Bureau schools and another ten thousand were receiving instruction through private schools or those supported by religious societies. The Constitution of 1868 required that the General Assembly at its first session provide for a system of free public schools for all the children of the state between six and twenty-one years of age. There was every reason to be hopeful about the future.

Back home in Pennsylvania, Grandfather began to wonder. Political war clouds gathered while he worked away on the farm, harrowing corn, cutting oats and hay, helping his father put a roof on the barn, and binding, hauling and threshing wheat. Storm warnings grew more ominous as the time neared for him to return to his teaching post. The Rebels had recovered from the first shock of their defeat and were now engaging in the undeclared War of Reconstruction under the cloak of the Democratic party. Wrote Grandfather:

Aug. 21. I saw an extract from a Missouri

journal declaring that the Rebellion had recommenced in that state and that the Democrat Rebels had armed themselves and gone to Wayne and other counties and closed all the civil and government offices and driven the officers off. That the sheriff with a detachment of soldiers had to go out to interfere and that a collision was expected. So much for the Democratic Party . . .

Sept. 4 . . . The colored members pronounced ineligible in the Georgia Legislature, and therefore expelled. The feeling upon this piece of treachery (from the white Democrats) is of deep well settled conviction of the deception of the Democrat Party.

None of his kinsfolk could understand why he was so dead set upon returning south. He was much too frail to stand the hardships of that Godforsaken country, they felt. Robbie had always been the kind of fellow who threw himself into things and worked too hard. That summer working in the harvest he had almost collapsed from the heat several times. Once he was laid up with fever and had to have the doctor in to see him. He got better from the fever but was left somewhat deaf. And they all knew his eyesight was getting worse. He was now helpless if he went anywhere alone after dark. Often he came home long after dawn, his clothes covered with mud or wrinkled from his taking refuge in a hayloft.

As Grandfather explained it to his parents, he was a soldier in a "second war," this time against ignorance. Unless the freedmen were educated they would lose the rights they had gained at such great cost. In North Carolina alone there were one hundred thousand Negro children who could not read and write, to say nothing of the grown folks. These children were the "seed corn" of the future. Until the common schools were established the Freedmen's Bureau and religious groups must fill the breach. There were only about five hundred teachers in the field and Grandfather felt it his duty to join them, for every school kept open even for a few months was a tremendous gain.

Looking at it that way, his parents could say nothing against his going, but they hated to see him go alone. They were not yet ready to sell out and follow him. Sorrowfully they watched him pack his books and clothes the Sunday before he left home, noting how carefully he had cleaned and polished his army pistol and laid it among his things. Great-Grandfather Thomas offered a special petition at family prayers for his son's safety and guidance and that he might have "that wisdom and understanding that the world knows not of." And Great-Grandmother Sarah Ann slipped him fifty dollars of her butter-and-egg money to help him with his new venture.

Yet the gloom which hung over the household that Sunday affected even Grandfather. He wrote: "Mother and Mary are baking a cake and other little necessaries for my journey. Oh, how endearing is the love of a mother. Evening cloudy and portends[9] rain on tomorrow the day I start for Hillsboro, North Carolina. It makes me feel sad and superstitious of evil to leave home on a cloudy or wet day."

9. portends: forecasts, suggests

Pauli Murray (1910–1985)

Pauli Murray's achievements would be remarkable for anyone. For a woman born when opportunities for women were limited, and for a black growing up in a segregated land where many doors were closed to blacks, those achievements are astounding.

Born in 1910 in Baltimore, Maryland, Pauli Murray had black, white, and American Indian ancestors. After her mother died in 1914, Pauli came to Durham to live with her aunt, her grandmother Cornelia, and her grandfather Robert Fitzgerald. Her grandfather had come to North Carolina after the Civil War to teach newly freed slaves and had stayed to establish, with his brothers, a successful brickyard. (Buildings constructed with their brick are still standing—including the Durham office occupied by the publisher of this text.)

From an early age, Pauli Murray loved books. She learned to read by attending the first-grade class taught by her aunt, and she was a frequent visitor to the Durham Colored Library. She graduated from Hillside High School.

However, this bright young woman was denied admission to the law school at the UNC-Chapel Hill because of her race, and to Harvard University because of her sex. After receiving her law degree at Howard University, she had a distinguished and varied career, serving as a lawyer, a professor, a college vice-president, and deputy attorney general of California. Very active in political affairs, she was a cofounder of NOW (National Organization for Women). She was presented with a number of honorary university degrees, and was named Woman of the Year by *Mademoiselle* magazine in 1947.

At 62, an age when many people are planning retirement, she entered seminary in order to embark on a new career. In 1977, she became the first black woman Episcopalian priest in this country. Somehow in the midst of all this studying and professional activity, she also managed to write several books, including *Proud Shoes*, the story of her ancestors, and a prize-winning volume of poetry.

With all of these achievements, it is no wonder that *Washington Post* writer Jonathan Yardley has called her "one of the greatest Americans of her time."

Reflecting

1. Pauli Murray points out that even though blacks were legally free in the years following the Civil War, they faced a number of difficulties. List the problems which she cites.

2. Usually the word "missionary" refers to someone who is undertaking religious work. Do you believe the word is used appropriately in Robert Fitzgerald's case? Explain your answer.

The Bouquet

Charles Chesnutt

Preview

During the Civil War, because of President Lincoln's Emancipation Proclamation, slavery was abolished. However, as you are aware, racial division did not end. It takes more than a legal document to change attitudes, habits, and customs.

One of America's first philosophers, Ralph Waldo Emerson, was at the height of his career and influence during the Civil War and the years immediately preceding it. Emerson fully supported the abolition of slavery. However, he also observed that even people who are legally free are often slaves to other things that control their lives and prevent their acting wisely and justly—ambition, fear, pride, tradition, ignorance, etc. In the following story, look for factors that "enslave" various characters: the little black girl, Sophy; her white teacher, Miss Myrover; or the teacher's mother, Mrs. Myrover.

Mary Myrover's friends were somewhat surprised when she began to teach a colored school. Miss Myrover's friends are mentioned here, because nowhere more than in a Southern town is public opinion a force which cannot be lightly contravened. Public opinion, however, did not oppose Miss Myrover's teaching colored children; in fact, all the colored public schools in town—and there were several—were taught by white teachers, and had been so taught since the State had undertaken to provide free public instruction for all children within its boundaries. Previous to that time, there had been a Freedman's Bureau school and a Presbyterian missionary school, but these had been withdrawn when the need for them became less pressing. The colored people of the town had been for some time agitating their right to teach their own schools, but as yet the claim had not been conceded.

The reason Miss Myrover's course created some surprise was not, therefore, the fact that a Southern white woman should teach a colored school; it lay in the fact that up to this time no woman of just her quality had taken up such work. Most of the teachers of colored schools were not of those who had constituted the aristocracy of the old régime;[1] they might be said rather to represent the new order of things, in which labor was in time to become honorable, and men were, after a somewhat longer time, to depend, for their place in society, upon themselves rather than upon their ancestors. Mary Myrover belonged to one of the proudest of the old families. Her ancestors had been people of distinction in Virginia before a collateral[2] branch of the main stock had settled in North Carolina. Before the war, they had been able to live up to their pedigree; but the war brought sad changes. Miss Myrover's father—the Colonel Myrover who led a gallant but desperate charge at Vicksburg—had fallen on the battlefield, and his tomb in the white cemetery was a shrine for the family. On the Confederate Memorial Day, no other grave was so profusely decorated with flowers, and, in the oration pronounced, the name of Colonel Myrover was always used to illustrate the highest type of patriotic devotion and self-sacrifice. Miss Myrover's brother, too, had fallen in the conflict; but his bones lay in

some unknown trench, with those of a thousand others who had fallen on the same field. Ay, more, her lover, who had hoped to come home in the full tide of victory and claim his bride as a reward for gallantry, had shared the fate of her father and brother. When the war was over, the remnant of the family found itself involved in the common ruin—more deeply involved indeed, than some others; for Colonel Myrover had believed in the ultimate triumph of his cause, and had invested most of his wealth in Confederate bonds, which were now only so much waste paper.

There had been a little left. Mrs. Myrover was thrifty, and had laid by a few hundred dollars, which she kept in the house to meet unforeseen contingencies.[3] There remained, too, their home, with an ample garden and a well-stocked orchard, besides a considerable tract of country land, partly cleared, but productive of very little revenue.

With their shrunken resources, Miss Myrover and her mother were able to hold up their heads without embarrassment for some years after the close of the war. But when things were adjusted to the changed conditions, and the stream of life began to flow more vigorously in the new channels, they saw themselves in danger of dropping behind, unless in

1. régime: a system of government

2. collateral: running side by side, supporting

3. contingencies: possibilities

some way they could add to their meager[4] income. Miss Myrover looked over the field of employment, never very wide for women in the South, and found it occupied. The only available position she could be supposed prepared to fill, and which she could take without distinct loss of caste, was that of a teacher, and there was no vacancy except in one of the colored schools. Even teaching was a doubtful experiment; it was not what she would have preferred, but it was the best that could be done.

"I don't like it, Mary," said her mother. "It's a long step from owning such people to teaching them. What do they need with education? It will only make them unfit for work."

"They're free now, mother, and perhaps they'll work better if they're taught something. Besides, it's only a business arrangement, and doesn't involve any closer contact than we have with our servants."

"Well, I should say not!" sniffed the old lady. "Not one of them will ever dare to presume on your position to take any liberties with us. I'll see to that."

Miss Myrover began her work as a teacher in the autumn, at the opening of the school year. It was a novel experience at first. Though there had always been negro servants in the house, and though on the streets colored people were more numerous than those of her own race, and though she was so familiar with their dialect that she might almost be said to speak it, barring certain characteristic grammatical inaccuracies, she had never been brought in personal contact with so many of them at once as when she confronted the fifty or sixty faces—of colors ranging from a white almost as clear as her own to the darkest livery of the sun—which were gathered in the schoolroom on the morning when she began her duties. Some of the inherited prejudice of her caste, too, made itself felt, though she tried to repress any outward sign of it; and she could perceive that the children were not altogether responsive; they, likewise, were not entirely free from antagonism. The work was unfamiliar to her. She was not physically very strong, and at the close of the first day went home with a splitting headache. If she could have resigned then and there without causing comment or annoyance to others, she would have felt it a privilege to do so. But a night's rest banished her headache and improved her spirits, and the next morning she went to her work with renewed vigor, fortified by the experience of the first day.

Miss Myrover's second day was more satisfactory. She had some natural talent for organization, though hitherto unaware of it, and in the course of the day she got her classes formed and lessons under way. In a week or two she began to classify her pupils in her own mind, as bright or stupid, mischievous or well behaved, lazy or industrious, as the case might be, and to regulate her discipline accordingly. That she had come of a long line of ancestors who had exercised authority and mastership was perhaps not without its effect upon her character, and enabled

4. meager: thin, deficient in quantity

174

her more readily to maintain good order in the school. When she was fairly broken in, she found the work rather to her liking, and derived much pleasure from such success as she achieved as a teacher.

It was natural that she should be more attracted to some of her pupils than to others. Perhaps her favorite—or, rather, the one she liked best, for she was too fair and just for conscious favoritism—was Sophy Tucker. Just the ground for the teacher's liking for Sophy might not at first be apparent. The girl was far from the whitest of Miss Myrover's pupils; in fact, she was one of the darker ones. She was not the brightest in intellect, though she always tried to learn her lessons. She was not the best dressed, for her mother was a poor widow, who went out washing and scrubbing for a living. Perhaps the real tie between them was Sophy's intense devotion to the teacher. It had manifested[5] itself almost from the first day of the school, in the rapt look of admiration Miss Myrover always saw on the little black face turned toward her. In it there was nothing of envy, nothing of regret; nothing but worship for the beautiful white lady—she was not especially handsome, but to Sophy her beauty was almost divine—who had come to teach her. If Miss Myrover dropped a book, Sophy was the first to spring and pick it up; if she wished a chair moved, Sophy seemed to anticipate her wish; and so of all the numberless little services that can be rendered in a schoolroom.

Miss Myrover was fond of flowers, and liked to have them about her. The children soon learned of this taste of hers, and kept the vases on her desk filled with blossoms during their season. Sophy was perhaps the most active in providing them. If she could not get garden flowers, she would make excursions to the woods in the early morning, and bring in great dew-laden bunches of bay, or jasmine, or some other fragrant forest flower which she knew the teacher loved.

"When I die, Sophy," Miss Myrover said to the child one day, "I want to be covered with roses. And when they bury me, I'm sure I shall rest better if my grave is banked with flowers and roses are planted at my head and at my feet."

Miss Myrover was at first amused at Sophy's devotion; but when she grew more accustomed to it, she found it rather to her liking. It had a sort of flavor of the old régime, and she felt, when she bestowed her kindly notice upon her little black attendant, some of the feudal condescension[6] of the mistress toward the slave. She was kind to Sophy, and permitted her to play the role she had assumed, which caused sometimes a little jealousy among the other girls. Once she gave Sophy a yellow ribbon which she took from her own hair. The child carried it home, and cherished it as a priceless treasure, to be worn only on the greatest occasions.

Sophy had a rival in her attachment to the teacher, but the rivalry was altogether friendly. Miss Myrover had a little dog, a

5. manifested: shown or demonstrated plainly

6. condescension: patronizing behavior or manner (To *condescend* is to behave toward someone as if you are better or wiser than they, but are coming down to their level.)

white spaniel, answering to the name of Prince. Prince was a dog of high degree, and would have very little to do with the children of the school; he made an exception, however, in the case of Sophy, whose devotion for his mistress he seemed to comprehend. He was a clever dog, and could fetch and carry, sit up on his haunches, extend his paw to shake hands, and possessed several other canine accomplishments. He was very fond of his mistress, and always, unless shut up at home, accompanied her to school, where he spent most of his time lying under the teacher's desk, or, in cold weather, by the stove, except when he would go out now and then and chase an imaginary rabbit round the yard, presumably for exercise.

At school Sophy and Prince vied with each other in their attentions to Miss Myrover. But when school was over, Prince went away with her, and Sophy stayed behind; for Miss Myrover was white and Sophy was black, which they both understood perfectly well. Miss Myrover taught the colored children, but she could not be seen with them in public. If they occasionally met her on the street, they did not expect her to speak to them, unless she happened to be alone and no other white person was in sight. If any of the children felt slighted, she was not aware of it, for she intended no slight; she had not been brought up to speak to negroes on the street, and she could not act differently from other people. And though she was a woman of sentiment and capable of deep feeling, her training had been such that she hardly expected to find in those of darker hue than herself the same suscep-

tibility—varying in degree, perhaps, but yet the same in kind—that gave to her own life the alternations of feeling that made it most worth living.

Once Miss Myrover wished to carry home a parcel of books. She had the bundle in her hand when Sophy came up.

"Lemme tote yo' bundle fer yer, Miss Ma'y?" she asked eagerly. "I'm gwine yo' way."

"Thank you, Sophy," was the reply. "I'll be glad if you will."

Sophy followed the teacher at a respectful distance. When they reached Miss Myrover's home, Sophy carried the bundle to the doorstep, where Miss Myrover took it and thanked her.

Mrs. Myrover came out on the piazza as Sophy was moving away. She said, in the child's hearing and perhaps with the intention that she should hear: "Mary, I wish you wouldn't let those little darkeys follow you to the house. I don't want them in the yard. I should think you'd have enough of them all day."

"Very, well, mother," replied her daughter. "I won't bring any more of them. The child was only doing me a favor."

Mrs. Myrover was an invalid, and opposition or irritation of any kind brought on nervous paroxysms[7] that made her miserable, and made life a burden to the rest of the household, so that Mary seldom crossed her whims. She did not bring Sophy to the house again, nor did Sophy again offer her services as porter.

7. paroxysms: spasms or sudden outbursts of emotion

One day in spring Sophy brought her teacher a bouquet of yellow roses.

"Dey come off'n my own bush, Miss Ma'y," she said proudly, "an' I did n' let nobody e'se pull 'em, but saved 'em all fer you, 'cause I know you likes roses so much. I'm gwine bring 'em all ter you as long as dey las'."

"Thank you, Sophy," said the teacher; "you are a very good girl."

For another year Mary Myrover taught the colored school, and did excellent service. The children made rapid progress under her tuition, and learned to love her well; for they saw and appreciated, as well as children could, her fidelity to a trust that she might have slighted, as some others did, without much fear of criticism. Toward the end of her second year she sickened, and after a brief illness died.

Old Mrs. Myrover was inconsolable. She ascribed her daughter's death to her labors as teacher of negro children. Just how the color of the pupils had produced the fatal effects she did not stop to explain. But she was too old, and had suffered too deeply from the war, in body and mind and estate, ever to reconcile herself to the changed order of things following the return of peace; and, with an unsound yet perfectly explainable logic, she visited some of her displeasure upon those who had profited most, though passively, by her losses.

"I always feared something would happen to Mary," she said. "It seemed unnatural for her to be wearing herself out teaching little negroes who ought to have been working for her. But the world has hardly been a fit place to live in since the war, and when I follow her, as I must before long, I shall not be sorry to go."

She gave strict orders that no colored people should be admitted to the house. Some of her friends heard of this, and remonstrated.[8] They knew the teacher was loved by the pupils, and felt that sincere respect from the humble would be a worthy tribute to the proudest. But Mrs. Myrover was obdurate.[9]

"They had my daughter when she was alive," she said, "and they've killed her. But she's mine now, and I won't have them come near her. I don't want one of them at the funeral or anywhere around."

For a month before Miss Myrover's death Sophy had been watching her rosebush—the one that bore the yellow roses—for the first buds of spring, and, when these appeared, had awaited impatiently their gradual unfolding. But not until her teacher's death had they become full-blown roses. When Miss Myrover died, Sophy determined to pluck the roses and lay them on her coffin. Perhaps, she thought, they might even put them in her hand or on her breast. For Sophy remembered Miss Myrover's thanks and praise when she had brought her the yellow roses the spring before.

On the morning of the day set for the funeral, Sophy washed her face until it shone, combed and brushed her hair with painful conscientiousness, put on her best frock, plucked her yellow roses, and, tying them with the treasured ribbon her

8. remonstrated: objected or protested

9. obdurate: stubborn to the point of being hard and unyielding

teacher had given her, set out for Miss Myrover's home.

She went round to the side gate—the house stood on a corner—and stole up the path to the kitchen. A colored woman, whom she did not know, came to the door.

"W'at yer want, chile?" she inquired.

"Kin I see Miss Ma'y?" asked Sophy timidly.

"I don't know, honey. Ole Miss Myrover say she don't want no cullud folks roun' de house endyoin' dis fun'al. I'll look an' see if she's roun' de front room, whar de co'pse is. You sed down heah an' keep still, an' ef she's upstairs maybe I kin git yer in dere a minute. Ef I can't, I kin put yo' bokay 'mongs' de res', whar she won't know nuthin' erbout it."

A moment after she had gone, there was a step in the hall, and old Mrs. Myrover came into the kitchen.

"Dinah!" she said in a peevish tone; "Dinah!"

Receiving no answer, Mrs. Myrover peered around the kitchen, and caught sight of Sophy.

"What are you doing here?" she demanded.

"I—I'm-m waitin' ter see de cook, ma'am," stammered Sophy.

"The cook isn't here now. I don't know where she is. Besides, my daughter is to be buried to-day, and I won't have anyone visiting the servants until the funeral is over. Come back some other day, or see the cook at her own home in the evening."

She stood waiting for the child to go, and under the keen glance of her eyes Sophy, feeling as though she had been caught in some disgraceful act, hurried down the walk and out of the gate, with her bouquet in her hand.

"Dinah," said Mrs. Myrover, when the cook came back, "I don't want any strange people admitted here to-day. The house will be full of our friends, and we have no room for others."

"Yas 'm," said the cook. She understood perfectly what her mistress meant; and what the cook thought about her mistress was a matter of no consequence.

The funeral services were held at St. Paul's Episcopal Church, where the Myrovers had always worshiped. Quite a number of Miss Myrover's pupils went to the church to attend the services. The building was not a large one. There was a small gallery at the rear, to which colored people were admitted, if they chose to come, at ordinary services; and those who wished to be present at the funeral supposed that the usual custom would prevail. They were therefore surprised, when they went to the side entrance, by which colored people gained access to the gallery stairs, to be met by an usher who barred their passage.

"I'm sorry," he said, "but I have had orders to admit no one until the friends of the family have all been seated. If you wish to wait until the white people have all gone in, and there's any room left, you may be able to get into the back part of the gallery. Of course I can't tell yet whether there'll be any room or not."

Now the statement of the usher was a very reasonable one; but, strange to say, none of the colored people chose to remain except Sophy. She still hoped to use her floral offering for its destined end, in some way, though she did not know just how. She waited in the yard until the church was filled with white people, and a number who could not gain admittance were standing about the doors. Then she went round to the side of the church, and, depositing her bouquet carefully on an old mossy gravestone, climbed up on the projecting sill of a window near the chancel. The window was of stained glass, of somewhat ancient make. The church was old, had indeed been built in colonial times, and the stained glass had been brought from England. The design of the window showed Jesus blessing little children. Time had dealt gently with the window, but just at the feet of the figure of Jesus a small triangular piece of glass had been broken out. To this aperture Sophy applied her eyes, and through it saw and heard what she could of the services within.

Before the chancel, on trestles draped in black, stood the sombre casket in which lay all that was mortal of her dear teacher. The top of the casket was covered with flowers; and lying stretched out underneath it she saw Miss Myrover's little white dog, Prince. He had followed the body to the church, and, slipping in unnoticed among the mourners, had taken his place, from which no one had the heart to remove him.

The white-robed rector read the solemn service for the dead, and then delivered a brief address, in which he dwelt upon the uncertainty of life, and, to the believer, the certain blessedness of eternity. He spoke of Miss Myrover's kindly spirit, and, as an illustration of her love and self-sacrifice for others, referred to her labors as a teacher of the poor ignorant negroes who had been placed in their midst by an all-wise Providence, and whom it was their duty to guide and direct in the station in which God had put them. Then the organ pealed, a prayer was said, and the long cortége[10] moved from the church to the cemetery, about half a mile away, where the body was to be interred.

When the services were over, Sophy sprang down from her perch, and, taking her flowers, followed the procession. She did not walk with the rest, but at a proper and respectful distance from the last mourner. No one noticed the little black girl with the bunch of yellow flowers, or thought of her as interested in the funeral.

The cortége reached the cemetery and filed slowly through the gate; but Sophy stood outside, looking at a small sign in white letters on a black background:—

"*Notice.* This cemetery is for white people only. Others please keep out."

Sophy, thanks to Miss Myrover's painstaking instruction, could read this sign very distinctly. In fact, she had often read it before. For Sophy was a child who loved beauty, in a blind, groping sort of way, and had sometimes stood by the fence of the cemetery and looked through at the green mounds and shaded walks and blooming flowers within, and wished that she might walk among them. She knew,

10. cortége: a procession, usually for a funeral or formal ceremony

180

too, that the little sign on the gate, though so courteously worded, was no mere formality; for she had heard how a colored man, who had wandered into the cemetery on a hot night and fallen asleep on the flat top of a tomb, had been arrested as a vagrant and fined five dollars, which he had worked out on the streets, with a ball-and-chain attachment, at twenty-five cents a day. Since that time the cemetery gate had been locked at night.

So Sophy stayed outside, and looked through the fence. Her poor bouquet had begun to droop by this time, and the yellow ribbon had lost some of its freshness. Sophy could see the rector standing by the grave, the mourners gathered round; she could faintly distinguish the solemn words with which ashes were committed to ashes, and dust to dust. She heard the hollow thud of the earth falling on the coffin; and she leaned against the iron fence, sobbing softly, until the grave was filled and rounded off, and the wreaths and other floral pieces were disposed upon it. When the mourners began to move toward the gate, Sophy walked slowly down the street, in a direction opposite to that taken by most of the people who came out.

When they had all gone away, and the sexton had come out and locked the gate behind him, Sophy crept back. Her roses were faded now, and from some of them the petals had fallen. She stood there irresolute, loath to leave with her heart's desire unsatisfied, when, as her eyes sought again the teacher's last resting-place, she saw lying beside the new-made grave what looked like a small bundle of white wool. Sophy's eyes lighted up with a sudden glow.

"Prince! Here, Prince!" she called.

The little dog rose, and trotted down to the gate. Sophy pushed the poor bouquet between the iron bars. "Take that ter Miss Ma'y, Prince," she said, "that's a good doggie."

The dog wagged his tail intelligently, took the bouquet carefully in his mouth, carried it to his mistress's grave, and laid it among the other flowers. The bunch of roses was so small that from where she stood Sophy could see only a dash of yellow against the white background of the the mass of flowers.

When Prince had performed his mission he turned his eyes toward Sophy inquiringly, and when she gave him a nod of approval lay down and resumed his watch by the graveside. Sophy looked at him a moment with a feeling very much like envy, and then turned and moved slowly away.

MEET THE AUTHOR:
Charles Chesnutt (1858–1932)

Charles Waddell Chesnutt has been called "the first Negro author to win the attention of nineteenth-century American critics." Born in Ohio, the son of a man who served as a teamster in the Union Army, Charles Chesnutt moved with his family to Fayetteville, North Carolina, soon after the Civil War. As a young man, he taught in Charlotte and at the State Colored Normal School in Fayetteville, where he served as principal. He then moved to the north and passed the bar examination.

Once he had established a successful legal stenography firm, he began writing humorous sketches, then essays on social issues, and finally, fiction. At the age of twenty-nine, he published his first story in *The Atlantic Monthly*—then, as now, one of the most prestigious magazines in the country.

For the next eighteen years he was considered one of the major fiction writers of his time. He published both short stories and novels and three of his novels are set in North Carolina. Another North Carolinian, Walter Hines Page, (see p. 142) helped him get his work published. Chesnutt also continued to operate a successful business and to participate in a number of programs dedicated to improving social justice.

Chesnutt has been called "a pioneer in treating racial themes." In 1928, he was

awarded the Spingarn Medal for "pioneer work as a literary artist depicting the life and struggles of Americans of Negro descent, and for his long and useful career as scholar, worker, and freeman of one of America's greatest cities."

Cleveland, where he spent most of his life, has recognized Charles Chesnutt's importance by naming a street and a school after him.

Language Alert

1. Although Charles Chesnutt wrote his narrative in eloquent standard English, some dialogue is difficult to read because, like many authors of his time, he used dialectal spellings, i.e., "lemme" for "let me," and "gwine" for "going." The nontraditional spelling slows down reading, but usually it isn't too difficult to figure out what words are represented.

2. As has been noted earlier, language changes. Some words are discarded as others are adopted. One such word is *darkey* (sometimes spelled *darky*), used often in Chesnutt's time to refer—usually politely—to blacks.

Reflecting

Suppose these major events in this story happened in your town and your school today.

1. A white woman from a socially prominent family becomes a teacher.
2. A black child develops a profound affection for the teacher.
3. The teacher dies.

If you, like Charles Chesnutt, used these events as the framework for your plot, what elements of the story would remain the same? What would be different? Think of matters such as the following:

1. Do women from socially prominent families teach school today?
2. Do children ever develop deep bonds with a teacher of another race?
3. Might a teacher feel condescending toward a student of another race?
4. Might a bitter old woman take out her grief by forbidding others to come to the funeral of her daughter?
5. Are black people admitted to white churches, and if they are, must they enter at a side door and sit in a special section upstairs?
6. Are cemeteries legally segregated?

Granny Younger's Mountains

Lee Smith

Preview

Lee Smith's writing is noted for its realistic dialogue that accurately reflects regional speech. She often lets her characters tell their own stories in their own voices. In the following short selection, Granny Younger, an old woman who lives on Hoot Owl Mountain in western Virginia, is describing her part of the world. It is 1898. Despite her name, "Younger," Granny is already an old woman who, as she says, "has lived for more years than I could tell you if I was to sit down and try to count them which I won't." She has lived a full life and is the woman neighbors and kinfolk call on when they have troubles. She knows the herbs and folk medicines to help them get over their ailments. She knows the Bible and the local superstitions. And she knows the people who live around her and their stories—both the true stories and the legends.

This selection is only two paragraphs long, but because Granny Younger speaks so directly and so specifically, we can learn a great deal. Look for information about:

1. Granny Younger herself—her spirit, her interests, her personality;
2. the physical details of Hoot Owl Mountain and Hurricane Mountain; and
3. the language.

Hoot Owl Mountain looks like how it sounds, laurel so thick you can't hardly climb it atall, in fact you plumb can't do it iffen you don't know the way. They's not but one trail up Hoot Owl Mountain and it goes on to the burying ground. So you start up that trail through the laurel and it's so dark in there you can't hardly see your way. You get through that laurel and then you're climbing, see, but climbing slow—it's a big mountain, and the trail goes round and round. They's trees up Hoot Owl biggern you ever saw in your life, they's ferns nigh as tall as a man. On up, they's caves in the rocky clift and one cave a man got lost in, so they say. They say you can hear him holler. Now the burying ground on the top of the mountain is a flat grassy bald, and it's real pretty. They's a wind that blows all the time. I like that burying ground. But I mislike Hoot Owl Mountain myself and don't go up it lessen I have to, but you can find yellow root there, and ginger, heartleaf and pennyrile, red coon for poison ivy. What I need. Hoot Owl Mountain is a dark mountain though, maybe it's all them pines, and it don't get hardly no sun. Fog will hang on the north side all day long, with that blue mist spread over the top. Moss grows everywhere under them pines, moss thick enough to sleep on if you cared to. Not me, mind you. They is something about Hoot Owl Mountain makes a body lose heart. If you laid down to sleep on that pretty moss, you mought never wake up again in this world. It's no telling where you'd wake up. They was never anybody knowed to court on Hoot Owl neither, you see for why. I keep a buckeye in my pocket, traveling Hoot Owl. I get right along.

But up on Hurricane, where I live, now that's as pretty a place as you please. Grassy Creek running down it, all them little falls, why it is music to your ears just a-walking up Grassy Creek. It is pussy-willow and Indian paint, Queen Anne's lace and black-eyed Susan. It is swimming holes with water so clear you can see straight down to the bottom. They never was any water bettern Grassy Creek. Then you get on up, you've got your oak, your chestnut, your tulip tree. Big old trees all spreaded out which lets the sun shine through. The mast under these trees is so good it's what they call hog heaven up here on Hurricane Mountain, everybody lets their hogs run here. Hurricane Mountain is a fine mountain and they's other folks lives here too, you can see for why. Now I've got my own holler, mind. Nobody ever lived in it but me and mama, and mama's dead. But I've got my neighbors up here on Hurricane. . . . They's a bunch of Horns, been here forever, and some Justices, some Rameys, Davenports. They is one-eyed Jesse Waldron lives all by hisself in the Paw Paw Gap. Rhoda Hibbitts not far from me with them two ugly mealy-mouth daughters of hern, and no man in sight. That wouldn't bother me none if I was Rhoda. I'd not put up with a regular man if you paid me. But it grieves Rhoda considerable. Take 'em to town, I says. Well, that's another story.

MEET THE AUTHOR:
Lee Smith (1944–   )

Lee Smith was born and grew up in the mountains of Virginia, but she has spent most of her adult life in North Carolina. Her interest in writing came early. "I wrote constantly when I was in junior high school: poems, songs, stories," she reports. She published her first novel while she was a still a student at Hollins College in Virginia. Since then she has published seven other novels and two collections of short stories. The novel *Oral History,* from which the selection below was chosen, has been adapted into a musical play, *Ear Rings,* which has been widely performed. A short story, "Dear Phil Donahue," was made into a short film.

Most of her stories are set in North Carolina or Virginia—frequently in the mountains. They are peopled with both old-fashioned country folk, many of whom are "set in their ways" and younger generations who are often moving out of the hills and leaving the old ways behind.

Students at North Carolina State University, where she is associate professor, know Lee Smith as a witty and warm woman as well as a famous writer willing to share her knowledge about the craft of writing. The state

has recognized her talent with the Sir Walter Award for Fiction and the North Carolina Award for Literature. She has also won national prizes: the John Dos Passos Award for Literature and two O. Henry Awards for Short Stories.

Language Alert

In her speech, Granny Younger breaks many of the rules of standard English grammar. Her language is also peppered with words reflecting her regional dialect. (For more about dialects, see "Some Words about Words," p. xvi.) Some terms have to do with regional pronunciation: she says *they's* instead of *there's* and *mought* instead of *might*. Others are variations on standard speech: *mislike* instead of *dislike*, *lessen* instead of *unless*. *Holler* is the regional term for *hollow*—a valley. (The word *mast* is not a dialectal term. It refers to an accumulation of nuts under the trees, used especially as feed for pigs.)

Granny Younger also uses phrases that we don't hear much in cities: "you plumb can't do it" or "something . . . makes a body lose heart." But if you take on the role of Granny Younger and read this selection in her voice, you will be able to understand what she says—and to enjoy her lively personality and the richness of her dialect.

Reflecting

1. Choose a section of Granny Younger's monologue and rewrite it in another voice. For example, you might use the way your own grandmother speaks; or the speech of a friend or relative; or even a television character with a distinctive dialect.

   Now use the same section and give Granny Younger's language the English-teacher treatment. Correct all the errors and change the language to standard American English.

   Share your rewritings and compare them to Granny Younger's version. What are the strengths of each version? The weaknesses? Which do you like best? Why?
2. If you were a historian doing research on life in the Appalachian mountains at the end of the last century, what could you learn from this brief segment?

The Bonnie Poet of Riverton

MEET THE AUTHOR:
John Charles McNeill (1874–1907)

Of all the poets in this state, John Charles McNeill was possibly the most beloved and popular. Although he was never given the title, he was informally referred to as North Carolina's "poet laureate."

Born in Scotland County in the community of Spring Hill, he later moved with his family to Riverton. Young John attended the Spring Hill School, then lived with his grandfather so that he could attend Whiteville Academy. Although he worked each afternoon after school, he earned honors in his classwork.

John didn't have enough money to handle the fees at Wake Forest University, but very quickly his talent was recognized and he was given the job of grading themes for Dr. Benjamin Sledd, one of the school's most distinguished professors. (For more about Sledd, see page 46.)

After obtaining master's degrees in English and law at Wake Forest, he began teaching school. Although highly regarded as a teacher, he was disappointed by uninterested students, so he left teaching. Turning to law, he practiced first in Lumberton, then in Laurinburg. He turned some of the court cases into stories that were published in national magazines. His legal career also led to his being elected to the state legislature, where he was known as both hardworking and fun-loving.

After he began publishing some of his poems, the *Charlotte Observer* made him an unusual offer: if he would publish with the

Observer, he could write whatever he wished and, for that matter, whenever he wished. The offer was a writer's dream, and McNeill quickly accepted. His works—paragraphs, essays, poems, fables, reports—usually appeared about twice a week. Rather than make profound observations on philosophical or social themes, he chose to write about common folk and everyday occurrences: swimming in the Lumber River, hunting opossums, or watching the trains go by.

Eventually his poetry was published in collections: *Songs, Merry and Sad* (1906), *Lyrics from Cotton Land* (1907), and, many years after his untimely death at the age of thirty-three, *Possums and Persimmons* (1977). He was the first recipient of the William Houston Patterson Award for literary achievement.

Preview

Although it's now rare to see a steam locomotive in action, perhaps you've been lucky enough to see one, or even ride one. (Tweetsie, in the western part of our state, is a steam locomotive.) Steam engines frequently appear in movies or television shows. You know the kinds of movements a steam locomotive makes: the shriek of the whistle, the chuffing of the engine just before the train moves from the station, and the roar as it thunders down the track in the open countryside.

In this poem, John Charles McNeill pays tribute to the fastest, most powerful transportation of his time. To make his poem dramatic, he uses a **metaphor**. That is, he compares the locomotive—in this case a mail train—to something else, without ever naming the thing to which he is comparing it. See how quickly you recognize the comparison. Which word or phrase gives you the first clue? Is the metaphor consistent throughout the poem?

"97": The Fast Mail

John Charles McNeill

Where the rails converge to the station yard
She stands one moment, breathing hard,

And then, with a snort and a clang of steel,
She settles her strength to the stubborn wheel,

And out, through the tracks that lead astray,
Cautiously, slowly she picks her way,

And gathers her muscle and guards her nerve,
When she swings her nose to the westward curve,

And takes the grade, which slopes to the sky,
With a bound of speed and a conquering cry.

From *Songs Merry and Sad,* by John Charles McNeill, first published by Stone and Burrage Co., 1906. Copyright 1906 by John Charles McNeill, © 1932 by J. I. Memory, Jr.

The hazy horizon is all she sees,
Nor cares for the meadows, stirred with bees,

Nor the long straight stretches of silent land,
Nor the ploughman, that shades his eye with his hand,

Nor the cots and hamlets that know no more
Than a shriek and a flash and a flying roar;

But, bearing her tidings, she trembles and throbs,
And laughs in her throat, and quivers and sobs;

And the fire in her heart is a red core of heat
That drives like a passion through forest and street,

Till she sees the ships in their harbor at rest,
And sniffs at the trail to the end of her quest.

If I were the driver who handles her reins,
Up hill and down hill and over the plains,

To watch the slow mountains give back in the west,
To know the new reaches that wait every crest,

To hold, when she swerves, with a confident clutch,
And feel how she shivers and springs to the touch,

With the snow on her back and the sun in her face,
And nothing but time as a quarry to chase,

I should grip hard my teeth, and look where she led,
And brace myself stooping, and give her her head,

And urge her, and soothe her, and serve all her need,
And exult in the thunder and thrill of her speed.

Reflecting

1. Discuss the terms and phrases that compare the train to a horse.
2. Consider how wonderful the train must have seemed to people who heretofore had relied on horses or oxen for land transportation.
3. Consider that the train was to McNeill's generation what the jet plane is to ours, carrying people, mail, goods, etc. Notice the factors which seem to impress the poet, such as speed, strength, and sound.
4. Write either a poem or a paragraph in which the jet plane is implicitly compared to something else. (An animal? An astronomical body?)

Steam locomotive at Tweetsie Railroad near Blowing Rock, NC.

Turning the Century

A lthough industry (mainly tobacco, textiles, and furniture manufacturing) continued to grow, North Carolina was still mainly an agricultural state as it moved into the twentieth century. Farming was not yet mechanized, so it required very hard work—with, in most cases, only modest rewards.

By 1900, the state had 3,800 miles of railroad, but roads were poor, so travel was limited. Most highways were maintained not by the state, nor even by the county, but by men who gave six days a year to work on local roads. Compared to today, most North Carolinians worked hard, traveled only short distances from their homes, and enjoyed simple pleasures such as gathering with the neighbors for a barn raising or corn shucking, or perhaps to swap tall tales.

A Christmas Long Ago

John Parris

Preview

It is Christmas. John Parris is preparing to celebrate by burning a large Yule log, as his family did for generations. We can assume that the John Parris who tells the story is about forty years old. (This story was published in Parris's collection, *Roaming the Mountains*, in 1955.)

Looking at the hickory stump his friend Nelse has just delivered, Parris recalls an incident which occurred many years earlier. He and his family were riding in a Model T—the Ford automobile that was made between 1908 and 1928. John was just a child, going with his parents to visit his aging grandparents. It was an ordinary-seeming day, but you will see the exchange of some very special gifts.

Aunt Ede's Grandson Nelse rode up in his wagon just at dusk with the big water-soaked hickory stump.

Grandpa Parris used to say there was nothing like a water-soaked hickory stump for a Yule log. Grandpa knew, for he was a mountain man. When he was a boy it was his job to fetch in the Yule log, and later when he had sons it was their job to search out the hickory stumps on Little Savannah.

By the time I came along we were living in town and our fireplace had a grate and we couldn't have a hickory stump. But Dad always took me to Grandpa's during Christmas, and there was the big hickory stump blazing and simmering in the big fireplace where Grandma did a lot of her cooking.

Looking at the stump Nelse had fetched down from the mountain, I thought that somehow it didn't look as big as the stumps I remembered at Grandpa's as a little boy.

I said, "Nelse, you sure this is the biggest hickory stump you could find?" and he looked at me and then at the stump.

"Why, that stump'll burn for a month of Sundays. It'll be all right. I reckon my grandmammy would've been proud to see such a stump as that. I've heard my mammy say back in olden times when her mammy was a slave that it was the custom for everybody to just rest and fold their hands long's the Yule log burned. The white folks lit it on Christmas Eve and sometimes, my mammy said her mammy said, that ol' Yule log'd burn for two whole days, maybe three. Times shore have changed, and that's a true fact."

Yes, times have changed, I said, thinking on the size of Grandpa's logs and sitting around his hearth on Christmas day listening to him tell about the Christmas he was snowed in and the other Christmases, some that sounded like fun and others that sounded pretty grim, even to a ten-year-old boy.

"Reckon I'll be gettin' on toward home," said Nelse. "It looks like it's fixin' to weather-up."

While we had stood there, flurries of snow had started blowing down from the peaks that towered dark above the valley.

"If this keeps up," said Nelse, "I reckon we will have us a shore 'nough white Christmas. My ol' bones start achin' when it snows."

I watched Nelse climb up into the wagon and ride off. The clop-clop-clop of the mule and the squeak of wheels were only a whisper from down the road when finally I picked up a couple of logs from the stack beside the door and moved on inside to mend the fire.

In the last few minutes darkness had come on with a suddenness, and the only light in the paneled room was that from the big fireplace. I tossed the logs on the fire, then sank down into a chair. Sitting there I watched the flames dance along the logs of birch.

The birch tossed flames to which you could attach a face, a figure, even a voice. And suddenly the flames etched into life a scene from out of the long ago. . . .

It was a snowy Christmas and Grandpa was eighty-seven. Mother and Dad and I had driven the eight miles out from town and parked the Model-T under the apple tree across the creek from Grandpa's. We carried presents for Grandpa and Grandma, who lived all alone since their sons had grown up and moved into town.

Standing by the Model-T while Mother heaped my arms with packages, I looked over toward the house which wore a shawl of snow and, watching the blue wood smoke curl up from the chimney, asked Mother did she think Grandma would bake me some johnnycake on the hearth and Mother said she guessed she might if I was real nice about it.

When we got to the house we found Grandpa sitting by the fire, all hunkered over the flames, and he said he couldn't seem to get warm. "Been havin' chills all day," he said.

Even before I took off my coat I went over to him and handed him a little package all done up in red paper and tied with a piece of green ribbon. He took the package and laid it down beside his chair but I said he was supposed to open it right then. He reached down and got it and opened it and smiled at me as he held

196

up the pocketknife I had picked out all by myself. He gave it to Grandma and told her to lay it on the mantel.

For a moment he just sat there staring into the fire and was all quiet, not like he usually was when I came to see him. Then he pulled me to him like he always did and hugged me and a little later he reached into his pocket and took out a bright, shiny silver dollar.

"I've been so poorly, son, I couldn't get into town to get you anything for Christmas. This is the best I can do."

And then he took my hand and put the silver dollar in it and closed my fingers around it. I thought it was the finest present I had ever had. I knew right then I never would spend it.

Grandma said she was about to fix supper and, of course, we would stay, but Mother said the weather was so bad we would have to get back before dark. Grandma said then why didn't we spend the night but Mother shook her head and said Santa Claus wouldn't know where I was and Grandma smiled and ran her hand through my hair.

Then Grandma said how would I like some johnnycake and sweet milk, knowing all the time I would, and I looked at Mother and she nodded and I said, please, then asked, "Would you bake it on the hoe like you sometimes do, Grandma?" and she said, "Why, bless you, honey, I will."

While Grandma was gone back to the kitchen to mix up the batter, Grandpa said this was the first time since he and Grandma had been married that they hadn't had a Yule log.

"It don't seem like Christmas," he said, and Dad nodded his head but didn't say anything.

Mother looked at Dad but he wasn't looking at her; he was staring into the fire.

And Grandpa said, "I'm not as young as I used to be and I've got no one to go out and fetch me a hickory stump," and he paused and looked at Dad, then went on, "Boy, remember them big hickory stumps you used to drag in?" And Dad nodded again, still not saying anything.

Then Grandpa was quiet, and he reached down and picked up a little bitty hickory log and tossed it on the fire.

Finally, Dad said, "Pa, has the mule been fed?" and Grandpa looked at him and said, "I reckon. Jim Pott's boy has been lookin' after him for me, though he's not been by the house yet."

"Think I'll have a look," Dad said, and I said I would go with him but he shook his head and went on back through the house toward the back door and the path that led out across the branch to the barn.

"Now why do you suppose he got interested all of a sudden in that mule?" said Grandpa.

Mother shook her head.

About that time Grandma came back. She had a bowl of batter in one hand and a hoe in the other.

Grandma said, "Where's John?" and Grandpa said, "Went to see about the mule."

Then Grandma bent down and dipped her hand into the batter and spread some of it on the hoe blade. With the edge of the hoe turned toward the fire she leaned the handle against the top of the fire-place. The batter started steaming and simmering and turning gold-like.

Grandma went back to the kitchen to fetch me a glass of sweet milk and when she came back the johnnycake was all brown. She handed me the milk, then bent down and broke off a hunk of the johnnycake for me. It was almost too hot to eat. I would take a bite of it and then a swallow of the milk to cool it off.

While I ate, Mother and Grandpa and Grandma talked about this and that, stuff that didn't interest me. Once Mother said she wondered what was keeping Dad, and then they talked about Grandma's other sons and their children and by that time I had stuffed down all of the first johnnycake and Grandma had cooked me another one.

By this time it was beginning to get dark and Dad had been gone over most an hour, Mother said, remarking that she was a little concerned. Grandpa said maybe he was talking to Jim Pott's boy and had plumb forgot the time. Mother said if he didn't come soon we would never get home. Then they went back to talking about something else.

Grandpa's clock on the mantel struck five and Mother said she was going out to see what had happened to Dad, but just then we heard a clomping and a stomping on the porch and the door opened and there was Dad, all covered with snow from head to feet.

Mother took one look at him and said, "Where've you been?" and Dad sort of grinned and shook the snow from his shoulders.

"Doing something that I used to do," said Dad, grinning again.

He called me to him and told me to hold the door open for him and then he went back outside. Grandma came to the door and said, "Land sakes!" and Grandpa said, "What is it?" and Mother started to get up but by that time Dad was backing through the door saying, "Easy does it."

Dad had ahold of one end of a big log and Jim Pott's boy had ahold of the other end. They toted it right into the room and right up to the fireplace and then they eased it down into the fire where the other logs had just about burned out.

"There's your hickory stump," said Dad, looking at Grandpa. "Now don't say you haven't got a Yule log. Of course, it's not like the ones I used to fetch when I was a boy but I didn't have much time to look around and in this snow besides."

Grandpa seemed to perk up for the first time and he smiled at Dad, then lowered his head and got out his handkerchief and blew his nose. "Reckon that hickory stump'll heat up this place and cure my cold," he said.

Dad gave Jim Pott's boy a dollar and told him to see that the mule was put up in the barn, and then we were all laughing and talking at once and watching the hickory stump begin to catch fire.

Mother said we'd better be going and Dad said he guessed so. She got up and helped me into my coat. Dad held open the door for us and it was dark as we said "Merry Christmas" to Grandpa and Grandma.

Both of them had come to the door and

both of them were smiling and Grandpa said he already felt better. Then we were out in the night, tramping through the snow to the Model-T.

Dad cranked up the Model-T and got in and Mother said to him, "You probably got your death of cold," but her voice wasn't sharp. There was something proud in it. She reached across me and touched Dad's arm and then looked back toward the house where Grandpa and Grandma sat before the fire that now was eating into the hickory stump Dad had fetched, like he had when he was a boy.

It had stopped snowing as Dad backed the Model-T out into the road and headed her for home. . . .

The scene faded from the flames of my own fire as Dorothy came into the room and said, "Asleep?" and I laughed and said, "Just dreaming."

"We'd better have some light," she said, and I said, "I guess so."

But before I got up and walked over to the wall switch, I said, "Nelse brought our Yule log but it doesn't look as big as the ones Grandpa used to have."

And then I felt in my pocket and my fingers caressed a silver dollar.

MEET THE AUTHOR:
John Parris (1914–)

Born in Sylva, a small town in the North Carolina mountains, John Parris has stated that he began writing as soon as he was big enough to hold a pencil. When he was only thirteen, he was already contributing articles to the *Jackson County Journal* and the *Asheville Citizen-Times*. At twenty, he was the youngest correspondent to cover news from the state capital for the United Press.

His career carried him to London and North Africa during World War II, and later to New York. By the age of thirty-three, he had returned to his native Sylva to become one of the best-known recorders of mountain life and lore. In 1958, his writing won him the Thomas Wolfe Memorial Award. His column in the *Asheville Citizen-Times* includes folk tales, personality profiles, and quick, but vivid, word-portraits of places and events in his beloved mountains.

Language Alert

Some words and phrases common to the mountain dialect:

1. "True fact" is a **redundancy**; that is, it re-peats needlessly. (Any fact is something that is known to be true; therefore "true" is unneeded.)
2. "It looks like it's fixin' to weather-up," says Nelse as he sees snow flurries begin to fall. "Fixing to" means preparing to. What does "weather-up" mean?
3. "I've been so poorly. . . ." Can you guess the meaning of these terms just from the context?
4. *Johnnycake*: A thin flat cake made from cornmeal—much like a pancake.
5. *sweet milk*: milk that has not soured
6. *plumb*: completely

Reflecting

1. Notice the gifts that were given and received on that long-ago Christmas. How does each fit the person to whom it is given?
2. John Parris tells the memory from a child's point of view. The child sees things, but doesn't quite know how to interpret what he sees. Can you explain the following?
   a. Why, after young John gives Grandpa his gift, is Grandpa "all quiet, not like he usually was"?
   b. After Grandpa says that "It don't seem like Christmas" without a Yule log, Mother looks at Dad. Why? Dad is staring into the fire and doesn't say any-thing—why?
   c. Dad stays away for a long time, supposedly "to have a look" at the mule. Does the boy suspect anything? Did you? Find the place in the story when you realized where Dad had gone. What clues did you have?
   d. Grandpa never says "thank you" for what Dad has done. How do we know that he appreciates it?
   e. How does Mother feel about what Dad has done? How do we know?

The Lost Boy

Thomas Wolfe

Preview

A sensitive child, a stern father, a money-grubbing old couple—these are the characters whose lives conflict in this story. If you have ever felt that someone was taking advantage of you, surely you will feel akin to Grover, the boy who has just finished delivering papers on a cool April evening in turn-of-the-century Asheville.

Light came and went and came again, the booming strokes of three o'clock beat out across the town in thronging bronze from the courthouse bell, light winds of April blew the fountain out in rainbow sheets, until the plume returned and pulsed, as Grover turned into the Square. He was a child, dark-eyed and grave, birthmarked upon his neck—a berry of warm brown—and with a gentle face, too quiet and too listening for his years. The scuffed boy's shoes, the thick-ribbed stockings gartered at the knees, the short knee pants cut straight with three small useless buttons at the side, the sailor blouse, the old cap battered out of shape, perched sideways up on top of the raven head, the old soiled canvas bag slung from the shoulder, empty now, but waiting for the crisp sheets of the afternoon—these friendly, shabby garments, shaped by Grover, uttered him. He turned and passed along the north side of the Square and in that moment saw the union of Forever and of Now.

Light came and went and came again, the great plume of the fountain pulsed and winds of April sheeted it across the Square in a rainbow gossamer of spray. The fire department horses drummed on the floors with wooden stomp, most casually, and with dry whiskings of their clean, coarse tails. The street cars ground into the Square from every portion of the compass and halted briefly like wound toys in their familiar quarter-hourly formula. A dray, hauled by a boneyard nag, rattled across the cobbles on the other side before his father's shop. The courthouse bell boomed out its solemn warning of immediate three, and everything was just the same as it had always been.

He saw that haggis[1] of vexed shapes with quiet eyes—that hodgepodge of ill-sorted architectures that made up the Square, and he did not feel lost. For "Here," thought Grover, "here is the Square as it has always been—and papa's shop, the fire department and the City Hall, the fountain pulsing with its plume, the street cars coming in and halting at the quarter hour, the hardware store on the corner there, the row of old brick buildings on this side of the street, the people passing and the light that comes and changes and that always will come back again, and everything that comes and goes and changes in the Square, and yet will be the same again. And here," the boy thought, "is Grover with his paper bag. Here is old Grover, almost twelve years old. Here is the month of April, 1904. Here is the courthouse bell and three o'clock. Here is Grover on the Square that never changes. Here is Grover, caught upon this point of time."

It seemed to him that the Square, itself the accidental masonry of many years, the chance agglomeration[2] of time and of disrupted[3] strivings, was the center of the universe. It was for him, in his soul's picture, the earth's pivot, the granite core of changelessness, the eternal place where all things came and passed, and yet abode forever and would never change.

He passed the old shack on the corner—the wooden fire-trap where S. Goldberg ran his wiener stand. Then he passed the Singer place next door, with its gleaming display of new machines. He saw them and admired them, but he felt no joy. They brought back to him the busy hum of housework and of women sewing, the intricacy[4] of stitch and weave, the mystery of style and pattern, the memory of women bending over flashing needles, the pedaled tread, the busy whir. It was women's work: it filled him with unknown associations of dullness and of vague depression. And always, also, with a moment's twinge of horror, for his dark eye would always travel toward that needle stitching up and down so fast the eye could never follow it. And then he would remember how his mother once had told him she had driven the needle through her finger, and always, when he passed this place, he would remember it and for a moment crane his neck and turn his head away.

He passed on then, but had to stop again next door before the music store.

1. haggis: a Scottish dish concocted of various meats and vegetables

2. agglomeration: cluster, collection

3. disrupted: upset, disturbed

4. intricacy: complexity, something very complicated

He always had to stop by places that had shining perfect things in them. He loved hardware stores and windows full of accurate geometric tools. He loved windows full of hammers, saws, and planing boards. He liked windows full of strong new rakes and hoes, with unworn handles, of white perfect wood, stamped hard and vivid with the maker's seal. He loved to see such things as these in the windows of hardware stores. And he would fairly gloat upon them and think that some day he would own a set himself.

Also, he always stopped before the music and piano store. It was a splendid store. And in the window was a small white dog upon his haunches, with head cocked gravely to one side, a small white dog that never moved, that never barked, that listened attentively at the flaring funnel of a horn to hear "His Master's Voice"—a horn forever silent, and a voice that never spoke. And within were many rich and shining shapes of great pianos, an air of splendor and of wealth.

And now, indeed, he *was* caught, held suspended. A waft of air, warm, chocolate-laden, filled his nostrils. He tried to pass the white front of the little eight-foot shop; he paused, struggling with conscience; he could not go on. It was the little candy shop run by old Crocker and his wife. And Grover could not pass.

"Old stingy Crockers!" he thought scornfully. "I'll not go there any more. But—" as the maddening fragrance of rich cooking chocolate touched him once again—"I'll just look in the window and see what they've got." He paused a moment, looking with his dark and quiet eyes into the window of the little candy shop. The window, spotlessly clean, was filled with trays of fresh-made candy. His eyes rested on a tray of chocolate drops. Unconsciously he licked his lips. Put one of them upon your tongue and it just melted there, like honeydew. And then the trays full of rich home-made fudge. He gazed longingly at the deep body of the chocolate fudge, reflectively at maple walnut, more critically, yet with longing, at the mints, the nougatines, and all the other dainties.

"Old stingy Crockers!" Grover muttered once again, and turned to go. "I wouldn't go in *there* again."

And yet he did not go away. "Old stingy Crockers" they might be; still, they did make the best candy in town, the best, in fact, that he had ever tasted.

He looked through the window back into the little shop and saw Mrs. Crocker there. A customer had gone in and had made a purchase, and as Grover looked he saw Mrs. Crocker, with her little wrenny face, her pinched features, lean over and peer primly at the scales. She had a piece of fudge in her clean, bony, little fingers, and as Grover looked, she broke it, primly, in her little bony hands. She dropped a morsel down into the scales. They weighted down alarmingly, and her thin lips tightened. She snatched the piece of fudge out of the scales and broke it carefully once again. This time the scales wavered, went down very slowly, and came back again. Mrs. Crocker carefully put the reclaimed piece of fudge back in the tray, dumped the remainder in a paper bag, folded it and gave it to the customer, counted the money carefully and doled it out into the till, the pennies in one place, the nickels in another.

Grover stood there, looking scornfully. "Old stingy Crocker—afraid that she might give a crumb away!"

He grunted scornfully and again he turned to go. But now Mr. Crocker came out from the little partitioned place where they made all their candy, bearing a tray of fresh-made fudge in his skinny hands. Old Man Crocker rocked along the counter to the front and put it down. He really rocked along. He was a cripple. And like his wife, he was a wrenny,[5] wizened[6] little creature, with bony hands, thin lips, a pinched and meager face. One leg was inches shorter than the other, and on this leg there was an enormous thick-soled boot, with a kind of wooden, rocker-like arrangement, six inches high at least, to make up for the deficiency.[7] On this wooden cradle Mr. Crocker rocked along, with a prim and apprehensive little smile, as if he were afraid he was going to lose something.

"Old stingy Crocker!" muttered Grover. "Humph! He wouldn't give you anything!"

And yet—he did not go away. He hung there curiously, peering through the window, with his dark and gentle face now focused and intent, alert and curious, flattening his nose against the glass. Unconsciously he scratched the thick-ribbed fabric of one stockinged leg with the scuffed and worn toe of his old shoe. The fresh, warm odor of the new-made fudge was delicious. It was a little maddening. Half consciously he began to fumble in one trouser pocket, and pulled out his purse, a shabby worn old black one with a twisted clasp. He opened it and prowled about inside.

What he found was not inspiring—a nickel and two pennies and—he had forgotten them—the stamps. He took the stamps out and unfolded them. There were five twos, eight ones, all that remained of the dollar-sixty-cents' worth which Reed, the pharmacist, had given him for running errands a week or two before.

"Old Crocker," Grover thought, and looked somberly at the grotesque little form as it rocked back into the shop again, around the counter, and up the other side. "Well—" again he looked indefinitely at the stamps in his hand— "he's had all the rest of them. He might as well take these."

So, soothing conscience with this sop of scorn, he went into the shop and stood looking at the trays in the glass case and finally decided. Pointing with a slightly grimy finger at the fresh-made tray of chocolate fudge, he said, "I'll take fifteen cents' worth of this, Mr. Crocker." He paused a moment, fighting with embarrassment, then he lifted his dark face and said quietly, "And please, I'll have to give you stamps again."

Mr. Crocker made no answer. He did not look at Grover. He pressed his lips together primly. He went rocking away and

5. wrenny: like a wren, small and brown

6. wizened: dried, shriveled

7. deficiency: lack, shortage, inadequacy

got the candy scoop, came back, slid open the door of the glass case, put fudge into the scoop, and, rocking to the scales, began to weigh the candy out. Grover watched him as he peered and squinted, he watched him purse and press his lips together, he saw him take a piece of fudge and break it in two parts. And then old Crocker broke two parts in two again. He weighed, he squinted, and he hovered, until it seemed to Grover that by calling *Mrs.* Crocker stingy he had been guilty of a rank injustice. But finally, to his vast relief, the job was over, the scales hung there, quivering apprehensively, upon the very hair-line of nervous balance, as if even the scales were afraid that one more move from Old Man Crocker and they would be undone.

Mr. Crocker took the candy then and dumped it in a paper bag and, rocking back along the counter toward the boy, he dryly said: "Where are the stamps?" Grover gave them to him. Mr. Crocker relinquished[8] his clawlike hold upon the bag and set it down upon the counter. Grover took the bag and dropped it in his canvas sack, and then remembered. "Mr. Crocker—" again he felt the old embarrassment that was almost like strong pain—"I gave you too much," Grover said. "There were eighteen cents in stamps. You—you can just give me three ones back."

Mr. Crocker did not answer. He was busy with his bony little hands, unfolding the stamps and flattening them out on top of the glass counter. When he had done so, he peered at them sharply for a moment, thrusting his scrawny neck forward and running his eye up and down, like a bookkeeper who totes up rows of figures.

When he had finished, he said tartly: "I don't like this kind of business. If you want candy, you should have the money for it. I'm not a post office. The next time you come in here and want anything, you'll have to pay me money for it."

Hot anger rose in Grover's throat. His olive face suffused[9] with angry color. His tarry eyes got black and bright. He was on the verge of saying: "Then why did you take my other stamps? Why do you tell me now, when you have taken all the stamps I had, that you don't want them?"

But he was a boy, a boy of eleven years, a quiet, gentle, gravely thoughtful boy, and he had been taught how to respect his elders. So he just stood there looking with his tar-black eyes. Old Man Crocker, pursing at the mouth a little, without meeting Grover's gaze, took the stamps up in his thin, parched fingers and, turning, rocked away with them down to the till.

He took the twos and folded them and laid them in one rounded scallop, then took the ones and folded them and put them in the one next to it. Then he closed the till and started to rock off, down toward the other end. Grover, his face now quiet and grave, kept looking at him, but Mr. Crocker did not look at Grover. Instead he began to take some stamped cardboard shapes and fold them into boxes.

8. relinquished: surrendered, gave up

9. suffused: spread through or over, saturated

In a moment Grover said, "Mr. Crocker, will you give me the three ones, please?"

Mr. Crocker did not answer. He kept folding boxes, and he compressed his thin lips quickly as he did so. But Mrs. Crocker, back turned to her spouse, also folding boxes with her birdlike hands, muttered tartly: "Hm! *I'd* give him nothing!"

Mr. Crocker looked up, looked at Grover, said, "What are you waiting for?"

"Will you give me the three ones please?" Grover said.

"I'll give you nothing," Mr. Crocker said.

He left his work and came rocking forward along the counter. "Now you get out of here! Don't you come in here with any more of those stamps," said Mr. Crocker.

"I should like to know where he gets them—that's what *I* should like to know," said Mrs. Crocker.

She did not look up as she said these words. She inclined her head a little to the side, in Mr. Crocker's direction, and continued to fold the boxes with her bony fingers.

"You get out of here!" said Mr. Crocker. "And don't you come back here with any stamps. . . . Where did you get those

Thomas Wolfe's home, run as a boarding house, "The Old Kentucky Home" by his mother. Located near downtown Asheville, it is open to the public as a memorial to Wolfe.

stamps?" he said.

"That's just what *I've* been thinking," Mrs. Crocker said. "*I've* been thinking all along."

"You've been coming in here for the last two weeks with those stamps," said Mr. Crocker. "I don't like the look of it. Where did you get those stamps?" he said.

"That's what *I've* been thinking," said Mrs. Crocker, for a second time.

Grover had got white underneath his olive skin. His eyes had lost their luster. They looked like dull, stunned balls of tar. "From Mr. Reed," he said. "I got the stamps from Mr. Reed." Then he burst out desperately: "Mr. Crocker—Mr. Reed will tell you how I got the stamps. I did some work for Mr. Reed, he gave me those stamps two weeks ago."

"Mr. Reed," said Mrs. Crocker acidly. She did not turn her head. "I call it mighty funny."

"Mr. Crocker," Grover said, "if you'll just let me have three ones—"

"You get out of here!" cried Mr. Crocker, and he began rocking forward toward Grover. "Now don't you come in here again, boy! There's something funny about this whole business! I don't like the look of it," said Mr. Crocker. "If you can't pay as other people do, then I don't want your trade."

"Mr. Crocker," Grover said again, and underneath the olive skin his face was gray, "if you'll just let me have those three—"

"You get out of here!" Mr. Crocker cried, rocking down toward the counter's end. "If you don't get out, boy—"

"*I'd* call a policeman, that's what I'd do," Mrs. Crocker said.

Mr. Crocker rocked around the lower end of the counter. He came rocking up to Grover. "You get out," he said.

He took the boy and pushed him with his bony little hands, and Grover was sick and gray down to the hollow pit of his stomach.

"You've got to give me those three ones," he said.

"You get out of here!" shrilled Mr. Crocker. He seized the screen door, pulled it open, and pushed Grover out. "Don't you come back in here," he said, pausing for a moment, and working thinly at the lips. He turned and rocked back in the shop again. The screen door slammed behind him. Grover stood there on the pavement. And light came and went and came again into the Square.

The boy stood there, and a wagon rattled past. There were some people passing by, but Grover did not notice them. He stood there blindly, in the watches of the sun, feeling this was Time, this was the center of the universe, the granite core of changelessness, and feeling, this is Grover, this the Square, this is Now.

But something had gone out of day. He felt the overwhelming, soul-sickening guilt that all the children, all the good men of the earth, have felt since Time began. And even anger had died down, had been drowned out, in this swelling tide of guilt, and "This is the Square"—thought Grover as before—"This is Now. There is my father's shop. And all of it is as it has always been—save I."

And the Square reeled drunkenly

207

around him, light went in blind gray motes before his eyes, the fountain sheeted out to rainbow iridescence[10] and returned to its proud, pulsing plume again. But all the brightness had gone out of day, and "Here is the Square, and here is permanence, and here is Time—and all of it the same as it has always been, save I."

The scuffed boots of the lost boy moved and stumbled blindly. The numb feet crossed the pavement—reached the cobbled street, reached the plotted central square—the grass plots, and the flower beds, so soon to be packed with red geraniums.

"I want to be alone," thought Grover, "where I cannot go near him. . . . Oh God, I hope he never hears, that no one ever tells him—"

The plume blew out, the iridescent sheet of spray blew over him. He passed through, found the other side and crossed the street, and—"Oh God, if papa ever hears!" thought Grover, as his numb feet started up the steps into his father's shop.

He found and felt the steps—the width and thickness of old lumber twenty feet in length. He saw it all—the iron columns on his father's porch, painted with the dull anomalous[11] black-green that all such columns in this land and weather come to; two angels, fly-specked, and the waiting stones. Beyond and all around, in the stonecutter's shop, cold shapes of white and marble, rounded stone, the languid angel with strong marble hands of love.

He went on down the aisle, the white shapes stood around him. He went on to the back of the workroom. This he knew—the little cast-iron stove in left-hand corner, caked, brown, heat-blistered, and the elbow of the long stack running out across the shop; the high and dirty window looking down across the Market Square. . . the rude old shelves, plank-boarded, thick, the wood not smooth but pulpy, like the strong hair of an animal; upon the shelves the chisels of all sizes and a layer of stone dust; an emery wheel with pump tread; and a door that let out on the alleyway, yet the alleyway twelve feet below. Here in the room, two trestles of this coarse spiked wood upon which rested gravestones, and at one, his father at work.

The boy looked, saw the name was Creasman: saw the carved analysis of John, the symmetry of the s, the fine sentiment that was being polished off beneath the name and date: "John Creasman, November 7, 1903."

Gant looked up. He was a man of fifty-three, gaunt-visaged, mustache cropped, immensely long and tall and gaunt. He wore good dark clothes—heavy, massive—save he had no coat. He worked in shirt-sleeves with his vest on, a strong watch chain stretching across his vest, wing collar and black tie, Adam's apple, bony forehead, bony nose, light eyes, gray-green, undeep and cold, and, somehow, lonely-looking, a striped apron going up around his shoulders, and starched cuffs. And in one hand a tremendous rounded wooden mallet like a

10. iridescence: a display of rainbow-like colors

11. anomalous: irregular, abnormal

208

butcher's bole; and in his other hand, a strong cold chisel.

"How are you, son?"

He did not look up as he spoke. He spoke quietly, absently. He worked upon the chisel and the wooden mallet, as a jeweler might work on a watch, except that in the man and in the wooden mallet there was power too.

"What is it, son?" he said.

He moved around the table from the head, started up on "J" once again.

"Papa, I never stole the stamps," said Grover.

Gant put down the mallet, laid the chisel down. He came around the trestle.

"What?" he said.

As Grover winked his tar-black eyes, they brightened, the hot tears shot out. "I never stole the stamps," he said.

"Hey? What is this?" his father said. "What stamps?"

"That Mr. Reed gave me, when the other boy was sick and I worked there for three days. . . . And Old Man Crocker," Grover said, "he took all the stamps. And I told him Mr. Reed had given them to me. And now he owes me three ones— and Old Man Crocker says he don't believe they were mine. He says—he says— that I must have taken them somewhere," Grover blurted out.

"The stamps that Reed gave you— hey?" the stonecutter said. "The stamps you had—" He wet his thumb upon his lips, threw back his head and slowly swung his gaze around the ceiling, then turned and strode quickly from his workshop out into the storeroom.

Almost at once he came back again,

and as he passed the old gray painted-board partition of his office he cleared his throat and wet his thumb and said, "Now, I tell you—"

Then he turned and strode up toward the front again and cleared his throat and said, "I tell you now—" He wheeled about and started back, and as he came along the aisle between the marshaled rows of gravestones he said beneath his breath, "By God, now—"

He took Grover by the hand and they went out flying. Down the aisle they went by all the gravestones, past the fly-specked angels waiting there, and down the wooden steps and across the Square. The fountain pulsed, the plume blew out in sheeted iridescence, and it swept across them; an old gray horse, with a peaceful look about his torn lips, swucked up the cool mountain water from the trough as Grover and his father went across the Square, but they did not notice it.

They crossed swiftly to the other side in a direct line to the candy shop. Gant was still dressed in his long striped apron, and he was still holding Grover by the hand. He opened the screen door and stepped inside.

"Give him the stamps," Gant said.

Mr. Crocker came rocking forward behind the counter, with the prim and careful look that now was somewhat like a smile. "It was just—" he said.

"Give him the stamps," Gant said, and threw some coins down on the counter.

Mr. Crocker rocked away and got the stamps. He came rocking back. "I just didn't know—" he said.

The stonecutter took the stamps and

gave them to the boy. And Mr. Crocker took the coins.

"It was just that—" Mr. Crocker began again, and smiled.

Gant cleared his throat: "You never were a father," he said. "You never knew the feelings of a father, or understood the feelings of a child; and that is why you acted as you did. But a judgment is upon you. God has cursed you. He has afflicted you. He has made you lame and childless as you are—and lame and childless, miserable as you are, you will go to your grave and be forgotten!"

And Crocker's wife kept kneading her bony little hands and said, imploringly, "Oh, no—oh don't say that, please don't say that."

The stonecutter, the breath still hoarse in him, left the store, still holding the boy tightly by the hand. Light came again into the day.

"Well, son," he said, and laid his hand on the boy's back. "Well, son," he said, "now don't you mind."

They walked across the Square, the sheeted spray of iridescent light swept out on them, the horse swizzled at the water-trough, and "Well, son," the stonecutter said.

And the old horse sloped down, ringing with his hoofs upon the cobblestones.

"Well, son," said the stonecutter once again, "be a good boy."

And he trod his own steps then with his great stride and went back again into his shop.

The lost boy stood upon the Square, hard by the porch of his father's shop.

"This is Time," thought Grover. "Here is the Square, here is my father's shop, and here am I."

And light came and went and came again—but now not quite the same as it had done before. The boy saw the pattern of familiar shapes and knew that they were just the same as they had always been. But something had gone out of day, and something had come in again. Out of the vision of those quiet eyes some brightness had gone, and into their vision had come some deeper color. He could not say, he did not know through what transforming shadows life had passed within that quarter hour. He only knew that something had been lost—something forever gained.

MEET THE AUTHOR:
Thomas Wolfe (1900–1938)

For decades, Thomas Wolfe has been by far the most famous writer from North Carolina. His novels won him a national reputation as a storyteller with a remarkable gift for poetic language.

Wolfe grew up in Asheville, NC, where his mother ran a boardinghouse and his father was a stonecutter. After completing high school, he enrolled at UNC-Chapel Hill. There he majored in English, acted with the Playmakers, and began his writing career by editing the college newspaper and writing folk plays. After graduation, he went on to Harvard to continue studying playwriting, but his plays never met with success, so he taught at New York University.

Look Homeward, Angel, his first novel, is an autobiographical story set in his native Asheville. In this novel, he depicts a boy's struggles in growing up and coming to terms with his strong-willed mother and a strife-torn family. Later novels are to some extent based on Wolfe's adventures in New York and Europe, but his first remains his most famous and possibly his best. It was made into a movie and adapted into a play which won awards on Broadway and later was filmed for television.

Wolfe's promising career was cut short in 1938 when a brain infection took his life. The Asheville boardinghouse in which he grew up is today open to the public, and the national Thomas Wolfe Society keeps alive interest in the man and his writing.

Reflecting

1. Why did Mr. Crocker refuse to give Grover his three stamps back?
2. Before Grover goes into the candy store, we are given a thorough and poetic description of the street, the fountain, and the passersby. When he comes out of the store, the description is repeated, and Grover thinks, "Here is the Square, and here is permanence, and here is Time—and all of it the same as it has always been, save I." In what way has he changed?
3. At the very end of the story, we are told that Grover "only knew that something had been lost—something forever gained." What had he lost? What had he gained?

From **The Summer Land**

New Broom in the Schoolhouse

Burke Davis

Preview

In North Carolina today there are no one-room schoolhouses where all students from first grade through high school are mingled into one classroom. However, such arrangements were fairly common during the early part of this century, especially in rural areas. In fact, according to Bill Peek of the North Carolina Department of Public Instruction, in 1950 there were still 408 one-room schoolhouses in the state, and the last one—Mt. Sterling in Haywood County—did not close until 1967.

To handle such a wide mixture of ages, abilities, and subjects required an unusual personality, and in a small community, the arrival of a new teacher was a major event—especially to a boy like Fax Starling, the narrator of this story. He tells us that "Papa always called me the odd whelp of the litter because I never minded going to school, and would sometimes read books if they didn't watch me." So as Fax says, "It made me feel better just to think of school, and of the new teacher who was coming."

We pick up this story at the end of July 1916. Fax is helping his father at the tobacco-curing barn. With them are Fax's older brother Jimroe, the mischief-maker in the family, one who claims to hate school "like poison." It is early in the morning, and the three of them, along with Tree, their cousin, are checking on the nearly cured tobacco.

While we stood around we saw dust on the road and somebody turned in at our lane. It was Shad Starling, the Negro who drove for our Aunt Ly Sue Poindexter, and he had come from town in Judge Bucktarrel's phaeton.[1] Aunt Ly Sue was great-aunt to Mama and Tree and about a thousand others, and was the only one in the family who put on any side. She lived in the biggest house in Corona Crossroads, almost hidden behind overgrown box bushes, and she kept Shad to drive for her.

We most often saw Aunt Ly Sue in a string hammock on her porch, fanning herself, with Shad's wife Poll to wait on her, and sometimes Judge Bucktarrel beside her, plinking his mandolin. Once when I had gone to her porch Aunt Ly Sue hugged me and she smelled of vanilla extract. I told Jimroe and he said she tippled all the time, but I couldn't be sure he wasn't making it up.

We waited at the barn and wondered what was going on, because it was a rare day that Shad came to our house. Mama sent Ivy down to us and she came out of breath.

"The schoolmarm's coming!"

Papa looked like he had heard better news in his day.

"Mama says you'll have to send for her."

"She picked a fine time. Why don't Shad fetch her?"

"Because Aunt Ly Sue is tailfeathers over teakettle, trying to get things ready for her—and you'll have to send. Mama said so."

"Of course, tobacco don't matter. Making a living is just some foolishness men-folks thought up. We've all got to go off to school and learn to spell cat." Papa was warming up in what Mama called his sourcastic vein, but he reined himself in and hugged Ivy. "All right, Sugarfoot. Where do we get here?"

"It's the noon train, and hurry."

Papa took a quick look to see who he could spare, and told Jimroe to go. My mouth popped open before I knew it and I wailed, "Papa."

He didn't say a word but knew what was wrong with me, and waved me on despite his itch to keep every hand at work every minute until the crop was finished. He yelled after us, "Take the buggy. She'll have a ton of traps and tricks. You'll have to squeeze 'em in."

Papa meant for us to hurry back as fast as we could, without wasting time. We had to cross the river and meet the train and take the teacher to Aunt Ly Sue's house in town. It was a long ride, but hers was the only place for a teacher to stay. The place was so big that the old lady and Shad and Poll rattled around in it, and Aunt Ly Sue was about the only woman in Corona with enough learning to make her decent for a schoolteacher to talk to. She had been off to school before her daddy died and left her all his money, a long time before. There was a story that some little girl had asked her once why she never got married, and Aunt Ly Sue said, "I was spoiled by Mr. Milton. I read *Paradise Lost* when I was young, and fell in love with the Devil and never found a man half so fascinating. I'm looking yet. Furnifold Bucktarrel

---

1. phaeton: a light, open four-wheeled carriage

comes close, but don't quite fill the bill." It was a tale Mama told sometimes.

Jimroe groused all the way to the river, where we left his old horse and the buggy. We got a free trip on the ferry with one of Tree's little boys.

"I ain't got all day to hang around for a fool schoolteacher," Jimroe said.

"Suppose she's prettier than Dumpling Kinnamon," I said.

"Shoot. She'll be as old as Methuselah and ugly as homemade sin. All them durn Virginia women are long in the nose and big in the foot."

We hung around the Atlantic & Redwine depot in Osmond until the noon train came, but there was no schoolteacher. We had only one other chance, the evening train, and we waited. The teacher was aboard. There was no trouble spotting her.

The conductor and brakeman came first, squabbling over who would set out her baggage for her. Then she came out, a woman about the size of a well-fed twelve-year-old, wearing a blue serge skirt that swept the gravel. She leaned on a steamer trunk while the old men worked. She was so pretty that she made me want to pin back her ears and swallow her whole.

We went up to say that we'd come after her, but she beat us to it and took both our hands. "I'm Cassie Carson. I've come to Corona School, and I expect you're some of my innocent victims."

Her blue eyes were the color of chicory flowers and as steady as the muzzle of a shotgun. Around the eyes she looked like she might be ready to laugh any second.

Jimroe pretended to be too busy to notice her. I tried to tell her about my reading and how fast I went in school and how hard I was going to study, but I made such a mess of it that she could hardly understand me. She smiled.

The trainmen called the livery-stable hack[2] to carry her things the hundred yards to the ferry landing and the train captain paid the hacker himself. Miss Cassie blew the captain a kiss and the old man barked his shins climbing back into his train. The train puffed off in the dark. . . .

It was only early fall, but it was like ending one year and beginning a new one when we had to quit fooling with tobacco for a while and go back to school. A gaggle of the least kids from our end of the country went by our house not long after sunup one morning, and we fell in with them. We trailed along pretty fast, thinking that we would get there before the teacher and play ball and get used to being on the school grounds again before we had to face her.

Miss Cassie was standing in the door. The room had been swept and there was fresh water in the bucket with a new dipper floating there. She was ready to go.

Our building was what we called an Old Field Schoolhouse, a shack perched on stilts on the mountainside with a fairly level yard around it, rough and weedy and surrounded by woods. Hunters often came by the door, chasing game. We couldn't see the village of Corona Crossroads because of the woods, but if we

2. hack: a carriage for hire; the hacker is its driver

214

climbed the bell tower we could have looked down the hill a mile or so away to see Biscoe Allen's store and the tobacco warehouse and the blacksmith's and the few houses in town. Corona Crossroads was so little that Tree said, "Town, heck. You'd poke it with a stick before you ever saw it."

We had one room and about forty children in our school, and we ran from the First to the Sixth Readers—all with Miss Cassie to teach us. Some were only five years old, and the worst boys ran up to more than twenty—but they didn't come at first. From our family, only Trout and Ivy and Cornelia and I went to school the first few days, because we could be spared from the work. Jimroe and the others couldn't come until later.

In the middle of the schoolhouse an iron stove squatted in a sandbox, where the big boys would spit their tobacco juice. Girls sat on one side of the room, with boys on the other, and we had homemade benches and desks. Up front was the water stand, and Miss Cassie sat at a table with a blackboard slate. There were two windows and only one door, and cracks in the walls wide enough to fling a cat through. Our necessary houses[3] were outdoors at the edge of the woods, with boys' and girls' about a hundred yards apart.

We read our lessons all at once, and until you got used to it the racket was fierce. Little five-year-old girls squeaked and the oldest boys growled like bumblebees in tar buckets. Miss Cassie sat as straight as an ironing board without touching her back to the chair, and took turns hearing our lessons while the other children hummed on. Her hair was pulled hard across her head and done up in little balls over her ears, about the size of biscuits and just the color of butter.

We opened with a Bible reading and everybody had to take a turn, so we passed the Bible around. Then we sang "The Star-Spangled Banner" and pledged allegiance to the flag—but without a flag in the room. When she caught one of us whispering or fiddling around, Miss Cassie popped him on the hand with her ruler, sounding like she was swatting a mosquito. When we miscalled words in the reading, we had to look them up in a big Page's Dictionary on her table and all of us tried to learn to spell them. None of us knew what they meant.

Miss Cassie began the first day to see how far she could go with us. "Children, what would you say if I asked you if you wanted to go home early today?"

"Yase, ma'am!"

She made my sister Ivy stand up.

"Did you say 'Yes, ma'am'?"

"Yase'm."

"Would you come up and write the word 'yase' on the slate?"

Ivy wrote it out for her, y-e-s, and Miss Cassie said that Ivy was a crackerjack speller.

"I guess it's a surprise to you children, but this word is pronounced *yes* just about everywhere else in the country. We don't say *yase*—and we don't say *naw* for *no*, either. If you went to other places and

---

3. necessary houses: outhouses containing toilets

talked like that, people would laugh at you."

While we tried to get that down, she said that there were places in the world where people didn't say *ma'am* every time they opened their mouths around a grown lady. She went on with the lessons, taking all of us in turn, and it was dinnertime before we knew it. We snatched our dinner pails and went out to eat and play. I went back in for a dipper of water and saw Miss Cassie open her lunch at the table.

Aunt Ly Sue was known to be stingy and the sorriest cook in Corona, and I could tell she had put up Miss Cassie's dinner herself. When the teacher opened the pail she had nothing but two hunks of light bread with a canned tomato slapped between, so that it was just a handful of pink sog. Miss Cassie made a tight little mouth and sent me to Biscoe Allen's store with a quarter, and I got her some potted meat and sardines and soda crackers. Afterward she stopped at Biscoe's every morning on her way to school and got something for her dinner. I was sorry she didn't let me run that errand for her so that I could be alone with her in the schoolhouse for a minute or two; she smelled like lemon verbena when you got near her.

I forgot about *yase'm* and *naw*, but the next day one of the little ones hobbled to school and told Miss Cassie that his papa had licked him for putting on airs and said it was none of the teacher's dang business what he learned at home. We heard no more of that from Miss Cassie, except that as an example she talked like

she wanted us to talk—but sometimes, in the heat of playing ball, she slipped and said *yase* herself.

We thought she must have noticed our smell in school. She kept somebody opening our windows even after cold weather came, and sometimes when she could no longer stand us she broke in on our lessons and turned us out for recess, no matter what the weather. Once or twice I saw her pat a little perfume under her chin when she finished eating, and I thought it might be so that she couldn't tell what all of us smelled like in there. At recess she was always getting out a little mirror and primping her hair, too.

At home Mama began teasing me when nobody else was around. I was getting up earlier every morning and hustling through my chores before the others stirred, and went into the kitchen for breakfast. Mama would say, "Where you off to in such a rush, boy? I know you're not old enough for a sweetheart." I would gobble corn mush and milk without waiting for bacon and eggs, and go to school. When I took the short cut through the woods I usually beat Miss Cassie there.

I did the sweeping then, or got fresh water, and lots of times did extra studying, and left my work on the slate so that she would notice. Then I went outside quick, before any of the others came and caught me.

When all of us went inside after Miss Cassie rang the bell, and we had finished the Bible reading and prayer, I watched to see who she would notice first in the crowd. I hated any other boy she looked at first, or called on to do his lesson before me.

But when Jimroe and the other big boys finally came to school, everything changed. Jimroe and I had begun to get away from each other at home, too. I hardly ever found him around. He worked with Papa and my older brothers, keeping watch over our tobacco and sometimes going to town with Papa to talk about the opening of the tobacco market. Jimroe was out late at night, and finally moved out of our big bed into the room with Creed and Damon. He had begun to dress in Damon's old clothes when he went into town, and wore his hair slicked down. Once before he went to school, Jimroe asked me lots of questions about Miss Cassie, but pretended to pay no attention to what I said about her.

It was late when the big boys came to school, for they wouldn't go until the very last minute, when they had run out of excuses. None of them would even talk about going until tobacco curing was over. But most of all they waited until they got baseball out of their systems for the year. Most of them played on our county league team, and Corona usually won the league, and people like our ballplayers didn't bother much with school. Baseball was played until late fall, since we had no other games. It didn't matter; we had no grades in school, and every year each one went as far as he could in the Readers, and took up in the place where he had left off when the next year came.

The big boys came to school for the first time one rainy, cold morning, about ten of them in a bunch, and right away they started cutting up and playing

tricks. I could see that they were just testing Miss Cassie, to set what they could get away with.

She kept the big boys after school that day. Some of us listened under the schoolhouse.

"Boys, I came to teach you a little something and not to run a circus. You're bigger than I am and lots of you are older, but I'm paid to handle the school and so long as I'm here, I'll do it."

They were quiet and she chirped again. "Some day it might come over you just how overgrown and ignorant you are. Maybe you'll have the grace to be ashamed of yourselves. But yes or no, you'll not break up school for the young ones who want to learn. You behave, or you're going home."

One of them growled and she shushed him. "You needn't treat me like I hadn't a grain of sense. I know we have some silly rules, but I didn't make them."

After that Miss Cassie paid more attention to Jimroe. She loaded things on him, so that he hardly had time for devilment. She made him captain of the lightard knot brigade, and about half of every day he had a crew of us in the woods hunting up old pine knots so full of resin that they would explode when you lit them in the school stove. They were the kindling for our fires.

That wasn't enough, so Jimroe had to fetch the water from a spring about a quarter of a mile away. He soon had that worked out so that he could boss, and two little kids lugged the buckets. When Jimroe fidgeted she sent him alone for water, even if the bucket was almost full.

I had to find new things to do in the early mornings before the teacher came. For a while I worked on handwriting. Papa said I already wrote like a girl, I had worked on it so much, but I kept practicing, and one morning Miss Cassie helped me. I was writing on the slate at my desk: "Raleigh is the capital of North Carolina," and all about Sir Walter Raleigh, from my Reader, when she leaned over my shoulder and touched me in several places without realizing it. The lemon smell was all around us and she covered my hand with hers and helped me make my letters smoother, straighter up and down. The other children came in while we were working and she moved her hand off, but it was a long time before the warmth of her palm went away, and I thought I could feel her pulse beating. During recess, when I took a dipper of water from the bucket, I got another whiff of her lemon perfume, because I had drunk just after her. The water had a different taste to me. Every time I saw her take a drink from the dipper I had to keep myself from running to be next to drink, for fear the kids would notice.

She worked to keep the rest of them busy and I helped her. When I had finished my Reader for the day, I would go into a corner with some of the youngest ones and help teach them. Once she bragged on me about that before the others, and that made me shy away for a few days.

Miss Cassie paired the smart ones with the dull ones and mixed the Indians with the whites on both sides of the room, and got the Indians interested by making them stand up and tell things about the way their people lived—almost anything she could think of. And so we got on together.

MEET THE AUTHOR:
Burke Davis (1913–   )
See p. 79

Language Alert

1. The title, *The Summer Land*, is taken from the toast to North Carolina, written in 1904 by Leonora Martin and Mary Burke Kerr, and adopted as the official state toast by the General Assembly in 1957. The toast goes as follows:

> Here's to the land of the long-leaf pine,
> The summer land, where the sun doth shine,
> Where the weak grow strong and the strong grow great.
> Here's to down home, the Old North State!

2. The title of this chapter, "New Broom in the Schoolhouse," alludes to an old saying: "A new broom sweeps clean."

Reflecting

1. How does Papa feel about the arrival of the new schoolteacher? Explain his reaction.
2. Aside from the fact that this is a one-room school, what other differences can you find in Fax's school and your own? What are the similarities? (Think of the building and other facilities, the equipment students use, attendance policies, activities in the classroom.)
3. From this excerpt, would you predict that Miss Cassie will succeed in handling the classroom? Explain your answer. In what way is she a "new broom"? Would you like to have her as a teacher? Why or why not?

The Corn Shucking

Paul Green

Preview

In the days before movies, radio, and television brought entertainment from across the world into every village and household, people concocted their own fun—and frequently they combined that fun with necessary labor. Thus a barn raising or a corn shucking became not just a chore, but an occasion for a community party, with everyone contributing time and energy and talent, and the host family providing a hearty feast. The adults not only worked, but swapped stories. The children played boisterous games and the teenagers (though they weren't called that then) made the occasion an opportunity to get in some "courtin'."

Through Paul Green's story, we can move back through time to get the flavor of this community party. As you read, think about any similar events that you may have experienced: perhaps a neighborhood July Fourth celebration, a potluck supper for a neighbor's birthday, or a dinner-on-the-grounds at your church. Pay attention, too, to young Paul, who is hoping to catch the eye of a special girl. How do his feelings and behavior resemble or differ from those of teenaged boys today?

In the old days when late October and early November came on, the farmers would haul the corn in the shuck from the fields, pile it in a horseshoe-shaped mounding around the barn door, and invite their neighbors in to help shuck it. This was always a joyous and festive occasion, and the housewives would cook up a storm of ham, barbecue, beef stew, chicken, pastry, pies, cakes, biscuits, and a multitude of things for good eating and fun. The shuckers usually ate in sequent groups—the oldest men first and the younger and yearling fellows last. Sometimes after the supper feeding was over, the girls would come out to the cornpile and find their respective sweethearts and snuggle down beside them and pretend to help shuck corn. After that, of course, the falling of the shucked ears toward the barndoor slackened down considerably. Now and then someone would find a red ear, and then a forfeit—or better, a reward—of a kiss would be taken by the young people—to the merriment and good spirits of all.

One corn shucking occasion I especially remember. I was about seventeen at the time and much in love with a country girl. I could hardly think of anything else, except maybe poetry. One cold October evening as the sun was going down in its great splurge of fire across our wide fields, I was out in the lot milking the cow, and the girl's little brother came by riding his father's black mule.

"Gonna shuck corn tomorrow night and want you all to come," the ruffian said, letting loose a squirt of tobacco juice at the gate post and eyeing me sternly from beneath his mop of tangled blond hair.

Keeping back my eagerness, I answered with due deliberation and judicial gravity that some of us would try to be there. Of course I'd be there if torment—if hell didn't freeze over.

I watched my time, and the next afternoon when everybody was out of the house, I slipped in and got my daddy's razor and took my first shave as best I could. Then I slicked down my hair and put on my Sunday suit—all for the girl's sake—and stood ready to ride. As a last measure I sprayed myself plentifully with my sister's cologne too. Then I hitched up my mule and drove through the country, feeling fit and ready as a man of God.

The corn shucking was in full swing when I got there. Young men, old men and boys were sitting and squatting around the horseshoe pile. In the dusk the stripped ears were pouring over toward the barn like a thick swarm of dancing bats.

I took my place among the sweaty overalls and ragged hats. Out of my vest pocket I fished my string-fastened shucking-peg, made of the hardest dogwood, seasoned by sun and fires, and coming to a fine point at the end. In a few minutes I was ripping the shucks open and shooting the ears over with the best of them. On and on we shucked, ear by ear, nubbin after nubbin, throwing the shuck behind with one hand and reaching forward with the other. And all the while there was a low drumming and seedy spattering of the corn falling ever toward the crib.

I was thinking about the girl in the house as I shucked, seeing her in my mind as she helped arrange the table, dishing up the stew and all the fine things to eat. It was almost time for supper now. The fields out by the barn were growing dim, and the open door to the hayloft above was a square of blackness, and looked lonesome. I gazed up at the sky and saw that the stars were coming out. The sky looked lonesome too. That was a trait I had—when I thought of something sweet and happy, I always thought of something sad and lonesome. One feeling seemed to bring on the other.

"Let's sing some," I said timidly to Laughing Gus Brown. "Sam Adams and Tim Messer's here."

Sam and Tim and Gus and I had been singing as a country quartet now for some time—round at corn shuckings, ice cream suppers, parties, and the like. We sure could make music, if I do say so.

Presently Tim and Sam left their places and came around. We made room for them.

"What shall it be?" said Sam, dumping his chew of tobacco into his hand and throwing it behind him.

"Oh, anything," I answered. "What would you like?"

"Sing about poor 'Omi," old Yen Yarborough spoke up in his chair a few paces away. Old Yen liked music, and he specially liked that mournful piece. He'd seen a lot of trouble in his time and now was dying from a bad sore that had eaten away most of his nose. Try doctors, herbs, salves, all that he might, including Miss Zua Smith's powerful plasters—nothing did him any good. But he still kept cheerful and wore his big bandage with dignity.

"Poor 'Omi it shall be," said Sam.

Thereupon we cleared our throats and settled our knees more firmly in the bed of shucks.

"Ta-la-la-la," said Tim, setting the chord. He was the first tenor and a good one.

"Do, sol, mi, do," growled Sam,

Then we let loose a harmony that shattered the twilight air and trembled the cobwebs in the hayloft. Out, around, and upward we sent the lady's plaintive story.

"O pity, O pity! pray spare your babe's life,
And I will deny it and not be your wife."
"No pity, no pity, no pity have I,
In yonder Deep River your body shall lie."

How we did make it chord, all with queer minor and mode! And when we'd reached the end where the poor lady's body, by desperate deed foredone, is found in the "drean" below the mill dam and the guilty George Lewis is captured and bound down in chains, there were grunts of approval and clapping of hands on all sides.

Then through the cool October evening I heard a voice that thrilled me to the bone.

"Come on in to supper, you all!" She was outside the lot fence with some other girls.

"Come on to supper!" the call was repeated.

The fellows around the cornpile craned their necks around, snickered and stirred with enlivenment. The older men would eat first, and seven or eight of them soon rose, dusted the corn silks from their clothes, and went on toward the gate.

"We need four more," old Yen called back.

And finally four middle-aged fellows followed the older ones to supper. The young girls in their white dresses and ribbons clustered around like beautiful butterflies beyond the fence.

"There she is," and Laughing Gus punched me in the side.

But I went on with my shucking as cold and indifferent as the old dummy that lived by the creek.

"You gals come over here and help us shuck this corn!" three or four voices called.

The group of girls beyond the fence were suddenly animated with a flurry of motion, and there were giggles and whispers among them. Finally little Cissy Tatum, who had a tongue like a scorpion's tail, shrilled out—"Who's that all dressed up in his wedding garments?"

A great shout went up around the corn pile, and I felt my face grow hot as fire.

"Come here, little Black-Eyes, and hold her hand!" cried Gus, who seemed to have gone crazy in his head. "Bring your handkerchief and an'int it, for she smells like the Queen of Sheby."

Sam Adams suddenly rolled over on his back and wallowed among the shucks with little squeals and whimpers of joy.

If only the ground would open and swallow me up, or if I might but burrow my way deep under the corn and hide myself from all human eyes! I remembered foolishly that Enoch walked with God and was not, for God took him. And so it was with Elijah—translated. I looked up at the sky and wished, as the Negroes sang—wisht I had-a wings for to fly. Then the girls went away, and she called back over her shoulder. "We'll all come and help you after supper."

"Do," shouted Gus, "and a kiss for every red ear!"

Soon the men came back and it was the turn of us younger ones to go to supper. Sam and Gus had just made a bet about who could eat the most, and there was much arguing as to the powers of each as we went out of the lot.

"Sam'll do it."

"No, Gus will. He's got more room 'twist his ribs and his waist and is ga'ntlike."

We shuffled on through the darkness and crowded around the pump outside the dining room. There we washed up with strong homemade soap and dried our hands and faces on towels hanging from the limbs of a pecan tree. The young girls hovered about in the gloom and waited upon us as if we had been lords.

"Here's some soap, Charlie," one said shyly to her husky sweetheart.

"And here's a towel," said another.

"Hurry up there," the sharp voice of Miz McLaughlin called from the kitchen.

Through the lighted window of the parlor I could see other girls gathered, one playing the organ and singing, and two or three sitting on the lounge looking through the family albums. Time would hang heavy on their hands until we boys were through at the corn pile. Like a herd of goats we trampled in through the dining room and seated ourselves at the table. All the while I had not seen her.

Mr. McLaughlin was noted for his closeness, but he hadn't failed to provide on this occasion. No farmer does. The table was loaded down with chicken stew, ham, collards, early pork, beef stew and steak, biscuits, muffins, cornbread, potato pie, and custards and cakes, and goodness knows what all. Two or three stolid Negro women moved about the room, handing the dishes on. And over it all Miz McLaughlin, with face as dried as a bean root, watched with hawklike eye. She was a stingy one, no doubt, but she did urge everybody to help himself. If she cared for her rations, as it was said, she was due to suffer this night. And so we began. I being so timid, and with my mind on something else, the girl, like a fool got a whole plateful of collards from the first Negro woman. I hated "greens" above all things, and in a few minutes my appetite was gone. It looked like a grimace of pleasure on the hostess's face when I soon had to say "no" to a proffered dish of stew.

After a few minutes the girl came in and shyly spoke to Sam.

"Are you going to play for us later?" she said.

"We are if we can tote our vittles," he answered.

A bit longer she stayed in the room and then went off along the porch toward the parlor. Not once had I looked up at her, but sat bent over my plate diddling with the hated greens.

"Come on there, Samuel, my son, how many cups of coffee does that make you?" queried Gus.

"Six."

"I'm two ahead of you. Undo your belt. Heigh, Mis' Sally," he called to Miz McLaughlin, "fire up the b'ilers and put on more coffee."

"You boys'll kill yourselves," she murmured.

"Huhp, not hardly," said Gus. "I ain't had a bite all day. Been laying up for these here vittles. Ain't that right, Sam?"

"Put on another pot of coffee, Ellen," she said resignedly. The Negro woman went out into the kitchen.

"Now for the 'tater custard," Gus chuckled.

By this time several of the boys had returned to the lot. But I waited around to see the fun and maybe to see her when she came in again. It was touch and go with Sam and Gus as to who would win. Sam was short and thick, Gus was long and stringy. While they devoured plate after plate of the good things, Tim Messer, who had long ago finished, sat with a stub of pencil and an old envelope keeping tally.

"You boys'll eat me out'n house and home," Miz McLaughlin laughed mournfully.

"Not hardly," Gus chortled. "Lord, your smokehouse is a-running over."

"How do they stand now?" she sighed presently. "And where is their raising?" she added spitefully.

Tim pored over his envelope.

"Purty nigh even," he answered, eyeing his scrawls with the air of the bookkeeper in the bank. "Sam has sunk away ten coffees, two plates of collards, three plates of stew, two pieces of ham, fourteen biscuits, a slab of steak, and nine whole custards."

"How's Gus?"

"Two biscuits ahead."

"Oh, my goodness gracious!"

A couple of custards later, Sam laid his knife down and sat looking at Gus with his mouth open.

"I got about enough," he murmured.

"Land a'mighty!" Gus cried in astonishment. "Where's your appetite? He's on the puny list, poor fellow."

"Bring on your custards," wheezed Sam. He took three in his hand, staggered out into the middle of the room and lay down on the floor. He lay there flat on his back, devouring them. Several of the girls came in and laughed at him, and Maisie Strickland, his shamed sweetheart, begged him to get up.

"I can't do no more for man nor country," he finally said. "Open the door there—I'm coming out." He crawled to his feet and stumbled from the room, his upper lip wrinkled back most sickeningly.

When Gus had emptied another pot of coffee and gone three biscuits and a custard farther, he pushed back his chair and stood up.

"Now that's what I call a sort of a supper," he said. He reared back his shoulders and strode from the room, never caring for Miz McLaughlin's sharp look that went after him. And the rest of us followed. We passed Sam leaning over the yard fence. "G'won, leave me alone," he spluttered.

Back at the corn pile we shucked and shucked. Presently the cold moon came up behind the barn and peered in our faces. Gus suggested another song, but I, who had grown mournful, said I didn't feel like it.

"And Sam's not here, anyhow," I said.

I was waiting and hoping she would come. Well, if she did she'd go and sit with somebody, not me, of course. The corn was dwindling away under our onslaught, we'd be through in a few minutes. Then I heard the tap of the latch in the gate, and

the shout that went up around the pile told me the girls were there. Through the edge of my eye I saw them come in. My heart pounded in my ribs and nearly stifled me, but I kept at my task, erect and with the gravity of a stolid Indian. I saw them settle themselves here and there along the pile with their different sweethearts. Ah, it was all so foolish anyhow. I didn't care, I didn't. Why'n thunder had I dressed up like a fool? Then a cool sweet voice spoke up behind me.

"Let me sit with you," she said.

I gripped the ear I was shucking. "There's maybe some room here," I answered casually, making a place for her.

"Uh-uh," Gus snorted, "red ears, where are you hiding!" And he went on making funny remarks, but I heard nothing now. Here she was, right here beside me, and she chose me before the rest. My head was swimming, and all the fine speeches I had planned were lost in a hazy dreaminess. Bless the Lord if a sort of sleepiness didn't soon come over me. What ailed me anyhow? Then I felt her soft hand against mine among the shucks. And fire raced all over me. But—well— she was reaching for an ear maybe, sure, that was all. We shucked away in silence. She would say nothing either. Once Gus stuck a red ear at me.

"Now's your chance," he said. But I made no reply and Gus threw the ear scornfully toward the barn.

"How's everything at your house?" she finally said.

"Well as common."

I wanted to talk out and laugh and cut up like the others, but something weighed me down like lead. I was happy, but something weighed me down. Once or twice she looked at me intently and then presently shivered and stood up. "It's cold here," she said, "and I better get my fascinator." She went out through the gate, and Laughing Gus lay back and roared with glee.

"What's all the fun?" a neighbor queried.

"The cat's got the bridegroom's tongue," he cackled.

Now if I but had a sledge hammer or rail-splitting maul I'd kill that Laughing Gus Brown. I wouldn't mind caving his head in, not a bit in this world. A flood of wretchedness came over me. I was the biggest fool that ever wore shoes, no doubt about it. Well, out I would go.

And I did. I stumbled up and went toward the lot gate. I would go home and go to bed where I belonged. Catcalls and merry gibes followed me out and cut me to the quick. With a sob in my throat I went toward the fence where my mule was tied. I began re-hitching him to the buggy. As I was ready to drive off, she came out of the gloom with her shawl around her.

"Where are you going?" she asked.

"They're about through now and I'd better go on."

"Don't go, we're going to play and have some music in a little bit."

"I better leave," I muttered, but I stood making no move.

She came closer and laid her hand on my arm. Mechanically I tied the mule again and stood by her, silent. There were no words to be had now, fool!

"The moon's so beautiful," she murmured, "let's go walking down the lane. We'll come right back."

We went along, and soon she took my arm.

"The wheel ruts make hard walking—so," she said.

The moon looked down with smiling face as we walked, and the fields lay wide and peaceful on either side. There in the hedgerow the flowers stood dead and sere from the early frost. The yarrow that Achilles knew held up its blistered hands, and the proud old mullein nodded its gray fuzzy dry head at us from the shadowy fence jambs. I felt it all rather than saw any of it.

"It's a beautiful night," she murmured again. "Look at the man in the moon!"

"And everything all around us," I answered foolishly and in a choking voice. At the turn of the lane we stopped and leaned against the fence. Presently she laid her hand on mine, and I caught it in a tight convulsive clutch.

"What's the matter?" she whispered. I looked down at her with shining eyes. "Oh, me!" she cried. And I put my arms gently around her then.

"That's all right, that's all right," I kept saying crazily. For a long while I held her so. Then more foolish words came stammering through my lips. "I've been thinking a whole lot. I'm gonna do something in this world, gonna be something somehow. I'll do it do it for you, you wait and see. They can laugh at me—I don't care—I'll—"

"They don't laugh at you." She leaned her head timidly against my shoulder and

I kissed her fabulous hair once.

"Let's go back," she said as if afraid. And I could feel her tremble. For a while we stood there, and then hand in hand we went up the lane toward the house. The music had already begun, the fiddle and banjo ringing out through the night. Boys and girls could be seen having fun on the porch. Near the barn I stopped and gestured around with a quick sweep of my arm.

"You know, I'm gonna do something."

"Yes, you will."

"I'm gonna write about all these things, make poems and such—tell 'em how purty—how beautiful it is—"

"Yes," she said, "yes, you will!"

And hand in hand again, we went on toward the house and toward our future together—as I foolishly believed.

MEET THE AUTHOR:
Paul Green (1894–1981)

No North Carolina writer is more revered than is Paul Green. A Lillington native, he grew up on a farm and first attended a one-room log schoolhouse "just across the creek" from his home. Green then walked each day to Buie's Creek Academy, three miles away, reading poetry "even as I marched." To earn money to attend UNC-Chapel Hill, he taught school. (In those days, a college degree was not required of teachers.) Once he got to the university, his education was interrupted by service in the U.S. Army during World War I, where he discovered "a lot of horror and waste and disillusionment."

Back at the university after the war, Green developed his writing skill, composing plays for the Carolina Playmakers under famed Professor Frederick Koch. An early play, *In Abraham's Bosom*, won the Pulitzer Prize. Other plays did well on Broadway, and eventually Hollywood recognized Paul Green's talents and called on him to write film scripts. He wrote over twenty, and called movies "one of the greatest means of story-telling ever invented."

Perhaps Green is best known for developing what he called "symphonic drama," or what we think of as "outdoor drama." His first was *The Lost Colony,* which has been produced at Manteo every summer since 1937 except for the World War II years. Blending historical fact, dramatic form, dance, pageantry, and music, *The Lost Colony* is produced in an open amphitheater during the summer season. Like most outdoor dramas, it is produced close to the site of the original historical event on which it is based.

Paul Green was also noted as an influential teacher and citizen. He lent his energies and his strong voice to many organizations and causes devoted to the arts and to social and economic justice. In addition to plays, he wrote five volumes of short stories. In 1965, he was presented the North Carolina Award for Literature.

Language Alert: Words and Their Kin

1. *sequent*: following in order (This is the adjective form of *sequence*, the noun which means "a following of one thing after another.")
2. *splurge*: to indulge in an extravagant or showy expense (We may speak of *splurging* all our money at the state fair, for example. We don't know the origin of this word. It's interesting that a number of verbs that begin with "spl" seem to have a similar mood. They all indicate lack of order and plan. Think of *splash, splatter, splat, splay, split,* and *splotch*.)
3. *stolid*: showing little or no emotion or sensitivity, unexcitable (We don't know the origin of this word, but it's interesting to note its resemblance to *stiff,* as in *stiff upper lip,* as well as to *solid*.)
4. *ruffian*: a tough or rowdy person (Although *ruffian* isn't derived from the same root as *rough,* don't you see similarities in meaning?)
5. *judicial*: having to do with courts of law (It's kin to *judge, judgment,* and *judicious*.)
6. *gravity*: seriousness. (Can you see *grave* embedded in *gravity*?)
7. *plaintive*: melancholy, expressing sorrow (This word is related to *complain*.)
8. *fascinator*: a scarf or shawl made of lace or net and worn by women, often on the head (Since it derives from the same word as *fascinate,* you can imagine what such a shawl is meant to do!)

Reflecting

From this story we get the flavor of the old-timey corn shucking. We know what it was like in the earlier part of this century—before World War I—to be a shy boy with big dreams and a crush on a girl.

We also get a good portrait of the young Paul Green—the things he did, his abilities, his dreams, his personality, his character. Reviewing both the story and the biographical profile, see what you can find about Paul Green the boy that shows us Paul Green the man.

Preview

Have you ever heard someone comment that "Mr. _____ has got a hard row to hoe"? That common North Carolina saying means that the person is going to have a tough time. In the following poem, the narrator describes what it was like to grow up on a mountain farm in the early years of this century—and the title gives us a clue.

The poem is written as a *dramatic monologue*—a poem in which a narrator tells a story. The speaker not only shows us how hard farm life was, but also how she schemed to make a better life for herself.

Twice, the son to whom she is speaking interrupts the mother's monologue—once at the beginning ("Did you like it?") and again near the end ("You really hated it then?"). Notice how his second question turns her thoughts in a different direction.

My Mother's Hard Row to Hoe

Fred Chappell

Hard, I say. Mostly I can't think how
To make it clear, the times have changed so much.
Maybe it's not possible to know
Now how we lived back then, it was such
A different life.
       "Did you like it?"
                I
Felt that I had to get away or die
Trying. I felt it wasn't me from dawn
To dawn, "slaving my fingers to the bone,"
As Mother used to say; and yet so bored
Because that world was just plain hard.

From *Midquest*, by Fred Chappell. Copyright © 1981 by Fred Chappell. Reprinted by permission of Louisiana State University Press.

Mother was always up at five o'clock,
Winter and summer, and jarred us out of bed
With her clanging milk cans and the knock
Of water in the pipes. Out to the shed
I went, and milked five cows and poured the milk
Into the cans—so rich it looked like silk
And smelled like fresh-cut grass. Then after that
The proper work-day started. I did what
She told me to, no never-mind how tired
I was, and never once did she run out,
Because that world was just plain hard.

Because from May through August we put up hay
And worked tobacco and, sure as you were born,
We'd find the hottest stillest July day
To start off in the bottom hoeing corn.
From the pear orchard to the creek's big bend,
Corn rows so long you couldn't see the end;
And never a breeze sprang up, never a breath
Of fresh, but all as still and close as death.
We hoed till dark. I was hoeing toward
A plan that would preserve my mental health,
Because that world was so almighty hard.

I'd get myself more schooling, and I'd quit
These fields forever where the hoe clanged stone
Wherever you struck, and the smell of chicken squat
Stayed always with you just like it was your own.
I felt I wasn't me, but some hired hand
Who was being underpaid to work the land,
Or maybe just a fancy farm machine
That had no soul and barely a jot of brain
And no more feelings than any cat in the yard
And not good sense to come out of the rain.
That world, I say, was just too grinding hard.

But I'd learn Latin and Spanish and French and math
And English literature. Geography.
I wouldn't care if I learned myself to death
At the University in Tennessee
So long as I could tell those fields goodbye
Forever, for good and all and finally.
—"You really hated it then?"
                          No, that's not true.
. . . Well, maybe I did. It's hard to know
Just how you feel about a place; a blurred
Mist-memory comes over it all blue
No matter if that place was flintrock hard.

There were some things I liked, of course there were:
I walked out in the morning with the air
All sweet and clean and promiseful and heard
A mourning dove— . . . *No! I couldn't care.*
You've got to understand how it was *hard.*

Fred Chappell (1936–   )

"I believe that writing is a sport like other sports; the more difficult the task, the more fun it becomes," Fred Chappell once remarked. He should know: he has published six novels, a collection of short stories, nearly a dozen volumes of poetry, and numerous book reviews and essays.

Fred Chappell grew up on a farm near Canton. In the eighth grade he began writing science fiction; the next year, he started writing poetry. Since receiving two degrees from Duke University, he has taught English and creative writing at UNC-Greensboro. His excellence as a teacher is praised by a large number of former students, including Kathryn Byer (p. 393), Stephen Smith (p. 391), Tom Hawkins (p. 567) and Anna Wooten-Hawkins (p. 439).

Many of Chappell's writings are based on experiences and observations made as he was growing up in the North Carolina mountains. His early interest in science fiction is reflected in some works which blend reality and fantasy in unusual ways. (See his story, "The Maker of One Coffin," p. 477.) His work has received nine state prizes, including the North Carolina Award in Literature, but recognition goes beyond this state. Chappell has also been honored with the

Bollingen Prize, one of the most important national awards for poetry, and even with a coveted international award from France. A book catalogue recently featured him as one of "America's Greatest Living Authors."

He is currently working on the fourth of a four-novel sequence which began in 1985 with *I Am One of You Forever*. In spite of his acclaim, he still strives to improve. "I'm trying to unlearn old habits—the worship of information rather than wisdom," he says. "I'm trying to read and listen more thoroughly and heighten my power to observe."

Language Alert

In his poetry, Fred Chappell often lets his characters speak in their natural mountain dialect. About that speech, he has said, "This is such a linguistic banquet for a writer. It's a regional speech that, if you work at it enough, has a real poetry to it." As you read this poem, notice the colloquial speech of mountain people—and how Chappell merges it with poetry.

Reflecting

1. <u>What</u> does the poem say?

   a. List the things that the speaker remembers as being "hard."
   b. How did she plan to escape?
   c. Perhaps you noticed how, in expressing her feelings, the speaker contradicted herself. First, she said that she didn't hate her early life, then admitted that maybe she did. She described some pleasant memories in serene, almost dream-like language, then broke into her reverie with an emphatic exclamation, arguing with her son, perhaps with herself, that "it was *hard*." It isn't unusual for people to have conflicting, even contradictory, feelings about a place, an event, or a person. Such feelings are called *ambivalent*. (Can you think of an experience or a place about which you feel ambivalent?)

2. <u>How</u> does the poem say it?

   a. Did you realize that the poem is rhymed? Sometimes the rhyme is very obvious, as in the second stanza when *milk* and *silk* end adjoining lines. Sometimes the rhyming lines are further apart (like *much* and *such* in the first stanza.) Sometimes the poet uses what is called *slant rhyme*: the words almost rhyme, but not quite—as in *how* and *know*, *dawn* and *bone*, or *bored* and *hard* in the first stanza. Because the rhyme is sometimes not quite perfect, the poem avoids a sing-songy sound, like a nursery rhyme. Instead, it sounds almost like natural speech.
   b. For emphasis, Fred Chappell uses a common poetic device: the repetition of a phrase or line at the end of a stanza, making what is called a **refrain**. The last line of every stanza has to do with "that world" being "hard." But to avoid monotony, no two lines are worded in exactly the same way. Do you like the variety?

A Blackjack Bargainer

O. Henry

Preview

This plot hinges on a situation that has inspired many a story or play: a feud between two families, leaving resentment and bloodshed in its wake. As a typical O. Henry story, it features a number of surprises, including the famous O. Henry ending—an ironic conclusion in which what happens is the opposite of what is expected.

As you read, watch for the moment when you begin to spot an ironic twist in the action. (Remember that readers not only absorb information from what they are reading at the moment; their minds are also busy predicting what will come next.)

The most disreputable thing in Yancey Goree's law office was Goree himself, sprawled in his creaky old armchair. The rickety little office, built of red brick, was set flush with the street—the main street of the town of Bethel.

Bethel rested upon the foot-hills of the Blue Ridge. Above it the mountains were piled to the sky. Far below it the turbid[1] Catawba gleamed yellow along its disconsolate valley.

The June day was at its sultriest hour. Bethel dozed in the tepid shade. Trade was not. It was so still that Goree, reclining in his chair, distinctly heard the clicking of the chips in the grand-jury room, where the "courthouse gang" was playing poker. From the open back door of the office a well-worn path meandered across the grassy lot to the court-house. The treading out of that path had cost Goree all he ever had—first inheritance of a few thousand dollars, next the old family home, and, latterly the last shreds of his self-respect and manhood. The "gang" had cleaned him out. The broken gam-

1. turbid: clouded, dirty

bler had turned drunkard and parasite; he had lived to see this day come when the man who had stripped him denied him a seat at the game. His word was no longer to be taken. The daily bouts at cards had arranged itself accordingly, and to him was assigned the ignoble part of the on-looker. The sheriff, the county clerk, a sportive deputy, a gay attorney, and a chalk-faced man hailing "from the valley," sat at table, and the sheared one was thus tacitly advised to go and grow more wool.

Soon wearying of his ostracism, Goree had departed for his office, muttering to himself as he unsteadily traversed the unlucky pathway. After a drink of corn whiskey from a demijohn under the table, he had flung himself into the chair, staring, in a sort of maudlin[2] apathy, out at the mountains immersed in the summer haze. The little white patch he saw away up on the side of Blackjack was Laurel, the village near which he had been born and bred. There, also, was the birthplace of the feud between the Gorees and the Coltranes. Now no direct heir of the Gorees survived except this plucked and singed bird of misfortune. To the Coltranes, also, but one male supporter was left—Colonel Abner Coltrane, a man of substance and standing, a member of the State Legislature, and a contemporary with Goree's father. The feud had been a typical one of the region; it had left a red record of hate, wrong and slaughter.

But Yancey Goree was not thinking of feuds. His befuddled brain was hopelessly attacking the problem of the future maintenance of himself and his favorite

follies. Of late, old friends of the family had seen to it that he had whereof to eat and a place to sleep, but whiskey they would not buy for him, and he must have whiskey. His law business was extinct; no case had been intrusted[3] to him in two years. He had been a borrower and a sponge, and it seemed that if he fell no lower it would be from lack of opportunity. One more chance—he was saying to himself—if he had one more stake at the game, he thought he could win; but he had nothing left to sell, and his credit was more than exhausted.

He could not help smiling, even in his misery, as he thought of the man to whom, six months before, he had sold the old Goree homestead. There had come from "back yan' " in the mountains two of the strangest creatures, a man named Pike Garvey and his wife. "Back yan'," with a wave of the hand toward the hills, was understood among the mountaineers to designate the remotest fastnesses, the unplumbed gorges, the haunts of law-breakers, the wolf's den, and the boudoir of the bear. In the cabin far up on Black-jack's shoulder, in the wildest part of these retreats, this odd couple had lived for twenty years. They had neither dog nor children to mitigate the heavy silence of the hills. Pike Garvey was little known in the settlements, but all who had dealt with him pronounced him "crazy as a loon." He acknowledged no occupation save that of a squirrel hunter, but he

2. maudlin: mushy, overemotional

3. intrusted: variant spelling of *entrusted.*

"moonshined"[4] occasionally by way of diversion. Once the "revenues"[5] had dragged him from his lair, fighting silently and desperately like a terrier, and he had been sent to state's prison for two years. Released, he popped back into his hole like an angry weasel.

Fortune, passing over many anxious wooers, made a freakish flight into Blackjack's bosky pockets to smile upon Pike and his faithful partner.

One day a party of spectacled, knickerbockered, and altogether absurd prospectors invaded the vicinity of the Garveys' cabin. Pike lifted his squirrel rifle off the hooks and took a shot at them at long range on the chance of their being revenues. Happily he missed, and the unconscious agents of good luck drew nearer, disclosing their innocence of anything resembling law or justice. Later on, they offered the Garveys on enormous quantity of ready, green, crisp money for their thirty-acre patch of cleared land, mentioning, as an excuse for such a mad action, some irrelevant and inadequate nonsense about a bed of mica underlying the said property.

When the Garveys became possessed of so many dollars that they faltered in computing them, the deficiencies of life on Blackjack began to grow prominent. Pike began to talk of new shoes, a hogshead of tobacco to set in the corner, a new lock to his rifle; and, leading Martella to a certain spot on the mountain-side, he pointed out to her how a small cannon—doubtless a thing not beyond the scope of their fortune in price—might be planted so as to command and defend the sole ac-cessible trail to the cabin, to the confusion of revenues and meddling strangers forever.

But Adam reckoned without his Eve. These things represented to him the applied power of wealth, but there slumbered in his dingy cabin an ambition that soared far above his primitive wants. Somewhere in Mrs. Garvey's bosom still survived a spot of feminity unstarved by twenty years of Blackjack. For so long a time the sounds in her ears had been the scaly-barks dropping in the woods at noon, and the wolves singing among the rocks at night, and it was enough to have purged her vanities. She had grown fat and sad and yellow and dull. But when the means came, she felt a rekindled desire to assume the perquisites[6] of her sex—to sit at tea tables; to buy inutile[7] things; to whitewash the hideous veracity of life with a little form and ceremony. So she coldly vetoed Pike's proposed system of fortifications, and announced that they would descend upon the world, and gyrate socially.

And thus, at length, it was decided, and the thing done. The village of Laurel was their compromise between Mrs. Garvey's preference for one of the large valley towns and Pike's hankering for primeval

4. "moonshined": made illegal whiskey

5. "revenues": revenuers, agents of the U.S. Department of the Treasury. They often were employed to seek out and arrest "moonshiners."

6. perquisites: extra benefits

7. inutile: useless

236

solitudes. Laurel yielded a halting round of feeble social distractions comportable[8] with Martella's ambition, and was not entirely without recommendation to Pike, its contiguity[9] to the mountains presenting advantages for sudden retreat in case fashionable society should make it advisable.

Their descent upon Laurel had been coincident with Yancey Goree's feverish desire to convert property into cash, and they bought the old Goree homestead, paying four thousand dollars ready money into the spendthrift's shaking hands.

Thus it happened that while the disreputable last of the Gorees sprawled in his disreputable office, at the end of his row, spurned by the cronies whom he had gorged, strangers dwelt in the halls of his fathers.

A cloud of dust was rolling slowly up the parched street, with something travelling in the midst of it. A little breeze wafted the cloud to one side, and a new, brightly painted carryall, drawn by a slothful gray horse, became visible. The vehicle deflected from the middle of the street as it neared Goree's office, and stopped in the gutter directly in front of his door.

On the front seat sat a gaunt, tall man, dressed in black broadcloth, his rigid hands incarcerated in yellow kid gloves. On the back seat was a lady who triumphed over the June heat. Her stout form was armoured in a skin-tight silk dress of the description known as "changeable," being a gorgeous combination of shifting hues. She sat erect, waving a much-ornamented fan, with her eyes fixed stonily far down the street. However Martella Garvey's heart might be rejoicing at the pleasures of her new life, Blackjack had done his work with her exterior. He had carved her countenance to the image of emptiness and inanity;[10] had imbued her with the stolidity of his crags, and the reserve of his hushed interiors. She always seemed to hear, whatever her surroundings were, the scaly-barks falling and pattering down the mountainside. She could always hear the awful silence of Blackjack sounding through the stillest of nights.

Goree watched this solemn equipage,[11] as it drove to his door, with only faint interest; but when the lank driver wrapped the reins about his whip, and awkwardly descended, and stepped into the office, he rose unsteadily to receive him, recognizing Pike Garvey, the new, the transformed, the recently civilized.

The mountaineer took the chair Goree offered him. They who cast doubts upon Garvey's soundness of mind had a strong witness in the man's countenance. His face was too long, a dull saffron in hue, and immobile as a statue's. Pale-blue, unwinking round eyes without lashes added to the singularity of his gruesome visage. Goree was at a loss to account for the visit.

8. comportable: agreeing with, supporting

9. contiguity: nearness

10. inanity: something that is stupid or pointless

11. equipage: a carriage, especially one with horses and uniformed servants

"Everything all right at Laurel, Mr. Garvey?" he inquired.

"Everything all right, sir, and mighty pleased is Missis Garvey and me with the property. Missis Garvey likes yo' old place, and she likes the neighborhood. Society is what she 'lows she wants, and she is gettin' of it. The Rogerses, the Hapgoods, the Pratts, and the Troys hev been to see Missis Garvey, and she hev et meals to most of thar houses. The best folks hev axed her to differ'nt kinds of doin's. I cyan't say, Mr. Goree, that sech things suits me—fur me, give me them thar." Garvey's huge, yellow-gloved hand flourished in the direction of the mountains. "That's whar I b'long, 'mongst the wild honey bees and the b'ars. But that ain't what I come fur to say, Mr. Goree. Thar's somethin' you got what me and Missis Garvey wants to buy."

"Buy!" echoed Goree. "From me?" Then he laughed harshly. "I reckon you are mistaken about that. I reckon you are mistaken about that. I sold out to you, as you yourself expressed it, 'lock, stock and barrel.' There isn't even a ramrod left to sell."

"You've got it; and we 'uns want it. 'Take the money,' says Missis Garvey, 'and buy it fa'r and squar'.'"

Goree shook his head. "The cupboard's bare," he said.

"We've riz," pursued the mountaineer, undeflected from his object, "a heap. We was pore as possums, and now we could have folks to dinner every day. We been reco'nized, Missis Garvey says, by the best society. But there's somethin' we need we ain't got. She says it ought to been put in

the 'ventory ov the sale, but it tain't thar. 'Take the money, then,' she says, 'and buy it fa'r and squar'.'"

"Out with it," said Goree, his racked nerves growing impatient.

Garvey threw his slouch hat upon the table, and leaned forward, fixing his unblinking eyes upon Goree's.

"There's a old feud," he said distinctly and slowly, " 'tween you 'uns and the Coltranes."

Goree frowned ominously. To speak of his feud to a feudist is a serious breach of the mountain etiquette. The man from "back yan' " knew it as well as the lawyer did.

"Na offense," he went on, "but purely in the way of business. Missis Garvey hev studied all about feuds. Most of the quality folks in the mountains hev 'em. The Settles and the Goforths, the Rankins and the Boyds, the Silers and the Galloways, hev al been cyarin' on feuds f'om twenty to a hundred year. The last man to drap was when yo' uncle, Jedge Paisley Goree, 'journed co't and shot Len Coltrane f'om the bench. Missis Garvey and me, we come f'om the po' white trash. Nobody wouldn't pick a feud with we 'uns, no mo'n with a fam'ly of tree-toads. Quality people everywhar, says Missis Garvey, has feuds. We 'uns ain't quality, but we're buyin' into it as fur as we can. 'Take the money, then,' says Missis Garvey, 'and buy Mr. Goree's feud, fa'r and squar'.'"

The squirrel hunter straightened a leg half across the room, drew a roll of bills from his pocket, and threw them on the table.

"That's two hundred dollars, Mr. Goree; what you would call a fa'r price for a feud that's been 'lowed to run down like yourn hev. Thar's only you left to cyar' on yo' side of it, and you'd make mighty po' killin'. I'll take it off yo' hands, and it'll set me and Missis Garvey up among the quality. Thar's the money."

The little roll of currency on the table slowly untwisted itself, writhing and jumping as its folds relaxed. In the silence that followed Garvey's last speech the rattling of the poker chips in the courthouse could be plainly heard. Goree knew that the sheriff had just won a pot, for the subdued whoop with which he always greeted a victory floated across the square upon the crinkly heat waves. Beads of moisture stood on Goree's brow. Stopping, he drew the wicker-covered demijohn from under the table, and filled a tumbler from it.

"A little corn liquor, Mr. Garvey? Of course you are joking about—what you spoke of? Opens quite a new market, doesn't it? Feuds, prime, two-fifty to three. Feuds, slightly damaged—two hundred, I believe you said, Mr. Garvey?"

Goree laughed self-consciously.

The mountaineer took the glass Goree handed him, and drank the whisky without a tremor of the lids of his staring eyes. The lawyer applauded the feat by a look of envious admiration. He poured his own drink, and took it like a drunkard, by gulps, and with shudders at the smell and taste.

"Two hundred," repeated Garvey. "Thar's the money."

A sudden passion flared up in Goree's brain. He struck the table with his fist.

One of the bills flipped over and touched his hand. He flinched as if something had stung him.

"Do you come to me," he shouted, "seriously with such a ridiculous, insulting, darned-fool proposition?"

"It's fa'r and squar'," said the squirrel hunter, but he reached out his hand as if to take back the money; and then Goree knew that his own flurry of rage had not been from pride or resentment, but from anger at himself, knowing that he would set foot in the deeper depths that were being opened to him. He turned in an instant from an outraged gentleman to an anxious chafferer[12] recommending his goods.

"Don't be in a hurry, Garvey," he said, his face crimson and his speech thick. "I accept your p-p-proposition, though it's dirt cheap at two hundred. A t-trade's all right when both p-purchaser and b-buyer are s-satisfied. Shall I w-wrap it up for you, Mr. Garvey?"

Garvey rose, and shook out his broadcloth. "Missis Garvey will be pleased. You air out of it, and it stands Coltrane and Garvey. Just a scrap ov writin', Mr. Goree, you bein' a lawyer, to show we traded."

Goree seized a sheet of paper and a pen. The money was clutched in his moist hand. Everything else suddenly seemed to grow trivial and light.

"Bill of sale, by all means. 'Right, title, and interest in and to' . . . 'forever warrant and—' No, Garvey, we'll have to leave out that 'defend,' " said Goree with a loud

12. chafferer: bargainer

laugh. "You'll have to defend this title yourself."

The mountaineer received the amazing screed that the lawyer handed him, folded it with immense labour, and placed it carefully in his pocket.

Goree was standing near the window. "Step here," he said, raising his finger, "and I'll show you your recently purchased enemy. There he goes, down the other side of the street."

The mountaineer crooked his long frame to look through the window in the direction indicated by the other. Colonel Abner Coltrane, an erect, portly gentleman of about fifty, wearing the inevitable long, double-breasted frock coat of the Southern lawmaker, and an old high silk hat, was passing on the opposite sidewalk. As Garvey looked, Goree glanced at his face. If there be such a thing as a yellow wolf, here was its counterpart. Garvey snarled as his unhuman eyes followed the moving figure, disclosing long-amber-coloured fangs.

"Is that him? Why, that's the man who sent me to the pen'tentiary once!"

"He used to be district attorney," said Goree carelessly. "And, by the way, he's a first-class shot."

"I kin hit a squirrel's eye at a hundred yard," said Garvey. "So that thar's Coltrane! I made a better trade than I was thinkin'. I'll take keer ov this feud, Mr. Goree, better'n you ever did!"

He moved toward the door, but lingered there, betraying a slight perplexity.

"Anything else to-day?" inquired Goree with frothy sarcasm. "Any family traditions, ancestral ghosts, or skeletons in the closet? Prices as low as the lowest."

"Thar was another thing," replied the unmoved squirrel hunter, "that Missis Garvey was thinkin' of. 'Tain't so much in my line as t'other, but she wanted partic'lar that I should inquire, and ef you was willin', 'pay fur it,' she says, 'fa'r and squar'.' Thar's a buryin' groun', as you know, Mr. Goree, in the yard of yo' old place, under the cedars. Them that lies thar is yo' folks what was killed by the Coltranes. The monyments had the names on 'em. Miss Garvey says a fam'ly buryin' groun' is a sho' sign of quality. She says ef we git the feud, thar's somethin' else ought to go with it. The names on them monyments is 'Goree,' but they can be changed to ourn by—"

"Go! Go!" screamed Goree, his face turning purple. He stretched out both hands toward the mountaineer, his fingers hooked and shaking. "Go, you ghoul! Even a ch-Chinaman protects the g-graves of his ancestors—go!"

The squirrel hunter slouched out of the door to his carryall. While he was climbing over the wheel Goree was collecting, with feverish celerity, the money that had fallen from his hand to the floor. As the vehicle slowly turned about, the sheep, with a coat of newly grown wool, was hurrying, in indecent haste, along the path to the court-house.

At three o'clock in the morning they brought him back to his office, shorn and unconscious. The sheriff, the sportive deputy, the county clerk, and the gay attorney carried him, the chalk-faced man "from the valley" acting as escort.

"On the table," said one of them, and they deposited him there among the litter of his unprofitable books and papers.

"Yance thinks a lot of a pair of deuces when he's liquored up," sighed the sheriff reflectively.

"Too much," said the gay attorney. "A man has no business to play poker who drinks as much as he does. I wonder how much he dropped to-night."

"Close to two hundred. What I wonder is whar he got it. Yance ain't had a cent fur over a month, I know."

"Struck a client, maybe. Well, let's get home before daylight. He'll be all right when he wakes up, except for a sort of beehive about the cranium."

The gang slipped away through the early morning twilight. The next eye to gaze upon the miserable Goree was the orb of day. He peered through the uncurtained window, first deluging the sleeper in a flood of faint gold, but soon pouring upon the mottled red of his flesh a searching, white, summer heat. Goree stirred, half unconsciously, among the table's débris, and turned his face from the window. His movement dislodged a heavy law book, which crashed upon the floor. Opening his eyes, he saw, bending over him, a man in a black frock coat. Looking higher, he discovered a well-worn silk hat, and beneath it the kindly, smooth face of Colonel Abner Coltrane.

A little uncertain of the outcome, the colonel waited for the other to make some sign of recognition. Not in twenty years had male members of these two families faced each other in peace. Goree's eyelids puckered as he strained his blurred sight toward this visitor, and then he smiled serenely.

"Have you brought Stella and Lucy over to play?" he said calmly.

"Do you know me, Yancey?" asked Coltrane.

"Our course I do. You brought me a whip with a whistle in the end."

So he had—twenty-four years ago; when Yancey's father was his best friend.

Goree's eyes wandered about the room. The colonel understood. "Lie still, and I'll bring you some," said he. There was a pump in the yard at the rear, and Goree closed his eyes, listening with rapture to the click of its handle, and the bubbling of the falling stream. Coltrane brought a pitcher of the cool water, and held it for him to drink. Presently Goree sat up—a most forlorn object, his summer suit of flax soiled and crumpled, his discreditable head tousled and unsteady. He tried to wave one of his hands toward the colonel.

"Ex-excuse—everything, will you?" he said. "I must have drunk too much whiskey last night, and gone to bed on the table." His brows knitted into a puzzled frown.

"Out with the boys a while?" asked Coltrane kindly.

"No, I went nowhere. I haven't had a dollar to spend in the last two months. Struck the demijohn too often. I reckon, as usual."

Colonel Coltrane touched him on the shoulder.

"A little while ago, Yancey," he began, "you asked me if I had brought Stella and Lucy over to play. You weren't quite awake then, and must have been dreaming you were a boy again. You are awake now, and I want you to listen to me. I have come from Stella and Lucy to their old playmate, and to my old friend's son. They know that I am going to bring you home with me, and you will find them as ready with a welcome as they were in the old days. I want you to come to my house and stay until you are yourself again, and as much longer as you will. We heard of your being down in the world, and in the midst of temptation, and we agreed that you should come over and play at our house once more. Will you come, my boy? Will you drop our old family trouble and come with me?"

"Trouble!" said Goree, opening his eyes wide. "There was never any trouble between us that I know of. I'm sure we've always been the best friends. But, good Lord, Colonel, how could I go to your home as I am—a drunken wretch, a miserable, degraded spendthrift and gambler———"

He lurched from the table into his armchair, and began to weep maudlin tears, mingled with genuine drops of remorse and shame. Coltrane talked to him persistently and reasonably, reminding him of the simple mountain pleasures of which he had once been so fond, and insisting upon the genuineness of the invitation.

Finally he landed Goree by telling him he was counting upon his help in the engineering and transportation of a large amount of felled timber from a high mountainside to a waterway. He knew that Goree had once invented a device for this purpose—a series of slides and chutes—upon which he had justly prided himself. In an instant the poor fellow, delighted at the idea of his being of use to any one, had paper spread upon the table, and was drawing rapid but pitifully shaky lines in demonstration of what he could and would do.

The man was sickened of the husks; his prodigal heart was turning again toward the mountains. His mind was yet strangely clogged, and his thoughts and memories were returning to his brain one by one, like carrier pigeons over a stormy sea. But Coltrane was satisfied with the progress he had made.

Bethel received the surprise of its existence that afternoon when a Coltrane and a Goree rode amicably together through the town. Side by side they rode, out from the dusty streets and gaping townspeople, down across the creek bridge, and up toward the mountain. The prodigal had brushed and washed and combed himself to a more decent figure, but he was unsteady in the saddle, and he seemed to be deep in the contemplation of some vexing problem. Coltrane left him in his mood, relying upon the influence of changed surroundings to restore his equilibrium.

Once Goree was seized with a shaking fit, and almost came to a collapse. He had to dismount and rest at the side of the road. The colonel, foreseeing such a condition, had provided a small flask of whisky for the journey but when it was offered to him Goree refused it almost with violence, declaring he would never touch it again. By and by he was recovered, and went quietly enough for a mile or two. Then he pulled up his horse suddenly, and said:

"I lost two hundred dollars last night, playing poker. Now, where did I get that money?"

"Take it easy, Yancey. The mountain air will soon clear it up. We'll go fishing, first thing, at the Pinnacle Falls. The trout are jumping there like bullfrogs. We'll take Stella and Lucy along, and have a picnic on Eagle Rock. Have you forgotten how a hickory-cured-ham sandwich tastes, Yancey, to a hungry fisherman?"

Evidently the colonel did not believe the story of his lost wealth; so Goree retired again into brooding silence.

By late afternoon they had travelled ten of the twelve miles between Bethel and Laurel. Half a mile this side of Laurel lay the old Goree place; a mile or two beyond the village lived the Coltranes. The road was now steep and laborious, but the compensations were many. The tilted aisles of the forest were opulent with leaf and bird and bloom. The tonic air put to shame the pharmacopæia. The glades were dark with mossy shade, and bright with shy rivulets winking from the ferns and laurels. On the lower side they viewed, framed in the near foliage, exquisite sketches of the far valley swooning in its opal haze.

Coltrane was pleased to see that his companion was yielding to the spell of the hills and woods. For now they had but to skirt the base of Painter's Cliff; to cross Elder branch and mount the hill beyond, and Goree would have to face the squandered home of his fathers. Every rock he passed, every tree, every foot of the roadway, was familiar to him. Through he had forgotten the woods, they thrilled him like the music of *"Home, Sweet Home."*

They rounded the cliff, descended into Elder Branch, and paused there to let the horses drink and splash in the swift water. On the right was a rail fence that cornered there, and followed the road and stream. Inclosed by it was the old apple orchard of the home place; the house was yet concealed by the brow of the steep hill. Inside and along the fence, pokeberries, elders, sassafras, and sumac grew high and dense. At a rustle of their branches, both Goree and Coltrane glanced up, and saw a long, yellow, wolfish face above the fence, staring at them with pale, unwinking eyes. The head quickly disappeared; there was a violent swaying of the bushes, and an ungainly figure ran up through the apple orchard in the direction of the house, zig-zagging among the trees.

"That's Garvey,"said Coltrane; "the man you sold out to. There's no doubt but he's considerably cracked. I had to send him up for moonshining once, several years ago, in spite of the fact that I believed him irresponsible. Why, what's the matter, Yancey?"

Goree was wiping his forehead, and his face had lost its color. "Do I look queer, too?" he asked, trying to smile. "I'm just remembering a few more things." Some of the alcohol had evaporated from his brain. "I recollect now where I got that two hundred dollars."

"Don't think of it," said Coltrane cheerfully. "Later on we'll figure it all out together."

They rode out of the branch, and when they reached the foot of the hill Goree stopped again.

"Did you ever suspect I was a very vain kind of fellow, Colonel?" he asked. "Sort of foolish proud about appearances?"

The colonel's eyes refused to wander to the soiled, sagging suit of flax and the faded slouch hat.

"It seems to me," he replied, mystified, but humouring him, "I remember a young buck about twenty, with the tightest coat, the sleekest hair, and the prancingest saddle horse in the Blue Ridge."

"Right you are," said Goree eagerly. "And it's in me yet, though it don't show. Oh, I'm as vain as a turkey gobbler, and as proud as Lucifer. I'm going to ask you to indulge this weakness of mine in a little matter."

"Speak out, Yancey. We'll create you Duke of Laurel and Baron of Blue Ridge, if you choose; and you shall have a feather out of Stella's peacock's tail to wear in your hat."

"I'm in earnest. In a few minutes we'll pass the house up there on the hill where I was born, and where my people have lived for nearly a century. Strangers live there now—and look at me! I am about to show myself to them ragged and poverty-stricken, a wastrel and a beggar. Colonel Coltrane, I'm ashamed to do it. I want you to let me wear your coat and hat until we are out of sight beyond. I know you think it a foolish pride, but I want to make as good a showing as I can when I pass the old place."

"Now, what does this mean?" said Coltrane to himself, as he compared his companion's sane looks and quiet demeanour with his strange request. But he was already unbuttoning the coat, assenting readily, as if the fancy were in no wise to be considered strange.

The coat and hat fitted Goree well. He buttoned the former about him with a look of satisfaction and dignity. He and Coltrane were nearly the same size—rather tall, portly, and erect. Twenty-five years were between them, but in appearance they might have been brothers. Goree looked older than his age; his face was puffy and lined; the colonel had the smooth, fresh complexion of a temperate liver. He put on Goree's disreputable old flax coat and faded slouch hat.

"Now," said Goree, taking up the reins, "I'm all right. I want you to ride bout ten feet in the rear as we go by, Colonel, so that they can get a good look at me. They'll see I'm no back number yet, by any means. I guess I'll show up pretty well to them once more, anyhow. Let's ride on."

He set out up the hill at a smart trot,

the colonel following, as he had been requested.

Goree sat straight in the saddle, with head erect, but his eyes were turned to the right, sharply scanning every shrub and fence and hiding-place in the old homestead yard. Once he muttered to himself, "Will the crazy fool try it, or did I dream half of it?"

It was then he came opposite the little family burying ground that he saw what he had been looking for—a puff of white smoke, coming from the thick cedars in one corner. He toppled so slowly to the left that Coltrane had time to urge his horse to that side, and catch him with one arm.

The squirrel hunter had not over-praised his aim. He had sent the bullet where he intended, and where Goree had expected that it would pass—through the breast of colonel Abner Coltrane's black frock coat.

Goree leaned heavily against Coltrane, but he did not fall. The horses kept pace, side by side, and the Colonel's arm kept him steady. The little white houses of Laurel shone through the trees, half a mile away. Goree reached out one hand and groped until it rested upon Coltrane's fingers, which held his bridle.

"Good friend," he said, and that was all.

Thus did Yancey Goree, as he rode past his old home, make, considering all things, the best showing that was in his power.

O. Henry (William Sydney Porter) (1862–1910)

At the turn of this century, no short story writer enjoyed more popularity than William Sydney Porter, a North Carolina native known to the world as O. Henry. Even today, more than eight decades after his death, his best stories are anthologized.

Porter's life was as interesting as any story he ever wrote. Born close to Polecat Creek near Greensboro, he left school at fifteen to work in his uncle's drugstore. Even at that early age, he had already developed an interest in writing and drawing, and enjoyed a local reputation as a cartoonist. When he was nineteen he went to Texas where he worked on a cattle ranch, then in a bank, then as publisher/editor/writer of a humor publication, *The Rolling Stone*. But then came a jolt. He was arrested for stealing funds from the bank where he had worked. Whether he was an embezzler or merely a poor bookkeeper is still a matter of some dispute, but he was convicted.

It was while in prison that "O. Henry" was born as a name under which Porter wrote and published a number of short stories. Released in 1901, he went to New York, where his fame—and his fortune—as a writer grew, and where he spent money almost as fast as he earned it. He died in 1910, and was buried in Riverside Cemetery near Asheville.

Language Alert

Although the plot is easy to understand, two factors may make this story harder to read than many contemporary stories:

1. When the uneducated Pike Garvey speaks, his language is spelled to reflect his pronunciation. (If you've ever seen a rerun of the old "Gomer Pyle" television series, you're familiar with the dialect, so try to read Pike's speeches as Gomer would.)

2. In contrast to Pike Garvey, William Sydney Porter himself had a very broad vocabulary and loved to use formal, even elegant language. Many of the unfamiliar words will become clear in context.

Reflecting

1. Many readers loved O. Henry's stories—especially the surprise endings. Others have criticized him for being too sentimental. Do you find the ending of this story unrealistic and sentimental—or realistic and inspiring? Be able to explain your reasons.

2. This can be called a story of *redemption*. Look up the word in a good dictionary and see if you agree.

O. Henry (William Sydney Porter) worked at W. C. Porter's Drug Store in Greensboro when he was a boy. This reproduction is now part of the Greensboro Historical Museum.

Tall Tales

Almost everybody loves a tall tale—a story so exaggerated and fantastic that there is no mistaking it for reality. Fishermen often compose tall tales about "the one that got away." (Since it got away, there's no way of telling how big it really was or what a fight it put forth!) In our early days, the tall tale was a favorite from of story-telling. Telling "whoppers" whiled away many a long evening by campfire or lamplight, and the exaggerated details often provided good comedy.

The following tales have been collected by two authors.

The Blizzard of '98

Ellis Credle

Preview

At one time or another, almost everyone exaggerates about the weather—the hottest day, the heaviest rainfall, the driest summer, the strongest wind, the deepest snowfall. Try to recall some of the fantastic claims you have heard friends or relatives make about the weather. "It was so cold that . . . ," "It rained so hard that. . . ."

Hank Huggins sat on the porch of his cabin one cold March day, with his feet propped on the rail. He was looking out over the long ranges of the Blue Ridge Mountains.

"Cold enough for you, Hank?" asked a neighbor who had stopped to borrow a pint of lamp oil.

"Why, no," said Hank. "My mind was just working back to the blizzard of '98. Folks that didn't see that blizzard haven't got any idea of what cold weather is." Hank settled himself for the following tale.

"It came on suddenly. One minute, it was near about as warm as summer. The next, everything was frozen stiff and hanging with icicles a foot long. Some cattle that were a-pasturing out on a hillside right near my cabin piled up on top of one another to get warm. They froze into a pyramid as hard as a rock. But the freakiest thing I ever heard of was what happened to my old lady.

"I was across the valley, where you see that cabin with the smoke a-rising from the chimney. A-walking, it's a mighty far piece over there. But as the crow flies, it's near, within hollering distance. Well, sir, when my wife saw the sky darkening all of a sudden and heard the wind whistling down from the high peaks, it scarified her half outen her wits. She ran into the front yard and yelled across the valley for me to come home.

"I was a-standing in the front yard across the way. I saw her come into our yard. I saw her jaws a-working like she was talking. But I never heard a sound. Anyway, one look at the weather told me I'd never get home before the storm broke. I hustled into the house with my neighbor and we slammed the door. Well, sir, just as I told you, it was a blizzard to end all blizzards.

"After the worst was over, the sun came out. I set off for home. Everything was coated with ice and a-glittering like crystal. I slid downwards through a glass forest and chipped my way up the other side. Everything you looked at was like an ornament to put on the mantelpiece.

"When I got home, the old lady was in a temper. 'Why didn't you answer when I called you?' she shouted at me as I came in the door. "Seems you could have said yes or no or something!"

" 'I didn't hear you say anything,' I threw back at her.

" 'Don't tell me you didn't hear anything!' she cried. 'I've been hollering across that valley too many years to think I couldn't make myself heard!'

"Well, we talked it back and forth, she claiming that she hollered for me, I allowing that she never made a sound. We were still at it hot and heavy when a queer noise in the air made us stop stock-still. At first it sounded like an old phonograph record starting off slow-like. Then it picked up. And out there in the blue air, between the two mountains, came a shout, 'Hank! You, Hank Huggi-i-ns! Look at the sky! It's a-going to snow! You come on right now before you get caught away from home!'

"It was my old lady's voice—to the life. And she hadn't said a word! We looked at each other, our eyes fairly popping. 'They're my very words!' she whispered as though she'd heard a ghost. 'They're the very words I hollered when the blizzard was a-blowing down!'

"Well, sir, for a minute there, my brains were fairly scattered. I didn't know what to think. Then it came to me.

" 'Why, of course,' I said. 'Can't you see what happened? That blizzard was so cold and it came up so suddenly that it froze your words in mid-air. They never got to the other side. Now, with the weather warming up, they've thawed out.' "

"Well, Hank," said the neighbor, picking up his bottle of lamp oil, and setting off down the path, "I agree with you. The folks that missed that blizzard don't know what cold weather really is!"

MEET THE AUTHOR:
Ellis Credle (1902–   )

Born in Sladesville in Hyde County, Ellis Credle has traveled far from her native eastern North Carolina. She has lived and worked in the Blue Ridge Mountains, New York City, and, most recently, in Mexico. An artist as well as a writer, she is noted not only for her books for young readers, which have been named Junior Literary Guild selections, but also for her illustrations. One book, *Down, Down the Mountain*, was the first picture book to feature Blue Ridge mountaineers. After World War II, it was translated into Japanese and was among the books used by General Douglas MacArthur's occupation forces to show the Japanese what American life was like.

Ms. Credle began creating her own books for young readers when she realized that the children for whom she was a governess preferred the stories she made up to the stories she read from their library. She first does research on the history and economic conditions of the location in which the story takes place—even for books written for children under six years old. "I find that plot and incident and action are often suggested by living conditions, economic problems, and local customs," she explains.

Over her long career she has created over twenty such books as well as a novel for adults. In May 1989, at the age of 87, she was working on another book, *Chicken Feed and Treasure*, set in Kitty Hawk, North Carolina, as well as a novel for adults. Recognizing her advanced age, she wrote, "This adult novel may never come off the press. If not, I can only say that I have had a good time writing it, so it hasn't been wasted time, has it?"

Language Alert

Ellis Credle lets mountain characters tell the tall tales in their own dialect. You won't find difficult words in the stories, but unless you and/or your family have lived in the Appalachian Mountains you may find some unfamiliar terms. Just try reading the story through, keeping in your mind (and ear!) the rural mountain accent, and see if the meanings don't come clear to you.

Reflecting

1. Can you mark the place in each story where realism fades and fantasy takes over?
2. It has been said that the heart of comedy is *incongruity*—that is, things are put together that don't belong together. (The old slip-on-the-banana-peel sight gag is most hilarious if a pompous, stuffy, conceited person does the slipping. It isn't funny at all if a crippled old woman slips.) What details in this story are incongruous—that is, they go against our expectations or our notion of what the real world is like?

Twelve Tall Tales from Wilkes County

John E. (Frail) Jones

Preview

In 1972, John Joines's son, Jerry D. Joines, collected twelve of his father's stories and submitted them to *North Carolina Folkore*, a publication from Appalachian State University. His collection won the first prize for student work submitted to the magazine that year. A native of Wilkes County, Jerry D. Joines attended the public schools there, then went to UNC-Chapel Hill, where he majored in zoology.

Jerry Joines recorded these tales just as his father told them to him, adding a preface about his father, the storyteller. As with Ellis Credle's tales, the colorful language adds a great deal to the plot and details. Notice that the stories deal with four different subjects:
1. Tales 1–6: smart dogs—first a bird dog, then a coon dog.
2. Tales 7–8: superhuman feats
3. Tale 9: the weather (Notice the similarity to "The Blizzard of '98.")
4. Tales 10–12: cats

John E. Joines, the source of these tales, is my father and a resident of Wilkes County, North Carolina. He was born 1914 in the Brushy Mountains community of Brocktown near Moravian Falls, a part of the county not until recent years approached by modernization. Brocktown is about ten miles south of Wilkesboro in the vicinity of Pore's Knob, highest mountain in the area and site of a lookout tower.

Many of the older people of the area grew up in genuine Appalachian mountain tradition. My father was and is a part

Collected by Jerry D. Joines. Published in *North Carolina Folklore*, February 1972.

of this tradition and retains a great many songs and stories that have come to his attention in the past. He enjoys talking and singing, and his stories and songs are so familiar to him that they are almost commonplace. He has heard most of them for as long as he can remember, and he has made no special effort either to learn or remember material.

In his early years, he worked at a number of jobs, including farming, sawmilling, orchard work, and horse-breaking. It is significant that his favorite pastime is, and has always been, hunting. His experience with dogs and game enables him to tell detailed stories which capture the listener's belief until the lie is revealed at the end.

The twelve tales which follow are given in precisely the order in which he related them to me in March and April, 1971.

ONE. Did I ever tell you about that old bird dog I used to own? I guess he's about the best old dog that anybody ever hunted after. I know one time I had 'im out goin' out through the field with 'im, and I had an old single-barrelled gun and he went into a briar patch and he pointed a covey of birds. I told him to flush 'em, and out come one bird and I killed it, and loaded my gun back, and when I got it loaded out come another bird. I shot it and loaded my gun back and out come another bird. And after I'd killed about five or six birds I got to wonderin' how he's a-lettin' one bird fly at a time, how he's a-flushin' one instead of the whole covey. So I got to lookin', and he'd pointed 'em in a stump hole and ever' time I'd load my gun he'd pull his foot off and let a bird fly out, and

then he'd slap his foot back over the hole till I loaded my gun back.

TWO. I's a-huntin' one day and a bunch of kids were playin' down on the bank and he [my old dog] run down to where they was a-playin' and come to a full point, and I thinks, "Why, you're crazy, they ain't no birds there, and them kids playin' there on the bank." I got to lookin', and one of the little old boys had on a shirt made out of a Bob-White flour sack, and he had the bob-white on his shirt pointed.

THREE. And when I's out one time it come a big rain and the creek was up pretty deep, and goin' up the creek bank and he [the bird dog] run up to the end of a log and pointed at the log. I kept searchin' around, and I couldn't find no birds and finally I looked down in the log and there was a nine-pound catfish. I got the catfish out, but I kept wonderin' why the dog pointed the catfish. He'd never tried to point no fish before, nor nothin' like that, and I got the catfish home and started to clean it that night and it had seven potteridges in it. The potteridges had evidently run in the log to get out of the rain and the creek got up and the catfish swum up in the log and eat the potteridges, and the old dog pointed the potteridges, and I thought he's a-pointin' the catfish.

FOUR. I finally lost 'im though. I took him out a-huntin' one day and he got gone, and I hunted and hunted and hunted and I never did find my dog. I knew he was a good dog. He wouldn't break a point if he ever pointed a covey of birds. He'd just stand and hold 'em until I came and told 'im to flush 'em. And the next year I went back and I found his bones where he's standin' at full point and he had nine piles of potteridge bones in front of him. He'd pointed a covey of birds and stood there and held them till they all starved to death, and he starved to death, too.

FIVE. Did I ever tell you about the coon dog I had a few year ago? I believe he was the best that I've ever been in the woods with and I've owned several good coon dogs. I know I went one night, settin' up on a ridge and there was a big chestnut tree over there on the side of the ridge there, right below me. And that old dog, when he run a coon that went inside of a den in a holler tree, he'd bark different than he did when it was on the outside of the tree, so I'd just call 'im, and he'd leave. Well, I set up on that ridge that night, and he just kept strikin' a coon, and he'd run it, and it'd make a big circle around over the mountain, and come back and go in that one old holler chestnut. I don't know how many coons he did run in there that night, and the next mornin' about daylight he treed in that old holler chestnut, and I went over there and he had so many coons in that tree that, ever' time the coons would draw their breath in, the crack in the chestnut would spread four inches and when they'd let it out, it'd go back together. I don't know how many they was; I didn't keep count of 'em, but they was several coons in that tree.

SIX. I know one night one of my friends had come up to go with me a-huntin', and we went over and set down on a stump. That old dog he just kept runnin' around all over the country, and he'd run back into the road about a mile below us, and then he'd go off and strike again, and then he'd run back into the road. My friend said, "I thought you had a coon dog," said, "I never saw a dog that'd run races and then quit; I thought they's supposed to tree when they run 'em up a tree." I said, "That dog ain't run none up a tree yet," I said, "You wait until daylight, and I'll show you what he's doin'." Well, he kept doin' that all night. Next mornin' we saw him comin' up the road and he had about fifty coons in front of him a-herdin' 'em along up the road. I says, "I told you I had the best dern coon dog in the South."

SEVEN. My Grandpa, when he got up about eighty-five years old, he had 'im a big mill rock, oh, it was about six foot across and about eight inches through. He'd always, ever' Christmas, he'd get him a gallon of apple brandy and he'd go out and pick that mill rock up and stick it up over his head. He'd done that ever' Christmas ever since he got married, so one Christmas he's about eighty-seven he got him a gallon of brandy, and he'd always wait till after dinner before he'd go out and stick the mill rock up. He got him a gallon of brandy, and he took 'im two or three drinks, and he eat dinner, and took 'im another drink or two, and he decided to go out and put the mill rock up over his head. And it'd been awful cold there for about six weeks, just real freezin' weather and the ground hadn't thawed nor nothin', and he went out there and he got down and he got a-hold of that mill rock and he couldn't even shake it. So he goes back in and drinks a little more brandy, and goes out and tries it again, and he couldn't move it again. He goes back and he sets down, and he looked awful bad. Granny said to him. "Grandpa," said, "What's the matter with you?" said, "What are you so down and out about?" He said, "I'm a-gettin' old and old fast, woman." said, "Last year that rock wadn't even heavy, and this year I can't even move it." He sat and studied a while and took in two or three more drinks of brandy, and went out and he got down on his knees and he got a-hold of that rock, and he grunted and groaned a time or two and give a heave and stuck it up over his head and he had nine acres of topsoil froze to it.

EIGHT. He built him an old gun, a great big gun, barrel I guess it was about fifteen or twenty feet long, and big around as a washin' tub almost; but he'd made it out of old pipe and stuff so he made it sort of like an old muzzle loader, you know. He put him a fuse in the back and then he'd pack in a great big load of powder. He'd usually put a keg of powder at one time, sometimes two kegs. And that summer ever' time he'd have a piece of scrap iron, any kind of an old broke clevis[1] or end or clip off a swingletree, or a grab or a piece of axe or a piece of broken glass or anything, he'd just drop it down in the gun barrel, and he'd do that till it come about three or four big frosts in the fall of the year. Then he'd pack him some waddin' on top of that junk and he'd shoot that gun. Then he'd send all of his children and grandchildren up on the mountain to get the game. It'd usually get enough to last till next year. He'd freeze and can meat and have enough to last 'im till the next year.

NINE. Did I ever tell you about the cold winter we had when I was a boy? I know one winter, sound was even froze. It was so cold everything just froze; you didn't hear a sound all winter, I know I had a pack of dogs and I got out there one day a-rabbit-huntin'. They jumped a rabbit and run away round the mountain and backwards and forewards for about an hour; and I noticed I couldn't hear 'em bark but I didn't think much about it, I'd got so used to not hearing no racket. Rabbit run by me and I killed it, and thought no more about it till the next spring. And it turned warm up in the spring after the game law had closed, and there wadn't no open season on rabbit, and the game warden happened to be a-passin' through and heard them dogs runnin' that rabbit around the mountain and the gun go off and shot it. And he come and arrested me for huntin' out of season.

TEN. I had a cat one time and I had two young dogs, and they was always chasin' that cat. And I had a stackpole down in the field where I'd had some hay stacked and got all the hay hauled off and left the pole standin' up. It was about three or four hundred yards from the house. These pups would get after that old cat and run 'im around the house a time or two and then he'd take off down

---

1. clevis: a U-shaped device used to attach or suspend parts.

in the field and climb that stackpole. They done that till the pups got up about grown, and they was pretty good-sized dogs, and gettin' so they was pushin' that old cat pretty fast to outrun 'em. So he's afraid they'd catch 'im and kill him, they's making him get up in high gear to get to that stackpole before they caught him. So I slipped down there in the field one day and I pulled that stackpole out, and laid it down. So the dogs got after the cat and around the house he went about twice, and he made a dive for that stackpole, and you know that cat run forty foot in the air before he even noticed that pole wadn't there.

ELEVEN. I had two old cats one time and they got into a fight in the backyard. They fit and fit and fit, and all at once they just started climbin' one another. Them fool cats climb one another, one would run up to the top of one, and then the other would run up him, and they that till they went clean out of sight and fur fell for three weeks. I never saw such a cat fight in all my life.

TWELVE. I know when I was a kid we had an old cat and wanted to get rid of 'im. My daddy he hauled him off to town. It was ten miles to town. We was ridin' in a wagon. We took 'im down to town and turned him loose. We carried him across the Yadkin River and over to the North Wilkesboro side and turned him loose. Well, when we got back home, the blame cat was settin' at home on the porch. And Dad said, "I will fix him," so he got him a sack and put him in it the next time he went to town, and he got him some big rocks, and he put the rocks in the sack, and tied the old cat up in the sack, and throwed him in the river. And when we got home, he's a-setting' on the porch, as wet as he could be, and I don't know how he got out of that sack. Dad told me, he said. "Well, you've got to see if you can't get rid of that cat." And I said. "Why, I can get rid of him easy." So I took the old cat way down in the woods. There's a big stump down there, and I took my axe with me. I just laid him down on that stump and chopped his head off. Went on back to the house, and in about an hour we's settin' there on the porch talkin,' and I looked out the road and there come that cat, come out of the woods and was trottin' out the road with his head in his mouth.

MEET THE AUTHOR:
John E. "Frail" Joines (1914–1982)

John E. Joines, known to his friends and family as "Frail" Joines, was a native of Wilkes County. He was so gifted a storyteller that a film, *Being a Joines*, has been made featuring him and his tales.

John Joines stayed on the family farm in Wilkes County until service with the U.S. Army Medical Corps took him to England, France, Germany, and beyond in World War II. He volunteered to leave the relative safety of wartime hospitals in order to go to the dangerous front lines to help the wounded. After the war, one of the soldiers he had treated wrote to the Joines family, commenting on John's hands: "They are so big and strong, they look like two clubs," he wrote, "but they are as gentle as any woman's hands."

Back in North Carolina, Joines managed apple orchards, did landscaping, and worked in a garage. Throughout his lifetime, he was known as an outdoorsman who hunted almost all game (except deer—he said they were too beautiful to kill) and a storyteller. Many of these yarns are old tales, which he enlivened with his own energetic language. Toward the end of his life, he also wrote a story.

His wife of many years, Blanche Clanton Joines, reports on the philosophy of life he shared with others—especially his children. "All people were the same to him," she says. "There were no higher-ups or little people. He told the children, 'Never look down on anybody. Never look up to anybody. God created us all the same. Look people in the face at eye level.' "

Reflecting

1. The first six tales all deal with dogs used for hunting. When this country was young, hunting was not merely sport; it was also a means of furnishing food for the family. Having a smart and skilled dog was a real plus, for it might mean the difference between having meat for supper or going without.

   Today we are much more likely to depend on machines than on animals to help us do our work. Can good tall tales be made featuring computers? Cars? Tractors? Dishwashers? Choose a machine and see if you can write a story like Mr. Joines's "smart dog" tales. Remember to begin rather realistically, then move into zany exaggeration.

2. Joines's tales are examples of oral history—stories passed down in the exact language of the person who tells them. Some oral history deals with facts: how to cure a ham, for example, or wash clothes over an open fire. Some, like Joines's tales, preserve old legends and stories.

The Calm Between the Storms

During the first half of the twentieth century, two different wars involved much of the civilized world. The United States was involved in World War I for only nineteen months, but almost 90,000 North Carolinians served in the armed forces. Over 800 died from wounds, over 1,500 from disease. (Most of the latter died from a severe influenza that swept the world during the fall of 1918, killing 15 million people worldwide and 13,644 in North Carolina alone!)

Twenty-three years later, after the bombing of Pearl Harbor, the United States entered World War II. This conflict was much longer—almost four years—and involved many more people.

Between these two wars another great disaster occurred—the Great Depression, which began in 1929. Once again, poverty became a familiar condition as many people lost their homes, their businesses, their life savings. Jobs were scarce, and "making do"—sometimes in very creative ways—became a way of life.

Many of the selections in this section center on people who are trying to survive during very hard times.

Wash Carver's Mouse Trap

Frederick Koch, Jr.

Preview

Today North Carolina prides itself on its good roads and highways, but such was not always the case. In fact, until the middle of this century, many of the roads were unpaved, and after rainy weather, ruts and pot-holes made travel jerky and uncomfortable—and sometimes even dangerous.

Fred Koch, Jr. drew the material for this play from his own experience. Living in the mountains as a social worker, he got to know the mountain people, whom he called "the most interesting people I ever met." Traveling with his puppet show in New England, he got to know the very different city dwellers of that part of the country. In his play, he brings both types together, with comic results.

CHARACTERS	SCENE
Wash Carver	Wash Carver's cabin on Mouse Branch road, off the scenic highway to the Great Smoky Mountains of western North Carolina.
Jen Carver, *his wife*	
Harry Goldstein	
Rosie Goldstein, *his wife*	

Originally published in *The Carolina Playbook,* December 1938. Copyright © The Carolina Playmakers. Reprinted by permission of the author.

TIME

Eight o'clock on a rainy summer night of 1934.

WASH CARVER'S *cabin is tucked away in a remote cove of the Great Smoky Mountains of western North Carolina. It perches high over Mouse Branch road, a rough, dirt road, passable in dry weather, in wet weather "not even jackassable," as* WASH CARVER *would say. A few miles away this straggling dirt road runs into the wide paved highway that takes tourists from Asheville into the Smoky Mountains Park.*

The scene is the living room of WASH CARVER'S *two-room cabin. There is a rough, but clean and homey, look about it. The smooth-worn planks that wall the room are well over a foot wide, having been cut long before the days of second-growth "toothpick" timber. A door in the right of the rear wall opens onto the* CARVERS' *front porch. To the right of the door a rough board ladder leads to the loft. To the left of the door is a home-made wooden bed. In the right wall is a fireplace hung with several strings of "leather britches" (dried string beans), some twists of home-grown tobacco, and strings of small red peppers. In the left wall, opposite the fireplace, is a door leading into the cook-room and a window overlooking the road. Under the window is an old-fashioned family trunk. The soft grey of the walls is brightened by gay-colored magazine pictures and the shifting lights of the wood fire.*

As the curtains open JEN CARVER *is seated in front of the fireplace, by the center table, mending by lamplight a bedspread of antique design. She is a sturdy, middle-aged mountain woman, dressed in a plain, loose-fitting cotton print. Standing and looking intently out of the window, with foot propped on the trunk, elbow on knee, and chin cupped in hand, is* WASH CARVER, *guardian of Mouse Branch road. He is a tall, lean, slow-moving and slow-talking man with weathered face and shrewd blue eyes. He wears a faded work shirt and dark cotton trousers, stuffed into mud-bespattered brogans.*

JEN (*righteously*). I'm a-tellin' ye, Wash Carver, ain't no good goin' 't come of it.

WASH (*innocently*). Kin I help it if they git stuck up?

JEN. I seen ye, Wash Carver, drivin' that load o' wood back'ards an' for'ards, a-geein' an' a-hawin', an' a-whoain' an' a-backin' till them wagon wheels had cut the bottom plumb out'n that road. Jist so folks 'u'd git stuck up.

WASH. Reckon a feller's got a right to haul his wood down the public road.

JEN. Well, ye sure picked a fine time to do it, an' the road plumb drownded with rain, an' all them tourist cars turned through here on that detour.

WASH (*a little irritated*). Reckon ye think I made it rain. Reckon ye think I put up that detour sign, jist so them cars 'u'd git stuck up.

JEN. I don't reckon nothin', Wash Carver. All I know is ye done got that bottom in sich a shape a hog couldn't git through 'thout gittin' mired up to the ears (*With disgust.*) Eight cars stuck up since dark!

WASH (*coming over to the table and pulling some bills and change out of his pocket, begins to count*). Well, I pulled 'em all out, didn't I?

JEN. Yeh, ye pulled 'em all out. An' ye charged 'em a-plenty fer it too.

WASH (*gloating, his spoils laid out before him*). Seven dollars an' sixteen cents cash money. And that last feller I pulled out give me a can o' smokin' terbaccer an' a *pearl-handled* pocket knife. That ain't a bad haul fer a little extry work, is it? (*Exhibiting the knife proudly.*) Ain't that pearl purty? Look at it shine! Always did love pearl.

JEN (*regarding it with disapproval*). Hope ye cut your throat with it. It 'ud serve ye right. A-stickin' folks in the mud an' a-chargin' 'em all that money to pull 'em out.

WASH. How come you to git so blamed sanctified? Last I recollect you warn't so bad at stickin' folks yerself—a-puttin' water in the milk, an' lard in the butter.

JEN (*without a wince*). Don't see as that's got a thing to do with this.

WASH (*with the wisdom of many such fruitless encounters*). Well, mebbe not. (*Pocketing his spoils.*) Ain't had so much luck since time I won that bedspread you're a-mendin' over to the Indian Fair. Jen, you ort to a-gone with me to that Fair. I remember same as yisterday how I won that spread. I kin see that feller now, standin' back there amongst all them purty doll babies and bedspreads, a-spinnin' that big, red wheel with the numbers on it round and round. (*He illustrates with his hand.*) Seems like somethin' jist told me to slap a dime down on that "thirteen." (*In his enthusiasm he whacks the table with his big hand, rocking the lighted lamp.*) Well sir, them—

JEN. I've heard ye tell it more times than they is fleas on a dog, Wash Carver—(*mimicking him*)—how them little nails went clinkin' around, how it stopped on "thirteen," an' how you won this here bedspread fer only a dime—an' you needn't go a-knockin' the lamp off'n the table to fresh up my memory on it neither! (*Squelched*, WASH *goes back to his post by the window.*)

JEN (*rising*). I don't know as ye didn't git stung a-payin' a dime fer it. (*Crossing to the bed she spreads the cover on it.*) I ain't never liked this spread. Hit's as coarse as a old feed sack. Ain't fitten to bed down a sick calf. Why, it already looks fer all the world like one o' them ol' wore-out homespun bedspreads. Ye ort to a-had sense enough to a-picked me out one o' them shiny, pink kind, like Lovey Crisp has got.—Talkin' about luck, now Lovey Crisp was lucky. Sold all her maw's old homespun bedspreads to one of them fancy tourist places in Asheville for five dollars apiece. It sore beats me how anybody'd give five dollars fer one o' them ol' homespuns when the mail order sells them shiny, pink kind with the ruffles fer only ninety-eight cents. (*With a sigh.*) I shore wish you'd git me one.

WASH (*excited*). Jen, yander comes another autimobile! He jist turned that first curve by the branch. (*Overcome with curiosity* JEN *goes to the window. The powerful beams of the automobile headlights shine through the window brilliantly illuminating their faces for a moment.*) Lord, his light's brighter 'n a June bug. Must be one o' them new cars. (*Turning suddenly, he catches* JEN *watching eagerly too.*) What you lookin' at?

JEN (*starts and turns away guiltily*). Wash Carver, I ain't a-studyin' yer doin's.

WASH. He's a-slowin' up fer that first bad place by the willer tree.... (*Breathlessly.*) Looks like he's got out o' the ruts. (*The excitement is too much for* JEN; *she cannot resist going to the window to see for herself now.*) God a'mighty, he's slidin' like a greased eel...look...look at him... look! He's stopped. (*A long blast from a high-powered horn breaks the spell.* WASH *slaps his knee and shouts gleefully.*) Listen at 'im holler. Mouse Branch road has trapped another'n! Wonder who it is this time, Jen. Hope it's one o' them rich fellers that wears diamond rings and smokes big, ten-cent seegars. (*With sudden inspiration he takes the lamp to the window, waves it several times, then sets it down on the window ledge.*)

JEN. Wash Carver, you bring that lamp right back here this minute an' set it on this table where it belongs. If it falls off'n that window and ketches the house afire, they'll see your house sure enough.

WASH. Aw Jen....

JEN. If you don't fetch that lamp back, Wash Carver, I'll—(*And he does! Then sits by the table, takes off his shoes, crosses the room barefoot, and conceals them under the bed.*)

WASH. Jen, fer Lord's sakes, don't ruin ever'thing. There ye stand slap in the middle o' the room like a preacher layin' fer the devil. Set down, and act natural!

JEN (*stubbornly*). I'll not be a partner in yer sinful doin's, Wash Carver.

WASH (*rushing to the bed, he pulls off the spread and forces* JEN *into the chair by the fireplace.*) Here, act like common. Make out like you're a-mendin' the bed-kivver.

JEN. You're as crazy as a slew-foot gan-der! Ye know I jist got done mendin' this bed-kivver.

WASH. Don't make no difference. Jist make out like you're a-sewin' on it. (*More gently.*) Come on, Jen. I'll give ye half o' what we git out'n this un'.

JEN *settles back with a snort.* WASH *takes up the Bible from the table, opens it at random and pretends to read. After a bit he looks at* JEN, *who now smiles triumphantly.*

WASH (*disappointed looks toward the window*). Don't look like they're a-comin'. Told ye the lamp ort to been in the window so's them pore folks could see where the house's at. Woman, you ain't got no heart at all! (*He gets up and tiptoes to the window.*) Them pore folks must a-sunk plumb to Chiney!

JEN. Well, I hope they got out. (*Voices are heard outside.* WASH *hurries back into his chair.*)

WASH (*motioning* JEN *frantically*). Set down, woman, set down!

JEN (*still standing*). If you think ye kin drive me around like one o' yer blamed mules, ye—(*The sound of footsteps on the porch checks her. Unwillingly she slips into her chair and begins her mending.*)

ROSIE (*outside, her whining voice unmistakably "East-Side-New-York"*). Harry... Harry Goldstein.... Wait for me, Harry!

HARRY (*outside, of the same species, his voice rasping with exasperation*). For Christ sake, Rosie, I told you to stay in the car!

ROSIE (*outside, wailing*). Oh, Har-r-ry. (*She draws out his name, accenting both syllables.*)

HARRY (*outside*). Rosie, will you shut

up! (*He knocks sharply on the door. Neither* JEN *nor* WASH *makes a move to answer.*)

ROSIE (*outside, innocently*). Why don't you ring the bell, Harry?

HARRY (*outside*). For Christ's sake, Rosie, 'cause there ain't any bell!—Why don't you go hop a street car? (*He pounds frantically on the door.*) Hello . . . hello there inside. . . . I want some help! My car's stuck!

WASH (*casually*). Jen, seems like I hear somebody at the door. (*Calling over his shoulder.*) Jist pull the latch an' push the door.

ROSIE (*outside*). What did he say, Harry?

HARRY (*outside*). How do you think I can hear what he said with you talking? Shut up, Rosie!—Hello there inside; I'm stuck in the mud.

WASH (*gets up at last and ambles to the door*). Why, come on in! Jist come right in!

HARRY *steps inside. His nervous movements, his unmistakable East-Side accent, and his oily, well-groomed appearance stamp him immediately as a city "furriner." He is obviously out of his element, as much out of place as the mud on his polished shoes and on his striped trousers.* ROSIE, *his wife, eases in behind him. She is considerably younger, or at least a certain silliness in her manner makes her seem so. She is dressed in ridiculous hiking togs. Both* ROSIE *and* HARRY *stand a moment struck by the strangeness of the room and the spectacle of* WASH CARVER *standing in his bare feet, his big toes upturned.*

WASH (*in the typical manner of greeting strangers*). Don't believe I know you. (*He studies a minute.*) Seems like I've seed your face som'ers, but I don't believe I can call yer name right off.

ROSIE (*eagerly stepping forward*). Goldstein—Mr. and Mrs. Harry Goldstein from New York. Harry and I are touring through your be-a-utiful Smoky Mountains. (*Aside to* HARRY.) Oh, Harry, isn't this romantic? It's just like that movie we saw at Radio City last week. Aren't you glad now we came to the mountains? (*Back to the* CARVERS.) Harry wanted to go to the seashore but I—

HARRY (*finally explodes*). Rosie, for God's sake—(*To* WASH.) Listen, I'm stuck.

WASH (*innocently*). What say?

HARRY. I'm stuck, *stuck!* My new car's sunk in the mud!

WASH (*incredulous*)! Stuck? Well, you don't say. Where at?

HARRY. Where? By that damn brook down there where the road is all wet. (WASH *looks puzzled.*) About two blocks from here.

WASH (*uncertainly*). Brook . . . two blocks. . . . Oh, yeah, you mean where Mouse Branch runs acrost the road through that bottom. You know, I was just a-telling' Jen here how them cars a-comin' through this detour had got that bottom mighty slickery. (*Hospitably.*) You all jist take chairs an' rest yerselves awhile.

HARRY. Good Heavens, man, rest? We haven't time to rest. We've got to make Asheville tonight.—How far is it to the nearest garage?

WASH (*scratching his head*). Garage, did ye say? Let me see now. Pap Wilkins runs a sort o' fillin' station like, if that's what ye mean. (HARRY *nods impatiently.*) Hit's jist yan side o' the gap o' Sugar Loaf Mountain. Ye remember that time, Jen, when me and Pap went bear huntin' up Little Snowbird and that derned cow almost—

HARRY (*in no mood for a mountain yarn*). The garage! How far is it?

WASH. Oh, let me see now. From here to Grady Mashburn's mill is about a quarter. Then on to Sweetwater church . . . that's another quarter, or maybe that 'u'd come nearer to bein' a half, don't ye think, Jen? Well, anyhow, I'd say from here to Red Hog knob is upwards of three mile. Now from Red Hog—

HARRY. Please! please! The garage? How far is it?

WASH. Makin' a chanc't guess I'd say it was ever' bit o' five mile from here. (HARRY *wails.*) Without you knowed the shortcuts it 'u'd take you upwards of two hours o' stiff walkin' to make it to Pap's. I reckon Pap's done gone ter bed by this time though, ain't he, Jen?

JEN. Hunh? I don't know nothin' 'bout Pap's bed habits.

ROSIE. Five miles! Oh Harry, that's entirely too far for you to walk with your blood pressure. . . . Maybe he'd let you use his telephone, Harry!

HARRY. Rosie, will you please shut up! (*To* WASH.) Has this Pap fellow got wrecker service?

WASH (*enjoying the game hugely*). Wrecker service? (*He pretends to be puzzled.*) Oh, he's got 'im a wife if that's what you mean! (WASH *guffaws loudly at his own joke, then seriously.*) Naw, Mister, Pap Wilkins ain't got nothin' but a T-model Ford an' a monkey wrench. You-uns just stay here and spend the night with us. They's a ex-

try bed up in the loft. (*He motions toward the ladder.*) Jen and I 'u'd be plumb glad to have ye stay, wouldn't we, Jen?

JEN (*sourly*). I reckon. . . .

WASH. Course we would! Course we would, plumb glad!

ROSIE. Oh, Harry, let's stay. (*Nudging him.*) Southern hospitality, Harry!

HARRY (*pacing the floor*). My God, Rosie! This is terrible. (*To* WASH) Listen, I've got to get out of here at once. I'll lose five hundred dollars worth of business if I'm late back to New York. (*In despair.*) Rosie, I told you we should have went to the beach. (*Back to* WASH.) Listen you've got to help me out. Great God, Rosie, I'd give ten dollars to get out of this dump!

WASH (*quickly*). Ten dollars?

HARRY. Yes, five dollars.

WASH (*sitting on the bed and scratching his head, he drawls.*) I was jist a-figgerin'. I got a team o'mules been pullin' chestnut stumps on some new ground top o' Old Whiteface. (HARRY *starts impatiently.*) Say ye had a Ford or a Chevrolet?

ROSIE (*irrepressible*). It's a Packard. It's the latest model—a blue one. Harry wanted a Buick but. . . . (HARRY *turns sharply and she stops. Innocently.*) What's the matter, Ha-r-ry?

WASH. Packard. That's one o' them big, high-priced cars, ain't it? (*Shaking his head.*) I'm afeard it 'u'd strain the mules. Ye know, that least mule o' mine's got a sore place on 'er back. I was jist a-tellin' Jen awhile ago that—

HARRY (*pacing the floor, stops abruptly*). Listen, you've got to help me. I've got to get out. My God, my business! Every minute is money to me. I'll pay you extra . . .

extra!

WASH (*shaking his head*). Them big cars is awful heavy.

HARRY. Listen, I'll give you ten dollars to pull me out, ten dollars!

WASH (*looking up*). Ten dollars? (*He pretends to study a minute. Then suddenly.*) You know, I just remember.—Jen, ain't there an old block 'n' tackle in the shed right under them feed sacks?

JEN (*with a snort*). Not as I know about.

WASH (*unperturbed*). Now, come to think on it, I know there is. (*He hauls out his shoes from under the bed and begins putting them on.*) You know, with that block an' tackle, them mules kin more'n like make it. Ye say ye'll give me ten dollars?

HARRY (*reluctantly*). Yes, ten dollars . . . if you pull me out.

ROSIE (*petulantly*). Harry, I think that's an awful lot of money to spend. . . .

HARRY (*with a wail*). Rosie, I suppose you think I want to spend it!

ROSIE. Harry Goldstein, if you spend ten dollars on your old car I'm going to buy one of those homespun bedspreads for Rachel's room. You know I promised Rachel I'd buy her a spread and here you go spending all the money on your old car.

HARRY. For cryin' out loud, Rosie!— We're stuck in the mud . . . stuck in the mud! We got to get out! You want to stay here all night?

ROSIE. Harry, you're so unreasonable. Yes, I'd much rather stay here than go with you. (*Mincing over to* MRS. CARVER.) You'll let me stay, won't you, Mrs. . . . Mrs. . . .

JEN. Carver. I reckon ye kin stay.

WASH (*going to the door*). Well, Mister Gold . . . Goldpine—

HARRY. Gold*stein*.

WASH. That's right, Goldsign.—Don't know as I ever heard that name before.— Well, Mr. Goldmine, I'll go put the gears on them mules, an' we'll jist see if they can't yank that big Packard o' yourn out'n the mud. (*He illustrates.*) Same as a stump. (*He goes out.*).

HARRY. Come on, Rosie.

ROSIE. I'll do no such thing, Harry Goldstein. It was you stuck that car in the mud; now you can just get it out yourself. I'm going to stay right here and talk to Mrs. Carver.

HARRY. Rosie, for—! (*His patience utterly spent, he gives her an annihilating look, turns and goes out, slammng the door in her face.*)

ROSIE (*with a hurt cry*). Oh, Harry! (*She turns and wanders down toward* JEN *with a puzzled expression.*) Now, what do you suppose I could have said, Mrs. Carver, to make Harry so angry? Harry is so unreasonable.

JEN. Reckon all men critters is that-a-way.

ROSIE. But your husband seems so nice, Mrs. Carver.

JEN. You just don't know him like I do.

ROSIE. But he's so quiet and country-like. You know, Harry don't appreciate the country. All he cares about is business. Sometimes I say to him, "Harry, why don't you give up the jewelry business and buy a nice little farm where we could settle down with a cow?" But Harry don't care about nothing but business. (*Contemptuously.*) Selling cheap ten-cent-store jewelry—(*she indicates a string of imitation pearls she is wearing*)—like these pearls.

JEN. You mean them pearls cost only ten cents?

ROSIE. Oh yes, Harry sells thousands of them to Ten Cent Stores. (*With pride.*) He's the best salesman the company ever had. Mr. Greenberg, he's the President, says Harry could sell trunks to elephants. (*She giggles.*) Mr. Greenberg is so funny. (*Sighing.*) Oh, I guess I shouldn't complain, but sometimes Harry is so unreasonable. Only yesterday, in Knoxville, I had a chance to buy a real homespun bedspread for only ten dollars, and Harry wouldn't let me.

JEN (*taking the spread over to the bed, she starts to put it on*). I reckon all men-folks is ornery an' hard to git along with. I been a-tryin' to git my old man to git me one o' them shiny, pink bedspreads fer the last five years. This old spread ain't fitten—

ROSIE (*noticing the spread for the first time*). Oh, Mrs. Carver, that's a beautiful bedspread! Do let me see it. (*She takes it from the bed and examines it eagerly.*)

JEN. I ain't never liked it much. It's too coarse an' common lookin'.

ROSIE. Oh, I know, but all homespuns are coarse. I think it's exquisite! Did you make it?

JEN. Why no, I didn't make it. Hit's jist an old spread I got—

ROSIE (*interrupting her*). Of course, you didn't make it. How stupid of me. It must be at least a hundred years old! I just love old antiques. (*Holding it up.*) You know, it's just the right color to match with Rachel's room—Rachel is my daughter, such a sweet girl! I'm furnishing her room in antiques, and this spread is just what I want. You'll sell it to me, Mrs. Carver, won't you?

JEN. Well, I'd like to sell it all right, but ye see—

ROSIE. Oh, I understand so well. It's awfully hard to part with old things. But I'll pay you well for it. You know, I wanted so much to buy one of these hand-woven bedspreads yesterday in the tourist shop in Knoxville, but Harry said it might not be genuine. He was afraid it might be like the pearls he sells. It's hard to tell them from real ones. You don't know how much it would mean to buy an antique spread where you know it's genu-ine! I'll pay you well, Mrs. Carver.

JEN (*struggling with her conscience*). I'm awful sorry to tell you, but that spread—

ROSIE (*insisting*). Mrs. Carver, I simply must have it! It's just the right shade for Rachel's room. (*Opening her purse.*) I'll give you ten dollars for it.

JEN (*thunderstruck*). *Ten dollars!* I'd like to sell it, but—

ROSIE. I know that's not enough but.... (*Looking in her purse and taking out the money.*) Here's three more dollars, thirteen dollars in all. Now I know you're going to be a dear and let me have it, aren't you? (*A long blast from the automobile horn.*) Oh, there goes Harry. He must be un-stuck. Wouldn't you think he'd be gentleman enough to come for me, instead of blowing? (*Persuasively.*) Can't I have the spread, Mrs. Carver?

JEN (*bewildered*). Ye kin have it all right ... but it ain't worth—

ROSIE. You just don't know what they charge in the stores. It's worth every cent

269

of it. And to buy it here in a real mountain cabin! (*A romantic sigh.*) When I look at it, I'll always think about the time poor Harry got stuck. Poor Harry! (*She folds the spread hurriedly and goes to the door.*) I'm sorry to hurry off. Thank you so much, Mrs. Carver. If you come to New York be sure to let me know. Good-by! Good-by, Mrs. Carver! (ROSIE *hurries out. Her voice can be heard trailing off.*) Harry . . . I'm coming, Harry! Wait, Ha-r-ry! . . . Ha-r-ry! . . .

JEN *looks at the money* ROSIE *has forced into her hand, then at the bed. Struck dumb at her good fortune, she sinks weakly onto the bed. She stares at the money, then at the door. She is undergoing a struggle. Suddenly she bolts for the door and calls.*

JEN. Mrs. Goldstein! . . . Mrs. Goldstein! . . . (*There is no answer. With a wide smile she closes the door, comes down to the table and resumes her seat by the fire still somewhat dazed as* WASH *comes stomping loudly onto the porch.*)

WASH (*entering*). Well, old woman, I pulled 'em out all right! (*Laughing.*) Easy as pullin' a blue tick off'n a hound dog. (*He looks out the window.*) Look at them lights move! Them folks sure is in a hurry. (*He sprawls on the bed.*) But ye cain't guess what I got.

JEN. There ain't no tellin'.

WASH (*gloating*). Jist seems like good luck's a-huggin' me tonight. That feller was a powerful good trader. He could out-talk a jaybird and trade the feet off'n a black snake. I sure had to talk 'im slick and trade 'im close. You got ter use yer

head, ol' woman. (*Chuckling.*) You'll have to figger out somethin' better'n puttin' lard in the butter.

JEN. You're a-feelin' powerful high an' mighty, ain't ye, Wash Carver?

WASH. Got a right to. Ain't had so much luck since that time I won that derned old bedspread at the Indian Fair. (*He notices that the bed is uncovered.*) What's come o' that spread? What ye done with it?

JEN. That 'ere swift-talkin' woman tuck a likin' to it. (*Holding up the money gleefully.*) She give me thirteen dollars fer it!

WASH (*incredulous*). Thirteen dollars! Fer that old thing? Didn't ye tell her it didn't cost me but a dime?

JEN. Mebbe I did, and mebbe I didn't. She talked so fast I couldn't git a word in edgewise.

WASH. By God, Jen, she must a-been blind as a hoot owl. —What got into 'er?

JEN (*cryptically*). She jist took a likin' to the color.

WASH. Well, I'll be damned! (*Generously.*) Well, Jen. It looks like I've learnt ye to be a good trader after all. Them pore folks sure got skinned. (*A pause.*) Reckon, bein's how I won that spread, a part o' that money's mine, ain't it?

JEN (*firmly*). Not nary a cent, Wash Carver. You *give* me that spread, an' you know it.

WASH (*exploding*). Well, I'll be a suck-eared mule! If that ain't jist like a woman. It don't pay to be nice to 'em; it shore don't. (*He looks out the window.*) Wish't now I'd a-took the money instead.

JEN. 'Stead o' what?

WASH (*turning angrily*). Blamed if I

give 'em to you now! I'll take 'em to Bryson City an' sell 'em, an' it'll serve ye right.

JEN. Wash Carver, what air you a-talkin' about?

WASH. Somethin', I was aimin' to give ye for a present.—Like a blamed fool I tuck to feelin' sorry fer ye.

JEN. Wash Carver, you're talkin' like a plumb fool!

WASH (*riled up*). Talkin' like a fool, am I? All right then, jist look! (*He digs into his pocket and pulls out a string of pearls. Triumphantly.*) Look at 'em! Pearls!

JEN. Pearls?

WASH (*holding them up, his eyes shining*).

A whole string of 'em—*pearls!* (*With a contemptuous snort.*) And that feller thought he was a good trader.—I'll bet they're worth twenty dollars!

JEN. And how much did ye give fer them pearls, Wash Carver?

WASH. Besides givin' 'im the ten dollars I got fer pullin' 'im out, I just had to give 'im that sixteen cents I had in my pocket extry.

JEN. Sixteen cents extry? Ten dollars an' sixteen cents for them pearls!

WASH. Yeh, why they ain't no tellin' how much they're worth! (*JEN bursts into laughter. WASH looks on, uncomprehending.*)

Meet the Author:
Fred Koch, Jr. (1911–)

Fred Koch, Jr., grew up in Chapel Hill, where his father was busy building the university drama program into national prominence. Frederick Koch, Sr., known affectionately as "Prof. Koch," had introduced a form known as "folk drama," in which plays focus not on kings and queens, the wealthy and powerful, but the common folk. Many of his students (such as Paul Green, Thomas Wolfe, and Frances Gray Patton, all included in this anthology) wrote plays about tobacco farmers, bootleggers, textile workers, and the like. Fred Koch, Jr. adopted this form also.

Young Frederick Koch began his career as a sociologist; a Phi Beta Kappa graduate of UNC, he spent four months in the mountains of Graham county investigating families who were on welfare during the Depression. Then he turned to drama. He toured

New England and Canada one summer with a puppet show, then took another show to the schools of North Carolina for the State Board of Health to help students learn better dental care. While doing graduate work in drama, he wrote "Wash Carver's Mouse Trap" and two other folk plays. In 1939 he went to the University of Miami, where he began the drama department which he chaired for sixteen of the thirty-five years he taught there. During that time he oversaw the design and construction of the Ring Theater at the University. He also spent summers directing plays at the Parkway Playhouse at Burnsville.

Currently retired, Fred Koch divides his time between Miami and Burnsville. He continues his professional interests by using his VCR to catch up on the good movies he had to miss while devoting so much time to teaching and directing dramatic productions.

Language Alert

This script is written in dialect. You will make the reading easier and more fun if you place yourself in the roles, take on that rural mountain dialect, and "ham it up."

Some terms you might not be familiar with:

1. *"a-geein' an' a-hawin"*: *Gee* and *haw* are two terms used to order mules or horses to turn right and left, respectively.
2. *plumb*: Used informally, this word means *completely*.
3. *sanctified*: Pure and holy.
4. *spoils*: Loot; the goods a thief or plundering soldier might obtain.
5. *slew-foot gander*: *Slew* is slang for *twisted*. A *gander* is a male goose; the word is also used as a slang term to refer to someone who is dim-witted.
7. *fillin' station*: A filling station, a term once used for service stations (where you could fill your car with gasoline).
8. *ornery*: Cranky; unpleasant.

Reflecting

1. The term *poetic justice* refers to a situation in which someone receives "just what's coming to him (or her)"—often because he/she has done something at least a little shady or dishonest. Explain how Wash's situation at the end of the play can be called "poetic justice."
2. Do you feel sorry for Wash for getting outsmarted? Why or why not?
3. Check in your newspaper or a catalogue to see what bedspreads cost today. Call a craft or antique store to see what a homespun bedspread—especially an antique—costs. Compare the prices you're given to the prices mentioned in this play.

The Journey

Bessie Willis Hoyt

Preview

In the following excerpt, "The Journey," young Bessie Willis is beginning her first teaching job in the North Carolina mountains in 1926. Before reading, answer the following questions, based on your knowledge of how things are *today*.

1. What kind of training is required in order for one to teach school? How many years of schooling does one need? Where can it be obtained?
2. If you need money to obtain that training, what might you do to get it?
3. Suppose you are in the eastern part of the state and you take a position teaching at an elementary school in the mountains. How will you get to your new location?
4. How big do you expect your school to be? About how many teachers will be employed there?
5. Suppose you rent a furnished room, at least temporarily. Describe it. How big is it? How is it heated? What furniture do you expect? How is it decorated? Where will you bathe?

Now remember that Bessie Willis Hoyt began her work in 1926. Go back over these questions and answer them in terms of what you think life was like *at that time*. Then, as you read, compare your answers to Bessie Willis Hoyt's experience.

"Howdy, are you'uns the new school marms?" the smiling brown eyes asked inquiringly.

"Yes sir, we are," as we rose from the seat on our trunks to greet him and introduce ourselves.

"I 'lowed as how you were," still smiling. "I'm Tillet Gryder and my rig is right outside if you'uns ain't above riding in it. Martha Cook sent me to fetch you'uns. She and my missus stopped off in Heaton to buy a few eats. We'll pick them up on the way."

Mary and I didn't know what a rig was, but if this friendly man rode in it we could too. The year was 1926. The place was the little mountain town of Elk Park, Avery County, North Carolina. We sized up this man who had come to meet us as a kind and friendly soul. He wore his clean overalls with pride. We liked him instinctively.

"You'uns go get in the wagon. I'm going to get somebody to help me load the trunks." The station master willingly made himself available.

"Did you hear him call us you'uns?" Mary asked as we walked toward the rig.

"I sure did. Guess they say 'you'uns' like we say 'you all.' We can learn to say that," I answered.

The rig was a two seated covered wagon, the cover being made of feed sacks sewed together. Two mules stood in the July sun ready to pull it.

"My gosh, Mary, it's just like the Oregon Trail," I gasped. "If somebody was to 'Whoop' I'd head for the hills."

"Shut up," she warned, "Don't get me tickled at a time like this." Both of us were thinking of the woman who got on the train between Johnson City and Elk Park. Under her arm she carried a shot gun. That was a little unnerving.

The trunks were lifted into the back of the wagon. We hoisted ourselves up and sat on the front seat, Mary on the outside.

"I'm going to ride shot-gun," she whispered. It was my turn to say "Shut up."

Mr. Gryder lifted himself easily on the seat beside us, leaned over and spat out a stream of tobacco juice as he flipped the reins. At the sound of "Giddup," the mules strained, threw back their heads, and were off. In that brief interval Mary and I knew that we had found the adventure we had been seeking.

"How'd you'uns like the train ride?" Mr. Gryder asked. "You'uns saw some of the prettiest sights around these parts if you'uns got on the train in Johnson City. That's one of the few narrow gauge trains left. It's the East Tennessee and Western North Carolina Railway."

We told him this was our first trip to the mountains. We had spent the past four days in Marion with college friends. The only way to get to Elk Park was to go to Johnson City, Tennessee, spend the night, and take the narrow gauge train for the last part of our trip. Mr. Gryder laughed when we told him that coming through the gorge we saw the engine from our observation car, the road being full of curves.

"You'uns are in for a lot more sights before we get to Dark Ridge," our new friend added.

The narrow, rocky road followed the course of the Elk River which tumbled and splashed its way through the valley. It was easy to talk to Mr. Gryder. He smiled a lot and his manner put us at ease. He must have sensed our apprehension at the newness of all this. It was as if he knew we had a sinking feeling in our stomachs.

The time was early July during the state of economic depression all through our land. Mary and I had finished our second year at East Carolina Teachers' College and found ourselves badly in need of money to go on. Both of us had worked in the dining room at school, but that was not enough. College friends from the mountains told us of schools that started in the summer time and closed at Christmas because the roads became almost impassable after that time.

Letters to several northwestern counties of our state had brought eager replies. The one from Mr. R. T. Teague, Avery County Superintendent of Education, sounded the best. He had a two-teacher school at Dark Ridge which was vacant. It was a grammar school with about forty pupils.

"That sounds just right," Mary had said. "There won't be anybody to see how ignorant we might be."

We had not yet studied teaching methods. This arrangement of starting school in the summer would mean we would miss only the fall term at college. We could make that up the next summer and still graduate with our class. So here we were. We had come to these mountains at that time of the year when the rhododendron was in full bloom and ox-eye daisies blanketed the hillsides. Buttercups overflowed the side of ditches. Butterflies flitted over the meadows of red clover, and

honey bees droned a steady hum over the buckwheat fields. I thought with Chaucer, "Here is God's plenty."

The four miles from Elk Park to Heaton gave us a chance to ask Mr. Gryder some questions about the community to which we were going, and also to get better acquainted with this man who was making a round trip of eighteen miles to meet us. We were appreciative and told him so. We had passed several wagons on the way, but no cars. The road was so narrow that sometimes one vehicle had to back to a wider place in the road to allow the other to pass. Sometimes only a few inches seemed to separate our wagon from the valley below. It was nerve racking and seat wrecking.

Heaton was a small, sleepy crossroad settlement with a cluster of wooden stores, the largest one being run by Mr. Jim Heaton. Around the lone gas pump in front several wagons had stopped. A model T Ford looked out of place in such a setting. One of the stores also housed the post office. Bags of feed, drums of kerosene and farm tools were displayed on the store porch. We pulled up beside the other wagons. Two women waited on the store porch, motioning to us. One was the missus of whom our host had spoken. She was a lean woman with a kind face and a shy manner. The other was Martha Cook, with whom we were to board. Both wore hats. Several people had written us, but we had chosen her home because it was closest to the school house and we liked the friendly tone of her letter. Mr. Gryder had told us that Mr. Cook was working in Detroit. We learned that many men from the ridge went to Detroit. Akron and Lockport, New York to work for a year or two. There was little cash to be earned in Dark Ridge, and many found jobs in distant cities necessary. Some had stayed.

Martha Cook was a woman in her early thirties, small in stature with flashing brown eyes and a ready smile. She gave us a hearty "Howdy." Both women put their packages beside the trunks in the back of the wagon. Mary and I slipped to the back seat. "You'uns don't have to move," Martha Cook laughed. "Hannah ain't the jealous kind." Mrs. Gryder allowed as how we shouldn't have moved.

"We're fine," we said, and stayed where we were.

At the end of the cluster of stores the road turned sharply up the mountain. From then on for the five miles to our new home the way was up. Narrower than the other road and rockier, it hugged the mountain side and overlooked broad sweeps of the valley below. Sometimes a small house amidst a cluster of trees was seen.

The July sun and the steep climb had made the mules sweat. Around one of the countless bends in the road and in a spot where the trees gave cool shade, Mr. Gryder stopped. I could hear running water but could see none. " 'Lowed as how you'uns would be wanting a cool drink," he said.

All of us got down. With his hands, Mr. Gryder cleared the leaves from a spring which flowed into a small hollow beside the road. We watched him as he cupped his hands and drank the cool water.

When my turn came, I not only drank but I washed my face to cool off.

The houses were few, but as we passed one of our new friends would point out where pupils lived. Mrs. Cook was eager to answer our questions, and we learned enough about our new home to make the knot in our stomachs smaller. With the exception of leaving for college, this was our first venture from home. As the wagon passed under some overhanging branches full of red berries, we stopped.

"These are sarvis (service) berries," Martha Cook informed us. "They're good to eat. Want to taste?" We did. The berries were tart but good. We were beginning to have a feeling for this place, which was to deepen as the months went by and we came to know the honesty, sincerity and goodness of these people. The wagon stopped. A house stood across a field. Several out-buildings were near.

"This is where me and my family put up," Mr. Gryder told us. "Leave your packages in the wagon, Hannah, I'll fetch them," he spoke to his missus.

"I'll see you'uns Sunday at meeting," she called as she went down the path to her home.

The Gryders ran this farm for Mr. Ben Farthing who lived in Boone. Mr. Farthing had once taught school in Dark Ridge. The house was larger than most and seemed to have more flat land around it. There were seven children in this family. We would have four of them in school. A son Gaither and a daughter Beulah had finished the seventh grade and were in high school at Cove Creek where they lived with a relative and helped with the work. This was a pattern for those who wanted to continue their education. Not all did. Four girls and two boys were working in Cove Creek homes in order to attend high school.

It was late in the day when we drew up in front of a small house hardly a yard from the road. Its vertical weather boarding was unpainted. Across the front ran a narrow porch. So steep was the slope on which it sat that I could stand on the road and almost spit down the stone chimney. Two small girls came onto the porch, followed by a lively, sprightly grandmother who gave us a warm greeting. The younger girl had the bright dark eyes of her mother. Her dark brown hair was cut in a straight bob. She had the friendly, outgoing manner of her mother and grandmother.

"Mary, these are the new teachers," Martha Cook told her as she came to greet us.

"My name is Mary, too," Mary Hocutt said. "Do you think we can keep ourselves straight?"

The older girl, Nilla, was a perfect Nordic maiden with fair skin and long flaxen braids that hung to her waist. She was more reserved and waited for us to greet her. Both would be in school, Mary, eight, in the third grade and Nilla, ten, in the fifth.

"Light down and come in. This is our home. It ain't fancy," Martha Cook seemed to apologize, "but it don't rain on us and we have enough to eat." She laughed.

"We make out fine," the older woman said as she laid a calloused hand on my arm.

"This is my mother," Martha Cook said. "She'll probably keep you jumping."

"I'll tell you right now you'uns can call me Aunt Elve."

"Thank you, Aunt Elve. We'd like that," we spoke up.

Her skin was bronzed and wrinkled as if a lot of her days had been spent in the sun. Her movements were quick and she seemed capable of taking command of any situation that faced her. She had evidently known hard work and liked it. Several strands of brightly colored glass beads hung around her neck and over a plaid gingham shirt waist. We were to learn that her sense of humor made the house a happy place. Already I was aware that in this family I would find a home.

Bessie Willis Hoyt (1906–   )

Bessie Willis Hoyt was born in Carteret County and grew up in Morehead City. She graduated from what was then East Carolina Teachers College and undertook graduate studies at two branches of the University of North Carolina—in Chapel Hill and in Greensboro. Her teaching career began with high school English classes in Dark Ridge in Avery County. Later she turned to teaching special education, first in Mt. Airy, then in Pittsboro.

Her writing career began early: she wrote poetry in grammar school, contributed poetry and short stories to her high school magazine, and served as editor of her college newspaper in 1927–28. Much later in her life she took creative writing classes at Johnston Technical College in Smithfield. Her poetry and historical writings have won both regional and statewide awards. Now retired from teaching, she lives in Elizabeth City.

Ms. Hoyt advises aspiring writers to "get all the grammar they can get" and to take

creative writing courses when they are available.

In her autobiographical book, *Come Where The Timber Turns,* Bessie Willis Hoyt not only tells us of her life as a young woman, but gives us the flavor of North Carolina in the years between the world wars.

Language Alert

This excerpt includes some words common to the rural mountain dialect. Make a list of terms used by the mountain folk in the 1920s, but relatively unused in your own area of the state today. (You should be able to figure out the meanings with little difficulty.)

Reflecting

Assume that you can take a voyage back through time and that you are accompanying Bessie Willis and her friend Mary Hocutt on this journey from the train station to the rooming house. In this short journey, what experiences would you have that now (more than sixty years later) you would not have?

Going Seining

Kate Rinzler et al.

Preview

It is the 1920s, a time when money is scarce. The Locklears, a Lumbee Indian farming family in Robeson County, are law-abiding folk who know that seining—fishing with a net—is illegal. However, they also are fully aware that, like most rural North Carolinians, they must depend on hunting and fishing to supplement their gardens and livestock. And today the children decide to help the family out—and have an adventure at the same time.

A play in three scenes

CHARACTERS (In order of appearance)

Winford Locklear, Jr.—oldest Locklear son, about 15 years old
Annie Lee—Locklear daughter, about 10 years old
Sarah—Locklear daughter, about 6 years old
Bracey—Locklear son, about 9 years old
Luther—Locklear son, about 13 years old
Kathyrn Locklear—Mama
Aunt Mary—Winford Locklear Sr.'s unmarried younger sister
Winford Locklear, Sr.—Papa
Sheriff Walter Smith

SCENE ONE: The New Seine

Curtain remains closed. Winford Locklear, Jr. enters, stage right, running. He crosses in front of the curtain, carrying a seine (fishing net) wrapped in brown paper, and exits, stage left.

Curtain opens. The scene is the front room/ kitchen and yard of the Locklear household. Mama and Aunt Mary are outside rinsing a pile of washed clothes and hanging them in the breeze. Sarah is pulling grass to neaten the yard. Indoors, Bracey is preoccupied, whittling on a stick. Annie Lee washes dishes and Luther dries.

ANNIE LEE: (*Calling out the window.*) Sarah, are you finished pulling the grass?
SARAH: (*Straightening and entering the house.*) Yeah, you can sweep the yard now.
ANNIE LEE: Bracey, Mama told you to help Luther fetch firewood for Sunday. Luther, when you've fed the hogs, bring Bessie in from the back field so's I can milk her.
BRACEY: Lord, listen at Miss Home Economics bossing everybody around.
ANNIE LEE: Everwhat I do, you pick at me, you aggravating lazy bones. Let's finish the chores so's we can play. (*Pushing Bracey up and out of the way.*) I'm going to scrub the floor. (*She throws the dishwater into the yard from the door, then takes a bucket of fresh water from the porch and starts scrubbing the floor with a long-handled scrub brush made of corn shucks set in a block of wood.*)
LUTHER: Come on, Bracey, help me tote the wood.
SARAH: (*Looking out the open door.*) Good

gracious alive! Here comes Winford running like he's going to a fire.
(*Enter Winford, running through the yard while making sure that their mother doesn't see him. He places his package outside the door and enters.*)
BRACEY: How'd you get back so fast? Where's Papa?
WINFORD: (*Breathing hard.*) I run all the way from Maxton. Papa's a-coming with the wagon.
LUTHER: If it was me, I'd have stayed to watch them pretty girls.
WINFORD: Hush, boy, you don't know what you're a-talking about. Anyway, guess what I brought you.
SARAH: Stick candy.
WINFORD: No-o-o, gal, that's too little. I got us something on sale at C. W. Carter's.
LUTHER: A shotgun?
WINFORD: Guns cost too much.
BRACEY: A bream-buster rod and reel?
WINFORD: No, it's something you set down in the water.
BRACEY: I know, I know! One of them steel traps with big teeth, so's we can catch beaver and muskrat!
WINFORD: Our box traps are good enough for that, boy! This here ain't for furs, it's for fish.
LUTHER: Say it is? (*Silencing the others.*) Let me guess. I bet you got a seine.
WINFORD: Well, go and see. (*They start noisily.*) But don't let Mama hear you.
(*Bracey and Luther discover the package by the door and bring it inside.*)
BRACEY: (*Tearing open the package.*) It *is* a seine! Buddy, look at it! (*They unfold the seine—six feet long, three feet wide with wood-*

en handles on each end. Bracey, approvingly.)
It's a short seine.
LUTHER: Yes, *we* can handle this one! Don't have to have Uncle John and them along!
SARAH: Looky here, it's got handles just like a big seine.
(As Sarah and the boys spread the net, Annie Lee admires it, then resumes her scrubbing.)
BRACEY: Hot dog! We can use it today. Sheriff Walter Smith ain't gonna be in them swamps and them snakes on a Saturday evening.
LUTHER: I'll bet he's clear across Long Swamp a-looking for stills.
ANNIE LEE: We could go, soon as we finish the chores!
BRACEY: We! Who you a-talking about, Miss Annie-Home-Ec-Lee?
WINFORD: Hush, Bracey. Annie and Sarah can go with us.
BRACEY: Now wait a minute y'all! It's against the law. Gals are like to get us caught.
ANNIE LEE: I can beat you a-running.
BRACEY: Gal, you wouldn't know what to do.
ANNIE LEE: I been a-muddying many a time. Ain't that like seining?
LUTHER: That's right. You muddy the water to make the fish rise and rush 'em into the net.
BRACEY: Well, Sarah can't help! She's afraid of everything.
SARAH: You lie! I ain't a-scared of nothing—'less it's a ghost.
ANNIE LEE: *(Joining forces with Sarah.)* We're a-going, Bracey. Or eitherways you ain't a-going at all. I'll tell Mama!
WINFORD: Let 'em go. Let 'em go. Sar-ah can watch for the sheriff. *(He carefully rolls up the seine as the others scurry around.)*
ANNIE LEE: I'm going to sweep the yard right now, so's I'll be done.
LUTHER: Let me finish getting in the wood. *(He exits.)*
BRACEY: I'll get Uncle John's shotgun.
SARAH: You can't tote his gun, Bracey.
BRACEY: Can, too, 'cause he won't know about it, dummy. And you better not tell. I'll get us some squirrels and cook 'em on a spit at the old pond. *(He exits.)*
SARAH: I'm going to wrap my feet in tow sack. I'm not going in amidst them snakes in my bare feet.
(Enter Luther with an armful of wood.)
LUTHER: Snakes can't bite you under water, Sarah. Hang 'em upside down and they can't bite you out of water neither.
SARAH: *(She grabs gunny sack scraps and ties them to her feet.)* I ain't a-taking no chances.
WINFORD: Put the seine in the tow sack so's Mama can't see it. I'll take this cornbread and sidemeat. *(He puts leftovers from the stove into a lunch tin. Bracey enters.)*
BRACEY: I got the gun. Where's the matches? *(He finds matches.)* Let's go. *(He notices Sarah's wrapped feet.)* Hot dang! Sarah, you like to get drowned with them things on your feet!
WINFORD: We'll go down Juniper Swamp to the old mill pond. We can more or less get us a big old blackfish.
BRACEY: If we catch a trout or a jack, I'll be real happy.
LUTHER: Don't count on it, Little Brother.
WINFORD: Grab the poles, Bracey, so's Mama won't see the gun.

ANNIE LEE: (*She has finished sweeping the yard.*) I'm done. Y'all ready to go? (*The girls go to Mama and stand masking Bracey and Luther, who are carrying the gun, fishing rods, lunch tin, and the seine in a tow sack.*)

WINFORD: Mama, we're through with the chores. We're a-going down Juniper Swamp a-fishing. Can the girls come with us?

MAMA: You girls finished the house and yard?

ANNIE LEE and SARAH: Yes, ma'am.

ANNIE LEE: Papa can slop the hogs. I'll milk Bessie when we get back.

(*Mama walks towards them. They pretend to look casual, hiding the tow sack.*)

MAMA: I could use your help with the ironing.

AUNT MARY: That's all right, Kathryn, let 'em go play.

MAMA: All right, but you boys watch out. Them snakes'll poison you in a heartbeat, them moccasins. If you get bit, you hustle for home.

BOYS: Yes, ma'am.

MAMA: And be careful. If you step on one of them snags in the water, you'll get blood poisoning.

BOYS: Yes, ma'am.

MAMA: Annie Lee, you take care of Sarah. And don't you go near that water, hear?

ANNIE LEE: Yes, ma'am.

AUNT MARY: Sarah, you bring me back some pretty stones. (*Sarah grins and nods.*)

MAMA: All right, give me some sugar.

(*Annie Lee and Sarah hang onto their mother's neck. Sarah hugs Aunt Mary, too. The others mask the tow sack.*) Run along, young'uns.

SARAH: (*To Winford.*) Where's Little Jack?

WINFORD: He ran along with Papa to Maxton. He ain't back.

BRACEY: We don't need no dog; Luther's a pure snake-killer. Let's go. (*They all traipse off as Mama and Aunt Mary walk toward the house.*)

CURTAIN FALLS

SCENE TWO: The Mill Pond

(*In front of the curtain, Bracey enters, followed by the other children. Sarah stoops occasionally to collect stones. Bracey aims his gun here and there. Suddenly he stops still, aims, shoots, and runs offstage, then back, holding up a squirrel.*)

BRACEY: Buddy, look-a-here. I got it. (*They nod, as he runs alongside each, showing off the squirrel.*)

ANNIE LEE: Winford, what's it like, seining at night? I know that the women go along, too, 'cause Mama told me.

WINFORD: That's right, Annie Lee, the women build a big fire to boil coffee and fry fish. The men go in, and the first fish we catch, well, the women cook them and the men eat them. Drink coffee and eat fish. It's cold in that water; that warms us up.

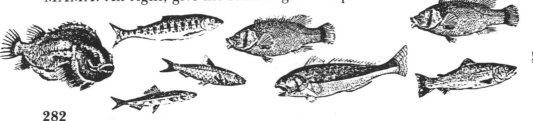

ANNIE LEE: How come you don't use boats?

WINFORD: We're working the holes and shallow places. We keep on till near 'bout day, dump the seines on the hill. We only take the good fish—trout, pike, blackfish, jacks, such as that; anything too small, we just leave 'em to die. Catfish and suckers, we leave them.

LUTHER: We get enough to take all y'all for a picnic on Saturday.

ANNIE LEE: Oh, that's where all those fish come from.

LUTHER: Yes, honey, we hide them in the river in a wire trap. Law comes along, they think we're catching everything with hooks. Have enough for the whole crowd. (*They all laugh.*)

SARAH: I ain't a-wanting to go seining at night. Tell about Uncle John and the haint.

BRACEY: Let me tell it.

LUTHER: Bracey, you weren't even there. Let Winford tell it.

BRACEY: There's another squirrel! (*He runs off ahead, exits.*)

WINFORD: See, we was going a-seining. But Little Jack treed a coon. Leastways we thought it was a coon, till Uncle John shone the lightered splinter up in the tree. Come to see it was a big old white thing.

ANNIE LEE: It was an owl.

WINFORD: Weren't no owl. Looked like a ghost! It took off through the trees and we shot at it. Little Jack was a-barking. He was scared. His hair was standing straight up on his back.

(*A shot is heard. They all jump, startled.*)

BRACEY: (*Offstage.*) I got it!

ANNIE LEE: Mrs. McNair says there ain't no such thing as ghosts, Winford. It's just superstition.

WINFORD: But Aunt Mary heard Uncle David's token, said it sounded just like him a-coughing. Didn't she know he was dead before anybody told us?

LUTHER: What you reckon causes tokens, Winford?

WINFORD: Sometimes I think about it. I believe that there's an ulterior world—I mean beyond what this world is meant to express. This world is our imagination. Hearing a token is like getting into the real world, something like that.

SARAH: You sure got some pretty words, Winford.

ANNIE LEE: Reckon since Mrs. McNair went to college she can't get into the real world?

LUTHER: I know she can't hear tokens.

SARAH: I ain't studying it. Annie Lee, why you reckon Mrs. McNair says I don't talk right?

ANNIE LEE: 'Cause it's not the way they got it in books, Sarah.

SARAH: Grandma says if we talk like that, we're trying to get above our raising.

LUTHER: Yeah, but we got to learn to read and figure sums, Sarah, so they can't cheat us on paper. That's what Papa says.

WINFORD: That's not the whole of it, Luther. I read for the love of it. Sometimes I study the dictionary just to see all those words.

SARAH: You'll go to college one day— and then you won't see the real world neither!

WINFORD: Nope, once I see something I can't unsee it.

BRACEY: (*Entering, holding up two squirrels.*) I got two squirrels!

LUTHER: Mmmm, mmmm—that'll make good eating!

BRACEY: They's lots of squirrels in here. Go on! I'll catch up!

WINFORD: All right, but don't stay too long. (*Winford, Annie Lee, Luther, and Sarah exit.*)

BRACEY: (*Stalking squirrels, talking to himself.*) I know you're up there. I'm a-gonna sit here still as water till you come out. (*He creeps along, his gun to his shoulder; exits.*)

(*CURTAIN OPENS into a scene at the swamp. A creek twists down the middle of the stage. The fishing poles and lunch tin in the tow sack lie on the bank. Winford is teaching Sarah how to catch fish. Luther and Annie are seining down the middle of the creek with the net half-rolled-up at the ends.*)

WINFORD: All right, Sarah, now feel around with your bare hands inside the cypress stump, and if you catch something, mash it under your foot. Then go for his gills and lift him up. (*He lifts a fish he has caught as he explained, takes a forked stick from the back of his pants, and puts the fish on it.*) He can't get away if you got him by the gills.

(*Luther and Annie Lee lift the seine and, find-ing they've caught nothing, climb the bank to watch. Winford and Sarah continue leaning over, feeling for fish.*)

SARAH: I'll go in here by this old cypress knee. I feel one, Winford! I feel one stir-ring! It's real slick, a jack or a pike!

WINFORD: Now step on it, Sarah. Mash it under your foot.

SARAH: Whoooeee, I got a pike, sure as you're born. Well, sir, let me get you by the gills. I can't find his gills, Winford. Where are your gills, you old feller? Hot dang! I'm gonna pull him up the way he is. I'll beat all of y'all a-fishing! (*Sarah pulls up the "fish" to find she has caught a water moccasin. Although terrified, instinc-tively she does as she is instructed.*)

ANNIE LEE: It's a moccasin! Sarah, hold still.

WINFORD: Hang it down so's it can't bite you.

LUTHER: (*He leaps to grab a large stick.*) Now dash it over here on the bank, Sarah! (*Sarah heaves the snake and Luther hits it smartly on the head.*) John Brown it, rascal! You'll never crawl again!

SARAH: (*Trembling with terror.*) Help! I'm stuck! Get me out of here. Them snakes will get me. Get me out of here.

ANNIE LEE: Hurry, Winford!

WINFORD: (*Walking towards Sarah through the water.*) Easy, Sarah. You ought not to have put tow sacks on your feet. (*Luther joins Winford in the water.*)

SARAH: (*Frantically.*) I'm sinking in the mud! Help! (*As the two boys grab Sarah, she gets pulled down into the water.*) You're pull-ing me down in the water. Let go of me! Annie Lee, help!

(*Bracey enters with the gun and four squirrels.*

He watches.)
ANNIE LEE: (*Picking up Luther's big stick and holding it out to Sarah.*) Here, Sarah, pull yourself in.
SARAH: (*Crying and pulling herself in.*) Luther tried to drown me!
ANNIE LEE: Hush your fussing. You want to get out, don't you? (*Sarah pulls herself to safety, but she is shaken.*)
BRACEY: Hark at the crybaby. What did you put them fool things on your feet for anyway?
SARAH: (*Crying profusely.*) I am not a crybaby.
ANNIE LEE: (*Reassuring Sarah.*) Bracey, leave Sarah alone. You'd be scared too, if you caught a water moccasin.
BRACEY: Anyway, look what I got—four squirrels!
WINFORD: Now don't be a-shooting that gun no more. We don't want to scare the fish. (*Bracey puts the gun down and reaches for some corn bread.*)
ANNIE LEE: (*Puts her arm around Sarah's shoulder, reaches for the lunch tin, offers her some cornbread, and nods towards the snake.*) You can skin that snake and Uncle John will make you a belt.
WINFORD: Come on, let's fish. I'll take anything we can get—cats, mudsuckers, anything. (*The boys go in the water with the seine.*) Come on, Annie, we need you to help rush.
ANNIE LEE: I'm coming. I'm coming.
WINFORD: Start out there in the pond, and when they try to escape in the creek, we'll catch 'em.
ANNIE LEE: Let me hitch up my skirt.
WINFORD: You muddy the water and cut off that section.

ANNIE LEE: Sure wish girls could wear short pants.
BRACEY: Hot dog! There're are some big ones down here. One just bumped into me. Rush 'em in, Annie Lee.
ANNIE LEE: I am.
WINFORD: Now, Luther, raise it up. We got us a netful.
LUTHER: Carry it up on the bank.
WINFORD: Get out of the way, Annie.
LUTHER: Grab it.
WINFORD: Pull it up, Sarah.
BRACEY: Watch out! Don't let 'em flip out!
LUTHER: Pull it!
WINFORD: Now turn 'em out. (*They turn the fish out of the net onto the ground.*)
LUTHER: Catch 'em, Annie Lee. Catch 'em before they flip back in the water!
ANNIE LEE: Ow!
WINFORD: Watch the cats don't sting you!
BRACEY: (*Chasing flopping fish.*) Look at those big old cats and mudsuckers.
LUTHER: Now hang 'em on the stick through their gills. See, like this. (*The children gather and string the fish.*)
ANNIE LEE: Keep still, you big old flopper. Catch him, Sarah!
BRACEY: They's more in there.
WINFORD: Come on.
BRACEY: Let me hold the net. Luther, you and Annie Lee rush the fish.
LUTHER: All right. I'm a-trying to get that blackfish.
(*The children take the seine in the water. Sarah inspects the fish on the stick. While they are absorbed in their tasks, Sheriff Walter Smith enters. Sarah has her back to him. When he speaks, Sarah jumps.*)

SHERIFF SMITH: What are you boys a-doing in here? (*The two boys drop the seine and turn their heads to look at the sheriff. They remain silent. Sarah quietly lays the fish beside her.*) Don't you boys know it's against the law to seine?

WINFORD: Yes sir, but our daddy told us that we could.

SHERIFF SMITH: What?

WINFORD: He told us to go on and catch some fish.

SHERIFF SMITH: Whose boys are you?

WINFORD: Winford Locklear's boys, sir.

SHERIFF SMITH: Winford knows you boys down here a-seining?

WINFORD: No sir, but he told us to go on and fish.

SHERIFF SMITH: Well, you boys get out of here with that seine. You go home. I'll talk to Winford in the morning.

(*The boys reach down in the water, bring up the seine and carry it out of the pond. EXIT Sheriff Smith. The children sit on the bank and begin to eat corn bread, talking in low voices.*)

LUTHER: Boys, we got to go back, they's a fish in there. It may be a big one—a blackfish or a trout. I ain't going home without him.

ANNIE LEE: (*Talking to Sarah.*) Luther and Sheriff Walter think we're boys.

BRACEY: (*Ignoring Annie Lee.*) You're right, Luther. I felt him running around my feet. I believe it's a big old blackfish.

LUTHER: Mr. Walter ain't a-coming back. He's looking for stills. Come on!

(*They all back in the water quietly, but Bracey immediately gets excited.*)

BRACEY: I feel him. I feel him! He hit my leg! He's in here!

(*Enter Sheriff Smith.*)

SHERIFF SMITH: (*Raising his voice to an authoritative command.*) You boys! You boys come back here. Now you listen to me!

(*The Locklears look up, startled.*)

WINFORD: Yes sir.

SHERIFF SMITH: You young'uns get out of this pond and go home. If you don't, I'm a-gonna carry you over to Maxton and put you in jail. It'd be a shame to put your sisters in jail. Now you get out, and I better not find you here again. (*The children take their seine, get their fish, and head for home. Bracey grabs the gun and the squirrels.*)

CURTAIN

(*The children walk again in front of the curtain, this time homeward.*)

BRACEY: Doggone it, we almost had that devil! I could see him. He's a big one, a big old blackfish. I could almost catch him with my hands.

LUTHER: I wonder what Mr. Walter's going to say to Papa.

ANNIE LEE: Did Papa know you got us the seine, Winford?

WINFORD: No, but he goes seining with the men at night just like everybody else.

ANNIE LEE: Well, he'll know you got it now.

EXIT ALL

SCENE THREE: The Visit

Scene: The home of the Locklear family. Everything is prepared for Sunday dinner. Mrs.

Locklear puts a tobacco-twine crocheted table-cloth on the table. A pretty quilt can be seen on a well-made bed. Aunt Mary arranges a bouquet of flowers and peacock feathers and stands it on a table in the corner. There is an orderly elegance in this simple household. Annie Lee is setting the table as her mother pulls bread and a cake from the oven. The boys throw a ball in the backyard. Winford Locklear, Sr. sits on a bench in front enjoying his pipe.

(Enter Sheriff Smith. Aunt Mary sees him from the window and, embarrassed, moves out of sight.)

PAPA: Well, sir, what brings you out this way today, Walter?

SHERIFF SMITH: Evening, Winford. I have a little something to talk over with you.

PAPA: Well, come on up.

SHERIFF SMITH: (*He comes to the bench, sits down beside Mr. Locklear.*) Been a-looking for stills. Jim and I found one and busted it up yesterday morning. You know of any here-abouts?

PAPA: No, Walter, I sure don't. Not in this here section.

MAMA: (*Coming outside to welcome the sheriff.*) Well, Mr. Walter, nice to see you. Vittles about ready. Such as we have, you're welcome to it.

SHERIFF SMITH: Thank you, ma'am, that's very hospitable of you. (*Noticing Aunt Mary approvingly.*) Evening, Miss Mary. (*Mary smiles, but says nothing.*)

MAMA: (*Calling to the other side of the house.*) Y'all children, come on, let's eat! Don't forget to wash your hands. (*The boys drop their play and run around the house to the pump. They stop short when they see the sheriff. As the sheriff speaks with the father*

and the boys, Annie Lee and Sarah at first merely look out the door; they finally emerge to join the others.)

SHERIFF SMITH: Well, hello, boys. I believe we met yesterday.

WINFORD: (*Lowering his eyes, speaking respectfully.*) Yes sir.

SHERIFF SMITH: What were you a-doing?

WINFORD: (*Eyes still lowered.*) We were seining, Mr. Walter.

SHERIFF SMITH: (*To the father.*) Winford, you knowed your boys was down at the mill pond a-seining?

PAPA: No, but they come home yesterday evening and told me you stopped them. Said they had to leave a big old blackfish down there.

SHERIFF SMITH: I had to tell them to get out of there two different times.

PAPA: Now, see here, Sheriff, children is children. I didn't bring my young'uns up to do wrong, and I don't think you ought to talk to them like grown folks. If they do anything, you bring it to me. It's not against the law for them to fish in that old pond. How come you a-running my boys out of that hole anyhow?

(*During this speech, Mrs. Locklear and Aunt Mary walk up to listen. Mrs. Locklear nods her head. Mary looks at Walter Smith with new eyes.*)

SHERIFF SMITH: Well, they had a seine.

PAPA: It's like this, Walter, my boys don't have much time for fishing and fooling around. They gets through with the chores on Saturday evening, you know boys are going to fish. Winford Junior bought that seine. He ain't harming nobody, minding his own business.

MAMA: Mr. Walter, them fishing laws are passed by rich people a-trying to keep the fish for themselves. They ain't a-wanting us Indians to catch them. My boys bring home everwhat they catch—cats, mud-suckers, such as that.

PAPA: Anyhow, scarcely a body lives up in this section 'cept me and my brothers. Rich folks ain't a-coming up in these swamps and these snakes nohow. And they're so full of fish, you can't never fish them out. (*Mrs. Locklear and Aunt Mary look at each other, nodding in agreement.*) We work hard trying to make an honest living. And the law lets rich folks by. My boys ain't a-breaking God's laws. Just trying to put vittles on the table.

(*Sheriff Smith, nods, considering what has been said. Mrs. Locklear and Aunt Mary go into the house to finish getting the meal ready.*)

SHERIFF SMITH: (*To the children.*) Now listen, boys. You know the problem with seining is turning the fish out on the hill and leaving half to die. I don't want you a-wasting fish.

LUTHER: We take them all, Mr. Walter.

BRACEY: We don't leave nary a one.

WINFORD: Mama cooked those fish. We're eating them for dinner.

MAMA: (*Stepping out of the house.*) Dinner is ready. (*She holds out her hands, indicating that her sons should show theirs, then sends them back to the pump to wash in a pail of water. She, the sheriff, and Mr. Locklear go indoors.*)

SHERIFF SMITH: (*Looking again at Aunt Mary. This time she returns his gaze with pride.*) How pretty you keep everything, Miss Kathryn, Miss Mary.

MAMA: (*Bustling with the meal. The children are entering and standing behind their places at the table.*) My children's good housekeepers. Sheriff, will you sit here? Children, you may sit down. Sheriff, will you ask the blessing?

SHERIFF SMITH: (*As they all bow their heads.*) Dear Lord, make us truly grateful for these blessings and for all the nourishment for our body, Amen.

FAMILY: Amen.

(*Mrs. Locklear passes the plates of food for the men to serve themselves.*)

PAPA: Now, tell us what you're a-doing in all these swamps on a Sunday.

SHERIFF SMITH: Well, you know, your cousin Claude's been a-making moonshine.

PAPA: Yep. Wish he'd give it up and try to make a decent living.

SHERIFF SMITH: He's going to give it up now, I reckon. He'll be on the chain gang for awhile. Revenuers caught him yesterday morning about daybreak, making moonshine. They run him right down through a patch of briars and down the other side of that canal yonder. And when he come out, his clothes were pure tore up.

PAPA: I'll tell you something, Sheriff, when we were boys, and used to play fox and hounds, Claude never did like to get caught.

CURTAIN: THE END

Kate Rinzler
aided by Wanda Locklear Kettlety and Johnny Bullard

Most good writings are derived from true experience, although characters, events, and settings are rearranged and enlarged through imagination. Most good writers also supplement their memories and personal experience by doing research and consulting with others. This play is an unusually good example of how writing can be a cooperative venture.

Kate Rinzler (1937–   )

Kate Rinzler, the playwright, "started writing poetry in elementary school and never stopped." Trained as a Shakespearean actress, she became fascinated by the idea of drama rooted in oral history. Since attending UCLA and receiving her master's degree in social anthropology from Goddard College, she has written a number of plays, some of which have been performed at the Smithsonian Institute in Washington. Currently she is coauthoring a history of the Smithsonian Festival of American Folklife. She wrote "Going Seining" while working in educational programs in Robeson County.

Wanda Locklear Kettlety

Wanda Locklear Kettlety grew up in a farming family in Robeson County and is now studying to become a registered nurse. As a native of the area, she provided advice on regional dialect to Ms. Rinzler for this and several other plays based on oral history and Indian legends.

Johnny Bullard (1909–   )

"Going Seining" is adapted from an oral narrative given by Johnny Bullard, a native of Robeson County. It deals with a personal experience from his own childhood. Bullard has been a farmer and educator and is now an assistant pastor at the Prospect Methodist Church in Robeson County. He is also widely known as a raconteur—one who tells stories and tales with skill and wit. Many of his stories deal with farming, hunting, and fishing—daily activities in his area of the state.

Language Alert

As with many stories and poems in this collection, the characters speak in a special dialect—in this case, the dialect of rural people with limited education. (This is not racial dialect. Notice that the language of the Indian family and the white sheriff are almost identical.) Some references are also made to things that are now rarely seen. Some special words and references to watch for:

1. *everwhat*: everything
2. *bream-buster rod and reel*: Bream are a kind of fish, so you can guess what *bream-buster* means.
3. *seine*: a net wrapped around two poles (When the poles are spread, the net sinks into the water. Then, after fish are entrapped, the net is pulled from the water. Larger seines might be ten to twelve feet long and drop as deep as five to six feet. Smaller ones might be only six feet long and drop about three feet.)
4. *sweep the yard:* Some rural folk preferred a dirt yard to grass. Often these yards were carefully raked and swept to keep them neat.
5. *like to*: sometimes used as short for *likely to*
6. *traipse*: to walk about casually
7. *lightered splinter*: a torch made of light wood that is full of resin
8. *token*: (pronounced "toe-un") This word refers to something that is taken as a sign of a person's death.
9. *stills*: short for *distilleries* (A still is an apparatus for distilling something, usually alcohol. Stills were—and sometimes are—used by "moonshiners" to make illegal whiskey (often called "moonshine" because the work was done mostly at night with equipment hidden in the woods). Until recent years, when the sale of alcoholic beverages was made legal, stills were rather common all over this state.
10. *vittles*: (non-standard spelling for *victuals*) food for human beings
11. *John Brown it!*: A byword or epithet, similar to *Doggone it* or *Dang it!* Variation (not in this play): "I'll be John Brown if . . ." meaning, "I'll be darned . . ." or "I'll be switched. . . ."
12. *revenuers*: Officers representing the U.S. Department of Revenue. They hunted and arrested moonshiners, who were making whiskey on which no taxes—revenues—were paid.

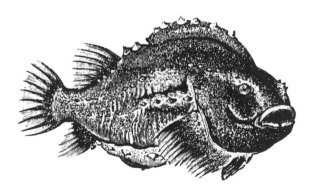

Reflecting

1. This family has five children, and although the play is not very long, we get to see each one distinctly. From the following list, choose a word or phrase that you believe applies to each child. Then choose two examples of his or her behavior or speech which support your choice. (Note: More than one word may apply to any one character and certain words may apply to more than one character.)
   a. adventuresome
   b. curious
   c. ambitious
   d. reflective
   e. shows leadership
   f. resourceful
   g. helpful
   h. kind
   i. responsible
   j. determined

2. Assume that you are Sheriff Smith. Would you handle this situation as he did? Consider these facts:
   a. It is against the law to seine in the river.
   b. These are children, not adults.
   c. The children use their seine, not in the river, but in backwoods swamps.
   d. Rural people are having "hard times"; it is difficult for them to make a good living.
   e. All of the fish that they catch will be used for the family's food. (Note: This is different from the situation in which the men go seining at night and sometimes waste some of the fish.)
   f. This is generally a law-abiding family, and the father and mother discipline their children.

3. In Scene Two, notice the conversation about language: what Mrs. McNair says about language, what Grandma says, what Papa says, and what Winford says. Evidently these people think a great deal about language and what it has to do with their well-being. Can you argue for each of these opinions? Can you argue against them?

Auction Day

Guy Owen

Preview

What's the most exciting day in your year? Your birthday? Christmas? The first day of summer vacation?

Those who farm tobacco would rank the day they take their crop to the warehouse for the auction as one of the most important days in any year. On that day, they find out whether the long hours they have devoted to planting, tending, cropping, barning, and curing tobacco have finally paid off—or whether they will end the year in debt, worrying about how to put food on the table and shoes on their children's feet until the next auction day a year later.

In this story taken from Guy Owen's novel, *Journey for Joedel,* we see that day through the eyes of Joedel Shaw, a part-Indian boy, in southeastern North Carolina. He and his family are tenant farmers. They don't own the land they farm, but share the profits with the owner, Mr. Eller. Today is especially exciting for Joedel, for this is the first time his father has permitted him to come along to the auction. He is even allowed to offer his own bundle of tobacco for sale. For a boy to whom money of his own is rare indeed, this is a splendid opportunity.

We pick up the story as Joedel wakes up after spending the night tending the fires in the barn where the tobacco is cured.

"Joedel." His father was shaking his shoulder. "Wake up. It's auction day, son."

It was only a little past dawn when the boy awoke the second time. He had been dreaming of a lost hoard of gold coins, but when he reached triumphantly for them, suddenly they turned to crumbly vanilla wafers. The mournful quaver of an owl was mixed in with his deep sense of loss. When he opened one eye, there was not the platinum beauty of Jean Harlow casting its radiance on him from above his cot. Instead, there was only the advertisement tacked on the log wall, the moon-face of John Barefoot, owner of the New Deal Warehouse.

"Joedel." Clint Shaw shook him roughly. "It's time. It's time to stir, boy."

For an instant fear gripped him, and he thought he had fallen asleep and let the fire go out, spoiling the tobacco. But as he sat up on the gritty quilt, he heard the reassuring roar of the furnace and the crackle of hot flues. The temperature would be over two hundred degrees now, the stems nearly all dried out.

Joedel stood up, rubbing the cobwebs out of his dark eyes. His shoulders were stiff and sore, for he had helped barn tobacco the day before for Mr. Eller, and he was not yet used to lifting the heavy crates from the mule-drawn sleds.

Just now Mr. Eller whistled shrilly from the Big House, and Joedel heard the Negro sharecroppers answer, as his father did, with a whistle or loud "Wahoo!" Across the flat fields and pastures he saw plumes of smoke coiling up from the scattered shanties. He imagined the little white-haired landowner standing near the magnolia tree at the two-story white house, whistling with two fingers stuck in his mouth. Cap'n Jim always went to bed with the chickens and was usually up at four o'clock, urging his tenants to the fields and barns.

Father and son waited under the open shelter as Mr. Eller sent a final importunate blast across the dew-drenched morning. Then Clint Shaw laced up his brogans.

"Listen at him. Ain't he something now, the Cap'n? Loud enough to wake up the devil." As usual, he spoke harshly, disguising his closeness to the old man whose farm he tended, the admiration and pride he would never articulate.

They grinned shyly at each other, fully awake now.

Joedel saw that Maddie's side of the bed was empty, only Sissie lay curled under the gritty sheet, close to the warm clay-daubed logs. His mother had already walked the two hundred yards to the tenant house to start their breakfast—and dinner, too, since they would be gone all day. He heard the rattle of the chain as she drew water from the well, and a pair of mourning doves in the pasture behind the Big House.

The boy turned to the door, then pulled the twine that his mother had braided from used tobacco string. When the thermometer bobbed against the dusty pane of glass, he peered at it, also noting how the middle flue was glowing a dull red from the heat.

"It's two hundred ten," he said, letting the warm twine slip smoothly through his fingers. He thought, If one of those sticks fell now across a flue—it would be the end of Papa's dream, forever.

"You climb up and check them stems. They ought to be pretty near dried out. They are, we'll let her cool down now, before we leave." His father blew the sooty lantern out, shaking it close to his ear to test how much oil remained.

Fully alive now at the possibilities of the day, Joedel climbed up on the dwindling stack of firewood, onto the tin shelter, then carefully up the ladder nailed to the side of the barn. When he reached the small wooden window under the gable, he paused for a moment. An ineluctable feeling of joy swept through him and he shouted a loud "Wahoo!" to the morning, his throat swelling like a rooster's. It was good to feel the old barn logs give under his weight. A chunk of clay came loose and thudded against the furnace below; a spurt of hot air shot out, tickling his patched knee.

He let his lungs fill with the dew-rinsed air, glancing across the wide, flat fields. There was enough light now to distinguish between tobacco, corn, and cotton, then, vaguely, the tall paper-shelled pecan trees at Mr. Eller's. He could see that the other tenants, all Negroes, were already scurrying about, preparing for opening day at the auction. He heard a trotting team and wagon on the clay road, headed for Clayton.

The boy's heart quickened, because for the first time he would have a basket of his own to sell at the auction, a gift from Cap'n Jim—even if it was damaged, slightly rotten. No, not really rotten, for he had picked out all the tainted leaves he could find. This day, he told himself, he would remember all the years of his life.

As the light of morning spread, he looked once again toward the tenant house, relishing the new perspective. He liked the old house, even though his mother did not, preferring the cotton-mill village they had left in Hoover times. Joedel felt as though he were looking down on the barns and sagging back porch from a great height, say, the red sawdust pile at Sam Eller's mill. The rail fence lot, smokehouse, and clay potato bank looked neat and clean; the hail-shredded sunflowers and sagging scarecrow in the garden seemed suddenly dwarfed.

He felt a surge of pride, for the weathered gray house was the biggest of all Mr. Jim Eller's tenant houses. The others were only three-room shanties with stunted outbuildings and small garden plots. Here was where the landowner had lived before the war, before he built the two-story "Big House" on the green rise, where soon the array of lightning rods would sparkle in the rising sun. Under the pecan trees a rooster crowed and, nearby, the boy's pet bantam answered.

"You, Joedel."

Quickly, he twisted the latch and opened the small board window, turning his face away from the blast of hot smothery air, his nostrils stinging with the scent of drying tobacco. His left arm broke into a sweat as he thrust it into the barn, his fingers fumbling above the top tier pole for leaves that were dry as locust husks. Each time he bent a stem end it broke with a snap, stiff as a dried twig. He broke three off to show his father, letting the window bang shut.

On the ground, Joedel wiped his face on his shirt sleeve, handing the three warm stems to his father. "They killed out. Those stems are dry as fodder."

"Yeah, they're dry as a old maid's kiss. We'll let her cool down now." Then he asked, "How does it look up there?"

"It's some kind of pretty, Papa. That tobacco's nothing but golden wrappers."

His father smiled and spat beyond the shelter. "Yeah. Cap'n Jim climbed up there yesterday, him at his age. Even he had to brag, though to be sure it's got no weight to it. Pretty as a guinea hen, but it's too light."

Joedel threw back the iron furnace door, and his father kicked open the two air holes on each side of the front door.

"Now we better get a move on. That market yonder ain't gonna wait on us." Already his father had heard the loaded wagons and trucks passing on the dirt road which led to the landing and ferry.

Clint Shaw picked his daughter up without waking her, holding her close to his blue denim jumper. Joedel watched as his gaunt father strode through the wet weeds toward the tenant house.

"I'll be on directly to milk, Papa."

"Get the doors. I clean forgot the doors."

The boy opened both doors of the barn and propped them with tobacco sticks. Papa's as excited as I am, he thought, but he won't let it show.

The sun was not yet up. Joedel milked the brindled cow slowly, for he enjoyed milking. In the next stall he could hear the two mules stomping, their teeth grinding the few weevily ears of corn his father had given them as a tribute to the special day. The cow slobbered as she switched her tail, chewing on nubbins that were more cob than corn. Nearby, a partridge called to its mate in the pine thicket.

The boy pressed his dark head into the cow's flank. Tilting the pail on his bare toes, he aimed the white stream toward the corner. He liked to hear the jet of warm milk hit the pail, then watch the quick foam as it rose steadily in the dented bucket. Joedel's nose quivered with the pleasure of the milk smell, as it did to green fennel or the cypress shingles he split to build pyramidal bird traps. He did not mind when the cow's tail, aimed at a buzzing horsefly, raked a cocklebur across his copper cheek.

"Soo, there, Bessie, soo, gal."

He had carved the cow in a bar of Octagon soap for the hobby and craft school fair last fall, idealizing her, for she had only one hooked horn. The carving had not won a prize, but his arrow collection had.

He had not even thought to enter the collection of arrowheads until Doctor Clay's wife asked him to. She was the sixth-grade room mother and she had driven over from Clayton to ask him about his arrowheads. She was a tall handsome lady with frank blue eyes, her auburn hair drawn back in a bun.

Joedel liked her immediately. She had not made him feel like an Indian, a stranger in an alien land. She had merely suggested that he mount his collection and she was almost sure it would win a prize, saying she had learned of his hobby from DeWitt, her son.

And he had done it, with Mr. Sam Eller's help. He had mounted the arrowheads—flints, slates, all kinds—in an old Barlow knife showcase, with a spearpoint at the center. At Mr. Sam's suggestion they had glued them in so as to make the design of a huge arrow, poised in flight. It had won a blue ribbon, and for the first time he had been pleased to acknowledge the Indian blood that had brought his family nothing but trouble in Cape Fear County.

Joedel had blushed under the stares of his classmates as he stood up to receive the ribbon. The doctor's wife praised him for taking pride in his heritage. "After all, Joe Dell has a right to a special sense of pride. The Indians were here a long time before the white men came. And we all know that the Croatans are descendants of the Lost Colony—the first white settlement in America."

Joedel took the ribbon, thinking of the theater in Lumberton, where the Indians sat separately from both white and Negroes.

Only a few clapped when he sat down, and Joedel noticed that the other judges were frowning at the homeroom mother, now presenting a ribbon to Trudy, a pretty classmate, for a slender vase modeled from red clay. He found himself staring at the red lips of Trudy's vase, and, blushing, looked at the back of the room-mother's head.

The doctor's wife had meant well, mentioning the widely known legend of the Lost Colony and tacitly accepting the theory that the boy's mother was descended from the mysterious Croatans. But, Joedel thought, she doesn't even know that we're no longer called Croatans. The

name had come to mean only a mongrel race to be looked down on with contempt, in the end shortened to Cro by the neighboring Negroes and white farmers. Finally, the beleaguered remnants of the Croatans had given up their claim to being descendants of the English colonists and petitioned the Legislature to be called the Cherokees of Robeson County. (Later they would be renamed Lumbees.) Most

people, like Mrs. Clay, were unaware of the new tribal name and the reasons for the change and went on calling them Croatans, the name the English found carved on the tree at Manteo when they discovered that the first colony had vanished into the wilderness.

His mother strained the milk through two layers of white cloth, pouring off the last into a half-gallon jar and screwing on

the bright lid which she kept spotless. It was Mr. Jim Eller's jar of milk.

"You take that milk on to the Big House. And don't you waste time, Joedel." Breakfast would be ready when he returned and then they would load the tobacco on the Hoover cart. "You know how your papa is, always in a strut on auction day." She smoothed the feedsack apron over her bulging stomach. "And don't forget he said ask Mr. Jim about the tarpaulin."

"Yessum."

As Joedel walked the worn path along the ditch to the white house on the little hill, the sun began to rise over the tall longleaf pines. A few birds were already up, towhees and sparrows, scrabbling on the ditchbanks among the sumac and trumpet vines. The heavy dew was cool on his bare feet, the warm milk sloshing in the jar in the crook of his arm. The boy began whistling.

Every morning for more than two years he had taken the jar of milk to Mr. Eller, not missing even once because of illness. He came to realize that the little Cap'n did not really need all that much milk, now that his nervous and childish wife had been taken to the State Hospital in Raleigh. No, Mr. Eller went on buying the same amount because he knew they needed the ten cents a day. Also, lately there was a growing family of cats that slept under his back porch, and the old man kept a permanent bowl of milk for them.

He knocked on the back door. The times must be bad for Mr. Eller, too. His large square house was scaling paint and

297

the screen on the wide back porch was rotting out, with unpatched holes open to the flies.

Mr. Eller had let things go after his wife was committed to the State Hospital. The chickens roosted in the walnut trees, their droppings falling on the hood of his old Studebaker. A brood of pigs had rooted up a crepe myrtle bush where the lightning rods were grounded on the south side. Inside, the floors were not always swept and the sagging furniture went half dusted, for the old colored woman had cataracts on both eyes and was a slovenly housekeeper.

The moment he knocked with his knuckles, calling "Mr. Jim," a half-dozen cats scurried from under the house, purring, and twining their tails around his patched overalls.

In the kitchen he heard Mr. Eller stirring around, eating his solitary breakfast. When he opened the door, Joedel caught the odor of bacon and coffee and the noise of the staticky radio.

Joedel saw that Mr. Eller had already put on his rumpled seersucker suit, white shirt, and black bow tie, his auction day dress that never varied, as though it were a uniform. There were snuff stains on his right sleeve, and his back shoes were unpolished and turned over at the heels.

Until a light stroke and his daughters joined forces to stop him, the little Cap'n had toiled with his Negro sharecroppers, sweating profusely, working harder than any of his hands in the hot, flat fields.

"I declare," his daughters would say, "Papa dearly loves to go perfectly filthy." And they hinted that Mrs. Eller's nervous condition could be blamed on her husband, who never took time off from his work for vacationing or entertainment.

On the other hand, the Negroes took a fierce pride in the little Cap'n. "He don't ask us to do nothing he wouldn't do hisself, that man." In the long cotton rows he would lead the field hands, his hoe setting a steady rhythm, sweat running off his prominent nose, staining his white dress shirt with salt. "Work? Do Jesus, look at that man go. Whooee! "And the Negroes would smile at each other, lift their hoes in the blazing sun and try to catch up with the white man leading them mercilessly under an old felt hat, pausing only to spit on his hands.

Now Mr. Eller opened the screen door and looked at the lanky boy on the back steps.

"I brought the milk, Mr. Jim."

"Come on in, son."

He took the half-gallon jar, slamming the door against the swarming cats and hitting Joedel's heel. For a moment he railed tenderly at the cats that threatened to inundate his home, asserting that the Lord had sent them as a curse on his head.

This was an early morning ritual and Joedel smiled. He watched as Mr. Eller poured out half the jar of milk into a cracked porcelain bowl and slipped it out the rusty screen to the hungry cats.

"There you are, sir. You greedy tom." Then to Joedel, "There's not a thing more pestiferous on God's green earth than a pack of mangy, ungrateful cats. They are a curse and a care."

"Yes, sir."

Joedel looked at the long table on the porch. It was piled high with vegetables brought by the tenants, now that Mr. Eller no longer tended a garden. Under the laden table were striped watermelons and warty orange squashes. At the end of the porch was a large blue vase with shedding sea oats in it and nailed to the wall a deer's antlers holding Mr. Eller's summer hats.

Aunt Mary Mape came out from the kitchen, an old woman with fierce hair and skin the color of a fig newton. She peered at Joedel through half-blind eyes, smiling.

"How're you, Aunt Mary Mape?"

"I'm fair to middling for a old woman, I reckon." She took the jar from Mr. Eller. Nodding at him, she said querulously, "You see he's going. He won't listen to Doctor Clay. He done told him he could miss one opening day in his life."

Joedel told her it wouldn't seem like an auction without Mr. Jim. Which was true; he hadn't missed an opening sale since before the war. And he had been the first farmer to plant tobacco in the whole township.

"You mind him to bring back my ointment from that yonder drugstore."

"Yessum."

Mr. Eller spoke. "You all got that curing ready to put on the floor?"

"It's ready, Mr. Jim. It's in good order."

Remembering Maddie's admonition, Joedel was turning away from the back door.

Mr. Jim asked, "What about your little basket? You gonna put it on the auction? His voice was less severe, his thin lips smiling.

Joedel looked across the overgrown privet hedge toward the scuppernong arbor. "It's ready. I got it picked out and disguised good now. Papa says you all reserved space for my pile."

"I hope you have a good sale, Joedel, your first one," Aunt Mary Mape said. "I done said a prayer for you."

Joedel was embarrassed. He could not look the old man in the eye. If he did, he knew that he would give himself away, maybe his lip would tremble.

"I'm much obliged to you, Mr. Jim."

Mr. Eller did not even nod, for that was his manner, brusque. But before Joedel had rounded the corner he called after him. "Wait. You tell Clinton I'm sending Shad on with my two-horse wagon. I'm sending him on directly, and I mean for him to use it, hear?" Mr. Eller said he never intended to take any chances with that one-horse Hoover cart. The use of the wagon would cost the tenant nothing.

Then he added, "Tell him I can't spare any tarpaulin now."

"I'll tell him for you, Mr. Jim."

But he was frowning, for he knew Clint Shaw had his mind set on going to market in his own cart. He was that prideful—one reason he had refused to load up on the International truck—though the extra cost was the main consideration.

Clint had built the Hoover cart himself, using the rear axle and wheels of the Model A Ford they had moved to the farm with, selling the rest for junk during the first hard winter.

Joedel lengthened his stride. Still, the two-horse wagon would be faster; it would give them more time to spend in Clayton before the auction began. Maybe, on the way back home, Clint would let him sit up there and drive the team of white mules by himself.

Suddenly he began running toward home, clutching the dime in his pocket.

But he could not pass the curing barn without looking inside again. He bent in the open doorway, feeling the escaping heat across his ribs, filling his lungs with the sharp, pleasant odor. He peered in at the heavily veined leaves hanging on sticks from the poles, rising in tiers above the cooling flues to the roof. Now brittle as fodder, they had colored up yellow and orange, and he knew his cropping would bring the top price at the New Deal Warehouse, even if there was a depression on. Even a depression could not diminish the beauty of tier on tier of the golden leaves. More, he knew that he had had a part in the raising of the tobacco, and that it would make a payment on the piece of land his father had set his heart and mind on owning.

MEET THE AUTHOR:
Guy Owen (1925–1981)

Guy Owen grew up on a tobacco farm near Clarkton, but after finishing three degrees at UNC-Chapel Hill, he never again worked on a farm or lived in a rural area. However, we might say that this writer/publisher/university professor plowed those fields forever. In his poetry and novels he repeatedly captured the work, beliefs, joys, and hardships of people who lived the life he had known as a boy.

While he was a student at Clarkton High School, his English teacher, Jean Lightfoot Newton, submitted some of his poems to an anthology. With this encouragement, he went to UNC-Chapel Hill to study English. His studies were interrupted by World War II, in which he served in the Third Army, but eventually he completed his formal education and began a career in college teaching. In addition to becoming one of the most beloved professors at North Carolina State University, he founded and edited what became a very influential poetry journal, *Southern Poetry Review.*

He also fulfilled his own writing ambitions, publishing many articles and essays, two collections of poetry, and five novels. One novel, *The Ballad of the Flim-Flam Man*, became a prize-winning and popular comic film. *The Flim-Flam Man* starred George C. Scott as a "con man" who swindled greedy and gullible people out of their money. Owen's books and writing career won him five awards, including the North Carolina Award for Literature.

As a writing teacher, he proposed two main principles. First, be as specific as possible. "Never say 'tree' if you can say 'pine' or 'willow,' " he would advise. "Never write 'flower'; write 'rose' or 'marigold' or 'chrysanthemum.' " The second principle was : "Make your reader comfortable." By that he meant that a writer should give enough information in a sufficiently clear style that the reader doesn't have to struggle to enter the writer's world of thoughts.

Language Alert

Allusions

1. In the second paragraph we are told that Joedel thinks of "the platinum beauty of Jean Harlow." He is referring to a beautiful blonde movie star who starred in many films during the 1930s and was considered the most glamorous actress of the day—much as Marilyn Monroe was in the fifties and sixties. (What film star would Joedel think of if this story were written today?)
2. You will see references to "Hoover times," and "the Hoover cart," both named for President Herbert Hoover who, fairly or not, was widely blamed for the Great Depression.

Vocabulary: Take a Hint!

Using the context of the sentence, can you recognize the meaning of the italicized words? From the three choices offered for each word, select the best definition.

1. Because I was so excited, I found it difficult to *articulate* my gratitude for her gift.
   a. figure out   b. express verbally   c. repay
2. In the barnyard, the *bantam rooster* was crowing loudly, as if to make up for his size.
   a. a breed of giant fowl   b. a breed of tall fowl   c. a breed of small fowl
3. Although she did nothing, the glance she gave me showed that she *tacitly* agreed with me.
   a. silently, without speaking   b. with great hope   c. grudgingly

4. Mindful of the massed enemy forces just over the hill, at last the *beleaguered* soldiers surrendered.
   a. surrounded, beseiged   b. without rations   c. without ammunition
5. When I saw the coffee stains on the tablecloth, the newspapers littering the floor, and the cigarettes dangling from the ashtray, I knew she was a *slovenly* housekeeper.
   a. sick   b. untidy   c. hot-tempered
6. After the concert, hundreds of requests for autographs *inundated* the pleased band members.
   a. bored   b. infuriated   c. flooded
7. Frowning, she turned to her husband. "You never take me out any more," she said *querulously*.
   a. in an angry manner   b. in a calm manner   c. in a complaining manner
8. After the captain had given the men their orders, he dismissed them *brusquely* and hurried away.
   a. abruptly, bluntly   b. in a comical way   c. angrily

Reflecting

In a news story or essay, writers frequently state their points directly—they make a statement, then support it with details. For example, a writer might start out by saying, "Auction Day is an exciting day in tobacco country." He or she would then tell how many farmers crowded the town when they came to auction; what they said about the prices; how the merchants looked forward to selling clothing and other merchandise; and how sellers and buyers alike were enchanted by the auctioneer's chant.

A fiction writer, however, usually gives us the details and lets *us* make generalizations—just as we live and observe in our own lives and then draw conclusions about what we've experienced and seen.

From reading this story, what conclusions can you draw about the following?

1. The way that people who work for Cap'n Jim Eller feel about him. (Include the black fieldhands, Clint and Joedel Shaw, and Aunt Mary Mape, the housekeeper. None of them state their feelings directly, but you can infer how they feel from what they say and do.)
2. Whether the farm owner and the tenants are hard working or shiftless and lazy.
3. How they feel about their tobacco crop.
4. How well-to-do the Shaw family and the Ellers are.

The Vanilla Man

Ruth Moose

Preview

You have probably heard your grandparents or other older people talk about the Great Depression which began in 1929. You may have listened to tales about how poor everyone was, how so many people were thrown out of work, and how they had to "make do or do without," since there was so little money to buy even the necessities of life. Many people still laugh sheepishly about how being a "child of the depression" has left them with certain thrifty habits: saving little dabs of leftovers in the refrigerator; refusing to part with outgrown garments or shabby furniture; or hoarding bits of string or rubber bands.

Unlike milder "recessions," which hurt only a relatively few people, the Great Depression affected most of the citizens of this country—and for that matter, of other countries, as well. But the pain was not merely physical or financial. Crippled pride can hurt as much as an empty stomach, and the pain sometimes spreads throughout an entire family.

In this story, you will meet a family and a peddler, all trying to survive these difficult times.

I was afraid of the man who couldn't talk. When he came to the door, dusty hat in hand, I ran for Mama. "He's here," I said. "That man with the handkerchief around his neck."

She held pie dough like a paper circle, fitted it into a glass dish.

I pinched off a mound from the remaining dough, popped it in my mouth. Sticky. It tasted like flour and made my mouth dry. I sneaked a slice from the bowl of peaches. Peaches were better raw, dough when it was baked, but I liked them together in a pie. Mama had peeled the fuzzy, freckled peaches. They were small, she said, and wouldn't have much flavor. The peach tree was old.

"Go tell Mr. Regis I'll be there in a minute." Mama rolled the rest of the dough. "Go on now."

I walked slow, my bare feet slipper soft on the cool floor. Maybe he would be gone. I peeked around the door. Still there, Mr. Regis squatted on the steps and rubbed Blackie, whose tail drummed in the dust sending up a tan cloud.

I cleared my throat.

He looked up and smiled stubby brown teeth.

"She'll be here in a minute."

His black coat pushed through the screen mesh and he nodded. It was July and he wore a coat. It was fuzzy on the sleeves and across the pockets, and his pants bagged, bunched over his shoes like too-long pajamas.

Blackie rolled over at Mr. Regis' feet, showed the white star on his stomach and waited to be tickled.

I motioned for Blackie to get up, go away, but he wiggled, four paws in the air, and made happy sounds. If Mr. Regis had some disease that took away his voice, Blackie might get it. Then he wouldn't be able to bark.

He rolled over and Mr. Regis rubbed him several more times before he wiped his hands on a tan handkerchief he pulled from his pocket. Tan, the color of coat linings, yet the handkerchief he wore around his neck was white as a bandage.

The small bag he carried rattled as he took out a pad, short yellow pencil.

I hoped Mama would not buy anything today. Maybe Mr. Regis drank his own flavorings and they burned his voice out. Vanilla smelled like perfume and it burned when you tasted it. Mint was cool on your tongue and tasted like candy, but you couldn't use it for many things, Mama said.

She came to the door. There was flour on her nose and her hair looked wispy and damp. "Mr. Regis," she said, "isn't it too hot for you to be out on a day like this? My goodness, let's go sit in the shade."

She didn't invite him in because Daddy didn't like it. If he came in and someone, even Mama's friend Gwen, had been visiting and smoking cigarettes, he would say who was here in an angry voice. And don't you let any salesmen in. You can't get rid of them if you do. I know, Mama said.

Mama and Mr. Regis went to the wooden chairs under the peach tree. She saw that peach tree when we rented this house and acted like it was a present. When it bloomed, she went to the window a dozen times a day and said how pretty it was. Daddy got so tired that Sunday, he said if she didn't shut up about the thing he was going to chop the darn peach tree down. Only one side had bloomed and now had a scattering of leaves.

Mr. Regis took the chair with the broken arm. Mama sat on the edge of the one with the broken board in the seat. She had begged Daddy to fix them. He said boards cost money and they were nothing but pieces of junk, not worth it. The people who lived here before had left them. Thrown them away, Daddy said.

"I haven't seen you in a while," Mama said to Mr. Regis. He smiled and nodded.

Daddy used to fix things, whistle while he worked and let me hand him the hammer. Since he lost his job and we had to move, he was always tired, left early and came home late. I wondered if Mr. Regis ever wanted to whistle.

He leaned over to show Mama the page with colored pictures of flavoring bottles.

"All I need is vanilla," she said.

He hit the paper with his pencil.

"No, I don't think I'll take anything but vanilla."

Mr. Regis hit the paper again, harder this time.

"I'm sorry," Mama frowned, "I really am. But vanilla is all I want. My family didn't like the others."

He hit the page so hard this time I looked to see if it had torn. It hadn't.

"Oh, I see what you want," said Mama. "You want me to read this."

He smiled, moved his lips as she read.

"For every two bottles of Wallace Flavoring purchased one necklace of beautiful simulated pearls will be given absolutely free."

Mr. Regis traced a circle on Mama's neck with the end of his pencil.

"I don't...."

He took two bottles of vanilla from his bag.

"I guess I can always use it." Mama went into the house for her money.

After Mr. Regis left, I took the pearls from their small envelope, lifted my hair in back so Mama could clasp them.

She put the two new bottles of vanilla on the shelf next to another new bottle.

"You had...," I started. "Daddy said we couldn't buy anything we absolutely didn't have to have."

"I know," she said, "But poor Mr. Regis is old and sick and out trying to make a living. I can help him out a little."

"Why can't he talk?"

Mama mixed sugar with the peaches, poured them into a crust. "He had some disease a long time ago and an operation."

"Is the disease catching?" I thought of measles, how my chicken pox had itched.

"No, no." She dotted the peaches with lumps of butter, sprinkled cinnamon and laid on the top crust. "I'm sure it's not." She jabbed slits in the pie and pink juice oozed out. "Poor Mr. Regis. He's lost weight, looks bad. I'm afraid...."

I held the oven door, Mama slid in the pie. "Won't the kitchen smell good when Daddy comes home?"

One pie, one good smell. Mama said the tree was so old and had quit bearing, we were lucky to get enough for a pie.

Mama combed her hair, put on the lipstick for the first time in days. I took off the pearls, clasped them on her. She laughed, rolled them between her fingers.

"They are pretty."

"Are they real?"

"What do you think?"

"They might be," I said.

"I've never seen real pearls before." Mama held an almost empty bottle of hand lotion high, waited for a drop to fall. "Since these were so expensive," she laughed, "I'm sure they must be real."

I giggled, looked at the two of us in the mirror. "Free," I said, "That's what kind of pearls they are."

•   •   •

Daddy wolfed down his macaroni and cheese and said the skin on his sliced tomatoes was tough and why didn't Mama peel them.

He was almost through eating when he noticed Mama's necklace. "Where did those come from?." He pointed with his fork, kept chewing.

"What?" Mama asked.

"That necklace."

She felt the pearls, "I'd forgotten I had them on. My expensive necklace. Where do you think? My boy friend gave them to me."

Mr. Regis wasn't Mama's boy friend. He wasn't even a boy. I started to giggle until I looked at Daddy's face.

"I'll just bet he *gave* them to you."

Mama hit her glass, almost knocked it over. "What makes you say something like that, Colin?"

"You get nothing *given* to you these days. I've got enough sense to know that much."

"They were free," I said, "He did give them to Mama."

"He who?" Daddy's hard dark eyes pinned me fast in my seat.

"The vanilla man."

"Colin, you're being silly," Mama said. "Can't you take a little teasing?" She took the plates to the sink. There was food left on hers. She fussed at me if I left food, said we couldn't waste things. "The pearls were free with two bottles of vanilla."

"And what else?" Daddy grabbed her arm as she went to the porch for the pie.

"And nothing else. "Don't you know me better than that?" She jerked away, went to the porch and came back with the pie. "Mr. Regis is old and I buy the vanilla to help him out. It's something I have to have anyway."

She cut the pie, lifted a large slice to Daddy's plate.

"Thank you Stella darling," said Daddy in a squeaky voice. "Is that what he calls you? Your Mr. Regis boy friend?"

"You're making a big fuss over a silly joke. He doesn't call me anything."

I couldn't eat. With my fork I moved a peach slice around in its juice. The top crust was burnt a little.

"Stella Sugar pie with your lipstick and pearls," said Daddy, scraping his plate. "Is that what he calls you?"

"Stop," Mama said in a wet voice. "For goodness sakes stop."

"Maybe he whispers in your ear," Daddy said. "Sweet words." He clasped her shoulder, made ridges in her dress.

"He doesn't say anything," Mama stared at her plate.

"He can't talk," I yelled. "Mr. Regis can't talk. He's got a hole in his throat and. . . . "

Mama jerked away and the pearls broke. She laid her head on the table, cried into her arms, her elbow in the butter dish.

The front door slammed behind Daddy. He would be back later, talking loud, my mother crying. In the morning her face would be swollen and red.

There were pearls scattered on the table, the floor, some under my chair. I picked them up, put them in a saucer. If they were restrung they would look the same, but they wouldn't be the same, not ever again.

Ruth Moose (1938–   )

In modern America, most people move about a good deal during their lifetimes, sometimes all the way across the continent. Ruth Moose, however, grew up in Albemarle, North Carolina, and she and her husband, artist Talmadge Moose, still live there. Her imagination, however, has roved far—winning her readers all over this country and abroad.

Encouraged by a teacher, she began writing in the eighth grade, winning third prize in a national contest on "Why I Love America." She reports that her teacher "read my stories which were written in green ink, and corrected the spelling and punctuation."

During her writing career, Ruth Moose's essays, short stories, and poems have appeared in many newspapers, popular magazines, and literary journals. She has also published two collections of poetry and two of short stories, and some of her work has been translated into other languages. Her writing has won a number of state and national awards, including a North Carolina Writer's Fellowship.

In addition to working on her own writing, Ruth Moose has been involved in a number of projects promoting the writing of others. For several years she edited *The Uwharrie Review*, a literary magazine focusing on writers of the region in and around the Uwharrie Mountains. More recently, she compiled and edited *I Have Walked,* an anthology of poems and stories portraying the poverty in this state. Currently, as a librarian at Pfeiffer College, she plans literary programs, often featuring North Carolina writers.

Meet The Artist:
Talmadge Moose

A native of Albemarle, Talmadge Moose is noted for his drawings, which move beyond realism to capture the spirit of the scene or person portrayed. He received his Bachelor of Fine Arts degree at Virginia Commonwealth University and has worked as a commercial artist and as an art teacher at the college level. His paintings and drawings have appeared in numerous exhibitions and have won a number of awards, including first prize in the Southeastern Print and Drawing Show.

Reflecting

This story is told from a little girl's point of view. She is so young that she is afraid that her dog might "catch" the condition that took Mr. Regis's voice away (probably cancer of the vocal cords—not an infectious condition). She also thinks that the simulated (imitation) "pearls" that Mr. Regis gave free with two bottles of vanilla flavoring might be real. Being so small, she doesn't try to explain what happens, but just tells the story as she experienced it. She does, however, give us enough details that we can explain such matters as the following:

1. How the father has changed—and why.

2. How the mother and the father react differently to their poverty—and to others in need.
3. Why the mother buys two bottles of flavoring when she already has some and has little money.
4. Why the father gets so angry about the pearls.
5. Why the pearls which the little girl picks up will never be the same, "not ever again," after she restrings them.

Pick out the details in the story which help us understand all these things.

Preview: Fifty Acres

Most people like to travel. Given free time and some money, they head for new horizons—the beach or mountains, a large city, a scenic spot such as the Grand Canyon, or a foreign land.

Many people, however, consider themselves "homebodies." Henry David Thoreau, a writer who spent almost his entire life in the little town of Concord, Massachusetts, once wrote that "I have traveled a great deal in Concord." He was referring to the travels of his alert and energetic mind, which seems never to have been idle.

Thoreau would have understood James Larkin Pearson's most famous poem, "Fifty Acres," in which Pearson claims that his homestead provides what ad writers would call a "variety vacationland" all by itself.

Fifty Acres

James Larkin Pearson

James Larkin Pearson stands outside his home on his beloved fifty acres.

I've never been to London,
I've never been to Rome;
But on my Fifty Acres
I travel here at home.

The hill that looks upon me
Right here where I was born
Shall be my mighty Jungfrau,
My Alp, my Matterhorn.

A little land of Egypt
My meadow plot shall be,
With pyramids of hay-stacks
Along its sheltered lee.

My hundred yards of brooklet
Shall fancy's faith beguile,
And be my Rhine, my Avon,
My Amazon, my Nile.

My humble bed of roses,
My honeysuckle hedge,
Will do for all the gardens
At all the far world's edge.

In June I find the Tropics
Camped all about the place;
Then white December shows me
The Arctic's frozen face.

My wood-lot grows an Arden,
My pond a Caspian Sea;
And so my Fifty Acres
Is all the world to me.

Here on my Fifty Acres
I safe at home remain,
And have my own Bermuda,
My Sicily, my Spain.

1. lee: the side (of a boat, a plot of land, etc.) that is sheltered from the wind

2. beguile: charm, captivate

James Larkin Pearson (1879–1981)

In his autobiography, James Larkin Pearson, the second officially appointed poet laureate of this state, reported that when he was only four years old, he was already speaking in rhyme. As he worked on the family farm, he continued to compose poetry. "I always carried my notebook and pencil to the field with me," he said, "and as I trudged between the plow-handles in the hot sunshine, my mind was busy working out a poem."

Born on Berry's Mountain in Wilkes County in 1879, Pearson, like many boys and girls of that era, went to school very little. When he was twenty-one, he left the farm to take a job in a printing shop, and he worked very hard not only to learn the printing trade, but also to educate himself. "I never let a day pass without learning something that would add a little to my general education," he once declared. Years later, at the age of forty-four, Pearson admitted his regret at having so little formal education.

He wrote constantly throughout his long life, publishing poetry, his life story, and monthly newspapers. When the last of his six books appeared in 1971, Governor Robert Scott dedicated April as "James Larkin Pearson Month." He died in 1981, at the age of 101.

Language Alert

1. Almost all of the places mentioned in the poem are famous foreign lands or sites. The exception is Arden. Pearson may have been referring to the forest of Arden, a magical woodland occurring in William Shakespeare's play *As You Like It*. You will be familiar with many of the place names. Usually the wording of the poem indicates whether a name refers to a country, a river, a mountain, or a region.

Reflecting

1. Why does the poet capitalize "Fifty Acres"?
2. If someone asked you how you could "travel here at home" as Pearson did, what would you answer? Think of places in your town or countryside which could compare to famous travel spots.

A Watermelon
Four Feet Long

Tom Wicker

Preview

We all like to feel important—to feel that we count, that people pay attention to us. Often we depend on what Doris Betts called "a mark of distinction," something that makes us stand out from the crowd (see Ms. Betts's story, p. 461). That mark may be a talent or skill (a high-scoring basketball record or the ability to play the piano by ear); an experience (a trip to some remote place, a life-threatening near-accident, or a meeting with a television or sports celebrity); or a possession (the fastest bike in the neighborhood, a Gibson guitar, or a large CD collection).

In this story, which takes place during the 1930s, the main character, Sandy, doesn't have much to brag about. His father has lost his business and is having a difficult time supporting the family. His mother is dead and the family lives in the part of town inhabited by people scorned as "white trash." When the family gets "the biggest watermelon in the whole world," it looks as if his moment of glory has come.

Published in *Short Stories from the Old North State,* ed. Richard Walser. Copyright © 1959 University of Carolina Press. Reprinted by permission of the author.

Father was touchy. He would go to work for somebody—I'm talking about after he had to close his cabinet shop, when Mister H. P. Henderson's bank went broke—and they would hit it off all right and then it would be payday and maybe whoever it was would say to Father, "I owe you twelve dollars." And Father would say, "That's right, but there was them two co-colas you bought me." And the man would say, "Oh, I ain't worrying about two co-colas." Then Father would rip off something like, "Durned if I'll take your charity." First thing anybody know, there went another job. Or maybe a man would say to him, "That's a pretty house over there, ain't it?" and Father would answer, "Well, you and me could have one like it if we was willing to lie and cheat poor folks like so-and-so done to get it." Of course, it would turn out every time that so-and-so was the other man's cousin. And one Christmas, Father even hit a fireman spang in the nose for bringing charity toys to our house.

My sister Estelle used to say Father wasn't a bit hard to get on with before my mother died. I don't suppose losing his shop did him any good, either. I was just a little fellow when I helped him take the sign down from over the door. *Edward Martin*, it said, *Cabinetmaker*. While we were getting it loose from the angle-iron, some men came up in a truck and carted the electric jigsaw away. We went home and Father took his sign out to the woodshed and chopped it up for kindling. Estelle cried but it didn't seem so sad to me; it had been just a little shop and I thought maybe Father would open

up a movie house and get rich.

I had about given that up by the time Brooks brought us the watermelon, two years later. I guess that was about 1934. Father hadn't been able to get a steady job, much less keep it, and his odd work building fences and repairing porch steps was all that kept us going. I don't reckon Estelle could have managed if Karo syrup and fat meat hadn't been so cheap.

"My land, Brooks," Father said, the day we got the watermelon. "You take that thing downtown and get what it's really worth. I never saw such a watermelon."

"I ain't either," Brooks said. "All summer I been meaning hit for you folkses, Mist Ed."

He had put the watermelon on the dirty gray floor of our front porch and knelt beside it, one dark hand still and tender on its green skin.

"I don't know," Father said. "Times are too hard for you to be letting me have a watermelon like that for two bits." He pushed open the screen door and went out on the porch, squatting by the watermelon and thumping it with his forefinger. It gave off the sort of hollow sound he had taught me to listen for in watermelons—the sound that meant it was ripe and red inside.

"That time we was building Mist John's new stoop and I step on that rusty nail," Brooks said. "Who was it load me in the car and drive me to the doctor?"

Even Alton Henderson never had a watermelon like that, I thought. Nobody in this old town ever had a watermelon like that.

"Who was it loan me the money for

lockjaw nockalations?" Brooks said. "You just give me a quarter now, Mist Ed, and take dis old watermelon for dis yere boy." He smiled at me, a gold tooth flashing in the summer-morning sun. Behind him, morning glories twined brilliantly on our porch rail. It was just past seven o'clock, and out on the street Brooks's wife was sitting patiently in the wagon while their motheaten mule cropped at the damp grass along the curb. The wagon was loaded with peck and bushel baskets of string beans and okra and tomatoes and field peas; when they left our house, Brooks and his wife would go along Oak Avenue, rapping on the porch floors of the big old houses there, and offering their fresh produce a lot cheaper than you could get such things downtown.

Father fished in his pocket and pulled out a quarter. "Well, I ain't going to argue," he said. "I take this kindly, Brooks."

Brooks took the quarter and stood up; his fingers lingered on the watermelon. "Hit ought to make some right smart eating," he said. "Mist Ed, you let me know when you need help on another job."

Father laughed. It was a sound I had come to dislike, harsh and high-pitched and faintly angry. "All the jobs I get these days, a man don't need no help to do, Brooks. I ain't had enough this summer to make one good day."

We took the watermelon out in the back yard after Brooks left. My sister Estelle was sitting in a kitchen chair under the wild cherry tree, shelling peas into a pan she clutched between her knees.

"Where's that old washtub?" Father said. "We got the granddaddy of all watermelons."

"My stars," Estelle said.

I ran for the washtub and carried it to the outdoor spigot and filled it half-full of water. "Pop," I called, "I bet we got the biggest watermelon in this old town."

"I bet so too," Father said. "That's enough water."

I twisted the spigot and he lowered the melon into the tub. It was so long only the lower part would go in the water. The rest of it stuck up over the rim. I stroked it gently and I can remember to this day how the smooth, firm skin made my hand tingle and a shiver go up my spine.

"It's not going to get cold that way," Estelle said. "That's the biggest watermelon I ever laid my eyes on."

"Let's take it to the icehouse, Pop." We'll have the walk through town, I thought. Right through town carrying the biggest watermelon in the world.

Estelle got up and put down her pot of peas and came over and thumped the watermelon with her forefinger. "We could eat it the way it is. It sounds like it ought to be cut right this minute." She thumped it again.

"I ain't eating no warm watermelon," Father said. "I'd as soon eat dirt."

"Well, you better not take it down to that icehouse." Estelle bent and sloshed water up over the green skin. "That old man'd skin his grandma for a dime."

"Alf? I never knowed him to cheat a man."

"They'll all cheat you," Estelle said. "You know that, Pa."

He heaved the watermelon out of the tub and up on his shoulder. "I reckon Alf ain't going to try to cheat Ed Martin," he said.

"All right." Estelle went back to her chair and sat down and picked up the pot of peas. "You go on then. I don't like watermelon anyway."

"Come on, Pop," I said. "She's just belly-aching like always."

We went down the driveway, where grass and weeds were coming up in the ruts the T-model used to make. The screens on the windows were rusty and torn and the lawn was patchy as a sick dog's coat. "I got to fix this place up," Father said. "It's beginning to look like a white trash house." We went on out to the sidewalk the WPA had staked off. Father had said he would be in hell with his back broke before those bums would lay it across his lot, but it looked like they were

going to do it. We went across it to the cracked and broken tar of the street and started toward town. Bird Dog Barnes came out of his house carrying an iron hoop and a piece of bent wire.

"Hey, Sandy," he called. I pretended I didn't hear him. Bird Dog trotted across the street, rolling the hoop in front of him with the piece of bent wire. He stopped suddenly, looking at the watermelon on Father's shoulder. He had staring blue eyes and a nose almost as wide as his mouth; it wiggled when he talked.

"Is that yours?" he said, his nose moving.

"Hello, Bird Dog," Father said. "You getting pretty good with that hoop, ain't you?"

Bird Dog stared at the watermelon. He was my age but he wore a pair of his fath-

er's cutdown overalls and they blossomed around him so that he looked much bigger. Bird Dog could handle a hoop better than any boy in town and he always seemed to have certain dark secrets I longed to share. But I had no use for him. Alton Henderson said Bird Dog was trashy and that was a good word for him.

"We better hurry," I said, pretending not to notice him.

"Yah," Bird Dog said, his nose wiggling furiously, "you got to hurry and muck up to Alton Henderson and them other pretty boys over to Oak Avenue. That's some watermelon you got there, Mister Martin."

"Maybe you can have a piece of it," Father said. "We'll see when we bring it back."

I looked over my shoulder. Bird Dog was still staring at the watermelon with his outsize eyes and I felt good about that. Over my dead body he'll get a piece of it, I thought. It's my watermelon, ain't it? The biggest watermelon in this town.

The tar was already hot and sticky under my bare feet and I picked my way along, looking for sandy spots I could step on. I thought about how I would announce the watermelon to Alton Henderson. I hoped Junior Fields and Billy Spencer and some of the other Oak Avenue boys would come over to Alton's so I could tell them about it, too.

"Maybe I'll ask Alton to come around and have a piece of it," I said.

Father looked down at me and his mouth worked curiously, as though he were tasting something sour. "We'll see," he said. "Maybe he won't want to come."

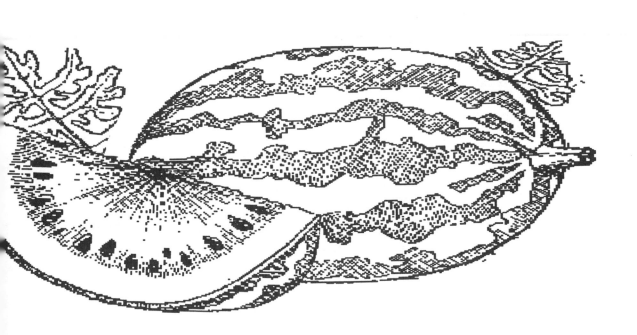

"Oh, I expect he'll want a piece of the biggest watermelon in town, all right."

We had to go right through town to get to the icehouse. Everybody we passed stared at the watermelon. I don't reckon another watermelon like that one has ever been seen in our county. Maybe not even in the whole state of North Carolina. Mister Cutlar Ray stopped us and said that himself and he was just about the biggest lawyer in town at that time. Mrs. Sadie Blue offered us fifty cents for it and I was scared to death Father was going to take it. I expect he might have if she hadn't been the richest woman in town. Mister Talking Billy Carrington called out to us when we were crossing Courthouse Square and wanted to know if it was a watermelon or a green shoat. Father said he sure-God wished it was a shoat but no such luck.

"I bet the boy don't wish it was a shoat," Mister Talking Billy said. "How 'bout it, boy?"

"I wouldn't take anything for it," I said. "I wouldn't even take a trip to Raleigh on the bus for it. You come around and have a piece of it with us this afternoon, Mister Talking Billy."

"I might do that," the old man said. "You got enough there to feed the whole dang town, look like to me."

We went on across the square and down Pine Avenue and three more people stopped us before we could get to the icehouse. By the time we got down to where the tobacco warehouses were getting ready to open for the season, Father had his chest stuck out like the rasslers we saw out to the fair one fall. He was walking so fast I almost had to run to keep up with him.

"I can't understand that Brooks," he told me. "Letting a thing like this go for a quarter when he could of got maybe a dollar just as easy."

Mister Alf was sitting on the loading porch when we came around the corner of the old whitewashed brick building of the City Ice and Fuel Company. Mister Alf had a colored helper named Joshua and he did all the work while Mister Alf just sat under the peg-board where the ice hooks hung, and gave directions. We stopped at the foot of the creaky wooden steps that led up to the loading porch and we could see that Mister Alf was napping. His straw sailor hat was pulled down over his eyes. The heavy wooden door that always looked like it was wet swung open and Joshua came backing out of the storage room, dragging a two-hundred-and-fifty-pound block of ice. He pulled it across the splintery porch floor to the crushing machine, then hung his icehook on the peg-board above Mister Alf's head.

"Hey, Alf," Father called.

Mister Alf rubbed a black-nailed hand over his face and all the way to the bottom of the steps I could hear it rasping against the gray stubble of his chin; then he pushed the sailor back and looked down at us. Joshua took an icepick out of a leather holster attached to his belt and began to pick at the block of ice.

"I be John Brown," Mister Alf said, "if that ain't the beatinest watermelon I ever laid my eyes on."

"How much you want to ice it down for

me?" Father said. "I ain't got a tub'll hold it."

"Lemme see that critter up close." Mister Alf allowed his cane-bottomed chair to come down on all four legs, and Joshua chuckled, looking at the watermelon, too. The block of ice between his legs broke precisely in two from his picking. Father carried the watermelon up the steps and I scurried up after him, bending and scooping ice chips from around the crushing machine. Mister Alf leaned over, grunting, and thumped the watermelon. Joshua picked up one of the blocks of ice and dropped it into the crushing machine, then kicked an old enamel pan under the spout. Beyond the storage room and the little office where Mister Alf kept the supply of ice picks he sold for a dime each, I could hear the steady rushing fall of the brine through the ice-maker.

"I tell you," Mister Alf said. "A man brings a watermelon like that into my place, I ain't going to charge him to ice it down. It's a right down pleasure to have it on the premises."

"Well, I take that kindly," Father said. "Ain't nothing I love less'n a warm watermelon."

"Tell you what I bet I could do, though, Ed. I bet I could sit right here and not move no more than a finger and sell that critter for at least a dollar."

"No!" I cried, and almost choked on a chip of ice that slipped to the edge of my windpipe. Joshua began to turn the handle of the crushing machine, grunting rhythmically, and a steady stream of crushed ice poured from the spout into the enamel pan.

"Is that a fact?" Father said. He pounded me on the back. The chip of ice came free and I swallowed it. "Dollar, huh?"

"He wouldn't take a dollar for our watermelon," I said. "We wouldn't take a hundred dollars for it."

"I guess not, Alf." Father put his hand on my shoulder. Mister Alf tipped the straw sailor down over his eyes again. "You, Joshaway," he said. "Carry that John Brown critter in the storeroom."

"YasSUH!" Joshua let go of the handle of the crushing machine. He looked delighted to be allowed to touch that green and glowing skin.

"We'll be back this afternoon," I called, as we went down the ricketing steps. "We'll be back for sure, Mister Alf." We went on back then past the warehouses and through town toward Alton Henderson's house. Father was still walking so fast I almost had to run to keep up. Good old Brooks, I kept thinking, good old Brooks, bringing us that watermelon. The biggest watermelon in this town.

Alton Henderson had his collection of model cars that was really fine. He had had to go all the way to Raleigh or Charlotte with his father to buy them. There were more than a dozen of them and all but two had real rubber tires. Alton would get the hoe out of the shed and take it and the box of cars out to where Mister Henderson had dug up one of his wife's flower beds and left this cleared space. Alton would draw off highways with the hoe-blade, a whole county full of highways right there in his backyard. He had this tin gas station he would put down at one crossing and he had a house or two that he took from his electric train set. He even had a place scooped out and lined with glass for a river, and there was a real drawbridge he could put down across it.

Father was tearing out the back of Mr. Henderson's garage that day, because Miz Henderson was just learning to drive. But Alton didn't even come out of the house until after dinner. He was carrying a pasteboard box full of cars.

"Junior and Billy are coming over in a little while," he told me. "Want to help get everything set up?"

I decided not to say anything about the watermelon until they arrived. Bird Dog would always try to pick a fight with either one of them, but I didn't feel that way. I liked Alton better—Alton would *talk* to you, most of the time anyway—but Billy and Junior were all right. They didn't mean to hog the cars. I was sure of that. But it did seem like every time they came, pretty soon there wouldn't be enough room for me around the little county in Miz Henderson's old flower patch. But that day, Billy and Junior even let me have the Willys-Knight Whippet model.

"Listen," I said, the first time I thought they all could hear me. "You know what we got at our house today?"

Junior hopped across the river, pulling a blue Olds over the drawbridge. "I'm taking a thick old lady to the hoth-pital. I'm breaking all thpeed laws but it'th a matter of life or death." He had had two front teeth knocked out in a baseball game and the tip of his tongue was always

poking out of the hole when he talked.

"I'm a speed cop," Alton said. "I'll see you when you cross that road down there and chase you."

"We got a watermelon four feet long!"

"I'm not going to thtop," Junior said. "You'll have to try to thtop me but it'th my Chrithtian duty to keep going."

Billy Carter looked up at me, shaking his head. He had funny brown eyes and he always looked as if he were going to cry. "Watermelons can't be four feet long, stupid. Anybody knows that."

"What was that?" Alton let Junior's speeding car pass the crossing unobserved. "What was that, Sandy?"

"I said old Brooks brought us a watermelon this morning and it was four feet long."

"Aw." Junior looked disgusted. "You mean four incheth?"

"Nosirree. Four feet. That long." I stretched my arms as wide as I could. "Mister Alf is icing it down for us at the icehouse. We didn't have a tub big enough to put it in."

"Aw," Junior said. "Leth go thee it, then."

"I ain't going to see it." Billy turned his back on me. "He's just talking. Who ever heard of a watermelon that big?"

"I tell you what." My voice was calm but I felt like jumping up and down. None of them had ever paid so much attention to me before. "Hows about if everybody came around to my house after awhile? We could all have a piece."

"No kidding?" Alton picked up his Dodge model and blew sand off the tires. "You really got a watermelon four feet long?"

"Hope to die." I started to run toward the garage. "I'll tell Pop you're all coming."

"Aw," I heard Junior say. "Why don't he bring it around here?"

But I didn't care. Father and I owned the biggest watermelon in town. We owned a watermelon Mister Alf could easily have gotten a dollar for. And Alton and Junior and Billy were coming to my house. They would see. They would find out that I wasn't like Bird Dog and the other boys on Cooper Street. They would find out I wasn't trashy.

The sun had dropped below the tree-tops when we got back to the icehouse. Its last harsh light flickered through the leaves of the big trees and just over the roof of one of the tobacco warehouses, making my eyes smart. Mister Alf sat in his chair under the pegboard, fast asleep. Joshua sprawled on the steps of the loading porch, sucking on a big hunk of ice he kept flipping from one hand to the other.

"Get me my watermelon, Josh," Father said. "No need to wake up Alf."

Joshua took the ice out of his mouth. "Mist Alf," he called softly. "Here's Mist Ed done come back."

"No need to wake him up, I told you. Just go and . . ."

Mister Alf's chair thumped down on the hollow floor. He pushed back his sailor hat and stood up. His shirt tail billowed out around his fat waist.

"What'd I tell you 'bout that John Brown critter you brung in here, Ed Martin?"

"You got it iced down for me, ain't you?"

Mister Alf thumped his hand down on the porch rail. "I ain't no fool, if you are. I sold that watermelon for you, Ed."

I felt a stab in my throat as real as though a lump of ice had gone down my windpipe.

"*Sold* it?" Father said. "Why, Alf Butler!"

"Sold it is right. For a *dollar'n a half*."

"You *sold* it!" Father said. "A dollar and a *half*?"

"Car drove up not an hour after you'd gone. This here woman's driving it and she says to me I'm looking for a goodsized watermelon. Wellsir . . . "

"You didn't have any *right!*" I ran up the steps, leaping across Joshua's long legs in their tattered old overall trousers. "It was *ours!*"

"Wellsir, I seen my chance and I wan't the man to miss it . . . not Alf Butler."

I pushed at his hip with both my hands. "But it was *ours*, Mister Alf . . . make him get it back, Pop! Make him!" I thought of Alton and Billy and Junior coming around to our house. I thought of the way Father had stuck out his chest carrying it through town that morning.

"Sure 'nough, the minute that woman laid eyes on that John Brown critter she like to shuck her skin. Hold on there, I says to her, quicklike. It'll cost you a dollar'n a half to take it out."

"A dollar and a *half!*" Father said. "I never heard of anything like that in my life."

"I tell you, Ed, a man in trade he gets to know just how far he can push a price. He shorely does."

"Leave off that, Sandy!" Father said sharply, as I pushed Mister Alf again. Tears scalded my eyes and my chest swelled as though it would burst. I looked down at him, but he was paying no more attention to me.

"Seems like you might of asked me, Alf."

Mister Alf slid one hand into the pocket of his old wool trousers. "Ed, I had to close that sale on the spot or maybe not at all. A man in my line ain't always got time to do things the way he wants."

"Make him get it back, Pop! He didn't have any right to sell our watermelon . . . make him get it *back!*"

"Where's the money?" Father said, still not looking at me. Mister Alf cleared his throat.

"I tell you what's a fack, Ed, just any and everybody couldn't of done what I done for you. You spring a dollar'n a half price for a watermelon on just *any*body and see what you get."

"Where's the money?" Father said. He came up two of the steps to the porch and Joshua moved to the other side of the ice-crushing machine.

"Make him get it back, Pop," I said. "We don't want his old money."

"Now I got the money right here." Mister Alf took his hand out of his pocket. "What I was going to say was that taking only just what seems right and fair for my commission it was going to leave you six bits."

"Why, you cheap old goat!" Father came up the rest of the steps to the porch. Mister Alf moved quickly behind me.

Father's face was white. I could see his teeth biting hard at his lower lip and he kept rubbing his hands on the front of his overalls. "You think I'd let you get away with that? Selling *my* watermelon without so much as a word to me and then trying to keep half the money?"

"Now listen here, Ed Martin . . . what you aim to do?"

"Do?" Father put his hands on my shoulders, still not looking at me, and moved me against the porch rail. Beyond him, Joshua slipped quietly off the porch. "*Do?* I aim to collect my due."

"I'll make it a dollar," Mister Alf said. "Nobody ain't never called me ungenerous in my life."

"Dollar'n a quarter," Father said. "You earned a quarter of it, skinflint."

"I'm surprised at you, Ed. I didn't think you'd treat a old man like he was dirt. I thought better of . . ."

"Dollar'n a quarter," Father said "Give it here."

Mister Alf looked in his hand and picked out a quarter, then stuck out his hand to Father. "It's a John Brown crime the way folks look on a man in trade," he said. "I was just doing honest business."

"Honest business," I said. "Selling our watermelon."

The tears spilled out of my eyes and down my cheeks. There was a great emptiness in my stomach. It was as though the bottom had fallen out of something I had not even known was a part of me. I couldn't think about what Alton would say, or Billy or Junior. I couldn't think about anything. All I could see was Father standing there on the porch counting the money he'd got for the biggest watermelon anybody had ever seen. All I could see was the way the skin stretched over his jawbones, and the way his eyes kept switching around, like a cat's do when you give him milk.

"Hush that whining, boy," Father said. "We can buy us a half a dozen watermelons with this here."

"I just want ours back," I said. "I don't want the old money."

Father looked away from the money, at Mister Alf, then at the peg-board over his head. "We can't get ours back anyway," he said. "You and me ain't had no business with anything that grand to begin with." He held out his hand. "Here."

He was offering me a dime. I hit his hand as hard as I could and the dime spun to the floor, flashing in the fading rays of the sun. Father's face went white again. His teeth clenched and the corners of his mouth pulled back and his eyes squeezed shut as though a sudden wind had blown sand in them. I stooped under the rail and leaped to the hard, rutted clay of the parking area in front of the icehouse. It was a long drop and I slipped when I hit the ground; small pebbles and cinders scraped the skin of my knees and hands. I heard Father cry out after me, but I scrambled up and ran around the corner of a tobacco warehouse. Joshua was peeping back around it, but I didn't stop. I ran with my face down, the sharp slap of my bare feet on the hot soft asphalt of Pine Avenue sending a jolt up my legs to my stomach and on to my head . . . *no right* I kept thinking *no right no right no right* but there was no right about any-

thing. I looked at my dirty bare feet running through my world of no possession and no pride and no right, and I hated it. I hated my world and myself and, most of all, blindly running down those quiet evening streets in the last red glare of the sun, I hated my father, who alone could have made us something else.

They were sitting on a pile of old lumber Father had saved from a chicken coop he had built for Mister Carson Maynard. It was stacked under the rotting old oak at the side of our driveway and they were perched on it like pigeons in a row, Alton is the middle, waiting for me.

I ran around the corner of the house and stopped, looking at them. Behind me, across Cooper Street, I could hear the rusty scream of the old screen door of Bird Dog's house and the sharp slap of it back against the siding of the porch.

"Where'th that watermelon?" Junior said. He had brought a ball and glove with him and he tossed the ball up above his head and caught it without looking, carelessly, the way he did everything. He tossed it up again but this time it fell all the way to the ground and rolled toward me. In the twilit silence I could hear somebody running across the street and the faint whir of a rolling hoop.

"Can't we have some of the watermelon?" Alton said.

I bent and picked up the ball, but taking my eyes off them. Billy looked a little scared and more than ever as though he was going to cry. He slipped off the pile of lumber.

"How 'bout somma that old watermelon?" Bird Dog said, behind me. "Your old man said I could have a piece of it, too."

"I thought you said you had a watermelon four feet long," Alton said. "That's what you claimed around at my house."

I don't care what they think about me, I told myself. I don't care. Just so they don't find out he sold it.

I looked from one to the other of them, then at Billy edging toward the street. "We gave it away," I said. "We gave it to some poor people."

"Aw," Junior said, "I bet you didn't even have any watermelon four feet long."

"Yes, he did too!" Bird Dog said. "He's just trying to cut us out of having any, he just wants it all hisself. I seen that watermelon this morning with my own eyes."

I whirled toward him, the shameful tears flooding into my eyes again: "You're a liar! A liar!" If they just don't find out, I thought. If they just don't find out he sold it.

"Fight!" Junior said. "Thick'im, Bird Dog!"

I looked at his grinning face with its careless gaptoothed mouth and at the worried frown on Alton's face and the furious working of Bird Dog's broad nose. All the muscles in my body went tight as wound-up rubber bands. With all the strength I had, I threw Junior's ball across the corner of our house and down Cooper Street.

"Hey!" Junior said. "That'th my ball!"

"Oh, come on," Alton said. "I guess there isn't any watermelon." He and Junior walked slowly out the driveway to where Billy was waiting for them. Then they set off at a trot down the street toward Junior's ball.

Bird Dog walked up very close to me, his fists cocked in front of him. His breath was bad and his nose was working and sniffing as though I had left a scent for him to follow.

"Nobody calls Bird Dog Barnes a liar," he said.

"I'm not going to fight." I was not angry any more. I listened to the shouting voices of Junior and Billy and Alton as they hunted for the ball I had thrown down the street. I hoped they would be able to find it. "I'm sorry I called you a liar." I turned away and went back toward the house.

"Of all the yellow-bellied rats," Bird Dog called after me, "you're 'bout the *yell*owest!"

I went around the house to where our old Ford was sitting up on its two sawhorses, I climbed up on one of them and into the back seat. I lay down on the floorboards. There were a couple of Big Little Books there from the last time I had hid out, but I didn't read them. I just lay there looking up at the sky going dark and the way the clouds moved across it. After awhile, Bird Dog quit yelling and went back across the street. Father's heavy footsteps came down the driveway. The back door slammed after him. Then it was dark and I couldn't see the clouds anymore; not even the stars. Pretty soon, the back door slammed again and Father's footsteps came out in the yard.

"Sandy?"

I didn't answer. He went over to the old chicken coop and called for me again.

Then I heard him coming toward the Ford. I shut my eyes.

"You out here, Sandy?"

I didn't say anything. I tried not to breathe. He was standing right beside the car. Maybe he was looking down into it. Maybe he could see me lying there on the floorboards.

"Don't you want some supper, Sandy?"

I could hear him breathing heavily and regularly, as though his chest hurt him. He stood there a long time. Then he went into the house.

After awhile, I got hungry and went in too. Father had gone by then; Estelle said she didn't know where. I had supper and went to bed.

That was a long time ago, of course, and Father is dead now. So is Alton Henderson, and I haven't seen Bird Dog Barnes or Junior Fields in ten years. Estelle is married and living in Chicago. Everything is changed. Everything keeps on changing. But I never have seen another watermelon like that one and I'll never forget the way Father looked counting that money on the porch of the icehouse. Maybe things would have been better for us if he and I had ever talked about that after I was old enough to understand. But we never did.

MEET THE AUTHOR:
Tom Wicker (1926–)

Thomas Grey Wicker has crowded three careers into one lifetime. He is a fiction writer with eight novels to his credit; a nonfiction writer who has authored five books about politics and social matters; and a nationally honored journalist.

Born in 1926 in Hamlet, NC, Tom Wicker graduated from Hamlet's public schools and from UNC-Chapel Hill. He worked on newspapers in Aberdeen, Lumberton, and Winston-Salem, serving as everything from sports editor to city hall reporter to Washington correspondent. His journalistic career was interrupted during the Korean War, when he was in the United States Naval Reserve in Japan for two years.

During 1957–58, he studied at Harvard University as a Nieman Fellow. In 1960, after working as associate editor of *The Tennessean* in Nashville, Tennessee, he joined the *New*

York Times, where he has covered the White House, Congress, and national politics. Even with such a busy journalistic career, he has continued to write books.

Tom Wicker has been honored with the University of Arizona's John Zenger Award for journalists and the North Carolina Award for Literature. You can often see him on television talk shows concerned with political matters, such as "This Week With David Brinkley," which appears on ABC-TV each Sunday.

Language Alert

1. *nockalations*: The speaker means *innoculations*—shots to prevent lockjaw (tetanus).
2. *WPA*: Works Progress Administration, a federal program sponsored by Franklin Roosevelt's New Deal to help end the depression. (Through this program, unemployed men were hired to work on projects of long-range value. They built roads, public buildings, parks, etc. The name was later changed to Works Projects Administration.)
3. *shoat*: a very young pig
4. *rasslers*: wrestlers
5. *premises*: land
6. *that John Brown critter*: When it is not a real person's name, *John Brown* is used as a term to belittle someone or something, similar to *darn* or *blasted*. *Critter*, of course, is a mispronunciation of *creature*.

Reflecting

1. In the first line Sandy declares that "Father was touchy," and we see firsthand how cross and touchy Father can be—and how it sometimes costs him work and friends.

   Sandy doesn't tell us (directly) what other characteristics his father has and he doesn't tell us how he and his father feel about each other. Reviewing the story, look at specific incidents and see what they tell us:
   a. about what Mr. Martin is like, and
   b. about his relationship with his son.
2. Sandy doesn't talk openly about social classes, but through the story we can tell that the town (Sandy included) is conscious of differences in social class. Who is considered "trashy"? Which of the boys are from well-to-do, respected families? How can you tell?
3. Sandy yells out his objection the minute Mr. Alf starts talking about selling the watermelon for a dollar. How does his father feel about it? How do you know? Similarly, Sandy reacts violently when he finds out what has happened to the watermelon. Again, how does his father feel, and how can you tell?
4. At the end of the story, Sandy tells us that "things would have been better for us if he and I had ever talked about that [the watermelon incident] after I was old enough to understand. But we never did."
   a. What "things" would have been better for them if they had talked?
   b. Why didn't they ever talk about the incident?

Preview

Although other sports are certainly popular, baseball has for generations been considered *the* national sport. Before city recreation leagues and Little League teams were even dreamed of, American kids were playing baseball, often with home-carved bats and balls made of almost anything that could be crammed into an approximately round shape.

In the following poem, Shelby Stephenson revisits his boyhood home. Leaning against the chimney which served as "home" for his boyhood baseball games, he is suddenly thrown into a memory of boyhood games. Notice how the memories pile fast on top of one another.

The Old House's Brick-Oven Chimney

Shelby Stephenson

Hair rubs on the baked brick chimney behind the planked house
and it is mine, coming into being
on the homemade sockballs we hit as kids.
Using the scooped-out grill as backstop
we slam homers a country mile, chase shadows where the ball
strikes branches falling on the mound.
A canopy of oaks keeps a dome
over our heads running the one oak, two, three trees
home to the chimney where Skeeter catches
without a mask to protect his nose
broken there when a snib gets him face-on
before blood and cowlicked hair
smear the worn brick oven in the chimney on Paul's Hill.

MEET THE AUTHOR:
Shelby Stephenson (1939–)

Music and conversations brought Shelby Stephenson to writing poems. As a child, he loved listening to people talk and hearing the stories they told. In the ninth grade, having been brought up on hymns and country music, he started writing country songs. His poetry reflects both influences. Many of the lines sound like the informal conversation of country folk sitting around a fireplace, and many of them are musical and rhythmical. Even today, when he reads his poems throughout the state, he often precedes his reading by singing country songs and hymns in his rich baritone, accompanying himself on the acoustic guitar.

After graduating from Cleveland High School in Johnston County, Shelby Stephenson earned degrees in English and law. He now lives with his family in Southern Pines and teaches at Pembroke State University, where he edits a nationally recognized literary journal, *The Pembroke Review*. His poetry, most of which reflects his roots in rural North Carolina, has been published widely and has won two state awards.

A gregarious person equally at home with farmers and artists, students and governors, he recommends that young people "Listen to the people—anybody—particularly the old people. Turn that peaking energy to capacity—to a state where you are neither superior nor inferior to even a stone, let alone a person." About writing, he declares, "There are no rules, though; there are no rules—just the blank page. The art is waiting—around us, in us, as we see and try to form what surrounds our lives."

Reflecting

The chimney in this poem was built in such a way that it had an oven facing the outside. Players running at top speed to make it "home" before the ball was tossed in might find themselves banging into the house, "smearing" blood and hair on the chimney. It sounds like a dangerous game—and we know that a fast pitch did break Skeeter's nose—but Stephenson's memory doesn't concentrate on those matters, or the fact that the ball was just a wound-tight wad of socks. No, the game may have been imperfect by some standards, but to the kids this was pure fun.

Did you have a childhood game or playtime that you still remember warmly? Write down the details—what equipment you were using (some of it homemade?), where you played, who was playing, what happened. See if you can capture that favorite time as Stephenson has in this poem.

CAROLINA BOY

Andy Griffith

Preview

There is something very appealing about success stories. Americans respond to such stories: the Horatio Alger tales of poor boys who through hard work and determination become successful businessmen and the *Rocky* films in which an unpromising boxer whips the toughest opponents.

Andy Griffith's true life story fits into that category. He was not poverty-stricken or abused or physically handicapped, but he had some very difficult obstacles to overcome before his life became satisfying. In 1982, he told his story to members of the North Carolina Literary and Historical Society. As you read his story, look for (1) the difficulties—both within himself and from outside—which young Andy Griffith faced; and (2) the things—again, both from within and from outside—which helped him along his way.

For many years I have entertained and done shows all over North Carolina, but I have never been able before to publicly say what North Carolina really means to me. For this reason, I am especially glad that you asked me to talk with you tonight.

First, though, let me mention a few things I *don't* love North Carolina for. I don't love North Carolina because we make beautiful furniture here, although my family made a lot of it. For that matter, I did too. And I don't love North Carolina because we grow tobacco here. I used to smoke four packs a day, and I think I've paid my dues on that. And I don't love North Carolina because we've got beautiful trees—you can go to Georgia for that—or because we have these wonderful outdoor dramas all over the state, where young people can get a start; or because we make the best barbecued pork

Published as "What North Carolina Has Meant to Me" in *Carolina Comments*, Vol. XXI, No. 3, May 1983.

in the world; or because of our fine sea-food; or even because of our beautiful, beautiful countryside, all the way from Manteo to Murphy. All of these things are important, but I love North Carolina for a much more personal reason.

My parents were both North Carolinians. Each of them gave me at least one special gift besides showing their love for me. My mother's family were all musical; all of them played guitars, banjos, fiddles, or other instruments. My father couldn't carry a tune, couldn't even whistle. But he had the best sense of humor of any man I ever met, and he was a great storyteller. So, you see, even though I didn't know it, and they didn't know it either, my parents started me out with two gifts right off the bat: singing and talking.

As I grew up in North Carolina, every time I needed help, and every time it looked like I wasn't going to make it, some person or some group or sometimes an entire area in this wonderful state looked my way and gave me a hand. I guess it began when I went to Rockford Street Grammar School in Mount Airy. There were only eighteen or twenty of us in each class, and in a small school like that you would think it would be hard to have a class idiot. But folks, you're looking at him. I did something stupid every day, or said something stupid; and I was funny-looking too, so people laughed at me, though I really didn't want them to.

One Friday our class was supposed to give the program at assembly. We hadn't planned anything, so a buddy of mine said he'd get up and sing if I would. I said that sounded all right to me; and since I was sitting next to the aisle, I got up to let my buddy out. But he didn't move—and there I was, already standing. I had to walk all the way down that long aisle and then up the steps to the stage; and when I got there I didn't say a word, just started right in singing the only song I knew. "Put on Your Old Gray Bonnet." I knew you were supposed to sing it through twice, one time slow and one time fast, so I started out slow. Man, they began to laugh; so I got faster: "Put-on-your-old-gray-bonnet-with-the-blue-ribbon-on-it." I'm telling you something, you could hear them laughing way out on the street. I could even see my teacher, down front, leaning back, her mouth wide open, just screaming with laughter.

I guess I should have learned something from that, but I didn't. Kids need somebody to make fun of, to laugh at; and I seemed to fit the role pretty well. As a result, I didn't have much self-esteem.[1] I wasn't doing very well in school, and I couldn't seem to do anything else right, so I stayed by myself a lot and kind of dreamed about being somebody else.

Things finally started to change about the time I went to high school. Swing music was big then, and I got interested in it. Every day I'd get out Spiegel's catalogue and look at the pages of musical instruments—just dreaming, I guess. Then one day in class I heard a boy say that his daddy had worked in the furniture factory all his life and that he was going to end up working in the furniture factory

1. self-esteem: respect for oneself (This is one of the most important words in the speech!)

all his life, so there just wasn't any reason for him to try to learn all the stuff in the school books. Whewwww. My father worked in the furniture factory all his life, and there was nothing wrong with that; but I didn't want to. And just at that time something else came along.

I was fourteen years old and I learned about a job with the NYA, the National Youth Administration. Sweeping out the school. Six dollars a month. You were supposed to be fifteen years old, but I lied about my age and got the job. I sent that first six dollars off to Spiegel's catalog and ordered me a slide trombone. We didn't have a band or anything, so I didn't know what I was going to do with it. But I really wanted that trombone.

When it finally came in the mail, I thought that trombone was the priettiest thing I'd ever seen. I still didn't know how to play it, but for two or three months I blew on it every day. My poor father. "Get out! Take that thing somewhere," he'd say. And then one day he came home and said a fellow at the furniture factory had told him there was a preacher up at the other end of town who taught boys how to play horns. I went right on up to see that man. He was a Moravian preacher— every Moravian church has a band, you know—and people in town knew him as Ed Mickey. Well, folks, that man taught me how to play that trombone—and how to read music. What a difference! What a difference! None of the boys I knew anywhere in town could play a trombone.

Before he was done, Ed Mickey taught me to play every horn in that church, baritone horn, E-flat alto, bass horn, valve trombone. Then he taught me to sing And soon I was singing all over Mount Airy—civic clubs, churches, everywhere. When we graduated from high school I sang—at the baccalaureate service, graduation, and at the senior dance—but this time they didn't laugh. And it was all because a fine North Carolinian, the Right Reverend Edward Timothy Mickey took his time, his talent, his knowledge, his effort, and his love and gave them all to me. (He is now bishop of the Moravian Church, Southern Province.) I later went on to the University of North Carolina and studied music, but if it hadn't been for him, none of that would have happened.

I had a *wonderful* time—and a *horrible* time—in Chapel Hill. I went through every day hoping, just hoping, they wouldn't find out how little I knew, but sometimes they did. I failed Political Science 41 twice. My counselor, a lady, called me in and said: "Andy, very few people fail political science once, but nobody fails it twice." I guess that was the only record I ever broke at Chapel Hill. But I got in a lot of singing. Sometimes I'd sing by myself, sometimes with small groups; and I suppose while I was there I sang with every choir and chorus in town. And I learned some wonderful music—Verdi, Brahms, Mozart, Handel, Beethoven, Bach. Even today I get a great deal of pleasure out of it, singing or just listening.

Chapel Hill offered me another new experience when I got a part in a play. On a stage. Acting. And you know something, I thought I was just having a good time, without even knowing that I was falling in love. The first play I did was by Gilbert and Sullivan. It was directed by Foster Fitz-simons, a fine, fine man who took extra effort and time and care with me. He brought people over to give me encouragement, who made me feel like I was ten feet tall when they talked to me.

All along the way at Chapel Hill I was getting help from a man named Paul Young, who was head of the Choral Department. One day he told me if I was going to be a singer I ought to be studying singing. When I told him I couldn't pay for it he said that that wasn't a problem. If I would take care of the Glee Club music—just patch it up and keep it together—he'd teach me for nothing. I studied music with that man for five wonderful years.

There was a graduate student there, a fellow named Bob Armstrong, who had written a three-act play that was going to be done by the Carolina Playmakers, I wasn't even a drama student, but Bob insisted that they let me play the male lead. Sam Selden directed it, and I guess it went pretty well. Ten or twelve years later, Bob Armstrong was in a stage play in New York called *Cat on a Hot Tin Roof,* directed by Elia Kazan. One night Kazan told Bob Armstrong about a picture he was going to do. It was about this bum from Arkansas who went on the radio and began to get a big following, and then went on television and got bigger and bigger and more and more powerful, and finally was about to control the government; and the only thing was, he was crazy. Kazan asked Bob Armstrong if he knew anybody who could play that part, or was like that, and Bob said, "Yeah, Andy Griffith's like that." As the result of my friend from Chapel Hill saying that, I got my first leading role in a major motion picture, a fine film called *A Face in the Crowd.*

The first man I ever met in Chapel Hill was Edwin S. Lanier, who was the self-help officer there at the school. He got me a job right away as a busboy in the cafeteria. Breakfast and eight dollars a week: five dollars for tuition, and three dollars to live on, more or less. I was a lot thinner in those days than I am now. That went on for a long time, but then I came down with some bad back trouble, so I went over to Duke and got my back X-rayed. The told me it was all out of line and I'd have to wear a brace, a big old leather thing with steel running up and down. It cost thirty dollars, so I went to Mr. Lanier to see if I could get my tuition deferred. He wrote down a man's name and told me to go over to see him in Raleigh. The man's name was W. Rea Parker, and he got me talking right off about what I wanted to do with my life. He couldn't really understand how a man with a major in music could make a living, but he told me the state of North Carolina had a program for indigent[2] students with physical disabilities and that they would help me out with my tuition and a few books.

I was astounded. I still am. And when I asked him how I was expected to pay back the money, all he said was: "You get a

2. indigent: poor, needy

332

good education, get a good job, and be a good taxpayer." Well, there are a lot of things I haven't done in my life. But I did get my education, I do have a good job, and I've been a wonderful taxpayer.

By then I was the dorm manager and got my room free, and I took up the laundry and got two dollars a week for that. I had some other jobs and got a little money singing here and there, and with the help the state of North Carolina gave me, I made it. But I'll tell you right now, if it had not been for the help from the state of North Carolina I would never have graduated from the University of North Carolina and I would never have achieved the success and found the happiness that I have found in my life. I will always be grateful for that.

There have been so many people here in Raleigh and around the state who have given me a handup—people like Bess Ballentine and John Fries Blair, and Jimmy Theim, and Ainslie Pryor, and Paul Hoover—and a lot of others down in Dare County. I first went down there, to Roanoke Island, in 1947 to be in *The Lost Colony*. I really don't know why, because I hadn't done that much acting. I'd never been there, either. Didn't even know where it was. In fact, I'd never been anyplace near the water. But boy, am I glad I went.

I played the part of the First Soldier that first summer in *The Lost Colony* and understudied the role of Sir Walter Raleigh; and I learned to swim, and had a sweetheart, and everything was just perfect. Later on in the summer a fellow named Ted Cronk said he was going to put on some nightclub shows over on the beach, and I tried out for the barbershop quartet. I didn't get it, but a little bit later he let me do a song called "The Preacher and the Bear," sung like a sermon—"The preacher went a-hunting, 'twas on a Sunday morn/ 'Course it was against his religion, but he took his gun along." I'd get the crowd shouting along with me, and then make some announcements—old . . . jokes, kind of, that could be used as announcements, . . . Sassy stuff! I'd stomp my feet and get the crowd going, and it became known as the "old preacher act." I later came to be called Deacon Andy Griffith because of it.

I did that preacher act a couple of times that summer and a couple of times the next summer, and I really enjoyed it. But then Ted Cronk left, and that put an end to the nightclub show. One day, though a local fellow came to me and asked if any of us in *The Lost Colony* and the choir would like to put on shows over at the Shrine Club. So eight or nine of us got together and put on a show—singers, dancers, quartets, and different things— with me as emcee. Finally I got the notion to do something out of *Hamlet*—"to be or not to be"—and do it funny; only I couldn't make it funny. So I asked that same friend of mine, Bob Armstrong, to tell me the story of *Hamlet*. He went through the whole thing while I wrote down the names of the characters, and that week I made up a monologue on the actual play. Only I told it as if it took place in the mountains of North Carolina.

I'll never forget that Saturday night when I did the *Hamlet* monologue. The place was packed, every table full, the floor full of people sitting in a big semicircle around the stage. The laughter came in rolls, just waves of it; and for the first time in my life people laughed at me, not because I was stupid, or seemed dumb, or looked funny, but because I wanted them to.

I wrote and performed a different monologue every week that summer and the next summer. Some were funny, and some weren't. But the people came anyway, those wonderful people from Dare County. They laughed when the monologues were funny, and they forgave me when they weren't. They gave me a special gift, those Dare County folks, and I'll always remember it. They gave me a chance to search for something—and to find it. They did it unselfishly and with great love, and I will be trying to repay them for the rest of my life.

I love being a North Carolinian. My mother and father, North Carolinians, gave me whatever talents I have. This state gave me a childhood that made me know I wanted more than what I had, and it gave me places to look for it and people to help me along the way. This state sustained[3] me when I couldn't sustain myself; and the people of this state accepted me and mine when we were good and offered forgiveness when we weren't good. That's what North Carolina has given me. And that's why I'm proud to be a North Carolinian.

MEET THE AUTHOR:
Andy Griffith (1926–   )

It's a long, long way from Mt. Airy, a small town in North Carolina, to Hollywood, the film capital of the world. But Andy Griffith made that journey. It's a long leap from sweeping out the school for six dollars a month to being the star of one of the most popular and long-lasting comedies in television history. But Andy Griffith made that leap, too.

Born in 1926, Andrew Samuel Griffith majored in music at UNC-Chapel Hill. After graduation, he taught music and speech at Goldsboro High School during the school

3. sustained: supported

year and appeared in *The Lost Colony* at Manteo in the summers. His "big break" came when his comic monologue "What It Was, Was Football" was recorded. It became a national hit which sold 800,000 copies, and brought fame and offers of television appearances to young Andy Griffith.

Not long afterward, Griffith was offered the leading role in a television play, *No Time for Sergeants*, which was adapted into a successful Broadway play and later into a movie which is still shown on late-night shows. He made other movies, but is perhaps best known for "The Andy Griffith Show," the comedy series which appeared on television for eight years and is still one of the most popular syndicated series.

Since then, Andy Griffith has appeared in more movies, given shows in Las Vegas, and starred in other television series—most recently, "Matlock." He often returns to Manteo, where he has a home and, as this selection proves, he still feels ties with North Carolina.

Language Alert

If you have heard Andy Griffith—and surely you have, at least on reruns!—you know that he is famous for his rural North Carolina dialect. As you read this address, try to hear his voice in your mind's ear. Notice how he sprinkles his speech with "down home" phrases, for example:

"right off the bat"; "But I got in a lot of singing"; and "so many people . . . have given me a handup."

This language has been his trademark— he knows both *how* to use it effectively and *when* to do so.

Reflecting

Looking at Andy Griffith

1. List the talents and abilities which enabled Andy Griffith to achieve his dreams.
2. List the people who helped him along the way—and what each did for him.

Looking at Yourself

1. List the talents and abilities which you can use to overcome obstacles and meet your own goals. (Be honest. You do not have to share this writing, so you need not be modest.)
2. List the resources outside yourself which (or who) have helped you in the past: institutions (churches, schools, clubs, social agencies) or people (friends, relatives, neighbors, professional people).
3. List the resources you can use in the present and the future. Are there any you are fearful of using? Why? Can you overcome that fear?

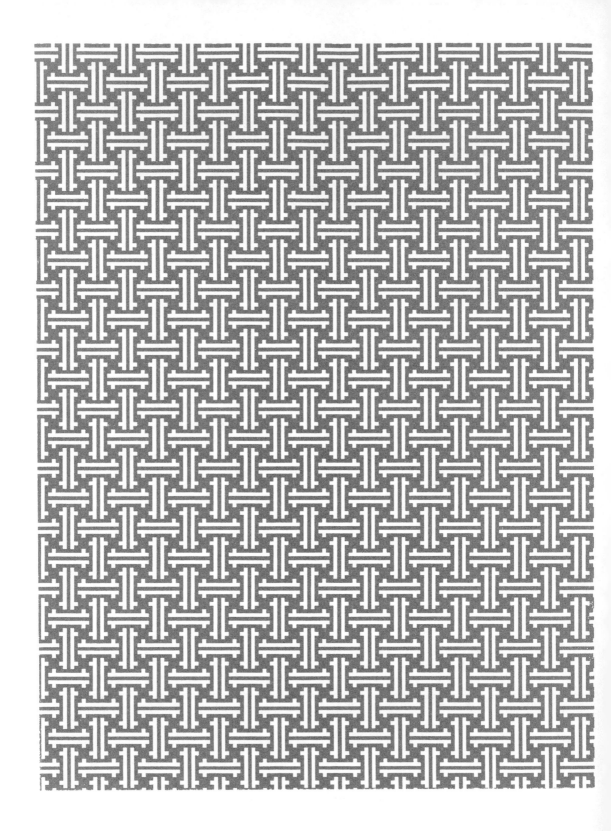

The Big War

The United States was involved in World War I only a short time. World War II lasted much longer—almost four years. It also involved many more people: around 360,000 North Carolinians gave military service and 4,088 were killed. Furthermore, it altered the lives of those who remained at home. Many goods, such as gasoline, coffee, meat, sugar, tires, and shoes, were in such short supply that they were rationed. Civilians were encouraged to plant "Victory gardens" to grow their own food. They were urged to collect any scrap materials that could be used in the war effort, such as rubber and metal. Even bacon grease, which could be used to make munitions, was to be saved! Everyone was asked to work together to produce goods—both food and manufactured goods—essential to the troops. The war touched everyone's life in one way or another.

The following writings provide both fictional and nonfictional glimpses of the war and what it meant both to those who fought and those who remained at home.

December 7, 1941

Vermont Royster

Preview

December 7, 1941—After the United States was caught by surprise by the Japanese attack on Pearl Harbor, President Franklin Roosevelt termed it "The Day of Infamy." Much has been said and written about the shock our nation experienced and how it took this country months to mobilize enough resources to begin to turn the war around. What we don't often think about is what a shock this event was to young soldiers and sailors, who had known that they might eventually have to fight, but who in their hearts hadn't really believed it. Suddenly, they found themselves with more responsibility than they had ever dreamed of.

Vermont Royster was one of those men. In 1941, he was serving on an old destroyer, expecting only a one-year tour of duty before returning to civilian life and the journalistic career he had already begun. Then suddenly—December 7.

The following excerpt is from his autobiography, *My Own, My Country's Time.*

On Sunday afternoon, December 7, 1941, I was the duty officer aboard the USS J. Fred Talbott, an old World War I destroyer known as a "four-piper," tied up at the Balboa docks, Panama Canal Zone.

In fact I was the only officer on board. The others, including the captain and the executive officer, were ashore enjoying a pleasant holiday after a week of routine maneuvering exercises[1] in the Bay of Panama. Some of them no doubt were sipping mint juleps on the veranda of the Ti-

---

1. maneuvering exercises: training exercises in which military men "fight" in mock combat

voli Hotel under the slowly revolving big-bladed electric fans. Two-thirds of the crew were also ashore, possibly enjoying the more exciting pleasures of Panama City.

On board the tropical heat and humidity were oppressive[2] even with the portholes open. Sweat rolled down my face, chest, arms, and legs. I was sitting at the wardroom table in my skivies, my cap and a rather rumpled uniform on a chair nearby. I was writing a letter to Frances, whom I had not seen in nearly a year, about the happy prospect that in a few short weeks my year's tour of duty would be over. I was writing of a grand reunion and of seeing my Bonnie again, now a year and a half old and already walking.

A little after 1330 (1:30 p.m. civilian time) the duty radioman stuck his head in the door and said something was going on at Pearl Harbor, judging by the radio traffic. I wearily told him to keep monitoring[3] and let me know if it was anything interesting.

About 1400 he came flying down the ladder from the radio shack and burst into the wardroom as if the devil were after him. He handed me the radio-file clipboard with a message on top.

It read: AIR RAID PEARL HARBOR X THIS IS NOT A DRILL.

It had been sent by Cincpac (commander-in-chief, Pacific Fleet) and forwarded by Navy radio Washington, information to all ships and stations. It had to be true. But I stared at it in disbelief.

The radioman and I were both paralyzed. I wiped some of the sweat off my face with a handkerchief trying to clear my head. Any such air raid had to come from the Japanese. The thought flashed through my mind that if the Japs had raided Pearl Harbor we might be next at the Canal. Obviously I should do something. But what?

I sent the radioman back to follow the traffic. In this situation it was unlikely any of the messages would need officer decoding; I put on my uniform and went out to the gangway. There I sent a messenger for the chief machinist's mate on duty. In about five minutes he arrived, sleepy-eyed and a bit grumpy at having been awakened from a nap. I told him to fire up the boilers and prepare to get underway.

He started to balk at such an unusual order from the most junior officer on the ship. I told him there was a war on and to get cracking. I was beginning to feel the authority suddenly thrust upon me.

I knew with our ancient boilers it would take an hour to get up steam unless we wanted to risk damage to the tubes, and possibly an explosion. So I next crossed over to the *USS Borie*, a sister ship tied up alongside flying the flag of our division commander. Several other duty officers were collected on her deck. Most, like myself, were ensigns, the lowest commissioned officer. The senior among us was a lieutenant, junior grade. We held a "council of war" and decided the best thing was to get underway and away from the docks.

I returned to my ship exhilarated.

2. oppressive: difficult to bear, harsh

3. monitoring: keeping watch over

Navy regulations were quite clear that in the absence of the captain the senior officer on board was in command. That was me. I had visions of getting the ship underway myself, steaming out to meet the foe at thirty knots, undoubtedly winning a Navy cross or something, posthumously or otherwise.

It was not to be. Word had already come from below that with the crew available we could only fire-up two boilers, giving us at most twenty knots. It also took longer than an hour to raise steam. In the meantime Lieutenant John Foster, our engineering officer, showed up, followed by Lieutenant Shallus Kirk, the executive officer. Some crew members also began to straggle aboard, alerted by announcements in all the movie houses, and elsewhere rounded up by the shore patrol.

So it was nearly 1600 by the time we cast off the lines and backed into the turning basin. As we straightened out for the channel a motor-whaleboat hove in sight with Lieutenant Commander C. M. Jensen, our captain, frantically waving. He scrambled up the portside ladder and came to the bridge still in his civilian sportswear.

Then we headed out into Panama Bay, turned right for Cape Mala and the open Pacific beyond. It was ridiculous. The *J. Fred,* built in 1918, was armed with old four-inch World War I guns that had to be aimed and ranged individually by eye, and they couldn't be elevated high enough for aircraft even if we had any antiaircraft shells for them, which we didn't. For the rest we had only a battery of infantry fifty-millimeter machine guns that couldn't have hit a plane at a thousand feet. We had no radar, not even any echo-ranging sound gear (sonar) to detect submarines. Neither had our sister ships. It was as absurd as the Charge of the Light Brigade.[4]

Fortunately we found nothing but an empty ocean. If there were U.S. fighter planes anywhere, we never saw any. The Japs had missed their chance. If they had the ships and the wit they could have bombed locks with impunity[5] and put the Canal out of commission for months.

All that night and the next day our division of old destroyers steamed nervously but aimlessly well out to sea. Then we got orders to return at best speed and transit the Canal to the Caribbean side. There had been reports of German submarines in the sea.

Normally a Canal transit takes seven to eight hours, deep water to deep water. When we reached the entrance we found that all other shipping had been cleared away; the locks were set for our transit, and we tore through it like epsom salts in a matter of four hours, hitting twenty knots in the cuts and sending sweeping waves on the banks from our wake. It was a record transit up to then and may still be.

4. The Charge of the Light Brigade: On October 25, 1854, during the Crimean War, a British cavalry brigade charged a strong Russian position. Less than 200 of the 600 men survived. It is considered a major military blunder—"absurd," as Royster calls it.

5. impunity: immunity from punishment

Japanese dive bombers, Pearl Harbor.

We found nothing on the Caribbean side, either, save one lone freighter on innocent business. It all proved much excitement about nothing, though in fairness to those directing the operation there was no way they could be sure of that.

So it was a week before I could visit the ship's office, find a typewriter and write a letter to the Bureau of Navigation, which then handled officer personnel. Since there had been no general directive from Washington about the one-year service people, I thought I would at least try, citing[6] my original orders, for a request to be transferred to inactive duty. By this time, however, I understood about going through channels. I took it with me to Captain Jensen for forwarding with his appropriate endorsement.

Captain Jensen looked at me as if I were crazy, which I probably was. Anyway, he quietly tore up the letter. That was strictly contrary to regulations but I knew a protest was futile. Although I never got any official extension of my one-year orders, I was in for the duration.[7]

6. citing: mentioning, calling attention to

7. duration: period of time during which something lasts

Vermont Royster (1914–   )

Born and reared in Raleigh, Vermont Royster has been one of our state's most distinguished journalists. A Phi Beta Kappa graduate of UNC-Chapel Hill, he began working as a reporter for the *Wall Street Journal* in 1936. Five years later, like many young men, he had to interrupt career plans in order to serve his country during World War II. Upon return to civilian life, he rejoined the *Wall Street Journal*, where he became editor-in-chief in 1951. Two years later he won the most important award given to journalists—the Pulitzer Prize—for his editorials. The Pulitzer committee announced that he won the award for his ability "to decide the underlying moral issue, illuminated by a deep faith and confidence in the people of our country."

In addition to hundreds of editorials, Vermont Royster is the author of a number of books dealing with social and political matters and with his own life. He has also served as president of the American Society of Newspaper Editors. When he retired in 1970, he returned to his native state to hold the William R. Kenan Professorship of Journalism and Public Affairs at UNC-Chapel Hill.

Reflecting

This account is only one man's story, yet it illustrates how unprepared America's military forces were on that day. Go through the story and pick out all the details which show that neither Royster, his shipmates, nor the nation at large were adequately prepared for war.

The U-Boats Return

David Stick

Preview

One of the best-kept secrets not only during, but long after, World War II was the fact that German submarines lurked close to the eastern coast of the United States and caused a great deal of damage there. In all, eighty-seven ships, not counting the German submarines, were destroyed off the North Carolina coast during the war—most of them by submarines, and most of them during the first six months. Not only was the citizenry at large unaware of the conflict in the Atlantic, but even eastern North Carolinians knew very little of the vicious battle going on in our coastal waters.

David Stick had to conduct long and careful research to get the full story of these seacoast battles. The results of his efforts are published in this chapter from his book, *The Graveyard of the Atlantic*. As you read, you will see that Stick's story reads much like a script for a television documentary. (This isn't surprising, since he spent a number of years as a journalist, both for newspapers and for radio.) Using your imagination, you can almost hear Peter Jennings or Dan Rather narrating. Try to picture the images that would provide background for their words and imagine cameras zooming in for an interview with a survivor.

During the first six months of 1942 residents of coastal North Carolina were closer to war than were most of our troops then on overseas duty, and the coastal Carolina war, during that period, was a one-sided affair, with the odds strictly on the other side.

Simply stated, the reason for this early success by Nazi submarine raiders was that the Germans had concentrated on the development of U-boat warfare while this phase of naval preparedness was relegated[1] to a comparatively unimportant status by the United States. Thus, the outbreak of the war in December, 1941, found Hitler with a large and fully trained underseas fleet, and when this fleet attacked shipping along our coast it had about as hard a time of it as a hunter shooting into a pond full of tame ducks.

The amazing thing is that we were able, during that otherwise disastrous six-month period, to so perfect our antisubmarine defenses as to almost completely thwart[2] the underseas raiders throughout the remainder of the war; for the records show that more than 90 percent of the ship sinkings on our coast during the nearly four years of submarine attacks, occurred in those six months between January and July in 1942.

One of Hitler's first actions after Pearl Harbor had been to order a submarine attack on our east coast shipping, and six of his five-hundred-ton U-boats had been assigned to the job. These five-hundred-tonners, constituting the bulk of the Nazi sub fleet, were 220 feet long and 20.3 feet in width; their top speed was 7½ knots submerged and 17½ knots on the surface; each had four torpedo tubes forward and one in the stern, carried a total of fourteen torpedoes plus deck guns, and was fueled for an average voyage of six weeks duration.

Other U-boats were shortly dispatched to the aid of the six sent out originally, and by January of 1942 some nineteen German underseas craft were operating in the western half of the Atlantic. To guard against them we had five sub-chasers, a nondescript collection of miscellaneous small craft, and a handful of shore-based airplanes. The situation, with one exception, was directly comparable to that in the early part of World War I. The sole exception was that this time the enemy had many times the number of subs to throw into the battle.

The war came to our coast in explosive fashion in the early morning darkness of January 18, 1942. Sixty miles off Cape Hatteras the Standard Oil Company of New Jersey tanker *Allan Jackson*, a single-screw vessel of 4,038 net tons, was proceeding northward in a calm sea. She was loaded with 72,870 barrels of crude oil, nearly capacity, which she had picked up a week earlier at Cartagena, Colombia, for delivery to New York. The crew of the 453-foot vessel consisted of thirty-five officers and men.

At 1:30 that morning Captain Felix W. Kretchmer was in his bunk, resting. Second Mate Melvin A. Rand had the duty on the bridge, Seaman Randolph H. Larson was at the wheel, Boatswain Rolf Clausen was in the messroom playing cards, and Seaman Gustave Nox was en route to the foc'sle[3] head to relieve Seaman Hamon Brown of the lookout duty there.

1. relegated: assigned—quite often to an unimportant or obscure task or position

2. thwart: to prevent from taking place, to frustrate

3. foc'sle: (forecastle) that part of the upper deck of a ship located in front of the mast nearest the bow (front of the ship)

At 1:35 a.m. two torpedoes struck the *Jackson* in quick succession. The first, hitting the forward tank on the vessel's starboard side, exploded beneath an empty cargo hold and caused only minor damage; the second struck even closer to the bow, exploding with such force that the tanker was split completely in two, her cargo of crude oil spewing out in all directions.

The second explosion threw Captain Kretchmer to the floor, and though flames filled his quarters he managed to escape through a porthole, falling to the boat deck on the lee side. Meanwhile both Rand and Larson were knocked overboard by the force of the explosion, Boatswain Clausen rushed on deck in search of a lifeboat, and seamen Nox and Brown, closer than the others to the actual point where the torpedo made contact, already were dead.

The scene, at that time, was one of despair for the crewmen yet alive, for in addition to the flames engulfing the sinking ship the entire surface of the water surrounding the vessel was covered with fiercely burning oil.

Boatswain Clausen, in his frantic search for a lifeboat, discovered that the No. 1 boat was a total wreck, the No. 2 boat was jammed in its chocks[4] and could not be budged, the No. 4 boat was surrounded by wind-driven flames, and only the No. 3 boat remained serviceable. This was immediately lowered away, and even before it struck the water Clausen and seven others jumped inside.

"When the boat was in the water and held in position by the painter we were 3 to 4 feet from the ship's side," Clausen said. "Around us, within a short distance, were the flames of crude oil burning on the surface of the sea. What saved us was the strong discharge from the condenser pump. The outlet happened to be just ahead of the lifeboat, and the force of the stream of water, combined with the motion of the ship, pushed the burning oil away."

"I unhooked the falls and cut the painter," Clausen continued. "At that time, the broken-off bow of the *Allan Jackson* was listing to port and the main part of the vessel was listing to starboard, over our lifeboat. After cutting the painter, I found in the excitement no one had unlashed the oars. By the time I cut the lashings and the oars were manned, the boat was being sucked toward the propeller."

The prospect of drowning or of being burned to death was bad enough, but now the eight men faced a third and even greater danger. For they were pulled directly beneath the great propeller, and with each revolution the huge blades struck the boat, threatening not only to crush the small craft, but to grind to pieces its human occupants as well. For seconds that lasted interminably the men stood helplessly while this giant grinder spiralled, with sickening regularity and force just above them. But finally, pushing against the stern of the ship with oars, the men managed to get clear of the propeller, were suddenly caught in its backwash,

---

4. chocks: blocks or wedges placed under something to keep it from moving

and driven this time straight at the great mass of burning oil astern.

Once again luck was with them, for this backwash from the propeller forced a clear path through the burning mass, and with oars properly manned, at last the boat proceeded down this turbulent path to safety.

Within ten minutes both sections of the tanker sank from view, but the men in the lifeboat remained near by, searching for other survivors, and they rescued one man, a radio operator, Stephen Verbonich.

"Then we saw a white light, low over the sea, which undoubtedly was on a submarine," Clausen said. "Putting up sails, we steered for shore in a westerly direction."

Two and a half hours later a second light was seen, a bluish searchlight, east of the lifeboat. Clausen started signalling with a flashlight, turning the beam on the white sail and beginning a message in Morse code, but his companions feared the light might be from a submarine, and he stopped signalling. For the remainder of the night the nine men—eight who had pulled away from the sinking ship in Boat No. 3, and Radioman Verbonich— proceeded westward under sail without incident. The night was comparatively warm and the Gulf Stream wind moderate; under other circumstances theirs could have been an enjoyable outing.

Captain Kretchmer was not having as easy a time of it. Finding himself on the boat deck after escaping through the porthole, he looked around for signs of life. He could locate none of his crew and so started up the ladder leading to the bridge. "The decks and ladders were breaking up and the sea was rushing aboard," he said. "As the vessel sank amidships, the suction carried me away from the bridge ladder. After a struggle I came to the surface, on which oil was afire a short distance away." He then managed, somehow, to grasp a couple of small boards and supported his weight on these throughout the remainder of the night as he drifted away from the scene of the disaster.

Meanwhile, both Second Mate Rand and Seaman Larson had also located pieces of wreckage large enough to keep them afloat, though in the immediate confusion they became separated. Rand later sighted another small raft, to which Third Mate Boris A. Voronsoff and Junior Third Mate Francis M. Bacon were clinging, and joined forces with them; but Bacon began to get cramps and lashed himself to the wreckage, where he died soon after.

Thus, as the first light of false dawn appeared in the sky that morning the tanker *Allan Jackson* had disappeared completely, with only an oil slick to mark her burial place beneath the waters of the Gulf Stream; nine of her crew were in the No. 3 lifeboat a considerable distance to the west; Captain Kretchmer was clinging to his two tiny boards; Mates Rand and Voronsoff were together on their comparatively seaworthy raft, and Seaman Larson was floating nearby on a small piece of wreckage.

They might all have remained thus until they either floated ashore or drowned, had it not been for Boatswain Clausen's brief attempt to signal with his flashlight against the sails. For his signals had been seen by a friendly vessel, the U.S. Destroyer *Roe*, which remained nearby until morning, picking up all of the survivors in turn.

That first submarine attack on the Carolina coast had proven costly in lives as well as cargo; for of the thirty-five crewmen on board the *Allan Jackson* only the thirteen listed above were saved. But the *Allan Jackson* was just one of many ships, and her crewmen but the first of many merchant seamen lost in what has since been referred to as the Battle of Torpedo Junction.

Eight more ships went to the bottom off the North Carolina coast by the end of January, including the British tanker *Empire Gem* and the American-owned combination ore and oil carrier *Venore*, both of which were sunk southeast of Diamond Shoals on January 23 with considerable loss of life. Only the captain and one crewman survived the sinking of the *Empire Gem*, and twenty-one men were lost on the *Venore*.

Another eight went down in February; four freighters, three tankers, and the Brazilian passenger ship *Buarque*. Of the survivors of these eight sunken ships, none were subjected to a more harrowing experience than the six crewmen from the Norwegian cargo ship *Blink*, who were picked up in a lifeboat at sea February 14. Twenty-three persons had left the sinking ship in the lifeboat three days earlier, but seventeen had died as the small craft floated on the wintry Atlantic.

The U-boat attacks in January and February had been relatively haphazard affairs, but by the first of March the Nazis had effectively organized their forces. For one thing, instead of operating singly as they had in World War I, they now cruised in packs, exchanging information as to convoy[5] locations by wireless and banding together, especially at night, for their lethal[6] attacks. In addition, two or three were permanently stationed off Diamond Shoals in all but the roughest weather, resting on the sandy bottom during the daytime, then surfacing at night as our ships attempted to dash around Cape Hatteras.

Night was most frequently the time of attack, not only because it was more difficult for the subs to be seen, but because our authorities had not yet ordered a blackout[7] along the coast. Consequently, the subs were able to surface beyond the shipping lanes, thus silhouetting the unwary tankers and freighters against the lights on shore.

These tactics paid off in royal fashion, for during the month of March the subs sank an average of almost one ship daily along the North Carolina coast.

One of the ships sunk during March was the American freighter *Caribsea*, which went down on the eleventh with a valuable cargo of manganese ore. On the

5. convoy: As a noun, *convoy* means a group of ships or vehicles traveling together for convenience or protection. As a verb, it means *to accompany.*

6. lethal: capable of causing death

7. blackout: the extinguishing or concealing of lights that might be visible to the enemy

Caribsea, as on most merchantmen, the licenses of her officers were prominently displayed in a special glass case, and one of the licenses thus exhibited was that of Engineer James Baugham Gaskill, whose birthplace was listed as Ocracoke, North Carolina.

Gaskill was one of the crew members killed when the *Caribsea* was sunk that night southeast of Ocracoke. On the island, today, the inhabitants will tell you that the glass case, with Gaskill's license prominently displayed, came ashore a few days later near the village; and if you visit the Ocracoke Methodist Church they will undoubtedly point out a special cross behind the altar, a cross said to have been made from the nameplate of the *Caribsea*, which the island residents claim drifted through Ocracoke Inlet and was found opposite Gaskill's birthplace on the sound shore.

Of all the merchant seamen set adrift off our coast during World War II, Seaman Jules Souza of the American cargo carrier *Alcoa Guide* was the luckiest. For

This cemetery holds the graves of four British sailors whose bodies washed ashore at Ocracoke, NC, during World War I.

the *Alcoa Guide* was sunk March 16, some three hundred miles off Hatteras, and from then until late April—more than a month—Jules Souza drifted on an improvised raft. Three companions on the raft with him died long before help came, but amazingly Souza stuck it out and lived to tell of his experience. . . .

For almost three months the Nazi subs had been going about their deadly business. In less than ninety days they had sunk some fifty large ships, most of them loaded with valuable cargo, yet there had not been a single documented instance of one of the attacking U-boats being destroyed. By mid-April, however, a change was in prospect, for we finally had started blacking out our coastal communities, the British had transferred a number of armed trawlers to submarine patrol duty off North Carolina, additional planes and patrol vessels had been made available, and a more efficient convoy system had been put in practice.

In addition, a mined and protected anchorage was being provided at Cape Lookout, making it possible for almost all coastal shipping to proceed at night, blacked out. For most ships could make it from Lookout to Hampton Roads (closest protected port to the north) or Charleston (closest to the south) between disk and dawn.

Pinning it down to actual dates, April 14, 1942, was the day when the tide of battle changed. For early that morning the destroyer *Roper* encountered a submarine south of Wimble Shoals, dodged one torpedo, and then opened fire with her deck guns at three hundred yards range (so close that her searchlights were played on the target). The gunfire seriously damaged the sub while she was in the process of submerging, and the destroyer's depth charges finished her off. A number of bodies were recovered from the sunken sub that morning, and the craft was definitely identified as the five-hundred-ton *U-85*. Thus the first submarine kill of the war off the North Carolina coast was recorded.

For a time it looked as if the *Roper's* success had been little more than an accident, for certainly the overconfidence of the submarine commander had been a contributing factor to the loss, and his cohorts,[9] becoming more wary as a result, were able to elude our defenders for the remainder of the month. During this period eight more vessels were sunk, including the British freighter *Empire Thrush*, loaded with phosphates and TNT. The *Empire Thrush* was torpedoed off Cape Hatteras the same day that the *U-85* went down, but fortunately for her fifty-five crewmen the explosive cargo did not ignite, and all reached port safely. Another vessel lost at about the same time was the British freighter *Harpagon*, loaded with planes, tanks, and 2,602 tons of explosives. The *Harpagon* was sunk off Cape Hatteras, April 19, and the following day the Panamanian freighter *Chenango*, bound from Rio de Janeiro to Baltimore, went down off Dare County with the loss of all hands except an Irish fireman named James Terrence Bradley, who

9. cohorts: a group of people united in some task

was picked up from a raft twelve days later with a dying companion.

The record for May demonstrates in the most dramatic fashion how effectively our antisubmarine defenses had been developed in such a short time. During the month the subs sank but three vessels, all British; two of them were armed trawlers serving on convoy or patrol duty. Meanwhile, during the same period, the Navy credited a destroyer with sinking a German submarine off Cape Fear on May 2; the Coast Guard cutter *Icarus* chased the *U-352* ashore near Cape Lookout, May 9, capturing most of her crew; and the Navy claimed two other kills, one on the eleventh and the other on the nineteenth. A four to three score, if the navy claims can be accepted, with our side at last on top.

Between the end of May and the middle of July twelve more of our ships went down, several from striking mines, while the Nazis were losing one of their own number in exchange. Among the vessels lost was the sugar-laden freighter *Manuela* which was torpedoed, remained afloat for several days, and was being towed into Morehead City when it was torpedoed a second time and finally sank; and the tug *Keshena* which struck a mine while towing a torpedoed vessel into port July 19.

From then until the end of the war the subs had poor pickings, getting only a handful of ships during the next three years; the most noteworthy were the Cuban freighter *Libertad*, sunk off Lookout on December 4, 1943, with a loss of twenty-five crewmen, and the freighter *Belgian Airman*, torpedoed eighty miles east of Nags Head, April 14, 1945, with the loss of one life.

The totals for the four years of war show eighty-seven vessels lost on the North Carolina coast, not including the German submarines. Of these, better than two-thirds were sunk by Nazi raiders, the remainder going down as the result of striking mines, stranding, or foundering at sea. In size and numbers of vessels sunk, lives lost, and cargo destroyed, the period from 1942 through 1954 was the worst on record; but it could have been multiplied many times had we not come up with effective antisubmarine facilities in 1942.

MEET THE AUTHOR:
David Stick (1919–   )

Although born in New Jersey, David Stick moved to Manteo, NC, when he was ten. Except for eight years immediately before, during, and after World War II, he has been a resident of the Outer Banks ever since.

David Stick's father, an illustrator and writer, gave him a secondhand typewriter when he was only fourteen. A year later, young David was writing for newspapers. He served as editor of the student newspaper at

Elizabeth City High School and he worked on local newspapers for two summers before entering college. Once at UNC-Chapel Hill, like most budding journalists there, he served on the staff of the *Daily Tar Heel.* After graduation he worked on several North Carolina newspapers and, during World War II, served for more than three years as a combat correspondent with the U.S. Marine Corps.

Since returning to the Outer Banks in 1947, he has operated a number of businesses: a craft shop, a bookstore, a motor lodge, and realty companies. He also has been involved in what amounts to two more full-time careers. As an author, he has published eleven books and many articles about coastal North Carolina. As a citizen-activist, he has supported tourism, storm rehabilitation, outdoor drama, historical celebrations, erosion control, libraries, recreation, and marine science. His efforts have won him seven local and state awards.

Reflecting

The stories of individual incidents—the extent of the damage, the heroic efforts which sailors made to escape burning or sinking ships, the coincidences that helped men to escape destruction—these are so interesting that we may not remember the important lessons about preparedness, cooperation, and defense which this article teaches. Take a moment to review so that you can complete the following:

1. List the factors that put the Germans at an advantage during the earliest months of the war. Then add what they did in March to increase their effectiveness.
2. List the measures that the United States and Britain took that eventually ended Nazi domination of the seas off our coastline.
3. Explain how this story shows the importance of cooperation in surviving. (Think of the cooperation of the Navy men when a ship was hit. Look at your second list and notice how different nations and agencies cooperated to successfully defend shipping against the U-boats.)

We Are Now Soldiers

Marion Hargrove

Preview

War is certainly a solemn matter, but human beings have found that humor often gives them the extra boost that enables them to face dark times. Hargrove's columns and book were popular precisely because they gave a comic edge to a very serious situation.

This column is from the early part of the book, when Private Hargrove has just arrived in Fort Bragg and is trying to deal with what to him is a brand new way of life. Before you read, just from what you know about the military, imagine what you yourself might find difficult to get used to.

This morning—our first morning in the Recruit Reception Center—began when we finished breakfast and started cleaning up our squadroom. A gray-haired, fatherly old private, who swore that he had been demoted from master sergeant four times, lined us up in front of the barracks and took us to the dispensary.

If the line in front of the mess hall dwindled as rapidly as the one at the dispensary, life would have loveliness to sell above its private consumption stock. First you're fifteen feet from the door, then (whiff) you're inside. Then you're standing between two orderlies and the show is on.

The one on my left scratched my arm and applied the smallpox virus. The only thing that kept me from keeling over was the hypodermic needle loaded with typhoid germs, which propped up my right arm.

From the dispensary we went to a huge warehouse of a building by the railroad tracks. The place looked like Goldenberg's Basement on a busy day. A score of fitters measured necks, waists, inseams, heads, and feet.

My shoe size, the clerk yelled down the line, was ten and a half.

"I beg your pardon," I prompted, "I wear a size nine."

"Forgive me," he said, a trifle weary, "the expression is 'I wore a size nine.' These shoes are to walk in, not to make you look like Cinderella. You say size nine; your foot says ten and a half."

We filed down a long counter, picking up our allotted khaki and denims, barrack bags and raincoats, mess kits and tent halves. Then we were led into a large room, where we laid aside the vestments of civil life and donned our new garments.

While I stood there, wondering what I was supposed to do next, an attendant caught me from the rear and strapped to my shoulders what felt like the Old Man of the Mountain after forty days.

"Straighten up, soldier," the attendant said, "and git off the floor. That's nothing but a full field pack, such as you will tote many miles before you leave this man's army. Now I want you to walk over to that ramp and over it. That's just to see if your shoes are comfortable."

I looked across the room to where an almost perpendicular walkway led up to and over a narrow platform.

"With these Oregon boots and this burden of misery," I told him firmly, "I couldn't even walk over to the thing. As for climbing over it, not even an alpenstock, a burro train, and two St. Bernard dogs complete with brandy could get me over it."

There was something in his quiet, steady answering glance that reassured me. I went over the ramp in short order. On the double, I think the Army calls it.

From there we went to the theater, where we were given intelligence tests, and to the classification office, where we were interviewed by patient and considerate corporals.

"And what did you do in civil life?" my corporal asked me.

"I was feature editor of the Charlotte *News*."

"And just what sort of work did you do, Private Hargrove? Just give me a brief idea."

Seven minutes later, I had finished answering that question.

"Let's just put down here, 'Editorial worker.' " He sighed compassionately. "And what did you do before all that?"

I told him. I brought in the publicity work, the soda-jerking, the theater ushering, and the printer's deviling.

"Private Hargrove," he said, "the Army is just what you have needed to ease the burdens of your existence. Look no farther, Private Hargrove, you have found a home."

Marion Hargrove (1919–   )

Born in Mount Olive, Marion Hargrove grew up in Charlotte. He wrote for the school newspaper at Piedmont Junior High School and at the age of thirteen won first prize (one dollar) for a short story in a contest held by *The Charlotte Observer*. He must have been encouraged in spite of the smallness of the prize, for he began working for the *Charlotte News* when he was in his third year at Central High School. By the time he was twenty-two years old, he had risen to the position of feature editor. Then came the war and the army career which brought him fame.

While in training at Fort Bragg, Marion Hargrove continued to send columns back to the *Charlotte News* detailing his adventures as a civilian trying to learn how to be a soldier. A collection of the columns, *See Here, Private Hargrove*, became a best-seller and later a popular movie.

During the war, Hargrove served on the staff of the army paper, *The Yank*. After his honorable discharge in 1945, he wrote novels and screenplays. In 1961, he won the Writers Guild Award for the best musical comedy screenplay for a film which is still frequently replayed on television, *The Music Man*.

Language Alert

Some of the comedy in these stories is based on the situation of a naive civilian dealing with the strict rules and no-nonsense attitudes of the military. Some is based on language. Hargrove sometimes chooses words or phrases that deliberately contrast with the situation. Notice how he uses the following:

1. "... life would have loveliness to sell ..."
   This line echoes a famous romantic poem by Sara Teasdale, one which lists lovely things.
2. Hargrove refers to "the vestments of civil life." Vestments are garments. The word usually refers to the official clothing of clergymen.
3. "The Old Man of the Mountain." In the White Mountains of New England is a mountain into which wind and rain have carved the natural profile of a man's face. This huge stone cliff would, of course, weigh tons.
4. An alpenstock (a staff used by mountain climbers), a burro train, and two St. Bernard dogs are all associated with serious mountain-climbing expeditions.

Reflecting

Try one of the following:

1. Think of a situation that was brand new to you—and therefore a little terrifying. Write about the experience in a comic way—exaggerating, finding funny comparisons, etc. Don't be afraid of poking fun at yourself.
2. Rewrite Hargrove's columns to make them "unfunny." Write seriously, like a factual report, or like a letter of complaint to a friend back home.

The *Terrible* Miss Dove

Frances Gray Patton

Preview

Remember the strictest teacher you've ever had? Remember the rules he or she laid down? The things you couldn't do in that class? The way your throat grew tight every time that teacher looked at you with eyes as cold as steel? Remember the tales you and your classmates told about that teacher—and how they got bigger and more outlandish every time someone repeated one?

It seems inevitable that every student will have a "Miss Dove" sometime between kindergarten and graduation. Such teachers become legends, or sometimes the central characters in horror stories! Years later, classmates meeting as adults laugh nervously as they recall the days they spent in THAT classroom.

Before you read this story, take a few minutes to think about your legendary "tough teacher." As you are reading, see how your teacher compares with Miss Dove.

Miss Dove was waiting for the sixth grade to file in for its geography lesson. She stood behind her desk, straight as the long map pointer in her hand. And suddenly she had the feeling of not being really alone. Someone or something was moving about the room. Over there, near the sand table where the first grade's herd of rickety clay caribou grazed at the edge of the second grade's plateau, it paused and looked at her. But even when the presence glided, like the shadow of a drifting cloud, along the wall behind her; even when she heard—or almost heard—a new stick of chalk squeaking on the blackboard, Miss Dove did not turn around. She knew, of course, that nobody was there. Her imagination was playing tricks on her again. It was something, she had to admit, humiliatingly close to nerves. Miss Dove did not believe in nerves.

Through the open door she watched the sixth graders come out of the music room down the hall. They came out with a rush, as if for two minutes of freedom between classroom and classroom they were borne along upon some mass exhilaration. They always left the music room in that fashion, but this morning they managed to be noisier than usual. It was the season, she supposed. The spring day was warm, and the children were restless as the weather. There was a sharp sound among them, as of a plump posterior being spanked with a book; there was a voice saying, "Double dare, Watty!"; there was a breathless giggling.

But as they approached Miss Dove's room their disorder began to vanish. They pulled their excitement in, like a proud but well-broken pony. One by one they stepped sedately across her doorsill. "Good morning, Miss Dove," they said, one by one, with the same proper lack of voice inflection, and went demurely to their places. At a nod from her they took their seats. Hands folded, eyes to the front, posture correct—they were ready for direction.

Jincey Webb, Miss Dove noticed without enthusiasm, had a permanent wave. Yesterday her carrot-colored mane had been neatly braided and pulled back from her serious, freckled face. Now it hung to her shoulders, a bushy mop of undulations and fizzy ringlets. It hung on her mind, too; that was plain to see. For Jincy's expression was one of utter and enviable complacency. It seemed doubtful that a long lifetime of repeated triumphs could again offer her an achievement so sublime with self-satisfaction.

Watty Baker, a pink boy of exceptional daring, wiggled his ears at Jincey. Miss Dove looked at him. Watty's pinkness paled. A glaze of innocence came over his round eyes. His ears grew very still.

Miss Dove kept looking at him, but she had stopped seeing him. Instead, she was seeing his brother Thomas, who had sat there at Watty's desk seven years before, with the same glaze over the mischief in his eyes. And then she saw Thomas on a raft in the Pacific. She did not see him as they had described him in the papers— skin and bones and haggard young face overgrown with a rough, wild beard. The Thomas she saw looked like Watty. He had braces on his teeth and a dimple in his chin. And he was all alone in the dismal gray mountains of the sea.

A wave of giddiness swept over her, but she did not sit down. It was nothing. It had been happening to her off and on all year, and it always passed. Miss Dove had a poor opinion of teachers who could not practice self-control.

For thirty years Miss Dove had taught geography in Cedar Grove Elementary School. She had been there before the brooding cedars had been chopped down by a city council that believed in progress and level playgrounds. She had seen principals and fads and theories come and go. But the school still squatted there, red brick, ugly, impervious. Inside it still smelled of wet raincoats and pickle sandwiches. Galahad still petted his charger on the left wall of the vestibule, and Washington still crossed the Delaware on the right. Every fall nervous six-year-olds had to be sent home in tears to put on dry drawers. Every spring there occurred the scandal of cigarette butts in the boys' basement. The same deplorable, old-fashioned words sprang up overnight like mushrooms on the cement walk. And now and then some hitherto graceless child could still surprise you with an act of loyalty or understanding. The school had not changed much. Neither had human nature. Neither had Miss Dove.

Each June some forty-odd little girls and boys—transformed by the magic of organdy ruffles and white duck pants into a group picture of purity—were graduated from Cedar Grove. They went on to the wider world of junior high and, beyond that, to further realms of pleasure and pain. In the course of time they forgot much. They forgot dates and decimals and how to write business letters.

But they never forgot Miss Dove.

Years afterward the mention of the Euphrates River or the Arctic Circle or the Argentinian pampas would put them right back in the geography room. They would see again the big map with its flat blue ocean and its many-colored countries. (India was pink, they would recall, and China was orange, and the Italian boot was purple.) They would see Miss Dove lifting her long stick to point out the location of strange mountains and valleys. And they would feel again the wonder of a world far-flung and various and, like themselves, entirely under control.

They would also feel a little thirsty.

"Remember Miss Dove?" they would smile.

But this green remembrance and the accident of her name's rhyming with a tender word should not deceive anybody about Miss Dove. She was no valentine. Miss Dove was a terror.

She had been young when she first started teaching. Her pupils would have hooted at the notion; they would have felt it more reasonable to believe Miss Dove had been born middle-aged with her mousy hair screwed into a knot at the back of her head and a white handkerchief pinned to her dark, bony bosom. Nevertheless, it is true. She had once been quite young.

Her father had died, leaving her little besides a library of travel books, an anemic violet-scented mother, and two young sisters yet in school. It had been up to Miss Dove. Older people had pitied her. She seemed too thin and pale and untried, they thought, to carry the burden alone. But Miss Dove never pitied herself. Responsibility was the climate of her soul.

The children of each grade came to her forty-five minutes a day, five days a week, six years of their lives. She saw them as a challenge. Their babyish shyness, their lisping pronunciation, their reckless forgetfulness—these evoked no compassion from Miss Dove. They were qualities to be nipped and pruned. Her classes were like a body of raw recruits that she was to toughen and charge with purpose. Miss Dove was the stuff that commanders are made of.

Other teachers had trouble keeping order, but not Miss Dove. Other teachers tried to make a game of their work—they played store and pasted gold stars on foreheads. They threatened and cajoled. Miss Dove never raised her voice. She rarely smiled. She laid before the children the roster of her unalterable laws. And the laws were obeyed. Work was to be done on time. There was to be no whispering, no hair chewing, no wriggling. Coughing, if indulged in at all, was to be covered with a clean handkerchief. When one of these laws was chipped, Miss Dove merely looked at the offender. That was all. If a child felt obliged to disturb the class routine by leaving the room for a drink of water (Miss Dove loftily ignored any other necessity), he did so to the accompaniment of dead silence. The whole class would sit, idle and motionless, until he had returned. It was easier—even if you had eaten salt fish for breakfast—to remain and suffer.

Miss Dove managed to introduce a moral quality into the very subject she taught. The first graders, who studied the animals of different lands, repeated after her, "The yak is a very helpful animal." And they knew she expected them all to be yaks. Later they learned a more complicated sentence. "The camel," they recited in perfect unison "is not a pretty beast, either in looks or disposition, but he is able to go many days without water." And they knew what was meant. "Above the fiftieth parallel," sixth graders wrote in their notebooks (keeping the margins even), "life requires hardihood."

Occasionally a group of progressive mothers would nearly rebel. "She's been teaching too long," they would cry. "Her pedagogy hasn't changed since we were in the third grade. She rules the children through fear." They would turn to the boldest one among them. "*You* go," they would say. "You go talk to her."

The bold one would go, but somehow she never did much talking. For under the level gaze of Miss Dove she would begin to feel—though she wore her handsomest tweeds and perhaps a gardenia for courage—that she was about ten years old and her petticoat was showing. Her throat would tickle. She would wonder desperately if she had a clean handkerchief to cough into.

And then there was the little matter of the state achievement tests. Cedar Grove always placed first in geography.

Occasionally, too, there would be an independent child who did not yield readily to group discipline. Miss Dove knew how to deal with him.

Once she had overheard two small boys talking about her at the drinking fountain. (They had no business at the fountain; it was their library period. But the librarian was lax.)

"I bet Miss Dove could lick Joe Louis," one of them had said.

"Who? That ole stick?" the other one had jeered. "I could beat her with my little finger."

He had glanced up then to see Miss Dove looking down at him. She had looked at him for a long time. Her light gray eyes were expressionless. Her long nose was pink at the tip, but no pinker than usual. At last she had spoken.

"Thomas Baker," she had said in the

tone of one making a pure observation, "you talk too much, don't you?"

"Yes, ma'am," Thomas had said in a tiny voice. He went off without getting any water. Seven years later he sweated when he thought of it. He could not know that Miss Dove also remembered. But she did.

Ever since Pearl Harbor Miss Dove had been troubled. She lived quite alone, for her sisters had married and her mother had departed for a place not on the map. (But decently, with every possible comfort. Miss Dove liked to remind herself of that.) And one evening while she was correcting papers she sensed, with that uncanny perception of the teacher, that something intruded upon her solitude. She turned quickly and looked about the room. A starched white curtain rustled in a puff of wind; her grandmother's rosewood whatnot cast a curious shadow on the polished floor; a finger of lamplight picked out the gilt titles of her father's old brown travel books. There was nothing else. But the red correction pencil was shaking in her fingers; for a moment her throat ached with a spasm of desolate, unaccountable grief, and—less familiar still—with a feeling of her own unworthiness. Miss Dove had never felt unworthy before in her life.

After that the thing happened frequently, until at last she saw who the intruders were. They were the children she had taught long ago.

War had scattered those children. There was a girl—a vain, silly little piece she had been—who was a nurse on Corregidor. At least, when last heard of she had been on Corregidor. One of the boys was dead in Tunisia. Others were on the Anzio beachhead, or in the jungles of New Guinea, or in the flak-brightened skies over Germany. But they came back to Miss Dove. She saw them as they had been at seven, at ten, at twelve. Only they had a beauty she had never seen in them then. They lifted her faces like starry morning flowers. Their limbs quivered with the unreasonable joy of childhood. And as Miss Dove looked at them they grew still. Their faces paled. Their eyes stopped dancing. They folded their little hands. They faded and were gone.

The child who came oftenest was Thomas Baker. The town paper had been full of Thomas. His ship had been bombed, his officers killed, and Thomas had taken over. A hundred men owed their lives to his presence of mind. For days he had floated on a raft with no food and only the water in his canteen. When they picked him up his tongue had protruded from his mouth, black and swollen with thirst. That was what got Miss Dove—he had run out of water.

The Thomas who came to stand before her now was a sturdy boy in knickers. He held his chin at a cocky angle, but the dimple in it trembled. He ran the tip of his tongue over his lips. He looked thirsty.

But they came only at night. When daylight returned Miss Dove could believe she had been imagining things. She would eat her customary boiled egg and her whole-wheat toast; she would take an extra vitamin pill with her orange juice; she would walk forth at her usual measured pace and assume her usual role of

unshakable authority. The children at the school would seem plain and ordinary. They would have little in common with those graceful and evanescent figures that haunted her. And no intruders dared come into the geography room. Or they never had until this morning.

A boy on the back row cleared his throat. One by the window followed suit. Soon the whole room was dotted with the sound, a rough "h-hrmph," like frogs in a distant marsh. Miss Dove knew what the sound meant. It was the school's traditional signal—a kind of dare. She had heard other teachers speak of it in exasperation. It had never happened in her room before.

Slowly Watty Baker raised his hand. The sounds stopped. Silence like a caught breath hung on the room. Miss Dove could see a fine dew pop out on Watty's brow; his open palm was damp and gleaming.

"Yes, Watson?" she said.

Watty stood up. Miss Dove's pupils always stood when they addressed her. He smoothed his round stomach with his hand. "I got a letter from Tom yestiddy," he said.

"*Received*, Watson," said Miss Dove. "You received a letter from your brother *yesterday*. That was nice."

"Yes, ma'am," said Watty. He paused. He was clearly floundering. "He sent me a dollar he won playing poker in the convalescent hospital."

"I am sorry to hear that Thomas gambles," said Miss Dove, "but we are all very proud of his war record. If you have nothing more interesting to tell us you may take your seat, Watson."

"H-hr-rmph!" went the boy behind Watty.

"He's been decorated," said Watty, "for bravery beyond the call of duty." The high words seemed to inspirit him. "He sent a message to the class."

"Did you bring the letter?" asked Miss Dove. "If so, you may read that part aloud."

Watty took an air-mail envelope from his hip pocket. Miss Dove noticed that Thomas' handwriting was as sprawling and untidy as ever. Somehow the observation pleased her.

The class stirred. The ghost of a titter rippled the air.

"Attention, please," said Miss Dove.

Watty opened the letter. The paper was smudged and crumpled. Obviously it had suffered many readings and many hands. Watty cleared his throat. The sound was not a link in the chain signal. Miss Dove could tell the difference. "It's sort of long," Watty demurred hopefully.

Miss Dove knew there was naughtiness afoot. The frog noises as well as Watty's hesitation had told her that. But she did not believe in avoiding an issue. She made a practice of facing impudence in the open—and facing it down.

"We can spare the time," she said.

Watty began to read. His voice was high and clear; it had the girlish sweetness that comes just before the breaking point.

"The funny thing about the world," Watty read, "is that it looks just like you think it does. When they flew me back to Cal. in a hospital plane I looked down

and, heck, I might as well have been looking at those diagrams on the geography board back in dear (ha, ha!) ole Cedar Grove. I spotted a peninsula just as plain. A body of land almost entirely surrounded by water. I saw some atolls too. And they really are made in rings like doughnuts, with palm trees sprouting out of the cake part and blue water in the hole in the middle. The water is the color of that blue chalk I swiped once and drew the picture of Miss Dove on the sidewalk with. Remember?"

So it *was* Thomas who had drawn that caricature. She had always suspected him. "Proceed, Watson," she said.

"You want to know if I was scared when the little yellow insects from"—Watty swallowed and went on—"from hell"—in his embarrassment he brought out the word with unnecessary force—"dive-bombed us. The answer is, you bet. But it came to me in a flash that I wasn't much scareder than I was that time ole lady Dove caught me bragging about how I could beat her up at the drinking fountain. 'I didn't run that time,' I told myself, 'so I won't run now.' Besides, there wasn't any place to run to."

The class laughed nervously.

"And later," read Watty, "when I was bobbing up and down like Crusoe on my raft, what do you guess I thought about? Well, it wasn't any pin-up girl. It was Miss Dove. I thought about that fishy stare she used to give us when we needed a drink of water. So to make my supply hold out I played I was back in the geography room. And even after the water was all gone I kept playing that. I'd think, 'The bell is bound to ring in a few minutes. You can last a little longer.' It took the same kind of guts in the Pacific it did in school. Tell that to the kids in Cedar Grove." Watty stopped abruptly.

"Is that the end?" asked Miss Dove.

Watty looked directly at her. For a fleeting moment she thought he was going to say yes. If he did, the incident would be closed, of course, for Miss Dove never questioned a child's word. That was why they generally told her the truth. He shook his head.

"No, ma'am," he said. "There's a little more." His face turned the color of a nearly ripe tomato. "He says here"—Watty gulped—"he says"—Watty took a deep breath—"he says: 'Give the terrible Miss Dove a kiss for me.' "

"Well, Watson," said Miss Dove, "I am waiting."

There was an electric stillness that was followed, as the full meaning of her words penetrated the children's consciousness, by a gasp. Watty folded the letter and put it back into his pocket. Then he began to walk toward her. He walked with the deliberate stoicism of a martyr going to the chopping block. Miss Dove inclined her head and turned her cheek in his direction. He did not come any closer than he had to. He leaned forward stiffly from the waist and placed his puckered lips against her cheek. (*He smells like a last year's bird's nest,* thought Miss Dove. It was strange. However frequently a twelve-year-old boy was washed, he always smelled like a bird's nest.) Watty smacked. His kiss resounded, a small explosion in the room.

"Thank you, Watson," said Miss Dove.

"You may give Thomas my regards. " She straightened up and faced the class. To her surprise, nobody was grinning.

Jincey Webb spoke. She did not raise her hand first for permission. She just spoke out. "It's like a medal," said Jincey softly. "It's like he pinned a medal on Miss Dove."

For a moment a lamp seemed to burn behind her face. Then over the light swept a shadow, a look of awe. It was as if Jincey had glimpsed some universal beauty—of sorrow, perhaps, or of nobility—too poignant for her youth to bear. She began to cry. She flopped her head down on her desk with her red hair falling forward and spreading out like a crinkly fan.

All the other girls were weeping too. All the boys were trying not to.

For the first time in her teaching career Miss Dove was at a loss. She wanted to make a speech. She wanted to say something beautiful and grateful about what life really meant to her, about the overwhelming generosity of children. No, not generosity. It was something better than that, something much harder to come by. It was justice. And Miss Dove did not know how to say what she felt. She had never thought it dignified to express emotion.

But as she stood there waiting for the words to form in her mind, she realized that she was neglecting her duty. The first duty of a teacher was to preserve order.

She fished a piece of string from a receptacle on her desk. She walked down the aisle to Jincey Webb. She took Jincey's hair, that marvel of art and nature, and bunched it in her hand. She tied it securely at the nape of Jincey's neck with the little bit of grocery string.

"Now it will be out of your way," she said.

At the sound of her voice, cool, precise and natural, the children rallied. They sat erect. They blew their noses on clean handkerchiefs. They folded their hands on their desks.

"Get out your notebooks, class," she said.

A transient mist came over her eyes. Through it, as through a prism, the children glowed. Freckles, cowlicks, pinafores and polo shirts seemed bathed in a rainbow iridescence. Her love flowed out to her children—to those opening their notebooks before her, and to those in the far places she had once helped them locate on the map. It did not flow tenderly like a mother's coddling love. It flowed on a fierce rush of pride and hope, as an old general's heart might follow his men into battle.

She went to the blackboard and picked up a piece of chalk. "Above the fiftieth parallel—" wrote the terrible Miss Dove.

MEET THE AUTHOR:
Frances Gray Patton (1906–   )

"I can hardly remember a time when I didn't consider myself a writer," says Frances Gray Patton, whose stories have been translated into seventeen languages. She composed her first "literary work," a poem, when she was three years old:

"The wind is blowing sof'ly.
The birds are singing awf'ly."

Frances Gray was born in 1906 in Raleigh. Her father and mother read so much to Frances and her two brothers that, as she says, "we felt most natural when we had a book in our hands." Her promise as a writer became evident when, while still in high school, she won first place in a national contest. She continued writing at Trinity College (which later became Duke University) and at UNC-Chapel Hill, where she worked with the Carolina Playmakers.

For a number of years after her marriage to Dr. Lewis Patton, a Duke professor, she

was mainly occupied with rearing their three children. As the children grew older, she again began to write. Eventually one story won second place in a national competition and was chosen for inclusion in the yearly volume of *O'Henry's Best Short Stories*. Her career had begun in earnest—but hers was not a smooth uphill path. She received many "tersely worded rejection slips" from various editors before the stories began gaining acceptance.

"The Terrible Miss Dove" is one of a number of stories about an eccentric schoolteacher. Appearing first in *The Ladies' Home Journal*, eventually the stories were rearranged into *Good Morning, Miss Dove*, which became first a best-selling novel, then a popular movie. Mrs. Patton has also published three collections of short stories and a number of articles and poems. Currently she continues to live and work in Durham.

Language Alert

Scenes of Combat

During the story Miss Dove recalls some of her students who have been serving in the following places during the war:

—Corregidor: A rocky, fortified island in the Philippines. There the American and Filipino troops made their last stand against the Japanese forces soon after Pearl Harbor. Not until February 1945, six months before the end of the war, was it freed from Japanese control. Then the prisoners, who had undergone dreadful ordeals during their captivity, were released.

—Tunisia: A small North African country on the Mediterranean Sea between Algeria and Libya. During World War II, it was an important naval base which was recaptured from the Germans by the Allies in 1943.

—Anzio: A small seaport south of Rome. Allied troops landed and established a beachhead (a position on the shoreline) there after heavy fighting in January 1944.

—New Guinea: The second largest island in the world, New Guinea lies just north of Australia. It was the scene of heavy fighting between the Japanese and Allied forces during World War II.

In Other Words . . .

The following sentences give you brief glimpses of the story, using some of the words you will encounter. For each italicized word, can you choose the correct answer from the three choices given in the question?

1. The children rush into the classroom with *exhilaration*.
   Are they disgusted, invigorated, or terrified?
2. When they step into Miss Dove's classroom, they always do so *sedately*.
   Is their manner serene and controlled? Sly and sneaky? Fearful and timid?
3. With a new permanent, Jincey Webb's hair is "a bushy mop of *undulations*."
   Does her hair have forms like corkscrews, like spiderwebs, or like waves?
4. Jincey's facial expression is marked by *complacency*.
   Does she seem excited, self-satisfied, or bored?
5. For a moment Miss Dove has a vision of a *haggard* face overgrown with a beard.
   Does the face appear ruggedly handsome, worn and exhausted, or angry and stern?

6. For a moment, the teacher is attacked by a wave of *giddiness*.
   Does she feel dizzy, strong, or furious?
7. The ugly red brick school building is referred to as *impervious*.
   Is it something which can't be affected, which is haunted by ghosts, or which is falling down?
8. To achieve better classwork, some teachers *cajole* their students.
   Do they spank them? Threaten them? Coax them?
9. At one point Miss Dove has an *uncanny* feeling that something has intruded into her room.
   Is this feeling strange and almost supernatural? Full of terror? Marked by frustration?
10. The child began to cry because the moment was so *poignant*.
    Was the moment touching? Frightening? Short-lived?

Reflecting

1. Throughout the story, Miss Dove acts tough, but we learn that there is another side to her, one that few, if any, students have suspected. Go through this story and note all the details that hint that Miss Dove isn't quite as terrible as she seems.
2. Can you explain why Miss Dove behaves as she does in the classroom?
3. This story, like the poems "Long Distance, 1944" and "Missing in Action," shows us how war affects those who are left "on the home front." Other works in this book that deal with this subject include "Casey and Dwayne," p. 424, and "A Marine Communications Man Leaving for Vietnam (1966)," p. 512.

If You Want To Write . . .

If I were advising young people who want to write I think I would tell them—but I really don't *know* what I *would* tell them except to cultivate their love and knowledge of words—the color and texture and sound and true meaning—and then to practice stringing them together on a thread of thought to make a sentence. And after a while the ones who *really* want to write will discover the magical gift that sentences have for clustering together and making little neighborhoods or even *worlds* of ideas and inventions.

A good way to begin a story, I think, is to find out what interests you most and let that be your starting place or frame. Is it character, plot, philosophy, or place that most stirs your imagination? I myself feel that I write a short story almost as if it were a one-act play so that if I visualize a room, a grove, a back yard—any small, contained space with a distinct character of its own—then conversation and plot fall into place easily. But occasionally it's a sense of character that gets me going.

Once, I remember, I saw a man in a shabby, rather threadbare coat go out from a worn country store into a winter day, and as he did I saw him raise one shoulder as if to ward off the cold wind—or more than the wind, all the troubles of the world. And the gesture told me what I needed to know about misfortune and courage.

I think it was Henry James who said an author should try to be "a person on whom nothing is lost."

—Frances Gray Patton

Those Who Wait at Home: Two Poems

During wartime, there are many kinds of pain: the physical pain of the injured; the despair of those who lose their homes; the distress caused by being uprooted; the grief endured by those whose loved ones are casualties; and the gnawing anxiety of those at home who live in fear of receiving word that one of their own has died or been seriously injured.

The following poems, by different poets, portray the pain not of soldiers, but of their family members back home. In each case, the pain is shown from the father's perspective. In our culture until recently, most men have traditionally felt less free than women to display their emotions openly. Notice how each father handles his pain.

Preview

In the following poem, we live for a moment with a father who is receiving a long-distance telephone call from his son. We hear only one side of the telephone conversation: the boy's, printed in italics. But we are also given insight into the dialogue going on within the father—another dialogue, between his heart and his brain.

Long Distance, 1944

James Boyd

Lift the receiver. Hear the young word, "Hi!"
Feel the old heart leap up and shout with joy,
Tumbling and crying to the brain: "The boy!
It's him! He has not had to die!"

"We just got in. . . .
Well, it was quite a trip. . . .
Oh, sure, I'm fine. . . .
She's a good ship. . . .
How's everything at home?
. . . That's swell . . . that's swell,
Maybe a liberty. . . .
We're not allowed to tell. . . . "

And all the while, old heart with his uproar
Keeps shouting, "Brain, why speak so calm,
    so slow?
Caper, you fool, and holler! Don't you know
That this is him? That he is back once more?"
Until brain answers low,
"Hush, hush. I know, I know.
Back from that Distant Shore,
Once . . . more."

1. liberty: for a soldier, like a short vacation or authorized leave from duty.

James Boyd (1888–1944)
See p. 64

Reflecting

1. This poem comes from a volume of James Boyd's poems, *Eighteen Poems*, which has been described as containing "the poet's feelings about the anguish of war." James Boyd knew how to use his imagination, but in this case he was writing directly from experience. His daughter, Nancy Boyd Sokoloff, gives us the background of the poem: "The subject is my eldest brother, Jim, serving on a weather ship in the North Atlantic, which was being heavily traveled by American troop ships—and German submarines." (Remember that James Boyd himself had seen battle firsthand during World War I. He knew the dangers and horrors of war.)

2. Think about the following:
   a. Why isn't the father's brain as overjoyed as his heart?
   b. "Distant Shore" is capitalized. Why?
   c. In the last line, why are there ellipses (three periods) between *Once* and *more*?

Preview

In "Long Distance, 1944," we saw in one man a difference between the responses of his brain and of his heart. In "Missing in Action," we see the difference between what people perceive and what is really going on inside a man.

Sometimes, in our hurry to get into a story or poem, we may pay little attention to a title. But titles are important, certainly in poems, which are trimmed to the bone. In poems, every word counts, and the title may be the key to our understanding. In the following poem the title gives us the background situation without which we wouldn't be quite sure what has happened.

Missing in Action

Stewart Atkins

"Joe takes it pretty well," the city said.
"He hasn't broken much that I can see;
Not knowing whether his son's alive or dead—
A thing like that would be the end of me."

Joe took it pretty well, the city thought.
He had a smile for friends just as before.
He went to business daily, sold and bought.
He didn't talk about it anymore.

If asked about it, he would always say
He hoped that better news would come some day.

The city thought his unconcern was strange
And marveled at his calm and even smile.
The city couldn't notice any change,
Though it had watched intently all the while.

It didn't know, of course, of the long night
(His knuckles beaten, bruised against the wall),
Nor of the hours when his face was white
And dawn seemed likely not to come at all.

The grief tears cannot soften nor relieve
Is worn within the heart, not on the sleeve.

Stewart Atkins (1913–1961)

The son of a newspaperman, Stewart Atkins was best known as advertising director of *The Gastonia Gazette*, but he had another writing life—that of a poet. He began writing at an early age—sometimes in class (even when he was supposed to be doing other assignments), sometimes on the staffs of the school paper or yearbook of the Darlington School in Georgia. After graduation, he held other jobs which required writing. He worked for an advertising agency and on the staff of Governor R. Gregg Cherry.

While Atkins earned his money doing other kinds of writing, he continued writing poetry. Many of his poems center on the "common people" and the oppressed. These include textile workers, such as he saw daily in Gastonia, a textile-manufacturing center, as well as farmers and blacks. In those poems, often written in first person, he tried to come to grips with the problems these people faced.

In addition to writing his own poems, Atkins encouraged the writing of others. He was one of a small group of poets who got together in Charlotte in 1932 and organized

the North Carolina Poetry Society. From 1933 to 1936, the heart of the depression years, he edited *The North Carolina Poetry Review*.

Reflecting

The first four stanzas let us see Joe only from the outside. We see only what "the city" sees. Not until the last two stanzas do we get an inner view.

Usually poets, concerned with being original and fresh, avoid clichés. This poem ends with an echo of the old cliché, "he wears his heart on his sleeve," which is usually spoken in reference to someone who is grieving publicly about a broken romance. Atkins uses the cliché to contrast the depths of this father's sorrow with lesser pain involved in frustrated romance.

Explain why Joe "had a smile for friends," "went to business daily," and "didn't talk about it." Do you believe he is handling his feelings in the best way? Explain your answer.

From Washington at War

THE PRESIDENT IS DEAD

David Brinkley

Preview

April, 1945: Franklin D. Roosevelt has just been inaugurated for his fourth term as president. (He has served so long—over twelve years—that to the younger generation it seems strange to think that anyone else could hold the position!) His jaunty personality and broad smile are familiar sights on newsreels. His confident voice, heard both in major speeches and less formal "fireside chats," has lifted the nation's spirits ever since 1933, when, in the heart of the Depression he declared, "We have nothing to fear but fear itself."

And now the Depression is over and the end of World War II is almost in sight. Citizens can expect that personality, that smile, that voice to join them in a victory celebration before too many more months have passed.

It is not to be. President Franklin Roosevelt, whose seriously failing health has been kept a secret from all but a few, dies suddenly of a cerebral hemorrhage.

In this account by David Brinkley, we get an inside view—a behind-the-headlines glimpse of what was going on in Washington at that time, of how Vice-President Harry Truman accepted his new and terrible responsibility—and of how the people reacted to this shocking news.

The president returned to the White House for a few days that were mainly spent receiving titled foreign visitors. With the war winding down, they were able to travel again, and they required substantial time and attention. Toward the end of the month Roosevelt, looking extremely tired, said he had had enough of entertaining visitors and would leave on Thursday, March 29, for Warm Springs, Georgia, for two weeks, maybe longer.

As he left, the day was pleasantly warm. The summer's heat and damp had not yet arrived. Washington's splendid cherry trees were in bloom, the wisteria was draping its lavender clusters over the fences and brick walls. His train to Warm Springs left the Fourteenth Street underground track at 4 p.m., crossed the Potomac into Virginia and headed south toward Georgia and his little wooden cottage and the warm spring water he had once hoped would help him strengthen his leg muscles and allow him to walk again.

Dr. Bruenn, always at his side now, listened to Hassett saying the president's health was deteriorating: "He is slipping away from us and no earthly power can keep him here." For months, Roosevelt had seemed simply not to give a damn about anything, even his own reelection. Had Dewey not started what he considered a particularly dirty campaign, the president might never have campaigned at all. Now, when Hassett gave his papers to sign, the bold, assertive signature of the past was gone. In its place was a feeble scrawl, trailing off into nothingness and ink splotches at the bottom of the page.

Dr. Bruenn was alarmed too. His patient had lost twenty-five pounds, had no strength and no appetite, could not taste his food, and looked worn, drawn, exhausted. But Roosevelt had enough strength to insist that even through everyone was trying to talk him out of it, he would be in San Francisco to address the opening of the United Nations conference on April 25. Nothing, he said, could stop him from going. . . .

In the press offices at the "Little White House" in Warm Springs and in the real White House in Washington, all was confusion. Jonathan Daniels was so distraught he could barely speak, so it was Steve Early, the old professional, who arranged a conference call to the three wire services and told them in a strained, quiet voice: "I have a flash for you."

A "flash" was the wire services' designation for news of the most shattering urgency. The International News Service got the news out first, at 5:47 p.m., perhaps the briefest news story ever written: "FDR DEAD."

Within minutes, the news was being relayed around the world. Editors worked frantically to reset their front pages and get out special editions. Radio stations cancelled their commercials. In Chicago, Colonel McCormick ordered his *Tribune* to report the death straightforwardly. McCormick himself had planned to have champagne served at dinner that night, but he did not want it said he had toasted the president's passing, so "we drank

Montrachet instead." Cissy Patterson had the *Times-Herald* fill its entire front page with a black-bordered photograph of Roosevelt, with no headline and no words. Inside, she ordered, the paper would turn its attention to the new president. "Truman's the news now."

From London came a message so phrased its author would have been evident even if he had not signed it:

I FEEL SO DEEPLY FOR YOU ALL AS FOR ME, I HAVE LOST A DEAR AND CHERISHED FRIENDSHIP WHICH WAS FORGED IN THE FIRE OF WAR. I TRUST YOU MAY FIND CONSOLATION IN THE GLORY OF HIS NAME AND THE MAGNITUDE OF HIS WORK. CHURCHILL.

For a while, Truman wandered about the west Wing almost aimlessly, waiting for his wife and daughter to arrive from their apartment on Connecticut Avenue, waiting for the chief justice to arrive, waiting for someone to find a Bible somewhere on the White House bookshelves—waiting to be sworn in as president of the United States. People began to gather in the cabinet room: the presidential staff, the cabinet, others, all stunned, many in tears. Most of them barely knew Harry Truman. A few had never met him. For a while no one seemed to notice him, a virtual stranger sitting alone in a big leather chair to one side of the room. One cabinet member later remembered glancing at the new president and thinking, "He looks like such a little man."

Less than an hour later, he held his first cabinet meeting and looked out on a group of officials about whose work he knew virtually nothing. He had been vice president for only two and a half months. Roosevelt had ignored him, told him nothing, seldom even spoke to him. The meeting was tense and awkward, and about all Truman could find to say to the Roosevelt Cabinet, now suddenly and strangely the Truman Cabinet, was that he intended to continue his predecessor's policies and that he hoped all of them would remain in office, at least for a while, because he needed their help. The meeting ended, and the members drifted in silence out into the night.

Secretary of War Stimson stayed behind. He had a "most urgent matter" to discuss with the new president. And that night, for the first time, Truman learned of the development of the atomic bomb.

The details of the president's death became public slowly over the next several days. He had been sitting at the rickety card table he always used as a desk in his modest wooden cottage in Warm Springs when he pressed a hand to his temple, said "I have a terrific headache," and collapsed. Dr. Bruenn had climbed out of the swimming pool, come running in and tired to revive him. Nothing worked. He had suffered a massive stroke, a "cerebral hemorrhage" the doctors called it. He was dead in the afternoon.

The plan was for Roosevelt's remains to leave Warm Springs by train the next day, Friday, to reach Washington and the White House for a funeral service in the East Room on Saturday and then to go on by train to Hyde Park for burial in the garden behind the family's house on Sunday. But the logistics were massive and difficult. Warm Springs, a tiny town, could not

Franklin Roosevelt—before he became President— stands with his friend and colleague, Josephus Daniels.

supply a coffin, an embalmer, an undertaker or a hearse. All these had to be ordered hurriedly from Atlanta. A hearse bringing the bronze coffin broke down with a flat tire on the highway. A coffin could not be carried in through the door of the railroad car—the turn inside was too tight. One of the car's windows had to be removed and then replaced. The coffin would weigh 760 pounds and would require some kind of wooden ramp to get it up from ground level to the railroad car window. Time was short. A local carpenter said he could build a ramp during the night if he could find some helpers. It was built. A train had to be put together in haste at the Southern Railway yards in Atlanta and brought to Warm Springs during the night, and had to come in backwards since in the little town where was no place to turn it around. The coffin would be so heavy it would take at least ten muscular men to lift it up the ramp and through the window and ten more in the car to pull it inside and set it in place.

In Washington, the U.S. Army chief of staff, General George C. Marshall, personally took charge and assembled a group of officers to organize a funeral. Some men would be needed in Warm Springs, they said. The little town could not handle this alone, nobody there could deal with all the complexities. The local people loved Roosevelt and would do anything for him, but this was too much for them. Within an hour the army had two thousand men from Fort Benning, Georgia, loaded in trucks and carrying their dress uniforms, guidons with black mourning bands added to their battle streamers, and tents and field kitchens for overnight on the ground at Warm Springs. The marines came with a detail from the navy. A military band arrived in town, its brass instruments glittering in the sun as they were unpacked on a too warm day.

The undertaker finished his work and asked, "Is there a bier?"

"A what?"

"A bier. A platform inside the railroad car for the coffin to rest on."

No. There was no bier. Nobody had thought of it.

Back to the carpenter who had already worked all night. For Roosevelt, he would go on working. He built a bier. They covered it with a blanket borrowed from the marines.

It was a strange-looking train that rolled in. A steam locomotive painted in the southern's green livery pulled it in rear end first. On the other end, soon to become the front end, were two other handsome steam locomotives. They had been pulled in backwards from Atlanta, and when the train was ready to leave for Washington they would pull it out, the engine on the rear end being uncoupled and left behind. No one in town had ever seen anything like this before, but there was no other way to get a train in and out.

The last car on the train, to carry the body, was a private car, the *Conneaught*, supplied by the Southern. It would carry the president's coffin and a four-man military honor guard standing at attention at the four corners of the bier. Immediately in front of it was the old, familiar car on which in life had had traveled thousands of miles, the *Ferdinand Magellan*.

Up through the south the train rolled at twenty-five miles an hour. The family asked that it be moved slowly because all along the way, throughout the afternoon and throughout the night, people lined the tracks to see it pass. In darkness, the *Conneaught* was softly lit, the shades raised, and people outside could see the American flag atop the coffin, the honor guard in dress uniforms and, occasionally, Mrs. Roosevelt sitting there. The people stood along the tracks beside tobacco and corn and peanut fields, in the cities and towns. Even at 3 a.m. they were out there. They held their children up to see. They cried. They knelt. They sang hymns. No one could count the people lining the track through town and country from Warm Springs to Washington. Some guessed two million.

The new president—accompanied by Henry Wallace and James F. Byrnes, either of whom, but for Bob Hannegan's maneuverings the previous summer, might himself have been president now— met the funeral train at Union Station. Many in the crowd outside the station recognized Wallace before they recognized Truman.

A slow funeral cortege—a horse-drawn caisson, a squadron of motorcycle policemen, armored troops, the marine band, the navy band, a battalion of midshipmen from Annapolis, a detachment of service women, a line of black limousines—moved through the streets of Washington between columns of soldiers at attention. Two dozen army fighters roared across the sky in tribute. An elderly black woman sat on the curb in front of the white House, rocked back and forth, and cried out as the procession went past her through the gates, "Oh, he's gone. He's gone forever. I loved him so. He's never coming back."

Two days later, Roosevelt left Washington for the last time, to be buried in his mother's rose garden in Hyde Park.

Meet the Author:
David Brinkley (1920–)

For nearly forty years David Brinkley's face has been a familiar one on the television screen. This Wilmington native began working with NBC radio in 1943; by 1951 he was the Washington correspondent for NBC television news, and for years he and his co-anchor, Chet Huntley, were among the most popular of all television newscasters. Currently he can be seen each Sunday on an ABC-TV news analysis show, *This Week With David Brinkley*.

Eager to begin his career, David Brinkley started working for the *Wilmington Star-News* when he was only seventeen. After a brief stint at college, he worked for the United Press for two years before being hired at NBC as a newswriter.

Although his fame rests mainly on his television appearances, Brinkley writes all his own scripts, insisting that "I'm a writer by trade. I'm not an announcer. I just can't take a piece of paper and read it on the air. I try

to write the way I talk." His broadcasting, which is especially noted for its sharp wit, has won many awards. In 1964, he and his high school English teacher from Wilmington, Mrs. L. Burrows Smith, were presented the Golden Key Award from the American Association of School Administrators: he was named as a "citizen who has contributed significantly to the national welfare;" she was praised as the teacher "who most influenced him at a formative stage in his life."

Language Alert

A. Characters in the Story

This is a segment from a much longer book. A number of people who are identified earlier in the book appear in this portion. They include:

—Hassett: William D. Hassett, secretary to the President
—Rayburn: Congressman Sam Rayburn, Speaker of the House
—Jonathan Daniels: Daniels was a North

Carolinian, editor of the Raleigh *News and Observer*, and son of Josephus Daniels (see p. 165).

—Colonel McCormick, Cissy Patterson: publishers of major newspapers

—Churchill: Winston Churchill, Prime Minister of Great Britain

—Henry Wallace: former Secretary of Agriculture and former Vice-President; he held both offices during Roosevelt's earlier terms as President.

—James F. Byrnes: Director of War Mobilization

B. In Other Words

1. Roosevelt had an *assertive* signature. (It was forceful.)
2. One room in the House of Representatives had a "*fragrant reputation*." (It was well-known, but its fame was somewhat "smelly"—as if something not-too-good were going on in there.)
3. Some legislators were *recalcitrant*. (They were difficult, stubborn, headstrong.)
4. Sometimes Speaker Sam Rayburn used *cajolery* to persuade representatives to change their vote. (He used sweet talk and flattery; he coaxed them.)
5. Cajolery is just one form of *coercion*. (It's just one way to persuade someone or to force them to do your will.
6. Politicians *coveted* invitations to Speaker Rayburn's meetings. (They strongly desired such invitations.)
7. The Vice-President was an *unprepossessing* man. (He failed to impress people; he wasn't very colorful.)
8. At one time Harry Truman had been a *haberdasher*. (He sold men's clothing.)
9. The *logistics* of a national funeral are very complicated. (The arrangements of persons, materials, dates, etc. are complicated.
10. People lined the streets to watch the funeral *cortege*. (They watched the procession of vehicles, persons, etc.)

Reflecting

1. Find some persons who were at least eight years old in 1945 when Franklin Roosevelt died. Ask them what they recall about the event. Do they remember where they were when they heard the news? How they heard the news? How people reacted?
2. President Roosevelt's casket was moved from Warm Springs, Georgia, to Washington, DC, on a train which moved slowly through the countryside, then was brought down the Washington streets in a memorial procession.

   Do you know how Abraham Lincoln's casket was moved from Washington to Springfield, Illinois, for burial? Do you know how President Kennedy's body was brought from Dallas, Texas, to Washington, DC? How the casket was taken to Arlington Cemetery?

Hiroshima: Two Views

On August 6, 1945, a United States bomber, the *Enola Gay*, dropped the first atomic bomb on Hiroshima, Japan, killing an estimated 70,000 persons and injuring at least that many more. When the first news was flashed over the radio, most people had no concept of what "atomic bomb" meant. The information that this one blast produced an explosion equal to 20,000 tons of TNT helped listeners get some idea of its power. However, it was months before the public recognized the awesome destruction—both immediate and longterm—caused by "the unleashing of the atom."

In the following works, we see how North Carolinians reacted to the use of this new and fearsome weapon.

"When the Wind Blows"

At Kill Devil Hills Hotel

10:15 A.M., August 6, 1945

Susan Rose

Across the Beach Highway the Memorial stands,
symbol of a dream—that they could fly,
no thought of anything but cycle parts,
wing struts, winter winds, sloping sand,
their goal—to keep the fragile craft in flight.

The flag blows out straight in the steady breeze.
The granite pylon reaches up, proclaims
that man has made a conquest over air
with "Dauntless Resolution, Genius, Faith."
Or such is the view we see from Nags Head beach

where the sun beats down on children holding back
the surf with fortresses. Their parents watch,
play porpoise with them, read in the shadow of the dunes.
We lean into our cars to hear the news
from Hiroshima, "Enola Gay." We stare

at sand that changes with a shifting wind
and tide, brings oil in shore from tankers hit
far off. Clouds darken the pylon, dim-out the scene;
we pick up shovels, pails, seize towels against
the chill, move close and take our children's hands.

pylon: tower, often
marking an
entrance

From *North Carolina's 400 Years: Signs Along the Way*, ed. Ronald H. Bayes. Copyright © 1986 by North Carolina Poetry Society. Reprinted by permission of the author and the North Carolina Poetry Society.

Preview

If you have been to, or even seen pictures of, the memorial at Kill Devil Hills, you know about the white granite tower that rises from a tall dune, honoring the Wright brothers. You may have read about the Wrights' persistent efforts to make their dream—that human beings could fly—a reality. A few hundred yards east is the shore, a favorite vacation site for families.

In this poem by Susan Rose, we become one of those families enjoying, in August 1945, the sunlit peace of the beach, then, over the car radio, hearing news we can't quite comprehend.

MEET THE AUTHOR:
Susan Rose (1915–   )

Reviewing Susan Rose's busy life, one can conclude that age is no excuse for not trying new things. Although she did not begin writing poetry until after her retirement from a business career in 1979, her poetry has won a number of awards and she has promoted creative writing in the state through her work with the North Carolina Poetry Society. Furthermore, in 1987, at the age of 72, she received her second degree from Duke University, a master of arts in liberal studies.

Born in Scotland Neck, Susan Rose received her first degree from Duke, then settled down to help her husband both raise a family and conduct a commercial stationery business. Her major creative outlet was music. She appeared many times as a soloist with her church, the Durham Civic Chorus, and the Durham Theater Guild. Through those years she was also dedicating herself to writing letters and making them as interesting as possible. So without consciously doing so, she had kept her language skills polished.

Susan Rose is probably best known for her "Effie" poems, a series of dramatic monologues in which a rural woman talks about her friendship with her neighbor Effie, and the moments they have shared. Rose has built them into a dramatic sequence which has attracted audiences in colleges, community centers, and the Eno River Festival.

Now, thinking back to her own school days, she reports that she wrote only the required work; "I was far more interested in reading poetry, fiction, the news, anything." She urges all students to read, "even if they don't like to, because if they read enough they will find something that will interest them, and they will grow from that discovery."

John Kincheloe

The drawing, "When the Wind Blows," is by Raleigh artist John Kincheloe, a media specialist at Meredith College. Born in Raleigh, John Kincheloe moved to Richmond, Virginia, when he was eleven. He received undergraduate and master's degrees in religious studies from the University of Richmond and the University of Virginia, respectively. In 1985, this drawing was used in "Living Double Lives," a Public Television documentary about citizens of Charlottesville, Virginia, who were directing their energies toward opposing nuclear weapons and war. John Kincheloe and his wife, Pat, now live with their two children in Raleigh, where they are still active in movements devoted to world peace.

Reflecting

Most of the first three stanzas emphasize the peacefulness of the scene and the innocence of the Wright brothers' ambitions. They wanted only to fly, not to destroy others. But the mood of the poem changes at the end of the third stanza, when the parents hear the newsflash about the *Enola Gay* bombing Hiroshima. Suddenly the speaker notices things she hadn't seen before—changes in the physical environment around her. Think about the following:

1. The speaker's mention of "a shifting wind" as soon as she hears the radio announcement suggests that with the development and use of this terrible weapon, something more than wind is shifting in the world. (Our security? Our values?)
2. As she hears the news, the speaker notices oil on the water. See David Stick's story (p. 343) of the naval war just off the North Carolina coastline. (By 1945, most of the naval battles were conducted farther offshore.)
3. We are told that "Clouds darken the pylon, dim-out the scene." What could these clouds signify?
4. Why do the parents pick up the shovels and pails and take their children's hands? Why do they feel a chill?

Preview

A year after World War II ended, John Hersey, then a young novelist, wrote a book entitled *Hiroshima,* a nonfiction account of what happened when the atomic bomb destroyed that city. In his book, Hersey did not simply gather statistics on injuries, deaths, and destruction. He may have realized that although numbers might shock us, they seldom move us emotionally. Instead, he interviewed many individuals who were in Hiroshima when the bomb dropped. He described what they underwent and often let them do the talking.

Guy Owen also gives us, in the first four stanzas, specific details illustrating the results of that blast. Then, in the last three lines, he states the American view of the blast, and what we (the Allied forces) decided to do thereafter.

When We Dropped the Bomb
(After John Hersey)
Guy Owen

When we dropped the bomb on Hiroshima
  it roasted pumpkins on the vine
  and baked potatoes nicely under the ground;
  deep in the vaults the x-ray plates were spoiled;
  men became sterile; women miscarried,
  but sesame and sickle throve in ashes and puke.

When we dropped the bomb on Hiroshima
  the soldiers' eyes ran from their sockets
  and smeared like honey down patient faces;
  unnumbered thousands lay in the streets
    in vomit and died politely
    under the darkened sky.

From *The White Stallion and Other Poems,* by Guy Owen, published by John F. Blair, Publisher. Copyright © 1969 by Guy Owen . Reprinted by permission of Dorothy Owen.

When we dropped the bomb on Hiroshima
     the wounded crawled to Mr. Tanaka's garden,
     retching among bamboo and laurel
     fouling the exquisite garden, the pools,
     staining the pools, the delicate bridges
          arching . . .
          (No one wept.)

All day the young wife rocked her swaddled
          corpse;
     a burnt horse walked on the dying,
          trailing its entrails
     while Father Kliensorge scratched in ashes,
          seeking his melted Christ.

When we dropped the bomb on Hiroshima
     it worked; it was altogether good.

So we turned to Nagasaki.

MEET THE AUTHOR:

Guy Owen (1925–1981)   See p. 300

Reflecting

Think about these things:

1. Assume that this poem is the only document that you can find about the bombing of Hiroshima. List what it tells us about the power of the bomb.
2. In each of the first three stanzas, there are references to people "throwing up," only Owen doesn't use that polite term. Since there are so many horrible things he could include, why do you think he focused three times on the same thing?
3. Hiroshima will forever be known as the city where the first atomic bomb was dropped. What do you know about Nagasaki?

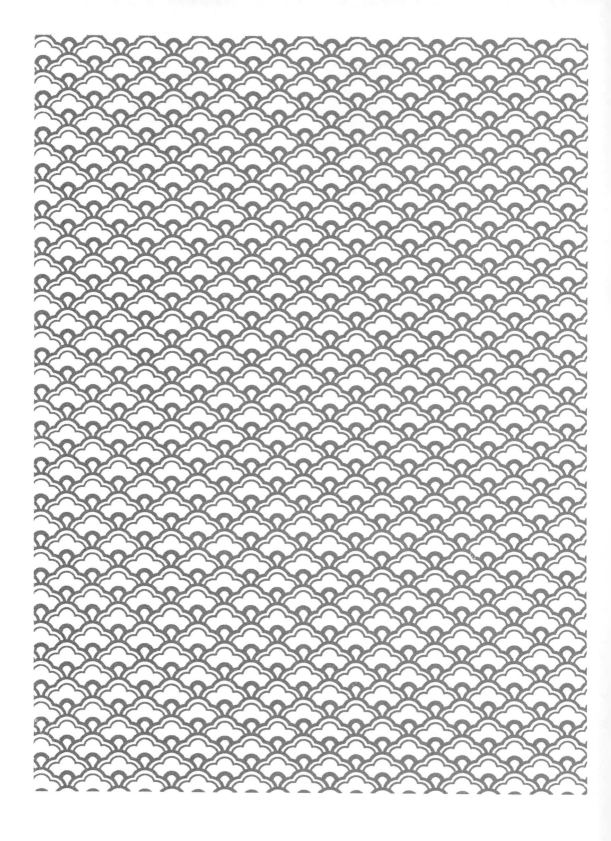

Thirty Tumultuous Years

World War II ended in 1945, but the years that followed were hardly quiet. There were smaller wars all over the world. Two of them—in Korea and Vietnam—involved our country. One—the Vietnam War—sparked dissent and violence within our country. The "cold war" caused tension between the Soviet Union and the United States and fear of communism here at home. Technology took off like a rocket, with television, space travel, computers (all of which had sounded like science fiction just a few decades earlier) becoming commonplace. There were startling scientific advances in almost every field. And one hundred years after they were freed from *legal* slavery, blacks demanded equal rights—an end to *social* slavery.

North Carolina felt the effects of all this tumult, and several of the works in this section deal with these events. Other works look at the important moments of daily life—driving a favorite car, getting a new dress, learning how to deal with other people—that go on among human beings no matter what is happening in the society as a whole.

Preview

People have always loved good stories and good storytellers. Jesus illustrated his sermons with stories called parables, and effective preachers still know the value of a lively story that makes a point. Mark Twain traveled the world telling tales that enchanted listeners of many nations. Many of today's stand-up comics—Bill Cosby, for example—are master storytellers.

In the days before television and night club comedy shows became popular, the man or woman who could take a minor incident and from it spin a fascinating yarn became a local treasure. Around the fireplace on a winter evening, or at the general store or gas station on a summer afternoon, the storyteller kept his or her listeners entertained for hours on end. Often the audience listened with rapt attention to stories they had heard many times before. It was not the content of the stories that so enchanted them; it was the way in which the stories were told.

In the following poem, Betty Adcock takes us to a country store marked by one old-fashioned gas pump, some wooden drink-crates to sit on, and one terrific storyteller.

Stories, 1940s

Betty Adcock

For example, Oscar Sawyer's store.
Out front the lone gas pump was red,
the kind already long past use,
a skinny sentry with a head of glass.
The store itself listened toward the road,
leaning by inches in the direction of news
without much more forward margin.

I don't have to tell you how old men
sat outside on wooden drink-crates in good weather,
how they watched. A boy might come by with a pup
or a sack of pecans to sell or trade.
You know what was on the shelves inside:
potted meat, sardines and crackers, rusty traps,
glass candy-jar clouded with sugar dust.

A mile or two back of the store,
Indian village and Spanish mission
slept together two centuries under
Jenkins' farm. That far down, the bones
of the Ays and the priests exchanged conversions,
heat-shimmer on green ears of corn.

Hosey Lucas was always there at Oscar's
He looked like a man made out of parched cornhusks.
People said that. People waited in the lull
when no car was passing. They knew he'd tell
again how he happened to have that sunk-in place
right in the middle of his forehead—
kicked by a mule when he was twelve
and the whole thing just healed over
without a doctor. Left him potholed
deep enough to set a teacup in,
and he still had good sense.

He might tell about the coon that jumped
straight out of a tree onto Garsee Johnson's back
and rode him home
Or about the time old man Burton found a track
in the dirt road by his house and thought a snake
that didn't ever wiggle must have made it,
so he got his gun and trailed the thing for miles.
Came up on a bicycle rider resting in the shade.
The old man, who'd never seen a town,
stayed mad a week. Hosey Lucas and his dog would sit.
And both of them could talk. . . .

MEET THE AUTHOR:
Betty Adcock (1938–   )

Louise Smith, formerly a fifth-grade teacher in St. Augustine, Texas, recalls that Betty Sharp, one of her students, sometimes held up her geography book as if she were studying earnestly—but when the teacher strolled the aisles, she would find that behind the cover of the book, young Betty was totally engrossed in scribbling a poem. Forty years later, Betty Sharp Adcock remembers and sighs: "I was quite incurable."

She also recalls that she began writing at the age of seven, hiding her poems in a secret compartment in her desk because she was quite sure that her family and friends would not appreciate them. She continued writing, however, and after coming to Raleigh, North Carolina, with her husband, Don Adcock, she enrolled in a creative writing class under Guy Owen (see p. 300). Almost immediately she began placing her poems in national journals. By 1989, she had published three collections of her poetry, each of them an award winner. After the publication of the third book, *Beholdings,* the United States poet laureate, Howard Nemerov, invited her to read at the Library of Congress.

Ms. Adcock has conducted workshops and

readings throughout the United States. Currently she continues to write and teach as Kenan Writer-in-Residence at Meredith College.

Language Alert

The Ays (mentioned in the third stanza) were a small tribe of Indians who lived in East Texas—in fact, on the very farm where Betty Adcock grew up. They died out by the time of Thomas Jefferson's presidency in the early 1900s.

Reflecting

1. In the third stanza we are told that under the Jenkins farm, "the bones of the Ays and the priests exchanged conversions/heat-shimmer on green ears of corn." *Conversion* means a change into another form or substance. Certainly missionary priests attempted to convert the Indians to Christianity. But what kind of conversions can be going on now, years after these persons are buried?
2. What does the last line mean?
3. Many families hand down certain stories through the generations—the way Grandma and Grandpa met, for example, or the time Uncle Ned went camping and found a rattlesnake curled up in his sleeping bag.

   Ask older members of your family or neighborhood to tell you a true funny or scary or exciting story. Write it down in their own words (or tape record it) and bring it to class to share. Afterward you might talk about what makes a good story—one that captures and holds a listener's attention.

Preview

All of us remember "firsts"—the first time we rode a bike, the first day at a new school, or the first trip away from home without the family. Stephen E. Smith remembers his first car—a 1953 Dodge which was in need of serious repair. Most importantly, however, the car was *his* and was part of his life at important moments. In this poem, he describes both the car and one of those moments.

For a '53 Dodge

Stephen E. Smith

That flathead six
got eight miles to the gallon
and the ball joints were so bad
my teeth rattled for thirty minutes
after we slapped the railroad tracks.
The stabilizer bar was bent
and the window cranks weren't connected
to anything and the seats were so sprung
I had to put two Coke crates
under the driver's side just to see
over the steering wheel.
Three times the brake lines ruptured
and sent me screaming into busy intersections.

Still, there was that rainy night
I kissed Nancy Simmons goodbye for good
and drove that Dodge into the dark.
The lights over South River blurred
like the eyes of an old lover turning away,
and I looked out through that cracked
windshield and believed, if only for a moment,
that the highway to anywhere
was wide open.

From *North Carolina's 400 Years: Signs Along the Way*, ed. Ronald H. Bayes. Copyright © 1986 by North Carolina Poetry Society. Reprinted by permission of the author and the North Carolina Poetry Society.

MEET THE AUTHOR:
Stephen E. Smith (1946–)

Stephen E. Smith was born and raised in Maryland, but he came to North Carolina to attend college (first Elon, then UNC-Greensboro) and stayed as a college teacher. Currently he directs the writing program at Sandhills Community College and serves as associate fiction editor of *Pembroke Magazine*.

Smith's poems, like his stories, tend to center on persons rather than places or things or ideas. Often they are told in first person by a character whose personality clearly comes through in his words, complete with slang. Some of his works are about childhood or the perils of the teen years. Others center on "the good ole boys" who hang around the service station bragging and swapping jokes.

Smith's poems and stories have been published widely, and his work has been recognized by awards: a Young Poet's Prize in

Stephen Smith and the '53 Dodge he and his son recently restored.

1981, and a writing fellowship from the North Carolina Arts Council in 1986. Currently he is writing and performing songs (in country-music style), as well as writing poetry and fiction.

Reflecting

One day a few years ago, Stephen Smith was traveling through the countryside when he saw an abandoned shell of a car rusting in a field. It was—you guessed it—the same model as the '53 Dodge he describes in this poem. (He admits that both cars were Chryslers, not Dodges, but he felt that Chrysler sounded too big and fancy. So, using what is called "poetic license"—the freedom to do something to create a special effect in the poem—he transformed the Chrysler to a Dodge.) After bargaining with the farmer who owned the abandoned car, he took a course in automobile mechanics and spent two years restoring it to a condition far better

than the car he had owned as a teenager. Since then he has found two other similar models and is currently restoring them, too.

Can you remember something you considered a treasure, though to anyone else's eyes it would look like a mess? The teddy bear you held onto when it was practically rags? The skateboard which was scuffed and scarred, but which to you seemed magical? A sweatshirt that was practically in tatters, but which held special memories?

Describe that object so that we see it as precisely as we see Stephen Smith's banged-up, barely working '53 Dodge.

Preview

In the following poem, Kathryn Byer recreates a time when a tornado struck at Christmastime, just as the children were singing "Adeste Fideles." The children, caught up in holiday spirit, could hardly be convinced to find refuge. As you read the poem, notice the mixture of real events and religious references.

Angels

Kathryn Stripling Byer

We sang Adeste Fideles while
clouds darkened over my grandfather's
farmhouse. What angels
we were, my three cousins caressing
their bride dolls, and I, the soprano
in front keeping time because
I sang the loudest. The nerve
of somebody (my deaf aunt?)
to whisper, "Tornado"! We wouldn't stop
singing till hailstones came
clattering down on the tin roof the way
in the movies Comanches charge out of a hill
like an avalanche. "Open a window,"
my grandfather yelled while we ran
for the root cellar, clutching our candles
like converts. The house howled
with wind as the Angel of Death thundered
on to the next town where (so
it's been told every year since that
Christmas night) two men were raised
by the whirlwind and set down
a mile away, babbling of light
at the end of a tunnel,
the buzzing of ten thousand angels.

From *The Girl in the Midst of the Harvest,* by Kathryn Stripling Byer. Copyright © 1986 by Kathryn Stripling Byer. Reprinted by permission of Texas Tech Press.

Kathryn Stripling Byer (1944—   )

When Kathryn Stripling Byer was growing up in Georgia, there wasn't much emphasis on creative writing in her school. However, she says, "Fortunately, I had to write lots of essays, and this taught me a great deal about the skill and discipline of good writing." She composed a few poems in high school, but didn't begin writing seriously until her sophomore year in college.

Since she began publishing her work, she has won a number of state and national awards, including the Creative Writing Fellowship from the National Endowment for the Arts and the Anne Sexton Poetry Prize, named for one of the most famous American poets of this century. Her second book, *The Girl in the Midst of the Harvest*, won the Na-

tional Associated Writing Programs Award.

For a number of years Kathryn Byer has lived in the mountain town of Cullowhee. She frequently teaches poetry in the school her daughter attends, encouraging students to find their own voices in writing. In 1990 she was named writer-in-residence at Western Carolina University.

Language Alert

Adeste Fideles: The Latin name for a popular Christmas carol, "O Come, All Ye Faithful"
Comanches: a tribe of Indians who inhabited the American western plains

avalanche: a fall or slide of a large mass of rock or snow down an incline
converts: people who have just accepted a new religious faith

Reflecting

1. Angels are referred to three times in this poem (besides the title), each time indicating something different. Explain each reference.
2. You probably have heard of unpredictable things that have happened during tornados. A rooftop may be wrenched from a house, twisted slightly, then set neatly back in place. A baby may be whisked out of a window, carried on the wind for blocks, then put down safely. One house may be torn into splinters while the home

next door suffers only minor damage from blowing debris. The fury and structure of a tornado cause unpredictable events.

In this poem, we are told that each Christmas people continue to repeat the story of the two men who traveled two miles in the tornado, then were set down safely. Does the fact that this occurred on Christmas have special significance to those who tell the story?

Dancing
Two Views

Anthropologists tell us that dancing is one of the oldest of the arts, one of the ways which persons in all cultures express themselves. In the two poems below, the authors deal with both the joy of dancing and the dancers themselves.

Preview

How many times have people asked you, "What do you want to be when you grow up?" When you've answered, has it always been the same answer? Did some of these dreams involve fame such as being President, a great actress, a rock star, or an all-American athlete?

Many people at least once in their lives dream of being a famous something. In the following poem, the speaker remembers her childhood dream of being a famous tap dancer. As you read, notice how the sounds of the words resemble the sounds of tapping feet.

Why I Wanted To Be a Famous Dancer

Judy Goldman

Young Judy Goldman preferred tap dance, but here she poses in her ballet costume.

Kafka: Franz Kafka, a famous Austrian novelist (1883–1924)

Understand I mean tap.
The dance of a stick
ticking off slats
in a picket fence.
The dance of a tongue
licking something cold
until it snaps.

You would watch me
enter the floodlight
of the stage,
thousands of tiny sequins
all over me
raising the temperature
to smoke.
Not even you
could follow my feet
as they trip over
roots of music,
clapping like stars
in fiery circles
from one side of the stage
to the other.

And then
at exactly the right moment
I would stop,
the silence lifting everyone
from their seats,
making them laugh and cry
at the same time
and of course
as Kafka predicted,
the world would begin
to roll in ecstasy
at my feet.

MEET THE AUTHOR:
Judy Goldman (1941 –   )

Judy Goldman started keeping diaries in the third grade and has been "holding onto memories in this way ever since." She can still recite one of the poems which she wrote in elementary school. Educated in Rock Hill (just across the South Carolina line from Charlotte) and at the University of Georgia, she and her family moved to Charlotte in 1967. For several years she taught poetry workshops at Queens College. Now she frequently works in the Poetry-in-the-Schools program and conducts poetry workshops for adults in Charlotte. She has also read her poetry and directed workshops all over the Southeast.

Ms. Goldman's first poetry collection, *Holding Back Winter*, was published in 1987 and is now in its third printing. Her work has been published in over one hundred literary

magazines throughout the country and has won a number of awards. Her advice to young writers: "If you like to write, then you *are* a writer. Honor your talent by writing and saving what you write. Also, read, read, read."

Reflecting

A. This poem is entitled "Why I Wanted to Be a Famous Dancer," yet the speaker never tells us directly her reasons for her ambition. She simply describes an experience of tap dancing on stage, and lets us figure out her reasons for wanting to dance. What are those reasons?

B. Think about how this poem gets its effect:
   1. It doesn't rhyme in a regular way, but notice the repeated sounds— including some rhymes—in the first stanza:
     a. The a sound in *understand, tap, dance, slats, snaps*
     b. The hidden rhymes in *stick, ticking, picket, licking*
These word echoes provide a kind of music for the dancer.
   2. Notice the ways the speaker fantasizes:
     a. The sequins on her costume are "raising the temperature to smoke."
     b. Her feet "trip over roots of music."
     c. And, of course, notice the final fantasy: Kafka's prediction coming true.

Preview

This poem is presented from the viewpoint of an observer watching a performance. What kind of dancing is being performed? What does the speaker enjoy and appreciate about the dancer?

Portrait of a Dancer

Zoe Kincaid Brockman

She moves, so fluid and so free—
Like light upon a shadowed wall,
Like moonlight on a darkened sea,
Or leaves that pause before they fall
To trace faint patterns on the air
That scarcely knew a leaf was there.

Her body is a pliant thing,
Mercurial, exultant, free—
Each slim foot harbors hidden wing,
The vibrant arms weave poetry.
And circling her, the spotlight's gleam . . .
A gold net spread to trap a dream.

From *Heart on My Sleeve* by Zoe Kincaid Brockman, published by Banner Press. Copyright © 1951 by Zoe Kincaid Brockman.

Zoe Kincaid Brockman (1893–1975)

Every autumn the North Carolina Poetry Society presents the Zoe Kincaid Brockman Award for the best book of poems published in this state during the past year. The award both honors the author of the current collection and keeps alive the name of Zoe Kincaid Brockman, a Gastonia native and first president of the North Carolina Poetry Society. Ms. Brockman not only wrote poetry; as associate editor of the *North Carolina Poetry Review*, she also encouraged the writing of others.

Zoe Kincaid Brockman began writing while still a child. When she was sixteen, her verses began to appear in *The Charlotte Observer*. Over the years her poems have won a number of state and national awards and appeared in many publications, including the *New York Times*. Remembering the advice of her University of North Carolina professor, Dr. Edwin Greenlaw, who said, "Don't publish your teething pains," she did not offer a book for publication until 1951. The fact that the collection, *Heart on My Sleeve*, went through five printings demonstrates how well the reading public received her poems. In addition to writing poetry, she helped edit *Skyland Magazine* at Hendersonville, wrote for *Everywoman's Magazine*, and served for a number of years on the staff of the *Gastonia Daily Gazette* (working with fellow journalist-poet Stewart Atkins (see p. 370).

Language Alert

1. If your body is *pliant*, it is easily bent; it is flexible.
2. Something *mercurial* is quick, it changes direction quickly. (Have you ever tried putting your finger on a drop of *mercury*?)
3. If you have ever felt joyful, you have felt *exultant*.
4. When we *harbor* something, we shelter or protect it.
5. Something that is *vibrant* is pulsing with energy or activity. (This word is related to *vibrate*.)

Reflecting

1. Notice how in her effort to capture the graceful movement of the dancer, Zoe Kincaid Brockman uses **similes** (comparisons that use *like* or *as*) and **metaphors** (comparisons without *like* or *as*). Most of her similes and metaphors are extended. That is, she builds them, not just saying that the dancer is "like light," but is "like light upon a shadowed wall."
2. To what might you compare a dancer? Try listing three things. Try expanding them as Ms. Brockman did.
3. Are Judy Goldman and Zoe Kincaid Brockman describing the same kind of dancing? How do you know?

Preview

Today many people shop by catalog because of convenience. (Catalogue, with a *ue*, is an alternate spelling.) They save themselves the time or trouble of going to stores. Earlier in this century, when people lived in more scattered communities, often many miles from the nearest department store, catalogs were the only way to obtain certain items. Furthermore, in those days without television, catalogs provided a window on a larger world.

In this poem, Robert Morgan describes how the catalog appealed to a farm boy very much aware of his own narrow experience.

Catalogue

Robert Morgan

Comes wrapped like a giant candybar
to be lugged from the mailbox.
I felt reverence in the incense
of its inks. What a Christmas
spread in the summer of its wings,
me dirty from the field and crouching
to its money-bright leaves.
Whole lifetimes of toys every page.
The models smiled at something
just out of the picture, happy
in a world without weather.
And the women in underwear laughed
unconcerned to be seen in their polished skin,
in the places to which my life
was a poor and shabby cousin.

Robert Morgan (1944–   )

Robert Morgan grew up on his family's farm near Hendersonville. "The most interesting thing that happened to me in the eighth grade was the country bookmobile that came out to my community once a month with hundreds of books," he says. "I tried to read them all, before and after working in the field."

He began writing for the high school newspaper. Then, after earning university degrees in Chapel Hill and Greensboro, he taught at Salem College. He also worked as a farmer and a housepainter near Hendersonville before joining the faculty at Cornell University, where he has taught creative writing for a number of years.

Many of his poems deal with the life he experienced as a boy in the North Carolina mountains and/or with the natural environment, which he knows both from personal experience and from studies in science. He has published six volumes of poems and a collection of short stories. Both poetry and fiction have won a number of major national awards, including four grants from the National Endowment for the Arts and a Guggenheim Fellowship.

Reflecting

1. In what ways is the catalog like a candy bar?
2. Why does he call the leaves "money-bright"?
3. Why does he call his own life "a poor and shabby cousin" to that of the models?
4. For his biographical profile in *Contemporary Authors*, Robert Morgan explained why he writes: "Writing has always given me a center and continuity." Reading this poem, explain how writing serves him in that way.

Aunt Bessie's Old South Sunlight Bread Recipe

Shirley Laws Moody

Early on hot sunny days about mid-July,
Bessie started filling her mail-order china teacups
with fresh milk she scalded with well water.
That cooled while she pinched salt and measured
corn meal, flour and sugar.

All this got stirred in an old chipped blue
bowl her grandma once bought from a Lumbee girl
she'd swum with in Cotton Creek.
White linen covered the stir settling
in sun-warmed water.

Never did kill the yeast. Bessie's water was ripe.
After lunch and a few more stirrings,
she'd see that it was rising right.

On a flour-sifted board, she sprinkled seasonings
and passed on stories and hymns;
working, rocking and kneading until my lids slid
heavy as lard used to grease the pan hugging the dough
rising out back in sunlight again by then.

The smell of fresh baked bread quietly
trimmed away the crust of afternoon sleep
in time for us to break it at supper.
Unless some clouds had come up, or rain.
It never worked then,
and she'd stop wherever she was
and chuck it all to the hogs.   stir: the dough mixture

Preview

If we had nothing to rely on but television, we might think that there are only two types of cooks in this country: those who toss pre-packaged foods into the microwave, and those who consider themselves gourmet cooks, equip their kitchens with hundreds of gleaming gadgets and processors, and measure each ingredient to the hundredth-of-an-ounce.

But there is another kind: the cook who has made certain favorite dishes so often that he/she doesn't need recipes, specially designed tools, or careful concentration. In your family or neighborhood you probably have just such a cook—one who can prepare favorite recipes almost in his or her sleep.

MEET THE AUTHOR:
Shirley Laws Moody (1947–)

Hundreds of North Carolina students know Shirley Laws Moody and her work, for she has served as writer-in-residence in over 200 schools during the past ten years. She herself began writing stories and keeping journals when she was a fifth grader in Raleigh. After her mother's death when she was twelve, she began expressing herself through poetry, and continued doing so through her graduation from Needham Broughton High School and Peace College. "Although I was relatively secretive about my writings," she says, " the encouragement of certain teachers was invaluable in boosting my confidence."

While working as a legal secretary, she

studied creative writing at North Carolina State University with Thomas Walters (see p. 513) and began publishing her work in literary journals. She is one of four writers whose work comprises *Four North Carolina Women Poets*, and St. Andrews Press currently plans publication of another collection, *Charmers*.

Reflecting

1. This poem is partly about how Aunt Bessie prepared bread, and partly how her niece enjoyed their comfortable time together. Notice how in the last stanza the crust of the bread and the "crust of afternoon sleep" merge in the speaker's memory.
2. Interview a cook you know who works as Aunt Bessie did, measuring with fingers and whatever utensils happen to be around, cooking and socializing at the same time. Ask your parents or other adults if they remember an "Aunt Bessie" in their past. Collect details about how she prepared her special dish. Try arranging those details into a story-poem as Shirley Laws Moody has.

From Rainbow Roun Mah Shoulder

1949

Linda Beatrice Brown

Preview

In this excerpt from *Rainbow Roun Mah Shoulder*, Linda Beatrice Brown wants the reader not only to know what happened to Ronnie, a little girl, but to get inside the child. She captures the excitement of a little girl celebrating her tenth birthday. Although Ronnie doesn't tell the story, we see it from her point of view, using language much like hers.

"1949" is set in that year, so you get an opportunity to see what it was like to grow up then. Our country was enjoying the brief space of peace between the end of World War II (1945) and the beginning of the Korean War (1950). The civil rights movement had not yet begun, so blacks and whites lived in a segregated society, and prejudice was often apparent. Prices were much lower than they are now, and styles were very different. However, the excitement of celebrating a birthday was the same then as it is now.

That day started with Mama's usual Saturday trip for groceries and Ronnie's usual job of breakfast dishes, and beds to be made, but it didn't end that way. Along about noon, Miss Florice rang the doorbell and opened the screen all at the same time. "Ronalda Jackson Johnstone, where you?" Ronnie knew it was play and not trouble even if Miss Florice was using her whole name cause this was her birthday and she knew it would be a good time ahead. "Yes, Mam?" she answered smartly.

"You know you heard me ring that doorbell, girl, you ain't finished those dishes yet? We got a place or two to go, *this* birthday what's here!"

There was always a trip of some kind. Mama and Miss Florice would cook up something, and then Daddy would come home for ice cream and cake and there would be Chinese checkers and lemonade later on.

Today she was ten. A full decade. And Miss Florice said anyone who lived a decade deserved a special surprise. Mama came down from the attic wearing her spring hat for the occasion and told Ronnie to get on her Sunday shoes. She knew it was special then. Sunday shoes were never allowed in the mid-week except for school programs, so it had to be special! They made a threesome, Miss Florice and her umbrella, Mama and her spring straw, and Ronnie in her black patent leather Sunday shoes. She could hardly stand not asking, but knew it was against the rules of the game, so she bit her lip, all the time trying to figure out where they were headed. As they neared downtown, she counted cracks in the sidewalk to keep from bustin out, "Where're we going?" They passed the colored library and the sweet shoppe, spelled "shoppe" and Ronnie thought for the thousandth time, "Wonder why its called a shoppie?" but she didn't even ask that. Finally they were there—at the corner of Elm and Washington and at the biggest department store in town. Ronnie held her breath as they went through the door. It smelled of powders, perfumes and richness and there was a kind of hum inside she always heard when there were lots of dressed up ladies together anywhere. She was very quiet. Mama had a little smile on her face, Miss Florice's eyes were secretive. The elevator made that queer jolt it had when it reached a floor and they got on, stepping to the rear, like the lady said.

She didn't like being smashed into all those white bodies but the excitement was enough to make that a minor annoyance. They were going to the girls' department. The Girls' Department, with its striped candy canes and pink ruffles and blue and white artificial flowers and rows and rows of otherworld fairytale dresses! As she stepped off the elevator and into the wishworld of GIRLS 7-12 Ronnie guessed that they were going to buy her a dress, a store-bought party dress. It was too much for her. She swallowed her gum. Elmer said if you swallowed your gum all your insides would stick together, but what did boys know? What did boys know indeed on this wondrous day? There was blue and yellow to be chosen from, not just blue and yellow, but cloud blue and yellow from buttercups, there was red velvet and white lace collar, and green taffeta with tucks and, oh my, white organza! Mama said not over six dollars. She edged up to each one and glanced quickly at the price tag to see if she could risk liking it. Miss Florice was glaring at the clerk who did the usual clucking in the nice nasty tone of "Can I help you girls," which told them they were Black and therefore might steal or at the very least contaminate these dresses which were really made for little white girls in golden curls. Miss Florice held her at bay with her umbrella and Ronnie took her sweet time. "Finally!" Mama said as Ronnie triumphantly turned with "This one." Then there was the trying on. The turning, the twisting, the checking, and the nod they knew all the time she would give—even before she put it on. The clerk stuffed it in the box,

Miss Florice had insisted on a box with a flourish of her umbrella—and she stuffed it with an incredible urgency as if to get them out of there as fast as possible.

Ronnie worried about her blue satin sash all the way home. She held murder in her heart in reserve for the clerk. If there was any damage to her powder blue lace dress and her satin sash when she got home, she would return to that store herself, and with a poison dart hide behind the nearest dummy and spit, hard.

The breath was held as they opened the box for Daddy. It was blue, it was lacy and it was not smashed. It was hers alone. Happy ten years, happy candles wrapped up in blue sashes, and ice cream dreams that night.

MEET THE AUTHOR:
Linda Beatrice Brown (1939–   )

Like many modern writers, Linda Beatrice Brown divides her work between writing and teaching. She has published a prize-winning novel, *Rainbow Roun Mah Shoulder* (under the name of Linda Brown Bragg), and many poems and articles. She has taught, both as a full-time faculty member—currently at Guilford College—and as a guest lecturer or writer-in-residence at many schools and colleges throughout the state. She is also well known as a speaker and workshop leader, often speaking on religion, racism, black concerns, education, or literature.

Linda Beatrice Brown recalls that being read to as a child inspired her to become a writer. She began writing when she was fourteen, publishing first in *Beyond the Blues*, a poetry anthology, when she was only nineteen. After completing high school in Akron, Ohio, she came to Bennett College in Greensboro, where she majored in French and English literature and graduated as valedictorian. She was then awarded a Woodrow Wilson Fellowship to pursue graduate studies at Case Western Reserve. She received her Ph.D. from Union Graduate School, focusing her studies in creative writing and black literature.

Her writing reflects her varied interests. She has published poetry in scholarly magazines such as *Black Scholar*, and children's magazines such as *Cricket*. Her nonfiction includes an account of her own writing career and *The Kid's Book About Single Parent Families*, published for the National Episcopal Church. She has read her work at churches, universities, city arts festivals, elementary and high schools, and senior citizens' centers.

Language Alert

1. Ronnie notices that the clerk acts as if she might *contaminate* the clothes—make them impure by being in contact with them. The clerk stuffs clothes into the box with *urgency*—meaning that she acts as if this is an important matter requiring immediate action.

2. Notice the special terms that mark the conversation of Miss Florice and the thinking of Ronnie: "this birthday what's here," "to keep from bustin out," and "nice nasty tone." Phrases like these give us the flavor of their speech and make the characters seem real and distinctive.

Reflecting

1. In the story, Mama and Miss Florice never tell Ronnie that they love her. They don't even say "Happy Birthday." How do we know that they love her, that they are almost as excited about her birthday as she is?

2. How does the celebration of Ronnie's birthday compare to the ways we celebrate a ten-year-old's birthday today? (Note both the differences and the similarities.)

3. Did you notice how dressed up the women and Ronnie were when they went shopping? In 1949 self-respecting women and girls wore hats and gloves when they went to town. When do women and girls wear hats and/or gloves now?

Polio Summers

Before 1955, poliomyelitis (often called polio or infantile paralysis) was one of the most dreaded diseases in this country. Caused by a virus that attacks the gray matter of the brain and spinal cord, this contagious disease causes paralysis in many cases and sometimes ends in death. Some persons recover almost entirely. Others are left permanently disabled.

Since the 1950s, vaccines—the first developed by Dr. Jonas Salk; the second by Dr. Albert Sabin—have been given routinely to children and thus have greatly diminished the number of cases in this country. However, before that time, whenever an outbreak occurred—usually in the summer—children were quarantined in order to prevent the disease from spreading. Many people who grew up in North Carolina during the 1940s and 1950s still refer to those seasons as "polio summers."

In the following poems, two writers recall their own polio summers. As you read, imagine yourself restricted to your own yard for two or three months—the very months you've looked forward to having free. Now, with the threat of polio, for you there will be no movies; no swimming in public pools or lakes; no neighborhood picnics or Fourth-of-July parades; no baseball or tennis or soccer; and no church or Scout meetings. You're not even supposed to be with the young people next door (though some will sneak and do so.) Imagine what emotions you and your family feel every time you get a headache or your throat gets scratchy.

That Summer

Claire Atkins Pittman

Swollen dreams escaped
into an atmosphere of illusion
like hot air balloons rising
on waves of heat.

We ate the dark, sweet cherries
stolen from old Mr. Shuford's
ancient tree. Played Kick-the-Can
at night in the still-hot street.
Caught lightning bugs in oily
mayonnaise jars. Kept them
in our rooms too long.

One of us got the first t.v.
in the neighborhood. Another one
came down with polio.

Even in the heat our parents
Shivered. Fear gnawed through
their plastic smiles.

We did not know what made
their eyes so strange.

Dog days came. News from the hospital
grew darker. Storm clouds bruised
the summer sky. Rain kept us
close on screened-in porches. One
cheated at Monopoly, wound up
with Boardwalk and Park Place
every time, a crime we ferreted
out years later.
We never forgave him.

Our boredom grew like weeds.
We formed clubs just to keep out
the younger kids. The rules we wrote
would chill the blood of a Zulu warrior.

When Linley died, only the grown-ups
could go to his funeral. We never
even talked about it.

Just walked from room to room
through our small lives or sat
long hours watching the rain
with eyes gone empty
and a little strange.

MEET THE AUTHOR:
Claire Atkins Pittman (1937–)

Claire Atkins Pittman's love for writing came naturally. She is the daughter and granddaughter of journalists, and her father, Stewart Atkins, was also a noted poet. (See page 370.)

When she was in the ninth grade in Gastonia, young Claire Atkins entered two state competitions: a poetry contest sponsored by the North Carolina Poetry Society, and an essay contest sponsored by the American Legion. She won second place in both. "Winning prizes was very inspirational," she says now. It must have been. Although her two degrees from Duke University are both in history, she has continued writing, publishing her work in many magazines, and continuing to win awards.

Like many poets, Ms. Pittman has given

readings of her work widely. Unlike most, she has also displayed her work visually, alongside paintings by her husband, artist Bob Pittman, in art exhibitions around the state. She has also served as literary editor of *Tar Heel* magazine. Currently, in addition to writing, she serves on the faculty of East Carolina University, where she directs the history lab and trains teachers.

Language Alert

1. *Dog days*: the hot, sultry days of mid-July to September (These days are so named because during that time Sirius, the Dog Star, the brightest star in the sky, rises and sets with the sun).
2. *Boardwalk and Park Place*: two areas on the Monopoly game board (They are the most expensive pieces of property, so whoever gets them has an advantage over other players.)
3. *ferreted*: searched and discovered (This verb derives from the noun *ferret*, the name of a polecat which is often trained to hunt rats or rabbits.)
4. *Zulu warriors*: tall, well-built natives of a province in South Africa (The warriors are famed for their bravery.)

Reflecting

See if you can figure out the following:
1. In stanza one, what dreams "escaped into an atmosphere of illusion"? Why are they swollen? Why do they rise "on waves of heat"?
2. In the fourth stanza, why do the parents shiver? Why are their smiles "plastic"?
3. Why could only the grown-ups go to Linley's funeral? Why do the children not even talk about it?
4. In stanza five, we are told that the parents' eyes are strange. Later—at the end—the children's eyes are "a little strange." Explain why, in each case.

Polio Summer

Mary Kratt

That summer I was twelve,
children were gifts
parents tucked out of sight,
hidden from crowds
lest we limp, die, or end up
like the newsreel lady
in her iron lung, that casket-tube
for her body breathing.
I saw my straight brown hair,
    my eyes looking out,
heard the great machine squeeze-gasp
my breath would make.
I imagined my leg, twisted and small
like Mother's from polio
when she was young.

It was the longest summer.
Tired of my brother,
I hid in trees.
Mother asked Cousin Janie Lucille,
the organist, Please.
And every Thursday with her
in the old, dark church
with glory windows,
it became the summer of whole notes.
I pedalled with short legs,
small feet. I stumbled sharps,
easy flats, and threw hymns
to empty pews.
Mighty crescendoes with all stops out,
my hands on the treble,
feet on the bass,
I pumped past organ pipes,
the white iron lung, past
the wall, the window, the road
high and far away.

MEET THE AUTHOR:

Mary Kratt (1936 –)
See p. 156.

Language Alert

1. The *iron lung* is a machine that was used for polio patients whose breathing muscles were paralyzed. A long metal tube, it encases all of the body except the head. Inside, pressure is regularly increased and decreased to provide artificial respiration for the patient.

2. An organ has varied *stops* that control the tone of the sound. If you play with all the stops out, you will get a very full, rich sound, like that of an entire orchestra.

3. An organ's sound is produced when air is *pumped* through pipes of various sizes.

Reflecting

1. Melodies are made up of notes that vary not only in pitch, but in duration. (In much music, a quarter note gets one beat; a half note, two; a whole note, four.) Why does the poet say "It became the summer of whole notes"?

2. Why, during this particular summer, might she play "with all stops out"?

3. Since the child is quarantined to her own neighborhood for the summer, what does she mean by the last four lines?

4. Compare these two descriptions of "polio summers." In what ways were the children's experiences similar? In what ways did they differ?

5. Read "A Matter of Trust" (p. 000), a story which is set during a polio summer. Again, compare the experiences of the various characters.

A Matter of Trust

by Suzanne Newton

Preview

Suzanne Newton's story is set in a small North Carolina town during a summer when all children were restricted to their home yards because of the polio epidemic raging throughout the state. (For more about this situation, read "Polio Summers," p. 407.) The main character, Josy, is a young teenager looking forward to a summer of fun and perhaps to her first romance. Understandably, having to stay home and remain away from her friends for three months seems like a prison sentence. But the summer turns out to be more eventful that she might have expected, and she learns some important lessons about friendship and trust.

I stood by Mother at the sink, drying dishes with an impatient swipe as she put them in the rack slowly, carefully, one by one. She had the radio on—her all-day companion—and both of us listened as the announcer spoke in a worried voice.

"...Three cases of infantile paralysis have been reported near Bailey in Jackson County. The victims, a nine-year-old girl and two boys, aged eleven and four, have been hospitalized in the Jackson City emergency unit. Public Health officials are trying to obtain information about the activities of these youngsters during the past two weeks. In addition, four other cases were reported today in widely separated areas of the State. Two deaths have been caused by bulbar polio—"

Mother turned pale and leaned on her elbows against the sink's edge. Her plump white hands dropped from the wrists like the heads of dead swans.

"Merciful heavens!" she breathed. "Josy, did you hear? It's jumped the line!"

"Sure, I heard it," I said, tossing the silverware into the drawer. "Wonder who it is?"

"Well, what *difference*!" Mother said indignantly. The sagging plumpness was at once all fire. She stood up straight and slopped at the dishes until the front of her apron was wet. "It's somebody's child, that's who. Somebody's poor child who— if he lives—may grow up a cripple with braces. Or live in one of those tanks."

She sighed and muttered on and I quit listening. I hardly ever listened any more, since we seldom agreed about anything. I daydreamed about Billy Turner and wondered whether he loved my best friend Anthy Willis better than he loved me. Anthy told me everything he said to her, and I told her everything he said to me, which wasn't much in either case. But both of us were fairly sure we knew what he was thinking. We had spent the better part of the previous afternoon matching his name with each of ours to see whose fitted better: Mrs. Josephine Turner—Josy Turner; Mrs. Anthia Turner—Anthy Turner. We wrote in our most elegant cursive on a sheet of Mrs. Willis' best linen stationery and felt compelled to agree, at last, that it was a draw.

"Well," said Mother, emptying the dishpan, "now that it's in the county I guess you know what that means."

"What?" I was already restricted to our street for the duration of the epidemic, the worst our state had ever known, and it seemed to me nothing else could happen.

"Why, it means you can't go out of the yard! Bailey is only forty miles away. You and Anthy will have to take a vacation from each other until this is over."

I put down the last plate with a bang that made her wince. "Not see Anthy? You mean not even *talk* to her?"

"I'm not willing to take chances with my only daughter," she said, ignoring my screech, "although Marlene Willis might feel differently . . ."

"I *know* you don't *like* Anthy," I blazed, "but this is ridiculous!"

"I like you both," she said evenly, "and I want you to stay healthy. You've seen the newsreels—girls and boys as old as you and Anthy, some even older, struck down, limp with paralysis—" she began to mutter again.

I hung up my dishcloth and started out of the kitchen.

"Now, you listen," she called after me. "I meant what I said. Another three weeks or a month and everything will be all right again. It won't hurt you to be apart for that little time."

I made a point of not replying.

We had no telephone. I went out to our picket fence and called Anthy. The people on the porches and sidewalks along our street scarcely turned their heads. After a while she came out on her porch at the other end of the block.

"Come over here!" I shouted.

"You come *here*!" she answered.

"I can't!"

I could see her shrug even from that distance. She tossed her long sun-bleached hair out of her eyes and came along the sidewalk, leggy and tanned, and with her back slightly arched so that her new figure showed to better advantage. I felt a twinge of envy, looking down at my own unpromising dimensions.

I met her at the gate. "Can't let you in," I said.

"Well, gee! What'd you call me all the way here for if you can't even let me in?" Anthy talked with shrugs and leaping eyebrows. "What goes? Did your mother find the cigarettes?"

I looked back hastily. "No! And don't talk so loud. It's the epidemic. Three cases in Bailey."

"Well, so what?"

"You know Mom," I said, trying to make my face elastic too. "She thinks the radio announcer spread germs all over Mellon just by talking about it!" I made little gasping noises that were supposed to be a sophisticated laugh. "She says you and I can't get together again until the epidemic is over. I've got to stay in *this yard*!"

Anthy was aghast. "Josy, your mother is impossible! Does she think we're going to *infect* each other?"

"I don't know," I said, ashamed. "You know how she is about germs."

"Don't I though!" Anthy groaned. "She nearly killed us both once for drinking out of the same glass, remember?"

I nodded gloomily. It was true: Mother was a nut about germs. Since they weren't out where she could see and fight them man-to-man, she waged a war against them that bordered on the irrational. If at one time her fear of germs had been based on sound reason, the passing years had blurred the true cause-effect relationship between germs and sickness. She was not willing to take any chances. I had to take a bath every day. I shouldn't dare use anyone else's comb for fear of catch-

ing lice. To use another's washcloth meant risking impetigo. There were typhoid shots every summer, daily cod-liver oil tablets in winter. Besides all that, I was not allowed to swim in Mellon Creek, the only swimming hole within twenty miles. "It is polluted," she told me when I was very young. "People who go swimming in it get sick and die." And then she added, as though to authenticate her statement for all time, "I have *seen* a drop of Mellon Creek under a microscope!"

As I grew older, I pondered sticking a toe in the creek, just to see if the skin would slough off and the bone dissolve outright. To know for sure would have been worth the loss of a toe. It was about that time that Dad and I, walking by the creek one Sunday afternoon, had rounded a bend and run smack up on a baptismal service. A long line of people dressed in white began on the high bank and went down to the creek's edge and out into the water. The clothes billowed and floated around their waists. I watched, horrified, as the preacher pushed a woman under the water. She came up again clinging to his wrist, and everyone praised God.

"They'll die!" I whispered to Dad, watching for the water-bound people to melt away or drown in agony.

"Of course they won't die," he had said. "What makes you think that?"

"Mother says."

"Oh, well," he said lightly, understanding at once. "She didn't mean it *that* way." He turned me around and we started back the way we had come. "She meant the creek's dirty. It could make a person sick."

I looked back at the rejoicing sinners. "Will all those people get sick?"

"Well," he said reluctantly, "I never *heard* of anybody getting sick from a baptism."

For a while afterward I clung to a belief that God suspended the rules of sickness and death for the Faithful. But later, when Anthy pointed it out to me, I saw that lots of people in Mellon swam in the creek with no noticeable ill effects. So began, with Anthy's encouragement, my private testing of Mother's rules of hygiene.

In the third grade I borrowed combs at recess. I did not get lice. In the fourth grade I drank soda pop out of the same bottle as Anthy. Neither of us got sick. In the fifth grade I started flushing cod-liver oil tablets down the john and did not get rickets. Then, one summer day between sixth and seventh grades, I sneaked off with Anthy and went swimming in the creek. In a town the size of Mellon no one has secrets, so when I got home Mother met me at the gate with a switch and a long list of restricted privileges. I hardly noticed. I had passed the ultimate test and was emancipated, thanks to Anthy, who was a perfect specimen of health without having been subjected to shots, pills, and rules.

While I did not openly declare my independence, Mother was nobody's fool. We had several heated arguments. Anthy was a frequent subject of contention between us.

"You're not going to pay any attention to her, I hope," Anthy said, pulling me back to the reality of the moment.

I hesitated only a second. "Naah," I said. "But we have to be careful."

We made plans to meet every day at one o'clock in a circle of bushes in Mr. Blakeland's back yard, next door to Anthy. Mr. Blakeland had gone to spend the summer in Vermont because of his asthma. Both of our mothers were after-lunch dozers, which mean it was pretty unlikely that we would be discovered. We parted at last after Anthy had shared with me Billy Turner's latest utterance, which was "Ain'tcha got nothin' better to do than lay around in a bathin' suit?"

"I saw you out by the gate talking to Anthy," Mother said when I went back inside. She was letting out the hem of one of my dresses. Her needle went rapidly in and out, little flashes of silver light.

"I didn't let her in," I said. "I had to tell her what was going on. I mean, I couldn't just stop seeing her without letting her know *why*." I practiced some shrugging and face-twitching.

"You are together too much anyway," Mother said absently. "I think it'll do you both good to be separated for a while."

"That *is* why you're keeping us apart, isn't it?" I accused. "It isn't the epidemic at all, is it?"

"Why, Josy, what a thing to say! You know that isn't it." Two little red spots appeared in her plump cheeks. There was a stricken expression in her soft brown eyes.

"Well," I said, "I certainly *hope* it isn't!" And I swept upstairs to my bedroom to write Billy Turner's latest words in my diary, even though he had said them to Anthy. I was a little ashamed for what I had said to Mother. She had an acute conscience where I was concerned, and I knew that she would sit and worry, going over in her mind all the years of my upbringing to determine where she might have failed.

Next day was Friday, Mother's Absolute Cleaning day, when she worked both of us half to death in order to have the house spotless for Dad's weekend homecoming. He was a salesman for a patent medicine firm and was on the road most of the time. In the middle of the morning she took her shopping bag and left me mopping the kitchen floor while she went to buy something for dinner. She was gone a long time, and came back worried and grumpy. I didn't pay much attention, as I was watching the clock and thinking about Billy Turner, wondering whether I could live through the rest of the summer without talking to him. Anthy was going to be way ahead in his affections, thanks to my own mother's edict. I felt betrayed.

Three minutes and a skinned knee after Mother trudged upstairs for her nap, I was sitting in the circle of bushes in Mr. Blakeland's back yard. Anthy soon scrambled in beside me.

"It took you long enough!" she grumbled. "I've been here three times already!"

"I had to wait for Mother to go up. She was late getting back from the store."

"I'll bet! She was at our house."

My mouth fell open.

"Boy, did she ever muddy the water!" Anthy's eyes rolled upward. "She was rushing up while I was sweeping the porch. 'Anthy, I must speak to your mother this instant.' *I* thought the *world* was coming to an end. So I invited her in and called Mum, and—oh, brother!"

Anthy flopped backwards in the little circle of grass.

"She told me she went to the store," I breathed.

"Well, maybe she did—afterward."

"Wh—what did she say to your mother?"

"Guess," said Anthy heavily. "She said, 'Marlene, I suppose you know that infantile paralysis has reached Bailey now.' Mum said yes, she had heard about it. Your mother said, 'I don't want our girls playing together any more until the epidemic is over in Jackson County.' Mum was just *startled*—I hadn't told her about yesterday, see—and she said 'Well, if you think it's best—.' Mum is *so* easygoing.

"When your mother got up to go, she said, 'I'm keeping Josy in our yard.' And then she just stood there like she expected Mum to say she was keeping *me* in *our* yard. But Mum didn't, thank goodness! Gosh—imagine not seeing Billy from now until school starts!"

"I don't have to imagine it," I said sullenly, plucking at a blade of grass.

"Poor you," Anthy said. "I don't know how you stand it with your mother like she is and all."

"I'm leaving home when I'm eighteen," I said, although the thought had only just occurred to me. "I might go out West."

"You mean you'd give up your half of Billy?" She gave me a crooked little smile. "Too bad. And your 'married' name looked so good, too. I showed that piece of paper to him—I mean the part *you* wrote on."

"Anthy, you didn't!"

"Well, I didn't think you'd *mind*," she said. "Mrs. Josephine Turner."

"All right, Anthy Willis, you wrote just as much as I did!" I said, full of fury and breathing hard. "How could you do such a thing? I think you're just aw—"

"Oh, come off it, Josy, I am just kidding. Can't you take a joke? You know I wouldn't show him." She was laughing at me, and I saw through her eyes how childish I must look, losing my temper that way. Of course she hadn't shown him the incriminating page. Or had she? That was the thing about Anthy: she was an awful tease.

She stood up and scratched her legs where the grass had pressed into the skin. "I'm going to Bailey this afternoon."

My mouth fell open for the second time. "To Bailey! But—"

"Oh, I know it," she said impatiently. "That's why I was so mad. Mom promised a month ago that I could go along when she and Dad went to the July square dance festival. I usually stay with Aunt Bess while they go to the dance. Well, after your mother left, Mum almost changed her mind. Boy, did I ever do some fast talking!"

I listened with a curious mixture of anger, envy, and unease as she rattled on.

"I reminded her how your mother is about germs. And I told her that as long as the car windows were rolled up I didn't see how anything could get in. And I told her there was really no worry about exposure—Aunt Bess is at *least* seventy."

"What's the use of going? You and your aunt will have to stay in the house," I said.

"I don't care. We can listen to the radio or play hearts or look at her picture albums. Maybe I'll tell her about Billy." She hummed under her breath and did a few dance steps.

"Somebody's going to see the top of your head," I said irritably. "Why don't you sit down?"

"*I* don't care if they see the top of my head. It isn't *my* Mum that's wanting all the kids in town to stay in their own yards!"

"I'm going home," I said, getting on my hands and knees to peer through the bushes. Anthy snorted.

"What's wrong?" I asked.

"You look so funny," she giggled. "Like some little first grader playing cops and robbers."

"Let me know when you get back," I said grimly as I began the crawl behind the backyard hedges. At that point I didn't really care whether or not she came back. The dry summer weeds crackled under my palms, and bugs skittered in front of me to vanish in the grass. I found myself hoping that something would happen to make Anthy's weekend a less-than-happy one.

I sat on our front porch in the middle of the afternoon and watched bleakly as Anthy and her parents drove away in their black Chevy. All during the weekend my father and mother listened to the newscast and talked gravely about the worsening epidemic. On Sunday morning when I went down to breakfast Mother had already finished and was drinking her coffee. Dad was still asleep.

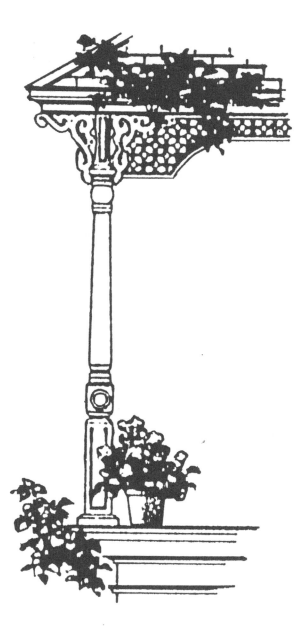

"It's really bad now," she said, laying the morning paper in front of me. The headlines read: FOUR NEW CASES IN JACKSON COUNTY. Underneath, it said that another Bailey child was in the emergency unit, and that the other three cases were scattered along a line about halfway between Bailey and Mellon.

"Looks like it just keeps coming," I said, my throat suddenly dry as I realized for the first time the seriousness of the thing. I thought of Anthy in Bailey.

Mother shook her head. I went over to the window and looked down the street.

"Their car isn't in the drive," Mother said, as though having read my mind. "They must be away for the weekend." She sighed. "I do hope they'll have sense enough not to take Anthy into an epidemic area."

I was seized by a violent fit of coughing. Mother was immediately concerned. "Are you feeling all right?"

"Yes—just swallowed the wrong way."

"You tell me, now, if you start feeling badly," she said. "If your head aches or you feel feverish. You will, won't you?"

"Sure," I muttered. "Don't worry so much."

"Somebody has to worry," she answered grumpily, going off down the hall to wake Dad.

I spent most of the day frantically running from our porch to the front gate to peer down the street. Finally, at twilight, the familiar black car pulled slowly into the Willises' drive. A great weight lifted from my chest. I beamed and waved. Anthy, in the rear seat, waved back, but not enthusiastically. I supposed that she wasn't wild to be home again, especially after the way I had acted. Nevertheless, I slept with clear conscience for the first time in two nights.

I arrived at our secret meeting place next day to find Anthy already there, sitting quietly on the grass. I flopped down beside her, feeling terribly self-conscious. "Tell me all about it," I said loudly, to cover up.

Anthy opened her mouth to speak, then unexpectedly dissolved into tears. I was flabbergasted; I had not seen her cry since we were in first grade together.

"I shouldn't have come here today, but I *had* to talk to somebody!" she blubbered. "You'd better not get near me, Josy—I'm scared I have infantile paralysis! I didn't stay with Aunt Bess," she gulped as I backed away from her. "I stayed with someone Mum used to know ages ago. A lady came visiting with her little boy, and he had a *fever*!"

"Aw, maybe it was just a cold or something," I offered hopefully.

She shook her head. "Did you see yesterday's paper? The little boy that went into the emergency unit?"

I gasped. "That little boy? The same one? Oh, Anthy!"

More tears welled up in her eyes and spilled down her cheeks. "I know how somebody must feel when the doctor tells them they have cancer," she whispered brokenly.

"But what did your mother and father say? Why, they ought to *sue*!"

"They don't *know*. I hid the paper from them. Josy, they'd *die* of worry. You're the only one I can tell."

I did not feel especially heroic. "How—how do you feel now?"

"Oh, I don't know. Sometimes I think I ache all over. And my head—"

"How long before you can know for sure?"

"It might be three days, or three weeks. I'll just have to suffer it out. And in the meantime I've got to make up some excuse for staying home without making Mum suspicious. It would be *terrible* to expose anyone else."

I backed away a little more, and a bush scratched me through my blouse.

"I'd die if anything happened to you because of me," she choked. "You mustn't come here again."

"What're friends for?" I said gruffly. "I'll meet you here every day."

She smiled at me tearfully. "You're a brick, Josy." This time she didn't laugh as I crawled away on hands and knees.

I was so blue that Mother was ready to call the doctor by bedtime, but I talked her out of it. Later, in bed, I lay on my back and looked out the window at the bright, full moon and clear sky. Anthy might not be able to enjoy the moon much longer. Did she, too, gaze out of her window at the still night? Tears trickled from the corners of my eyes and dripped into my ears.

One thing I could do would be to show Anthy that I had faith in her future even if she didn't. I decided to give her my brocade evening bag, a Christmas present from a great-aunt who had thought I was a lot older. It was the only possession I had that I cared about—or that Anthy cared about. I kept it tucked away in pink tissue paper against the day when I could carry it to my first formal dance.

I thrust it at Anthy the next day.

"Josy—no!" she squealed. "You simply can't give away your brocade bag. Why, you've never even had a chance to use it! Besides," she added, looking away, "I doubt that I'll ever be able to use it either."

"Sure you will," I croaked.

She shook her head and sighed, and in the heavy silence I saw a vision as Scrooge must have done with the Ghost of Christmas-yet-to-Come. I imagined the shadowy forms of Anthy, Billy Turner, and me, as Anthy held out the handbag with her last ounce of strength. "Take it, Josy," whispered Anthy's shadow, "and— thanks for everything. Just—remember me—when you and Billy are—dancing." And my shadow, beautifully gowned and tearful, took the bag, as Billy's shadow stood by with bowed head.

The real Anthy took the brocade bag from the real me. "On one condition," she said, looking at it hungrily. "If anything happens to me, it's yours again."

"I hope I never see it again, then," I said with emotion, "except when you're taking it to a dance."

The days dragged by. Every afternoon I asked Anthy how she was feeling. "Pretty well," she would reply, but it seemed to me that each day she was a little paler than the day before, and that her eyes were dark and hollow.

One morning Anthy's mother came over to borrow a cup of flour.

"I haven't seen Anthy out much," Mother said inquisitively as she handed the cup back. I held my breath.

"No, that's true," said Mrs. Willis, "but, then, it's awfully hot to be out *much*." And she took the cup and went home.

That was when I made up my mind that Anthy had to tell her folks. She needed help. I decided to persuade her that very afternoon—threaten her if necessary. But when I went to our place, Anthy was not there.

I had thought I was prepared for whatever might come, but the sight of the empty circle unnerved me. I sat weakly on the grass.

Anthy never came. I was not conscious of time passing until I heard Mother calling. Panicked, I ran around behind everybody's back yard and came up beside our garage, to emerge on our lawn sweating and scratched.

"Where in the world have you been!" Her voice was sharp with fear.

"Behind the garage—thinking," I panted.

"Let me smell your breath."

I went over and puffed in her face.

"Hmmmmph!" She turned and went into the house, muttering, "Funny place to think."

She eyed me the rest of the afternoon. I tried to pretend that nothing was wrong, but my conscience refused to cooperate. Besides the anxiety about Anthy, I now had a burden of guilt, having lied and been caught at it, but not accused. Mother's soft eyes were sad, but she said nothing. Her tact angered me. It was, after all, her fault for imposing rules that no normal human being could ever obey.

When our silent supper was over I dried the dishes and went out on the porch where I could keep my eye on Anthy's house. After a while I heard our radio come on with the beginning of Mother's favorite mystery play. She wouldn't move for the next thirty minutes.

I flew down our driveway to the back yard, to the back of the garage, along the rows of hedges to Mr. Blakeland's. A low brick wall enclosed his front and side yards. Callously, I gave thanks for the asthma that had sent him to Vermont. On hands and knees I crept beside the wall to the front corner, in order to hear what was going on next door in Anthy's house and yard without being seen.

The doors and windows were open wide. There were voices inside, and the clattering noise of plates being stacked. Shortly I heard the screen door open and close, and footsteps came along the walk.

Far down the street the sound of off-key whistling came rapidly nearer. As it approached I heard the whir of wheels and then the screech of bicycle brakes almost directly in front of me on the street side of the wall.

"Well, where've *you* been?" boomed Billy Turner's voice. I was petrified, thinking he spoke to me. I looked around anxiously. Was the top of my head showing? Or was there a hole in the wall?

"I've been right here," Anthy answered. It was the old Anthy, not the pitiable, soft-voiced girl that I had cared for during the past days. Somehow, she had recovered! I almost leaped from my hiding place.

"I've been right here," she said again. "I can't come out."

"Whassa matter? Mama catch you smoking?"

"No, silly! I'm con*fined* because Josy's mother has to poke her nose into everybody's business!"

"Haven't seen Josy, either," Billy volunteered, while I was trying to comprehend Anthy's words and tone.

"I guess not," Anthy said. "Her mother made her stay in their yard because of the epidemic. And she had to come over and scare Mum half to death, too. Mum got to thinking about it and the next thing I knew, Wham! I was stuck in this yard for the rest of the summer!"

"Tough," Billy said.

"I could die! You know the day we were going to Bailey to the square dance festival? Mum even changed her mind about *that*. We spent two and a half days in a stupid cabin in the mountains. There wasn't a person within sixteen miles!"

Crouched in the corner of the wall I listened, tight and shocked.

"Tough," Billy said again.

"I raised you-know-what," said Anthy, sounding pleased with herself, and without even seeing her I knew that her eyebrows and shoulders were getting a workout. "I told Mum that if she *dared* tell Josy's mother that I had to stay home, I'd run away!" She gave out one of those gasping laughs that only a month ago I had thought so clever. Billy joined in with a loud, uncertain bray. I almost threw up in the corner.

"It hasn't been so dull, though," she went on when she had gotten her breath. "For some reason, Josy thinks that I've been exposed to infantile paralysis and could come down with it any day. She even gave me her *evening* bag. I mean, she's just waiting for me to *die!*" She went off into another spasm of laughter. "I didn't really tell her any such thing—she always jumps to con*clus*ions—"

Her mother called her just then and Billy's bicycle moved off down the street. I stayed where I was while the hurt raged and shame consumed me. I recalled the past days—how Anthy had looked and what she had said. The trouble was that I was too used to Anthy's overdoing everything.

The sun went down, and Mother came out on our porch looking for me. She called and called, but I did not move. My legs had gone to sleep before I finally got up and limped out of Mr. Blakeland's front gate and came along the sidewalk to our house. Mother was sitting in the swing. Her feet barely touched the porch. She did not ask where I had been.

"Come sit beside me," she invited.

I shook my head, holding my face together, but knowing I was about to let go and ashamed of it.

"Summer's going to be over soon," she said gently, misreading the pain, "and you and Anthy can be together again."

I shook my head. "Never! The best thing you ever did was to separate us. I hate her! I wish she had gotten sick! I wish she was dead!"

And of course the dam broke and I fled through the door to the stairs and the safe stillness of my room.

Mother never prodded me for particulars, accepting my severance from Anthy the same as she accepted the coming of the seasons and the existence of germs. Nor did she say that people who betray a trust can expect sooner or later to be betrayed. I don't think she believed it, having forgiven me already that day before the sun went down.

MEET THE AUTHOR:

Suzanne Newton (1936–   )

When her children were very small, Suzanne Newton began writing stories. With four small children, spare time was very precious, so she began by vowing to write at least fifteen minutes a day. She began selling stories and articles to periodicals like *The Christian Home* and *Parents Magazine*. Finally, in 1971, her first novel, *Purro and the Prattleberries*, was published.

The seven novels Ms. Newton has written since Purro are usually labeled "young adult" novels, although the author says she never consciously writes for any age group. All the novels have main characters in their teens, usually living in small towns. The teenagers are always confronting the kinds of problems that teenagers today have to face: moving to a strange town, working out satisfactory family relationships, dealing with overly strict parents, taking a first job, or helping troubled friends.

Her novels have received many awards, and have been Junior Literary Guild selections. *I Will Call It Georgie's Blues* was named as a *New York Times* "Best Book" for 1983, and was recently listed among the National Top Ten Best Young Adult Books for the 1980s.

Suzanne Newton not only writes, but she helps others develop their writing skills, both in North Carolina schools (with the Poets-in-the-Schools program) and, as Kenan Writer-in-Residence, at Meredith College. She finds writing a very practical tool: "We all need to tell our stories," she points out, "because doing so helps us to make sense of our lives, to put a fence around them so we can handle them better." To become better writers, she urges students to read for fun—not just what's assigned. "That's how you learn to use words well," she observes.

Language Alert: In Other Words

1. Her argument was *irrational*. (She wasn't thinking straight or making good *rational* sense.)
2. When his mother called, Jack answered *sullenly*. (He was in a gloomy mood—in a bad humor.)
3. The policeman asked me to *authenticate* the signature as that of my mother. (I had to prove that it was really hers—that it was *authentic*, real.)
4. She slid her coat off like a snake might *slough* off its skin. (The snake sheds its skin—slips right out of it.)
5. It was the last day of school; we were *emancipated* from classes for three long months. (We were freed from having to go to class.)
6. The privacy of my room is always a subject of *contention* between me and my brother. (It's a subject about which we fight or argue.)
7. My father was always laying down stern *edicts* for his children. (He was giving commands.)
8. The police found several kinds of *incriminating* evidence. (The evidence was sufficient to involve someone or charge someone with a crime or wrongdoing.)
9. While her friend dissolved in tears, Jeannine watched *callously*. (She watched without feeling. She was tough and insensitive. [Notice this word's kinship to *callous*—a tough thickening of skin, usually on the hand or foot.])
10. When Miss Brooks asked who had broken the bowl, I remained quiet, but I was *consumed* by guilt. (I felt eaten up by guilt.)

Reflecting

1. If you could choose only two adjectives to describe each of the main characters—Josy, Anthy, Josy's mother—what would they be? Give evidence to support each choice.
2. Reread the last paragraph, then think of the title. Who has betrayed trust and how?
3. Many stories show us how someone learns an important lesson. What does Josy learn? Will her new knowledge change her in any way?

Casey and Dwayne

Sue Ellen Bridgers

Preview

It is 1950. Casey Flanagan's father has just been sent to Korea to fight "his second war"—World War II having been his first one. Casey has come to spend the summer with her grandparents while her mother works. She loves her grandparents and Uncle Taylor, but she longs to be back with her friends at home, and always hovering at the back of her mind are fears for her father's safety.

As for Dwayne, he is a thirty-year-old retarded man who builds his life around baseball. He listens to radio sportscasts and even "announces" his own, as he plays all nine positions by himself.

On a summer afternoon they meet.

Casey came unwillingly. So, when the bus pulled into the station after six hours of farmland, sky, and trees seen through the gray tinted glass that made everything look artificial, she sat still while the people around her got up, stretching, sighing, lifting down packages from above their heads. She sat there, hands folded in her lap, unable to look out the window, unable to reconcile[1] herself to a summer away from home even though she knew that when she did look, a familiar face would be there to greet her.

Perhaps her grandfather with his summer hat pushed back on his balding head, rimless glasses slipped beneath the hump of his thin nose. Maybe her grandmother in her black lace-up Sunday shoes, her pocket-book like a weapon at her side, her hand raised against the sun in her eyes. Or Taylor, off the job for a few minutes to

1. reconcile: adjust, settle

deliver his niece home, in shirt sleeves and with pants bagging at the knees, grinning at her, his hand out to pull her off the roaring bus like a knight rescuing a lady from a belching dragon.

It was her grandmother. Jane Flanagan stood there with her hand shading her eyes, the solitary welcomer in the empty bus station, waiting for a granddaughter who would be her child for the summer because her real child, Casey's father, was off in Korea fighting his second war.

Jane waited for a child's face, a girl's face, to appear at the window and look down at her as the bus spewed exhaust on the splotched concrete. But there was no face. The bus shuddered, growled, died. The door opened, and passengers started out. Moses from down the street, back from visiting his sister; the Farmer girls, home from a shopping trip; two strangers.

Her heart rose just like it had when she'd heard her mother was dead twenty-two years ago, just like it had when the lumberyard burned in 1938 and she hadn't known for hours if her husband and son were safe. Like it did when she knew David would be flying in yet another war. Her heart rose, pushing in her chest, cutting off her breath. And then a head appeared, tiny it seemed to her, like an infant's head, smooth with short shiny brown hair. A cheek, a profile[2] that made her heart stop, then two eyes turning toward her hesitantly. David's eyes. Deep set, wrapped in shadows of their own making. Her husband's eyes, her son's.

My goodness, she's shy, Jane thought, opening her arms. That's the difference between eleven and twelve, between Christmas and summertime. Long legs and arms, gangliness, a face turned away from kisses.

She was wearing pants, too. Long pants to hide in, as if dresses exposed too much. A boy's shirt opened at the neck. And saddle oxfords that looked the size of Taylor's.

It was a mistake to call her Casey, Jane thought as she held the thin body close to her. She knew that only she held on; Casey merely stood in her embrace resolutely, doing her duty. It's too much a boy's name, Jane said to herself.

"Sweetheart, I'm so glad you're here at last! I almost had a fright when you weren't the first one off the bus!" She turned the girl away from her but kept her arm about her.

"I have to get my suitcase," Casey said uneasily.

"Of course you do," her grandmother said. "What am I thinking? The truth is, Casey, I'm not at all accustomed to meeting buses. Usually I send your grandpa or Taylor on errands like this. But then there's never anyone quite so important to meet as a granddaughter coming by herself all the way from South Carolina." Jane hugged Casey again while the driver unloaded the baggage. "Which one is yours, honey? Can you carry that big old thing all the way home? Why, goodness gracious, it weighs a ton! I should have brought the car, but it's such a nice day and I thought you'd like to stretch your

---

2. profile: shape (as in the shape of a face seen from the side)

legs a little." Jane pretended to tug at the suitcase.

"I can carry it," Casey said.

And with the suitcase banging against her leg, they went down the walk toward the edge of town and the tree-shaded street where the Flanagans had always lived. Her grandmother talked on and on about how glad they were she had come and how her grandfather and Taylor would be home at suppertime.

Casey watched the street silently, looking for familiar signs, a tree she remembered, a house she'd once visited in, some obvious signal that she should be here at all. The houses were large and looming and very quiet at mid-afternoon. She wished she hadn't come. The wish almost brought tears to her eyes when she remembered how, at home, she'd be in the club pool right now or riding her bike to her best friend's house, where they'd eat ice cream off sticks and catch bees in pint jars or make clover chains.

She could see the edge of the Flanagans' yard and then the walk curving up to the porch, familiar but not dear to her. It wasn't her house.

"Well, we're almost home," Jane said as if she knew what Casey's silence meant.

Just then Casey heard a noise, a metallic ring, the thump of something hard and solid striking metal, the pounding of dirt, and then the voice, an announcer's voice, singsonging a mental picture she could not yet visualize.

"What's that?" She stopped to peer through the trees on the other side of the street, searching out the source of the chatter. The metallic clatter echoed again. A long swish—somebody sliding—a dusty voice sputtering.

"That's Dwayne Pickens, playing ball," Jane said, walking on.

"Who's he playing with? Is he new? I don't know Dwayne Pickens, do I?" Casey asked, heartened by the prospect of another kid in this neighborhood of ancient houses and, it seemed to her, even older occupants.

"Of course you don't. He just moved here. Dora Pickens and her family lived for years and years over on Plum. Dr. Pickens was a fine man, a good dentist, too, but he died a few years ago, not long after their other children were married. One of them lives in the big house on Plum now. Dora didn't see much point in keeping such a big place for her and Dwayne, so she bought that little house across the street from us a year ago. It's small, but there's an empty lot with it and a garage for Dwayne." Jane sighed.

"As for Dwayne," she continued, "he's in his thirties, your daddy's age, but he's got the mind of a twelve-year-old. Retarded but harmless. He likes baseball and toys just like a boy would. He goes all over town on his own. Everybody knows him so he never gets into any real trouble. Once, though, a while back, they sent him off to a home, an institution I reckon it was, but Dora got him back as soon as she could. She's a saint, but he's a burden on her any way you look at it. Makes me thank God every day my two boys were born healthy and right in the head." Jane turned up her walk, leaving Casey on the sidewalk.

Through the thin line of trees she

could see a figure on the dusty vacant lot. He stood in the middle of the field, slightly elevated on what must be the pitcher's mound. He was adjusting his black cap over his eyes.

"Reese steps into the box, ready to see what Dickson will give him this time. Pee Wee's oh-for-three so far today. He's flied to left, walked, and grounded to third," he yelled to his invisible audience.

Casey could see the yellow baseball in his hand as he flipped it with short snaps of his wrist. He looked hard toward the plate, set the arch of his right foot firmly across the rubber, and swung both hands behind himself while sliding his left leg back and dropping his head down. Then he swung both hands high over his head, where they met and were hidden somewhere behind his black cap. He pushed off with his left foot onto his right, swung his left leg into the air in front of him, dropped his right arm behind his back while balancing his left hand high in the air, swung his glove down, and followed it in a windmill motion with the right hand.

"Here's the windup and the pitch!"

The ball flew high toward the plate, then darted to the left and dropped suddenly across the outside edge of the plate. It whammed into the bottom half of the empty oil drum behind the plate and bounced back sharply between first and second base.

"It's a curve! Pee Wee swings and hits a hard ground ball toward second!"

Balanced on his toes like a diver, his right arm still across his chest in the follow-through, the man sprang to the left after the bouncing ball, then threw himself headlong at it.

"And Basgall can't get it! Pee Wee rounds first and holds up there for a single!" he shouted from the ground.

"What's he doing?" Casey asked her grandmother, who was waiting for her halfway up the walk.

"I told you, honey, he's playing baseball."

"By himself?"

"Does it look like he needs anybody else? He's got the Dodgers and the Pirates already." Jane came back to where Casey was standing. Together they watched as Dwayne picked himself up off the ground and trotted out into right field after the ball. Reaching down, he flipped the ball up into the webbing of his glove, tossed it into the air, and caught it in his bare hand. He was grinning when he walked back to the pitcher's mound.

"Hey boy, atta way to go, boy!" he called.

Jane stood watching him through the trees as if he were something from another time, something dear and familiar and yet lost to her. "Do you ever go out by yourself, Casey, maybe to sit in a tree or on the porch swing or just to wander around, and out there, all by yourself, things happen to you? You imagine wonderful, exciting times. You dream in your head with your eyes wide open till you forget it isn't real. Well, Dwayne's like that, except he doesn't know enough to keep his dreaming quiet. He doesn't see people laughing at him. Or maybe he doesn't care. He's gullible,[3] you see, and

---

3. gullible: naive and trusting

"more honest than most of us."

"Maybe he'll let me play with him," Casey said almost to herself. "I could run the bases."

"I doubt it," Jane said, hoping to squelch any such notions before they had time to settle. "He's like a twelve-year-old boy, you remember. He won't have anything to do with girls. Besides, there's plenty of young people around for you. Not that I object to Dwayne. He's respectful and good-natured. But still . . ." Her voice trailed off, not knowing what else to say.

Run the bases, she was thinking. No matter how she tried, there seemed little hope of having a girl in her house. Two sons and now a granddaughter in pants and saddle oxfords who wanted to play baseball with Dwayne Pickens.

"Let's get you settled," she said to Casey, who was finally following her around the house to the kitchen door. "I thought you'd like to have your daddy's room. Oh, Casey, we had the nicest letter from him yesterday. I'll let you read it. Of course, he doesn't know you've come for the summer yet. We'll have to write him all about it. I know it'll make him feel better. You know, he seems so close when a letter comes, like he's right down there in South Carolina and not all the way in Korea. Who'd have thought there'd be another war, Casey?" They pushed through the screen door and stood in the middle of the kitchen. "Who'd have thought there wasn't enough learning done the last time?" She sighed, conjuring up memories of sad times, of Dwayne Pickens and her David growing up together and then

leaving each other—at twelve, one mind slipped past the other—and now her David at war while Dwayne pitched baseballs at an oil drum. . . .

After lunch Casey slipped out the back door, passed the broken geraniums, and went around the house toward the vacant lot where she'd seen Dwayne Pickens. Crossing the street toward the trees in the Pickenses' yard, she wondered vaguely if she should have asked her grandmother's permission, or at least told her where she was going. She wasn't used to telling anyone where she was going at home. With both parents working, she had learned early what would do and what wouldn't, and she enjoyed both her independence and her parents' confidence in her. Besides, being around so many people in uniform had given her a special, if misplaced, sense of safety. It was like meeting a policeman on every corner. You never expected to be hit on the head midway the block.

She heard the ball hit the metal drum.

"And here's the pitch. Robinson *bunts!* Holy cow!"

Dwayne dashed to the plate, picked up the ball with his bare hand, turned and made a throwing motion toward first base, although he still held the ball in his hand. He raced off toward first himself.

"Garagiola's off with the mask! He grabs the ball and fires it to first! Is it in time?"

At first base, Dwayne toed the bag and then snared the ball from its invisible flight with a flick of his gloved wrist.

"They've got him. Garagiola throws

out Robinson on a beau-ti-ful play! And that's all for the Dodgers! In the top of the ninth, it's three up and three down!"

Casey was at the fence now. She wrapped her fingers around the wire and leaned into it for a better look. The man was on his way back to the mound. He was wearing khaki work pants and a T-shirt to which dirt clung in sweaty patches. He was short, although still a head taller than Casey, and his body was hard and muscular. Casey tried to make out his face from under the bill of his cap, but she could see only his chin and cheeks, a rugged jaw without a hint of the weakness she'd expected him to expose.

It must be in his eyes, she thought. That's where his stupid look must be.

But just then he took off his cap to wipe his forehead with the back of his hand. She saw a full head of thick dark hair, a wide clear forehead, and then the eyes. She couldn't see their color, but even from that distance she knew they weren't wild.

He knocked his cleats on the mound and moved a wad of tobacco to his cheek, then sent a squirt of brown juice straight in front of him, right toward her.

"Hey boy," he called in a voice more gruff than his announcer's tone, but just as loud. "Whatcha doin' here, boy?"

Casey felt her stomach lurch. She loosened her fingers from the wire and moved back a step.

"Hey boy! Hey you! Whatcha doin'?" Dwayne was coming toward her, trotting like players do when they're heading for the dugout.

"Just looking," Casey said, still backing away. The gate to the fence was farther down, but she knew he could jump the chicken wire to get to her if he wanted to.

He stopped, leaned into the same spot where she'd stood, and looked out from beneath his cap at her.

"I've come to stay with my grandparents," she said, desperate not to show fear in her voice. It's like talking to an animal, she thought. I can't let him know I'm scared. "You know the Flanagans across the street, don't you?" Surely he knew and liked them. He'd been her father's friend years ago. Or could he remember after all these years of being twelve?

"Miss Jane?" He began to grin. "I like that lady. One time a boy, he come by here and pitched to me. I hit one clean across the street right up on Miss Jane's porch. Boy, I can tell you I was scared! How about if I broke something? What would Mama say? And Alva? You know my brother Alva? He gets so mad at me! Really *mad!* Anyhow, 'nothing broken.' That's what your grandma says to me. She says, 'It's all right, Dwayne Pickens. And you come see me sometime.' " He was beaming at her, having remembered the conversation so vividly that it gave him pleasure again. "I like that woman."

Now she looked right into his eyes. They were gray eyes, and although he squinted against the sunlight at her, Casey could see that they were clear, unshadowed by his slow-moving brain. He didn't look retarded at all. Only his speech betrayed his childishness, for he slurred over words, bobbing his head as if to help himself think.

"What's your name?" he was saying. "Hey boy, what's your name?"

Casey moved a step closer to him and took a deep breath. She had never done what she was now thinking to do. She had never lied, at least not a big lie, a gigantic lie, one that could change her summer. Yet the proportions of her dishonesty didn't scare her, for it seemed right, both for her and for Dwayne Pickens, that she should say the words that could give them both so much pleasure.

"K.C. Flanagan," she said slowly, testing the sound she made. "K.C.—I'm David Flanagan's kid. I'm spending the summer right across the street."

"Hot dog!" Dwayne was shaking the fence in his excitement. "You like baseball?"

"Yeah," Casey said, remembering girls' softball games. She knew baseball wasn't all that different.

"What position?" Dwayne wanted to know.

"Most anywhere. Not much of a hitter, though."

"Don't need a hitter," Dwayne said. He moved his tobacco against his cheek and spit on the ground at his feet. "Need a outfielder. Run myself ragged out there. You don't want to pitch, do you? 'Cause I'm the pitcher."

"Never been much on the mound," Casey said, gaining confidence. If she had already convinced Dwayne Pickens that she was a boy, surely she could convince him she knew baseball.

"Casey!" It was her grandmother. "Casey, where are you?"

"That's Miss Jane right there," Dwayne said. "She's a-callin' you for something."

"I got to go," Casey said. "Maybe I'll see you tomorrow."

"Yeah." Dwayne looked a little disappointed that she was leaving so soon. Then he brightened and slapped his cap on his thigh. "Tomorrow we'll go downtown. I can show you everything." His face seemed to expand as he envisioned the sights in store for them. "Maybe we'll go to the show."

"Well, 'bye, Dwayne," Casey said.

" 'Bye."

Casey started across the street to her grandmother.

"Hey boy!" She could hear Dwayne calling. "See you tomorrow, boy!"

"So you met him already," Jane said when Casey reached her.

"Yes," Casey panted, out of breath from excitement as much as from running. "Grandma, he thinks I'm a boy," she said softly.

"Now just how did that happen?" Jane wanted to know. She started down the sidewalk with Casey trotting after her.

"I just didn't say I was a girl," Casey said breathlessly. "Casey could be a boy's name, too, you know. He just never thought any different."

"Not telling him is the same as lying, Casey," Jane said slowly.

"I know, Grandma, but it won't hurt anything. How can it? When school starts I'll be gone. Besides, I don't intend to spend my whole summer with Dwayne Pickens."

"I should hope not." Jane walked on ahead, trying to decide what she should say. If Casey were one of her own boys, she knew what she'd do—send him packing across the street to tell the truth—but this was her grandchild, a little girl with a father fighting a war and her mother at work—an abandoned child was one way of looking at it—who'd come here to have a family. How many more summers would there be for her to enjoy herself? And if she wanted a retarded person for a friend, why should this poor stumbling mind and opinions stop her? "I won't tell Dwayne," Jane said finally.

"Thanks, Grandma," Casey said, and Jane saw her smile for the first time. . . .

She heard the metallic slap of the baseball slamming against the drum and ran farther ahead of her grandfather. "Dwayne! Hey!" she shouted toward the lot behind the trees. 'Dw-ay-ne!"

She saw him pause on the mound and then watched while he scooped up something from the ground, jumped the fence, and trotted across the street with a package under his arm.

"Hey boy! Hey, I got you a present! Guess what I got you! Betcha can't guess!" He had arrived at her side and was pointing at the package wrapped in brown paper. "Betcha can't guess in a million, trillion years what I got in there."

He was grinning. Casey thought she'd never seen him so happy, not even at the racetrack or when he'd thrown Duke Snider out at third. Still she couldn't help feeling embarrassed.

"You shouldn't be getting me a present," she said. "It's not my birthday or anything."

"That don't matter," Dwayne said, undaunted by her lack of enthusiasm. "It's a real good present, the best present I ever

bought anybody." He thrust the package into her hands. "Open it up, boy! Let's see it!"

Casey tore the paper away from the taped edges and let it fall as she stood staring at the gift in her hands. It was the most beautiful baseball glove she'd ever seen.

"It's a fielder's glove," Dwayne yelled, as if he were as surprised as she. "It's a fielder's glove, Mr. Ben," he called to Casey's grandfather, who was coming up behind him. "I went down to the hardware store this morning and I says to Mr. Wilson down there, I says, 'I wants to buy a fielder's glove,' and he says to me, 'They cost a lot of money, boy. How much money you got?' And I says, 'Ten dollars and fifty-two cents because Mama helped me count it out this morning,' And Mr. Wilson says, 'Well, that'll do her, all right.' And so I tried them all and I pounded them some and this was the best one!" He was dancing with excitement. "Hey boy, put it on! Put it on!"

Casey slipped her hand into the glove. The leather was solid and raw against her fingers as she worked them into place and then sunk her fist into the palm. Her hand was swallowed up and she worked her fingers slowly, flexing the leather. First she cradled the glove against her chest, then reached out her arm to see it better, turned her hand slowly to study the golden grain and to inspect the web stitching and the stamped signature of Ted Williams. She curved her index finger over the top of the glove and squeezed the pocket shut.

"We got to oil it," Dwayne said. "We got to loosen it up so it fits you right. Make it soft and easy on your hand so you can pick up them ground balls like they was dandelions. I tell you, that's a fine glove you got there. See, I told you I got you something good! I told you!" He pounded her on the back and then pulled the glove off her sweaty hand and put it on himself. "See it, Mr. Ben. Ain't it a fine one?" He shoved his baseball into the webbing of the glove again and again, methodically slapping the leather into shape. "We got to work it, though. Got to do some good work on it. Come on. Let's do it!"

"Casey's got to eat dinner, Dwayne," Ben said.

"I'm not really hungry, Grandpa," Casey had an urgency in her voice that made Ben want to give in to her.

"So you want me to offer your apologies to your grandmother, huh?"

"Would you?"

"It does seem like a special occasion to me," Ben said. What could one missed meal hurt? "You two go ahead then. But don't expect anything from the kitchen before supper, Casey. You know how your grandmother is about folks not eating at mealtime."

"I won't," Casey said, already starting across the street. "Thanks, Grandpa."

Ben bent down to pick up the paper they'd dropped and when he looked up again they were disappearing between the trees on their way to Dwayne's baseball diamond.

"Let's break it in some!" Dwayne called, running ahead of her. He sailed over the fence and trotted to the mound where he'd dropped his own glove. "I'll throw you some! A few light ones is all. Why, that thing swallows your hand up. You got a little hand for a boy, you know that?" He pulled his cap down closer to his eyes, bit off a plug of tobacco which he worked carefully in his jaw, then sent the ball flying in Casey's direction.

It sank into the pocket of the new glove. Casey flipped it out, curving her palm against the sting, and tossed the ball back to Dwayne, who fired another straight at her. She caught the hot missile in the webbing, then the next in the pocket, trying to alternate the stinging palm with the hot stretching fingers that still hunted a comfortable position between their stiff leather casings.

The noon sun was white around her. She wiped her arm against her forehead, blinking to see Dwayne, who seemed to shimmer beyond her like he was doing an exotic dance. She felt lightheaded, sunstruck with heat, and hungry—but she refused to quit. She couldn't let him know that her hand was on fire, that her fingers were swelling tight in the glove fingers, or that her shoulder motion seemed to rub bone against bone. The ball kept coming, and she returned it as vigorously as she could, although she knew Dwayne was not at all taxed. He was enjoying himself, congratulating himself on his purchase while Casey picked up the grounders he occasionally sent toward her and pushed herself into the hot sunny air, her head light and burning, to grasp the frequent high balls in the webbing of the new glove.

Finally she heard a voice coming through the trees. "Casey! Casey!" It was Taylor. She followed his voice across the street and into the lot. "What are you two doing?" He leaned against the fence.

"I got K.C. a good present," Dwayne said. "Go ahead and show it to him, boy. Go ahead."

He sent a black stream of tobacco juice between his teeth while Casey gratefully tugged the glove off her steaming hand. Her fingers were as red and swollen as she'd imagined and she rested them limply behind her, out of Dwayne's view.

"Mighty fine," Taylor said, examining the glove. "Mighty fine present you got there, Casey."

"Ten dollars," Dwayne said happily.

"Big spender," Taylor agreed. "Really big."

"Yeah." Dwayne grabbed the glove himself. "I got to oil it some. Loosen it up. That boy's got a little hand, you know that?"

"Yes, well," Taylor said, seeing the need to change the subject. "It's Wednesday afternoon, you know, and I was thinking what with the lumberyard closed and all, we just ought to go somewhere. I was thinking, how about the arcade? You been there yet, Casey?"

"No. What do you think, Dwayne?" she asked hopefully because she didn't want to abandon him when he'd just given her the glove.

"*Wowee!* Them machines you're talking about!" Dwayne turned his head to spit again. "Them cars to drive. *Var-oo-om!*" His face fell. "But I ain't carrying much money," he remembered. "Spent it all on that glove there."

"I've got two dollars," Taylor said. "You can play till it's gone and then we'll call it a day."

They piled into the front seat of Taylor's Chevy and went downtown to a little building that had housed a local market before the chain grocery set up business nearby. The building had been stripped of its produce bins and refrigerators and its raw ripped walls were lined with pinball machines bulging with shiny glass and blinking lights.

Casey's empty stomach rose into her chest as she stood peering at the mass of jangling, sliding slots, flashing lights, and metal pinging metal.

"What you want to try first?" Taylor asked her.

"That one!" Dwayne shouted. He was holding out his hand to Taylor. "Gimme some money."

"You got to get change from that man over there. See him at the counter making change for people," Taylor said, slipping a dollar to each of them. "Now don't race around here wasting this, you two. Watch the games people are playing the most and try them. And make sure you don't put your money in a machine that says *Out of Order*. See that sign right there, Dwayne. You'll be throwing your money away if you put it in that one."

Dwayne was nodding enthusiastically, hardly able to contain himself until he was free to run loose in the room.

"Now I'm going down to the five and dime to see Gwen a minute," Taylor continued. "I won't be long, so you two stay right here until I get back. You got that, Casey? Right here."

Casey nodded. She didn't care where Taylor went as long as he stopped lecturing them. Nothing was more irritating than being given money and then having to hear how to spend it.

"O.K. then," he was saying. "You're all set." He could see they weren't listening to him anymore. "O.K. now. I'll see you in a little while."

Dwayne took off for the change counter, but Casey moved more slowly, wanting to take in the place, machine by machine. She still felt dizzy from having skipped lunch and having played baseball in the hot sun. The arcade was air-conditioned, and she stood in front of the blower for a minute feeling the cool breeze through her jeans on the back of her legs.

"Ain't you gonna play?" Dwayne asked. He was bobbing his head toward the machine nearest them and he jangled his fistful of coins at her. "I got the money."

He pushed a nickel into the slot and they watched the glass interior light up. The game sent a mechanical bear across the face of a woodland scene. Dwayne sighted through the rifle attached to the case and fired at the electric eye on the bear's side. The bear rose on its hind legs, glared at them, and then started down on all fours when Dwayne fired again. The bear rose again and slumped back onto the track, his light blinking. "I got 'im," Dwayne yelled. He fired again and again. The bear raised up and fell as if he were being pumped, his electric eye blinking furiously like a gaping wound until the lights went out.

"Let's do that one, boy!" Dwayne yelled over the noise of other machines. The place was getting crowded with boys off work for the afternoon. "This one!" Dwayne had arrived in front of a machine with two steering wheels. "Let's drive these cars!"

They inserted the money and watched the double-lane highway tremble. Then the landscape jerked into motion as trees spun by, rivers disappeared around the cylinder, and a little town blurred in the distance.

"Drive," Dwayne yelled. He gripped the wheel like a maniac, his jaw working, face set in dire concentration. "I'm gonna pass you!" he shouted. "Looka here, boy! I passed you. *Wooooo-ee!*"

Casey pushed hard on her accelerator and maneuvered into the lane ahead of him.

"That ain't fair," Dwayne said. "I'm gonna bump you offa this road, just like them drivers do out at the track!"

He gave her a spiteful grimace and then looked back into the machine to see his car wobbling on the road. "My car's broke!" He pressed on the accelerator with all his might but the car was coming to a gradual, defeated halt behind Casey's. Dwayne twisted his wheel angrily and let it spin back into place. "It quit," he said mournfully. "Just when I was gonna beat you good!"

"Let's try another one," Casey suggested, wanting to get his mind off defeat. He seemed truly angry with her. "I've got to get some change. You go ahead and pick one. Pick a good one now."

With change in her pocket, Casey turned back to see Dwayne across the room, beckoning to her. He was playing one of the flipper games and she went to the machine next to him and inserted her coin. The playfield lit up and she snapped the lever, sending the steel ball up the shoot and into the field of thumper bumpers and bells. The ball eased through the maze, racking up points, and she worked the flipper buttons eagerly as if she were galvanized, part of the machine that sparkled and clanged with her winnings.

"I'm gonna do another one," Dwayne said and left her while she inserted another nickel to play the flipper game again.

"Over here, boy!" she heard Dwayne calling over the bells as the ball rounded the posts. "Come see this 'en!"

By the time she reached him, he had already pushed his coin into the slot and the interior of the machine had shown a faint light on a dark blue background. It was a night sky and Casey saw small lights flickering across it. They were the targets toward which Dwayne was aiming a machine gun.

"What is it, Dwayne?" she heard herself asking incredulously, although even then, at her distance, she knew what it must represent. A sky of planes. Tiny flickers of light appearing on the wingtips of animate aircraft. She knew, too, as she was rushing toward the machine and Dwayne was aiming down the sight, his finger clicking the trigger *ra-ra-ratt-t-t,* that she couldn't let him go on. She stood there, despising his inability to understand what she would mean if she told him to quit, to leave this easy victory and go back to killing bears. How could he understand? She stood behind him, unable to focus on the havoc[4] inside the glass but looking instead at Dwayne's back, that crouched man's body leaning into his terrible task. He was so strong. His muscles moved under his khaki shirt, his arms flexed their bound-up strength. He could be a soldier, he could be any one of the thousands of men in uniform she'd seen in her life. He could have been someone who'd been to war and never spoke of it, someone who had flown beside her father, his eyes watchful for the plane that would spin out of the clouds to bring them down.

But he wasn't a soldier, no more than the plane he'd just hit contained the spattered, sinking remains of her father. It was a game, and a boy was playing it. Still, her ineptness[5] to stop him astounded, even fightened her. She had no words to tell him her fear, the swift aching panic that had paralyzed her so that she could only stand staring at him with tears in her eyes. A boy crying in an arcade.

"Dwayne," she said softly, putting out her hand to touch his shoulder. "Dwayne."

He heard her over the din of his own gunfire and she saw that her voice, just the sound of it, must mean something to him because he released the trigger and turned to her. He knew something had hurt her and he must put all his strength into fixing it.

"My daddy flies in the war," she said, feeling her tears. She didn't want to cry. What would he think?

Dwayne was staring at her. His brain worked slowly through what he knew about this person. David's kid. The name stumbled into place. This was David's boy. David was in the war, and here was his kid in the arcade scared of something.

He wasn't sure of what. What in the arcade could scare a boy like that? He rubbed his head under his baseball cap. He could see tears in Casey's eyes. He could tell they were tears because his eyes were too shiny. Too round. Well, it was all right to cry. He'd cried when they took him to that place a few years back. Now Casey was in a new place, too, feeling maybe the same as him. If he just knew what to do about it.

"Let's don't play that game anymore," he said. "I don't like that one."

Casey wiped her face on her sleeve and came up with a dingy smear across her cheek.

"Boy, you got a dirty face," Dwayne said, handing her his handkerchief, which was permanently stained with baseball grime. He grinned, glad to be doing something for his friend.

"Thanks." Casey rubbed the handkerchief against the smear and then stuck the cloth in his hand. "You want to run those cars again?"

"I'm gonna beat you this time! I'm gonna beat you so bad! I'm gonna turn you every way but loose!"

"You don't know nothing about driving," Casey said, shivering back her tears. She headed for the steering wheels with Dwayne, but deep in her body the fear remained open and oozing. It would be as easy as Dwayne's aiming that fake machine gun, she knew. It would be that easy to have her daddy never come home, to have her life forever different.

4. havoc: confusion, chaos
5. ineptness: awkwardness, clumsiness

MEET THE AUTHOR:
Sue Ellen Bridgers (1941 –   )

Even when she was growing up in Winterville, a small town in Pitt County, Sue Ellen Bridgers knew that she wanted to be a writer. As early as first grade she was writing poetry, and soon she began writing stories, too. Her first stories were published in literary magazines even before she graduated from Western Carolina University. Six years later, "when all three children were out of diapers," she published her first novel, *Home Before Dark*.

Her novels—all listed as young adult books—have won major awards both within this state and nationally. *All Together Now* (from which the excerpt below was taken) won the Christopher Award; *Permanent Connections* won the AAUW Award for the best novel for young people written in North Carolina in 1987; and in 1985, the National Assembly for Literature for Adolescents presented Ms. Bridgers with an award recognizing her entire body of work.

Ms. Bridgers, who now lives in Sylva, has also published short stories in *Redbook, Ingenue,* and other magazines. In 1989 her story "Life's a Beach" appeared in *Connections: Short Stories by Outstanding Writers for Young Adults.*

Reflecting

1. Why do you think Casey is willing, even happy, to run the bases for Dwayne? Why does she introduce herself as K. C.? (What do you think of this "lie" about her name?)
2. Reviewing the story, trace the way Casey's ideas about Dwayne as a retarded person change. Can you explain *why*, as well as *how*, they change?
3. Other writings in this collection deal with relatives of military men at war. Compare this story to works by James Boyd ("Long Distance," p. 367), Thomas Walters ("A Marine Communications Man Leaving for Vietnam," p. 512), and Stewart Atkins ("Missing in Action," p. 369).

The Change Coat

Tom Hawkins

Preview

"Clothes make the man" goes an old saying. Most of us don't like to think that our clothes completely determine who and what we are, but we must admit that what we wear affects the way people see us and even the way we see ourselves.

Can you recall having to wear something in which you felt entirely uncomfortable—something that didn't seem right for you at all? If so, you'll sympathize with the boy in this story who must wear a coat chosen for him by his father, a coat very different from what all the other boys at school are wearing.

My father took me to a department store downtown to buy me a coat—a coat like this, full-length wool, such as bankers wore over a suit, Puritan stern and altogether warm as if to hold in abeyance my juvenile ardor. I went along, as if in a trance, to see.

We found it in the department for young men, ironically, a gentleman's coat such as rich grandfathers buy for grandsons they expect will be rich. No one at school wore a coat like that—only one math genius who lived with his elderly aunt and also wore to school red plaid vests and broad silky neckties.

Young dudes in black jackets or athletic letter jackets, moved to an uncharacteristic, softspoken tone by the incongruity and by pity, called me "the undertaker." My younger sister's friends called me "the spy." Ashamed I had not expressed my own desires in coats, I wore it without complaint, and it *was* warm, and it *did* last, and last and last, like the shrewd banker it was styled to clothe.

It gave up a button now and then, but had its own supply stitched inside, and it never gave up thread, held all in its fierce herring bone weave, accrued interest and dealt hard.

I bore it like a cross, my false identity. For what was I being groomed? Neither a rising young banker, nor entirely now a kid. I wandered about with my jumbled thoughts like a displaced Russian count. Neither undertaker nor spy, I played my role as simply odd, an odd lot, a foreigner with foreign ideas.

And though it never became me much, I found that I became the coat. Its strange pretensions for me, and I myself, lived locked in ambiguity, like a restless poor man in an inherited house. This grand front demanded some unique inside, some longing pretense of expanded powers, as if by the coat's mere effect, I could slightly change the world.

Only musicians, bankers, poets and thieves wore such coats. Vagrants wore two or three.

In my mind I rehearsed a speech a thousand times that went something like this: "Dad, I've worn this coat for a year and a half, and it really is warm. But I would like something more informal, less expensive, just to wear to school. People think I'm strange wearing this coat. It would be like you wearing a leather bomber pilot's jacket to the office. It seems eccentric."

The words never passed my lips. I couldn't punish my parents for dreaming, even if it seemed sometimes to be the ruin of my life. And merely wearing an inappropriate coat, even when it became the object of fun—when I was the burden, the difficult project for them—it was too much to ask, for anyone with such iron pride, pride enough to wear a coat like that to school.

After all, I was like no other human being.

MEET THE AUTHOR:
Tom Hawkins (1946–   )

Like many writers, Illinois native Tom Hawkins started writing early, beginning with a story about pirates when he was in grammar school. At the University of Missouri he majored in journalism. Later, after serving in the Navy during the Vietnam War, he came to North Carolina to study creative writing at UNC-Greensboro. While there, he not only received a master of fine arts degree, but he met another student writer, Anna Wooten from Kinston (see p. 567). Now married, they live in Raleigh, both still actively writing.

Tom Hawkins currently works as a public affairs writer and editor for the National Institute of Environmental Health Services in the Research Triangle Park. His poems have been published in periodicals both here and abroad, and he has given readings of his work throughout the state. He has also served on the Board of the North Carolina Writers' Network. "The Change Coat" is from his first book, *Paper Crown*, a collection of short-short stories published in 1989.

Language Alert: Words and Their Uses

1. to hold *in abeyance*: to temporarily set aside (We might be angry with someone, but hold *in abeyance* our feelings in order not to cause a scene.)
2. *ardor*: strong feeling (Frequently *ardor* refers to romantic love.)
3. *incongruity*: a state in which things don't go together well; they are inconsistent or illogical (It seems *incongruous* for a princess to marry a beggar.)
4. *accrued interest* and *dealt hard*: These phrases are familiar to the business world. Money that grows through investment may be said to have *accrued interest*. a tough businessman who drives a tight bargain will be said to have *dealt hard*. Using these phrases, Hawkins is comparing his banker's coat to the ways of the banking business.
5. *vagrants*: wanderers without fixed homes or incomes, tramps (*Vagrants* often beg in order to get food or shelter.)
6. *eccentric*: odd (Literally this word means "off center." An *eccentric* action is not in the usual center of things; it is "off in left field.")

Reflecting

1. In this story, Tom Hawkins uses the word *ambiguity,* which has to do with our being uncertain in our understanding. He might also have used the word *ambivalence,* which has to do with our having uncertain feelings, or perhaps having two conflicting feelings at once. Do you see evidence that the boy feels two very different ways about wearing this coat? Explain both of those feelings.
2. Was the boy foolish to wear such an odd coat, even if his father did buy it for him, or do you admire him for doing so? Why or why not?

The Well

Clyde Edgerton

Preview

This story, "The Well," began when Clyde Edgerton realized that his kitchen floor had a soft spot which squished every time he and his wife walked across it. Crawling under the house, he saw that the soft spot was caused by moisture coming up from an old well directly under the kitchen floor. Back inside the house, he wrote a sentence which eventually turned into his first published short story. It was published in *Just Pulp*, a little magazine published in Vermont. More important, it was the seed from which his third novel, *The Floatplane Notebooks*, developed.

I swear, Meredith.

I seen this thing with him and the well coming. If you told me somebody was going to fall down the well—the open well under the rotten spot in the kitchen floor—I could have told you it would be Meredith. Anybody could—from the way he pushed on the spot all the time. To make it creak. It creaked like a little moan. Day or night, he'd be standing over there pushing down with his foot, making them noises.

He came in, pushed on the floor one time too many and there he goes like a rope had jerked him straight down through the floor, turning his head to look at me—his face following his shoulders on down through the floor, and down into the well. Swallowed up.

Served him right.

We abandoned that well six, eight years ago because he threw a litter of kittens down it. Papa told him to put them in a potato sack and drown them in the pond, but oh no, not Meredith. Too much trouble. So he just drops them down the well, one at a time. Then Mama comes along, pulls up the well bucket, and there's a drowned kitten in there—looks like a soggy black sock—and I bet you could have heard her scream a mile away. She swore off cooking with that water and said there was no choice but to dig a new well and put in regular plumbing. Everybody else had regular plumbing and it was time we had it too, she said. Papa said plumbing won't nothing but a passing fad. And Mama wanted a new kitchen added on to the house over the old well.

So anyway, Papa got a new well dug, tore down the old well shed, covered the hole, built the new kitchen over that hole.

The problem of the floor getting rotten was because of several things. For one, the joists were four instead of two feet apart. Mr. Hoover told Papa about that but he didn't pay no mind. Another thing was that the kitchen had about a five degree slant down toward the backyard, so that if something leaked, like the sink or refrigerator, the water ran to a spot in the floor which happened to be right over that open well.

Then there was this post stuck in the middle of the floor. It was supposed to be there for support, but it was nailed about a foot off the nearest joist and didn't support nothing.

Another problem was that Meredith kept crawling up under the kitchen, throwing things down the well, and leaving the top off—which made the floor damp right in front of the refrigerator. See, Meredith was using that well as a place to get rid of things.

So the dampness coming up from the well, and the fact that people stood right there in front of the refrigerator a lot,

sort of suspended between those far-apart joists, and the fact that the sink and refrigerator leaked—all this worked together, and that place in the floor got to be like the soft spot on a baby's head, and Meredith just couldn't get enough of making it creak and moan.

On the night it happened, two, three weeks ago, I'm standing at the kitchen sink washing arrowheads. Mama, Papa, Meredith, and Noralee, my little sister, are in the living room watching "I've Got a Secret."

Papa has his teeth out, which makes him lisp. "Thun," he says, "go get me thum buttermilk." Mama hates it when he talks with his teeth out.

Well, Meredith mumbles something, then comes on back. He's in his pajamas. And while he opens the refrigerator door, he pushes down with his bare foot on the rotten spot, just to make it groan. Then he gets the buttermilk, steps back on the rotten spot, and the floor, all of a sudden, sort of crunches open with a loud crack and there he goes—turning his face to look at me with this "Lord, it did it" look; there he goes right on out of sight *still holding on to that jar of buttermilk.*

You hear this deep splash, with a kind of a bathtub-bottled sound.

I stood there. I was in no hurry.

Papa, Mama, and Noralee come running in and Papa bends over the hole and yells, "You down there?"

"Where you think I'm at?" The echo hangs in the well.

Then there's this little splashing around, like he's moving. I walk on over to the hole.

"Joists were too far apart," I said to Papa.

"I could have told you them joists were too far apart," Meredith yells up.

Mama stood up straight, looked at Papa, and then bent back over the hole. She was scared. Didn't scare me. I knew Meredith was too hard-headed to get hurt falling down a well.

Papa told me to get the flashlight, but I couldn't find it, so he struck a match, got on his knees, and reached down into the well with the match as far as he could. Didn't do no good.

"I'm going to shinny up," yells Meredith.

About then Papa found the flashlight in the pantry, came back, shined it down the well, and we all saw Meredith. He was coming up, pushing with his hands and knees against the well casing—one hand, one knee, the other hand, the other knee. Down below him you could see the dark water reflecting the flashlight. And his pajamas, the blue ones, printed with the crossed rifles, were all wet and stuck to his shoulders—the wet making the skin show through. He wears that same pajama top to baseball practice.

"Wait a minute and we'll throw you a rope," says Papa.

"Never mind," says Meredith, grunting. "I can make it like this."

"Whereth a rope?" says Papa, looking around, still shining the light down on Meredith.

Meredith looks up at us and his face is all splotchy white and red, and he tells Papa to turn off the flashlight because he can't see how far he is from the top. So

Papa clicks off the flashlight and lays it down and that flashlight just slowly rolls right into that black hole before anybody can grab it and when it hit Meredith it sounded solid, like a hammer hitting a tree—got him right on the head. Then there is this heavy, scratchy scrambling followed by a short silence, then this loud, deep splash.

Meredith goes through his teeth: "What the hell was that?":

"The flathlight. Can you uth it?"

"You dropped the flashlight?"

"Look around. It'th suppoth to float."

"Meredith cussed," said Noralee. "You're not supposed to cuss in the house," she says down to Meredith.

"I ain't in the house. I'm in the well."

Mama tells Noralee to go call the fire department. Papa said we didn't need no fire department, and then he remembered the rope under the front seat of the truck and told me to go get it. I told him that rope was only five or six feet long. Meredith was a good twenty-five feet down.

But Papa gets this idea: add sheets onto the rope. So I went out to the truck, got the rope, came back, and Mama had collected a few sheets from the beds.

In a minute Mama and Papa were passing these tied-together sheets, one at a time, down into the well. About the time the sheets were out of sight and just the rope was left above the floor, Meredith yells up, "Okay, tie that end to something. I've got aholt to this end."

Well, we look around for something to tie the rope to.

The post.

Papa gets positioned on the side of the post away from the well, wraps the rope around the post, ties it into a knot, braces his foot against the post, and wraps what's left of the rope around his hand. I had my doubts, but I didn't say anything. Noralee says, "What if that post comes loose?"

"Poth ain't coming looth," says Papa. Then he does his jaw motion. He's got this habit of—with his teeth out—bringing his lower jaw right up under his nose, in this chewing motion, so that the whole bottom half of his face disappears up into the upper half. And he needed a shave.

"It could come loose," says Noralee.

Papa don't pay her no mind at all. He just yells down to Meredith, "All right, climb on up."

"You got that end tied to that post?" Meredith wants to know.

"The rope is thanchioned, Meredith," says Papa. "Climb on up."

"It's what?"

"Thanchioned."

"What?"

I didn't know what it meant either.

"Thanchioned! Thanchioned! Now climb on up like I told you!"

The rope tightened and squeaked on the post—which held. It held for a right good while, as a matter of fact, until Meredith was about halfway up, and then it snapped free real loud there at the bottom, jerked the rope out of Papa's hand, shot to the hole and wedged there. The knot held. And Meredith held on to the sheets. I guess he dropped about five feet. Papa can tie a knot. I'll say that.

"What happened?" Meredith yells up, shaky.

Papa says, "Nothing. Keep climbing." He hadn't no more than got the words out of his mouth when this little bitty rip starts somewhere in one of them sheets, sort of speeds up, then goes real fast, and there goes old Meredith again. Right back where he started from. Another loud, bottled splash sound.

Noralee says, "He ain't gonna ever get out of there."

Mama turns on Papa. "Albert, this kitchen has gone all this time rotting through. And now something like this happens. This floor ought not to ever got like this in the first place. Joe Ray Hoover told you about this kitchen."

Papa's mouth dropped open and his eyes darted around all over Mama's face. Then he did his jaw motion, turned, and walked out the back door.

"Papa, I could of told you that post would pop out," Meredith yelled up.

"He ain't up here, Meredith," I said.

The fire truck drove up. We could hear the loud idle of the engine. The fireman hit the siren for a low growl.

"We don't need no fire truck," said Meredith.

I walked out onto the back door steps and saw the firetruck headlights shining on Papa, sitting on the ground beside the well house, spotlighted, his head in his hands. The firemen, a tall one and a short one, walked up to him. Papa pointed to the kitchen, and they came on in and dropped the rope ladder down the well, hooked the end to the well curb, and in a minute out climbed Meredith, his pajamas dripping water. A red bump was on his hairline in front. Served him right.

"Where's Papa?" he said.

"He's out in the backyard," I said.

"Y'all didn't have to come," says Mere-dith to the firemen. " I could have got out."

"Then jump back down there and get out," I said.

MEET THE AUTHOR:
Clyde Edgerton (1944–   )

When Clyde Edgerton was growing up in Bethesda, a small community near Durham, he heard his family telling stories about themselves, their neighbors, their families. His novels have come from that storytelling tradition. Their conversational, colloquial flavor is one reason they have been so successful, not only locally, but nationally.

While in high school, Clyde Edgerton wrote humorous articles for his school newspaper. Later he spent five years in the air force. He piloted reconnaissance planes during the war in Vietnam. Once back home he received degrees at UNC-Chapel Hill and became a college teacher.

After he began writing, he collected 202 rejection slips and only six acceptances for short stories before he put some of those stories together into his first novel, *Raney*. All three of his novels have been well received both by the general public and by critics, and in 1989 he was awarded a Guggenheim Writing Fellowship.

A disciplined writer who can compose on word processors or with pencils, he writes every day. He does not plan his stories from beginning to end. Instead, he begins with characters, then lets the story flow, almost as if the characters have taken over. He also revises extensively—and likes doing so! "I enjoy revising my stories until they are exactly like I want them," he has said. He also writes

songs, most of which would be characterized as country music. He often performs and records his songs with his wife, Susan Ketchin—also a writer—and/or other musician friends.

445

Language Alert

1. Anyone who lives in eastern North Carolina probably knows that *won't* is sometimes used to mean *wasn't,* as in "He *won't* going nowhere, sick as he was." This is, of course, a colloquial term, but it is used so often that you will frequently see it in fiction set in the South.
2. *Joists* are parallel beams set horizontally from wall to wall to support a floor or ceiling.
3. When Papa tells Meredith that the rope is *thanchioned,* he is trying to say *stanchioned.* A *stanchion* is a post used as a support.

Reflecting

1. Because this story is told from Meredith's brother's point of view, the only details we get are those which he notices, and he states only one opinion—that Meredith is "hardheaded." However, we become fully acquainted not only with Meredith, but with the narrator, Noralee, and their parents before the story is over. What are they like? Find the details which support your description of them.
2. Think of an odd detail about some place with which you are familiar—for example, a carport with a bent support, a door which doesn't open into a room, a porch with no steps leading to it. Choose an interesting—perhaps somewhat odd—character to associate with this place. Build a story around this detail and this person.

From Shift to High

Crate the Great

Peggy Hoffman

Preview

What does a car represent to you? Mobility—the ability to get around when and where you want to? Power—the potential for high speed? Status—an opportunity to show off a sleek model with all the trimmings? Sociability—a way to get friends together?

To the Regan brothers, Crate the Great, the car assembled by Tork and his friends, represents two very different things. Tork, the designer and builder, views his "hot rod" as evidence of his mechanical genius. Rufus, Tork's younger brother, sees it as a door to adventure, a means of seeing the world outside his hometown—*if* he can talk his reluctant brother into letting him join the trip Tork is planning with his friend Dru.

Rufus Regan sat on the front steps, letting the March sunshine warm the back of his neck as he bent over a school book. Its protective paper wrapper indicated that it was the property of the Aycock Adams Senior High School, Raleigh, North Carolina. With reasonable care, the wrapper might be expected to last until the end of the semester, but not one minute longer. The book had been given hard wear, or at least the jacket had, but on this windy Saturday morning, it was being used only as a blind.

Open to approximately the middle, the ponderous *Modern Biology for Sophomores* lay across Rufus' knees convincingly enough, but it was upside down. The bowed head above it appeared to be that of an earnest scholar quietly pursuing a career of education. Instead, the tumbled locks of sandy hair covered a resourceful and scheming mind that was at the moment extremely active, darting into unexplored and tantalizing byways.

The gaze that should have been directed toward the printed page, especially since there was a tough quiz coming up on Monday, was angled toward a small bit of activity some ten or fifteen yards away. There was a noticeable touch of green in Rufus' normally brown eyes.

For the past half hour he had been sitting there pretending to study, but actually watching his brother Tork, two years his senior, and Tork's lifelong friend, Drury Wingate Carruthers III. The two older fellows, paying no more attention to Rufus than if he had been a heap of pine straw on the steps, were talking together out near the street. Tork lay sprawled on his stomach on a gravel parking space beside the driveway, working on a sign. Watching him idly but making little effort to help, Dru sat on a low brick retaining wall, now and then giving forth a small tune on the wooden flute he held in his hand.

Tork's sign was a thin board, roughly twelve by twenty inches. He had given the wood a preliminary coat of white paint, hoping to cover up the stenciled letters that still remained from an identifying label. The camouflage was not a complete success, so he was planning the sign with considerable care in order to eliminate all evidence of the true source of the wood.

"CRATE THE GRATE," he lettered industriously. "DESINED AND BIULT BY TORK REGAN. NOT FOR SALE."

Tiring from the demands of this unaccustomed type of skilled labor, he rolled onto his back and slid his long frame under the magnificent hot rod sitting near him. Its low-slung body had such a limited clearance from the ground that only the most determined mechanic would care to work underneath it. The car was parked as close to the road as was safe, in order that all who passed by might see and admire it.

In almost every way Crate the Great was a car of distinction. Certainly there was no other exactly like it anyplace. In spite of its great individuality and style, its ancestry and family relationships were obscure. At some distance it looked like a vintage Chevrolet four-passenger coupe—but smaller. The hard top, with roll-up front windows that could be opened and closed in spite of their obvious antiquity, made it a quite practical conveyance if the weather happened to be bad. The back seat was hardly wide enough for two persons, since the body narrowed gracefully someplace back of the waist. Actually, there was no seat in the rear of Crate the Great, a matter to which Rufus had given considerable thought.

Any closer look would soon show that the car bore no real resemblance to a Chevrolet at all, new or old. There was something about the chassis that suggested a 1932 Ford, reasonably enough. Tork Regan had begun the construction, or the reconstruction, of Crate the Great with just that model. An unbelievable amount of work had ensued and was still going on.

The unique quality of his masterpiece did not stop with the bumblebee body or the multiple-use manifold. The four wheels, two of them with very good salvaged Chrysler tires, sat high at the corners, giving the craft the look of a Ferrari or some other sleek racing car. An Alfa Romeo, perhaps. This effect was tremendously heightened by distance or dim light. After the body had been channeled to suit him, Tork put on full fenders, making the car look lower than ever, and also making it legal for driving in any state, an important consideration for his summer plans.

To a connoisseur, the various but relatively minor details of outward charm of the creation were soon forgotten in wonder at the motor. Left uncovered so that its glory could be more fully revealed, Crate the Great boasted eight gleaming cylinders in perfect order, waiting to leap into vibrant life. The air cleaner from the same Chrysler's motor gave all-weather protection to the carburetor. There was no risk of damage from rain or snow.

Extending back from each side were four exhaust pipes collected into a single larger pipe lying between the body and fenders. Those headers were brightly chrome-plated and had marked a major item of expense.

This was the spot at which Dru Carruthers had made a substantial contribution to the project in return for certain considerations of being allowed to drive the car. Dru's father, off on another foreign assignment, was always willing to send money for almost anything within reason, as long as he was not pestered to stay home.

The back ends of the headers were plugged up, a small pipe leading off them midway, carrying the exhaust fumes under and out. If he could ever race it—oh, if only he could!—Tork would remove these plugs so that the car would be in top racing form. The chrome-plating was absolutely necessary, he insisted. The headers must not rust out.

The other parts of the motor were painted a shiny black, scrubbed and polished to perfection. The road-and-track camshaft, the rings, the bearings, and the eight streamlined cylinders all added up to a motor in top-notch condition, made more so by love and labor.

The view of the rear was puzzling. The smooth, if somewhat abrupt, conclusion of this modern chariot might have done credit to a Manx cat if the car had fur. Since the body was painted a delicate brilliant orange-red, the stubby tail also suggested a foreshortened cardinal, caught in winter's severest freeze. Beneath the tail was considerable storage space, reached only from the inside.

The two bucket seats in front were at the moment awaiting upholstering. They were to be done in red velveteen. This luxurious decor, fit for a sultan, was going to be possible because a local fabric shop had had a fire and the damaged goods were on sale. Tork's quick eye had spotted the bargain instantly.

The hand brake, salvaged from an old MG, was between the two seats. The gearshift, rearing upward from the floorboards near the brake, seemed to be reaching for the roof. The driver was required to do some tricky maneuvering to be able to wrap himself around the post supporting the steering wheel and arrange his feet on the swinging brake and clutch pedals, but the feeling of power was well worth the effort, once accomplished.

Rufus had tried it several times, in secret. Since he was smaller than his brother, he fitted in neatly. He gripped the wheel with an air of authority and held his head high, sitting straight and tall in order to be able to see ahead from the low seat. The top curve of the steering wheel cut directly across his line of vision. If he ever did get to drive the car, unless he experienced a sudden spurt of growth to make him much taller, he would have to be stretched up like an ostrich to see out. At the moment the situation offered no problems on that score. He wasn't old enough for a license and he didn't know how to drive. And Crate the Great belonged to Tork, body and soul.

Tired of pretending to study when the car and the two boys were drawing him so strongly, he laid his book aside and began to amble across the lawn. The wind ruffled the tattered paper jacket as he got up from the steps. He went back to close the book more carefully and stick it inside the door to preserve it for a few more weeks.

Diffidently he picked up Tork's half-finished sign and read it aloud. "Hey, this spelling's wrong! You can't put up a sign like this. It's wrong!"

"Wrong? What's wrong with it?" Tork hauled himself out from under the car. "It looks all right to me." He got to this feet, brushing the gravel from his sweat shirt and worn blue jeans.

"Why don't you look at it real careful-like, huh? Study each word."

Dru ignored the two brothers and began playing a sad little tune on his flute, not bothering to recognize Rufus in any way. Tork rubbed his sleeve across the chalked letters and began redoing them. "It's g-r-e-a-t, huh? Not g-r-a-t-e?"

"Well, then, that makes it right." Tork made bold new strokes across the board.

"Just for the fun of it, how do you spell axle?" Rufus asked him.

"A-x-e-l, of course."

"No! It's a-x-l-e. We talked about that last week."

"Listen, if you don't put the "l" at the end of the word, you don't have anything for the rest of the word to lean on. That's stupid." He went back to his lettering. "I think I'll make this line bigger."

Finally he stood back to admire his work.

CRATE THE GREAT
DESIGNED AND BUILT
BY TORK REGAN.
NOT FOR SAIL.

"That certainly does look better. Thanks for helping me, Rufe."

"You changed the wrong word!" Rufus snorted. "Not for *sail*! Who'd want to sail it? Marco Polo?"

"Let's leave it off," Tork suggested. "People know that, anyway."

"Why put a sign on it at all?" Rufus inquired. "People don't wear signs telling other people their names."

Dru stopped playing long enough to growl, "Lay off it, Cupcake."

"My name is Rufus. Remember?"

"O.K., Goofus. But lay off." Dru wiped the mouthpiece of his flute and tucked the instrument into the leather pouch fastened to his belt. "Maybe we ought to put a sign on you. Rewfoot the Slewfoot. How does it sound?"

Rufus turned back to his brother. "Look, when you're driving, the sign might blow off or get in your way. You sure don't want anything to go wrong when you're on your big trip."

"Yeah." Tork studied the sign again, experimenting with setting it inside, propped against the windshield, or trying to find a place on either back or front where it might be fastened to the fame. "I'd better make it smaller so it can be put here on the dashboard. Everyone who looks at the car always looks at the dashboard."

"Speaking—that is—speaking of the—of the trip—" Rufus moved so that he was facing Tork with his back to Dru.

"No."

"Why not?"

"*No*! That's why not!" Tork tore up some scraps of paper on which he had been experimenting with his lettering. "Go along and get rid of this junk." He pushed the pieces into Rufus' hand. "And of yourself too. I'm busy."

"Busy? You're just messing around, same as usual." He headed for the house, then shot back from a safe distance, "You guys are going to be sorry if you go off on that trip without *someone* along that's got some *sense*. Me, that's who. Me!" . . .

For the next two months, Rufus schemed and planned and kept up the pressure on Tork. One obstacle was money: he had to be able to pay his own way on the expedition. First he talked his

mother into giving him money equal to what she would pay for his food if he were at home. He also squirreled away every cent he could spare from his small allowance and the money he earned doing odd jobs for the neighbors. He even started searching the furniture for change that dropped out of pockets when Tork's pals draped themselves over chairs or flung themselves onto the sofa.

By mid-May he had enough money, so, having stalked his prey with great care and precision, he moved in for the kill. There was a heavy rainstorm and he and Tork had been set at the unpleasant task of cleaning out the garage. Most of the mess was admittedly of Tork's creation, but Rufus had been given orders to clear out everything else, gather up the soft-drink bottles, assemble the trash for the trash collector, and most of all, keep Tork at it until the work was finished. Tork did a man-sized job of grumbling about taking the time away from his studies when the semester exams were so close, which gave Rufus a chance to insist that he work fast and get it over with. He watched for the moment when Tork stopped to mop the perspiration from his face and look around at the discouraging amount of work still to be done.

Sweeping up a pile of dirt into the dustpan, Rufus asked guilelessly, "How'd you like that soup we had last night?"

Tork fell into the trap. "Say, you know, that was terrific stuff. I wish we'd have that again."

"You liked it, huh?"

"Sure did. Why?"

"I made it. I just wondered how you

liked it." He went on with his sweeping.

"You're lying in your teeth."

"Scout's oath. I made it."

"You can't cook! You don't know the first thing about cooking."

"I wouldn't say that."

Tork made a face. "I can still remember that horrible fried chicken you foisted off on us when you were trying to get the cooking merit badge in Scouts. Ugh! I always thought that was why the troop folded up. Afraid you'd kill 'em off."

"That was a long time ago!" Rufus protested. "And you said you liked the soup. I can make good soup."

"Just because you did it once and tricked me into saying I thought it was good, you think you're a cook. How do I know it wasn't out of a can?"

"It was not out of a can. Ask Mom. And I wrote down everything I put in. Lots of celery, that's one of the secrets. And don't forget pepper as well as salt. And plenty of onions."

Tork went back to his work, straining to finish it in a hurry so he could escape from a situation that was getting out of hand. "Don't talk recipes to me, boy. I'm not the least bit interested in cooking. Only eating."

"That's the way I had it figured," Rufus told him cheerfully. "How's Dru's cooking?"

"Dru? All he does is read poetry and play flute music."

"Then you'll be chief cook as well as driver and trail boss?"

"We can eat out of cans, bub. No problem. And scrounge stuff from home."

"You hate eating out of cans, and you know it," Rufus reminded him. "And the stuff scrounged from home will last about two days, maybe only one. What are you characters planning to eat, day after day? Or have you got so much dough salted away that you can eat in fancy restaurants?"

"Baked beans, hamburgers, peanut butter sandwiches."

"Sounds a little monotonous to me." Rufus carried a basket of bottles to the garage door and set it down. "How'd you like the barbecued pork chops we had Monday night when Mom and Pop went to the P.T.A. banquet?"

"Hey, those were good!" Tork forgot to be wary. "Only there weren't enough. I could have eaten three or four."

"I made those too," Rufus admitted modestly. "You've been eating my cooking about half the time all week and you never complained once. And you seem to be in good health. Of course I never told you, so you wouldn't be suspicious or manage to develop one of your poor li'l ole tummy aches." He saw that his quarry was beginning to weaken. He moved in swiftly. It was now or never.

"Don't you think those pork chops would taste pretty good after you've been driving all day and you were tired and cross and hungry? I'd get the fire going and put baked potatoes in foil into the fire and pork chops on the top and get some fresh tomatoes from some farmer—makes me hungry to think about it. And you wouldn't have to do a thing but rest your great big carcass on the ground and wait for it to come to you."

"Aw, shut up. I'm tired of listening."

Tork dumped a stack of old magazines into the trash barrel with a huge, muffled, dusty *Thr-r-r-romp!* and brushed his hands together in a gesture of dismissal.

"I make that soup with hamburger. It doesn't cost much and I could make enough for two meals at once and we wouldn't have to do anything the second time but heat it. It tastes better then, too. And it's a whole meal in one pan." Rufus' freckled face was glowing.

"Any more bright ideas?" Tork inquired glumly.

Rufus put his final question. "If I do the cooking, all the cooking, can I go along? I've got three more weeks to practice and Mom will help me. Pop too. He's got a couple of specialties he likes to show off. And I'd be paying my share—"

"And wash the dishes." It was more a statement of fact than a question.

"I don't know about that—" Rufus started to protest but thought better of it in an instant. "O.K. Wash the dishes too."

"Well, all right. Now get busy on that stack of junk in the corner. Most of it's yours anyway. And don't say another word to me about the whole trip. Not one cotton-pickin' word! *Hear?*"

MEET THE AUTHOR:
Peggy Hoffmann (1910–   )

A native of Ohio, Peggy Hoffmann moved to Raleigh early in her adult life and has remained there ever since. Her professional life has been divided between music and writing. For a number of years she served as a music therapist and a church organist. She also published sixteen collections of choral and organ music, some of them arranged for choirs of children and youth.

Peggy Hoffmann's first books were written with her children in mind. She authored two "how-to" books on cooking and sewing, using her six-year-old daughter as the intended reader. When her sons were teenagers, she used them for resources as she wrote novels focusing on their interests. And when her children were grown, she turned to other kinds of fiction, including a historical novel. Her writing has won two Junior Literary Guild Awards and the Raleigh Medal of the Arts.

Ms. Hoffmann, who believes that writing

should bring joy to the writer as well as to the reader, gives the following advice: "Read. Write freely, anything you want to read aloud to get the full benefit of the sound of words. Read. Then write some more, for fun."

Through her teaching in public schools and at Meredith College, she has influenced many young writers. One fourth-grade student, after writing poetry for a week under Ms. Hoffmann's direction, wrote her, "Thank you for helping me find what was in my heart."

MEET THE ARTIST: Dot Stell

Dot Stell grew up in Sanford and studied art at Ferree Studios in Raleigh. She has been an artist for The News and Observer publishing company for twenty-nine years.

Language Alert: In Other Words

1. Rufus is a very *resourceful* young man. (He finds his own ways of handling matters.)
2. The possibility of a trip with the older boys is *tantalizing*. (The hoped-for trip is very tempting—very attractive, but possibly out of reach.)
3. My father drove a *vintage* Chevrolet. (It was old, but considered excellent—even classic.)
4. The Chevy had some dents and scratches, but it was a practical *conveyance*. (It offered us a means of getting from one place to another.)
5. Concerning cars and motors, Tork can be considered a *connoisseur*. (He is very well informed and can make good judgments about them. *Connoisseur* comes from the French word which means "to know.")

6. The boys are interested in the *decor*, as well as the mechanical condition, of the car. (They are interested in the style, the *decor*ations, the way it looks.)
7. In talking with the older boys, Rufus tries to keep his voice well *modulated*. (He tries to keep it under control.)
8. Like most brothers, these two have an occasional *skirmish*. (Now and then they have a minor conflict or dispute.)
9. Like many big brothers, Tork sometimes tries to seem *omnipotent*. (He tries to look as if he is all-powerful. Notice the root words: *omni* means *all*, *potent* means *powerful*.)
10. At the end of the story, Rufus makes a *magnanimous* offer. (His offer is generous and noble. Again, notice the roots buried in this word: *magna* means *great*, *anima* means *soul* or *spirit*.)

Reflecting

1. Interest in cars is not limited by state boundaries, but it does seem that North Carolinians are especially involved with cars, both with their own personal vehicles and with events such as sports car racing. (See Sylvia Wilkinson's story of a stock-car racing star, "Dirt Tracks to Glory," p. 455, and Stephen Smith's love song to the car of his boyhood, "To a Fifty-Three Dodge," p. 390).
2. You might like to know that although this is fiction, the Regan boys are modeled after Ms. Hoffmann's two real-life sons. Ted

(Tork) built thirty-seven cars from junk parts, "always in our front yard," while he was still a Raleigh teenager. After graduating from NCSU with a major in product design, he opened T. Hoff, a shop specializing in repairing and selling parts for foreign cars. While his mother was writing this book, he kept close watch to make sure that her mechanical details were accurate. David (Rufus) is now an insurance executive in Charleston, SC. Like Rufus, he has always enjoyed cooking.

Bobby Isaac

Sylvia Wilkinson

Preview

Someone has remarked that North Carolina is probably the only state where Richard Petty's name is more familiar than the current governor's. Petty is, of course, only one of a number of North Carolina stock-car drivers who have become sports heroes. The color and fanfare of the cars and the racing ring, the spirit that makes these men zoom their vehicles around the oval track at death-defying speeds—these have caught the popular imagination for decades.

In the following excerpt from *Dirt Tracks to Glory*, a history of stock car racing as told by participants in the sport, Sylvia Wilkinson begins with a quotation from Richard Petty, then introduces us to Bobby Isaac, one of the fabled pioneers of the sport. At the same time, she gives us a look at the origins of stock-car racing—how it developed from a minor attraction at county fairs to a national sport that attracts dozens of would-be champions and thousands of fans.

It ain't the money. Nor the glory. I just like to drive. It's that simple. Some cats, they like to watch cows eat grass. That's their thing. Me, I like to drive. It's my thing. I like the feel of metal around me, the feel of tires under me.—*Richard Petty*

Bobby Isaac came from the mill town of Catawba, North Carolina, and drove his way from dirt tracks to glory on NASCAR's Grand National circuit. Grand National racing, a series for late model American cars, is today the most popular, yet the youngest auto racing sport in the world. Stock car racers never knew the meaning of gradual evolution;[1] they emerged in one lifetime from childhood rags to young adult riches. A '34 Ford, modest as a pumpkin, was Bobby Isaac's first golden carriage. It rescued him from the misery of blue-collar Southern poverty.

1. evolution: a gradual process during which something changes into a different (and probably more complicated) form

"I hated working in that cotton mill," Bobby Isaac remarked. "I remember the first time I saw a stock car. I was lying on the side of a hill one afternoon and saw this tow car come past with a stock car behind it. I said that day that someday I was going to drive a stock car."

Bobby Isaac was a winner on the dirt track when he was a teenager. After World War II when southern America had the biggest new car boom, country boys all over the South were banging fenders throughout the forties on tiny fairground horse tracks. While the horse tracks doubled for car tracks, many of the race drivers and their cars led double lives too: racing during the day and running bootleg whiskey at night.

In 1948, a group of racing people got together in Daytona Beach, Florida, and decided to make some order out of this wild and woolly sport that had been born accidentally. Under the leadership of Bill France, Sr., a former driver and mechanic, the National Association of Stock Car Auto Racing (NASCAR), an organization that would grow into the most successful racing group in the world, was formed. When the name was suggested, someone thought it sounded too much like Nash-car, and might be confused with the popular automobile. Nash car is dead; long live NASCAR.

With the fifties came a new era: longer paved oval tracks were built for stock car racing only. New cars, not battered old jalopies, took to the race track, many with sizable financial backing from the Big Three American automobile manufacturers: Chrysler, General Motors and Ford.

Bobby Isaac went on to make the crucial transition[2] that hundreds of country boys-turned-race drivers were unable to make: he thrived on the speeds of the high-banked, paved tracks that came to be known as the superspeedways—Daytona, Darlington, Charlotte, Rockingham and Atlanta. When new showroom cars, the forerunners of today's late model or Grand National cars, thrilled the fans for the first time in Charlotte in 1949, the rugged flathead Ford was shoved aside. When the superspeedway at Darlington, South Carolina, opened in 1950, dirt track racing took the backseat. Bobby became one of the few who rode the new wave with success.

"If you're brave enough or foolish enough," Bobby said, "you can near about drive Daytona flat out, wide open all the time. Most of the drivers who are quitting didn't want to run the speeds we're running now. The speeds don't bother me. I feel safe in my car at 200 miles an hour."

When pressed about the obvious adjustment that many drivers didn't choose to or couldn't make, he added: "Physically the driving isn't too hard on you, but the tension wears you down. The heat is a problem, but if you roll your windows down a little, it will slow you up. You have to drive so far ahead of yourself and stay right on top of things every second."

No amount of safety equipment could guarantee that a driver would survive a

_____

2. transition: the process of changing from one form or place to another

crash when cars were travelling at the speeds they reached in the sixties. Racing had never been a safe sport even with dirt to slow down the cars: there were deaths in the first Indy 500 in 1911 when cars hit chuck holes and tossed the drivers out or rolled over on drivers and riding mechanics. Men died racing on the unpredictable sand of Daytona Beach. During the sixties, incidents at Indy and Charlotte made it apparent to racing people that the safety of their heroes had to be given strong consideration. In stock car racing, Fireball Roberts was fatally burned when his overturned car became a tub of burning fuel in front of his adoring fans at Charlotte. "I never went to another race after that," a friend of mine told me recently, "I could hear Fireball trapped inside and screaming." In that other form of racing unique to America, Indianapolis, Davie MacDonald, a promising rookie, and Eddie Sachs, a popular driver who went from a dishwasher at the track restaurant to a champion driver, both were killed in the same holocaust.[3] MacDonald crashed and caught fire, then Sachs, unable to see because of smoke and flames, collided with MacDonald, exploding the gasoline in the nose of his own car. Also in 1964, everyone's favorite clown, Little Joe Weatherly, died when his head went out the window as he hit the wall in turn six at Riverside. Something had to be done.

3. holocaust: total destruction, often caused by fire

For stock cars, no-leak fuel bladders were developed for the gas tanks, roll cages around the driver were strengthened, a net was put in the driver's window to keep his head inside. At Indianapolis, the cars were equipped with bladders, the bulk of the fuel was moved away from the wall side of the car, and gasoline was banned. Even so, the smaller, faster Indy cars are inherently[4] more dangerous. After World Champion Sir Jack Brabham arrived in 1961 with his rear-engined racer and made the bulky American-built Indy roadsters "resemble Mack trucks," as one famous car builder noted, Indy cars began to be more like the international Formula One or Grand Prix cars. Built for racing only, the Indy cars would simply never have the bulk and structure to be as safe as stock cars. Their construction became more like that of airplanes. Stock cars, on the other hand, remained committed to what makes them unique today—the American passenger car converted into a race car. Indy cars made one appearance at Darlington in 1951, but the fans didn't like them. Indy racing ceased to attempt to be all-American, while stock car racing never strayed from the course it embarked on in 1949 at Charlotte, when Lincolns and Packards and Chevrolets took to the oval.

In the sixties, factory involvement changed stock car racing both technically and financially. Bobby Isaac drove for the Ford team. Bobby grew as a driver through the sixties and in 1970 became *NASCAR* Grand National Champion. During his active years he was always one of stock car racing's top ten drivers. In 1972, when he claimed to be thirty-eight, Bobby said, "I'm too young to retire. Besides, what else could I do? Of course, at some of the shorter tracks, I get tired a lot quicker than I used to. I can't run as long at some of the places, but at places like Daytona and Talladega, the speeds still don't bother me at all."

Bobby took up golf and the stories of his temper outbursts on the greens were commonplace. He wrapped golf clubs around his legs, around his golf cart, trees—even threw a whole bag of clubs into a lake. But on the track he backed away from violence. When the legendary Curtis Turner dragged Bobby from his car after the two had tangled on the track and shouted, "Were you trying to wreck me?", Bobby supposedly answered, "No, I wasn't trying to wreck you. Why, fellow, I don't even know you."

Bobby was one of the best. He won a lot of races. He drove a lot of good cars. But then he started having a lot of crashes. He became more of a risk than an asset. Younger drivers were after his seat. His name dropped out of the current record book because he didn't make it to enough checkered flags. He seemed to be drawn to crashes like steel to a magnet. Even the men who fired him called it bad luck. Bobby talked publicly of strange voices that told him to get out of race cars. Then one day, he drove his race car into the pits at Talladega, got out, walked to his street car and went home.

He said later: "I have nothing to prove to myself or anybody else. I know how it

4. inherently: basically

458

feels to be a champion and I know how it feels to quit."

What was this man who wasn't afraid of driving 200 miles an hour afraid of?

Bobby didn't stay out of race cars. After he fell from the big time, he went back and drove Sportsman cars, older, less prestigious[5] cars than the late model Grand Nationals he had driven. Race drivers often have trouble retiring. Many of them retire and unretire several times. They compete against their children and still refuse to quit.

In 1977, Bobby died in a race at Hickory Speedway, the track where he ran his first race. But he didn't die in a crash. At the age of forty-eight, five years after he said he was thirty-eight, Bobby's heart failed.

MEET THE AUTHOR:
Sylvia Wilkinson (1940–   )

It's a long way from riding horses in Durham County to keeping score for Paul Newman's Can-Am Team on the auto racing circuit, but Sylvia Wilkinson has traveled the whole route—and published over two dozen books!

Born in Durham in 1940, Sylvia Wilkinson began writing when she was only six, recording interesting facts and the family stories her grandmother told. She wrote the first draft for what was to be her first novel, *Moss on the North Side,* when she was in the seventh grade, but she didn't finish it until she was twenty-five, a graduate student at Hollins College. From first writing to publishable copy, she composed eleven drafts.

Two of her four novels have won the Sir Walter Award for Fiction. However, vying with fiction writing for her attention is her love for cars and sports car racing. For years her career (not as a driver, but as a crew member for famous drivers) has taken her all over this country and abroad.

Not surprisingly, Ms. Wilkinson has joined her two interests, serving as motorsports cor-

respondent for *Autoweek* and writing eighteen books—fiction and nonfiction—about racing.

5. prestigious: having prestige, being considered important

Reflecting

1. About Stock Car Racing

a. Notice who helped finance the development of stock-car racing into a major sport. Why would they be interested in doing so?

b. Describe the changes developed to make stock-car racing safer.

2. About Bobby Isaac

a. Why does Sylvia Wilkinson compare Bobby Isaac's first racing car, a '34 Ford, to a pumpkin?

b. After telling about Bobby Isaac's simply driving his car into the pits, getting out, and going home, Sylvia Wilkinson asks this question: "What was this man who wasn't afraid of driving 200 miles an hour afraid of?" Can you provide the answer?

A Word from Doris Betts

Many of Doris Betts's stories include characters who refuse to let life get them down—who manage a dignified life in spite of difficulties. These characters reflect an attitude expressed by Ms. Betts in an interview: "If society says you're a second-class citizen and you believe it, you're pretty dumb. If society says you're second class and you say back, 'Who says so?,' then you're as liberated as you're ever going to be. . . . It never occurred to me when I was young that life was fair, and it hasn't been. It's not fair; it's not fair to men or women. What is so amazing is that so many men and women manage in spite of that to be intelligent and kind and responsible human beings. That's what is worthwhile."

A Mark of Distinction

Doris Betts

Preview

During this century, textile manufacturing became a major industry in this largely agricultural state. In some areas, that industry was so dominant that certain communities were called "mill towns"—Statesville, Gastonia, Concord, Albemarle, and Kannapolis among them. In such towns, the mills owned whole neighborhoods and rented the houses to their workers.

In this story you meet the Orlons, who live in a mill house just like all the other mill houses on their street. But Henry Orlon is a man of distinction and he wants his home to have a mark of distinction, too.

As you read, keep in mind the words of Doris Betts about "second-class citizens."

Number 209 Millwood was just like number 207 on the corner, or the house directly above it, number 211. In fact, all the grayish houses on both sides of Millwood Street were exactly alike—just so many identical, dingy boxes lined up at exact intervals all up and down the street, with exactly the same number of windows showing the same green window shades, and exactly the same four porch posts and the eight green steps that went up from every dusty walkway.

Mr. Orlon found this uniformity very depressing. Every time he walked down Millwood Street (that was a silly street name, he thought, it sounded so elegant) he would discover afresh that his own house was no different from a dozen other houses, and no matter how cheerful he had been before, this left him very grumpy.

"I wish you'd plant some flowers." Mr.

Orlon had told Sarah that just last spring.

"I thought you didn't like flowers," she said. That was just like Sarah, as if his liking them had anything to do with it.

"I don't," he'd answered shortly. Besides, no self-respecting flower would take root in the thin dust along Millwood Street, and even an experiment with grass had proved a failure. Henry Orlon's house continued to be an exact duplicate of Si Parker's which stood next door on the corner, and George Blane's, number 211.

Once Mr. Orlon had thought about knocking off the unsightly front porch, but after he crawled around under the house looking at timbers one Saturday afternoon, he found that as nearly as he could judge, this would bring the whole house down.

He was especially angry that night at supper. "You'd think from common sense, wouldn't you," he complained to Sarah, "you'd think it was downright impossible to build a house so that every board was nailed to every other board."

"Yes, I would," said Sarah. That was one thing about Sarah; she was long on common sense.

Mr. Orlon grunted. "Well, as far as I can tell, if I take a brick out of the foundation, the roof'll fall in."

"Really, Daddy? Will it really?" This was from Martha, the youngest, aged seven.

"Pass the potatoes," Sue said. Rachel ate her supper quietly, not saying much of anything.

"You've a spiderweb in your hair," Sarah added.

When you came right down to it, the only thing that made number 209 Millwood any different from the corner Parker house or the Blanes' next door was that Henry Orlon and his family lived in it.

This was no small distinction. There were Henry and Sarah Orlon and their three daughters, Rachel sixteen, Sue thirteen, and Martha seven. Besides that, Mr. Orlon had the reputation of being a smart man. It was he who generally represented the other millworkers when they had a grievance, which wasn't very often, since they were fairly easily contented. The Kyles family, which had owned and operated the mill for the last fifty years, tolerated no talk of unionizing the workers, which, they said, "sowed the seeds of unnecessary unrest."

The only member of the Kyles family who was very active in the mill any more was Charlie Kyles, a plump bachelor of about forty, who was always walking around trying to be friendly with the men. He'd once taken a college course on personnel relations and had never gotten over it. The workers were, as a body, contemptuous of him.

"Charlie Kyles is a half-wit," Mr. Orlon was fond of saying, and in the evenings the other Orlons would hear whether or not "that half-wit Charlie Kyles" had been "bungling about the mill today."

Still, Charlie Kyles seemed to consider Mr. Orlon some kind of "diamond in the rough," and was always being very friendly to him, which embarrassed Mr. Orlon greatly. Sooner or later he was always forced to make some subtle remark that would put Charlie Kyles in his place at every interview, and all day long the word would be passed by grinning workers from loom to loom. "Hey, did you hear what Henry Orlon told old Kyles today?"

Mr. Orlon was a hero. There was really no question about that; he was a man among men; he did his work quietly and well; and in the Millwood community he was liked and respected by everyone.

That's why the house bothered him so. He never came home from work in the evenings but what the sight of it was a nagging annoyance to him, and over supper he would be still and moody.

"I wish we could move uptown," he'd mutter.

"Away from your work and at three times as much rent?" Sarah would demand. She was such a practical woman. There was no argument to use against a practical mind like Sarah had, and Henry Orlon knew it. But that didn't mean he accepted her point of view; he simply let it wash over him and pass by and then he went back to thinking about a distinctive house somewhere uptown, maybe even with a telephone.

As far as Mr. Orlon could tell, his three daughters were completely undisturbed about the appearance of the house. This, he felt (almost bitterly), was because he had given Sarah such a free hand in the raising of them, and she had turned them out very reasonable girls, but without a sense of values. If there had been only one son . . . ah . . . that would have been a different matter.

Of course (and even Mr. Orlon realized this dimly, although he could not have put it into words), the trouble with Mr. Orlon was that he had been misborn. His allegiance was to another and more vivid age, where a man's honor was something to duel about, and the questioning of a man's rights might set off a nationwide revolution. Yet, here he was, Henry Orlon, aged forty-four and rapidly losing his hair, without banner, sword, or Crusade to ride forth upon. Here he was, stuck incongruously in Lincolntown, S.C., at 209 Millwood Street, along with four placid women in a house that was just like every other house, and for eight hours daily running a machine that was like eighteen other machines. It would have dampened the soul of King Arthur; it would have bored Thomas Paine to tears.

Their life on Millwood Street was quiet. On summer evenings, Mr. Orlon and his wife and the two younger daughters would sit on the green front steps (Rachel was always out with some boy; she was too young, thought Mr. Orlon) and they would speak pleasantly to some of the people that passed, or maybe they'd go over to the Parkers' for a beer and a radio program. (Mr. Orlon had taken his own radio to the mill where everybody could hear it while they worked, a generosity which Sarah had accepted quietly but did not wholly approve of.)

There had been some difficulty with Charlie Kyles about the radio, but Mr. Orlon had been well prepared for that. As a smart man, he was a great reader and his mind was always swarming with facts and statistics. Of course, sometimes his memory wasn't too good, but everybody admitted Mr. Orlon was a smart man and

A mill village in Roxboro, NC.

nobody doubted his word; so when he became forgetful he just made up some statistic that would do just as well. It always made his conversations very impressive.

That morning when that half-wit Charlie Kyles approached him about the newly installed radio, Mr. Orlon was ready and waiting for him.

"Now see here, Henry" (Mr. Orlon always flinched when Kyles had the audacity to call him by his first name), "about that radio . . ."

Mr. Orlon shut off his machine with an impatient frown. He always did this when Charlie Kyles addressed him in the mill, and it gave the impression that Kyles was a troublesome fellow who was always holding up production in his own plant by disturbing his efficient workers. Several of the other men grinned and dug each other in the ribs when Mr. Orlon switched off his machine.

"Statistics say," began Mr. Orlon thoughtfully, "that music creates a definite rhythm and increases efficiency by 87 per cent."

"That so?" blinked the half-wit.

"Yep. That's what statistics say."

From Mr. Orlon's reverent tone of voice, Statistics was conjured up as being an infallible, rather ill-tempered old man—a kind of second lieutenant to God—who had been let in on the secrets of the universe. Charlie Kyles had a vast and growing respect for statistics, which had been carefully fostered during his acquaintance with Mr. Orlon.

Still, Kyles tried to shift the victory to himself by putting on a patronizing smile. "Well, anything that keeps our workers happy," he said blandly, laying a friendly hand on Mr. Orlon's machine. At this time, Mr. Orlon flicked the switch and Kyles snatched his hand away barely in time as the wheels whirred into action.

"That's right," said Mr. Orlon politely.

Kyles searched his face for a smile or a sneer, but there was none; and finally he stalked off—the personification of a wicked and ousted archduke, the oppressive Redcoat army, or the defeated Huns of World War I.

All day the men grinned to themselves about Mr. Orlon's mastery over that half-wit Charlie Kyles, and in that way, the radio became a permanent fixture of the Kyles Textile Plant.

Still, Mr. Orlon had never been in serious trouble with the management. He went quietly along, undermining the Kyles superstructure with deft little nips at the most vulnerable places, but there was no open clash between them. Mr. Orlon was respected as a shrewd but restrained leader of the mill's employees, and the Kyles family felt that if he should be cast down, some less civilized rabble-rouser with communist leanings would spring up to take his place.

All this was before Mr. Orlon decided to build a fence.

April was always the most dangerous part of the year for Mr. Orlon. During that month his very blood and bones seemed to awaken and vibrate within him, and he would take to baiting Charlie Kyles more openly out of nothing but pleasure. It was as if he had been suddenly set upon by violent spirits—Joan of Arc and Sir Galahad and Paul Revere, for instance—and as if any minute the submerged centuries might break loose in him and set him to nailing these to the door of the Kyles Textile Plant.

It was one April afternoon as Mr. Orlon was walking home from work, averting his eyes from the rows of monotonous little houses, that the idea came to him. He stopped before 209 Millwood and examined the house thoughtfully, turning his head first on one side and then on the other. Yes, it would do perfectly. It was just what the place needed. Mr. Orlon wondered why he had not thought of it before.

When he came in to supper that night, he was humming happily "The Battle Hymn of the Republic," and Sarah and the three girls stopped their talking and looked at him. He grinned and broke suddenly into song while washing his hands:

I am trampling out the vintage where the
     grapes of wrath are stored,
I have loosed the fateful lightning . . .

"Sit down, Henry," said Sarah. "Everything's getting cold."

He sat down docilely. After all, he had no time to argue about trifles.

"I'm going to build a fence," he announced, smiling.

Sarah stopped with the dish halfway to the table and stood there eying him. "A fence?" she said.

"Where?" said Martha.

"What kind of a fence?" put in Sue.

Rachel didn't say anything; she just sat looking at him, waiting. Although she was the oldest, she didn't talk very much. Mr. Orlon still had hopes for her.

This was the sort of moment Mr. Orlon loved. "We got any butter?" he asked.

"No," said Sarah shortly.

Mr. Orlon put beans on his plate, picked up a fork, examined it, moved it in the air unnecessarily. "Just a fence," he said.

"Out front?" asked Rachel. This was the first sensible question of the evening. It showed the girl could think. Mr. Orlon looked at his oldest daughter with some interest, and showed his respect for her direct question by giving it a direct answer.

"Yes," he said. Sensibly enough, he observed, Rachel began quietly to eat her beans.

"What for?" asked Sarah. Mr. Orlon was profoundly irritated at that—what was a fence usually for? He did not even look at her. "Where's the pickles?" he retorted. It was an expression of obvious disapproval. Sarah, never very sensitive, put the jar on the table in front of him.

Mr. Orlon looked at his daughter Rachel with a new warmth and addressed himself to her as if they were alone. "What do you think of a white picket fence?" he asked pleasantly. She looked up at him (that's good, he thought. Always look squarely at people you talk to) and he noticed with pleased surprise that her eyes were pale brown too, very like his own.

"That'll be handsome," she said.

Content ran smoothly throughout Mr. Orlon's body like syrup. Now there was an answer for you. It was somehow just right. He sighed with pleasure.

Sarah brought in the jarring note. "I thought Mr. Kyles didn't want the outside of the houses changed."

Mr. Orlon got up from the table. He suddenly felt three inches taller. "I've finished," he said stiffy, "excuse me," and

went to read the paper.

The next day was Saturday, and in the afternoon Mr. Orlon went uptown to pick the lumber. He was so outraged by the prices that he very nearly decided to cut his own, but something of Sarah's sensibleness saved him.

"That's much too high," said Mr. Orlon, fingering the boards, "to pay just for a picket fence."

"All wood's high these days," shrugged the man. "It's good lumber."

"I know it," said Mr. Orlon shortly, who had never bought lumber in his life before. He tapped a board thoughtfully with his forefinger, having some idea that you tested its greenness as if it were a watermelon. He added, "Lumber's 78 per cent higher than it was in 1939."

The man squinted. "How's that?"

"Nothing," said Mr. Orlon. "Give me enough to make a picket fence."

"How big of a fence?"

Mr. Orlon was startled. He had not realized how exact a science this could be. He looked at the man in annoyance. "I'll let you know," he said.

In the end it was Rachel who went back and ordered the lumber after Mr. Orlon measured how many feet of yard he was going to fence. There was nothing to use for this but an old tape measure belonging to Sarah, and crawling around at three-foot intervals was a long process.

"You're getting it dirty." Sarah kept coming to the front porch to watch the measuring operation.

"Yes," snorted Mr. Orlon. It didn't seem to him that hers was an observation worthy of his notice.

They bought white paint too, and the fence was due to be started the following Saturday afternoon.

"I still don't see what it's for," Sue said.

Rachel silenced her. "To keep the grass in the yard," she said. Mr. Orlon grew even fonder of his oldest daughter.

During the week, Mr. Orlon was cheered daily by the prospect of his yard being surrounded by a trim white picket fence. Maybe Sarah could plant blue morning-glories; they said morning-glories would grow anywhere.

He couldn't resist mentioning it at the mill, and the men immediately accepted it as his right and privilege, just as in an older age they would have accepted without question the chieftain's having a more durable tent. It was inevitable that news of Mr. Orlon's venture should eventually get around to that half-wit Charlie Kyles, and on Thursday afternoon, Mr. Orlon saw him coming. One of the workers was tiptoeing along behind him, imitating the mincing movements of Kyles' plump buttocks, but Kyles never looked behind him and probably wouldn't have believed it if he had. He was sure all the men adored him.

Mr. Orlon switched off his machine with an air of patient resignation. "Yeah?" he said.

Kyles was jovial, "Hear you're planning some building over at your place." Mr. Orlon, his face expressionless, looked at him and waited. "Gonna put up a fence, I hear."

Still Mr. Orlon waited. These preliminaries he brushed aside without interest. He believed in a man saying what he had come to say, and then moving on.

"Well, I wish you wouldn't do that, Henry," said Charlie Kyles finally, putting on his best one-man-to-another expression.

Mr. Orlon winced at the first name. "How come?" he said.

"Well, you know how we feel about changing anything on the outside of the mill houses. Leads to competition that all the workers can't afford. Makes the men unhappy, you know."

Mr. Orlon watched him.

"Now I let you paper the hall, didn't I? I mean, the inside—now that's your business." He dropped a friendly hand on Mr. Orlon's shoulder and Mr. Orlon looked down his nose at it as if it were an open sore.

"Afraid we're going to have to ask you not to build that fence, Henry. You understand...."

"That all?" said Mr. Orlon.

"Why ... why I guess so. I just wanted you to understand how it was...."

"Well, I'm getting behind then," said Mr. Orlon, and the machine came back to life noisily. Kyles blinked a few times and then walked away, nodding affably to the other employees, none of whom responded.

Mr. Orlon was seething. He worked at a furious pace all day, and the other angry men who were friends of his did the same. Production climbed, but Charlie Kyles was uneasy. He hung around all afternoon until the shift changed, and was standing at the door when the men filed out.

"Gonna build that fence Saturday, Orlon?" one of the men called, as they were leaving.

Mr. Orlon squared his shoulders. "Sure am," he said firmly. He did not even look at Kyles.

On Friday, Rachel went to work in the women's section of the mill, in one of the sewing rooms. On Friday too, Charlie Kyles came through the mill with two of his relatives that nobody had seen in years and handed Mr. Orlon a long blue piece of paper. It was the rent contract, and one of the paragraphs forbade exterior changes to the mill houses without special permission from the owners.

"You see that, don't you, Orlon?" said Kyles. He looked very angry. Mr. Orlon nodded quietly. The two old men with Kyles nodded their heads too, more vigorously. Looked like everybody's neck was loose, Mr. Orlon said later.

Just then Tod Clan walked up, not paying any attention to the three representatives of the Kyles family. "Just wanted to tell you me and my brother Sam'll be over to help with the building tomorrow." Tod and Sam were the tallest men in town.

"Fine," said Mr. Orlon. "Thank you."

Charlie Kyles had gotten red in the face and his plump lower lip had begun to tremble with rage. "Now see here, Orlon, you'll be violating the law if you put up that fence."

Mr. Orlon studied him thoughtfully.

"The way I figure it," he said quietly, "a man's got a *right* to a fence."

The three Kyles men walked away. Every line of their backs said that Henry Orlon was no longer a man to be tolerated, patronized; he had become a quiet

kind of menace. He must be fought. Charlie didn't even speak to any of the workers when he left.

It was probably just as well. By quitting time, nearly everyone on Millwood Street had cut himself in on the fence building.

Sarah didn't understand what all the fuss was about. "It ain't as if we needed a fence," she protested at supper that night.

Mr. Orlon tried to explain it to her. "It's just that we got a *right* to a fence," he said. "It's just that I can put up a fence if I want to be different from my neighbors."

"So who wants to?" argued Sarah. "Have the Blanes next door got a fence? Have the Parkers got a fence?"

Mr. Orlon tired to be patient. "They don't happen to *want* a fence," he explained seriously.

"But they're still gonna help us put up ours," put in Rachel.

Mr. Orlon smiled. "That's it. They're going to help us anyway. You see, Sarah?"

"No."

Mr. Orlon sighed. You just couldn't do much with a practical woman. They couldn't understand about things like fences.

That night a truck pulled up in front of Mr. Orlon's house, and it turned out to be the man from the lumberyard. He came up on the front porch and stood on one foot and then the other as if neither of them were his, he had just borrowed them for the evening and they didn't fit very well.

"Uh..." said the lumberman, "we're running kind of short up at the yard on material. Uh, thought you might sell that lumber back at a nice profit to yourself."

"Rachel," Mr. Orlon called sharply. When his oldest daughter appeared, he nodded toward the door. "You go set out on that lumber pile and keep an eye on it," and she glanced at the lumberman and went.

The man from the lumberyard came on into the house to discuss the business over a glass of beer, and Mr. Orlon found the price had gone up about one third over what he paid for it. He told the man all about the fence and about Charlie Kyles, and by the fifth glass of beer, they had both gotten very angry about it.

The lumberman ended up giving Mr. Orlon the check for the wood anyway. It was made out to cash and it had Charlie Kyles' signature on it.

"If I was you, I'd cash it pretty early in the morning," said the lumberman.

"And what're you going to tell Kyles?"

The man giggled. "Don't nobody but me look after small lumber. I'll say I bought it, just like he said, and dumped it back on the pile at the lumberyard. Guess you must of bought some more someplace else."

Mr. Orlon was so pleased that he wouldn't let the lumberman go home. They went out and sat on the lumber pile with Rachel, and the three of them sang all the verses of "The Battle Hymn of the Republic" several times.

The lumberman had a good tenor.

On Saturday afternoon, the fence went up. Half the mill was there to help, and it took shape as if it had been altogether prefabricated. Midway in the afternoon, the lumberman drove over with a barrel of apple cider, and Rachel let him kiss her.

All in all, it was a very gala affair. Once the three Kyles men drove by, just to see if it were true, but they didn't stop their shiny car anywhere on Millwood Street. They had evidently decided in the face of such unanimous support that it was better not to openly cross Henry Orlon.

"After all, this is better than some co-operative workers' union," said John Kyles hopefully. John was seventy-nine. Charlie just glared at him.

As it turned out, not even morning-glories would take root in the dusty Orlon front yard, but this didn't dim the glory of the fence. You could tell which was his house from blocks away. And strangely enough, not one of the other workers built a fence. It was like Mr. Orlon said, "Some folks want a fence, and some don't." Sarah never did. She said it took half her time putting down packages to unlatch the gate.

MEET THE AUTHOR:
Doris Betts (1932–   )

Doris Betts was only a sophomore at UNC-Greensboro when her first book, a collection of short stories, won a national prize and was published. Since then she has written eight books, and one of her short stories, "The Ugliest Pilgrim," was made into an Academy Award-winning short film, *Violet*.

Her success does not surprise those who

knew her as a child, already writing poems and stories in elementary school; or as a teenager, editing her high school paper and working for the *Statesville Record*; or as a college student, working on both newspaper and literary magazine staffs while holding a part-time job and taking a full load of courses. After college, she continued a very active life as wife, mother of three, and newspaper staff member—and writer of fiction that has won several major awards, including the North Carolina Award for Literature.

While continuing to develop as a writer, Doris Betts has also managed to develop a second successful career as a faculty member at UNC-Chapel Hill. A beloved teacher, she was the first woman to be named Alumni Distinguished Professor of English, and the first woman to chair the faculty senate.

Reflecting

1. This story was published thirty-five years ago. Conduct some research, either through books or through interviews with people in the textile industry to find out what has changed or not changed concerning the following:
   a. mill housing (Do workers still rent homes built and maintained by mills?)
   b. the coming of unions to textile mills
   c. radios (either private or company owned) used in factories
   d. the hiring of sixteen-year-old workers in the mills.
2. We are told that Henry Orlon is "a hero . . . a man among men." His distinction comes from the way he handles other people. Notice how he deals with
   a. Sarah, his wife
   b. Charlie Kyles (about the radio and about the fence)
   c. the lumberman
3. Suppose someone were going to Henry Orlon's town and wanted to meet him. What could you tell him about Orlon—aside from the fact that he has the only fenced-in yard on Millwood Street—that would help the visitor pick out Henry Orlon from the other mill workers? (What "marks of distinction" can you find in his personality and behavior?)

Sharecropper

Stewart Atkins

This was his life—overalls, cotton, sweat,
Long hours of gossip at the village store,
Hours of picking cotton, hunger, debt.
This was his life. There wasn't any more.
He never knew—Civilization, note!—
That there was any more to life than this.
Life's singing early died within his throat.
He spent his days in poverty's abyss.
He's buried in the blue serge Sunday suit
He wore to church to hear the preacher say
That wanting things he couldn't have was root
Of evil for which God would make him pay.
He's buried with no smile upon his face.
His sons? they're picking cotton in his place.

From *The Halting Gods*, by Stewart Atkins, published by Banner Press. Copyright © 1952 by Stewart Atkins. Reprinted by permission of Claire Atkins Pittman.

Preview

For most of our history North Carolina was a rural state. Before modern machinery, human beings provided most of the labor on farms—and even a relatively small farm required more labor than a single family could provide. The farmer might therefore rent out part of his or her farm "on shares." The "sharecropper" would work the land and pay rent by returning to the farm owner a large percentage of the crop.

In the poem below, the speaker is attending a sharecropper's funeral. Through his eyes we get a picture of what the dead man's life was like.

(Hint: This is a **sonnet**—a fourteen-line rhymed poem. In a sonnet, the final two lines, called a **couplet**, often act as a "clincher" to sum up the poem. Pay special attention to those lines.)

MEET THE AUTHOR:
Stewart Atkins (1913–1961)
See p. 370

Language Alert

abyss: a bottomless, chaotic pit
serge: a strong, serviceable, but respectable material used frequently for men's dress clothing; not as elegant as linen, silk, or flannel

"root of evil": A biblical saying states that "the love of money is the root of all evil."

Reflecting

This poem gives us a great deal of information:
1. Details about the sharecropper's everyday life.
2. Explanations about why he remained a sharecropper.
3. Evidence of how he himself felt about his life.
4. Information about his family. (Many poor people have worked hard all their lives so that their children will lead better lives. What is the outlook for the children here?)

Using every bit of information you can glean from the poem, first give the sharecropper a name and then write the following:

You are the dead man's neighbor; you liked him a great deal. You are writing a letter to a friend in another state, one who does not know the dead man, nor does he/she know much about the sharecropping system. In your letter, explain your reaction to your neighbor's death—and, even more important, to his life.

Penny Show

Reynolds Price

Preview

Sometimes experiences that seem trivial when they occur leave lingering and important effects. In the following account, Reynolds Price remembers just such an incident from his childhood, and he examines its impact on his life.

Though I've lived in the country continuously for twenty-four of my adult years, I'm thought of by my friends as the Great Indoorsman—one who loves nature from behind glass most of the time, the ideas and images of nature more than its touch and smell. As a child, however, I was different and better. We only lived in close contact with a relatively wild environment for some two years, when I was age six to eight; but in that time, wandering without brothers or sisters or regular playmates, I was lured quickly into an intense harmony with our suburban woods, creeks, and small animals. It was a harmony amounting to mystical union with the vital[1] intelligence I suspected in nature; and while I knew nothing of Words-

worth then, I later found in his poems numerous close parallels to my own early raptures and faiths—a conviction that the inhuman world took benevolent[2] cognizance[3] of me in what seemed to be silence but was surely a secret code, decipherable[4] with patience (one of my methods was to plunge my hunting knife into live wood, then to bite the thrilling[5]

1. vital, vitality: essential, having to do with life

2. benevolent: good, kind, humane

3. cognizance: recognition, understanding, awareness

4. decipherable: can be solved or decoded

5. thrilling: exciting, vibrating, quivering

blade and feel the tree's message).

The great majority of these moments were solitary; and perhaps of necessity, they did not long survive puberty. The flood of physical maturation tears a child's attention from its old objects—and deposits it forever on other human beings, freshly magnetized poles of inexplicable[6] love. Seldom thereafter can many adults, barring saints or lunatics, plumb[7] the deep blissful well of singularity.[8] All the stranger then that one of my own clearest, most resonant, and most refreshing memories of such a moment involves two other people—my mother and (near-sister) Marcia Drake.

My cousin Marcia and I were seven or eight, which means that my mother was in her mid-thirties. Someone in her family had died. Maybe it was Uncle Brother, one of her father's two bachelor brothers who'd survived into his eighties (stone-deaf, asthmatic, but neat as a bridegroom) in the back bedroom of the Rodwell home in Macon, North Carolina. In any case, Rodwells, Drakes, Rowans, and Prices were gathered for a funeral in comfortable weather. The memory of flowers is strong—banks of cut flowers in the big dining-room, traditional pausing place for family coffins—and contagious tears from my mother's old sisters and my mother herself (my own continuing lachrymosity[9] is almost certainly the result of a Rodwell gene). Marcia and I caught the prevalent tone of lament and were soon disconsolate,[10] demanding some sign that the day's heavy air would break and not last the rest of our lives.

My mother took the challenge and, not changing her funeral dress, led us outside. The house in those days stood on two-foot brick posts, no underpinning; and the visible dirt expanse beneath was a warehouse of disused implements patiently awaiting new purpose. By one post were jagged panes of glass, removed from windows but never quite discarded. Mother crouched and found a piece the size of a platter. Then she found an old garden-trowel and led us far forward in the shady front yard. One of the big oaks near the road had a bowl-shaped arrangement of roots above ground. Mother crouched again there, laid her glass down gently, and (with us watching speechless) began to dig a small basin in the earth in the oakroot harbor. When she had its boundaries clearly sketched, she stood, brushed her hands, and passed me the trowel—"You and Marcia dig it deeper. I'll be back soon."

The funeral air still kept us silent—no complaints or questions. We dug on in peaceful turns, unsure of the depth prescribed for this mystery, and were working when Mother returned with her hands full of flowers. At the time, we didn't ask where she'd got them; now I

6. inexplicable: mysterious, cannot be explained

7. plumb: to determine the depth of something

8. singularity: the quality of being distinctive, something uncommon

9. lachrymosity: tendency to weep

10. disconsolate: heartbroken, cannot be consoled or comforted

see they must have been discreetly[11] removed from memorial sprays. Yet my memory of their color is mostly purple (purple flowers at a funeral? what could they have been?). She approved our dig, then bent and slowly arranged her flowers in a nest on its floor. Then she told us to turn our backs for a minute.

When she called us to look, she had risen and was standing by the site of our dig—vanished now. Still neither of us questioned her. "Ask me what happened," she finally said.

So Marcia asked her (maybe I was prevented; isn't "What happened?" the primal[12] unaskable child-parent question?).

Silent, Mother bent and with a clean hand swept at what had seemed firm-packed dirt. It slid back easily and showed her secret; she beckoned us toward it. The pane of glass, only lightly dusted, was a window again. What it showed was flowers under the ground, a garden buried under the earth. Mother covered it again. "It's a penny show," she said. "When people pay a penny, brush back the dirt and show it."

We had a few cents, and were happier, by the end of the day.

Only now, more than forty years later, have I asked any questions of the memory. In a recent random search, I could find no other friend or acquaintance who'd heard of a show like my mother's. For all her surging vitality, she was not unusually inventive or handy. Was the idea of small subterranean gardens a family invention, passed down to her? Or had her own pronounced periodic melancholia[13] responded so strongly to an old man's death, and her own son's distress, as to give her this tangible poetic invention?— a brief consolation, to be shared with others for a nominal[14] fee: the reward of your inventiveness.

Whatever, she'd quietly given me one of her largest gifts. An adult I trusted had confirmed my suspicion—from that day, a conviction—that the ground itself, the earth and its products, was inhabited in hidden ways. That many of the ways were hurtful, I'd known from the start; any infant knows danger. What she'd shown me, at the edge of a family death, was the fact of veiled beauty, discoverable by hand and of some small profit. It's by no means the least of the thanks I owe her.

11. discreetly: carefully, cautiously

12. primal: early, primitive, original

13. melancholia: depression, gloom

14. nominal: existing in name only, not real

Reynolds Price (1933–)

Few contemporary authors in North Carolina, or in the nation, for that matter, have been so highly regarded as Reynolds Price. His first novel, *A Long and Happy Life,* published in 1962 when he was only twenty-nine years old, won instant national attention. From then until the present, he has been considered one of the most talented writers of our time, noted especially for his lyrical language which weaves an almost hypnotic spell on the reader.

Born in Macon, in Warren County, Reynolds Price very early demonstrated a love for reading and talent in three arts: music, writing, and art. Writing teachers at Broughton High School in Raleigh and at Duke University immediately spotted his writing ability and encouraged him to develop it. While a senior at Duke, he won a Rhodes Scholarship to study at Oxford University in England. He stayed there for three years, then returned to Duke. There he completed his first novel, which immediately gained him notice as an unusually gifted and promising writer. Since 1962, except for travels abroad, he has taught at Duke, where he is a popular and admired professor.

Reynolds Price has been a very productive writer; by 1989 he had seven novels, several plays, two volumes of poetry, two of short stories, one of essays, and one of memoirs to his credit. He has also won many state and national awards (including, of course, the North Carolina Award for Literature), and in 1988 he was inducted into the American Academy of Arts and Letters.

Reflecting

1. Looking back, Reynolds Price finds it surprising that his mother set up this "penny show." Reread the next-to-last paragraph to find out why he considers this behavior unlike her.
2. The "penny show" helped two confused children—Reynolds and his cousin Marcia—deal with the sadness at the funeral gathering. But the last paragraph of this memoir shows us that it also had a long-lasting effect on Reynolds Price. Explain what it has meant to him. (Hint: Remember that he has become a noted writer.)

The Maker of One Coffin

Fred Chappell

Preview

Most of us know someone—perhaps a relative or a family friend—whom we would call weird or eccentric. (Notice how the word *eccentric* resembles the word *center*. Actually the two are derived from the same root, and eccentric literally means "off-center." It has come to refer to someone whose behavior or personality is so strikingly different from the rest of the group that he/she seems set apart.)

In Fred Chappell's novel *I Am One of You Forever,* Jess, the young narrator describes a number of eccentric uncles who visit his household. None is more of an oddball than Uncle Runkin.

Get ready to meet a very interesting man who carries some decidedly strange baggage with him wherever he goes. (You'll find out about that in the first sentence.) This man's attention seems fixed permanently on one thing—it won't take you long to discover what.

Fred Chappell occasionally allows fantasy to enter what has heretofore been a realistic story. Watch for any details that seem to come from Jess's imagination more than from his memory. Watch, too, for the humor: some derives from the situation, some from Jess's father's wry comments.

When Uncle Runkin came to visit he brought his coffin and slept in it, laying it across a couple of sawhorses we carried into the upstairs bedroom. But I could never imagine him sleeping. If I crept in at midnight, wouldn't I find him with his bony hands crossed on his chest and his weird eyes staring, staring into the dark? I didn't care to find out; I was frightened of him, and maybe my father was too at first, though he'd never let on. He treated Uncle Runkin lightly, loosely, banteringly, but surely he was bemused by our odd visitor who must have spent the majority of his years preparing to lie forever in his cold grave.

We often hosted wandering aunts and uncles, all on my mother's side, and they intrigued my father endlessly and he was always glad when one of them showed up to break the monotony of a mountain farm life. Especially glad for Uncle Runkin; he had a reputation which preceded him as twilight precedes darkness, and we were not to be disappointed.

He was slight, about five foot eight, and frail looking because he carried no fat and not much muscle. "All skin and bones"; Uncle Runkin was the only person I ever met who fit the description. The bones in his hands and head were starkly prominent beneath parchment-colored skin as tight on him as a surgeon's glove. His head was entirely hairless, and not pink but yellowish. His beaky nose drooped sharply. His eyes were black as coffee grounds and large and sunken in his skull and surrounded by large circles as dark as the great pupils. These eyes looked quite past you, and Uncle Runkin made you feel he saw you without looking; and that was another unsettling sensation.

His motions were grave and deliberate and I never saw him smile. His skin was dry as wood shavings and when he touched any surface there was a slight raspy whisper, like a rat stirring in a leaf pile. Or like a copperhead snake skinning over the edge of a table. Or like a black silk pall sliding off a coffin. I never got used to it; each time I heard it was like looking down into a bottomless well.

I never got used to anything about Uncle Runkin. It wasn't that he tried to discomfit[1] us; I think indeed that he tried not to. But whenever I was in his presence I felt like I was standing with my back to a cliff and couldn't remember where the edge was.

The same uneasiness affected my father, but he hid it pretty well. He teased Uncle Runkin and joked, but it was easier to be sociable with the midnight wind. His jollity went out into the void and no laughter returned. And we were not certain we wanted to hear the kind of laughter that might return; it wouldn't be what you call comradely.

Still my father kept on, gibing[2] and bantering ever more recklessly, his gestures growing ever more strained and awkward. Waving his hands about at the supper table, he tipped over the salt shaker.

Uncle Runkin gave the spilled salt a solemn glance and uttered his most characteristic sentence. "That means that somebody is going to die."

"What? Spilling the salt?" my father said. His desperation was obvious now; he snatched up the shaker and began sprinkling salt all over the green tablecloth. "Fine and dandy," he said. "We'll do away with the whole German army."

"It never is somebody you'd want to die," Uncle Runkin said.

My father gave him a wild look. "Well

1. discomfit: to make uncomfortable

2. gibing: taunting, mocking

478

then, who? Who's going to kick the bucket?"

But he didn't answer; his voice box had silted up again with crematory ashes.

Uncle Runkin found lots of signs for coming death. A black cat crossing in front of you, the new moon seen over your left shoulder, a flock of crows taking flight on your left-hand side, one crow flying against the full moon, sunset reflected in a window of a deserted house, an owl hooting just at dark, a ladder leaning oddly in a corner, the timbers of our old house creaking at night: he knew all these as indications that somebody was going to die, and the way he said *somebody* made you want to reconsider your plans for airplane trips and bear hunts.

My father scoffed. "It would take Noah's flood and the Black Plague to carry off as many victims as he's seen signs for." But I could hear in his voice a shaky bravado.

Uncle Runkin's silly prognostications[3] affected us all, but me—eleven years old—most. I found myself calculating where the new moon was in relation to my left shoulder, and I wouldn't look at the full moon because who knows when the crows might fly? And I began to operate mighty gingerly with the salt shaker. . . . He affected us in other ways as well. I'd never remembered my dreams before, but after Uncle Runkin arrived I couldn't forget them, much as I wanted to.

I thought he would say No, but when I asked to look at his coffin he seemed pleased I was interested. Coffin or no, it was an impressive piece of handiwork, though a monstrous huge thing, as we'd discovered in wrestling it up the stairs. Eight feet long and four feet wide, it was much too large for Uncle Runkin, and he must have lain lonesome in it like a single pearl in a jewel case. The corners were so tightly mitered[4] and joined that I could hardly find the seams with my fingertip. The wood, he told me proudly, came from an enormous black walnut, and the bottom and sides of the coffin were cut from whole slabs. There was a triple molding as elegant as ever you could see at the base of the coffin, and an elaborate cornice at the top with a crisp dentate design. The lid was to be attached with no fewer than eight brass butterfly hinges, and he looked forward to its completion.

It wasn't complete because the lid wasn't finished. Handsome as the box was, it wasn't a patch on what the lid was going to be. The unfinished lid sat on the long worktable out in our woodshed, covered with two blankets of heavy green felt and the weathered old tarpaulin he secured the coffin in when he hauled it in his open pickup truck.

He peeled the wrappings back so I could have a look at his hand carving. Along the edges ran a garland of grape and apples, rose and lilies, intricately intertwined and delicately incised, down to the leaf veins. In the center was a largish death's-head, and it was interesting how much this skull resembled a self-portrait,

3. prognostications: predictions

4. mitered: fitted (A miter joint is made of two pieces whose joined ends are at equal angles, such as the corner of a picture frame.)

only having an ominous hole where he had a beaky nose. Otherwise it was Uncle Runkin to the life. Or death. There was a blank entablature below on which he was going to engrave a motto, as soon as he could decide whether it was to be *Come lovely Angel* or *Sweet Death comes to Soothe* or *How glorious our Final Rest*. Or a phrase that destiny hadn't yet thrown in his way. He was still searching out mottoes. Beneath the blank he'd carved what he called a sleeping lamb, which looked to me like it would dream no more forever. Not quite completed, though the great work had taken him twenty-five years so far. The lid alone cost him seven years, but easy to see it was going to be worth it, rubbed and oiled and varnished and polished until it was as smooth as the inside of an eggshell and dark and satiny.

My father suggested that the motto ought to be *Death, where you been all my life?* But he too admired the coffin and complimented Uncle Runkin. Later he changed his motto suggestion to *Opus 1*[5] because, he said, making that coffin was the sole lick of work the old man had ever struck.

We talked about Uncle Runkin sleeping in his coffin, and we tried to imagine what that would be like. I thought it would be scary but exciting, and I didn't think it would be stuffy in there, but as cool and dark as eternity. I imagined that after you got accustomed to it, you would have peaceful winter dreams and hear voices from beyond the grave.

"What do you think the dead folks are saying?" my father asked.

"I don't know," I said. "I can't imagine that part. What do you think they're saying?"

"I don't know," he said. "But every time I imagine lying in the grave my rear end starts to itch."

I wanted to try it. I wanted to sneak into Uncle Runkin's room some hour when he was away and lie down in the coffin and see what I thought about it.

"I wouldn't do it," my father said. "I'm no great believer in signs, but there can't be much good luck in lying around in coffins all the time. I don't much look forward to death myself; it's like knowing you have to go to the dentist."

"I don't think it's like that. I think it would be real quiet." (I made noise in the company of dentists.)

"Well, if quiet is what you desire, you're going to have a riproaring time after you're gone. The graveyard eats up noise like Uncle Runkin eats his supper."

I knew what he meant. Uncle Runkin cleaned his plate so thoroughly that it was surprising to see the design still on it, the little blue Chinese bridge with the lumpy tree and long necked bird. Everything was gone, including the chicken bones, and not even a smear of grease remained. But I never saw him eat, never use a knife or fork or spoon. The plate would be steaming full before him and then the first time I noticed, it would be spotless, and Uncle Runkin wouldn't be chewing but looking at me, or rather beyond me,

---

5. Opus 1: *opus* means "a work" (A composer often uses the term *opus* to indicate the number of his/her composition, i.e., Opus 3, Opus 24, etc.)

with unearthly speculation.[6]

"I know what we can do," my father said. "We can steal that coffin."

"What in the world for?"

"Don't you have any curiosity? I'd just like to see what the old man would do when he couldn't find it."

I had mixed feelings about the idea. It was all right to look at the coffin and even to touch it, but when I thought about stealing it, it took a different shape in my mind. Became bigger and blacker and heavier and deeper. I felt we would be tampering with dark forces we knew nothing about, distressing some of the bones of the universe. "I'm not so sure," I said.

"Why not?"

"Too heavy," I said. "The three of us like to never wallered it up the stairs. Two of us wouldn't get it to budge an inch."

"I guess you're right," he said. "I'll think of something, though."

"Maybe you oughtn't to. Maybe Uncle Runkin is one uncle we ought to leave plumb[7] alone."

"Yeah?" He gave me an amused look. "That old man hasn't got you buffaloed,[8] has he, Jess?"

"He's a different kind of uncle from what we're used to."

"Don't worry," he said. "I just now figured out what we'll do." But when he chuckled softly, I had to feel uneasy.

I don't know what supernatural spell my father was able to exercise over my mother. It had to be one of nearly unthinkable power for her to aid him. Probably there was nothing more sinister about it than the fact that she too had a sense of mischief, usually dormant, which he was able to arouse on urgent and suitable occasions.

And this occasion was, for my father, an urgent one. The family had undergone gradual but significant changes since Uncle Runkin came. There was less casual talk, less casual touching, and less laughter. We were not absorbed in gloom, all day thinking morose[9] thoughts, but we had surely darkened and a quiet seriousness began to prevail over us.

It was just the sort of atmosphere my father couldn't abide, and he may well have felt that he was struggling for psychic survival.

Whatever means he used, they were successful. My mother brought home one Friday afternoon the skeleton from the health classroom at her high school. I know she didn't steal it; she wouldn't stray so far from the straight and narrow. Probably she just asked to borrow it for the weekend. "I don't know why," she would say. "My husband imagines he's got some use for it."

So we had a skeleton, and a lovely object it was too, properly wired together, all white and smooth, and its teeth intact. I was curious about where the high school

6. speculation: serious consideration or reflection upon some subject

7. plumb: completely, absolutely (This is an informal, or colloquial, usage.)

8. buffaloed: intimidated

9. morose: gloomy, melancholy

believe that story in a jiffy. And you know what he'd say?"

"He'd say, *In the midst of life we are in death.*"

"That's it exactly," my father said.

He had no very elaborate plans for the skeleton. He was merely going to lay it out in the coffin where Uncle Runkin slept. "That ought to give him something to think about." Then, as an afterthought, he decided to remove from the fuse box the fuse which controlled the upstairs bedroom lights so that Uncle Runkin would have to clump up in the dark to meet his unannounced bedfellow. "I'll tell him something's wrong with the wiring on that side, but that I'm working to fix it. Meanwhile, take every candle in the house and hide them."

This was one of my father's less complicated ruses, and the details were easily arranged. We ate our Saturday night supper in what had become our habitual bemused silence, and Uncle Runkin practiced his usual legerdemain,[10] disappearing every scrap and nitlet of food from his plate. He took his whispery-silent leave of us to go up to his room. My father had already lied about the wiring, and we made an ostentatious[11] search for the candles that I'd stuck away in a feed bin in the barn.

We couldn't hear our uncle, but we sat at the table without talking and felt his progress through the house on our skins.

had got hold of it, and my father said it was a former fullback on the Black Bears who had run the wrong way in a game and scored a safety for the Hiawasee Catamounts. "Huh," I said. He then told me it was a woman's skeleton, an axe murderess who had chopped up her mother-in-law, her husband, her eleven children, and the family poodle and then, realizing what she'd done, turned the axe on herself and committed suicide.

"I don't believe that one, either," I said.

"That's the difference between us and Uncle Runkin," my father said. "He would

10. legerdemain: trickery, such as hocus-pocus, sleight of hand

11. ostentatious: showy, intending to attract notice

We knew when he opened the hallway door upon darkness and went touching his way down the hall. We knew when he mounted the first step of the stairs and grasped the banister in his dry hand. We could feel every step upward he took and the pause he made at the top in order to get his bearings in pitch darkness. We felt how he inched down the upstairs hall and opened the door to his room and slid in the dark over to the edge of the coffin and began to disrobe.

But after that we knew nothing. Our heightened senses and imaginations failed us at this critical point, and we couldn't say what would happen, but sat hushed, waiting.

We sat a long time in silence. We looked at one another. I don't know what we expected from Uncle Runkin, a bloodcurdling scream, or a crash and shouted curses, or maybe the sight of the old man fleeing naked and bony-shanked out into the October night. Now it seems unlikely that we would have been treated to any of these edifying spectacles; the old man's attachment to the Black Deliverer was more profound than we could fathom, and there was nothing about death that was going to surprise him.

We sat a long time.

Finally my mother said, "Well, Joe Robert, this is one of your little pranks that didn't work out."

He sighed. "I didn't care what. As long as *something* happened, I would have felt better."

"And after all the trouble I went to to get that pile of bones," she said. "You boys go right up to his room in the morning and get that skeleton. I'll be in hot water if I don't get it back to school first thing Monday."

"Yes ma'am," my father said. His voice rang hollow with defeat.

Next morning Uncle Runkin came down to breakfast, all polished and ready for church. He'd tracked down some minor sect of strange Baptists yon side of Turkey Knob, with a preacher who gave sermons on the utter and awful and final power of death over life, and this little cinder block church drew Uncle Runkin the way a rosebush draws Japanese beetles.

During breakfast my father made a couple of feeble attempts. "Did you sleep sound last night, Uncle Runkin?"

He answered Yes in that voice that was like a breath of dying desert wind.

"No trouble with bedbugs—or anything like that?"

He told us No in that same sepulchral[12] voice and my father bent to his plate and took a mouthful of gloomy eggs.

After Uncle Runkin departed for church, my father pushed his chair back from the table and said, "Well, Jess, let's go up and rescue our skeleton." He looked as cheerless as a bloodhound.

Then it got worse because the skeleton was not there in the coffin. Nor anywhere else in the room. Nor in any other upstairs room, not in the bedroom, nor in the storage room. And in no downstairs room. We searched and searched again every nook and corner of every room of

---

12. sepulchral: pertaining to the grave (sepulcher)

the house, and there was no trace of it, not the least little finger bone.

"What in the world could he have done with it?" my father asked.

"I don't know," I said.

He looked at me with a glazed expression. "Look here, Jess, you don't think he ate it, do you?"

"I don't think so," I said, but I had to remember all the squirrel and rabbit and chicken and pork chop bones that were never left on Uncle Runkin's plate.

"I believe he did. I believe the old man ate that skeleton."

"Is that what you're going to tell Mama? So she can tell them at the high school that our uncle ate the skeleton from the health class?"

"I purely don't know," he said.

That was what she asked when she heard. "What am I going to tell them at the high school?"

"I think you'd better lie to them," my father said.

"Lie?" she wailed. "I can't lie to them. I don't know how."

"Nothing to it," he said. "We'll stay up late tonight and I'll teach you."

That afternoon Uncle Runkin made me go with him to look at a graveyard he had discovered. It was an old one, disused and grown up in weeds and sawbriars. Thick mosses and peeling lichen flooded the stones and some of the markers were just thin slabs of shale with the names and rude designs etched in with farm tools, cold chisels and axe bits and the like.

"What did we come here to see?" I asked.

He looked at me in surprise. "Why—everything," he said, and he swept the air to indicate the universe that interested him, the graves and weeds and briars and, I suppose, the grubs and worms munching away underground. "Don't you feel at peace here? Ain't it a shame people have let this beautiful spot go to ruin? Wouldn't this be an awful nice place if you wanted to build a house close by?"

Maybe it was beautiful, but for me it was a graveyard, and I wasn't ready to invest in that brand of real estate. Chill bumps rose on my forearms. "I don't know," I said.

"Let's go around and look at some of the stones," he said, and his voice was dreamy and intimate.

So that's what we did, with Uncle Runkin pausing before each hacked stone in rapt contemplation. He would stare at the stone, read off the inscription silently, stare at it some more, and then wag his head solemnly and pace up the hill to the next. He clasped his hands behind his back like a philosopher.

I wandered with him, feeling bored and dreary.

"Keep an eye out for any good motto I might could put on my coffin lid," he said.

"Well, how about this one here? *Gone but not forgotten.*"

"Look at the name on it," he said. "*Rodney Walsh.* You ever hear of Rodney Walsh?"

"No," I said, "but they buried him in 1910."

"You know any Walshes in this county?"

"No."

"Well, see, he's gone all right, but he's

plumb forgotten too. You see that motto a lot, but it just ain't going to do. People don't remember you after you're dead. That's why you have to do it all yourself beforehand."

"How about this one?" I asked. "*She done what she could.*"

"Well, but don't that make it clear she done a right piddling job?"

"Here's one. A *brighter day awaits.*"

He snorted. "What they mean by that? Next Thursday?"

We meandered on among the markers, and each time I would read off the writing he would be right there with a telling critique. I finally had to admire his expertise; he'd pondered on it until he was a connoisseur. And I admired the way he never got depressed by it; in fact, the more gravestones we looked at, the mournfuller the inscriptions became, the better he liked it; and if it was anybody but Uncle Runkin I would have said he was bright and cheerful.

"*Gone to a better place,*" I read.

"How do they know that?" he said. "I bet this William Jennings done a whole lot of meanousness they just never heard about."

"*Grave, where is thy victory?*"

"Suppose this here where we're standing is the battlefield where death and the living had a fight. Who would you say won?"

"*Gone to lighten the dark.*"

"Now that one might have possibilities," he said. "I'll be thinking about that one." He took a little notebook and carpenter's pencil out of his overalls bib and wrote it down. I thought he must have a hefty backlog of that kind of writing by now, and I was pretty sure it was his favorite reading matter, along with Job and the obituary page and the Lamentations of Jeremiah.

The motto he took the brightest shine to was, *In Life's full Prime Is Death's own Time*; he was positively gleeful when we struck on it and wrote it down and underscored it twice. "There's a lot of wisdom on these stones, if people would just take the opportunity," he said, and he was happy enough to be willing to leave for home, which didn't exactly break my heart.

At home he headed directly into the small room off the kitchen hallway where the coal stove and radio were. There was a radio program on Sunday afternoons called "Meditations" that he never missed. It was all slow organ music playing behind a fellow who read passages out of a book of dejected thoughts and it was just the thing to brace Uncle Runkin up.

I went upstairs, hoping against hope that I might locate the lost skeleton, though I knew my father had searched the place over again while Uncle Runkin and I were out. I went into his room and poked about quietly, but found no trace of Mr. Bones. I was attracted at this moment by his imposing coffin there on the sawhorses and went over to it and laid my cheek against its smooth side to enjoy the cool and polish of the wood. I pulled up a chair and looked over into it, and now it seemed inviting, sweet, and peaceful. I'd never been much interested in coffins before, but prolonged exposure to Uncle Runkin had begun to change my outlook, and I thought it might not be such a bad thing to be dead, not having to get up on frosty mornings to milk crazy old cows, not having to learn multiplication or the capital of North Dakota, not having to eat cold fried grits when my grandmother felt trifling.

I tugged off my high-topped shoes and stepped over into the coffin and lay down. It was marvelous at first. The black satin plush was not cool, as I'd thought, but warm and soft; he'd cushioned it with cotton batting. The black plush sides rose up steep in my vision, giving me a view of the ceiling in a box, and the perspective caused me to feel I was sinking down and down, that the world outside was receding. I waited for the sensation to pass but it never did; the ceiling, the room, the house, the farm, the sky kept pulling back from my sight, floating away to some unreachable forever. And I began to think of the coffin as being like the bathysphere[13] of William Beebe, except that the coffin sank not through water but through solid substance, would drop through the floor of the room, down through the foundations of the house, and dive into the earth; and I would be able to look upon creatures never seen or imagined before, animals made of glowing mineral that swam the veins of the world and traced their mysterious lives to mysterious destinies.

Then I fell asleep.

As soon as my eyes closed I was assaulted by a barrage of fleeting dream images. A sky full of stars arranged itself in an unreadable tombstone motto. A great silent galleon with black silk sails lifted off an ebony ocean and floated into the sky, straight into the full moon. A flock of crows flew through a snowstorm, then changed into a rain of blood and fell, staining the snowy ground scarlet. A sinister monk opened the orange-lit door in a mountain and stepped out; he was dressed in a loose black robe and made arcane gestures with his bony hands, causing a spiky crop of skeletons to rise out of the ground and giggle.

But none of these visions was frightening; they were comforting, and I began to know that death was the Meadow of Vision, where dream was wrested from the marrow of stars.

One vision, though, was not comforting but disturbing. That was the sight of Death himself. In my dream I was standing in a narrow doorway, which had no building to belong to, in the middle of a barren plain. Nothing was before or behind me but blank wind. His pinched, intense face appeared suddenly out of the air, his sunken eyes burning dementedly, and he recognized me there in my constricting doorway and reached out his paw of lightning and caressed my cheek. I jerked and quivered from the shock of his touch, and yelled an awful yell, a soul-shaking screech.

Death yelled too and leapt back away from me, and it was obvious that he also had been frightened. Death and I had met face to face and scared the pee out of each other. And then it was obvious that I wasn't asleep and dreaming of Death and

13. bathysphere: a spherical chamber in which men and women explore the depths of the sea

a doorway; instead, I was awake in Uncle Runkin's coffin and the old man, not expecting to find me there, had cried out in surprise. What he cried was *Yipes!*, just like Dagwood in the funny paper.

Yipes! That's the only time in my life I heard anyone say that word.

Then I heard Uncle Runkin rush out of the room and fly down the stairs. I sat up slowly, groggy from sleep and my harsh awakening, and took my time clambering out of the coffin and finding my shoes and putting them on in the dusk-dim room. From downstairs in the kitchen came the ruckus sound of heated conversation, and it was a sure thing that Uncle Runkin had not enjoyed finding me asleep in his coffin and was down there stirring up the family against me.

I sat in the straight chair and stared at the floor. I knew I was in for some kind of punishment, but I didn't care. I was dazed. After all, I had been out to visit the afterlife and had found it an entrancing place, and so a few licks with a hickory switch held no terror for me, and a month of Saturdays without cowboy movies not much disappointment. If death was as entertaining as it had been there in the promise of the coffin, I could always hang myself and have forever a free show that was better than any cowboy movie.

The noise downstairs went on and on, and I sat there and looked at my shoes until the noise stopped and I heard my father and Uncle Runkin coming up the stairs. When they entered the room my father switched on the light and all the strange thoughts that had been bemusing my mind flew away like a flock of birds at a gunshot.

"Jess," my father said, "Uncle Runkin has decided he can't stay with us any longer. He's got some pressing business in hand and needs to move on."

"That so?" I said, and I looked at Uncle Runkin but he wouldn't look back. He went over to his coffin and smoothed out the plush where I had been lying and inspected all over the wood for damage.

"Yes, he says he's afraid he'll have to be leaving," my father said. "So if you wouldn't mind giving us a hand with the coffin."

"Not at all," I said. "Be glad to."

It was much less a chore to get the coffin down the stairs and out of the house than it had been to get it upstairs. We slid it onto the truckbed and Uncle Runkin went to the shed and got the lid and placed it carefully over the box. We left him there, blanketing his treasure and roping it down tight. We went in and sat at the kitchen table, and my father poured coffee for himself and my mother.

In a few minutes the old man came in. My father stood up and they shook hands. Then he turned to my mother and offered her a slow, dry half-bow. He gave me one soulful burning glance and then stepped out and closed the door and was gone. Didn't utter a syllable. We heard the truck start up.

My father sat down and sipped the coffee. He blinked his eyes. "Whew," he said. "*A load off my mind.* I never knew what that sentence meant till right this minute."

My mother and I nodded. The old brick house felt lighter around our shoulders now that coffin was out of it.

"I have to admit I feel better too," she said.

My father yawned and stretched. "I don't know about you-all," he said, "but Uncle Runkin kind of took it out of me. I think I'll mosey on to bed, no matter how early it is."

That sounded good to me too, even though I'd already had a nice nap not so long ago. I went into my room and read a Hardy Boys for a while, then turned out the light. I was hoping that I would have more of those interesting dreams I'd had in the coffin. But I didn't. I slept lightly, peacefully, dreamlessly.

Until about six o'clock in the morning.

Then I was awakened abruptly again by the sound of someone yelling. This time it was a piercing shriek, a real true blood curdler, and it took a moment for me to realize that it was my mother who had screamed, out in the kitchen. I slipped into my pants and ran shoeless, shirtless, to the noise.

My father had just got there before me, rumpled and unbuttoned. "What in the world?" he asked.

She couldn't speak. She leaned white-faced against the doorway of the alcove and pointed a trembling finger.

There, sitting in the open icebox on a plate garnished with lettuce, was a skull. Two chrysanthemums glowed red in its eye sockets. A dead corn snake dangled out of its pearly teeth.

My mother cowered in my father's embrace. "I was just getting milk for our *oatmeal*," she said.

"I can see how it would give you a turn," he said. "I wonder what he did with the rest of it?"

We came to find out that Uncle Runkin had dismantled the skeleton and hid the pieces everywhere around the house. When you went looking for a Mason jar rubber or a length of string you would turn up a toe bone or a metacarpal. There are 206 bones in the adult human body and Uncle Runkin found 3,034 hiding places for them. Just the other day—twenty years afterward—I found in an old tackle box a kneecap. It brought back tender memories.

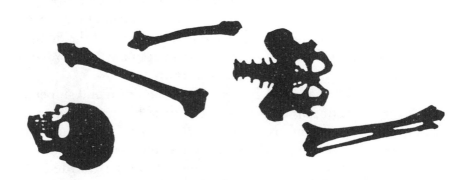

MEET THE AUTHOR:
Fred Chappell (1936–)
See p. 232

Reflecting

Do you feel as if you know Uncle Runkin now—that if he came struggling in, pulling his most prized possession behind him, you would recognize him immediately? From this one story, you can learn how he looks, what interests him, how he talks, what he has, and what he does. Fred Chappell gives us all this information, although he never once out-and-out declares, "Uncle Runkin was a _____ [fill in with an adjective] man." He just provides a host of details, and we add them up to discover what the man is like.

1. Choose six adjectives that you would use to describe Uncle Runkin. Then look back through the story and find details (description, action, dialogue) that support your choices. Share your choices with your classmates. Did you agree on what kind of person Uncle Runkin was?

2. Think of someone you would consider eccentric—someone whose behavior is so different as to set him/her apart from the remainder of the family or neighborhood. Jot down the details—actions, appearance, etc.—which make that person so different. What do those details tell us about the person's character?

The Oxford Philosopher

Choosing some from Thad Stem's many poems is like choosing a few pieces from a vast array of chocolates—all tantalizing, all different. The two below give us some idea of the variety of his work and the way his imagination worked.

MEET THE AUTHOR:
Thad Stem (1916–1980)

Peanut butter and jelly.
Romeo and Juliet.
Summer and baseball.
Thad Stem and Oxford.
Some things always seem to be paired—they appear to be incomplete if mentioned alone. Thad Stem, Jr., one of this state's most productive writers, is almost always paired with the town where he was born and where he spent almost all of his life.

Thad Stem left Oxford just long enough to earn a degree at Duke University, to write for newspapers in the North Carolina mountains and Florida, and to serve in the U.S. Army during World War II. Then he returned home to the same street on which he had been born, and settled into the life of a writer, publishing sixteen books and hundreds of editorials for the Raleigh *News and Observer*.

Stem was admired for his sharp wit, his lively imagination, and his ability to juggle words like a champion acrobat. People also remarked on his astoundingly broad knowledge: he could quote a wide variety of writers, refer to obscure historical events, and comment on scientific facts, all without hesi-

tation. His ability to draw meaning from these bits of knowledge won him a reputation as a local philosopher.

Thad Stem's poetry twice won the Roanoke-Chowan Award, and in 1974 he was honored with the North Carolina Award for Literature. His efforts to support and expand library services earned him an award from the National Trustees of Libraries.

Preview

In "Old Hup"—one of Stem's few rhymed poems—we meet the kind of person who used to be called a "ne'er-do-well." In the first two stanzas we see what a sad state he has come to. In the third, we get a glimpse of the man he used to be.

Old Hup

Thad Stem

Old Hup comes tottering down the street
Leaning on his cane;
He calls to mind a rusty tool
Left standing in the rain.

And all along the village square,
The lads all laugh to see
Old Hup going, God knows where,
On another spree.

I often wonder, my scarecrow friend,
If you recall the times
You picked my Ma wild roses
And courted her with rhymes?

Reflecting

1. In what way is Old Hup like "a rusty tool"?
2. Why is he now a "scarecrow friend"?

Preview

"December" uses a poetic device called **personification**—that is, something nonhuman is treated as if it were a human being. In this poem, December is an old man. Notice how many qualities of December are portrayed in the poem—always in connection with an old man.

December

Thad Stem

December rattled into town
With two white mules pulling an iron-gray wagon.
He clapped his bony hands together for warmth
So powerfully the church steeple cavorted around
As tantalizingly as a hoochy-koochy dancer.

Then he greased his wagon
And drove silently about our streets after dark
To confuse us by obliterating all our landmarks
With a host of goose feathers his gnarled wife
Spent many a long, lonesome night plucking.

Reflecting

What elements of winter are being represented by:
1. The two white mules pulling an iron-gray wagon?
2. The clapping of bony hands?
3. The host of goose feathers?

Language Alert

1. cavorted: pranced
2. tantalizingly: teasingly
3. hoochy-koochy dancer: dancer in a "girlie" show at a carnival or fair
4. obliterating: destroying without leaving a trace
5. gnarled: knotted, misshapen

From *The Jackknife Horse,* by Thad Stem, Jr., published by Wolf's Head Press. Copyright © 1954 by Thad Stem, Jr. Reprinted by permission of Marguerite Stem.

Edward R. Murrow

Charles Kuralt

Preview

The following selection is like a "two-for-the-price-of-one" bargain. In this speech, which Charles Kuralt presented at the annual banquet of the North Carolina Literary and Historical Association in 1971, you will learn how Charles Kuralt got started in journalism. You will also learn about Edward R. Murrow, whom North Carolinians are proud to claim as their own, even though he lived here only a short time during his childhood. (Murrow Boulevard in Greensboro is named for him.)

Like Kuralt, Edward R. Murrow worked for CBS News. He was already a well-known radio broadcaster when World War II began. His reports from London, always beginning "*This* (pause) is London," and often spoken against the thunder of dropping bombs, made him famous. After the war, he entered television. Some of his documentaries are still considered classic efforts at awakening people to social and political problems.

As you might imagine, the great and famous Edward R. Murrow became a model and mentor to young, ambitious Charles Kuralt.

I speak here of a man who, it seemed to me at the time I knew him, was the best man I had ever known. Nothing has happened since then to make me alter that judgment. Others, who knew him far better than I, shared that feeling. He was not the most courageous man I've ever known, nor the most honest, I suppose, nor the best writer—not by far—nor the best thinker . . . though courage and honor he had in full measure, and he was a fine thinker and writer. What lifted him above his fellows, I believe, was the one principle that seemed to light his life: the

Published in *North Carolina Historical Review,* Vol. XLVII, No. 2, April 1971.

search for truth, his belief that freedom *depended* on people willing to search for truth, his single-mindedness about that. That is the thing that elevated him and all who knew him. On his death, the unemotional Eric Severeid spoke on the air that shattering, emotional farewell of Shakespeare's:

 . . . Good night, sweet prince,
And flights of angels sing thee to thy rest!

And those who knew Edward R. Murrow felt that benediction appropriate.

You will pardon me if I speak personally at first. I was nine or ten, and I remember my parents listening to the radio, waiting for his broadcasts from London during the war. "This is London. Early this morning, we heard the bombers going out. It was the sound of a giant factory in the sky. . . . It seemed to shake the old gray stone buildings in this bruised and battered city beside the Thames. . . ." The radio was on all the time, but when Edward R. Murrow reported from London, the kids at our house didn't talk, even if we didn't always listen.

And then I was fourteen and the winner of a schoolboy speaking and writing contest, and with my mother in a hotel room in Washington, where I had gone to receive my prize. Somebody called to say, "Be sure to listen to Murrow tonight." We did, and at the end of his broadcast there was that same voice, quoting a few lines from my speech. I met the president of the United States that same day, but when I woke up the next morning, the thing I remembered was Edward R. Murrow saying my words.

And then I was fifteen, and Ed Murrow was to make a speech in Chapel Hill. A friend called me in Charlotte to ask if I would like to come up to hear him. I sat in the audience at the Carolina Inn and I remember thinking, "Look how close I am to him, right here in the same room with him," the kind of thing star-struck fifteen-year-olds think. He spoke about the job ahead for television news, to develop the same kind of tradition of courage that the best newspapers had long enjoyed. Afterward my friend said, "We're taking him to the airport in the morning, would you like to come along?" So I skipped another day of high school to ride to the airport with Edward R. Murrow. I wanted to know about London and New York and the world, but he would not speak, except to ask questions of the university student driver and—horror of horrors—of *me*. He questioned us in turn. So I worked on the high school newspaper, did I? What was its name? I wanted to say the *Times* or the *Herald* or the *World*, but I was forced to listen to my own voice saying, "The *Rambler*, that's its name, the *Rambler*." Do not ask any more questions about Central High School, I remember thinking, tell us about the blitz, tell us about CBS, and Ned Calmer, and Robert Trout. But he went on, looking out the window at the cotton fields that used to line the back road to the Raleigh-Durham Airport, remarking that it was pretty poor-looking cotton. I thought, hysterically, "Please do not spend this whole trip this way. Nobody

War correspondent Edward R. Murrow typing one of his radio reports.

cares about the *Rambler*, or the opinions of that kid who's driving, or the damned cotton." But that was how he spent the whole trip. I am sure he enjoyed that drive, in a passive way. But I *actively* hated it, was actually relieved to see him climb the steps of the plane, so as not to have to suffer any more of his questions. The student driver, by the way, who waved Mr. Murrow into his plane was Bob Evans, who was also to become a CBS News correspondent. I went back to the car, miserable, embarrassed, wishing I had never come along, too young and inexperienced to realize that I had spent an hour with a consummate[1] reporter, who, facing an hour with nothing more to dig into than the opinions of a couple of kids and noth-

1. consummate: complete, skilled

ing more to study than the state of the cotton crop, dug into, studied, what there was at hand.

And then I was twenty-two and walking into the CBS newsroom in New York, on invitation, to talk about a job. It was just a little room, I was surprised by it, a few people working at typewriters, a bank of wire machines against the far wall. And then I saw him, from the back, in shirt-sleeves, his galluses about to slip off his oddly small shoulders, his head bent over the AP machine, unmistakably, there he was. And for me that little room became a great hall. A few minutes later an executive was offering me $135 a week to work in that room as a writer, from midnight 'til 8:00 A.M. Yes, yes, I said. I would have said yes if I had had to pay *them* to work there.

It was hero worship, but what a hero he was! It dawned on me in the months that followed that it was not only the young, impressionable beginners who felt this way about Ed Murrow. It was everybody who knew him. "Well," he would say sometimes at the end of the day, "we have done as much damage as we can do. How about a drink?" The invitation was for everybody within the sound of his voice. And we would all go down to Colbee's on the ground floor of the CBS building, and pass an hour, the well-known correspondents and the seasoned editors and the young kids, all together, all *drawn* together, by Murrow. It was very nearly the best camaraderie[2] I have ever felt, and it helped me survive in New York on $135 a week. (He always bought the drinks.)

There came a day when I wrote for him—an appalling idea, but that was the way radio worked. I actually wrote the news portion of his radio broadcast a few times, while he worked on the commentary. He would toss what he had written across to me to read over, while he timed and edited what I had written. Once, I found that he had written the expression "including you and I." I debated with myself before pointing out that it should be "you and me," wondering what he would say. What he said was "Good catch." It was such a little thing, all these are such little things, but it is a measure of what we all thought about Murrow that I remember to this day Murrow saying to me, "Good catch."

Well, he said other things. He wrote me notes, complimenting me on something I had done, or quarreling with something I had said on the air, or with the way I had said it. He did the same for many others at CBS News, especially the young correspondents, and he did it even after he had left the network. He was, until the end of his life, gracious and generous beyond all hope of explanation.

When he died, Janet Murrow received a card from Milo Radulovich and his wife. He was a young Air Force lieutenant who had been classified as security risk until Murrow and "See It Now" turned a spotlight on the case and forced the Air Force to back down. "Wherever men cherish human freedom and dignity," Milo Radulovich wrote, "Ed Murrow's spirit will stand. To him, we owe what life and freedom are ours." To those of us

2. camaraderie: good will among friends

who worked with him, he gave something like that—a deeper understanding of what life, and freedom, mean. He left none of us unchanged.

It gave me pride in those days, and it gives me pride now, to think of Ed Murrow as a North Carolinian. It gave *him* pride. He always considered himself a Tar Heel from Guilford County, though as his recent biographer, Alex Kendrick, points out, his family moved to the state of Washington before he was six and at that time he was "obviously too young to be whistling Dixie."*

No matter, he loved to refer to his upbringing on Polecat Creek, and more than once, I heard him explain that Guilford County was where Andrew Jackson "came from." On such occasions, I was a silent Mecklenburger, having ridden my bicycle past the nearby monument which marks the spot where Andrew Jackson came from in Union County—and past the other monument a few miles away in South Carolina marking the spot where Andrew Jackson came from.†

Where Ed Murrow came from, there is no such doubt. It was the Center Community of Friends, Guilford County, North Carolina. He was born there, April 25, 1908, the youngest of the three sons of Roscoe and Ethel Murrow, and he was christened Egbert Roscoe Murrow, which seems to me to have been two strikes against him. (It must have seemed so to him, too. He had changed his name by his senior year in college. His mother wrote, "I think Egbert is not happy with his name. If I had known how it looked when written out, I wouldn't have given it to

him. It didn't look pretty.")

Ed Murrow's roots in Guilford County went back more than a hundred years. He came, on his father's side, from a line of Whigs, antisecessionists, Quakers. His grandfather, Joshua Stanley Murrow, had a 750-acre farm, served as a Republican state senator, and helped establish what is now A & T University. His maternal grandfather, George Van Buren Lamb, on the other hand, fought in the Civil War with the Twenty-second North Carolina regiment, meaning he fought at Manassas, Seven Pines, Harper's Ferry, Gettysburg, and so on and on to Appomattox.

The son of Joshua Stanley Murrow and the daughter of George Van Buren Lamb, Roscoe and Ethel, were neighbors and were married, and Ed Murrow's first memories were of a comfortable house made of poplar and walnut, with a wide porch and a great fireplace. From his father, Ed Murrow inherited the habit of long silences, practiced before that fireplace. From his mother, he learned a striking manner of speech, a kind of old-

* Alexander Kendrick, *Prime Time: The Life of Edward R. Murrow* (Boston: Little, Brown and Company, 1969), 81. Acknowledgment and appreciation is expressed to author and publisher for use of background material from *Prime Time* for this address.

† Murrow was apparently referring to the year (1787) that Andrew Jackson practiced law in Martinsville, where the first courthouse in Guilford County was located. The seat was later moved to the center of the county and named Greensboro. The site of Martinsville is at Guilford Courthouse National Military Park. John Spencer Bassett, *The Life of Andrew Jackson* (N.P.: Archon Books [two volumes in one], 1967), 12–14.

fashioned precision with inverted phrases like "this I believe" and verb forms like "it pleases me" which, as Alex Kendrick points out, Ed Murrow used, on and off the air, all his life.

It was a strict household. Ed Murrow's mother forbade smoking, drinking, card-playing, and work, or play, on Sunday. A chapter of the Bible as read in the house each evening and several chapters on the Sabbath. Ed Murrow grew up to be a smoker, a drinker, an enthusiastic poker player, and not much of a Bible reader. But some of Ethel Lamb Murrow's other precepts took better hold of his life. She taught her sons to be responsible, to be in control of their lives, to respect other people, including the opinions of other people, to love the land, and to keep the peace.

His family moved to the Puget Sound in 1913, lived in a tent before they found a house, and Ed Murrow grew up in the Northwest, working in logging camps, playing on the school baseball team. He became a debater and president of the student body. He went to Washington State University, where he was fortunate enough to have a great teacher, Ida Lou Anderson. It was she who taught him to love words and thoughts, and especially the thought of Marcus Aurelius,[3] who counseled, "following right reason seriously, vigorously, calmly . . . if thou holdest to this, expecting nothing, fearing nothing, but satisfied with thy present activity . . . *and with heroic truth in every word and sound which thou utterest* . . . thou wilt live happy. . . ."‡ At Washington State he again became president of the student

body and, later, president of the National Student Federation. He began to consider the international student movement as a career. His mother, who wanted him to be a preacher, began to fear that he was going to be a politician instead.

After graduation Ed Murrow went to New York as president of the student federation and spent his early twenties immersed in international student affairs. He worked his way to Europe more than once, married his Janet Brewster, and in 1935 accepted a job as CBS "director of talks," which meant that he was in charge of rounding up speakers for the network, in America and in Europe. Then, less than three years later, in 1938, he got a chance to speak for himself. In the previous year he had been made CBS European director, and he had gone to Vienna to arrange for a program of Christmas music. He was still there when Austria fell into Hitler's embrace in March. By intricately arranged broadcast lines to the United States, he reported: "Hello, America. . . . Herr Hitler is now at the Imperial Hotel. Tomorrow, there is to be a big parade. . . . Please don't think that everyone in Vienna was out to greet Herr Hitler today. There is tragedy as well as rejoicing in this city tonight. . . ."

His broadcasts from Vienna that month were his first. He had no formal

3. Marcus Aurelius: Roman emperor and philosopher

‡ The quotation is from the *Meditations* of Marcus Aurelius, Book III, No. 12. See George Long (translator), *The Thoughts of the Emperor M. Aurelius Antoninus* (London: George Bell & Sons, 1901), 91.

news background or training. Those broadcasts were models of careful, accurate journalism. When people say that Ed Murrow was born to do what he did in life, that first month in Vienna may be taken in evidence.

And so that was how it all began. By some miracle, it seems to me, the time and the place and the man came together. The birth of serious broadcast journalism can be said to be Ed Murrow's radio reports from Vienna in 1938. It was a long way from Polecat Creek, by way of Puget Sound logging camps and international student meetings—but he got there in time.

Many people in this room remember what followed. Night after night, "This is London." Thirty years ago this month:

Christmas Day began nearly an hour ago. The church bells did not ring at midnight. When they ring again, it will be to announce invasion. . . . This is not a merry Christmas in London. This afternoon. . . one heard such phrases as, "So long, Mamie," and "Goodnight, Jack," but never, "A merry Christmas." It can't be a merry Christmas, for those people who spend tonight and tomorrow by their firesides in their own homes realize that they have bought this Christmas with their nerve, their bodies and their old buildings. . . . I should like to add my small voice to give my own Christmas greeting to friends and colleagues at home. Merry Christmas is somehow ill-timed and out of place, so I shall just use the current London phrase, goodnight, and good luck.

And that was how the phrase originated, the one with which he was to close his broadcasts after the war.

It was after the war that he made his greatest contributions to broadcasting, in my opinion, and to his country. If you doubt that he spoke to the enduring issues, or that his clear voice is needed now, in this day, then listen to some of the words he said. (Remember, for example, the recent attack of Vice-President Agnew upon the news media. Murrow was not around to answer him. He answered him in 1945:)

Our system of broadcasting . . . is loud, occasionally vulgar . . . and not always right. But the man who is wrong has his chance to be heard. There is much controversy[4] and debate, and some special pleading, but frequently the phonies are found out. There is no conspiracy to keep the listener in ignorance, and government does not guide the listening or thinking of the people. There is much talk, and you may think that it only contributes to confusion. . . . A loud voice that reaches from coast to coast is not necessarily uttering truths more profound than those that may be heard in the classroom, bar or country store. But there they are. You can listen, or leave them alone. . . . [We] must hold a mirror behind the nation and the world. If the reflection shows racial intolerance, economic inequality, bigotry, unemployment or anything else, let the people see it. . . . The mirror must have no curves, and must be held with a steady hand.

If you doubt that Ed Murrow saw things clearly and often perceived the heart of a matter somewhat sooner than his countrymen, listen to what he said about Indochina in 1954.:

4. controversy: dispute

Advocates[5] of intervention[6] are unrealistic if they assume that the problem in Indo-china is primarily military. Actually, it is much more political. The victory in Indo-China is not to be won by more foreign group troops or guns, be they French or American . . . It is not to be won by the capture of strongpoints. The Vietminh have no strongpoints. It is to be won first of all in the realm of convictions. Only if the people of Indo-China believe that the fight against Communists is the fight for their own freedom will they turn the present tide of the conflict.

And when you hear new phrases like "stop and frisk," "no-knock laws," and "preventive detention," you might remember some older words. Murrow sixteen years ago:

> We must, for our very lives, remember that freedom will reside and flourish here in this generous and capacious[7] land, or it will survive nowhere on this minor planet. . . . Nations have been known to destroy their freedom while preparing to defend it. . . . Too many people have mistakenly thought it was necessary to be undemocratic to deal with the emergency. They have thought there wasn't time to be both safe and free. No more fateful mistake can be made. . . . For if we emerge from the long crisis undevastated by total war but no longer free, we have but chosen the cheapest and least heroic way to give tyranny the victory.

Ed Murrow's inquiring mind led him to do his great documentary, "Harvest of Shame," years before the national conscience was aroused to any kind of war on poverty. . . . He was the first on network television to report on cigarettes and lung cancer, years before the surgeon general's first report on that subject. And, after the national political campaign we have all lived through, it may cleanse your soul to hear the words he spoke on March 9, 1954, the night of his "See It Now" broadcast devoted to Senator Joseph McCarthy. He might have been moved to say them again in 1970:

> We will not walk in fear, one of another. We will not be driven by fear into an age of unreason if we dig deep in our history and our doctrine and remember that we are not descended from fearful men, not from men who feared to write, to speak, to associate and to defend causes which were for the moment unpopular. . . . The actions of the junior senator from Wisconsin have caused alarm and dismay. . . . And whose fault is that? Not really his; he didn't create this situation of fear; he merely exploited[8] it, and rather successfully. Cassius was right. "The fault, dear Brutus, is not in our stars but in ourselves."

He died in the spring, five years ago, before his time. His ashes were scattered at his farm in Pawling, New York. But to me, he will always belong to Guilford County. I am southerner enough to believe that there really is something born into a man that helps determine what he will become, and if that is so, then there was a century of good earth and hard work and woods and creeks and wild flowers born into Edward R. Murrow.

5. advocates: (verb) arguing for a cause; (noun) someone who argues for a cause

6. intervention: coming between two things

7. capacious: roomy, spacious

8. exploited: used selfishly or immorally

And a Scotch-Irish and English Quaker dignity and decency and respect for the truth.

At his death, he had been director of the United States Information Agency and an adviser to presidents and prime ministers. He was holder of fourteen honorary degrees and all the prizes of his profession, honorary Knight Commander of the Order of the British Empire, Chevalier of the Legion of Honor, an officer of the Order of Leopold.

But we don't remember him for his honors. We remember him, finally, for his deep and abiding belief that we could take it; that there was never any excuse for insulating the people from reality; that escapism was the eighth, and deadliest sin; that the American people were wise beyond the comprehension of those who would trick us or delude us or tell us lies; that we were decent and responsible and mature and could be counted on every time if only we could be supplied our fair measure of the straight facts.

We don't remember him for his honors. We remember him for how he honored us.

MEET THE AUTHOR:
Charles Kuralt (1934–)

For decades television watchers have enjoyed programs featuring North Carolinian Charles Kuralt. Early in his career he covered political happenings and major news stories. In more recent years he has devoted himself mainly to features, including human interest stories. At one time he and his crew traveled the country, interviewing interesting people, telling colorful tales, reporting unusual tidbits of the news—all to be included on a segment of CBS News called "On the Road with Charles Kuralt." More recently he has served as host of the CBS show "Sunday Morning," which is something like a magazine of the air.

Born in Wilmington, Charles Kuralt grew up in Charlotte. Later, at UNC-Chapel Hill, he earned a degree in history and served as editor of the *Daily Tar Heel*. Upon graduation, he began working for the *Charlotte News*. He was only twenty-three years old—

and one year out of college—when his writing won the Ernie Pyle Memorial Award, named for the most famous war correspondent of World War II. Receiving a letter of congratulations from CBS News, he wrote back asking if they wouldn't like to hire him. Indeed, they did, first as a writer for CBS News, then as a correspondent.

In addition to writing for television, Kuralt has authored five books, some of them collections of his television features. One of his most recent books, *North Carolina Is My Home*, is a poetic tribute to his home state. Some of the poems have been set to music by Charlotte composer Loonis McGlohon, and a television version of the show is frequently shown on public television.

Reflecting

We are told that Edward R. Murrow's mother taught him and his brothers "to be responsible, to be in control of their lives, to respect other people, including the opinions of other people, to love the land, and to keep the peace." Reviewing this speech, find evidence that Edward R. Murrow did indeed learn these lessons. (Hint: Sometimes Charles Kuralt openly praises Murrow, but just as often, like a good reporter he merely reports about something Murrow did or said and lets us, the readers, make up our own minds what this behavior shows us about Murrow.)

Martin Luther King, Jr.

Few persons in our century have so captured the imagination of Americans as did Martin Luther King, Jr. It is possible, perhaps even likely, that the time was ripe for the cause of civil rights and that changes would have occurred even without his influence. However, almost anyone—historian or citizen—will name King as the catalyst who moved civil rights further and faster than would have been the case without him.

When an assassin's bullet found him on a motel balcony in Memphis, Tennessee in April 1968, the country was stunned. As was the case in the assassinations of Abraham Lincoln one hundred and three years earlier and John F. Kennedy less than five years earlier, it seemed that anyone who had ever put pen to paper had to express the shock and grief in words. Editorials, feature stories, and poems appeared by the thousands. Decades after his death, analyses of, and tributes to, this remarkable man continue to be written.

Three such writings follow. The first, written by columnist Kays Gary, appeared in the *Charlotte Observer* immediately after King's death. The second and third are poems by two poets—Jaki Shelton Green and Gerald Barrax. They were written after the first shock had lapsed and reflect on King's lasting influence. Notice the mood and the central concern of each piece.

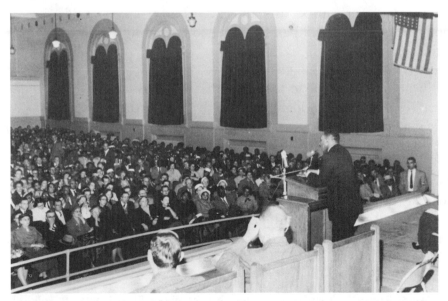

Martin Luther King, Jr., addressing an audience at Broughton High School in Raleigh.

Martin Luther King, Jr.

Kays Gary

Preview

Kays Gary's column focuses not so much on Martin Luther King himself as on the reactions people were having to King's death. It also touches on the way people had reacted toward King during his life. Notice the many strong feelings which are mentioned and described.

What is left to say, now? The grief and guilt pour out and into one great vessel of man's confession of his inadequacy. They are poured and they boil and steep[1] then in agonies.

There are screams and shouts and curses and prayers and mutilations[2] of our souls and passions in another midnight of our life and times.

But there is more.

The vilification[3] that came to Martin Luther King, as it comes to all spiritual revolutionists, suddenly stuck in the throats that once so open were now constricted.[4]

There came, perhaps slowly, a realization among multitudes—dim and inadequate as it might be—of who and what he was and who is left and what is left to take his place.

Because of this, it can be desperately hoped that Martin Luther King in death will serve mankind even greater than he did in life. This is the history of the great martyrs.[5] The terrible truth in death will not be denied nor is there any hiding from it.

Thousands and tens of thousands and millions now will read his words in depth and will come to know the man and his mission as never before.

Those among us, and they were legion, who knew Martin Luther King only as a Negro leader in the midst of multitudes and strife and thus ascribed[6] to him all manner of self-serving, destructive and demagogic[7] intents, now are forced to face the blinding martyr's light.

I was most struck by the flood of calls, particularly from mothers and the young, which followed the assassination. They were not calls of fear but instead were calls of deep sadness. "What can we do?" was the question most often asked. "I am so busy with the children, the PTA, the church, committee meetings. Maybe I attended the wrong meetings. Maybe I, like so many others, failed to speak my mind when we should have spoken."

That is the way it went and from the tone it would seem that these were not merely the temporary spasms of a cataclysmic[8] hour.

As for the violence, the complete antithesis[9] and—in truth—revilement[10] of the central purpose of Martin Luther King's life, it must be stopped. But just as importantly it must be understood. And it can be understood if we place ourselves in some common time and circumstance of cruelly assaulted innocence and feel again the mindless savagery that seemed to burst our vessels and our brain.

Martin Luther King is dead but in death he breathed life into the central truth of our creation so powerfully that neither white nor black shall ever be able to conquer it with guns or knives, bombs or flames.

Sadly, tragically, men will try to do this.

Joyfully, certainly, they will fail.

---

1. steep: to soak
2. mutilations: severe damages, as in severed parts of the body
3. vilification: open, deliberate, and forceful tearing down of someone's character
4. constricted: squeezed tightly
5. martyrs: persons who sacrifice and suffer for a cause
6. ascribed: assigned
7. demagogic: characteristic of leaders who appeal to emotions and prejudices in order to obtain and keep power
8. cataclysmic: relating to a violent and devastating upheaval, disastrous
9. antithesis: the exact opposite
10. revilement: abusive language

Kays Gary (1920–   )

For decades, readers of the *Charlotte Observer* looked forward to the daily column of Kays Gary. Usually those columns centered on the things that mattered in the daily lives of Charlotteans—the people and events in that rapidly growing community. Often they were personal: the story of a narrow escape on a busy highway, or a tribute to the beloved wife he called "Miss B." Frequently they focused on community needs, and ended with a gentle reminder of where people could send contributions.

Kays Gary's newspaper career began in the 1930s when, as a student at Fulleton High School in Cleveland County, he became community correspondent for the Shelby *Daily Star*. Later he honed his writing skills at Mars Hill Junior College and UNC-Chapel Hill. He served on the staff of the *Charlotte Observer* for thirty-eight years. Now retired, he still publishes an occasional column there.

His advice to young people: "Read. Read. Read. Sublimate television to the theater of the mind."

Reflecting

1. Reviewing the essay, list the kinds of reactions which people had to Martin Luther King's assassination.
2. Reread paragraph 9, which begins "Those among us. . . ." Gary described a way that some people perceived King during his lifetime, and predicts that they will now have a new view of him. What are these two very different views?
3. Toward the end of his essay, Gary says that "Martin Luther King is dead, but in death he breathed life into the central truth of our creation. . . ."
   a. What do you think Gary means by "the central truth of our creation"?
   b. When we say two things which seem to be contradictory but aren't, we have stated a **paradox**. For example, it is sometimes said that "If you have something important to do, ask a busy person to do it." (It would seem that busy people wouldn't have time to take on important tasks. However, the truth of the matter is, busy people are often not only well organized, but eager to do things, so they are indeed likely to tackle big jobs.) It is a paradox to say that in his *death* King "breathed *life* into the central truth of our creation." Can you find a way to explain this statement so that it makes sense?

Preview

In this poem, the only punctuation Ms. Green uses is one dash. However, if you read it aloud, you'll probably have no trouble at all figuring out how the phrases and sentences fit together. The effect is something like a cheer or a chant, rather than a formal speech. You might even imagine it being set to music. Would that music be rock or gospel or blues?

From *Dead on Arrival,* by Jaki Shelton Green, published by Carolina Wren Press. Copyright © 1983 by Jaki Shelton Green. Reprinted by permission of the author.

A birthday tribute III

Jaki Shelton Green

Martin
you are a master light
a black cat
jumping out of freedom's coffin
floating
crossing slavery's path
you are a master light
spirit glowing
spirit shouting
a master light
turning nights deep red
deep red
is the color of freedom
brilliant
burning
pulling the strings
of your own spiritual universe
you are deep red screams
loud—
you are a man
who is loud
on the birth
of his ways
you redefine lives
souls
predict their worlds
your song is heard
your sun rays chime
your coming

Jaki Shelton Green (1953–   )

When we look at the variety of work she has accomplished, it is evident that Jaki Shelton Green is a well-rounded person. A former teacher, she is now a community economic development specialist in Mebane, volunteers her service and professional advice in such issues as day care, and conducts writing workshops in homeless shelters. She has won two awards for her poetry, recognition as Orange County "Career Woman of the Year," and designation as Orange County NAACP Mother of the Year. She serves on boards with the North Carolina Writers' Network and the North Carolina Humanities Council. In 1983 she published a poetry collection, *Dead on Arrival.*

A native of Efland, a small community near Durham, she graduated from the George School, a Quaker school in Pennsylvania, then earned a degree at Carleton College in Minnesota. "Pre-teen, I began keeping extensive diaries, which I have maintained as a lifetime ritual," says Ms. Green, and she advises other students to do the same: "Keep journals and write in them consistently. Discipline yourself to 'feel' through smell, taste, hearing, touching, and seeing, and then begin to catalogue those feelings through writing."

This busy mother of three can readily explain what writing means to her: "It balances

who I am as a person," she says. "It's an energy form, a drive—as important to my spiritual and emotional life as food and water are to the physical. If I didn't write," she adds, "I would dance."

Reflecting

1. Jaki Shelton Green solves the problem of being sincere and being original at the same time by comparing Martin Luther King to several different things. Make a list of those comparisons.

2. One might expect a poem written in the aftermath of assassination to express moods of grief or outrage. What is the primary mood of Ms. Green's poem? Can you explain that mood?

Preview

Sometimes when we want to make a point, it's best to state it directly—to come right out in no uncertain terms to say what we mean. But sometimes we can be more effective if we tie our meaning to some specific thing—something concrete that becomes a **symbol** for readers and makes them feel as well as think.

In 1986 Gerald Barrax was asked to write a poem for North Carolina State University's first observance of Martin Luther King's birthday. Instead of merely talking about King's life and death, he took his theme from a quotation by Richard Wright, which has to do with uniforms. Then he wrote about various kinds of uniforms worn by blacks and whites throughout our history.

MEET THE AUTHOR:
Gerald Barrax (1933–)

It took Gerald Barrax a long time to get to North Carolina, but once he came—in 1969—he stayed. Born in Alabama, when he was ten years old he moved to Pittsburgh. After earning degrees at Duquesne University and the University of Pittsburgh, he served in the U.S. Air Force for four years. He lists a wide variety of "Occupations—Things I Have Been": steel mill laborer, cab driver, mail carrier and postal clerk, substitute teacher, encyclopedia salesman, and awning hanger. Eventually, however, he turned to college teaching—first at North Carolina Central University in Durham; then, since 1970, at North Carolina State University, where he teaches literature and creative writing.

His writing—especially poetry—has won a number of major national awards. His poetry appears not only in his own collections, but in a number of journals and anthologies. He has also served as poetry editor of *Callaloo*, a well-known literary periodical, and since 1987 has edited *Obsidian*, a major literary journal dedicated to works by black writers.

Gerald Barrax wrote his first poem when he was a sixteen-year-old junior in high school. When asked what he would tell students now he declared, "I owe everything that I am, including being a poet, to READING. Without READING, I'd be nobody. I started READING very early in my life and READ everything I could get my hands on. Everybody should."

Uniforms

Gerald Barrax

"Again we say, of the North as of the South, that life for us is daily warfare and that we live hard, like soldiers. . . . the color of our skins constitutes our uniforms."—Richard Wright, *12 Million Black Voices* (1941)

They have never died in our uniforms
as we have in theirs.
It was easier to die in battle,
in the uniform of the United States Colored Troops,
than on the plantations,
easier even at Fort Wagner, or Fort Pillow
when the gray demons shot and burned us
in our blue, prisoners of war.
We didn't want to die, but did.
All we ever wanted was to be free.
We died for that freedom, and theirs, too,
at Verdun, in the Argonne Forest,
and came back to familiar Chicago, Knoxville, Omaha
where they lynched us in khaki
dishonored their own uniforms
made a nightmare of their dream.
We didn't want to die at the Bulge,
at the Rhine and Arno Rivers,
on Pork Chop Hill, at Danang and Hue,
but we did,
becoming less sure whose freedom we were dying for.
For still, in places with familiar names
hooded men shame their faith as Christian Knights
of burning crosses,
enhance with sheets the color of the faces
that we often would die not to see, for just one day.

He didn't want to die in Memphis,
not because of a dream
not even for a dream,
but he did, in uniform,
in daily warfare,
and free, free of hate, because all he ever wanted
was that they could be as free as we are.

For Martin Luther King, Jr.
18 January 1986

Language Alert

This poem includes a number of references to battles fought in various wars.

1. Fort Wagner, Fort Pillow: engagements in which black soldiers fought; those who were captured were executed by Confederate troops
2. Verdun, Argonne Forest: famous battles of World War I
3. The Bulge: The Battle of the Bulge, one of the most famous battles of World War II
4. The Rhine River, the Arno River: rivers, scenes of conflict during World War II
5. Pork Chop Hill: battle of the Korean War
6. Danang, Hue: battles of the Vietnam War

Reflecting

1. Explain the meaning of the quotation by Richard Wright.
2. What kinds of "uniforms" does Barrax speak of in this poem? (Don't forget what was worn by the "hooded men.")
3. Does the ending surprise you? Can you explain it?
4. State the point—the message or theme—of this poem in one clear, concise sentence.

Preview:
A Marine Communications Man Leaving for Vietnam (1966)

In this poem, Tom Walters shares with us the true experience of talking on the telephone with his brother, Dwight, just before Dwight leaves for service in Vietnam. We are given some of Dwight's conversation, either directly or indirectly. However, most of the poem deals with the frightening sounds and pictures that flash, one after the other at a furious rate, through Tom's mind during this final call from the brother he knows faces a deadly task.

As you read, notice how the spaces between phrases and the wording itself gives a breathless effect, as though the speaker of the poem is almost dizzy with anxiety. The effect is like that of a television ad splashing one image after another on the screen.

A Marine Communications Man Leaving for Vietnam (1966)

—for Dwight Walters—

Thomas Walters

Your already   longdistance   voice
Laughs frail   laughs beneath blasting
Flights of jets   tarmac   squawks
"By noon, I'll be eating in Chicago
And unpacked in California before three."

Knowing your marrow must quake with bombs
We talk only of the past   of hikes   of bikes
Your voice controlled as time ticks out
Comes   arcing the crackling air   casual
As though by walkie-talkie   trained

Shouting postcard assurances   I   seem
To hear   near your glassed-in   booth
A cry   "On target. Fire for effect."

And you plunge in newsreel dash
Among casualties   utilitied   pistoled
Bone ivory pale beneath the bouncing steel
Desperately camouflaged   determinedly communicating
Help us   Help us   Help us
Your heart crossed   with bandoliers

With you hung up   it is a job to breathe.
Call again   Brother   so we may laugh.

---

1. tarmac: a paved area around a hangar

2. marrow: the soft material that fills bones, often used to mean the inmost part of something

3. arcing: forming an arc, like the discharge of electric current crossing between two electrodes

4. bandolier: a belt outfitted with loops for carrying cartridges worn across the soldier's chest

Thomas Walters (1935–1983)

People lucky enough to know Tom Walters before he died an untimely death at the age of forty-seven often called him a "Renaissance Man"—a term used to refer to people with wide knowledge and many talents. In addition to writing poems, fiction, and articles, Tom Walters painted, sculpted, made films, and illustrated books. He was also much beloved as a teacher—both at NCSU, where he taught English and trained English teachers, and in the public schools, where, as a writer-in-residence, he helped students try their hand at composing poetry and stories. His teaching excellence won him election to NCSU's Academy of Outstanding Teachers.

Tom Walters's first piece to be published was a story about Tokyo written for a sixth-grade teacher and printed in the Tarboro newspaper. After growing up on a farm in Edgecombe County in the eastern part of the state, he won a scholarship to UNC-Chapel Hill. He served in the Marine Corps, then worked in advertising before returning to graduate studies at Duke University and embarking on a career as college professor and writer. His books include a scholarly study, two volumes of poetry, and a novel for young readers.

Reflecting

1. In the poem above, Tom Walters doesn't tell us how he felt when his brother called him just before going to war. Instead, he gives us the experience in such a way that we know how he felt.

   Did you notice that this poem contains no commas and only five periods—and that it isn't always easy to see how words are joined? For example, in the third line, *tarmac* seems to connect to no other word. It is followed by *squawks*, which refers to the brother's voice coming over the telephone.

   Ordinarily we expect poems to follow regular English order, but in this case the confusion seems appropriate. The language is disconnected on purpose to make us experience what the speaker is undergoing. Knowing the danger and horror his brother will face, he cannot think logically, so his mind is flying off in many directions at once.

   Can you recall a time when you felt similar fear or dread or worry? Can you capture your mind's confusion—and all your feelings—in lines of poetry like these?

2. See "Long Distance, 1944" (p. 367), which presents a similar situation. In James Boyd's poem, a son, back on shore after being aboard a warship, calls his father.

HOME

Now we have come to our own time. Social and scientific change is still occurring at a rapid rate, with no slowdown in sight. North Carolina is no longer primarily an agricultural state. In fact, it is becoming increasingly urban, with large metropolitan centers such as the Research Triangle of Raleigh, Durham, and Chapel Hill; the Triad of Greensboro, Winston-Salem, and High Point; and the Charlotte-Mecklenburg area. In a more affluent culture, tourism has become one of our main industries, and ads in national magazines herald North Carolina as "Variety Vacationland."

In the following selections, we look around us—at our families and friends and neighbors, at our natural environment, at the things we do and the things we think about. Some of the works are celebrations of the good things of our lives. Others contemplate problems which we face, both as individuals and as a community.

Preview

The South is known as a region where family (including distant cousins and great-aunts and great-uncles) is very important. (Some say that if you introduce two Southerners, in five minutes they will have investigated each other's families enough to find out that they are second cousins.) In this poem, Jim Wayne Miller takes us to a family reunion, where kinfolk come from far and wide to eat a shared dinner-on-the-ground and swap stories and memories.

Family Reunion

Jim Wayne Miller

Sunlight glints off the chrome of many cars.
Cousins chatter like a flock of guineas.

In the shade of oaks and maples
six tables stand
filled with good things to eat.
Only the jars of iced tea sweat.

Here the living and dead mingle
like sun and shadow under old trees.

For the dead have come too,
those dark, stern departed who pose
all year in oval picture frames.

They are looking out of the eyes of children,
young sprouts
whose laughter blooms
fresh as the new flowers in the graveyard.

1. guineas: pheasant-like birds which are sometimes raised on American farms.

2. departed: those who have died

Jim Wayne Miller (1936–)

"I know of nothing greater than to be able to say exactly what you mean," writes Jim Wayne Miller. He has been doing that for many years, thus far turning out six collections of poems and one novel.

Born in Leicester in the North Carolina mountains, he began writing while in elementary school there. He reports that "I wrote in imitation of poems and stories I read. I even imitated radio dramas I listened to." Later he received degrees at Berea College and Vanderbilt University. Since 1963 he has lived in Bowling Green, Kentucky, and has taught at Western Kentucky University.

His works, which often reflect either events and trends of current life or his roots in the Appalachian Mountains, have won a number of awards, including the Thomas Wolfe Award and the Alice Lloyd Memorial Award for Appalachian Poetry. He has read his work in numerous settings, including the Folger Shakespeare Library in Washington, DC.

His most recent poetry collection, *Brier, His Book*, won the Zoe Kincaid Brockman Award in 1989. Miller's newest book, *Newfound*, is a novel in which a boy tells his own story of growing up (from age 11 to 17) in the Appalachian Mountains. He has also edited *I Have a Place*, an anthology of Appalachian literature.

Reflecting

1. Assume that you are a reporter from a foreign culture, and you don't know anything at all about a family reunion—even what one is. Look back through the poem and list all the information you can find about such a reunion:
   a. How many people attend? (You don't need exact numbers, but are there many or few?)
   b. What do they do?
   c. Where is it held?
   d. In what season is it likely to be held?
2. The last three stanzas talk about how "the living and dead mingle." How can the poet claim that "the dead have come too"?
3. "Young sprouts" is a term rural people often use to refer to children. Notice how the poet has expanded this old term so that it isn't just a cliché.

Preview

Ronald Bayes has noted that he first became attracted to "fun poems." In just five short lines in the following poem he draws a quick sketch of a four-year-old child at play.

Four-Year-Old

Ronald Bayes

Teddy Bear
and a stick
behind clump-weed and wild rye
he charges the evils of
the world.

Ronald Bayes (1932–)

Poets don't always begin writing in order to present great messages about serious topics. "Fun poems about athletic events and about animals whetted my imagination in grade school and high school," explains Ronald Bayes. He began writing limericks in the seventh grade. Now a noted editor, poet, and scholar, he has published eleven collections of his poems—many of them as playful as those early limericks, others quite serious explorations of important issues.

A native of Oregon, Ronald Bayes came in 1968 to St. Andrews Presbyterian College in Laurinburg, NC, as poet-in-residence. More than twenty years later he remains there as Distinguished Professor of Creative Writing. During those years he began a major literary magazine, *St. Andrews Review,* and founded a press which has published over one hundred volumes of poetry and short fiction.

In recognition of his writing, Bayes has been awarded the Woodrow Wilson National Fellowship, the Roanoke-Chowan Award, North Carolina Arts Council writing grant, and the North Carolina Award for Literature.

Reflecting

Good poets know that poems should be concrete: the details should appeal to our senses, helping us to see, hear, smell, feel, etc. They also know that poems should do their work in as few words as possible.

In "Four-Year-Old," Ronald Bayes captures the spirit of a four-year-old: energetic and daring to tackle anything. (Of course a four-year-old is very innocent and naive. He doesn't recognize that he can't really charge "the evils of the world" with just a stick.)

Choose another age: eight, ten, sixteen, forty, or eighty. What kind of mood or attitude or spirit do you think is typical of this age? Put a character that age into your own poem, and with just a few details let him or her show us that spirit.

Preview

If you have a brother or sister, you know that no matter how much you love each other, occasional teasing, scuffling, and arguing is almost bound to occur. But somehow when you face a common threat, the differences seem unimportant.

The Gingham Boy and the Calico Brother

Ardis Hatch

All day they spat insults,
Hit, tattled on, tortured each other.
One broke the other's red crayon;
The other bent the one's blue truck.
"I'll never speak . . ."
"I'll never plan . . ."
"That's mine . . . no, mine"
On into the shadows and beyond.

Last night it lightened and it roared.
This morning I found
That politics is not the only thing
That makes strange bedfellows.

MEET THE AUTHOR:
Ardis Hatch (1937–)

When Ardis Hatch was a sixth grader in "Little Washington" (Washington, NC), she began writing, and she kept on doing so until she had graduated from high school.

Then her attention turned elsewhere: first toward earning a degree at Duke University, and then toward rearing three active boys. Talent and interest rarely stay suppressed forever, however, and when she was thirty, she began writing again.

In addition to publishing a collection of her own poems, she has published a book about poetry in the classroom, basing it on her work as coordinator of the state Poetry-in-the-Schools program. Later, she directed a statewide conference on using arts in the public schools.

Presently she is president of Ardis Hatch and Associates, Inc., a company which helps organize and manage special events such as conferences. She still writes and teaches poetry, and passes along this advice to students: "Keep a journal and put it up someplace safe. You are at a pivotal point in your life,

and everything is wonderfully complex and interesting. Keeping it all recorded will give you a treasure beyond value."

Language Alert

Writers often use **allusions** (indirect references) to make their point. They may allude to persons, titles, slogans, or events. For example, someone may state, "Karl thinks he's a regular Superman." The allusion to Superman, the hero of comic strips and movies, makes us realize that Karl thinks he has superhuman powers and can achieve anything. In her poem, Ms. Hatch uses two allusions:

1. "The Gingham Boy and the Calico Brother" echoes the title of another poem, "The Gingham Dog and the Calico Cat," made famous by Lewis Carroll. Perhaps you

have read his poem and remember that the two stuffed animals fought so ferociously that they ate each other up.

2. An old saying goes, "Politics makes strange bedfellows." It refers to the fact that sometimes politicians who disagree on a number of matters (and perhaps even personally dislike each other) will work together when it suits their political purposes to do so. Notice how Ms. Hatch gives this old saying a new twist at the end of her poem.

Reflecting

1. In the last stanza, what "lightened" and "roared"?
2. What is this mother telling us about the ways brothers (and/or sisters) get along together?

From *The Illusion of Water* by Ardis Hatch (Kimzey), published by St. Andrews Press. Copyright © 1978 by Ardis Kimzey. Reprinted by permission of Ardis Hatch.

The Best Byline

A. C. Snow

Preview

Have you ever had a special place you considered your own—one which you could use as a hideaway perhaps, or a place that others knew about but did not come to unless invited? It may have been a bedroom, a corner of a room shared with others, an abandoned building, a shady corner outside, or a tree house.

In this column, A. C. Snow tells of building a tree house for his two daughters, ages five and eight. He tells the story from the father's point of view, but with the dialogue and details he provides we get the children's viewpoint, too.

For several years now, the children have wanted a tree house, wanted it with futile desperation. They know of their father's handicap with the hammer.

There exists in every earthbound creature an inborn desire to escape, to rise above it all—to cross over to Shangri-la, or walk the Yellow Brick Road. Or, yes, even to climb a tree.

A tree house, only four or five feet off the ground, can be a great escape for children.

I know a mother who cheerfully clambers up to her son's tree house some twenty feet off terra firma, for mother-son conferences in moments of stress. "It's only fair," she said, "that I make an effort to meet him on his ground now and then. After all, children for the most part have to meet us on OUR ground."

So on Friday, I took off the day I'd saved for a cold January. A quiet promise I'd finally elicited from my neighbor for aid in this undertaking materialized when the phone rang at 8:30 and he said cheerily, "O.K., man, let's go build that tree house!"

When he sank the first sixteen-penny nail into the tree house beam, the excitement of the beginning of our house some twelve years ago flashed through my mind. There's nothing like building a home.

It was apparent from the beginning that I was the apprentice and Ed Green was the master. But it was the first tree house for both.

We worked hard. And the house had taken form by noon when I drove over to pick up the five-year-old from kindergarten.

"Little girl, have we got a surprise for you when you get home!" I said. "Guess what's happening!"

"Oh Daddy, you've brought the circus to our house" she said in typical five-year-old misconception that all Daddies are miracle workers.

"Of course not, honey," I said irritably. "It's better than that. You're getting a tree house."

After a moment of silence she said softly: "Daddy, that makes me feel so happy I'd cry if I had time."

The second-grader was equally surprised when she came skipping home from school in mid-afternoon. They sat in the sun and planned and planned while we worked feverishly to get the doors and windows done before dark.

As we moved out—me weary with new aches and a new tiredness not born of pushing a typewriter carriage back and forth all day—the children moved in.

"We'll need shag carpet," said the eight-year-old to her sister. And she called out to me: "Daddy, when are you going to put the lights in?"

"Use fireflies!" I yelled back as I complained to my wife: "You see, the new generation is never satisfied. Electric lights and shag carpet. Next they'll want indoor plumbing!"

They finally came in to eat. The little one asked to say grace. "God," she said reverently, "we sure do thank you for Ed Green and our tree house—and Daddy." I didn't mind being the afterthought.

Next day, a list of club members had been posted in the tree house—with the name of "Gracey Snow" (the four-pound poodle) last to be added.

A crudely lettered sign on the dogwood out front said "No Trasspassing. Check before walking by."

Club rules posted in a prominent spot inside included:

1. Do not shout in club except when necessary.
2. Do not stick your body out the windows.
3. Do not jump out of the club. Use steps.
4. No jumping up and down.
5. Safety first.

As I left the tree house, I noticed that the maple and the dogwood nestling close against the windows were heavy with buds. Soon foliage and shade would add even more enticement to the little house.

Then I spotted my daughter's lettering on the side of a two-by-six timber under the tree house. "By Ed and A.C."

It was the first byline I'd shared in years. I've never had one I was more proud of.

MEET THE AUTHOR:
A. C. Snow (1924–)

The North Carolina Press Association has honored A. C. Snow, former editor of the now defunct *Raleigh Times*, many times for his writing. His columns now appear weekly in the Raleigh *News and Observer*. What perhaps indicates his skill even more than awards is the way readers who are familiar with his work will turn to his column first, even before skimming the headlines. In contrast to his editorials, which discuss important social and political problems, his columns deal with the personal side of life: selling a car, going to a funeral, mending the roof, or visiting the old home place.

A native of Dobson, a small town in Surry County "in the shadow of the Blue Ridge Mountains," A. C. Snow completed high school just after Pearl Harbor, graduating in the courthouse because the high school had burned down. During the war he served in the Pacific as a member of an Air Force troop carrier squadron. Safely home again, he graduated from both Mars Hill (then a two-year college) and UNC-Chapel Hill, where he earned membership in Phi Beta Kappa. He worked for seven years on the Burlington *Times-News* before moving to Raleigh.

Language Alert

1. A *byline* is a line of type appearing just under the title of an article which gives the name of the author. (Reporters consider it a mark of distinction to have a *byline* accompany a story.)
2. Something that is *futile* is useless.
3. *Shangri-la* and the *Yellow Brick Road* both refer to perfect places. Shangri-la is the imaginary ideal land in James Hilton's novel, *Lost Horizons*. The Yellow Brick Road is the path down which Dorothy and Toto skip in *The Wizard of Oz*.
4. *Terra firma* is a Latin phrase that means firm earth or solid ground.
5. If you *elicit* a promise, you have drawn the promise from someone.
6. Something that *materializes* takes shape. It is no longer just an idea or a plan; it appears.
7. An *apprentice* may be an amateur who is just beginning to learn something or he/she may be an assistant, a helper.
8. If you have a *misconception*, you have the wrong idea, you fail to understand.
9. An *enticement* is something that lures or attracts attention.

NOTE: On the sign at the tree house is one misspelled word. Can you spot it?

Reflecting

A. Thinking About Writing

1. Notice that the story is written in much shorter paragraphs than usual. Material that is going to be published in a newspaper usually appears in short paragraphs. Newspaper columns are so narrow that regular paragraphs look very long on the page.
2. The children never thank their father directly for the tree house. How do we know how happy they are—and how grateful?
3. Notice, too, that except for the last line, when he mentions his pride, A. C. Snow doesn't tell us directly about how he felt about building this retreat for his children. Which of his words and details show us how he felt?

B. Writing

Describe a place that is very special to you, as the tree house was to the Snow children. Let us know what it looks like, what you did there, when you used it. Try to make it so real that readers will feel as if they've been there.

From The Finishing School

Stronger and Smarter

Gail Godwin

Preview

Moving from one community to another is often difficult. It's especially difficult when the move is preceded by the shock of loss and grief and when money is scarce and choices are limited. Thirteen-year-old Justin and her mother and brother have recently come from the South to New England to live with Justin's Aunt Mona and cousin Becky. Justin doesn't accept Mona and Becky. She doesn't even accept the fact that the move was necessary.

As I went downstairs, I passed Becky coming up. She gave me a quirky[1] raise of her eyebrows, which could have meant "Hi," or "How dare you be on my stairs," or "Isn't life exasperating."

My mother was sitting on the living-room sofa. She already had Becky's sundress and was picking out the seam. My cousin certainly hadn't wasted any time.

My mother was wearing her new, martyr's look as she bent over Becky's sewing. But she was a very pretty martyr,[2] and something about the way she held her head made me think she saw herself now in the role of a person who is determined to make suffering noble and beautiful.

"I'm going up to that old empty farmhouse for a while," I said from the doorway.

She raised her light blue eyes from her work and smiled at me. I thought I glimpsed the ghost of the look she had rewarded me with occasionally in the old days, a flirtatious look that said: Something about you pleases me right now, but

1. quirky: peculiar
2. martyr: a person who endures great suffering, often as a sacrifice for others

I'm not going to tell you what it is.

Maybe it was not too late yet: maybe I could still say or do something to persuade her to pack up our things and take the train south again. I had made no new friends at school yet. There was nothing in this new place that I would be sad to leave behind. Emboldened by this flicker of her old self that I had spotted, I made a wry face at Aunt Mona's clear plastic runners, which led, in three directions, from the doorway to the main places one was expected to sit in the living room. This way, her seafoam-green wall-to-wall carpeting would be protected forever from a dirty footstep.

"What's she waiting for?" I said. "It's like those women you see downtown with their hair in rollers. You wonder what the special event would have to be for them to take them out."

In the old days, my mother would have giggled and said, "Justin, don't be naughty," but in a way that signified that the nonmotherly part of her, the part that was not required to instill respect in me, approved of the truth in my "naughty" observation. But now she only said gravely, "Come and sit by me a minute." She patted a place beside her. "I won't keep you long."

I crossed Aunt Mona's plastic bridge to the sofa and sat down beside my mother. She resumed picking out Becky's errant[3] seam with her nail scissors. The early-evening light was still strong, and, as she bent over her work, I noticed a new little line along the edge of her chin. It was nothing very awful, but it had a strange effect on me: it made me angry with her.

I felt, unreasonably perhaps, that, in her present way of life, she was encouraging such lines, that she was purposely trying to transform her whole being as a way of avenging herself on her unhappy fate of losing all her supporters and protectors. But wasn't I still here? Wasn't Jem? And we needed her as she had been. This new image of her made it seem as if our glamorous, carefree mother had died along with everybody else.

"You know, Justin," she began slowly, picking diligently at Becky's seam, "everyone in the world isn't going to have Honey's taste in furniture and rugs." Honey was our name for my late grandmother.

I sat silently, knowing I was in for a reproach.[4]

"But we're going to have to go on living in that world. I'm not saying we'll never have a home of our own again, with our own things, but right now this is the best I can do for you and Jem."

"Is it?" I could not resist replying bitterly.

"Justin. Do you remember, after we buried your father . . . and . . . " She picked out the next few stitches in silence. " . . . and Mr. Fowler at the bank came to the house to explain to me what my choices were, you remember the talk we had afterward, you and I?"

"Yes, ma'am." Of course I remembered it: how could I ever forget it? That was when she had told me we had to sell the

---

3. errant: wandering, especially straying from a proper course
4. reproach: disapproval

house. And, just as I had been able to accept that, just as I had gotten us comfortably and bravely settled into a smaller house I was sure we could find somewhere in town where everybody would still know who we were, who would remember what we had been—she had dropped her bomb: we were to go north, to live with Aunt Mona and Becky, the cousin I had never seen.

"I thought you understood why this was the only sensible choice. Frankly, Justin, I don't know what we would have done if Mona hadn't invited us to share her home."

"If she hadn't invited us, we would have found a way. If she and Mr. Mott hadn't gotten separated, we would still be at home. You know we would."

"Yes, perhaps. And it would have been terrible. I don't think you have imagined just how painful it would have been to have gone on living there with all those reminders. I mean"—and she put her scissors down upon the cloth, and a savage edge came into her voice—"did you imagine us taking *walks* every Sunday from our dinky little house over to Washington Avenue, so we could see how the new people were enjoying living in our old home? And what, exactly, did you imagine me doing to bring in an income, to bring in money so that your future and Jem's could lie safely in the bank collecting interest, so you could have your chance when the time comes?"

"You could have found something. Everyone would have wanted to help you. Granddaddy helped so many people. And I told you I was willing to get a job after school." I had to keep a tight hold on myself; tears of frustration were threatening to spill. We had been through this before.

"Justin, honey. You are *thirteen years old.* You can't even get a real job till you're sixteen."

"I could have baby-sat my way out of poverty and shabbiness, like Aunt Mona."

"Sarcasm doesn't become you, Justin. Mona may not do everything in the style you've been accustomed to, but she is making an effort to become self-sufficient. I admire that." My mother picked up the nail scissors and went back to Becky's seam. "God knows I admire that," she said with a sigh.

"Well, you could do it, too. You could get your realtor's license, like Aunt Mona is doing. She said, once she had it, she could make money hand over fist."

"Sooner or later I will have to train for something. I'll have to get some practical education. But, don't you see, my hands are tied until Jem's in school next fall. Until then, I just have to do what I can to help Mona out, and . . . and take the consequences for the kind of person I have been."

"What do you mean?" I said. "I don't understand."

"I'm just beginning to understand, myself," she said in a wistful, *humble* tone I had never heard her use before. "You see, all my life, I got to do exactly as I wanted. When I chose to run off and get married rather than go to Sweet Briar, I did it. There was some fuss made, but what could they do? I was their only child and they had raised me to believe I was a law unto myself. And when your father had to go to war three months later, and I was already expecting you, I was welcomed home like the prodigal daughter. After you were born, I got to go off to Mary Washington every day and take what courses I wanted while someone looked after you at home. And I took art, and courses like "The History of Furniture,' things like that. Nothing so boring as shorthand or typing or anything that would help me get a job later. Who needed a *job*? I had three people to take care of me. And then, when the war was over, and your father wanted to go off to Charlottesville and get his education, I got to go off with him and lead a carefree young college married life, while Honey and Father felt privileged to keep you at home and begin to spoil you as they'd spoiled me. And when we decided it was time to have another child, even though your father hadn't found the career that suited him yet, my loving parents encouraged us to come right home ... there was plenty of room for everybody in that house ... and I suppose it could have gone on like that for decades if Honey hadn't got cancer and then, on top of that, Father his stroke.

"And, you know, we still thought we could make it, your father and I, if we mortgaged the house to pay the staggering medical bills, and having those round-the-clock nurses for your grandfather. It wouldn't have been easy, but Rivers was doing real well selling college jewelry for Balfour. I mean, it wasn't the kind of profession I had hoped he'd have, but it suited his personality. Your daddy

had more personality and charm than any man I ever met. He was just a marvelous salesman.

"But what I had never counted on— after all, he had come home without a scratch from the *war*—was one little rainy night and his car skidding on a slick road." She put down the scissors and folded her hands tightly on top of Becky's dress. "So there you have the story of the little girl who got her own way for thirty-two years. Recently I have been thinking ... well ... that it would have been better if I hadn't had my own way quite so much. And I've been thinking about you, too. I know there are lots of things you don't like about our new life, but ... pardon me if I sound hard ... I think you may grow up to be a better ... certainly a more useful person than I am because of the very things you suffer now. You'll have to develop strengths I never bothered to. Does that make sense?"

"You make it sound like you brought us here so we could suffer." As soon as the words were out of my mouth, I knew they were unfair. I had said them as a defense against the bleak life she seemed to be holding up to me. Who wanted to spend the rest of their youth developing strengths from suffering? But my pride kept me from retracting them.[5] And also something else: something about her whole penitential[6] speech had upset me profoundly.

5. retracting: withdrawing, retreating, taking back
6. penitential: expressing remorse for one's misdeeds or sins

"Then you have misunderstood everything I have been trying to say," she replied sadly. "Oh well"—she started ripping Becky's wrong seam with renewed vigor—"maybe I didn't say it well enough. I have only just barely thought it out for myself."

Now I knew what it was that hurt so, as I watched her rip the seam. Her renouncement[7] of the way she had been was ripping out some vital thread that had run through my whole childhood. In our other life, my mother had always starred as "The Daughter." I was left with the role of the sturdy little soul, the companion of the grandparents, who colluded[8] with them in allowing Louise to go on being herself. "We must let Louise have the rest of her college," my grandfather would say. "We must let the young couple have the honeymoon that the war interrupted," my grandmother would say. Leaving me feeling, almost as far back as I could remember, like a prematurely aged little parent myself, who must exercise self-restraint and empathy[9]—the two chief virtues of my grandmother and grandfather, respectively—so that my mother could prolong her life as a girl.

And now she was saying she wished we hadn't allowed it, she wished that self had never been. Where did that leave me? In some kind of limbo,[10] with a lost childhood on either side. There was no reason for me to go on being the kind of person I had been in Fredericksburg; in fact, I couldn't be, even if I wanted to, because it had been in my role as granddaughter that I had excelled, and my grandparents were dead. And as for the few years of childhood left to me now, hadn't my mother just implied that those must be devoted to the art of suffering?

I sat on miserably, in uncomfortable silence with my mother. Even now, the old responsible adult-child self was asserting itself in me. I knew I should say something "wise," or at least gracious, in order to take away some of the sting of my previous remark. But what could I say? Then I recalled the words of the woman I had met today, as we had been walking back toward the sunny fields from the hut, when she had her hand on my shoulder.

"Money does lurk in the plot of everybody's life, then," I heard myself saying. "Even more than passion, probably."

My mother stopped what she was doing and gave me a strange look. "What a deep thing to say. When I was your age, I wouldn't have been capable of such a thought." She laughed bitterly. "Up until a *year* or so ago, if someone had said what you just said, I would have tossed my head and retorted. 'Don't be an old fogey, passion is what makes the world go around!'" In the act of saying this, she tossed her head and became the old Louise for a moment: the girl-mother I worshiped and admired and was jealous of, all at the same time, and was so proud to show off to my friends.

It was this mother I allowed to hug me, and whom I hugged back. "You see," she

7. renouncement: rejection, giving up
8. colluded: plotted, schemed
9. empathy: sympathy and understanding
10. limbo: a condition of neglect, a region where one is forgotten

said, as she let me go, "that's what I'm talking about. Already you are becoming a much stronger and smarter woman than I'll ever be."

But I went outside feeling her triumphant words had been more a threat than a compliment.

MEET THE AUTHOR:
Gail Godwin (1935–)

Before Asheville-native Gail Godwin had even begun school, her mother was typing the stories little Gail made up and submitting them to *Child Life* magazine. They were not accepted for publication, and neither was the novel she wrote while a student in Chapel Hill. But by 1990, Gail Godwin was a famous author who had published two short-story collections and seven novels, several of them best-sellers. *A Mother and Two Daughters* sold over a million copies, and her most recent novels, *The Finishing School* and *A Southern Family*, have also been well received.

Gail Godwin always wanted to be a writer. She began keeping a daily journal at the age of thirteen. Her ambitions were supported not only by her mother, but by teachers at St. Genevieve's School (in Asheville), Peace College, UNC-Chapel Hill, and the University of Iowa. For a time she worked as a journalist, writing obituaries and feature stories for the *Miami Herald*, then as a travel consultant in London, and later as a university faculty member.

Now a nationally acclaimed writer, she lives in Woodstock, New York. She still fits the description given in the *Lotus*, the Peace College yearbook, in 1957: "Gail Godwin is a unique combination of wisdom, talent, and beauty. She is the perfect contradiction of the popular theory that an intellectual girl must be minus charm. . . . Vivacious and witty, too, she is an outstanding senior who will be an example of the modern American woman."

Reflecting

1. Justin's mother argues that after her husband's death, moving in with Aunt Mona was the only reasonable action for her to take. Examine her reasoning. Is she right, or did she take the easiest way out of her situation? Explain your answer.

2. Justin's mother tells her, "I think you may grow up to be a better . . . certainly a more useful person than I am because of the very things you suffer now." Explain why you do or do not disagree.

Ben Owen: Master Potter

Jerry Bledsoe

Preview

Pottery is one of the oldest arts in the world, and one for which North Carolina is especially well known. In this profile you meet one of the most famous North Carolina potters, a man who carried on a family tradition that goes back hundreds of years—at least as far back and as far away as eighteenth-century England.

I t was quite a sight when the kilns were fired. All that smoke churning up through the trees. He had two kilns out behind the log workshop, big groundhog kilns. He never switched to oil, the way most of the other potters did. He always fired with wood, the old way, the way his father did before him, and his father before him.

And what excitement it was when the kilns were opened! In all of his years at it, that was one thing Ben Owen never got over. You never knew how a piece of pottery would take the heat. There were endless surprises, some good, some bad. He always felt the excitement, like a kid with a box of Cracker Jacks, as he put it.

The smoke no longer rolls from those kilns. It has been . . . what? . . . could it have been two years since he last felt that twinge of excitement on opening the kiln?

Ben Owen sits now in a rocking chair on the screened front porch of his modest white house. He lives halfway between Seagrove and Robbins on Highway 705, which once was the old plank road. A big man, Ben Owen. He has cataracts[1] and wears thick glasses. His hair is thinning but still black, although he is now 69.

The walker, built of aluminum and plastic, stands before the chair, and Ben

1. cataracts: a condition in which the lens of the eye becomes cloudy and opaque, causing partial or total blindness

From *Visitin' With Carolina People,* by Jerry Bledsoe, originally published by Fast & McMillan Publishers, East Wood Press, 1980. Copyright © by Globe-Pequot Press. Reprinted by permission of the author.

Owen leans forward in his gray-striped pajamas to rest his arms on it and remember . . .

"My father was a potter and so were my brothers; and my grandfather, he had a shop there in front of the home when I was a little boy, and my father turned pottery there some back in those days. But I would help my father when I was growing up, you know, a boy, fixing his clay, helping him lift his pottery off the wheel, kneading his clay for him."

Because of the clay that could be found in the area, a small community of potters had settled near Seagrove as early as 1740. Ben Owen's ancestors were among them, having come from Staffordshire in England. Their pottery was plain and utilitarian:[2] crocks, jugs, churns, bowls, dishes. Occasionally they would load their wares into covered wagons and set out to peddle them.

The Seagrove area potters were still making the same kinds of pottery when Ben turned his first pieces as a boy, practicing at the wheel after his father had finished his day's work. By age 18 he had learned the basics, and something happened that changed his life. A man named Jacques Busbee saw a pie dish Ben Owen's father had made and consequently became interested in the Seagrove area potters.

Jacques Busbee was an artist, a native of Raleigh who operated a small shop in New York. He had been commissioning[3] potters to produce work for his shop but was dissatisfied with what he was getting. He wanted to start a pottery of his own so he could supervise the work and was thinking of getting one of the Seagrove area potters to work with him.

There was a problem. Jacques Busbee was interested in pottery for its artistic merit, as well as for its practical purposes. None of the older Seagrove area potters were interested in working with him. But Ben was young and eager to learn, and the two formed a partnership.

Jacques Busbee was not a potter, but Ben credits him with being an excellent teacher. Together they visited museums in New York, Washington, New Orleans, studying and photographing classic works from master potters throughout the world.

Jacques Busbee built his pottery in Moore County and called it Jugtown, and for 35 years Ben Owen worked there. In that time, he became one of America's master potters, and his work spread throughout the country—indeed, the world. It was exhibited in the Smithsonian Institute, the Metropolitan Museum of Art, and many other museums.

Simplicity was Ben Owen's guide. He was deeply influenced by the oriental masters. He once wrote that quietness, modesty of form, and harmony were the elements he strived to achieve in a piece of pottery. His work was beautiful and highly prized. It was, in fact, so highly prized that he had trouble keeping up with demand.

"I couldn't keep anything," he says with a chuckle. "They would keep me bought up, cleaned out as fast as I could get it finished."

2. utilitarian: practical, useful

3. commissioning: ordering, authorizing

Despite the demand, he never took advantage. He always kept his prices low. "Everybody fussed at me that come here and bought, said I ought to get more for it. Well, I says, I wanted to keep it so that everybody who would like to have some could get it."

Jacques Busbee died in 1947, and Ben Owen stayed on, working for his widow. He remained until 1959, when Jugtown was sold. Then he built the kilns out behind the workshop next to his house and began working for himself. The demand for his work remained constant.

"I could've sold a lot more than I did," he says. "There was somebody there wanting something about every day, and on Saturday it was one sight, people coming out from everywhere."

No crowds come anymore. Ben fought hard to keep working. Arthritis had bothered him for years but he continued working, although the pain was often severe. He kept working even as he watched his hands losing control, gradually drawing inward, crippling him. Finally, when he could no longer walk, and his hands could no longer form the clay, against his will, he had to quit.

He had an operation on his knee and it has improved enough for him to get around with the help of the walker. But his crippled hands will never again be able to produce the beautiful forms they once did.

"I haven't been in my shop in over a year," he says, leaning back in his rocking chair. "I miss being out there, meeting the people and seeing the people and . . . you know . . . working. It's taken me quite a while to get adjusted."

October, 1973
Seagrove, North Carolina

MEET THE AUTHOR:
Jerry Bledsoe (1941 –)

Some writers begin thinking of themselves as writers while still very young—as early as elementary school. Others take a more gradual route. Jerry Bledsoe was not at all interested in writing while in school. In fact, beginning in eighth grade, when he made his first U (unsatisfactory grade), he became disinterested in school altogether. It became, he said, "a downhill slide."

After graduation from Thomasville (NC)High School, he became a soldier, serving in Okinawa and Japan. The army, he says, "sort of pushed me into writing, and once I was trapped I couldn't get out." During his military career he became a writer of such skill that twice he won the Ernie Pyle Memorial Award—a prize given in memory of Ernie Pyle, a World War II reporter who won fame by writing columns about the ordinary fighting men and their daily lives.

After leaving military service, Bledsoe worked for newspapers, notably the *Greensboro Daily News*, for which he wrote human interest stories and humorous columns. He has published several collections of his articles and columns, as well as *Bitter Blood*, the true account of a sensational crime. He is editor/publisher of Down Home Press, a pub-

lishing company which specializes in books about the Carolinas and is currently working on another book.

To students like the young Jerry Bledsoe, "the failing capable student," he gives the following comment: "I would only offer the solace that failure in school doesn't necessarily translate to failure in life, but it makes success a lot more difficult."

Reflecting

1. We know that Ben Owen was a skilled potter. From what you have read, what kind of *person* do you think Ben Owen was? What facts support your opinion?
2. You may be interested to know that the Owen family continues the tradition which Ben Owen was carrying on. Although the original Ben Owen is dead, his grandson, Ben Owen III, still makes and sells pottery in the shop managed by Ben Owen, Jr.

Old Man

Grace Gibson

He wore smiles and workman's gloves
though now he watched the morning
traffic pass and always waved.
The orange bus filled with laughter
rolled by on cold October
days when leaves were bright as paint.

Winter weather on a bike
wavering toward town, he
perilously raised one hand.
"Hold on, old man!" we yelled from
a thicket of arms waving
back to him. When the trees came
into bud, then bloom, we missed
him.
Little is left of his
house that stood behind a screen
of second growth just outside
town. Only its chimney stands,
smokeless now with empty hearth.

Preview

As we go about our daily rounds, we encounter people who become almost like part of the landscape. These people seem always to be in their accustomed places, doing their usual tasks. We may wave or nod briefly, but without taking much note of them.

In this poem, Grace Gibson presents an old man whom students see on their way to school each day. It is a very quiet poem. Nothing much seems to happen—or does it?

MEET THE AUTHOR:
Grace Gibson (1919–)

When Grace Evelyn Loving Gibson was a child in Drakes Branch, Virginia, she began writing for a children's page in the *Richmond Times-Dispatch*. She has been writing ever since, and her poems have been widely published. Her first collection, *Home in Time*, sold out its first printing in just one month.

After obtaining degrees at UNC-Greensboro and at Duke University, Ms. Gibson worked as a reporter on the *Durham Sun* and taught high school English. In recent years she has taught at Pembroke State University and St. Andrews Presbyterian College in Laurinburg. She has also led workshops and participated in many readings. Upon her retirement from Pembroke, a scholarship fund was begun in her honor.

"Writing is fun!" she declares. She recommends that students write "all you can, keeping a diary or a journal, writing for your school (or other) paper."

Reflecting

1. When a story or poem has little action, we are forced into our imaginations to figure out what it is about—what the author is trying to say. The man in this poem seems not to be kin or personal friend of anyone on the bus. The students seem to know little about him except what they observe each morning on their way to school. From their observations, what can you gather about him?
2. One day they miss him. What do you think has happened to him?
3. Why do you think the speaker remembers this old man? What feelings does she have?

Grandmothers: Two Views

Family is important to each of us. In the following poems, two poets each write of grandmothers. The first is written from the point of view of a child thinking of the "nana" she's going to visit; the second, from that of an adult, remembering the "grandma" she once visited.

On My Way to Nana's House

Linda Beatrice Brown

I'm on my way to Nana's house,
Can you come?
Nana has candy, a big box full
Nana has taffy you can pull
Won't you come?

I'm on my way to Nana's house,
Won't you come?
Nana has turnip greens and candied yams
Nana has turkeys and country hams
Won't you come?

I'm on my way to Nana's house
Can you come?
Nana has a feather bed high and light
Nana has kisses when you yawn goodnight

But best of all,
Nana has a nice big lap
For snuggling in tight
Won't you come?

for grandma

Jaki Shelton Green

I heard your voice this morning
speaking from the foot of the bed
your quilt crawled to the
floor
as I lay down in the
first whisper of dawn.
I heard your voice this morning
the sound of cloth
a casual sound
a sunday morning
preparing to visit your lord
sound
half your life
half my life
half my daughter's life
we all dream of landscapes
romantic deserts
white sands
connecting us together
a half dozen roses
I play out my life
listening every morning
for your voice
at the foot of the bed.

MEET THE AUTHOR:

Linda Beatrice Brown (1939–)
See p. 405

MEET THE AUTHOR:

Jaki Shelton Green (1953–)
See p. 508

Reflecting

1. Look for details or words that indicate how the speakers in the two poems feel about their grandmothers. Are their feelings similar or different? Explain.

2. Think of someone you admire a great deal—a family member, a neighbor, a teacher, a friend. Try writing a tribute to that person, using one of the poems above as models.

   a. In "On My Way to Nana's House," the speaker doesn't say "It's great being at Nana's house." Instead, she just tells us what is there, and we add it all up: "Hey, this is a warm, welcoming place to be." Think of a household you consider warm and welcoming—like Nana's house. What specific things make it so? Include them in your poem.

   Follow the form Linda Beatrice Brown has used—the statement, the invitation, the description of what the speaker knows is at the house.

   b. Before writing a poem like "for grandma," prewrite by listing things—articles, animals, scenes—which remind you of the person about whom you are writing. Be sure to include some of these in the poem. Notice Jaki Shelton Green's form: unrhymed very short lines, giving an almost breathless effect of one thought tumbling after another. Arrange your details in just such lines.

Granner Weeks

Jill McCorkle

Preview

Every person is unique—one of a kind. Some people, however, have so many colorful features—perhaps the way they speak, the clothes they wear, their habits, or odd ways of behaving—that they seem more distinctive than others. Granner Weeks is one of these distinctive persons—the kind of person about whom people say, "When she was made, they threw the mold away."

In the following excerpt from Jill McCorkle's novel, *July 7th,* we meet Granner Weeks on the morning of her eighty-third birthday. Although she is not telling the story herself, much of the story is told in her language. As you read, list her distinctive language and behavior that let us know that she is "one of a kind."

Granner Weeks has tossed and turned ever since she went to bed at nine-thirty, she is so excited. Now it is July 7th; it is her birthday and at seven a.m., give or take a few minutes if her Mama's memory was correct, she will be eighty-three years old. She just wishes that she could get a little rest so that she won't be slam wore out when her party starts mid-afternoon. It's two o'clock now, so she only has about twelve to thirteen hours to wait. She has already gotten up once for warm milk, once for a cup of hot water so that her body will perform first thing when she gets up so that she won't have that full uncomfortable feeling. Now she is eating a bowl of Product 19 because she has found that that seems to help the system as well. She knows she needs to get a good night's sleep, but every year it's this way. It's more exciting than being a child and listening for Santa's deer and sleigh bells.

More exciting than even thinking you hear that fat man creeping out of your fireplace, like she did as a child once and she didn't even have any kind of big Christmas like most children nowadays. She was lucky if the fat man left her some fruit and nuts and maybe some shoes and socks, and it was still exciting. Lord knows, if she had ever had a Christmas like her great-granddaughter, Petie Rose Tyner, with all those talking and wetting dolls, she would have tossed and turned all year long waiting. But now she's old; she's just about eighty-three and times have changed since she was a girl. People buy nice presents, or at least they got the money to. The actual niceness comes down to whether or not they got any taste about them. It's gonna be a nice birthday this year, with lots of nice presents, Granner can feel it in her feeble bones.

Imagine, Granner Weeks, formerly Irene Turner of Flatbridge, turning eighty-three years old! She can't stand it. It really is just like waiting for Santa Claus to come! She has baked a big coconut cake just like she does every year, and has already pulled out a big box of fireworks and her flags that she hangs out every year on her birthday. She has a North Carolina flag that she hangs in the kitchen, the American flag of 1776 that was a gift to her in the Bicentennial year that she drapes over the dining room buffet, her American flag (the modern one that includes Alaska and Hawaii) that she hangs in the entrance hall, and of course the Christian flag that she waves out of her bedroom window, but the real treasure is the great big Confederate flag that

her granddaddy passed down to her. She can just see him, just hear his voice! He was sitting out on his front porch swing, with one leg of his pants just sort of hanging limp and swaying back and forth. "They took away my leg, yes sirree, but they can't take away this flag. Wave it proud, girl. Do it right!" Granner Weeks does do it right. She always has done it right, and every July 7th she hangs that flag out on the front porch and lets it wave all day long. It makes her weep every time.

Her custom of flag-waving started way back, back when her husband Buck was still alive, back when little Kate was just a tot and had never laid her eyes on Ernie Stubbs. Back when her son, Harold Weeks, was still a nice child. She had thought it was silly to have two holidays right there together; it just made things too hard on her, having two big parties in one week. She had said to Buck, finally, after years of being pooped out on her birthday, "Let's combine the holidays, Buck. Let's celebrate this country's birth with my own birth."

"All right by me," Buck had said, because he was a very agreeable person, unlike his son Harold Weeks. "You won't mind gettin your presents three days early?"

"I ain't thinking of changing my day," she had said. "I was thinking it would be easier to change the country's day, so that I'll have three extra days to plan."

"All right by me," he had said and it has been that way ever since. It's a big celebration, with the flags waving, red white and blue Uncle Sam hats, and balloons. You name it. All the family comes and Granner always likes to pause for a few minutes to think over the guest list to see if there are any additions or subtractions. Lord, that was a sad July 7th when she had to cross Buck out; every year it's sad when she has to cross Buck out. Let's see, she thinks, and pushes away her half-eaten bowl of Product 19. She is too nervous to eat. There's her daughter Kate, and Kate's husband, Ernie Stubbs, who has made quite a name for himself around here as a real estate salesman, especially since he was raised over there on Injun Street, which as far as Granner can remember has always been a rough, cheap part of town. Ernie has done so well that he built them a fine house out in the country, a house with two and a half bathrooms and four bedrooms, even though there's just the two of them now. What's more, he can afford to run his air-conditioner all summer long. Of course that doesn't mean much to Granner, because she's cool natured now that her blood has slowed, but still that's sign of somebody with money to burn. It bothered Granner a little when she heard that they were building themselves a house in the country, because used to people with money moved to town, just like she and Buck had done.

Her yard right here on Main Street is a far sight bigger than Kate's and prettier, too. Ernie chopped down all of their trees to make room for that big house. Still, he's done all right by them, built that big brick patio off of that house just so he'd have some place to put up those Tiki torches when they have a party.

"I don't see you too much now that you've moved to the country," Granner said one day.

"Not country, mother," Kate had said. "It's called Cape Fear Trace." Granner just calls it "out there" because an old woman can't be expected to remember everything. That Kate always did take it in her head that she was a notch or two better than everyone else; pitched a pure fit when she wasn't asked to be a debutante up in Raleigh. Granner explained time and time again that Buck hadn't come from such fine lines, though he was the best looking man in all the county. But no, all Kate wanted was to be in high cotton, and how did she get there but to marry somebody off of Injun Streeet! Even if he has done well, he still came off of Injun Street and all that money don't change that, don't change the fact that his Mama died poor as a churchmouse. Granner is happy that Kate is happy and got just what she wanted, because for the longest time she had had her doubts, due to Kate not being the best looking thing. "She's a real plain Jane," Buck said one time when Kate entered herself in a beauty pageant and nobody had the nerve to tell her that she didn't stand one bit of a chance, and it hurt Granner's heart to hear that about her very own child, although she knew that it was the dead truth. Buck Weeks, rest his soul, wasn't the smartest man around, but he always told the dead truth.

MEET THE AUTHOR:
Jill McCorkle (1958–)

Jill McCorkle made publishing history that gained national notice: her first two novels were published on the same day. The fact that she was only twenty-six years old at the time also caused quite a stir.

Of course she had been writing for a long time—ever since she was a very small girl, when she composed what she has called "lousy" poetry. At seven, she wrote her first story: "The Night Santa Failed to Come." (She reports that it did have a happy ending.) After completing degrees at UNC-Chapel Hill and Hollins College, she began working as a medical secretary during the daytime and writing novels on weekends. It took her two years to complete *The Cheer Leader*, and eighteen months to write *July 7th*, both of which were published in 1984. She has since published a third novel, *Tending to Virginia*.

Some writers like to polish each part as they go along, but not Jill McCorkle. "I write very fast and don't scrutinize what I put

down," she declares. "I go back later and fix it." She doesn't like to talk much about her stories while she's writing them, but when she finishes, she shares them with others, including family members.

Reflecting

1. Here is a list of adjectives and/or phrases that someone might use to describe Granner Weeks. Choose one and find details and examples that support it.
   a. childlike
   b. mature
   c. creative
   d. imaginative
   e. proud
   f. family-oriented
   g. interested in tradition
2. Although we don't meet Granner Weeks's family, we catch glimpses of them through Granner Weeks's thoughts. Explain what we know about these characters, including what Granner Weeks thinks of them: Buck, Harold, Kate, Ernie.
3. Compare this selection to "1949" (p. 403), Linda Beatrice Brown's story of a little girl on her tenth birthday. How are Ronnie's and Granner Weeks's attitudes similar? How are they different?

Haiku

The haiku, an Oriental form, is a very short poem, just three lines long, with each line containing a set number of syllables: five, then seven, then five. Modern poets sometimes take liberties with these limits, adding or subtracting a syllable or two here or there, but they follow another of the haiku's demands: that it concentrate on an **image**—an appeal to the senses. The haiku poet tries to present that image so precisely that it begins to take on special meaning.

Haiku are not meant to be zipped through swiftly like ads or comic strips. We are expected to think about each image, let it work on our imagination, allow it to create a mood.

MEET THE AUTHOR:
Lenard Moore (1958–)

Born in Jacksonville, North Carolina, Lenard (pronounced with an accent on the second syllable) Moore began writing short stories while he was in high school. He continued writing—this time, poems—during the three years he served in the U.S. Army. Currently, he serves as writer-in-residence in public schools and writes poetry, essays, and reviews. His work has been anthologized and published not only in this country, but in India, New Zealand, Japan, Canada, and Nigeria, and has been translated into Spanish, Italian, Japanese, and Chinese. He has read his poetry in formal programs and on the radio across this country and in West Germany.

Lenard Moore's writing has been honored several times, including an award from the Haiku Museum of Tokyo and the 1989

Emerging Artist Grant given by the City of Raleigh Arts Commission. He has four pieces of advice for the students whom he teaches in North Carolina schools: "Keep a journal, and list ideas for writing in it. Read as much literature as possible. Write about what you know. Listen to the way people talk."

The Open Eye

Lenard Moore

Old deserted farm;
spring whirlwind twirls peach petals
over sunlit hills

In the moonlit breeze
slowly falling one by one:
white dogwood petals . . .

Summer sunset—
old oak's shadow lengthening
on the sunken grave

another deer
everywhere deer   leaping
through autumn night-fog

Winter stillness—
old barn's splintered remnants caught
in a crescent moon

Preview

It seems appropriate that Lenard Moore would entitle his collection of haiku *The Open Eye*. Each poem deals with a single image, presenting in very few words a remarkably sharp picture. The book is organized according to seasons and the poems are untitled.

Reflecting

1. The first two haiku both deal with springtime blossoms from trees. Both poems even use the word *petals*. But notice the differences:
   a. The first deals with fast action—twirling—while the second emphasizes the leisurely motion of falling dogwood petals. Notice how the second line slows the motion down, just by the words that are chosen and the way they are arranged.
   b. The first mentions sunlit hills; the second, a moonlit breeze.
2. The first haiku uses *word echoes*—repeated sounds such as the "w"s in *whirlwind* and *twirls*—to make the poem musical. Can you find other examples in this haiku? In the third one? In the fifth?
3. The third haiku doesn't have a single word in it that deals with feeling, yet it is certainly a serious, even sad, poem. What words give it a sad mood?
4. Try these substitutions for the fifth haiku:
   quiet for *stillness*
   antique for *old*
   broken for *splintered*
   remains for *remnants*
   shown for *caught*
   quarter for *crescent*

   What differences do the substitutions make? Do any of them work as well as Lenard Moore's original choices?
5. Choose an image which you find interesting and try your hand at capturing it—and a mood—in a haiku. Stick to the three-line, 5-7-5 form as best you can, but, like Moore, feel free to modify it if you need to.

WRYMES

Preview

You're probably familiar with **puns**—plays on words achieved by using a word so that it suddenly takes on two meanings at once or by using the similar sounds of different words. A good deal of humor is based on just such word tricks: twisting a word so that suddenly we see double meanings.

The title of Mae Woods Bell's collection, *Wrymes,* is itself a pun, combining the words *wry* and *rhymes.* (*Wry* means amusing or droll—the kind of dry wit for which Ms. Bell is noted.)

Each of the poems below takes a familiar saying and uses it as a basis for a pun.

Unmedical Opinion

Mae Woods Bell

There's an ironic twist to the fact
That many an unhappy bloke
Goes to a psychiatrist 'cause he's cracking up,
And leaves there completely broke.

bloke: British
slang for fellow

Lottery Luck

Mae Woods Bell

On the subject of lotteries,
I'll say this, and then I'm done;
Money can be lost
In more ways than won.

Mae Woods Bell (1921–)

Mae Woods Bell came all the way from the far western United States—New Mexico and California—to become a Tar Heel, but once she got here, she established herself firmly as a major contributor to the literary and cultural life of the state. In 1951, she became founding director of the Rocky Mount Children's Museum, and during the thirty-five years she continued as director, she also published writings in newspapers and literary magazines. She is perhaps best known for her four-line poems which take a humorous and often ironic look at life.

Ms. Bell began writing while still in elementary school, contributing a column on scout news to the local newspaper and rewriting the endings of favorite books such as *Treasure Island* and *The Wizard of Oz*. In high school, she worked on the paper and entered essay contests. She has won the Samuel Talmadge Ragan Award for her writing, the James Short Award for her museum work,

and the Silver Fawn/Silver Beaver Award for her work on behalf of the Boy Scouts of America.

Reflecting

Try writing your own **quatrain** (four-line poem) based on a pun. You might begin with a cliché or an old saying such as

1. Two heads are better than one.
2. A rolling stone gathers no moss.
3. He who laughs last laughs best.
4. A bird in the hand is worth two in the bush.
5. A penny saved is a penny earned.

You can also use a commercial slogan or the title of a popular song on which to base your poem. (The saying, slogan, or title must be very well known so that people will catch on to your trick.)

Preview

A. R. Ammons's poetry is quite varied. He writes very long poems as well as very short ones. Some are personal, based on his life in rural North Carolina. Others, very intellectual and philosophical, spring from his knowledge of the natural and scientific universe. Many of them are marked by playfulness, as he performs tricks with words, their meanings, and their sounds.

The following is one of his playful poems. Watch for the tricks A. R. Ammons plays in these five lines (including title).

Small Song

A. R. Ammons

The reeds give
way to the

wind and give
the wind away

A. R. Ammons (1926–)

In an interview, A. R. Ammons once told a Winston-Salem reporter, "I never dreamed of being a Poet poet. I think I always wanted to be an amateur poet." But he has come a long, long way from being an amateur. Today he is considered one of the most important poets in the nation, and he has won almost every national award available to writers.

Born in 1926, Ammons grew up on a tobacco farm and graduated from Whiteville High School. After serving in the U.S. Navy during World War II, he earned a degree in science from Wake Forest College (now Wake Forest University). He served as principal of an elementary school in Hatteras before moving north, where he eventually became an executive of a firm manufacturing biological glassware. Since 1964 he has been on the faculty of Cornell University.

Ammons did not begin writing poetry until his service with the Navy in the South Pacific, when he began keeping a log. His career did not blossom overnight. He submitted poems to poetry magazines for seven years before two were finally accepted. In 1955, he paid a company to publish his first book. Since then, he has published over a dozen collections, most with major publishing companies, and his work has been translated into at least five languages.

He has clearly explained why he writes poetry: "If a poem works out, the feeling is so wonderful, whether you get to share it with someone else or not, just to get the poem right feels so good that it's practically its own reward. . . . And then, if you get something else, wonderful, but you don't have to get something else."

Reflecting

1. Can you think of two meanings for the title?
2. What is the difference in meaning between "give way to" and "give . . . away"?
3. In this poem, notice the word music:
   a. all the sounds which are "breathy"— and thus make us think of wind.
   b. sounds which echo one another.

Preview

Basketball is a favorite pastime in North Carolina, both as an activity and as a spectator sport. After all, this state is home to a number of national stars: for example, James Worthy and Michael Jordan, whose dazzling court performances have become legendary.

Michael McFee takes a look at a boy so completely absorbed in shooting baskets that he forgets himself entirely until he becomes one-and-the-same with the activity.

Shooting Baskets at Dusk

Michael McFee

He will never be happier than this,
lost in the perfectly thoughtless motion
of shot, rebound, dribble, shot,

his mind removed as the gossipy swallows
that pick and roll, that give and go
down the school chimney like smoke in reverse

as he shoots, rebounds, dribbles, shoots,
the brick wall giving the dribble back
to his body beginning another run

from foul line, corner, left of the key,
the jealous rim guarding its fickle net
as he shoots, rebounds, dribbles, shoots,

absorbed in the rhythm that seems to flow
from his fingertips to the winded sky
and back again to this lonely orbit

of shot, rebound, dribble, shot,
until he is just a shadow and a sound
though the ball still burns in his vanished hands.

Michael McFee (1954–)

A native of Asheville, Michael McFee began writing in grade school, encouraged by his mother. Now he is a poet of growing reputation, with two collections already published: *Plain Air* and *Vanishing Acts*. His book reviews appear in a number of newspapers, as well as on weekly broadcasts on WUNC radio out of Chapel Hill.

After graduating from T. R. Roberson High School in Buncombe County, Michael McFee earned two degrees at UNC-Chapel Hill. He has been awarded fellowships in creative writing from the National Endowment for the Arts and the North Carolina Arts Council. His poetry has won a number of national awards, and he has taught as a visiting professor at a number of major universities. He has also given readings of his work widely—not only in North Carolina, but at the Poetry Center in New York City and the Folger Shakespeare Library in Washington, DC.

McFee recommends that anyone seriously interesting in writing take a business-like approach to developing that interest. "You've got to set up your life so you can write," he says, suggesting such means as taking creative writing courses and workshops, joining writers' groups, and disciplining oneself to write each day, perhaps setting aside certain hours to do so. Currently residing in Durham, he has made it a habit to write something daily—poems, reviews, letters—"to keep the tools sharp."

Reflecting

1. Why do you think McFee's poem is just one long sentence? Why doesn't he break it up?
2. Notice that every line has the same rhythm—four beats to a line. Why did McFee choose to have four beats instead of three or five? Notice also that one certain phrase is repeated four times in the six stanzas. (There are variations in the word-forms. For example, the verb *shoots* occurs instead of the noun *shot,* but the order never varies.) What is the effect of this rhythm and repetition?

From *Vanishing Acts,* by Michael McFee, published by Gnomon Press. Copyright © 1989 by Michael McFee. Reprinted by permission of the author.

Preview

Do you ever feel that no matter what you achieve, someone else will manage to top your record—that you'll never make it to "Number One"? If so, you will feel sympathy with the speaker of "Up-One."

Up-One

Emily Herring Wilson

If I ride my bike with no hands,
someone can always ride standing
on the seat. If I walk a fence,
someone can always walk it backwards. Balance a broom on my
middle finger, and someone else
can balance it on his nose.
Today I'm going to climb a tree
and twist the tail of the first
squirrel who gets in my way!

MEET THE AUTHOR:
Emily Herring Wilson (1939–)

When Emily Herring Wilson was eleven years old, her grandmother gave her a journal, in which she began to write poems, just as her grandmother had. She has been writing poems ever since, and has published two volumes, *Down Zion's Alley* and *Balancing on Stones*. She has also worked as a journalist and published nonfiction.

Although Ms. Wilson grew up in Columbus, Georgia, she has spent her adult life in North Carolina, beginning with her years at UNC-Greensboro and Wake Forest University. She has worked in the Poetry-in-the-Schools program, and has taught at Salem College.

Emily Wilson advises students, "Keep your journals and diaries to read later. Type up some of your favorite work, and keep it in a manuscript."

Reflecting

1. How does the speaker of the poem seem to feel about always being outdone? (Is he/she defiant? Discouraged? Depressed? Determined?)
2. Think of three other examples of feats you might try—only to be outdone by someone else. Try using Emily Herring Wilson's poem as a frame into which you fit your own examples. End as she did with an example of something you would like to do to prove your determined spirit.

Trees

Trees seem to have caught the human imagination ever since we started stringing words together. A tree figures prominently in the Garden of Eden story in the Bible. A favorite legend about George Washington features a cherry tree. A favorite song of soldiers in World War II was "Don't Sit Under the Apple Tree with Anyone Else But Me." In the jungle, Tarzan is said to have made his home in a tree. Tying yellow ribbons "around the old oak tree" (as the song goes) has become a symbol of welcome to people who have undergone some difficult ordeal.

Trees also often provide hideaways for kids. Sometimes they become supporting structures for tree houses; sometimes the tree itself becomes a house, a retreat where a youngster can take a friend or a book—or just his or her imagination.

Here are three poems about trees, all written by North Carolina poets, and each treating the subject differently.

Mimosa

Mary C. Snotherly

When I was born,
my father planted a mimosa sapling
to grow with me,
for me to climb when I was ten.

I climbed those limbs—
was Tarzan, Jane, sometimes Boy
and where two branches bent
I hid a tin—a Prince Albert tobacco box.
Inside, a ruby ring—the prize from Cracker Jacks—
one bluejay feather, silver-tipped and thin,
two glass marbles bright as suns,
a yellow satin ribbon.

I'd skin-the-cat,
swing the low limb upside-down—
my hair tumbling, sweeping the ground.
Once, I climbed so high
my father drove—
all that way from his office—
home, to bring me down.

Summer nights,
when dishes rattled in the sink
and windows lit
and planes and fireflies speckled skies,
I'd sit on my favorite limb—
pick soft pink puffs to buff my nose,
to catch my hair, a crown.
The whippoorwill might come
to roost, to sing.

I still climb high
when I need someplace to go,
still love things with wings—
planes and birds,
giant butterflies and gypsy moths
and leaves that spin—
and still have trouble sometimes
coming down.

From *Weymouth*, ed. Sam Ragan. Copyright © 1987 by St. Andrews Press. Reprinted by permission of the author.

Preview

In the preceding poem, Mary Snotherly tells of a mimosa tree which even in adulthood continues to have a special meaning for her. Mimosas, which in this country grow best in the South, are covered in summer with feathery leaves and blooms that resemble pink ballerina skirts. Because their limbs are sturdy and wide spreading, they are usually fairly easy to climb.

MEET THE AUTHOR:
Mary C. Snotherly (1938–)

When Mary Snotherly's grandmother died, among the treasures she left behind was a poem in white ink written on red construction paper, illustrated with drawings of deer and snow falling. It was one of the poems young Mary had written, encouraged by her mother.

When she went to Needham Broughton High School in Raleigh, Mary Snotherly found another encourager: teacher Phyllis Peacock, whose influence was felt by others who went on to become writers, including Reynolds Price (p. 476). Although at Meredith College she majored in home economics and natural science, Ms. Snotherly continued writing, contributing her poems to the literary magazine, *The Acorn.*

Busy with career and family life, Mary Snotherly stopped writing for several years, but began again in the 1970s, "when I felt a need to express my feelings and explore the changes in my life." Now she has published two poetry collections and written children's stories, fiction, essays, and reviews.

For seventeen years, Ms. Snotherly worked for Eastern Airlines, where she "did everything." Currently as writer-in-residence with Wake County Schools, she takes deep pleasure in helping students learn to love poetry and write their own "pure poetry." She is a past president of the North Carolina Writers' Conference.

558

Another tree frequently associated with the South is the magnolia, famed for its broad, creamy, velvet-petaled blossoms and their sweet fragrance. When the petals fall from the blossoms, slender ivory pistils are revealed, rising like candles from the green foliage. Because its large glossy leaves are evergreen and because it can grow to magnificent heights, the magnolia has been a favorite tree in formal gardens and lawns.

Below are two entirely different poetic treatments of the magnolia.

Preview

In this poem, Michael McFee uses a **metaphor** comparing the magnolia to a girl at a cotillion (a formal ball at which girls are presented to society). See how many ways this metaphor works.

MEET THE AUTHOR:
Michael McFee (1954–)
See p. 553

See p. 553

Cotillion

Michael McFee

Stately as a southern belle
in the bald room of winter,
the glossy magnolia gathers
a court of birds in her skirt,

choking the air with chatter
thick as memories of the smell
of her luscious candles
in summer's open window.

From *Plain Air,* by Michael McFee, published by University Presses of Florida. Copyright © 1983 by Florida Board of Regents. Reprinted by permission of the author.

Preview

Like Mary Snotherly, Margaret Boothe Baddour writes about a tree that was important to her during her childhood. As you read, compare her poem both to Ms. Snotherly's memory of the mimosa and to Michael McFee's very different perception of magnolias.

Wild Magnolias

Margaret Boothe Baddour

Wild memories
of riding the black-barked magnolias
me and Kitty Wallace
attacking the tree
gripping the trunk
to hoist up
and straddle a tangled limb
and ride feverishly
the wild magnolias

My mother's wrath
at her blackened child
at the already dirty
urchin, Kitty,
and the torn blossoms
strewn on the ground
booty from a mighty good time
upon the high seas
on the riding bronc
riding the wild magnolias

      My genteel mother
      my pale, light mother
      caught me
      riding the wild magnolias.

Published in *Wind,* 1975. Reprinted by permission of the author.

Margaret Boothe Baddour (1949–)

Audiences who have seen and heard Margaret Boothe Baddour at a poetry reading seldom forget the experience: she *performs* her poetry, sometimes with high drama, often with high good humor. Her dramatic readings reflect her training at Stephens College, where she received an associate degree in theater arts. She also earned two degrees at UNC-Chapel Hill.

A native of Greensboro, she completed high school at Salem Academy in Winston-Salem, where a teacher encouraged her in writing both poetry and prose, and where she joined the Scribblers Club. Her varied career includes newspaper work (the Burlington, NC *Times-News*) and teaching, as well as a stint directing the Goldsboro Community Arts Council. Her poetry has been widely published in both literary magazines and anthologies.

Margaret Boothe Baddour is as noted for teaching writing and for her support of the arts as for her own writing. She has taught poetry writing in varied settings (workshops, public schools, colleges) and to every population from kindergarten students through senior citizens. Currently she teaches a creative writing class at Atlantic Christian College. Her column on the arts appears in several North Carolina newspapers, including the Goldsboro *News-Argus*, and has won state awards, as have her poems. She has served a large number of arts organizations and was a founder of the North Carolina Writers Network.

Reflecting

1. Count the ways Mary Snotherly used the mimosa tree her father planted for her.
2. How does the tree continue to influence her, now that she is an adult? (Can you figure out two different meanings for "I still climb high/when I need someplace to go" and "still have trouble sometimes/coming down"?)
3. What differences are there in the way Mary Snotherly played in her mimosa tree and the way Margaret Boothe Baddour played in her mother's magnolia? Are there similarities? (Notice, for example, that in each case, the trees are associated with the child's parents.)
4. Michael McFee's and Margaret Boothe Baddour's poems differ considerably in mood. Notice how Ms. Baddour's form leaps over the page, while McFee's is in regular four-line stanzas. Think about the elegant sounds of *stately, glossy, gathers, luscious*. Contrast these words with the lively and more informal *attacking, hoist, straddle, booty*.

Preview

Now that our state is so thickly populated, it is unusual to see bands of wild animals of any kind, but for years people have been intrigued by the wild ponies that occupy the Outer Banks. In recent years, with so many tourists and cars on the island, the ponies have had to be enclosed in fenced pastures to assure their survival.

In the following poem, the poet describes an encounter with these beautiful animals.

Ocracoke Ponies

Ellen Johnston-Hale

We scanned the beach
for sight of them galloping
along the surf,

searched marshy grasses
for flash of tail,
glimpse of flowing mane.

We came upon it then:
Beside the road—a pasture
encircled by a fence.

There they were—the ponies,
penned,
grazing as gently as lambs.

Tourists stood outside
the rail
and fed them sugar lumps.

I reached out
to one that trotted up and
licked my hand

and tried to picture him
racing wild and free again
along a wind-swept shore.

MEET THE AUTHOR:
Ellen Turlington Johnston-Hale (1929–)

It is very possible that as a student you have been influenced by Ellen Johnston-Hale. As a poet-in-residence in many schools throughout the state, she has helped thousands of students discover that they are capable of expressing themselves and touching others through their own poetry. Furthermore, through dozens of teacher workshops, she has helped many teachers find creative ways of teaching both the reading and the writing of poetry. "Poetry Alive!," her award-winning video program, has been presented repeatedly on national public television stations.

Writing came naturally in her family, possibly because her mother was a journalist. When her parents went out for the evening, they often left poems under the children's pillows. "It was better than the tooth fairy!" Ms. Johnston-Hale declares. As a little girl, she wrote poems for holidays and birthdays, and, with her sisters, dictated stories which their mother typed.

After graduating from Sidwell Friends High School in Washington, DC, she earned a degree at UNC-Chapel Hill and another at

UNC-Charlotte. She taught for eleven years in public schools in Statesville and Mecklenburg County. In recent years she has published five books of poetry and served as president of the North Carolina Poetry Society.

Reflecting

In the middle stanzas (3–6), the poet gives us a picture of the ponies as they live today. She surrounds that view with her inner vision of how the ponies once lived, free to run unrestrained across the entire island. In a sense, she "frames" the current situation with word-snapshots of how things used to be.

Think of a place which you have seen change: perhaps a field or woodland which

has become a shopping center or housing development, or an old service station which has been replaced by a supermarket. Perhaps although you have not seen the change take place, you know about it: a town now sits where once Indians had a village, for example. Use Ms. Johnston-Hale's form—imagination, then reality, then imagination again—to give your reader a "double vision" of the place.

Preview

Almost everyone would name the cockroach as one of the most despised creatures. Anna Wooten-Hawkins says that she decided to write "The Roach" to see if she could find any way to sympathize with it. "If I could identify with a cockroach," she says, "I could identify with anything or anybody." She chose to write about the American cockroach, which is large and black, instead of its smaller brown cousin, the German roach, because the former looks uglier and more ferocious.

The Roach

Anna Wooten-Hawkins

Three a.m., my American friend,
I pad into the kitchen for a glass of milk,
throw on the light, and there you are.

　　　　Hearing me,
you've paused on the stainless steel strip
by the sink, thinking what to do. I'm thinking
of the filthy germs you've planted on my counter-
tops, thinking I can't let you live. Steering
the craft of millenia, you shift cautiously
to a better position sideways, a diminutive ocean-
liner, your hideousness when you turn, sublime—
the various oily headparts, alert and culpable,
the razorback "hair" rigid on your legs. Without
friends, it is not the light you wished. Yet you
admirably scramble past the spigots, freeze in
the shadow under the toaster. Believing yourself
hidden, you're unaware your slick chitinous rump
protrudes beneath the black broil button.

Published in *Pembroke Magazine,* No. 14, 1982. Reprinted by permission of the author.

Many times I have waited
as you wait now, in half-shadow,
for the end—the crushing thumb,
the bilious shoe. Soul crouched,
heart flattened on a tabletop.

Once, before the paperboy, I came on a crowd
of you, a Fiddlers' Convention—one of you working
some cellophane in the trash, another knitting
feelers in a pot, another on hind legs propped against
a cracker packet. You were so many you didn't even
run, just craned your necks to the indifferent light
and carried on. But now you are alone. Now the shoe
is on the other sticky foot.

What you are thinking under the toaster,
what it is you feel, if you remember
your life in walls, in drains, if
fear is what you feel, I do not know.

Once in another house I lived alone,
clamped clamshells over your kind
to stop their traffic in my bedroom;
for days crept around the mounds, nights
slept fitfully. Then lifting the cream
and purple weights nearly flush with the
floor, not one, *not one of you* was there.
I did admire it.

Even so, the sight of you shoots horror
to my blood. I have pointed the Raid can
at you like any killer, and writhed as you
died in cruel positions. No one can wish
you away. The crunch you make when mashed
is nightmare, the poison in hors d'oeuvre
trays more gruesome still. The first summer,
a holocaust of strewn bodies in the kitchen.
When I woke next morning my lethal dainties
had not killed the largest of you, hideous
and half-dead, heaving yourselves across
the orange warp-woof of placemats, dragging
like dazed addicts. The smallest of you had been
dismembered on the stove by larger brethren.
Our Armageddon. After that I had dreams.

How still you keep. As if you know to move
would frighten me to mayhem, nor do I move.
I do not want to smoke you out, to make you
scutter in crazed patterns over cabinets.
I do not want to kill you ever. I like
the quiet and our communion—how you are so
well-behaved, how you do not lunge straight
at me out of fear, how well you listen, for you
cannot see me. Were I to step forward, without
sound, you would know, back turned to me,
and you too would step forward. Were I to stop,
you too would stop. I learn well
this manner of surviving.

One can kill, but never conquer you.
You steer your way through mazes,
bilk scientists who pluck your eyes
by *knowing* not to stir till night.

In blight blizzard drought
you would outlive us all who stand
upright at the kitchen's lightswitch,
playing God. So you have thrived
in the interstices of the universe,
since the first breakfast of time,
digesting nearly all.

They who said beauty is not everything were right.

By way of bowing to
your ancient cunning,
I crook my finger.
I give you back
your needed dark.

MEET THE AUTHOR:
Anna Wooten-Hawkins (1948–   )

Kinston native Anna Wooten-Hawkins began writing poems at the age of seven. She continued writing throughout high school and college (Hollins College and UNC-Greensboro). Today she is still writing poetry and has published a prize-winning book, *Satan Speaks of Eve in Seven Voices, After the Fall,* an imaginative treatment of the story of the Garden of Eden. At St. Mary's Junior College in Raleigh, she teaches creative writing, advises the literary magazine, and organizes Muse Week, an annual literary forum featuring North Carolina writers. For her contribution to literary arts, she was awarded the first City of Raleigh Arts Commission Award for Excellence in Writing.

When she was earning a master's degree at UNC-Greensboro, she met fellow poet Tom Hawkins (see p. 439) in a class. Soon after they met, he commented, "Two poets

can't marry." They did, however, and now both live in Raleigh, where they work and encourage each other in their writing.

Language Alert

1. The cockroach has inhabited the earth for *millennia* (thousands of years).
2. A beetle looks like a *diminutive* (little) car.
3. A culprit is *culpable* (responsible for doing something wrong).
4. Some insects have outer coverings that are *chitinous* (tough, like horns or shells).
5. *Bile* is a bitter liquid secreted by the liver. Something *bilious* is bitter.
6. An *hors d'oeuvre* (pronounced *or-derve*) is an appetizer or snack served before the meal.
7. A *holocaust* is a widespread destruction of people or property.
8. According to the Bible, *Armageddon* will be the scene of a final battle between the forces of good and evil, to take place at the end of the world. Today we use the term to refer to any decisive and terrible conflict.
9. The scene was one of *mayhem* (terrible destruction).
10. No one wants to be *bilked* (swindled, cheated).
11. In buildings, bugs often thrive in dark *interstices* (small spaces between things).

Reflecting

1. In the first two stanzas, the speaker talks to a roach she has discovered when she turned on the light. As they both hesitate, she describes him in great detail. At one point, she says that his hideousness (ugliness) is sublime (noble, majestic, inspiring awe). How can this be?
2. The speaker in the poem remembers several other times when she has encountered roaches—usually in groups. Notice what she compares the roaches to; how she has fought them; how they behaved.
3. In stanza three, she remembers being in a situation like that in which the roach finds himself now. In what ways are they similar?
4. In stanza eight, she says "I do not want to kill you ever." Why not? In the final stanza, she turns out the light. Why?
5. Do you think Anna Wooten-Hawkins met her goal of being able to sympathize with or identify with the cockroach? Find some passages that support your answer.

Southern Style

Lois Holt

When I die—if indeed I do,
I want to be laid out in my natural state
in a white coffin
wearing a green dress that matches my eyes.
I want a wreath put on the door
and neighbors to bring food in,
old friends to stand over me crying and carrying on
like I was one of their own,
saying, "Lord, don't she look good."
I want the Porter sisters to sing
"Precious Memories"
and "When the Roll Is Called Up Yonder"
'cause it gets 'em every time,
brings tears to the eyes
of the most hard-hearted heathen.
I want the minister to read
"Crossing the Bar" and
the Twenty-third Psalm
and call me a dearly beloved soul.
I want my next of kin
to walk up the aisle with their heads hanging down
leaning on one another, weeping and wailing
while my sisters from Sunday School
carry wreaths to a long, black limousine
that's driven real slow down the street
behind a policeman on a motorcycle.
I want people to pull their cars over to the side
of the road and hold their hats over their hearts
while the cars with headlights on
pass in slow motion.
I want to see that "Great Beyond"
whether it's in Heaven or Hell.
When I die—if indeed I do—
don't throw my ashes off the nearest bridge
or fling them into a summer breeze or winter wind
to settle on some unplowed plot
God only knows where.
I want a proper funeral—Southern Style.

Preview

Every culture has certain distinctive ceremonies for important occasions, such as birth, marriage, inauguration into political office, graduation, and death. In this poem, Lois Holt describes the kind of funeral that was traditional throughout the South in earlier times—and is still customary in some communities.

As you read, think about which of these customs are still observed in your community. You might also take this poem home so that older members of the family could read it. (Hint: It is most effective if read aloud in a marked southern accent.)

MEET THE AUTHOR:
Lois Holt (1935–)

A native North Carolinian, Lois Holt credits her interest in poetry—and for that matter in reading and writing generally—to two influences. Her mother read to her daily from volumes of English and American poetry and had her recite the lines she had memorized. Later, when she was studying at Durham High School, her eleventh-grade English teacher encouraged her to write and submitted one of her poems to a national anthology.

After receiving a business degree from East Carolina College (now University), she reared two sons and developed a busy career in real estate, insurance, and property management in Durham. Currently she also is involved in a number of civic activities, including the Durham Chamber of Commerce and the Friends of the Durham Library. She still writes frequently, however, and publishes her

poetry widely. She finds her writing to be "an entirely different life from my structured professional life; when I write, it's as if I enter another world."

Ms. Holt has also been very involved with the North Carolina Poetry Society, and has served as president of that group, which has over two hundred members. Her poems have been anthologized in *Weymouth* and *Bay Leaves*.

Language Alert

1. "Precious Memories" and "When the Roll Is Called Up Yonder" are old favorite gospel hymns.
2. *Heathen* refers to persons who have not become converted to major religions, such as Christianity or Judaism.
3. "Crossing the Bar," a poem by Alfred Lord Tennyson, was often read or sung at funerals. It asks survivors not to weep for the deceased, who has simply "crossed the bar" to eternal life.

Reflecting

1. Assume that the year is 2190—about two hundred years from now. You are a historian who is writing a book about funeral customs in the southern United States. From this poem, what facts would you gather?
2. Is there any evidence that the speaker in the poem is not entirely serious? (Look at the final four words of the first line, repeated near the end of the poem. Consider the fact that the corpse's eyes are closed, so no one will know that the green dress matches her eyes. Are there any other indications that she's halfway joking? On the other hand, do you see any evidence that she does indeed treasure this kind of ceremony?)
3. Fred Chappell's story, "The Maker of One Coffin" (see p. 477), also centers on someone who is thinking about his own death. Compare these two selections.

A Word from Suzanne Britt

On all occasions of academic accountability, students are fond of asking, "Will this count?" My answer is rock bottom and hard: "Everything counts." The same is true of writing. Everything counts. Despair can be excellent. Misery is fine. Ecstasy will work—or pain or sorrow or hilarity or indignation. The only thing that won't work is indifference.

I hold with Wordsworth: the writer is simply a supercharged version of a regular human being. The writer is not necessarily brilliant or scholarly or refined, but she has a nameless longing—a hunger . . . —a need to report what she sees and a passion far deeper than mere curiosity. Raymond Carver says the writer needs to be able "to just stand and gape at this or that thing—a sunset or an old shoe—in absolute and simple amazement." The writer presumes to believe that sunsets or old shoes matter. She doesn't know why or how, but she keeps looking, sighing, writing. And she is never full.

Beach People/Mountain People

Suzanne Britt

Preview

If someone were to offer you a choice of a week in the Smoky Mountains or a week on the Outer Banks, which would you choose? Suzanne Britt's essay claims that your choice will tell a great deal about what kind of person you are. She contrasts what she calls "beach people" and "mountain people," not only according to where they like to be, but according to tastes, pastimes, habits, and personalities.

Some people think my theory does not entirely hold up. Well, neither does Plato's. I know that I have occasional mountain leanings. I like a cold day and a hot fire as well as the next person. But I wouldn't live out my life in the high black shadow of a mountain peak. I need to be taller than the land I stand on. I need to see farther than the blue edge of the ocean.

On the first hot day, as I walked across the huge black parking lot into the fragile air, the smell of honeysuckle smacked me in the face, and I was transported to the beach. Why the odor of tar, the honeysuckle and the thick, satisfying sizzle of the pavement should carry me away to oceans I don't know. But there I was, deep in sand; my hand sifting through cool, clean mud; feeling for periwinkles; whitecaps building toward tomato sandwiches and afternoon naps. I am a beach person.

It's dangerous, I know, to love places. Most of the time you won't be there, so most of the time you'll be miserable. People seldom live in the territory they long for. So I keep an eye on myself, knowing that life legislates against what we want and human nature is such that what we can have, we don't want. In other words, I am a cagey beach person.

My sister-in-law is mountains. Naturally, she's stuck on the coast, in the humidity, under the live oaks. Mosquitoes lope along her forearms. She looms up beside the water. But she tries. Her tan, her boat, her bare feet prove the effort. Still, she makes a big deal out of Christmas and secretly prays for snow.

I don't know whether psychologists ever did a study, but the differences between mountain and beach people are as big as the climb from sea level to Mt. McKinley's peak, with this important qualification: beaches and mountains, like their admirers, are not better than each other, only different. Beauty is not the kind of thing you can have a contest about. Neither, for that matter, is ugliness.

Beach people have big pores and no plans. They live in and through their skins, taking life in, letting it go, picking up here, leaving off there. They are evocative and given to evocation: the smell of suntan oil or low tides carries beach people, wherever they are, into porch swings and wet bathing suits. They can land, when a foghorn blows, in the middle of an inner tube on the green Atlantic.

Beach people love wind, salt, sensuality. They seek peace, freedom, conviviality. Their idea of fun is the whole family gulping down oysters over spread-out newspapers. When the beach is there, they never stay by concrete pools, don't care much about their hairdos and wouldn't consider fixing a big meal in the middle of a gorgeous day. A cucumber or fifty-seven chocolate chip cookies will hold them until supper. Beach people are wrinkled, dark-skinned, big-stomached,

frowsy, funny and given to dissipation. The only thing that keeps them from falling apart is the brevity of vacations, plus close, regular, unremitting contact with a mountain person.

Mountain people are firm, pale and traditional. They love fires, sweaters, hot drinks, leather books and holidays. They are maple trees, blue china, church, plaid and sunrise. The closest they get to a high passion is the spot of color in their cheeks after a jog through the bitter cold. They are prone to invigoration, not rest; solitude, not sociability; abstinence, not indulgence. The drama of the landscape is all the thrill they need. They like a place bigger than they are. Beach people, in contrast, want to be the only bright splash on the clean, white horizon.

Mountain people count on nature to tell them where they are and what time it is: they are up with the sun, chopping down trees, piling up mulch. They watch the seasons, live in anticipation, stand apart, give a grade to things. They are at the picture window, cozy and enchanted but ever objective. They do things right if they do them at all. They don't go far, but neither do they go astray.

Beach people are just out there, one with the universe, willy-nilly. They are having a snooze at lunch, scrambling eggs at dusk, raring to go at midnight. Beach people are hit or miss, but when they hit, they sometimes hit big.

The world needs all kinds, but lovers of mountains work better for daily life. From them we get memories of home, shelter from storms, warmth against dark, order against chaos, dry instead of wet. They send us out with hot breakfasts under our belts and solid ground under our feet.

Beach people are, of course, in constant mortal danger. If beauty doesn't get them, truth will. The undertow, the bright beating sun, the broken shells, the buttered lobster, the shifting sand could be their undoing. But then beach people would almost always rather be hot and undone than cold and certain. And they usually are, at least until the first sharp lash of winter comes to put them in their places once again.

MEET THE AUTHOR:
Suzanne Britt (1946–)

Although Suzanne Britt majored in English and studied creative writing while at Salem College and Washington University (St. Louis, MO), she didn't begin writing seriously until she was almost thirty. Then she won national attention with several "My Turn" essays in *Newsweek*. Other essays and articles have appeared in such national publications as the *New York Times* and *Reader's Digest*. Several of these essays, noted for their humor and fresh angles on familiar subjects, have been included in anthologies and college textbooks.

In recent years she has written regular columns for various publications including *North Carolina Homes and Gardens*. In addition to two collections of her essays and columns, Ms. Britt has published a college textbook on how to write entitled *A Writer's Rhetoric*. Ms. Britt currently teaches English at Meredith College in Raleigh and is in demand as a speaker for various public occasions.

Language Alert

1. *periwinkles*: small snails found in the ocean, or the cone-shaped shells of these snails
2. *cagey*: careful and shrewd (Instead of answering directly, he gave me a *cagey* reply.)
3. *lope*: to run at a steady, easy gait (Enjoying the breeze, we *loped* along the beach.)
4. *evocative*: having the power to call forth feelings or ideas or memories (The scent of hot cocoa is *evocative*. It brings back

memories of long winter evenings in front of a fire.)

5. *sensuality*: having to do with the senses (The professor spent most of his time on intellectual matters; his brother was more interested in *sensuality*.)

6. *conviviality*: sociableness, good company (I enjoy nothing more than an evening of *conviviality* with my friends.)

7. *dissipation*: wasteful consuming or indulging in pleasure (He was a talented man, but he ruined his career through *dissipation*.)

8. *unremitting*: persistent, never slackening (The headache gave me *unremitting* pain.)

The following two words mean almost the opposite of each other:

9. *abstinence*: doing without, denying the appetites; and *indulgence*: giving in to one's own desires, especially to an extreme degree (Some people's lives are marked by *abstinence*; others, by *indulgence*.)

Reflecting

A. What Suzanne Britt says:

Divide a piece of paper with a vertical line down the middle. Use one column to list traits which Suzanne Britt says are common to beach people. On the other column (headed "Mountain People," of course) list those traits which are exactly the opposite.

Do you think Ms. Britt is accurate? Which is she trying to write: a precise scientific report or an entertaining piece that exaggerates sometimes to make her point?

B. How Suzanne Britt says it:

1. Notice how Ms. Britt uses **concrete language**. Instead of saying, "Beach people snack a lot," she writes, "A cucumber or fifty-seven chocolate chip cookies will hold them until supper." What does she mean when she says that mountain people are "maple trees, blue china, church, plaid, and sunrise"?

2. Ms. Britt's style is noted for her **parallel phrasing**; that is, she uses combinations of two or sometimes many more phrases all structured in the same way. Examples:
   a. [Mountain people] are prone to invigoration, not rest;
   solitude, not sociability;
   abstinence, not indulgence.
   b. [Beach people] are having a snooze at lunch,
   scrambling eggs at dusk,
   raring to go at midnight.

Notice how easy it is to follow the ideas in sentences with parallel phrases.

For Him, School's Out and the Road Is Winding

Dennis Rogers

Preview

Do you ever get tired of school—so tired of homework and classes and schedules that you'd like to just toss your books and papers and just get on with life outside the classrooms? In the following column from the Raleigh *News and Observer*, we meet a sixteen-year-old boy who, having done precisely that and lived more or less on his own for a year, has hitched a ride to Kinston. The driver of the car is columnist Dennis Rogers, who of course makes the most of this opportunity to get a human interest story.

What can you predict about this boy and his life just from reading the title?

Dobbersville—He was on his way to Kinston when I picked him up here at this crossroads. He looked so young with his grocery-bag luggage.

His name, he said, was George Dupree, and he was "from the western part of the state."

He was lonesome and wanted to talk.

"I'm going to Kinston to get a job with the fair," he said. "I want to get me one of them traveling jobs running a ride or something. Man, you can't find no decent jobs in this place."

He said he was sixteen.

"I quit school last year," he said. "I wasn't learning nothing. I didn't like school, all that reading and math and teachers yelling at you. I swore if I ever got sixteen I'd quit, and I did. That stuff in school don't do you no good."

How was it, being out of school and on your own?

"It was all right," he said. "When I first got out I wasn't quite sixteen, but I turned it during the summer. I got my license, and me and my guys used to get one of them's ride and party a lot. But they're all gone now. One of them joined the Army and some of them went back to school when it started.

"I decided to take off. I couldn't find a job to make me some money and there wasn't much to do at the house."

So he headed north, catching the bus when he had money and hitchhiking when he didn't. He worked in a slaughterhouse in Virginia, shoveling up the bloody leavings when the butchers were finished. Then it was south again, this time signing on with a migrant crew.

"I couldn't stand that," he said. "I lived in the city and I couldn't work all day like they did. Everybody says you can't leave them places, but I did. I just walked out one night. They ain't nobody going to keep me somewhere."

That was somewhere near Benson, he thinks, and now he wants a job with a carnival.

Does he ever think of home?

"Yeah, sometimes, but it wouldn't do no good," he said. "My sister is there with her baby and Mama is kind of sick. The check and the stamps ain't enough to do nothing on. I was always fighting with my sister and her boyfriend, anyway.

"I sure do hope I can get on with the fair. They say they pay pretty good, and it's a steady job for a while. I don't know how to run a ride, but I can learn stuff like that.

"It was just that stuff in school I didn't like. I used to skip a lot and the principal didn't care. She said it was all right with her if I quit. None of my teachers liked me, and I didn't like them either.

"I didn't get along too good with the white kids. They were always kissing up to the teacher and mess like that and it made me mad, man. They got good grades just because the teacher liked them. That stuff wasn't right, so I quit."

About that time we passed a gaudy poster tacked to a telephone pole advertising the fair. I pointed it out to him and asked if that was where he was going.

"What's it say?" he asked. "I can't read very good. I can read funny books pretty good, but I don't like regular books."

The bravado was fading. The jiving and laughter in his voice gave way to resentment, it seemed. There was a chill in the car on that hot afternoon.

"That's another reason I didn't like school too good," he said. "I couldn't read as fast as they could and they acted like it took so much trouble for me to read out loud that they quit calling on me. I got tired of just sitting there.

"It'll be all right if I can get a job with the fair. I bet they don't make you read. . . ."

MEET THE AUTHOR:
Dennis Rogers (1942–)
See p. 159

Reflecting

1. George gives several reasons for quitting school and leaving home. List all of them, just the way he said them. Are some of these reasons just excuses? Decide which are real reasons and which may be what we call "rationalizing"—saying things just to build a good argument for what has been done.
2. We only have one short interview—not enough evidence to make firm judgments about who is right, who is wrong. Even from this short piece, however, we feel that although George is partly responsible for his situation, other people are also to blame. How have other people let him down? How has he let himself down?
3. Pretend you have a crystal ball. Predict George's future if he continues to think and act as he has been doing. Or pretend you have the power to change three things about George's life. What changes would you make—and why?

Preview

"Back Roads" is the prize-winning poem Kaye Gibbons wrote when she was in the tenth grade. In literature, the road or highway is often used as a **metaphor** for the journey of life. If your life journey were on a back road, what would it be like?

Back Roads

Kaye Gibbons

On the road to nowhere
That's everywhere I've been.
The traces, the lines, the tracks of my past
Haunt my humble den.

I unpack my bags and out come the guilt,
the shame, the tears.
I slam the door on the stale, the black,
the cruel,
    the frightening years.
I pull off the shoes that walked the roads
Where nobody knows I've been.

On the road to nowhere,
That's everywhere I've been.

From *Emerging Voices*, 1977. Reprinted by permission of the author.

Kaye Gibbons (1960–   )

In 1987, when Kaye Gibbons's first novel, *Ellen Foster*, appeared, it won high praise from some of the most highly respected authors in the nation. Eudora Welty, the Mississippian whom many consider the finest living American writer, praised this first novel for "the life in it, the honesty of thought and eye and feeling and word!" Walker Percy, another distinguished author, wrote, "It's the real thing. Which is to say: a lovely, breathtaking, sometimes heart-wrenching first novel."

While *Ellen Foster* went on to become a best-seller in France, Kaye Gibbons, still only in her mid-twenties, went on to publish her second novel, *A Virtuous Woman*, and a third, *A Cure for Dreaming*.

Kaye Gibbons credits her mother with starting "this writing urge" back when Kaye was growing up in rural Nash County. She declares that writing has always been something she "needs to do," just as reading is. When she was eight, she was reading *Jane Eyre*. In the fourth grade she became a devoted fan of Edgar Allan Poe. "I have always eaten literature," she admits. "Some people snack on it. I eat it and clean my plate."

Since she was in elementary school, she has "felt destined to write." When she was in

high school, one of her poems won an award in the Emerging Voices poetry competition sponsored by Peace College and the North Carolina Arts Council. She continued writing throughout college, but did not begin her novel until she was married. Now she balances writing with home life, scheduling her writing time on Tuesdays and Thursdays when a babysitter takes care of her three children.

Reflecting

These song-like lines capture the feelings of someone whose life has been marked by frustration. Notice the different phrases which the speaker uses to describe that life. All of them include concrete images that we can envision in our mind.

Try thinking of another image to represent an unsatisfactory life—something besides "road to nowhere." See if you can build a similar poem around that image.

Bound North

Marsha White Warren

The Silver Star
echoes its way north
through Southern Pines
each morning at 7:56
glides down the main street
effortlessly
past horse farms
virgin pines
pecan groves
moans through the same state
where bloodhounds once
sniffed slaves
down from trees
out of hay wagons and barns
before they could get underground.

A locomotive prepares to leave the Southern Pines depot.

Preview

Have you ever looked at a scene and wondered what was going on at that same place ten, twenty, a hundred, or two hundred years ago? Perhaps while on the coast you've imagined a ship wrecking where sunbathers now lie; or, picking up an arrowhead, you've realized that early Native Americans once lived where you now walk.

In this poem, Marsha White Warren has a double vision: a scene in Southern Pines today and an imagined scene of what she knows went on in that area more than a hundred years ago.

MEET THE AUTHOR:
Marsha White Warren (1938–)

Many writers grow up knowing that they want to be writers. Others might have been nudged by a teacher who noticed their talent and encouraged their desire to write. But Marsha White Warren didn't become interested in writing until she was an adult.

"I didn't particularly write as a student— only assignments," she says. "It was the death of my mother that *required* me to write as a release, as if my senses were awakened—on edge—noticing everything around me. I was hearing and seeing as I'd never experienced before."

Since her interest was awakened, Ms. Warren has not only written her own poetry, but helped edit two major anthologies: *North Carolina's 400 Years: Signs Along the Way* and *Weymouth*. Furthermore, since 1987 she has served as executive director of the North

Carolina Writers' Network, an organization that helps promote writers and writing throughout the state. It now boasts over 1,300 members—writers of all kinds, from novelists and poets and playwrights to freelancers who write articles for varied publications and technical writers who document computer software. Ms. Warren also has served as chair of the oldest writers' organization in the state, the North Carolina Writers' Conference (begun in 1949).

Reflecting

1. The Silver Star is a fast passenger train that offers a comfortable ride. Think about the difficult, dangerous journey runaway slaves had to make, hidden under loads of hay or skittering on foot across fields by moonlight, the baying bloodhounds just behind them.

2. Notice how certain words not only describe, but have an emotional impact: *glides* and *effortlessly* in connection with the commercial locomotive, *moans* and *sniffed* in connection with the underground railroad.

Birdsong Quieter Every Spring

Ann Berry

Preview

In 1962, Rachel Carson's best-seller, *The Silent Spring,* awoke us to the fact that many forms of wildlife were suffering from the effects of pesticides and other poisons being dumped into our air, soil, and water. Since then we have come to recognize many serious environmental problems: for example, damage to the ozone layer which protects us from harsh solar rays, danger from the disposal of hazardous wastes, and pollution caused by too many vehicles spewing fumes into the air along our highways.

Ann Berry looks at the same problem Rachel Carson discussed—not by conducting a scientific study, but simply by observing in her own yard in Raleigh. Is what she describes in any way similar to what you experience in your own neighborhood?

To the eye, nothing has changed much in the quiet dead-end-street vicinity of our house. The trees are taller, the ivy thicker than 25 years ago. The camellias and azaleas the Big Freeze killed back a couple of years ago are slowly rising again.

Across "our" creek, scarlet-tied stakes outline an impending episode of urban infill that will soon swap 10 houses' worth of sawed deadwood for the tall jungly cathedral of living sweet gum, tulip, hickory, oak and what-have-you. For those woods this spring is probably the last.

But for now, we have as many trees around as ever. Though life in the creek's waters has nearly vanished while we've lived there, it still flows, and its banks are

still hospitable.

Last Sunday, on the phone, I glanced out and happened to meet the sharply curious eyes of the fat grandmother of all raccoons, peering up toward the living-room window from a creekside tree trunk 15 yards away. But there've always been raccoons down there; they've adapted better to city life than many people.

What has changed, where we live, is the sound effects. A couple of decades ago, by this mid-March stage of the annual awakening, you couldn't sleep past 5 a.m. for the trilling, shrilling, screaming, stomping cacophony outside.

Flickers battered our gutters. The street was alive with mockingbirds, each with its assigned family tree, where the males sang themselves silly all night. Then they fought themselves punchy all day in the side mirrors of parked cars, when they weren't fighting each other over some disputed dogwood.

Similarly deluded cardinals fenced with reflections in our windows. We had back-yard wrens and front-yard wrens. Bluebirds and orioles would drop in.

Now the entire March bird chorus is scarcely loud enough to trouble the lighter slumber of our middle age. We have doves, a wren or two, the occasional mocker, tough robins, some others. But the total feathered population has shrunk to an echo of its former self.

Saturday morning, a couple of hairy woodpeckers deigned to do an elaborate courting ballet in the front-yard dogwood for an hour. We were so tickled to see them we tiptoed around and kept the cat in.

I could blame it all on cats, of which our short street has at least its fair share. But cats don't eat insects, and there aren't as many insects as there used to be, either. The houseflies that plagued our first years have become rare. We hardly ever see the big, slow, fuzzy carpenter bees that once dug dimples in the deck supports.

When the children were little, we had to warn them away from the haunts of small, yellow-striped, ground-dwelling stinging bees. Today you can go barefoot all summer in our yard and not get stung by anything worse than a sweet-gum ball.

I'm not sure why that is either. As a rule, we don't use chemicals to kill yard weeds or bugs. A lot of people in the area do; we enjoy their velvet lawns and flowers, much finer than any we'll ever grow.

As for us, we've put out plenty of chemical fertilizer in our time. Several times I've gotten desperate enough over roaches to call in exterminators, who always assure me that whatever potion they're using is the very latest thing and perfectly safe.

And in a quarter-century of do-it-yourself building and tinkering, a certain amount of gasoline and acids and detergent and petroleum byproducts has been added to our lot's soil. I'm sure insects don't thrive on any of those.

Meanwhile, up in Virginia a couple of lawsuits have been filed against "Otto the Orkin man" alleging chemical damage to health.

Meanwhile, they're spraying the ground and air over Hialeah, Florida with malathion against a new medfly outbreak.

Meanwhile, a state senator from downstream tells a reporter how today you'd "take your life in your own hands" to venture into the lower Neuse with an open sore or cut—the same Neuse whose water was clean enough to help heal cuts when he was a boy not many years back.

Meanwhile, pelicans in the Florida keys strangle on plastic fishline or choke on pellets of plastic they can't help eating with their salt-water food.

Meanwhile, roadsides by any suburban, Raleigh-Wake stoplight show how much slow- or non-rotting junk gets tossed every place where Homo Sapiens has to idle his motor for a minute.

Not all the news from the environment front is bad. There's real hope now for a phosphate detergent ban in North Carolina—and if we get it, Tar Heel clothes, I'll bet, will still get clean enough. The state is cracking down on many forms of poisoning. And we're slowly realizing we really do have to have places to treat and process and burn all the filthy, toxic killer junk we generate every day.

But the responses come so slowly. And the birds and the bugs keep declining. Maybe we'll do enough, soon enough, to keep our old mother the earth in business. I hope so. It's not a sure thing.

MEET THE AUTHOR:
Ann Berry (1930–)

A resident of Raleigh since 1962, Ann Berry began her journalistic career while she was still in high school in Manhattan, Kansas. Later, at Kansas State University, she persuaded the college newspaper editor to run her personal column. This experience, she says, "turned me on to commentary-style journalism." Currently, at the Raleigh *News and Observer* she writes editorials each day, five days per week, year-round—no easy task! Her editorials and columns have won her three first-place and two third-place awards from the North Carolina Press Association.

How did she achieve her skill? "I learned to write more by reading than by writing," she declares. "Do read—greedily, widely, addictively!—if you have any notion of becoming a writer." She also recommends volunteering for the school paper—and her own experience shows that such activity can lead to a successful career.

Language Alert: Substitutions

From the list beneath the sentences, choose the word which can substitute for the word or phrase in *italic* in each sentence.

1. If you're in the *area surrounding* our house, do stop by for a visit.
2. As the thunder crackled, I worried about the *approaching* storm.
3. This was just one more weird *happening* in my life.
4. In the 1980s, cities like Charlotte, Raleigh, and Greensboro experienced a great deal of construction on *vacant land between buildings* within the city.
5. When the orchestra is tuning up, I have fun listening to the *discordant clash* of sounds that are not in harmony with one another.
6. Because the speaker was so charming, I was *fooled* into believing him.
7. My neighbor sued my father, *claiming* that our fence was located on his property.
8. After three weeks of aerobics, they decided to *attempt* the climb up Looking Glass Rock.
9. We Americans *produce* tons of garbage each day.

a. venture   d. impending   g. alleging
b. vicinity   e. episode   h. cacophony
c. generate   f. infill   i. deluded

Reflecting

1. Interview a family who has lived in their house for at least twelve years. Find out what changes they have noticed in the environment: building, street construction, erosion or buildup of land, flooding or drying up of streams, planting or destroying of trees, or effects on wildlife. Compare their stories to Ann Berry's.
2. Notice the series of "meanwhile" paragraphs toward the end of Ms. Berry's essay. We use *meanwhile* to mean *at the same time*. Each of these paragraphs tells us of something that is happening to the environment somewhere else at the same time that Ms. Berry notices that the birds and bugs are disappearing from her yard. Construct some "meanwhile" paragraphs of your own, describing environmental damage that is going on somewhere outside your own community.

Preview

"Where were you when—?" This question is asked many times—especially concerning events that are important either nationally or personally. People who were alive can often tell you exactly where they were and what they were doing when they got the news of the bombing of Pearl Harbor, of the death of a famous person (or of someone personally close to them), or of the explosion of the space shuttle *Challenger*.

In this poem, Gladys Owings Hughes recalls the circumstances under which she heard the news of five important events.

Remembering News Bulletins

Gladys Owings Hughes

Dunkirk
bulletins blare
the man in the shop
lifts a small gray mouse
twisted in a trap.

Pearl Harbor
Sunday Symphony
of violins
brashly silenced
by war drums.

Hiroshima
shimmers in summer sun
with fragrant rows
of Carolina peaches
on my kitchen porch.

Dallas
shatters magic of Storytime
black shock blurs
faces of students
riding with a Prince.

Memphis
a morning walk
by the willow tree
the mockingbird lay
ants tearing at eyes and tongue.

From *North Carolina's 400 Years: Signs Along the Way,* ed. Ronald H. Bayes. Copyright © 1986 by North Carolina Poetry Society. Reprinted by permission of the author and the North Carolina Poetry Society.

Gladys Owings Hughes (1913–)

Gladys Owings Hughes's writing of poetry sprang from her father's discipline. When she was a child and complained, her father would direct her to go off alone and make a list of her blessings. She would begin with God and the heavenly bodies, move to the natural wonders of the earth, then to family, and conclude with those objects and animals on the farm on which she lived. Eventually she became bored with making this list over and over, so one day she made a rhymed poem.

"It must have been terrible, but Dad praised me for the effort," she reports. "The next time, I tried an unrhymed poem—with blessings hinted at and strung together with new words. This was my first poem. It was not a 'famous' one, but it was mine. It opened the door to the joy of words for me." She began keeping a journal. Then, after graduating from Western Carolina University, she composed plays for her first-grade students to perform.

She didn't write for publication until just before retiring after thirty-five years of teaching in Alamance County classrooms. However, she has made up for lost time, publishing in many magazines and winning both local and national awards. Her collection, *A Cell, A Door*, was published in 1989. For two years she served as president of the North Carolina Poetry Society. She has lived for many years in the small Piedmont town of Elon College.

Language Alert

Each stanza begins with the name of the place where the event occurred. Just looking at those you can probably guess what the event is, with the possible exception of the first: Dunkirk. In late May 1940, 350,000 Allied soldiers were surrounded by German troops in Dunkirk, a seaport town in France. A fleet of nearly 1,000 British and French ships rescued them and brought them to England. It was not only naval ships that carried out the rescue, which took several days. Heeding a call for help, people with private yachts—and even rowboats—came to carry the soldiers across the channel. This has been called one of the most remarkable military movements in history.

Reflecting

1. Notice that in each case there is some detail which seems either particularly appropriate or particularly inappropriate—and therefore ironic—when it is paired with the important event. For example, in the fourth stanza, students are reading about riding with a prince (perhaps the story of "The Little Lame Prince"?) when they hear the news of the death of John Kennedy—who, as President, could be compared to a prince. What is the significance of:
   a. The mouse in the first stanza?
   b. The musical instruments in the second?
   c. The two "shimmering" summer scenes in the third?
   d. The dead mockingbird in the fourth? (Is there something symbolic about ants tearing at the body? About their tearing at eyes and tongue?)

2. Think of an event which shocked you—perhaps one of national or international importance, perhaps one involving people you know personally. How did you hear the news? Can you, like Gladys Hughes, recall very specific details about what you were doing, where you were, etc.?

And Now Farewell...

In reading the works in this book, you have taken a literary and historical journey through our state. You have followed its development through several very different stages: from wilderness to colony to new-state-in-a-new-nation. You then read about a region struggling through defeat and poverty which has now become a thriving state. You have glimpsed North Carolina's varied landscapes, met some of its people, and heard their voices proclaiming their concerns.

So now perhaps you can identify with what Thad Stem (see p. 490) says in the following poem:

News from Home

Thad Stem, Jr.

When I'm an angel, I'll covet news from North Carolina
As wildly as an old soldier asking after some comrade
Who didn't make the regimental reunion this time.
But I'll be as exquisitely subtle as a faded man
Patiently sifting years of trite home-town history
For some small word of an old sweetheart long married.

When each boat docks, I'll stand on the fringe
Of relatives kissing, shaking hands, and being garrulous
As folks spreading lunch at a country church meeting.
When I've heard how the school house has new paint,
That Castleberry won for Congress by two to one,
I'll ask, as if I were the late landlord,
How the elms on Settle's Lane stood the winter?
If the brook yet hums at night like a spinning top?

A Showcase of Other North Carolina Writers

The 102 writers whose works are included in this collection are among this state's best, but it would require more than one volume to include all the good writers this state has produced. Furthermore, new authors appear on the literary scene every year.

Below are brief introductions to more of this state's long roster of distinguished authors. Just skimming, you will be able to find a number of writers from your own region. As you read your daily newspaper and listen to television, be alert to still others as their careers develop.

I. FROM THE DISTANT PAST

Seven years before the Civil War began, **Mary Bayard Clarke**, a poet, wanted her fellow citizens to recognize the literary work produced in this state. She edited and published the first anthology of North Carolina poetry: *Wood Notes: or Carolina Carols: A Collection of North Carolina Poetry*

In his own day—during the Reconstruction after the Civil War—**Thomas Dixon,** a native of Cleveland County, was an immensely popular writer. His novel *The Clansman* became first a play and then the first major full-length film, *The Birth of a Nation*. Today we recognize that his stories, including *The Clansman,* were not only melodramatic, but racist. In fact, some critics have dismissed that novel as mere propaganda.

In contrast, Davie County-native **Hinton Rowan Helper** in 1857 wrote a book about slavery that so outraged his native state that he never felt comfortable about returning to North Carolina. In *The Impending Crisis of the South* he argued that slavery slowed economic progress in the South by limiting opportunities for poor white workers. Slaveholders were so angry that the book was banned in the South.

Although born in Greensboro, **Wilbur Daniel Steele** grew up outside this state. Then, after winning a national reputation as a fiction writer, he lived in Chapel Hill for several years. Several of his short stories are set in North Carolina.

Henry Jerome Stockard from Chatham County became a scholar, poet, and, from 1907–1912, president of Peace College. His poetry was collected in *Fugitive Lines*. In 1911 he also collected and edited *A Study of Southern Poetry*.

United States Senator **Robert Strange** of Fayetteville wrote *Eoneguski, or The Cherokee Chief* (1839), based on his experience as a superior court judge in western North Carolina. This, the first novel written with a North Carolina setting, was critical of the way Native Americans were treated.

Calvin Henderson Wiley was not only the first state superintendent of public schools in this state, but a writer as well. He wrote historical novels and various religious pieces. In 1851, believing that students should be familiar with their own state, he compiled *The North Carolina Reader,* which included a brief history and description of North Carolina as well as a number of works by North Carolina authors.

II. FROM THE RECENT PAST

Arthur Talmadge Abernethy wrote fifty-three books and pamphlets as well as a weekly column for *The Charlotte Observer.* In 1948, Governor R. Gregg Cherry appointed him the first poet laureate of North Carolina. He also taught for seven years at Rutherford College (beginning at the age of seventeen, as one of the youngest professors in the nation), and held positions as a journalist, minister, and mayor of the town of Rutherford College.

Born in Mt. Olive in 1908, **Sam Byrd** became a noted Broadway actor; for his performance in *Tobacco Road,* he won the *Literary Digest* award for Best Young Actor on Broadway. He also produced a number of plays. His book *Small Town South* (1942) received the Houghton Mifflin Life in America prize. He was also author of a novel *Hurry Home to My Heart* (1945), set during World War II. He died in 1955.

Wilbur J. Cash, who lived and worked in Charlotte, is known best for a remarkable book, *The Mind of the South* (1941). In this nonfiction study, he attempted to explain southerners—their traditions, their philosophies, their attitudes. Although not all of his findings have proven to be accurate, this is still considered to be a remarkable analysis of a region and its people.

Jonathan Daniels, son of Josephus Daniels, carried on the family tradition by editing the *News and Observer* for a number of years. Like his famous father, he, too, led an active political life, serving as press secretary to President Franklin Roosevelt and adviser to President Harry Truman. He wrote many books, including *A Southerner Discovers the South* (1938), and biographies of both Roosevelt and Truman. He won a number of awards, including the North Carolina Award for Literature in 1967.

Born in Kentucky, **Olive Tilford Dargan** lived in the North Carolina mountains for many years and published fiction, poetry, and plays. She was awarded the Roanoke-Chowan Award for poetry in 1959. Some of her fiction was published under the pseudonym (pen name) of Fielding Burke.

Born in Savannah, Georgia, in 1900, **Willie Snow Etheridge** did not move to North Carolina until late in her life, but several of her books—collections of humorous essays—deal with her experiences here. Ms. Etheridge was presented the North Carolina Award for Literature in 1982, the year before she died.

California-native **Inglis Fletcher** came to this state after she got interested in her Tyrrell County ancestors. She and her husband bought a plantation on the Chowan River, where she lived and wrote until her death in 1969. She is best known for the Carolina Series: twelve historical novels she wrote about the settlement and early development of North Carolina. Like James Boyd, she based her novels upon very careful research. In 1964, she was presented the first North Carolina Award for Literature.

Many North Carolinians have Scottish ancestors. **Ina Forbus** came directly to this country from Scotland when she was eleven years old. She attended the university at Chapel Hill and became an American citizen soon after her marriage to Sample Forbus, director of Watts Hospital in Durham. They settled at an old gristmill on Cane Creek outside Chapel Hill, and she began writing poems and fiction. In 1958, her novel *The Secret Circle* won the AAUW Award as the best North Carolina book for young readers.

Carl Goerch is remembered not only for beginning *The State* magazine in 1933, but also for the chatty columns he published there. He also became widely known for the folksy stories he told on regular radio appearances. Many of his columns and radio talks were published in collections.

In 1905, at the age of three, **Harry Golden** came from Europe to New York; in 1941 he moved to Charlotte and began a small newspaper, *The Carolina Israelite*, which grew to a national readership of 30,000 in the 1960s. Many of his columns were reprinted in best-selling collections.

Raleigh resident **Ben Haas** penned more than one hundred books—many of them thrillers and fantasies—under half a dozen pseudonyms. However, he will be best remembered for a number of fine novels published under his own name and focusing on matters important to North Carolina. *Look Away, Look Away* deals with racial strife; *The Last Valley* focuses on the destruction of mountain forests in North Carolina; and *The Chandler Heritage* centers on the textile industry, much like Cannon Mills in Concord and Kannapolis.

Born in Alamance County, **John Harden** was a journalist for two North Carolina newspapers, directed public relations for two governors and a senator, and became an executive at Burlington Mills Corporation. He also collected and published two collections of tales: *Tar Heel Ghosts* and *The Devil's Tramping Ground and Other North Carolina Mystery Stories*.

Born at the turn of the century, Wake County-native **Bernice Kelly Harris** graduated from Meredith College. Like Frances Gray Patton, Thomas Wolfe, and Paul Green, she wrote folk plays while studying with Professor Frederick Koch in Chapel Hill. After her marriage she spent the remainder of her life in Seaboard, writing a number of novels about rural and small town North Carolina. *Purslane,* her first novel, was published in 1939. She won the North Carolina Award for Literature in 1966.

A native of Tennessee, **Randall Jarrell** (1914–1965) spent many years at UNC-Greensboro, where he was a beloved professor, and he considered that city his home. He became famous for his poems concerning World War II, especially "The Death of the Ball Turret Gunner." His poetry collection *The Women at the Washington Zoo* was given the National Book Award. He also wrote a novel, many essays, and a well-received fable, *The Bat-Poet.*

Born in Riverton in Scotland County in 1890, **Gerald Johnson** was a cousin of John Charles McNeill (see p. 188). He produced biographies of three American presidents: Andrew Jackson, Woodrow Wilson, and Franklin D. Roosevelt. He also wrote a number of novels and, for young readers, several books on American history and government. In 1965, he was presented the North Carolina Award for Literature.

Weldon native **Ovid Pierce** taught English at East Carolina University for many years. He wrote four novels and a collection of short stories. His fiction won many awards, including the North Carolina Award for Literature in 1969.

Wilmington-native **Robert Ruark** had an adventurous life as journalist, seaman, columnist, and novelist. He lived and wrote all over the world—Washington, DC, Africa, Spain, London—but he once said that "the best writing I will ever do" was in his book *The Old Man and the Boy.* Based on his own boyhood, that book describes the adventures of a boy (Ruark himself) whose wise grandfather teaches him the arts of hunting, fishing, and training dogs.

North Carolinians like to claim **Carl Sand-**

burg, who moved to a farm near Flat Rock when he was sixty-seven and spent his last twenty-two years there. However, we must admit that long before he came to this state he had completed most of his best work (poetry such as "Chicago" and "The People, Yes," and his famous biographical study of Abraham Lincoln). Furthermore, although he loved his mountain home, his work does not reflect that region. He died in 1967. His home, Connemara, is now open to the public.

Another famous writer who made North Carolina her home was **Betty Smith.** Born in New York in 1904, she came to live in Chapel Hill in 1938, when Paul Green arranged for her to receive a scholarship to the Federal Theater Project there. Her best-known novel—and her first—*A Tree Grows in Brooklyn,* was published in 1943. It became a major best-seller and a popular motion picture. Although she spent the remainder of her adult life in Chapel Hill and continued to write and publish novels, her stories continued to reflect the New York experience she had known in earlier years.

What Price Glory?, a prize-winning play and one of the most famous works to emerge from World War I, was coauthored by North Carolinian **Lawrence Stallings** and Maxwell Anderson. Stallings also wrote a well-received novel, *Plumes,* which was set on the old Wake Forest campus in the town of Wake Forest.

Richard Walser will long be remembered as Mr. North Carolina Literature. A Lexington native, he devoted his professional life to studying and recording the development of North Carolina writing. He published a number of anthologies of short fiction, poetry, and plays by North Carolinians, as well as a biography of George Moses Horton. He was also noted as one of the most authoritative Thomas Wolfe scholars. For many years he taught English at North Carolina University.

One of the most prolific writers this state has known was **Manly Wade Wellman.** He sold his first story when he was only a junior in college, and by the time he was eighty years old, he had written eighty books, many of them for boys. His novels were varied. He wrote science fiction, detective stories, history, biography, adventure stories, and tales based on folklore. In 1978, he was presented the North Carolina Award for Literature.

When he was a boy, **Charles Whedbee** spent every summer at his family's cottage at Nags Head and listened to mysterious tales told around the campfire. When he was a man, he followed a six-generation tradition by becoming a lawyer and served nearly sixty years as a judge. He also recalled those tales and published them in five collections which have become popular not only in this state but in other countries.

III. THOSE CURRENTLY WRITING

Davidson College professor **Anthony Abbott** has won awards for both fiction and poetry. He has also helped organize writers' programs and conferences throughout the state. His poetry collection *The Girl in the Yellow Raincoat,* appeared in 1990.

Without question, **Maya Angelou,** who has only recently lived in this state, is considered one of the foremost writers in the United States today. Born in St. Louis in 1928, she grew up in Stamps, Arkansas. She has been an actress as well as a writer, and has won acclaim both for her Broadway performances and books such as *I Know Why the Caged Bird Sings* (1970), her story about growing up in Stamps, Arkansas. More recently she has continued her autobiography with *All God's Children Need Traveling Shoes.* She has also published several collections of poetry, including *Shaker, Why Don't You Sing?* Currently she is a distinguished professor at Wake Forest University.

Like his classmates, Fred Chappell and Reynolds Price, **James Applewhite** studied at Duke University, where he now holds a distinguished professorship. A native of Wilson County, he has published eleven collections of poetry, several of which have won major honors, including the Roanoke-Chowan Award. Many of his poems center on the land and people and customs of his native region.

Born in 1923, **Daphne Athas** has spent most of her life in Chapel Hill. Her novel *Entering Ephesus,* published in 1973, is set in that town during the Great Depression. Of Greek descent, she set her 1978 novel, *Cora,* in Greece. A member of the faculty at the university in Chapel Hill, she won the Sir Walter Raleigh Award for *Cora* in 1979.

A native of Washington, DC, **Ellen Bache** graduated from the University of North Carolina in Chapel Hill. She and her family have lived in Wilmington for many years. She has published articles in *The Washington Post, New York Times,* and other periodicals, as well as over thirty short stories in such magazines as *McCalls, Seventeen,* and *Young Miss.* Her novel *Safe Passage* was published in 1988. Her book *Culture Clash,* based on a diary about her experience sponsoring a Vietnamese refugee family, has been used by many voluntary agencies and church groups involved in refugee resettlements.

In 1976 **Joseph Bathanti** came to North Carolina from his native Pennsylvania to serve as a VISTA volunteer working with prison inmates. Since then he has taught at several North Carolina colleges. *Anson County,* the most recent of his three collections of poetry, was written during and after his term as artist-in-residence at Anson Community College. Currently he teaches at Mitchell Community College in Statesville.

After authors **Corydon** and **Thelma Harrington Bell** moved to this state, they wrote a number of books, some together, some individually, for young readers. Among their best known: Mr. Bell's *John Rattling-Gourd of Big Cove: A Collection of Cherokee Indian Legends* (1955); and Mrs. Bell's *Mountain Boy* (1947) and *Captain Ghost,* which won the AAUW Award for books for young readers in 1959.

Legette Blythe of Huntersville has written a number of historical novels. Several are set in North Carolina; some are based on biblical stories. In 1961, his nonfiction work *Thomas Wolfe and His Family* won the Mayflower Award. With a collaborator he wrote *Hornet's Nest: The Story of Charlotte and Mecklenburg County* (1968).

Mebane Burgwyn, a native of Rich Square, has written a number of novels for young readers. Her books are noted for combining realistic characters with lively adventure. Some of her best known are *True Love for Jenny* (1956) and *The Crackajack Pony* (1969), which won the AAUW Award for books for young readers in 1970.

Betsy Byars of Charlotte has written over two dozen books; their excellence has been recognized by the Newberry Award, one of the most respected national prizes given to books written for young readers. Among her works: *The Not-Just-Anybody Family, The Golly Sisters Go West,* and a series of books about the Blossom family.

Mary Belle Campbell from Whispering Pines writes poetry, manages two publishing endeavors (Scot's Plaid Press and Persephone Press) and leads workshops on journal writing. She is the author of two collections of poetry: *The Business of Being Alive* and *On the Summit.*

A native of Utah who became a Greensboro businessman, **Orson Scott Card** has been writing science fiction novels since the 1970s. His 1984 novel *Ender's Game* concerns military geniuses who try to save the planet from invading aliens. It won the Nebula and Hugo Awards for Best Science Fiction and was named a Best Book for Young Adults. His most recent novel is *Seventh Son* (1987).

Richard Chase, a native of Alabama, is

one of this country's best-known collectors of folk tales and folk music. From his home in Beech Mountain, he has compiled a number of collections, including *Old Songs and Singing Games* (1938), *Jack Tales* (1943), and *Grandfather Tales* (1948).

To many who live in or who love the North Carolina mountains, *Where the Lilies Bloom* is a favorite novel. Written by **Vera** and **Bill Cleaver** after they moved to Watauga County, it was made into a well-received motion picture. The Cleavers have set several of their later books—including *Trial Valley* (1977), a sequel to *Where the Lilies Bloom*—in that same mountain region.

Charlottean **Judy Simpson Cook** is one of an up-and-coming generation of playwrights in this state. She has written twelve one-act plays and a full-length comedy set in the western Piedmont, *Country Songs* (1986). It has been produced regionally and has been well received by audiences.

A resident of Durham, **Elizabeth Cox** grew up in Tennessee, then studied writing at UNC-Chapel Hill. She has published a number of highly praised short stories and one novel, *Familiar Ground* (1984). She teaches creative writing at Duke University.

Lucy Daniels (Inman) of Raleigh and **Elizabeth Daniels Squires** of Weaverville represent the third generation of the writing Daniels family; both are granddaughters of Josephus, daughters of Jonathan. Lucy Daniels (Inman) entered the literary scene in 1956 with a novel, *Caleb, My Son*, about the conflict of generations among blacks. Elizabeth Squires, a journalist, has recently published a mystery, *Kill the Messenger* (1990).

Like the Daniels sisters, Greensboro-native **Angela Davis-Gardner** is also from a writing family. Her father, **Burke Davis** (see p. 79), and her younger brother, **Burke Davis III,** are fiction writers, and both her father and her mother, **Evangeline Davis,** have published nonfiction. Ms. Davis-Gardner taught in Japan and worked as a reporter for the *News and Observer* before she began writing fiction. Her first novel, *Felice,* won enthusiastic critical praise and was a Book-of-the-Month selection. Her second, *Dance of the Honeybees,* is to be published by Random House in 1991. She currently teaches at North Carolina State University.

Paxton Davis, who grew up in Winston-Salem, has taught journalism at Washington and Lee University and served as writer and book editor for the *Roanoke Times and World-News.* In his book *Being a Boy* (1988), he recounts his boyhood in Winston-Salem in the years before World War II. The sequel, *A Boy's War,* covers his experiences as a young soldier during World War II.

Ann Deagon, a professor of classics at Guilford College, has won recognition not only for her writing (poetry and fiction), but for her support of writers and literature with the Poetry Center Southeast and the North Carolina Writers' Network. She has won a number of awards, including a literary fellowship from the National Endowment for the Arts.

Rebecca McClanahan (Devet) teaches poetry to students of all ages in the Charlotte-Mecklenburg schools, where she serves as poet-in-residence. She has coedited an anthology of children's poetry and published a collection of her own poems, *Mother Tongue.*

Charlotte readers perhaps know **Harriet Doar** best as a journalist; for years she was editor of the book page of the *Charlotte Observer.* In 1983 *The Restless Water,* a collection of her poems, was published by St. Andrews Press.

In 1979 **Hilda Downer** published a collection of poetry, *Bandana Creek,* named for the Appalachian community in which she grew up. Her poems reflect her love of the mountains and her Native American heritage.

Born in Winston-Salem in 1916, **Charles Edward Eaton** has lived for many years in Chapel Hill. He has published a number of volumes of poetry and several of short fiction, and has won a number of prizes, including the 1989 North Carolina Award for Literature.

Durham writer **Georgann Eubanks** has published numerous essays and articles as well as short stories, in national publications. She also manages Word Works, a company which deals with writing and design.

Foster Fitz-Simons, now retired, taught in the drama department at the UNC-Chapel Hill for many years. In 1948 he wrote *Bright Leaf,* a novel which traces a family as they make their fortune in the tobacco industry—a family much like the Dukes of Durham.

Candace Flynt was born, raised, and educated in Greensboro, where she still resides, and all of her novels are set there. Her short stories have appeared in popular magazines, and she has published three novels since 1980. Her most recent, *Mother Love,* has been published in England and Sweden as well as in this country.

Another Greensboro writer, **Marie Gilbert,** has published several volumes of poetry; the most recent is *Myrtle Beach Back When* (1990). She also serves as president of the North Carolina Poetry Society.

Marianne Gingher, also of Greensboro, has published short stories both in popular magazines and in a collection, *Teen Angel.* Her novel *Bobby Rex's Latest Hits* (1986) was both a popular and a critical success, and won the 1987 Sir Walter Raleigh Award for Fiction. Ms. Gingher also writes book reviews for major newspapers. She has taught writing at UNC-G and at Hollins College in Virginia.

Laurel Goldman grew up in New York and attended college in Indiana before moving to Durham in the late 1970s. She has published two novels—*Sounding the Territory* and *The Part of Fortune*—and is recognized as an exceptionally talented teacher of creative writing. Currently she also teaches fiction courses in the continuing education department at Duke University.

Lucinda Grey and her husband **Robert Waters Grey** are both poets and editors. Lucinda's poems appear in many periodicals and a collection, *Letter to No Address.* Robert, a professor of English at UNC-Charlotte, has not only written and published a number of his own poems, but has also edited anthologies. Both work with *Southern Poetry Review,* one of the best-known literary magazines in the South—Robert as editor and Lucinda as associate editor.

After growing up in Rocky Mount, **Allan Gurganus** served in the navy during the Vietnam War before beginning to write seriously. He has published stories in major magazines and taught creative writing at Stanford and Duke universities. His first novel, *The Oldest Living Confederate Widow* (1989), was immediately a national best-seller.

A Virginia native, **William Hardy** has taught drama and worked with theater at UNC-Chapel Hill for many years. He has also published a number of novels as well as an outdoor drama, *The Sword of Peace.* Produced each summer at Snow Camp, this play tells the story of Quakers during Revolutionary times.

William Harmon, a native of Concord, also teaches at UNC-Chapel Hill. As well as publishing a number of volumes of poetry, he has edited a major anthology, *The Oxford Book of American Light Verse* (1979).

Since 1980 **Robert Hedin** has been poet-in-residence at Wake Forest University. He has published five collections of poetry, a collection of essays, and an anthology. He has taught in Alaska and Paris, France, and has read his work in many states.

Robert Hemley of Charlotte is a young writer of fiction. His first collection of short stories is *The Mouse Town* (1987).

G. C. Hendricks builds houses and writes fiction. He was born in the community of Olive Chapel near Raleigh, then grew up in Wake Forest. After three years of college, he joined the marines as a private and worked his way up to become a commissioned jet pilot; he flew many missions in Vietnam. His first novel, *The Second War,* covers twenty years in the life of a young man, including experience as a pilot during the Vietnamese war.

A native of Troy, **Phil Hines** was formerly director of the North Carolina Writers' Network. A number of his plays have been produced in North Carolina and have won awards. His most recent play, *Serving Time in a Dixie Diner,* opened in an "off-off Broadway" theater in New York in Spring 1990.

Judy Hogan of Chapel Hill has edited anthologies and published both fiction and two collections of poetry. Many North Carolina writers especially respect her work in founding and directing Carolina Wren Press. This small publishing company has given a number of writers their first publishing opportunity and, in so doing, has produced a number of fine books for both adults and children.

David Hopes, who teaches at the University of North Carolina at Asheville, intended to study biology when he began college, and his interest in science and nature is evident in his work. He has published poetry, fiction, essays, and plays. Two of his plays, *Timothy Liberty* and *Phantom of the Blue Ridge,* won the Southern Playwrights Prize.

Statesville-resident **Belinda Hurmence** has written a number of novels for young readers. She also edited a collection of interviews with former slaves: *My Folks Don't Want Me to Talk About Slavery* (1965). Since then she has published two books based on the oral histories and plantation records of actual slaves: a novel, *A Girl Called Boy* (1982), and a nonfiction book, *Before Freedom, When I Just Can Remember* (1989).

Charlotte-native **Paul Jones** works with computers in Research Triangle Park and directs the Poets Exchange at the Art School in Carrboro. His poems have won numerous awards.

H. G. Jones, originally from Caswell County, can be called the caretaker of North Carolina's words and ways. As curator of the North Carolina Collection in the Wilson Library at the University of North Carolina in Chapel Hill, he oversees the collecting and proper use of all records by or about North Carolina or North Carolinians. The collection includes books, recordings, maps, videos, historical documents, genealogy, theses, etc. Jones, who formerly served as director of the North Carolina Department of Archives and History, is himself an author; his best-known work is *North Carolina Illustrated: 1525–1984.*

One could say that Salisbury-native **John Justice** is carrying on two writing careers simultaneously. As communications officer for the Episcopal Diocese of North Carolina, he edits *The Communicant,* a periodical for Episcopalians. As playwright, he won the Thompson Theatre Award for an original play, *Bury Me Not.* His adaptations of two of Clyde Edgerton's novels—*Raney* and *Walking Across Egypt*—have been produced by major state theaters.

Since her graduation from UNC-Chapel Hill, Charlotte native **Susan Katz** has been a free-lance writer publishing articles and poems in national newspapers and magazines. Currently she lives in Los Angeles, where she is writing television scripts.

John Kessel grew up in Buffalo, New York. In 1982, he moved to Raleigh to join the faculty at North Carolina State University, where he teaches American literature, fiction writing, and science fiction. That same year, his novella, *Another Orphan,* won the Nebula Award of the Science Fiction Writers of America. His most recent novel is *Good News from Outer Space.*

Burgess Leonard of High Point has written a number of novels for young readers. His fiction, which centers on sports, is often set on the campuses of North Carolina colleges and universities. *Victory Pass* (1950) was his first novel.

C. Eric Lincoln, professor of religion and culture at Duke University, spent thirty years building a reputation as a scholar. During those years he wrote or edited nineteen nonfiction books. When his first novel, *The Avenue, Clayton City,* appeared in 1988, it immediately won high praise as a gripping story and a realistic portrayal of the life of blacks in a small Southern town. It was awarded the 1988 Lillian Smith Book Award for best Southern Fiction.

Boone resident **Romulus Linney** has written a great deal about his region. He began his career with novels, then turned to playwriting. His plays often involve folklore. Among his plays are *Appalachia Soundings,* written in commemoration of the nation's bicentennial anniversary in 1976.

Susan Ludvigson of Charlotte has published a number of poetry collections, including *Northern Lights* and *The Swimmer.* In 1985 she was awarded major national fellowships to live and write in Paris.

Robert Long grew up in Wilmington and was educated at Davidson College and Warren Wilson College. He was the first executive director of the North Carolina Writers' Network. His first volume of poetry is *The Power to Die* (1987). Currently he lives and writes in Massachusetts.

A Raleigh native, **Michael Malone** has written two novels, *Handling Sin* (1986) and *Time's Witness* (1989). Both are set in the south, and both are noted for their vivid characters and lively wit.

Margaret Maron, a resident of Smithfield, might be called North Carolina's Jessica Fletcher. Like the heroine of the television series *Murder She Wrote,* Ms. Maron writes mysteries. She is the creator of Bantam Doubleday Dell's Detective Sigrid Harald series.

Agnes McDonald has taught writing at several North Carolina colleges and universities, as well as in workshops for public schools and the North Carolina Correctional Center

for Women. She is now a member of the English faculty at UNC-Wilmington. Her poetry has appeared in many journals as well as *Four North Carolina Women Poets* (1982), and she is compiling an anthology of contemporary southern women's journals, *Journey Proud*

Tim McLaurin grew up in Fayetteville and served in both the Marine Corps and the Peace Corps before completing a journalism degree at UNC-Chapel Hill. There he studied writing under Max Steele and Doris Betts. He has published two well-received novels, *The Acorn Plan* (1988) and *Woodrow's Trumpet* (1989).

Ben Dixon MacNeill is known best for his book, *The Hatterasman* (1958), dealing with life on the Outer Banks. He lived on the coast for over a decade, and this book is a blend of history, legend, and poetry. MacNeill's novel *Sand Roots,* published after his death in 1960, deals with a young man who rejects his family heritage as an Outer Banks seaman.

Stanly County-native **Heather Ross Miller** is carrying on a family tradition by becoming a writer. Her father, **Fred Ross,** and her uncle, **James Ross,** are both novelists; her aunt, **Eleanor Ross Taylor,** is a noted poet; her uncle, **Peter Taylor,** is a Pulitzer prize-winning novelist who once taught at UNC-Greensboro. Ms. Miller, who studied with Randall Jarrell at UNC-Greensboro, has published both novels and award-winning poetry, and has taught creative writing at Pfeiffer College in Stanly County and at the University of Arkansas in Fayetteville, Arkansas. Her second novel, *Tenants of the House,* won the Sir Walter Award.

Another writer from Stanly County, **Fred Morgan**, has added to our collection of folklore. A native of Albemarle, he has published two collections: *Ghost Tales of the Uwharries* (1968) and *Uwharrie Magic* (1974).

After studying at UNC-Chapel Hill and winning two national awards for his writing,

Charlotte-native **Lawrence Naumoff** spent ten years building houses. Then in 1988 he won acclaim with his first novel, *The Night of the Weeping Women*. Two years later, his second, *Rootie Kazootie*, won critical praise and was published in Sweden, England, and Japan. He lives in Chatham County.

Although he is a native of Chicago, **Paul Baker Newman** has for many years lived in Charlotte and taught at Queens College. He has published six volumes of poetry; his most recent is *The Light of the Red Horse* (1881).

David Payne, who grew up in Henderson, published his first novel, *Confessions of a Taoist on Wall Street,* when he was twenty-nine. It was the 1985 Houghton Mifflin Literary Fellowship Award. His second novel, *Early from the Dance,* was published in 1989.

A native of Wilmington, **Peggy Payne** built a solid reputation as a travel writer. Journeying all over the world, she published travel articles in many newspapers and magazines. In 1988, she published her first novel, *Revelation.* Her short story "The Pure in Heart," from which *Revelation* was developed, was published in *New Stories from the South, 1987,* and was cited in *Best American Short Stories* for that year. She has also published stories in literary magazines and *YM*.

T. R. Pearson used his experiences growing up in Reidsville and the stories he heard there as the basis for three comic novels. In the first, *A Short History of a Small Place* (1985), a boy narrates the story of the zany goings-on in the small town of Neely—a place not unlike Reidsville. Two later novels also center on life in Neely.

Catherine Petroski, who lives in Durham, has won a number of awards and fellowships for her fiction. A short story was included in the O. Henry Prize Stories for 1989, and her novel *The Summer That Lasted Forever* won the AAUW Award for the best novel for young readers in 1985.

Greensboro-native **Bruce Piephoff** is a poet who has also made a name for himself as a songwriter. He has written over one thousand folk songs and poems, publishing many poems in literary magazines and producing two albums, *Razor's Edge* and *Doctor River.* Recently he has served as visiting artist at Brunswick Community College and Pitt Community College.

William Powell has been called "the leading authority on the history of North Carolina." Although now retired from active teaching at the UNC-Chapel Hill, where he was professor of history for many years, he continues his studies and writings in the history of his state. His most recent books include two state histories: *North Carolina Through Four Centuries* and *North Carolina: The Story of a Special Kind of Place,* a text written for eighth-grade students.

Wayne County-native **Eugene L. Roberts, Jr.,** is another North Carolina journalist who has won national attention. In fact, a *Newsweek* article stated that "Within the business, Roberts was probably the nation's most respected newspaper editor." His career carried him from North Carolina to *The New York Times* and finally to *The Philadelphia Inquirer,* which, during his eighteen years as editor, won seventeen Pulitzer Prizes.

Nancy Roberts of Charlotte was writing for a newspaper when Carl Sandburg, who had read some of her articles, encouraged her to write a book. The result: *An Illustrated Guide to Ghosts and Mysterious Occurrences in the Old North State* (1959). Since then she has published a number of other books, many of them dealing with ghost tales and legends. Among her best known are *This Haunted Land* (1970) and *Appalachian Ghosts* (1978).

Love or a Reasonable Facsimile (1989) is the remarkable autobiography of a remarkable woman, **Gloree Rogers**. Born in Bladen County, she overcame both a number of birth defects, and parental abuse. She earned a nursing degree and has lived an active life. Not only does she work and write, but she also contributes time and talents to community organizations.

Glen Rounds was born in South Dakota in 1906, but for many years he has made his home in this state. An artist, he has said that he began to write books "since no one would let me illustrate theirs." Using his own observations, he has written and illustrated a number of books about nature, directing them to an audience of young readers and using his own observations. He has also written fiction. Two of his best-known books are *Beaver Business* (1960) and *The Day the Circus Came to Lonetree* (1973).

Louis Rubin, Jr., can be said to wear at least four literary hats. He is a writer himself, having published both fiction and studies of literature. He has taught literature at Hollins College and the university in Chapel Hill. He is recognized as one of the foremost critics and authorities on southern literature. He also founded and manages Algonquin Press, which has brought to public attention a number of major writers, including Clyde Edgerton, Jill McCorkle, and Kaye Gibbons.

Detroit-native **Larry Rudner** has lived in Raleigh since 1978, when he began teaching American literature and modern fiction at North Carolina State University. Some of his short stories have won national awards. His first novel, *The Magic That We Do Here*, centers on a Polish child caught in the Holocaust during World War II; it was the winner of the Sir Walter Raleigh Award for Fiction in 1988. Currently he is completing a second novel, set in eastern Europe.

Born in Raleigh, **Anne Russell** has worked as a newspaper reporter and a college faculty member at Pembroke State University and the University of North Carolina at Wilmington. She has published poetry, nonfiction, and, with coauthor Marjorie Megivern, *North Carolina Portraits of Faith* (1986), a pictorial history of the many kinds of religions that have been practiced in North Carolina. Several of her plays, including *The*

Porch, have been produced in Wilmington and Raleigh. She now lives and writes in Wilmington, where as a child she spent many summers with her grandparents.

Louise Shivers grew up on a tobacco farm. She attended Meredith College, then moved to Georgia with her husband. Her novel *Here to Get My Baby Out of Jail* (1983) is set in rural tobacco-growing country much like her own region. It gained immediate national attention and was made into a motion picture.

Bland Simpson and **Jim Wann** became friends while living in Chapel Hill. They collaborated on a musical play, *Diamond Studs* (1974), based loosely on the life of outlaw Jesse James. After being produced locally, it moved on to New York. Since that time, Simpson and Wann have cowritten several other musicals, including *Pump Boys and Dinettes* (1981) and their most recent, *The Merry Wives of Windsor, Texas* (1989). Several of these plays have been produced in New York and other metropolitan centers; *Pump Boys and Dinettes* was also produced on television.

R. T. Smith is a native of this state, but has taught for a number of years at Auburn University, where he helps edit *Southern Humanities Review*. He has published several collections of poetry and has won the Zoe Kincaid Brockman Award.

Max Steele grew up in South Carolina, then moved to Chapel Hill when his first novel, *Debby*, won the $10,000 Harper Prize Novel Competition. He has directed the creative writing program at UNC-Chapel Hill and continued to publish both novels and short stories.

Bruce Stone, an English teacher at Chapel Hill High School, has published two novels for young readers: *Half-Nelson, Full-Nelson* (1985) and *Been Clever Forever* (1989). Both deal with the adventures of teenaged boys, and both are noted for lively plots, humor, and word-play. *Half-Nelson, Full-Nelson* was named an American Library Association

Best Book for Young Adults.

The poetry of Charlottean **Julie Suk** has appeared in many magazines as well as in her collection, *The Medicine Woman* (1980). She has also assisted in editing *Southern Poetry Review*.

Born in Atlanta, **Nancy Tilly** has spent most of her adult life in Chapel Hill. In 1986 her novel *Golden Girl* won the AAUW Award for the best North Carolina novel written for young readers.

Helen Tucker, a resident of Raleigh, has written many novels, several of which are set in this state. *The Sound of Summer Voices* (1969) is about a boy growing up in Louisburg. *The Guilt of August Sterling* (1971) takes place at old Wake Forest College (in Wake Forest, near Raleigh, not Winston-Salem, where Wake Forest University is located). Her historical novel *Bound by Honor* (1984) is set in Bath during the early 1700s.

Anne Tyler is considered one of today's most gifted fiction writers. In addition to short fiction, she has published eleven novels. *The Accidental Tourist* was made into a major motion picture, and her most recent, *Breathing Lessons*, won the Pulitzer Prize. Although she is not a native Tar Heel and she has spent her adult life in Baltimore, North Carolinians are proud that she was encouraged as a writer while a student here: first at Broughton High school in Raleigh, then at Duke University, where she studied under Reynolds Price.

The son of a Wilkes County sharecropper, **John Foster West** has published two volumes of poetry. In addition, he is the author of several novels, including *Time Was* (1965), and a biography, *The Ballad of Tom Dula* (1970). His most recent novel, *The Summer People,* won the first Appalachian Fiction Award. For twenty-two years he taught creative writing at Appalachian State University.

Samm-Art Williams grew up near Burgaw in Pender County, then developed a remarkable career as actor, director, and playwright. His play *Home* (1979) received national acclaim when it was produced both on and off Broadway. He has also written television scripts.

Warrenton-native **Ira David Wood** is known best as actor and producer-director of Raleigh's Theatre-in-the-Park. He is also a playwright and composer-lyricist; a number of his plays have been produced not only locally but in other locations, including New York. His musical adaptation of Dickens's *A Christmas Carol* is annually produced in Raleigh and has been taken abroad to England and France.

Edwin M. Yoder, who was born in Mebane and grew up in Greensboro, wrote editorials for the *Charlotte News* and the *Greensboro Daily News* before moving to Washington, D.C. He now writes a column on national affairs for *The Washington Post*; it is syndicated and appears in newspapers all over the country.

Lee Zacharias was born in Chicago in 1944. Since 1975 she has lived in Greensboro and coordinated the writing program at the university there. She has published a collection of short stories and a novel, *Lessons,* which won the Sir Walter Award in 1982.

Glossary of Literary Terms

Allusion: a brief, meaningful reference, usually to a historical or literary figure, event, or object. For example, the novel *All the King's Men* is about a political figure who falls from power; the title is an *allusion* to the nursery rhyme, "Humpty Dumpty," about an egg which falls, and "all the king's horses/and all the king's men/couldn't put Humpty Dumpty together again." The nonfiction account of the fall of President Richard Nixon was entitled *All the President's Men*—alluding to both the nursery rhyme and the novel. Another example, included in this book, is Ardis Hatch's poem, "The Gingham Boy and the Calico Brother."

Ambiguity: an expression or statement which may be understood in more than one way.

Ambivalence: the presence of two or more conflicting feelings at the same time. For example, one may at the same time feel both love and anger toward another person. Or one may feel both fascinated and revolted by a violent scene, such as an automobile wreck.

Analogy: a comparison of two things which are similar in some ways but not in others. For example, one may explain a camera by analogy to the human eye; or the human mind by analogy to a computer. Writers often say that writing a book is *analogous* to giving birth.

Cliché: an expression that is so overused that it is considered to be dull or trite. Examples: *tip of the iceberg, sweet as sugar, free as a bird.*

Coined words: words that have consciously been made up for a particular occasion or item.

Connotation: the emotions or ideas associated with a word or phrase, going beyond its dictionary definition. For example, the adjectives *chubby* and *obese* are both used to refer to persons who are overweight, but *chubby* implies that the fat is not excessive, whereas *obese* indicates extreme fatness, repulsiveness—even a serious medical condition.

Context: the circumstances in which an event occurs. In language, the term *context* refers to the part of the speech or writing in which a word or passage or issue occurs.

Couplet: a pair of rhyming lines, usually the same length and meter.

Dialect: a variety of a language common to a particular group, location, or time. Dialects may be distinguished from the standard language of the culture by differences in pronunciation, vocabulary, grammar, and/or sentence structure. (For discussion of dialects, see "Some Words About Words.")

Dramatic Monologue: a poem in which a narrator tells a story. Some of the most famous dramatic monologues are Robert Browning's "My Last Duchess" and T. S. Eliot's "The Love Song of J. Alfred Prufrock."

Haiku: a Japanese lyric poem consisting of three lines with a set number of syllables: 5-7-5. The haiku centers on an image (usually visual) either to present it forcefully or to suggest something else—perhaps an emotion or a spiritual insight.

Humor: the quality of being comical; something which arouses laughter or amusement.

Image: in literature, a word or phrase which appeals to our senses by calling up mental pictures, sounds, scents, etc.

Incongruous: inconsistent; made up of parts which do not seem to logically go together. Incongruity is often the basis of humor.

Inference: something which has been inferred (decided or deduced from evidence).

Irony: recognition of the difference between reality and what seems to be the case.
a. verbal irony: the use of words to convey the opposite of their literal meaning. For example, someone looking outside at a downpour says sarcastically, "What a great day." Both he and his listener know that he means the opposite.
b. irony of situation: a condition in which there is a great difference—sometimes even the opposite—between what is expected and what actually happens, or what seems to be the case and what really is the case.

Legend: a popular story handed down from earlier times. Often it is based on some historical figure or event. It may include mysterious or exaggerated elements, but it usually does not include supernatural elements. (Sometimes the words *legend* and *myth* are used interchangeably, although they are different; see *myth*, below.)

Metaphor and **Simile:** Both terms refer to figures of speech in which one thing is compared to another. A *simile* makes the comparison directly by using *as* or *like*, as in "Her smile was as bright as sunshine," or "Her smile was like sunshine." A metaphor omits *like* or *as* and therefore it implies the comparison, as in "Her smile was sunshine."

Myth: a traditional story dealing with supernatural beings, ancestors, or heroes. Myths are used to explain what is unknown—matters concerning both the natural universe and human behavior. For example, some myths deal with how the world was created or how humanity came to use fire (the Prometheus myth) or why we have both night and day.

Ode: a long, stately lyrical poem spoken in praise of a person, thing, or quality. The style is usually quite formal.

Paradox: a statement which seems to be contradictory, but in the deepest sense is nonetheless true. Examples: "The child is father of the man" (Wordsworth). "He who would save his life must lose it" (Jesus).

Parallel structure: two or more phrases or clauses, used in the same or adjoining sentences, and using the same form and frequently some of the same words. Examples " . . . that government of the people, by the people, for the people shall not perish from the earth" (Abraham Lincoln's Gettysburg Address).
"Ask not what your country can do for you; ask what you can do for your country" (John F. Kennedy's Inaugural Address).
"It was the best of times, it was the worst of times, it was the age of wisdom, it was the age of foolishness . . ." (Opening lines from *A Tale of Two Cities* by Charles Dickens).

Poetic justice: the rewarding of virtue and the punishing of wrongdoing. We use the term when a person or character receives a fate which seems particularly appropriate (and sometimes ironic).

Point of view: the position from which something is observed. In literature, this term often refers to the perspective from which a story is told.

Propaganda: material prepared to present one point of view or proclaim one doctrine. Examples: Adolph Hitler's regime used propaganda to stir up resentment against the Jews. Many political advertisements can be considered propaganda.

Pun: a play on words. Often it is based on different meanings of the same word. Sometimes it is based on similar meaning or sound of different words.

Quatrain: a stanza of four lines, usually rhyming.

Redundancy: unnecessary repetition.

Refrain: a phrase or line repeated at intervals throughout a song or poem—usually repeated at the end of each stanza.

Sonnet: a traditional fourteen-line poem. Usually it is arranged either into three **quatrains** (four-line stanzas or groupings) and a **couplet** (two-line pair), or into an **octave** (eight-line stanza) and **sestet** (six-line stanza).

Symbol: something that stands for or represents something else; especially a material object used to represent an abstraction or something invisible. For example, the rose often is a symbol of love; the color white symbolizes purity and/ or innocence.

Tall tale: a humorous story marked by a great deal of exaggeration. It is often told in a conversational style—perhaps a dialect.

Tone: in speech, *tone* refers to the quality of the voice—pitch, duration, etc.— often expressing feeling or attitude. Writers try to achieve a similar tone by choosing words, phrasing, etc., which *express* their attitude. We may speak of the tone of a work as being serious, playful, ironic, somber, condescending, etc.

Word music: similar or corresponding sounds in words which are fairly close together and thus echo one another. There are several different kinds of word music:

Alliteration: two or more words having the same initial sound. Examples: the **wh**istle of the **w**ind; **sp**ring casts a **sp**ell over the land.

Assonance: two or more words sharing the same vowel sounds. Example: the dr**u**m of th**u**nder; "the m**e**lons (which no one thought would surv**i**ve)/ball**oo**n to pr**i**ze s**i**ze,/r**i**sing like green whales."

Consonance: two or more words sharing the same consonant sounds. Example: "**r**oses, thei**r** pu**r**e co**r**al/**tr**embling the quiet ai**r**."

Onomotapoeia: use of sounds that mimic the sound being named: examples: *crash, buzz, creak.*

Rhyme: matching sounds in the final words or syllables in two lines of poetry. With **pure rhyme**, the match is exact: i.e., *night/flight/cite*. With **slant rhyme** (often called **off-rhyme** or **impure rhyme**), some of the sounds match, but not all. (Examples: *night/meet; night/fit; rain/sheen; rain/mate.*)

Word play: wit or cleverness based on irony, double meanings, or similar sounds of words. **Puns** are examples of word play.

Index by Author and Title

Acknowledgments

IN APPRECIATION

Compiling a collection like this and preparing it for classroom use is a monumental task, one which could not be accomplished alone. From the moment I began this work, I solicited information and advice from knowledgeable people whose cooperation was unfailing andinvaluable. I owe deep appreciation to the following.

Educators who helped with selections, made suggestions for classroom use, and/or tested materials in their own classrooms:

Nancy Banks, Mary Evelyn Jackman, and Sarah Jordan—Martin Middle School, Raleigh; Barbara Broadwell and Margaret Isenberg—Daniels Middle School, Raleigh; Betsy Clark—Norlina Middle School, Norlina; Cindy Clark—Cooper Middle School, Clayton; John Ellington, Betty Jean Foust, and Mike Frye—North Carolina Department of Public Instruction; Caroline Jacobs and Shirley Highfill—Githens Middle School, Durham; Sue McDowell and Carolyn Rogers—East Cary Middle School, Cary; and Deborah Pendleton—Ligon Middle School, Raleigh.

Scholars, historians, writers, and friends who helped me locate works, writers, information, and other resources:

Ed Buckner—Department of Forestry, University of Tennessee; Jim Clark—Humanities Extension, NC State University; John Crossno—Department of History, Peace College; H. G. Jones—Wilson Library, University of North Carolina at Chapel Hill; Mary Kratt—Writer and historian; Lucinda MacKethan—Department of English, NCSU; E. T. Malone—NC Department of Archives & History; Elizabeth Reid Murray—Writer and historian; Sallie Nixon—Writer; Sam Ragan—Writer, editor, publisher; Bes Spangler—Department of English, Peace College; Marsha Warren—North Carolina Writers' Network; and Rhoda Wynn—Paul Green Foundation.

Special appreciation goes to Travis Wester, who provided an eighth-grader's honest appraisal; to Dorothy Owen, whose knowledge of writing and network of writers is a superb human data bank; and to Bob Buckner, whose support made the completion of this work possible.

And of course my deepest gratitude to all the fine writers whose work is represented here. They have not only provided a rich treasure house of writings, but have given generously of time and support throughout this project.

Photo Credits

Chapter 1: p. 5 Oconaluftee Village: Photo by Clay Nolen. NC Travel and Tourism Division; p. 8 Great Tortoise Receives Sky Woman: Mrs. F. Roy Johnson; p. 10 F. Roy Johnson: Mrs. F. Roy Johnson; p. 16 Raven Rock State Park; Photo by Clay Nolen. NC Travel and Tourism Division; p. 18 Black Jack and Fleet Deer Drop Raven Over the Cliff. Drawing by Eugenia Johnson. Mr. F. Roy Johnson; p. 22 Early Map: NC Collection, University of NC Library, Chapel Hill; p. 26–27 Elizabeth II: Photo by Clay Nolen. NC Travel and Tourism Division; p. 28 Rebecca Rust: Rebecca Rust; p. 30–31 Scene from *The Lost Colony.* NC Travel and Tourism Division; p. 32 Kate Kelly Thomas: Kate Kelly Thomas; p. 40 The White Doe: Illustration by May Louise Barrett. From original publication. NC Collection, University of NC Library, Chapel Hill; p. 44 The Mother Vine: NC Collection, University of NC Library at Chapel Hill; p. 45 Sallie Cotten. NC Archives and History; p. 47 Benjamin Sledd: Wake Forest University; p. 48 Outer Banks Seen From Outer Space. Photo Courtesy of National Geographic Magazine. NC Travel and Tourism Division; p. 49 John Lawson Captured by Indians. NC Archives and History. This drawing appeared in *The Early History of the Southern States* (Philadelphia, 1932) by Lambert Lilly (Francis Hooks); p. 52 Native Americans. Engraving by Theodor de Bry. NC Collection, University of NC Library at Chapel Hill.

Chapter 2: p. 59 Helen Goodman: Helen Goodman; p. 64 James Boyd: *The Pilot,* Southern Pines; p. 72 Nell Wise Wechter: NC Archives and History; p. 74 General Nathanael Greene: NC Archives and History; p. 76 Helen Bevington: NC Archives and History; p. 79 Burke Davis: Burke Davis.

Chapter 3: p. 84 Grave of Nathaniel Macon. NC Archives and History; p. 85 Sam Ragan: Sam Ragan; p. 91 Native American and soldier: Scene from *Unto These Hills.* NC Travel and Tourism Division; p. 92 Felix Alley: Betty Jean Alley; p. 93 John Sevier: NC Archives and History; p. 97 Cherokee Chief. Scene from *Unto These Hills.* NC Travel and Tourism Division; p. 104 Sequoyah and His Alphabet. NC Archives and History; p. 108 Julia Montgomery Street: Julia Montgomery Street; p. 113 The Falls. Lithograph by Oscar M. Lewis. NC Collection, University of NC Library at Chapel Hill; p. 118 Wilma Dykeman: Wilma Dykeman; p. 126 Harriet Jacobs: Photo reprinted by permission of the owner and the publishers from *Incidents in the Life of a Slave Girl* by Harriet A. Jacobs, edited and with an introduction by Jean Fagan Yellin. Copyright © 1987 by the President and Fellows of Harvard College; p. 130 George Moses Horton: Illustration for *The Black Poet* by Richard Walser. NC Archives and History.

Chapter 4: p. 142 Walter Hines Page. NC Archives and History; p. 149 Re-enactment of the Battle of Bentonville: Photo by Clay Nolen. NC Travel and Tourism Division; p. 152 John Ehle: John Ehle; p. 153 Statue of Henry Wilson Wyatt, Capital Square, Raleigh, NC: NC Travel and Tourism Division; p. 155 John Richard Hood: Mary Kratt; p. 156 Mary Kratt: Mary Kratt; p. 159 Dennis Rogers. *The News and Observer,* Raleigh, NC.

Chapter 5: p. 165 Josephus Daniels. *The News and Observer,* Raleigh, NC; p. 171 Pauli Murray: NC Collection, University of NC Library at Chapel Hill; p. 178 The Bouquet: Illustration from original publication. NC Collection, University of NC Library at Chapel Hill; p. 182 Charles Chestnutt: NC Archives and History; p. 186 Lee Smith: Lee Smith; p. 188 John Charles McNeill: NC Archives and History; p. 191 Tweetsie Railroad: Photo by Clay Nolen. NC Travel and Tourism Division.

Chapter 6: p. 206 Thomas Wolfe Home: Photo by Clay Nolen, NC Travel and Tourism Division; p. 211 Thomas Wolfe: NC Archives and History; p. 218 Village School: NC Archives and History; p. 227 Paul Green: NC Archives and History; p. 231 Field Workers: NC Archives and History; p. 232 Fred Chappell: Fred Chappell; p. 240 North Carolina Mountains: NC Archives and History; p. 246 O. Hen-

ry: NC Archives and History; p. 247 W. C. Porters' Drug Store: NC Archives and History; p. 251 Ellis Credle: NC Archives and History; p. 258 John E. (Frail) Joines: Blanche C. Joines.

Chapter 7: p. 296 Tobacco Auction: NC Travel and Tourism Division; p. 270 Fred Koch, Jr.: Fred Koch, Jr.; p. 278 Bessie Willis Hoyt: Bessie Willis Hoyt; p. 289 Kate Rinzler: Kate Rinzler; p. 300 Guy Owen: Dorothy Owen; p. 309 Ruth Moose: Ruth Moose; p. 311 Pearson Home: James Larkin Pearson Library, Wilkes Community College; p. 312 James Larkin Pearson: James Larkin Pearson Library, Wilkes Community College; p. 325 Tom Wicker: photo by Gene Maggio, *The New York Times, The Pilot,* Southern Pines, NC; p. 328 Shelby Stephenson: Shelby Stephenson; p. 334 Andy Griffith: *The Pilot.*

Chapter 8: p. 341 Pearl Harbor: NC Archives and History; p. 342 Vermont Royster: NC Collection, University of NC Library at Chapel Hill; p. 348 Graveyard at Ocracoke: Photo by Clay Nolen. NC Travel and Tourism Division; p. 351 David Stick: *The Pilot,* Southern Pines, NC.; p. 363 Frances Gray Patton: News Service, Duke University; p. 370 Stewart Atkins: Claire Pittman Atkins; p. 374 Roosevelt and Daniels: In 1913, young Franklin Roosevelt and Josephus Daniels watch the dedication of a memorial at the White House. NC Archives and History; p. 376 David Brinkley: Photo by Hugh Morton. *The Pilot,* Southern Pines, NC; p. 379 Wright Brothers' First Flight. NC Travel and Tourism Division.

Chapter 9: p. 388 Betty Adcock: Photo by K. D. Zotter Photography. Betty Adcock; p. 389 Mast General Store: Photo by Clay Nolen. NC Travel and Tourism Division; p. 380 Susan Rose: Susan Rose; p. 391 Stephen Smith: Stephen Smith; p. 393 Kathryn Byer: Kathryn Byer; p. 395 Dancer: Judy Goldman; p. 396 Judy Goldman: Judy Goldman; p. 400 Robert Morgan. Photo by Hank De Leo. Cornell University; p. 402 Shirley Laws Moody. Photo by Mandy Moody. Shirley Moody; p. 405 Linda Beatrice Brown: Linda Beatrice Brown; p. 408 Claire Atkins Pittman: Claire Atkins Pittman; p. 423 Suzanne Newton: Viking Press; p. 437 Sue Ellen Bridgers: North Carolina Writers' Network; p. 440 Tom Hawkins: Tom Hawkins; p. 445 Clyde Edgerton: North Carolina Writers Network; p. 447 Hot Rods: Drawing by Dot Stell. *The News and Observer,* Raleigh, NC; p. 453 Peggy Hoffman: Peggy Hoffmann; p. 457 Charlotte Speedway. NC Archives and History; p. 459 Sylvia Wilkinson: NC Archives and History; p. 464 Mill Village. NC Archives and History; p. 470 Doris Betts: News Service, University of NC at Chapel Hill; p. 471 Sharecropper: NC Archives and History; p. 476 Reynolds Price: News Service, Duke University; p. 490 Thad Stem: Photo by Linda Walters. Marguerite Sten; p. 495 Edward R. Murrow: NC Archives and History; p. 501 Charles Kuralt: NC Travel and Tourism Division; p. 503 Martin Luther King at Broughton: NC Archives and History; p. 506 Kays Gary: Kays Gary; p. 507 Martin Luther King: NC Archives and History; p. 508 Jaki Shelton Green: Photo by Jodi Anderson. Jaki Shelton Green; p. 509 Gerald Barrax: Gerald Barrax; p. 513 Thomas Walters: Linda Walters.

Home: p. 517 Jim Wayne Miller: Photo by David Stephenson. Western Kentucky University; p. 519 Ronald Bayes: Ronald Bayes; p. 521 Ardis Hatch: Photo by Karen Tam. Ardis Hatch; p. 524 A. C. Snow: Photo by Karen Tam. *The News and Observer,* Raleigh, NC; p. 531 Gail Godwin: Photo by Jerry Bauer. Peace College; p. 532 Ben Owen: NC Archives and History; p. 534 Jugtown Pottery: NC Travel and Tourism Division; p. 535 Jerry Bledsoe: Jerry Bledsoe; 537 Grace Gibson: Grace Gibson; p. 544 Jill McCorkle: Algonquin Books of Chapel Hill; p. 545 Lenard Moore. Photo by Tom Olsen. Lenard D. Moore; p. 549 Mae Woods Bell: *The Pilot,* Southern Pines, NC; p. 552 A. R. Amons: Media Services, Cornell University; p. 553 Michael McFee: Michael McFee; p. 554 Emily Wilson: Emily Herring Wilson; p. 558 Mary Snotherly: North Carolina Writers' Network; p. 561 Margaret Boothe Baddour. Photo by LaVerne H. Clark. Margaret Baddour; p. 562 Ellen Johnston-Hale: Ellen Johnston-Hale; p. 567 Anna Wooten-Hawkins: Anna Wooten-Hawkins; p. 570 Lois Holt: Lois Holt; p. 574 Suzanne Britt. Photo by Snyder Photography, Inc. Suzanne Britt; p. 580 Kaye Gibbons: Photo by Sarah Durant. Kaye Gibbons; p. 581 Southern Pines Railroad Station: NC Archives and History; p. 582 Marsha White Warren: North Carolina Writers' Network; p. 585 Ann Berry: *The News and Observer,* Raleigh, NC; p. 588 Gladys Owings Hughes; Gladys Hughes.

Burke Davis

Wilma Dykeman

Bessie Willis Hoyt

Kaye Gibbons

Fred Chappell

Ovid Holt

Lenard D. Moore

Helen ____

Tom Hawkins

Ellis Credle

Lee Smith

Emily Wilson

Jaki Shelton Green

Marion Hargrove

Fred Kirk

Mary C. Smathers

Guy Owen

Sallie Southall Cotten

Sue Ellen Bridgers